Educational Psychology
FIFTH EDITION

Anita E. Woolfolk
Rutgers University

Allyn and Bacon

Boston • London • Toronto • Sydney • Tokyo • Singapore

*To my students
    and to their students—the children of the 21st century.*

Editor-in-Chief: Nancy Forsyth
Developmental Editor: Mary Ellen Lepionka
Series Editorial Assistant: Christine Nelson
Production Administrator: Susan McIntyre
Production Assistant: Cheryl Ten Eick
Text Designer: Dale Beda/Proof Positive
Photo Research: Photosynthesis/Gloucester, MA
Cover Administrator: Linda Dickinson
Composition Buyer: Linda Cox
Manufacturing Buyer: Megan Cochran

Library of Congress Cataloging-in-Publication Data

Woolfolk, Anita.
    Educational psychology / Anita E. Woolfolk. — 5th ed.
        p.   cm.
    Includes bibliographical references and index.
    ISBN 0-205-13810-1
    1. Educational psychology.   I. Title.
    LB1051.W74   1993
    370.15—dc20   92-24872
                                                   CIP

Printed in the United States of America
10 9 8 7 6 5 4 3   97 96 95 94

Text Credits: p. 3 F. Ruopp and M. Driscoll, reprinted with permission from the *Harvard Education Letter,* January–February 1990 (vol. VI, no. 1, p. 5). Copyright President and Fellows of Harvard College. All rights reserved. pp. 278–279 Reprinted with permission from the *Harvard Education Letter,* March 1986 (vol. II, no. 3, p. 6). Copyright President and Fellows of Harvard College. All rights reserved. p. 476 From Charles Anderson (1989). The role of education in the academic disciplines in teacher education. In A. Woolfolk (Ed.), *Research bases for the graduate preparation of teachers* (pp. 88–107). Reprinted by permission of Allyn and Bacon. pp. 489–490 Reprinted by permission from A. R. Baroody and H. P. Ginsburg (1990), Children's learning: A cognitive view. In R. Davis, C. Maher, and N. Noddings (Eds.), *Constructivist views on the teaching and learning of mathematics* (pp. 51–64). Monograph 4 of the National Council of Teachers of Mathematics, Reston, VA. pp. 491–492 P. Peterson, E. Fennema, and T. Carpenter (1989), Using knowledge of how students think about mathematics. *Educational Leadership, 46,* (4), p. 45. Reprinted with permission of the Association for Supervision and Development. Copyright © 1989 by ASCD. All rights reserved. p. 493 Reprinted by permission from N. Noddings (1990), Constructivism in mathematics education. In R. Davis, C. Maher, and N. Noddings (Eds.), *Constructivist views on the teaching and learning of mathematics,* p. 18. Monograph 4 of the National Council of Teachers of Mathematics, Reston, VA. pp. 556–557 D. Wolf, J. Bixby, J. Glenn III, and H. Gardner (1991), To use their minds well: New forms of student assessment. *Review of Research in Education, 17,* p. 71. Copyright 1991 by the American Educational Research Association. Reprinted with permission of the publisher.

Photo credits are on p. 644 which constitutes an extension of the copyright page.

Contents

CHAPTER 13   EFFECTIVE TEACHING/EFFECTIVE LEARNING   472

Student Preface

Many of you reading this book will be enrolled in an educational psychology course as part of your professional preparation for teaching, counseling, speech therapy, or psychology. Others of you, while not planning to become teachers, are reading this book because you are interested in what educational psychology has to say about teaching and learning in a variety of settings. The material in this text should be of interest to everyone who is concerned about education and learning, from the nursery school volunteer to the instructor in a community program for handicapped adults. No background in psychology or education is necessary to understand this material. It is as free of jargon and technical language as possible and many people have worked to make this edition clear, relevant, and interesting.

Since the first edition of *Educational Psychology* appeared, there have been many exciting developments in the field. This edition incorporates new insights and current trends and at the same time retains the best features of the previous work. The fifth edition continues to emphasize the educational implications of research on child development, cognitive science, learning, and teaching. Theories and applications are not separated but are considered together; the text shows how information and ideas drawn from research in educational psychology can be used to solve the everyday problems of teaching. To explore the connections between knowledge and practice, there are many examples, case studies, guidelines, and practical tips from experienced teachers. Professors and students who used the first four editions found these features very helpful. But what about the new developments?

In this revision, there is a new chapter on the impact of culture and community on students and the classroom. In schools all over the United States and in other industrialized nations, there are students from many different cultural backgrounds. Often several languages are spoken. What are the challenges and opportunities for teachers working with such diversity? This book examines this question.

Another area of critical importance to teachers is the growing body of research on the psychology of teaching and learning. Over 300 new citations have been added to this edition to bring prospective teachers the most current information. Topics include Vygotsky's theory of cognitive development, cultural differences, multicultural education, effective teaching for students placed at risk, sexism in teaching, Bandura's social cognitive theory, cognitive behavior modification, critical thinking skills, teacher planning, the ecology of the classroom, self-esteem, metacognition, schema theory, studies of expert knowledge, and expert classroom managers, cognitive/constructivist approaches to teaching, cooperative learning, learning styles, cognitive views of intelligence, motivation to learn, authentic assessment, portfolios, and changes in the SAT, to name only a few.

The Plan of the Book. The introductory chapter begins with you, the prospective teacher, and the questions you may be asking yourself about a teaching career. What is good teaching and what does it take to become an excellent teacher? How can educational psychology help you to become such a teacher? **Part One,** "Human Development: A Framework for Teachers," focuses on the students. How do they develop mentally, physically, emotionally, and socially, and how do all these aspects fit together? **Part Two,** "Individual Variations," addresses questions such as: Where do individual differences come from, and what do they mean for teachers? How can teachers adapt instruction for students with special needs? What does it mean to create a culturally compatible classroom, one that makes learning accessible to all students? **Part Three,** "Learning Theories and Teaching Practice," looks at learning from two major perspectives, the behavioral and the cognitive, with an emphasis on the cognitive learning theories. Learning theories have important implications for instruction at every level. Cognitive research is particularly vital right now and promises a great fund of ideas for teaching in the immediate future. **Part Four,** "Motivation and Classroom Management," discusses the ever-present, linked issues of motivating and managing today's students. The information in these chapters is based on the most recent research in real classrooms. **Part Five,** "Planning and Teaching," has chapters on designing instruction, choosing and using effective teaching strategies, and fitting the teaching approach to the goals of instruction and the abilities of students. **Part Six,** "Evaluating Students," looks at many types of testing and grading, providing a sound basis for determining how well students have learned.

In addition to the 15 chapters, an **Appendix,** "Research in Educational Psychology," discusses basic vocabulary, concepts, and methods of psychological research. The appendix takes you through the processes of planning and evaluating a study. You will probably find the Appendix worthwhile reading, whether or not your instructor incorporates the appendix into your regular class work.

Aids to Understanding. At the beginning of each chapter you will find an **Outline** of the key topics with page numbers for quick reference. An **Overview** provides a chapter "orientation" along with a list of **Learning Objectives** (also useful for review later). Then a new addition to the text asks, **"What Do You Think?"** Before you read each chapter, take a moment to reflect on the questions raised.

Within the chapter, headings point out themes, questions, and problems as they arise, so you can look up information easily. These can also serve as a quick review of important points. When a new term or concept is introduced, it appears in boldface type along with a brief **margin definition.** These **Key Terms and Concepts** are also listed alphabetically at the end of each chapter with page references and are defined in the **Glossary** at the back of the text.

Throughout the book, graphs, tables, photos, and cartoons have been chosen to clarify and extend the text material—and add to your enjoyment.

Each chapter ends with a **Summary** of the key ideas in each main heading. With the information from the chapter as a base, you are ready to solve the problems posed in the **"What Would You Do?"** application exercises at the end of each chapter. These questions treat both elementary and secondary classrooms and also include a cooperative learning activity.

Other Text Features. As in the previous editions, every chapter in the fifth edition includes **Guidelines** and the **Teachers' Casebook.** And because educational psychology is developing so rapidly today, I have added a new element in every chapter: **Point/Counterpoint.**

Guidelines: An important reason for studying educational psychology is to gain skills in solving classroom problems. Often texts give pages of theory and research findings but little assistance in translating theory into practice. This text is different. Included in each chapter are several sets of Guidelines. These are teaching tips and practical suggestions based on the theory and research discussed in the chapter. Each suggestion is clarified by two or three specific examples. Although Guidelines cannot cover every possible situation, they do provide a needed bridge between knowledge and practice and should help you transfer the text's information to new situations.

Teachers' Casebook. This highly acclaimed and popular feature from the first four editions is back in revised form. At the end of each chapter, master teachers from all over the country, including many Teacher of the Year award winners, offer their own solutions to many of the diverse problems you are likely to encounter in the classroom at every grade level. Their ideas truly show educational psychology at work in a range of everyday situations. The Teachers' Casebook brings to life the topics and principles discussed in each chapter. This edition emphasizes real rather than hypothetical cases and how expert teachers handle them.

Point/Counterpoint. New to this edition is a section in every chapter called Point/Counterpoint, a debate that examines two contrasting perspectives on an important question or controversy related to research or practice in educational psychology. Many of the topics considered in these Point/Counterpoints have "made the news" recently and are central to the discussions of educational reformers.

Student Supplements. Packaged with your text you will find a special edition of *TEACHER* Magazine Reader, which contains articles that relate to educational psychology. A **Study Guide** designed to help you master the material in the text is available. The *Study Guide* includes concept maps, case study applications, lists of key points, exercises with key terms and concepts, practice tests, and explanations of why answers are correct.

Student Responses. You are invited to respond to any aspect of this text. We welcome your feedback. You may wish to criticize the solutions in the Teachers' Casebook, for example, or suggest topics or materials you think should be added to future editions. We would also like to know what you think of the text features and student supplements. Please send letters to:

Woolfolk
EDUCATIONAL PSYCHOLOGY, 5/E
Allyn & Bacon
160 Gould Street
Needham Heights, MA 02194

ACKNOWLEDGMENTS

During the years I have worked on this book, from initial draft to this most recent revision, many people have supported the project. Without their help, this text simply could not have been written.

My writing was guided by extensive and thoughtful reviews from the following individuals:

Stephanie Blecharczyk
Keene State College

Kay Alderman
University of Akron

Rebecca Bardwell
Marquette University

James Turner
University of North Texas

Fintan Kavanagh
Marywood College

Patricia Haensley
Texas A&M University

Helen Botnarescue
California State University, Hayward

Francine Smolucha
Moraine Valley Community College

Joseph Philbrick
California Polytechnic, Pomona

Dale Schunck
University of North Carolina

Richard Craig
University of Maryland

Lois Draina
Marywood College

Manuel Darkatch
Glassboro State College

Mary Hauser
Western Michigan University

Venu Gupta
Kutztown University of
  Pennsylvania

Peter Denner
Idaho State University

James Short
Ohio University

Janet McCowin
California State University, Hayward

Sabrina Mims
California State University,
  Los Angeles

Many classroom teachers across the country contributed their experience, creativity, and expertise to the Teachers' Casebook. I have thoroughly enjoyed my association with these master teachers and am grateful for the perspective they brought to the book: Karen Beechy Kreider, Laura Atkinson, Bruce D. Fisher, Sarah Gustafsen, Stephen C. Ellwood IV, Candice J. Gallagher, Julie A. Addison, Joanne S. Groseclose, Brenda M. Lloyd, Betty Garner, Roseanne O. Newell, Marc Gray, Jan Reynolds, Jane C. Dusell, James D. Kraft, Darlene A. Walsh, Ida Pofahl, Kathryn Daniels, Lawrence Leebens, Dori Hoffman-Latter, Kathy Andrews, Carolyn R. Cook, Kathy A. Minniear, Linda Stahl, Marie Vachon, Bonnie Hettman, Don Knies, Simone Wharton, Sharon Klotz, Louise Harrold Melucci, Malcolm Jarrell, Deborah H. Platt, Phyllis N. Marshall, R. Chris Rohde, Marcia E. Miller, Eileen D. Akers, Harriet Chipley, Donald Falk, Nancy R. Gonzalez, Ruth Ann Dearth, Joan H. Lowe, and Carol Gibbs.

In a project of this size so many people make essential contributions. Jo-Anne Naples, the Permissions Researcher and Barbara Tsantinis, the Permissions Editor worked diligently to obtain permissions for the material reproduced in this text and the supplements. Laurel Anderson guided the collection of new photographs. The text designer, Dale Beda, and cover coordinator, Linda Dickinson, gave the book a completely new, colorful look. Susan McIntyre, Production Administrator, and Elaine Ober, Production Manager, coordinated all aspects of the project, including the *Annotated*

Instructor's Edition, with skill and thoroughness. Somehow they brought organization to the overwhelming complexity of the project. Now the book is in the able hands of Sandi Kirshner, Vice President and Director of Marketing, Ellen Mann, Marketing Manager, Nancy Costa, Marketing Assistant, and their staff.

On this edition, I was privileged to work with an outstanding editorial group. John Isley, President of Allyn and Bacon, gave the support needed to make this edition a significant improvement over all the previous editions. Bill Barke, Vice President and Editorial Director, and Mylan Jaixen, Executive Editor, were with the project from beginning to end, providing good ideas and wise counsel. Sean Wakely was an inspired and inspiring editor. His dedication to producing excellent books, his sweeping knowledge of the field, and his unfailing good humor made the difficult work both easier and more fun. Nancy Forsyth, the Editor in Chief for Education, brought energy, creativity, style, and intelligence to the project. It has been a pleasure working with such a strong and capable friend. The editorial assistants, Carol Chernaik and Christine Nelson, kept everything running smoothly. On this edition I was fortunate to have the help of Mary Ellen Lepionka, a remarkably talented developmental editor. She guided this revision in all its many aspects, keeping the quality of the work always as her prime concern. The greatly expanded supplements package and the excellent pedagogical supports would not exist without her tireless efforts. Jay Howland is responsible for the outstanding copyediting on this edition. Thanks, Jay, for improving my prose.

Finally, I want to thank my family and friends for their kindness and support during the long days and nights that I worked on this book. Again, to my now-almost-grown daughter, Liz, thanks for your insights about teachers and students, shared over the years. When I began this project, you were a tiny baby and now you are in college. You have been my greatest teacher. To my family, Anita Wieckert and Marion, Charlie, Bob, Claudia, Lucas, Geoffrey, Eric, and Suzie, you are the greatest. A final word of appreciation is due to a very special friend—thanks for what is and all that will be.

A. E. W.

Connections

1 EDUCATIONAL PSYCHOLOGY AND THE CLASSROOM TEACHER

$\mathbf{I}$f you are like many students, you begin this course with a mixture of anticipation and wariness. Perhaps you are required to take educational psychology as part of a program in teacher education, speech therapy, nursing, or counseling. You may have chosen this class as an elective because you are interested in education or psychology. Whatever your reason for enrolling, you probably have questions about teaching, schools, students, or even about yourself that you hope this course may answer. I have written *Educational Psychology* with questions such as these in mind.

In this first chapter we begin not with educational psychology but with education—more specifically, with the state of teaching today. Only when you are aware of the challenges teachers face can you appreciate the contributions of educational psychology. After a brief introduction to the world of the teacher, we turn to a discussion of educational psychology itself. We will consider what educational psychology is and why you should study it. How can principles identified by educational psychologists benefit teachers, therapists, parents, and others interested in teaching and learning in our society? What exactly is the content of educational psychology, and where does this information come from? By the time you have finished this chapter, you will be in a much better position to answer these questions and many others such as:

- Would teaching be a good career for me?
- What do expert teachers know?
- What are the greatest concerns of beginning teachers?
- Why should I study educational psychology?
- What roles do theory and research play in this field?
- What specific kinds of problems will the study of educational psychology help me to solve?

> ## WHAT DO YOU THINK?
>
> *Take a minute to remember the names of the best teachers you ever had. What characteristics do you associate with these expert teachers?*

Let's continue by considering the most basic, and perhaps the most difficult, question: What is good teaching?

WHAT IS GOOD TEACHING?

There are hundreds of answers to this question, including ideas based on your own experience. This question has been examined by educators, psychologists, philosophers, writers, mathematicians, scientists, historians, policy makers, and parents, to name only a few groups. And good teaching is not confined to classrooms—it occurs in homes and hospitals, museums and sales meetings, therapists' offices and summer camps. In this book we are most concerned with teaching in classrooms, but much of what you will learn applies to other settings as well.

Inside Five Classrooms

To begin our examination of good teaching, let's step inside the classrooms of several outstanding teachers. All the situations that follow are real. The first two teachers work with my student teachers in local elementary schools. I have chosen them because one of my colleagues at Rutgers, Carol Weinstein, has written about them in her book on classroom management (Weinstein & Mignano, 1993). The next three are secondary-school teachers who have been studied by other educational psychologists.

A Bilingual First Grade. There are 25 students in Viviana's class. Most have recently emigrated from the Dominican Republic; the rest come from Nicaragua, Mexico, Puerto Rico, and Honduras. Even though the children speak little or no English when they begin school, by the time they leave in June, Viviana has helped them master the normal first-grade curriculum for their district. She accomplishes this by teaching in Spanish early in the year to aid understanding, then gradually introducing English as the students are ready. Viviana does not want her students segregated or labeled as disadvantaged. She encourages them to take pride in their Spanish-speaking heritage while using every available opportunity to support their developing English proficiency.

Viviana's expectations for her students are high, and she makes sure the students have the resources they need. She provides materials—pencils, scissors, colors—so no child lacks the means to learn. And she supplies constant encouragement. "Viviana's commitment to her students is evident in her first-grade bilingual classroom. With an energy level that is rare, she motivates, prods, instructs, models, praises, and captivates her students. . . . The pace is brisk and Viviana clearly has a flair for the dramatic; she uses music, props, gestures, facial expressions, and shifts in voice tone to communicate the material" (Weinstein & Mignano, 1993).

Viviana's expectations for herself are high as well. She continually expands her knowledge of teaching through graduate work and participation in special training programs. To know more about her students each year, she spends hours in their homes. For Viviana, teaching is a not just a job; it is a way of life.

A Suburban Sixth Grade. Ken teaches sixth grade in a suburban elementary school in central New Jersey. Ken emphasizes "process writing." His students complete first drafts, discuss them with others in the class, revise, edit, and "publish" their work. The students also keep daily journals and often use these to share personal concerns with Ken. They tell him of problems at home, fights, and fears; he always takes the time to respond in writing. The study of science is also placed in the context of the real world. The students use a National Geographic Society computer network to link with other schools in order to identify acid rain patterns around the world. For social studies, the class played two simulation games focusing on the first half of the 1800s. They "lived" as trappers collecting animal skins and as pioneers heading west to search for gold.

Throughout the year Ken is very interested in the social and emotional development of his students—he wants them to learn about responsibility and fairness as well as science and social studies. This concern is evident in the way he develops his class rules at the beginning of the year. Rather than specifying dos and don'ts, Ken and his students devise a "Bill of Rights" for the class, describing the rights of the students and of the teacher. These rights cover most of the situations that might need a "rule."

An Inner-City Middle School. Another excellent teacher is described in the *Harvard Education Letter.*

Robert Moses, founder of the Algebra Project at the Martin Luther King School in Cambridge, Massachusetts, teaches students the concept of number and sign through a physical event: they go for a ride on a subway. Choosing one subway stop as a starting point, students relate inbound and outbound to positive and negative numbers. They translate their subway ride into mathematical language by considering both the number of stops and their direction. By giving students such experiences before introducing the formal language of algebra, Moses . . . has made math more enjoyable and accessible. (Ruopp & Driscoll, 1990, p. 5)

Two Advanced Math Classes. Hilda Borko and Carol Livingston (1989) describe two expert secondary-school mathematics teachers. In one lesson for her advanced mathematics class, Ellen had her students identify any three problems about ellipses from their text. She asked if there were any questions or uncertainties about these problems. Ellen answered student questions, worked two of the problems, and then used the three problems to derive all the concepts and equations the students needed to understand the material. Ellen's knowledge of the subject and of her students was so thorough that she could create the explanations and derive the formulas on the spot, no matter which problems the students chose.

Another teacher, Randy, worked with his students' confusion to construct a review lesson about strategies for doing integrals. When one student said that a particular section in the book seemed "haphazard," Randy led the class through a process of organizing the material. He asked the class for general statements about useful strategies for doing integrals. He clarified their suggestions, elaborated on some, and helped students improve others. He asked the students to tie their ideas to passages in the text. Even though he accepted all reasonable suggestions, he listed only the key strategies on the board. By the end of the period, the students had transformed the disorganized material from the book into an ordered and useful outline to guide their learning. They also had a better idea about how to read and understand difficult material.

What do you see in these classrooms? The teachers are committed to their students. They must deal with a wide range of student abilities and challenges: different languages, different home lives, different needs. These teachers must understand their subjects and their students' thinking so well that they can spontaneously create new examples and explanations when students are confused. They must make the most abstract concepts, such as negative numbers, real and understandable for their particular students. And then there is the challenge of new technologies and techniques. The teachers must use them appropriately to accomplish important goals and not just to entertain the students. The whole time that these experts are navigating through the academic material, they also are taking care of the emotional needs of their students, propping up sagging self-esteem and encouraging responsibility. If we followed these individuals from the first day of class, we would see that they carefully plan and teach the basic procedures for living and learning in their classes. They can efficiently correct and collect homework, regroup students, give directions, distribute materials, collect lunch money, and deal with disruptions—while also making a mental note to check why one of their students is so tired.

Viviana, Ken, Robert, Ellen, and Randy are examples of expert teachers—the focus of much recent research in education and psychology. For another perspective on the question "What is good teaching?" let's examine this research on expertise in teaching.

Teaching is one of the few professions in which an individual is expected to assume all the responsibilities of an experienced "pro" during the first week on the job. In this situation, a veteran teacher can be a real source of support and guidance.

Expert Teachers

What do expert teachers know that allows them to be so successful? How do they differ from beginners? Researchers are investigating how expert teachers think about their students, the subjects they teach, and the process of teaching itself. They are finding that expert teachers differ from novices in much the same way that expert physicists or chess masters differ from beginners in their field. **Expert teachers** have more elaborate systems of knowledge for understanding problems in teaching. **Novice teachers,** on the other hand, have limited knowledge. For example, when a beginning teacher is faced with students' wrong answers on math or history tests, all the wrong answers may seem about the same—simply wrong. The inexperienced teacher cannot connect other facts or ideas with the students' wrong answers. But for an expert teacher, wrong answers are part of a rich system of knowledge that could include how to recognize several types of wrong answers, the misunderstanding or lack of information behind each kind of mistake, the best way to reteach and correct the misunderstanding, materials and activities that have worked in the past, and several ways to test whether the reteaching was successful (Leinhardt, 1988; Floden & Klinzing, 1990).

Experts also work from integrated sets of principles instead of dealing with each new event as a new problem. They look for patterns revealing similarities in situations that seem quite different at first glance. Experts focus more than beginners on analyzing a problem and mentally applying different principles to develop a solution. In one study of solutions to discipline problems, the expert teachers spent quite a bit of time framing each problem, forming questions, deciding what information was necessary, and considering alternatives (Swanson, O'Conner, & Cooney, 1990).

Expert teachers have a sense of what is typical in classrooms, of what to expect during certain activities or times of the day. Many of their teaching routines have become automatic—they don't even have to think about how to distribute materials, take roll, move students in and out of groups, or assign grades. This gives the teachers more mental and physical energy for being creative and focusing on their students' progress. They also waste less class time. For example, one study found that expert math teachers could go over the previous day's work with the class in 2 or 3 minutes, compared to 15 minutes for novices (Leinhardt, 1986).

Even though these experts may have different ways of understanding their subject matter or different class routines, their knowledge is solid and thoroughly developed, enabling them to handle most questions or situations easily. They have experienced similar problems before and have noted what works. We saw with Ellen and Randy that expert teachers can improvise explanations and create new examples on the spot. They can turn students' confusion into understanding by helping the students organize and expand upon what they know. Finally, many experts continue their education, adding to their knowledge (Borko & Livingston, 1989; Sabers, Cushing, & Berliner, 1991).

So it seems that expert teachers, like expert dancers or gymnasts, have mastered a number of moves or routines that they can perform easily, almost without thinking. But they also know a great deal about their subject, so they can create new moves, improvise, and avoid trouble. And they are analytical; they can take a situation apart, diagnose the source of the problem, consider alternatives, and make decisions about what will work. Peterson and Comeaux (1989) argue that it is the quality of teachers' professional knowledge and their ability to be aware of their

Expert Teachers
Experienced, effective teachers who have developed solutions for common classroom problems. Their knowledge of teaching process and content is extensive and well organized.

Novice Teachers
Inexperienced teachers just beginning their career. They may be excellent teachers but have not yet developed a repertoire of solutions for common teaching problems or systems of well-organized knowledge about the many aspects of teaching.

FIGURE 1.1   **Expert and Novice Teachers Think about a Discipline Problem**   Experts and novices think about classroom problems in different ways. For example, an expert goes through a series of problem-solving stages that allow the expert to apply extensive knowledge about students and teaching. Novices, on the other hand, often "leap" to the first solution that comes to mind.

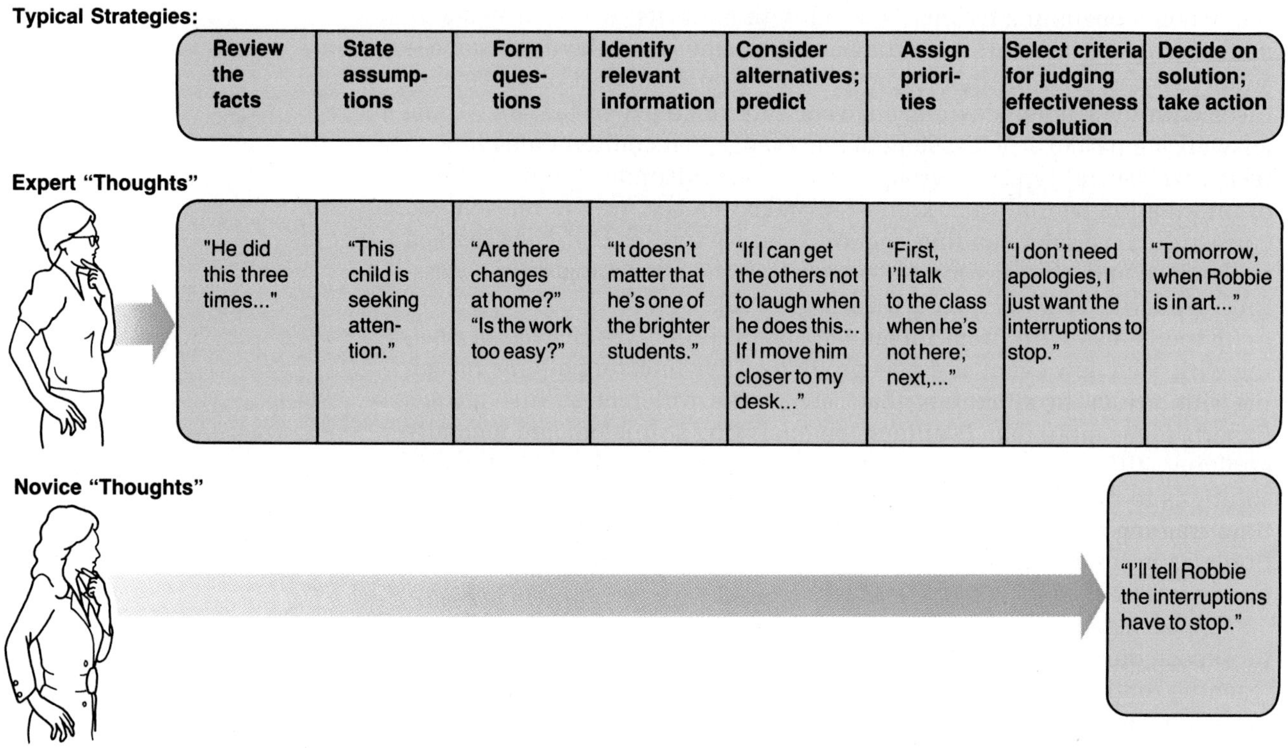

Typical Strategies:

Review the facts	State assumptions	Form questions	Identify relevant information	Consider alternatives; predict	Assign priorities	Select criteria for judging effectiveness of solution	Decide on solution; take action

Expert "Thoughts"

"He did this three times..."	"This child is seeking attention."	"Are there changes at home?" "Is the work too easy?"	"It doesn't matter that he's one of the brighter students."	"If I can get the others not to laugh when he does this... If I move him closer to my desk..."	"First, I'll talk to the class when he's not here; next,..."	"I don't need apologies, I just want the interruptions to stop."	"Tomorrow, when Robbie is in art..."

Novice "Thoughts"

"I'll tell Robbie the interruptions have to stop."

Source: Adapted from H. Swanson, J. E. O'Conner, and J. B. Cooney (1990). An information processing analysis of expert and novice teachers' problem solving. *American Educational Research Journal, 27,* Appendix B. Copyright 1990 by the American Educational Research Association. Adapted by permission of the publisher.

own thinking that makes them expert. Figure 1.1 contrasts the problem solving of experts and beginners by presenting the "thoughts" of two teachers. These thoughts are based on the findings of Swanson and associates (1990) and the experiences of my student teachers. Let's look for a moment at the knowledge of expert teachers.

Expert Knowledge

Lee Shulman (1987) has studied what teachers know, and he has identified seven areas of professional knowledge. Expert teachers know:

1. the academic subjects they teach;
2. general teaching strategies that apply in all subjects (such as the principles of classroom management, effective teaching, and evaluation that you will discover in this book);

3. the curriculum materials and programs appropriate for their subject and grade level;

4. subject-specific knowledge for teaching—special ways of teaching certain students and particular concepts, such as the best ways to explain negative numbers to lower-ability students;

5. the characteristics and cultural backgrounds of learners;

6. the settings in which students learn—pairs, small groups, teams, classes, schools, and the community;

7. the goals and purposes of teaching.

This is quite a list. Educational psychology will help you gain knowledge about general teaching strategies, learners, and settings; educational psychology is also somewhat concerned with goals and subject-specific knowledge for teaching. Obviously, one course cannot give you all the information you need to teach. In fact, a whole program of courses won't make you an expert. That takes time and experience.

How do you grow from beginning teacher to expert? Can you *learn* to be an expert teacher, or are really great teachers just "born"? Is good teaching an art or a science? Answers to this last question provide another perspective on good teaching.

TEACHING: AN ART, A SCIENCE, AND A LOT OF WORK

For years it was a favorite indoor sport of educators to debate whether teaching is an art or a science. Today, most people agree that teaching has both artistic and scientific elements. As an art, teaching calls for vision, intuition, talent, commitment, and creativity—very little of which can actually be taught. As a science, however, teaching requires knowledge and skills that can indeed be learned. Almost three decades ago, Charles Silberman described teaching this way:

> To be sure, teaching—like the practice of medicine—is very much an art, which is to say, it calls for the exercise of talent and creativity. But like medicine, it is also—or should be—a science, for it involves a repertoire of techniques, procedures, and skills that can be systematically studied and described, therefore transmitted and improved. The great teacher, like the great doctor, is the one who adds creativity and inspiration to that basic repertoire. (1966, p. 124)

Silberman's analogy to medicine is still useful today. A doctor treating a patient must use judgment, intuition, and creativity in solving the many medical problems for which there are no guaranteed answers. But the modern practice of medicine is also based on scientific theory and research. The same is true in education. The teacher who does not know what scientists have discovered about learning and instruction is like the physician who does not understand the principles of biochemistry and drug dosages. Both could make decisions that would lead inevitably to failure.

Whose Classroom Is It Anyway?

The Carnegie Forum on Education and the Economy report, *A Nation Prepared: Teachers for the 21st Century* (1986), introduced a new word to the vocabulary of educational reform—*restructuring*. The report argued that we must "restructure schools to provide a professional environment for teachers, freeing [teachers] to decide how to best meet the state and local goals for children" (p. 57). Is this recommendation becoming a reality? Is the structure of schools changing so teachers can use their expertise in deciding how to teach their students?

Point: Teachers have a bigger say.

The National Governors' Association, the National Education Association, and the National Association of Secondary School Principals have issued reports supporting teacher participation in school decisions. The National Governors' Association (1989) states that restructuring should involve (1) modifying curriculum to support higher-order thinking and problem solving, creativity, and cooperation; (2) bringing together teachers, administrators, and parents at each school to make instructional decisions; (3) creating new staff roles to make better use of the teachers' expertise; and (4) holding schools accountable for students' achievement.

The April 1990 issue of *Educational Leadership* describes many elementary and secondary schools that have radically altered curriculum, decision making, roles, and accountability systems. For example, the staff of Central Park East Secondary School decided to limit the number of class periods for its students to allow more in-depth study:

A typical week for students in grades 7–10, for example, includes several two-hour blocks of humanities and math-science, daily one-hour classes in Spanish, two to three hours of com-

Technique and Reflection: A Balance

Today the discussion about art and science in teaching has taken a new turn. Because researchers have identified a number of effective teaching techniques, some educators argue that all teachers should learn these practices and be tested on them to earn or to keep their teaching certificates. This view is consistent with an emphasis on the scientific side of teaching. Other educators believe that the mark of an excellent teacher is not the ability to apply techniques but the art of being **reflective**—thoughtful and inventive—about teaching (Schon, 1983).

Educators adopting this view tend to be more concerned with how teachers plan, solve problems, create instruction, and make decisions than they are with the specific techniques teachers apply. They believe teaching is a complicated, demanding activity that requires careful, creative thinking and a commitment to lifelong learning (Borko, 1989; Peterson & Comeaux, 1989).

As with the debate over the art and science of teaching, most people agree that teachers must be *both* technically competent and thoughtful. They must be able to use a range of known strategies, and they must also be able to invent new strategies. They must have some simple routines that work for managing classes, but they must also be willing and able to break from the routine when the situation calls for change. Without the technical skills required to give clear explanations, plan a lesson, organize and manage class rules and procedures, frame a question, lead a

Reflective Thoughtful and inventive. Reflective teachers think back over situations to analyze what they did and why and to consider how they might improve learning for their students.

munity service, and several advisory periods. During an extended lunch period and after school, students may participate in clubs, music, physical education, sports, and other activities. (O'Neil, 1990b, p. 7)

In 119 Dade County, Florida schools, administrator/teacher/parent councils have been created to redesign the schools. Three of the innovations established by these councils are Saturday classes providing extra help, enrichment, and even ballet instruction; satellite schools in local businesses; and lead teachers who receive extra pay to support and guide their colleagues.

Counterpoint: Restructuring is not working.

In 1987 the Carnegie Foundation for the Advancement of Teaching surveyed teachers across the United States to see if they felt involved in decisions at their schools. Most teachers—about 79 percent—participated in choosing textbooks, and a good number (63 percent) felt they were involved in shaping the curriculum. But only 47 percent helped to set standards for students' behavior, only 43 percent participated in designing staff development programs, and a mere 20 percent had a say in school budgets. Another finding of the survey was that participation varied greatly by state. For example, 85 percent of the teachers in Vermont helped to shape their schools' curricula, but only 40 percent of the teachers in Louisiana were involved in curriculum decisions.

Some researchers suggest that teachers must be so focused on their classrooms and students that they have little time or energy for participating in schoolwide decisions (Lortie, 1977). Other researchers suggest that teachers and administrators have a kind of agreement not to interfere in each other's "territory." In return for leaving school-level decisions to the administrators, teachers get to be autonomous in their classrooms (Corwin, 1981). Some critics fear that restructuring will require teachers to take on more responsibilities without giving them more time or resources to meet these new obligations (Conley, 1991).

discussion, or write test questions, teachers would be hopelessly ineffective. But good teachers also understand that teaching does not happen in a vacuum. New problems arise all the time, and when the old solutions do not work, something else is needed.

With the growing understanding that teaching is a complex problem-solving activity has come a call to give teachers more freedom and responsibility. A number of educational reform movements seek to involve teachers in designing the curriculum and making the decisions for their own students, as you can see in the **Point/Counterpoint** section above.

You may be thinking that all this talk about expert teachers and expert knowledge, art and science, technique and reflection, is a bit idealistic and abstract. Right now, you may have other, more down-to-earth, concerns about becoming a teacher. You are not alone!

Concerns of Beginning Teachers

In the first few years of "real" teaching, most people are concerned about their own competence. New teachers tend to lack confidence in their teaching skills, and they worry about being liked by peers and students, making a good impression, and generally surviving from day to day and from week to week. They are also enthusiastic about applying their technical skills in inventive and creative ways in their classrooms (Calderhead & Robson, 1991; Cooke & Pang, 1991; Veenman, 1984).

Beginning teachers everywhere share many other concerns as well. A review of studies conducted around the world found that beginning teachers regard maintaining classroom discipline, motivating students, accommodating differences among students, evaluating student work, and dealing with parents as the most serious challenges they face. Many teachers also experience what has been called "reality shock" when they take their first job and confront the "harsh and rude reality of everyday classroom life" (Veenman, 1984, p. 143). One source of shock may be that teachers really cannot ease into their responsibilities. On the first day of their first job, beginning teachers face the same tasks as teachers with years of experience. Student teaching, while a critical experience, does not really prepare prospective teachers for starting off a school year with a new class. And schools usually offer little chance for helpful contact between novice and experienced teachers, making mutual support and assistance difficult. Accepting that you are bound to have difficulties and worries when you start out, however, may prepare you better for the first phase of your career.

With experience, most teachers meet the challenges that seem difficult for beginners. They develop routines for making assignments, checking work, and setting rules so they don't have to spend too much time on (or even think about) these tasks. They have more time to experiment with new methods or materials. Finally, as confidence grows, seasoned teachers can focus on the students' needs. Are my students learning? Are they developing positive attitudes? Is this the best way to teach the slower learners to write a persuasive essay? At this advanced stage teachers judge their success by the successes of their students (Feiman-Nemser, 1983; Fuller 1969). Table 1.1 summarizes two views about the stages in teachers' development.

TABLE 1.1   Two Views of Stages of Teacher Development

Theorist	Fuller and Bown (1975)	Sacks and Harrington (1982)
Stages	Preteaching concerns	Anxiety
	Early concerns about survival	Entry
	Teaching situation concerns	Orientation
		Trial and error
	Concerns about pupils	Integration/consolidation
		Mastery

Theorists: F. F. Fuller & O. H. Bown, "Becoming a Teacher," in K. Ryan (Ed.), *Teacher Education,* 74th Yearbook of the National Society for the Study of Education (Chicago: University of Chicago Press, 1975), part 2, 25–52. S. R. Sacks & C. N. Harrington, *Student to Teacher: The Process of Role Transition* (Paper presented at the meeting of the American Educational Research Association, New York, March 1982).

Source: Reprinted with the permission of Macmillan Publishing Company from "Teacher Development," by Paul R. Burden, p. 317. In *Handbook of Research on Teacher Education* by W. Robert Houston, editor. Copyright © 1990 by the Association of Teacher Education.

Will I be able to control the class? This is a major concern for beginning teachers and a constant challenge for experienced teachers. Good classroom management requires energy and attention—all day long.

Of course, all experts were once beginners. How can educational psychology give you a basis for being a good beginning teacher? And can educational psychology provide the knowledge and skills needed for beginners to become experts?

THE ROLE OF EDUCATIONAL PSYCHOLOGY

We begin our consideration of the role of educational psychology by defining the term. For as long as **educational psychology** has existed—about 80 years—there have been debates about what it really is. Some people believe educational psychology is simply knowledge gained from

Educational Psychology
Discipline concerned with teaching and learning processes; applies the methods and theories of psychology and has its own as well.

psychology and applied to the activities of the classroom. Others believe it involves applying the methods of psychology to study classroom and school life (Clifford, 1984; Grinder, 1981). Many people argue that educational psychology is a distinct discipline, with its own theories, research methods, problems, and techniques. According to this view, which is generally accepted today, educational psychology is concerned primarily with (1) understanding the processes of teaching and learning and (2) developing ways of improving these processes. Educational psychologists examine learning and teaching in the laboratory, in preschools and in the home, in elementary and secondary schools, in colleges and universities, in the military and industry, and in many other settings. Whatever the situation or subjects studied, however, educational psychologists are especially concerned with applying their knowledge to improve learning and instruction.

Educational psychologists make an important distinction between learning and teaching. Much of what is known about how people learn is based on controlled research in laboratories. But knowing how people learn in the controlled environment of a laboratory does not tell us how to teach those people in the often unpredictable environment of the classroom. Theories and methods of teaching, which are based on theories of learning, must be examined and tested *outside* the laboratory. So studying how people learn is only half of the equation; the other half is studying how to teach them. Educational psychologists do both.

THE VALUE OF RESEARCH AND THEORY

Does educational psychology really have anything new to say to future teachers? After all, most teaching is just common sense, isn't it? Let's take a few minutes to examine these questions.

Is It Just Common Sense?

In many cases, the principles set forth by educational psychologists—after much thought, research, and money spent—sound pathetically obvious. People are tempted to say, and usually do say, "Everyone knows that!" Consider these examples:

Taking Turns. What method should a teacher use in selecting students to participate in a primary-grade reading class?

Commonsense Answer: Teachers should call on students randomly so that everyone will have to follow the lesson carefully. If a teacher were to use the same order every time, the students would know when their turn was coming up.

Answer Based on Research: Research by Ogden, Brophy, and Evertson (1977) indicates that the answer to this question is not so simple. In first-grade reading classes, for example, going around the circle in order and giving each child a chance to read led to better overall achievement than calling on students randomly. The system does let students figure out when their turn is coming, which gives them the opportunity to practice their own lines. This very practice, with teacher feedback, may

How should teachers select students to read out loud? Is oral reading an effective practice? Research provides some surprising perspectives on these questions.

be a more important aspect of learning to read than paying attention while others are reading, at least in the early grades. Research suggests that requiring everyone to "follow along"—to read silently as one student reads aloud—is not a good strategy for teaching reading. There are better alternatives for teaching reading than going around the circle, but if teachers choose this alternative, they should make sure that everyone has the chance for practice and feedback (Tierney, Readence, & Dishner, 1990).

Classroom Management. What should a teacher do when students are repeatedly out of their seats without permission?

Commonsense Answer: The teacher should remind students to remain in their seats each time they get up. These repeated reminders will help overactive students remember the rule. If the teacher does not remind them and lets them get away with breaking the rules, both the out-of-seat students and the rest of the class may decide the teacher is not really serious about the rule.

Answer Based on Research: In a now-classic study, Madsen, Becker, Thomas, Koser, and Plager (1968) found that the more a teacher told students to sit down when they were out of their seats, the more often the students got out of their seats without permission. When the teacher ignored students who were out of their seats and praised students who were sitting down, the rate of out-of-seat behavior dropped greatly. When the teacher returned to the previous system of telling students to sit down, the rate of out-of-seat behavior increased once again. It seems that, at least under some conditions, the more a teacher says "Sit down!" the more the students stand up!

Skipping Grades. Should a school encourage exceptionally bright students to skip grades or to enter college early?

Commonsense Answer: No! Very intelligent students who are a year or two younger than their classmates are likely to be social misfits. They are neither physically nor emotionally ready for dealing with older students and would be miserable in the social situations that are so important in school, especially in the later grades.

Answer Based on Research: Maybe. According to Kirk and Gallagher (1983), "From early admissions to school . . . to early admissions to college . . . the research studies invariably report that those children who were accelerated made adjustments as good or better than did the comparison children of similar ability" (p. 105). Whether acceleration is the best solution for a student depends on many specific individual characteristics, including the intelligence and maturity of the student, and on the other available options. For some students, skipping grades is a very good idea.

Lily Wong (1987) demonstrated that just seeing research results in writing can make them seem obvious. She selected 12 findings from research on teaching; one of them was the "taking turns" result noted above. She presented six of the findings in their correct form and six *in exactly the opposite form* to college students and to experienced teachers. Both the college students and teachers rated about half of the *wrong* findings as "obviously" correct. In a follow-up study, another group of subjects was shown the 12 findings and their opposite and asked to pick which ones were correct. For 8 of the 12 findings, the subjects chose the wrong result more often than the right one.

You may have thought that educational psychologists spend their time discovering the obvious. The examples above point out the danger of this kind of thinking. When a principle is stated in simple terms it can sound simplistic. A similar phenomenon takes place when we see a gifted dancer or athlete perform; the well-trained performer makes it look easy. But we see only the results of the training, not all the work that went into mastering the individual movements. And bear in mind that any research finding—or its opposite—may *sound* like common sense. The issue is not what sounds sensible but what is demonstrated when the principle is put to the test (Gage, 1991).

Using Research to Understand and Improve Teaching

Conducting research to test possible answers is one of two major tasks of educational psychology. The other is combining the results of various studies into theories that attempt to present a unified view of such things as teaching, learning, and development.

The Research Guide at the end of this book provides an extensive discussion of research in educational psychology. The next few pages summarize many of the key ideas and terms that you will find in the Research Guide. Your instructor may ask you to read this Research Guide before continuing to the next chapters so you will have a better understanding of how to interpret the research results you encounter throughout this course.

Descriptive Research. Educational psychologists design and conduct many different kinds of research studies in their attempts to understand teaching and learning. Some of these studies are "descriptive"; that is, their purpose is simply to describe events in a particular class or several classes. Reports of **descriptive research** often include survey results, interview responses, samples of actual classroom dialogue, or records of the class activities.

One descriptive approach, classroom **ethnography,** is borrowed from anthropology. Ethnographic methods involve describing the naturally occurring events in the life of a group and trying to understand the meaning of these events to the people involved. For example, the descriptions of expert high school mathematics teachers in the opening pages of this chapter were taken from an ethnographic study by Hilda Borko and Carol Livingston (1989). The researchers made detailed observations in the teachers' classes and analyzed these observations, along with audio recordings and information from interviews with the teachers, in order to describe differences between novice and expert teachers.

In some descriptive research, researchers carefully analyze videotapes of classes to identify recurring patterns of teacher and student behaviors. In other studies the researcher uses **participant observation** and works within the class or school to understand the actions from the perspectives of the teacher and the students. Researchers also may employ case studies. A **case study** investigates in depth how a teacher plans courses, for example, or how a student tries to learn specific material.

Correlations. Often the results of descriptive studies include reports of **correlations.** We will take a minute to examine this concept, because you will encounter many correlations in the coming chapters. A correlation is a number that indicates both the *strength* and the *direction* of a relationship between two events or measurements. Correlations range from 1.00 to −1.00. The closer the correlation is to either 1.00 or −1.00, the stronger the relationship. For example, the correlation between height and weight is about .70 (a fairly strong relationship); the correlation between height and number of languages spoken is about .00 (no relationship at all).

The sign of the correlation tells the direction of the relationship. A **positive correlation** indicates that the two factors increase or decrease together. As one gets larger, so does the other. Height and weight are positively correlated because taller height tends to be associated with greater weight. A **negative correlation** means that increases in one factor are related to decreases in the other. For example, the correlation between outside temperature and the weight of clothing worn is negative, since people tend to wear clothing of decreasing weight as the temperature increases.

It is important to note that correlations do not prove cause and effect. Height and weight are correlated—taller people tend to weigh more than shorter people. But gaining weight obviously does not cause you to grow taller. Knowing a person's height simply allows you to make a general

Descriptive Research Studies that collect detailed information about specific situations, often using observation, surveys, interviews, recordings, or a combination of these methods.

Ethnography A descriptive approach to research that focuses on life within a group and tries to understand the meaning of events to the people involved.

Participant Observation A method for conducting descriptive research in which the researcher becomes a participant in the situation in order to better understand life in that group.

Case Study Intensive study of one person or one situation.

Correlations Statistical descriptions of how closely two variables are related.

Positive Correlation A relationship between two variables in which the two increase or decrease together. Example: calorie intake and weight gain.

Negative Correlation A relationship between two variables in which a high value on one is associated with a low value on the other. Example: height and distance from top of head to the ceiling.

prediction about that person's weight. Educational psychologists identify correlations so they can make predictions about important events in the classroom.

Experimentation. A second type of research—**experimentation**—allows educational psychologists to go beyond predictions and actually study cause and effect. Instead of just observing and describing an existing situation, the investigators introduce changes and note the results. First a number of comparable groups of subjects are created. In psychological research, the term **subjects** generally refers to the people being studied—such as teachers or eighth graders—not to subjects like math or science. One common way to make sure that groups of subjects are essentially the same is to assign each subject to a group using a **random** procedure. Random means each subject has an equal chance to be in any group.

In one or more of these groups, the experimenters change some aspect of the situation to see if this change or "treatment" has an expected effect. The results in each group are then compared. Usually statistical tests are conducted to see if the differences between the groups are significant. When differences are described as **statistically significant,** it means that they probably did not happen simply by chance. A number of the studies we will examine attempt to identify cause-and-effect relationships by asking questions such as this: If teachers ignore students who are out of their seats without permission and praise students who are working hard at their desks (cause), will students spend more time working at their desks (effect)?

In many cases, both descriptive and experimental research occur together. The study by Ogden, Brophy, and Evertson (1977) described at the beginning of this section is a good example. In order to answer questions about the relationship between how students are selected to read in a primary-grade class and their achievement in reading, these investigators first observed students and teachers in a number of classrooms and then measured the reading achievement of the students. They found that having students read in a predictable order was associated or correlated with gains in reading scores. With a simple correlation such as this, however, the researchers could not be sure that the strategy was actually causing the effect. In the second part of the study, Ogden and her colleagues asked several teachers to call on each student in turn. They then compared reading achievement in these groups with achievement in groups where teachers used other strategies. This second part of the research was thus an experimental study.

Theories for Teaching. The major goal of educational psychology is understanding teaching and learning, and research is a primary tool. Reaching this goal is a slow process; there are very few landmark studies that answer a question once and for all. Human beings are too complicated. Instead, research in educational psychology examines limited aspects of a situation—perhaps a few variables at a time, or life in one or two classrooms. If enough studies are completed in a certain area and findings repeatedly point to the same conclusions, we eventually arrive at a **principle.** This is the term for an established relationship between

Experimentation Research method in which variables are manipulated and the effects recorded.

Subjects People or animals studied.

Random Without any definite pattern; following no rule.

Statistically Significant Not likely to be a chance occurrence.

Principle Established relationship between factors.

two or more factors—between a certain teaching strategy, for example, and student achievement.

Another tool for building a better understanding of the teaching and learning processes is theory. The commonsense notion of *theory* (as in "Oh well, it was only a theory") is "a guess or hunch." But the scientific meaning of **theory** is quite different. "A *theory* in science is an interrelated set of concepts that is used to explain a body of data and to make predictions about the results of future experiments" (Stanovich, 1992, p. 21). Given a number of established principles, educational psychologists have developed explanations for the relationships among many variables and even whole systems of relationships. There are theories to explain how motivation works, how differences in intelligence occur, and, as noted earlier, how people learn.

Few theories explain and predict perfectly. In this book, you will see many examples of educational psychologists taking different theoretical positions and disagreeing on the overall explanations of such issues as learning and motivation. Because no one theory offers all the answers, it makes sense to consider what each has to offer.

So why, you may ask, is it necessary to deal with theories? Why not just stick to principles? The answer is that both are useful. Principles of classroom management, for example, will give you help with specific problems. A good theory of classroom management, on the other hand, will give you a new way of thinking about discipline problems; it will give you tools for creating solutions to many different problems and for predicting what might work in new situations. A major goal of this book is to provide you with the best and the most useful theories for teaching—those that have solid evidence behind them. Although you may prefer some theories over others, each can be considered as a way of understanding the challenges teachers face.

THE CONTENTS OF THIS BOOK

Now that we have explored the role of theory and research, let us turn to a consideration of the topics studied by educational psychologists.

A Quick Tour

Part One of this text focuses on the students—or, more specifically, on the ways in which students develop. Human development is an important topic in educational psychology. As you will see, students of different ages bring a wide range of abilities and ways of thinking to the classroom. Besides having their own characteristic styles of thinking, students of different ages also face distinct challenges in social and emotional development. As a teacher you will want to take into account the mental, physical, emotional, and social abilities and limitations of your students. To do this, you must know something about the general patterns of development in these areas.

Part Two examines variations in development—particularly variations in learning abilities and learning styles. Classrooms today are be-

Theory Integrated statement of principles that attempts to explain a phenomenon and make predictions.

TABLE 1.2   **What Would You Like to Know? Educational Psychology Can Help**

Sample Questions	Sources of Information
■ What is good teaching? ■ Why study educational psychology? ■ How can a teacher use research and theory?	Educational Psychology and the Classroom Teacher, xxviii
■ How might my students' thinking processes differ from my own? ■ What is the emotional and social world of my students like? ■ How can I help my students develop self-esteem? ■ What can I do when a student is terribly upset about his or her parents' divorce?	Part One: Human Development: A Framework for Teachers, 24
■ What is intelligence and how can it be improved? ■ What if I am assigned a student who is mildly retarded? ■ How do I teach science to students who don't speak my language? ■ How can I help students from different cultures feel at home in my class?	Part Two: Individual Variations, 108
■ What causes some students to develop fears about school? ■ Should I use punishment in my classes?	Part Three: Learning Theories and Teaching Practice, 192

coming more and more diverse. Teachers are expected to work with students with learning disabilities and visual or hearing impairments, for example, and with both the retarded and the gifted. And most classrooms today are multicultural, with students who speak different languages and come from a variety of cultural backgrounds. Teachers need to understand and appreciate these differences.

Having introduced the students, we will move to one of the most important topics in both educational psychology and the classroom: human learning. Part Three explores the two main approaches to the study of learning, the behavioral and the cognitive perspectives. We will also see how these approaches can be applied in a number of very practical ways, including strategies for classroom management and instruction in various subject areas.

Having covered the dual foundations of teaching; the students and the processes of learning, we can concentrate in Parts Four, Five, and Six on actual practice. Part Four examines theories of motivation and their applications to teaching and then takes a careful look at how to organize

TABLE 1.2 continued	

Sample Questions	Sources of Information
■ Why do students remember some things and forget others? ■ How can I study more effectively and help my students do the same? ■ How can I encourage students to be creative? ■ Will students use what I teach them?	Part Three: Learning Theories and Teaching Practice, 192
■ Can algebra ever be as interesting as sex education? ■ How can I help students to take charge of their own learning? ■ How can I deal with a really defiant student? ■ What should I do when angry parents accuse me of treating their child unfairly?	Part Four: Motivation and Classroom Management, 334
■ Where do I start in planning my first class? ■ Is lecture better than discussion or individualized instruction? ■ What makes a teacher effective?	Part Five: Planning and Teaching, 434
■ How can the results of standardized tests help me teach? ■ Are grades really necessary? ■ How should I test my students?	Part Six: Evaluating Student Learning, 504

and manage a classroom. Since teachers deal with individuals as well as groups, we will spend some time discussing communication and interpersonal relationships. The focus is on creating conditions that keep students involved and learning.

In Part Five we look at instruction: how to set goals, select methods, plan activities, arrange the setting, group students, and teach effectively. We will draw heavily from research about how effective teachers actually operate.

In Part Six we consider how to evaluate what has been taught. Here we will look at standardized tests, teacher-made tests, grading systems, and various alternatives to the traditional systems of evaluation.

How This Book Can Help You

In Table 1.2 you will find a list of sample questions drawn from different parts of this book. The questions do not begin to cover the many topics that will be included in each part, but they will give you a sense of the kind of information you will encounter. You will find a more extensive list of questions with page references at the front of this text following the student preface.

The study of educational psychology involves both content and process. The content of facts, principles, and theories adds to your professional knowledge for teaching. The process aspect of educational psychology helps you think critically about teaching so you can become a researcher on your own effectiveness.

Becoming an expert teacher takes time and experience, but you can start now by becoming a good beginner. You can develop a repertoire of effective principles and practices for your first years of teaching so that some activities quickly become automatic. You can also develop the habit of questioning and analyzing these accepted practices and your own teaching so you can solve new problems when they arise. You can learn to look behind the effective techniques identified in research to ask why: Why did this approach work with these students? What else might be as good or better? The answers to these questions and your ability to analyze the situations are much more important than the specific techniques themselves. As you ask and answer questions, you will be refining your personal theories of teaching.

My goal in writing this book is to help you become an excellent beginning teacher, one who can both apply and improve many techniques. Even more important, I hope this book will cause you to think about students and teaching in new ways, so you will have the foundation for becoming an expert as you gain experience.

SUMMARY

In this introductory chapter we have examined good teaching by looking in the classrooms of expert teachers and considering the research on what distinguishes experts from beginners. You also saw an overview of the field of educational psychology.

What Is Good Teaching?

It takes time and experience to become an expert teacher. For experts, accomplishing many classroom tasks has become automatic, so that routines are smooth. Less class time is wasted. Experts can apply well-practiced solutions or readily invent new ones. They have a rich store of well-organized knowledge about the many specific situations of teaching. This includes knowledge about the subjects they teach, their students, general teaching strategies, subject-specific ways of teaching, settings for learning, curriculum materials, and the goals of education.

Teaching: An Art, a Science, and a Lot of Work

Teaching is both an art and a science. Effective teaching requires an understanding of research findings on learning and instruction as well as knowledge of effective techniques and routines. Teaching also calls for the creativity, talent, and judgment of an artist.

Learning to teach is a gradual process. The concerns and problems of teachers change as they progress. During the beginning years, attention tends to be focused on survival. Maintaining discipline, motivating students, evaluating students' work, and dealing with parents are universal concerns for beginning teachers. The more experienced teacher can move on to concerns about professional growth and effectiveness with a wide range of students.

THE ROLE OF EDUCATIONAL PSYCHOLOGY

The goals of educational psychology are to understand and to improve the teaching and learning processes. Educational psychologists develop knowledge and methods; they also use the knowledge and methods of psychology and other related disciplines. Two very important aspects of educational psychology are its scientific approach and its concern with the practical application of research findings to the classroom.

THE VALUE OF RESEARCH AND THEORY

Both descriptive studies and experimental research can provide valuable information for teachers. Correlations allow you to predict events that are likely to occur in the classroom; experimental studies can indicate cause-and-effect relationships and should help you implement useful changes.

Educational psychology involves content and process. The findings from research offer a number of possible answers to specific problems, and the theories offer perspectives for analyzing almost any situation that may arise. The process of analyzing research and theory will encourage you to think critically about teaching.

KEY TERMS AND CONCEPTS

case study, p. 15
correlations, p. 15
descriptive research, p. 15
educational psychology, p. 11
ethnography, p. 15
experimentation, p. 16

expert teachers, p. 5
negative correlation, p. 15
novice teachers, p. 5
participant observation, p. 15
positive correlation, p. 15
principle, p. 16

random, p. 16
reflective, p. 8
statistically significant, p. 16
subjects, p. 16
theory, p. 17

WHAT WOULD YOU DO?

It is your second year as a teacher in Ben Franklin Middle School. The district has just received money from the state and a private foundation to give three awards in your school for "excellence in teaching." You have been assigned to a committee that will make recommendations to the principal about how to choose the recipients of these awards. You have a week before the first meeting. How would you prepare? Draft a position paper listing your ideas for the selection criteria. How would you back up your recommendations?

COOPERATIVE LEARNING ACTIVITY

With four or five other members of your class who plan to teach the same grade level as you, develop a procedure and criteria for giving an "excellence in teaching" award. Present your group's plan to the class and be prepared to explain why your system is appropriate.

TEACHERS' CASEBOOK

Why did you choose teaching as a career? Would you choose it again?

TO BECOME A VALUED PROFESSIONAL

I recommend the teaching profession to both my high school students and student teachers. First, teaching is never dull. Each year we meet an entirely new cast of characters, individuals who are unique and who represent both challenge and opportunity. Certainly at the secondary level, to observe the development from gawky adolescent in 9th grade to young adult at graduation is gratifying. To observe the concomitant development of the mind is even more rewarding. Yes, it is tiring, hectic, and often frustrating, but time flies. Second, teaching allows for continual refinement of our own techniques. Good teachers do not do things the same way each year and with each class. We are regularly provided with the opportunity for which researchers in the hard sciences must continually write grant proposals. We have the freedom to function professionally as teacher-researchers, exploring diverse ways to stimulate and discipline young minds. Third, teaching allows us to do what we ask of our students; that is, continue to learn. Much has been written concerning the deadly and debilitating boredom that accompanies jobs consisting primarily of repetitive tasks. Our profession not only encourages, it requires continuous self-education. Every history book I read is professional preparation. However, this reading also brings with it personal edification and enjoyment. We must be living models of the importance of lifelong learning, and that, indeed, is a professional perk. Finally, teaching can be hailed as one of the most gender liberating of the professions. The past decades have seen women make enormous gains in the battle to be accepted as men's equals, intellectually and professionally. Yes, teaching is demanding; it requires many hours beyond those of the school day. Yet its schedule does not force men and women to choose between a career and a family. While in the 1950s teaching was a trap to hold women back, in the 1990s it offers both men and women the liberating opportunity to both raise a family and be part of an intellectually stimulating and respected profession.

Karen Beechy Kreider, *Pennsylvania 1991 Teacher of the Year*
Central High School, Philadelphia, Pennsylvania

TO INFLUENCE AND GUIDE

The profile of a "typical" teacher frequently presents him or her as overworked, underpaid, frustrated, tired, and lacking recognition. All human beings, teachers included, need to feel valued, respected, fulfilled. As a human being, I sought a profession that would challenge and fulfill me at the same time. A summer as a counselor at a camp for handicapped boys convinced me that these youngsters had minds that needed healing as well as nurturing. That summer led me to conclude that two important components of health are attitude and knowledge. The knowledge that I had the opportunity to influence the intellectual, emotional, physical, mental, and psychological development and well-being of my students, as well as their attitudes and values, challenged me to expand my own horizons. Perhaps teaching is not financially rewarding; but would I still make it my career choice if I had to choose again? You bet—in a heartbeat! Why? Because I anticipate tomorrow knowing that today I gave my students my best—knowing that I made a difference today—knowing that despite the fatigue and the frustration, I'm valued, I'm respected, I'm fulfilled.

Laura Atkinson, *Special Education Teacher*
Chapel Hill, North Carolina

BECOMING AN EXPERT

Did you reach a point after you had been teaching for a while when you realized that you had learned to "think like a teacher"? What helped you become more expert in making decisions about teaching?

RELYING LESS ON COMMERCIAL TEXTS

My initial awareness that I had begun to "think like a teacher" occurred when I realized that textbooks and teacher's guides were not the panacea for classroom instruction. I discovered that the textbooks were guides or road maps, but not the vehicles for student learning. I began to seek additional sources of curriculum and to develop materials to increase motivation and to explore the interrelationships among subjects. Working collectively and cooperatively with colleagues enhanced my decision-making expertise concerning teaching. Additional in-service training was instrumental in my development as a professional educator.

Bruce D. Fisher, *California 1991 Teacher of the Year*
Fortuna Elementary School, Fortuna, California

CREATING CURRICULUM CONTENT

After several years of teaching straight from the textbooks, I began to realize that in many cases, my students were able to learn more information and retain it better when I trusted my own judgment about how and what to teach. I began to use textbook manuals as guides to the curriculum and textbooks as one resource. I learned to create units of study around the same topics, but I was able to bring content alive for my students, to involve them in the learning process, and to make learning more meaningful. It took several years for me to develop the self-confidence necessary to take control of the curriculum and learning process. However, that experience allowed me to use my gifts as a teacher fully and to regain the excitement of learning for myself and my students.

Sarah Gustafsen, *Florida 1991 Teacher of the Year*
The Okeechobee Center, Okeechobee, Florida

METAPHOR FOR TEACHING

What metaphor for teaching would you use to complete the following sentence: "Good teaching is _____"? Why did you choose this metaphor?

LIKE GOOD LIVING

"Good teaching is like good living"

During my late teens and early twenties, I had to have many surgical procedures requiring lengthy hospital stays. After one of these procedures, I landed in intensive care with a serious complication. Fearing death, I vowed to make the most of my life when and if I recovered. In my quest for the most meaningful life I could live, I found teaching! Teaching is the metaphor of my life. It is the very opportunity to create and share my love of life. My life has meaning because I can give it away, and therefore, receive it back in every student I touch.

Recently, I had a conversation with a student with whom I had lost contact. She had moved on to high school and was preparing to graduate. She told me that she was going on to college to become a math teacher due to my inspiration. She thanked me for inspiring her to make something out of her life. Ultimately, therein lies the reward for teaching—I made a difference! Knowing this, I am charged and inspired to touch and influence, over and over again.

Stephen C. Ellwood IV, *Maine 1991 Teacher of the Year*
St. Francis Elementary School, St. Francis, Maine

2 COGNITIVE AND LANGUAGE DEVELOPMENT

How does the mind of the average 8-year-old work? What about the mind of the average 14-year-old? Can you explain geometry to second graders? Can you explain existentialism to seventh graders? The material in this chapter will help you answer these questions and many others about how young people think and how their thinking changes over time. These changes in thinking and understanding are called cognitive development.

In this chapter we will begin with a discussion of the general principles of human development. Then we will examine the ideas of two of the most influential cognitive developmental theorists, Jean Piaget and Lev Vygotsky. Piaget's ideas have implications for teachers about what their students can learn and when the students are ready to learn it. But there are important criticisms of his ideas that we will examine as well.

The work of Lev Vygotsky, a Russian psychologist, is becoming more and more influential today. His theory highlights the important role played by teachers and parents in the cognitive development of the child. Finally, we will explore language development and discuss the role of the school in developing and enriching language skills. One approach to language development is through holistic language programs. These programs emphasize learning language by using it to solve personally relevant problems.

By the time you have completed this chapter, you should be able to do the following:

- State three general principles of human development and give examples of each.
- List Piaget's four stages of cognitive development.
- Explain how children's thinking differs at each stage of development.
- Summarize the implications of Piaget's theory for teaching students of different ages.
- Contrast Piaget's, Fischer's, and Vygotsky's ideas about cognitive development.
- Describe briefly the stages by which children learn language.
- Suggest ways a teacher can help children expand their language use and comprehension.
- List possible elements for a whole-language program.

WHAT DO YOU THINK?

Think for a moment about how you would explain the concept of "symbol" to a 6-year-old and to a 14-year-old. Would you use words? Pictures? Specific examples? What kind? What do you know about how younger and older children differ in their thinking?

A DEFINITION OF DEVELOPMENT

The term **development** in its most general psychological sense refers to certain changes that occur in human beings (or animals) between conception and death. The term is not applied to all changes, but rather to those that appear in orderly ways and remain for a reasonably long period of time. A temporary change due to a brief illness, for example, is not considered to be a part of development. Psychologists also make a value judgment in determining which changes qualify as development. The changes, at least those that occur early in life, are generally assumed to be for the better and to result in behavior that is more adaptive, more organized, more effective, and more complex (Mussen, Conger, & Kagan, 1984).

Human development can be divided into a number of different aspects. **Physical development,** as you might guess, deals with changes in the body. **Personal development** is the term generally used for changes in an individual's personality. **Social development** refers to changes in the way an individual relates to others. And **cognitive development** refers to changes in thinking.

Many changes during development are simply matters of growth and maturation. **Maturation** refers to changes that occur naturally and spontaneously and that are, to a large extent, genetically programmed. Such changes emerge over time and are relatively unaffected by the environment, except in cases of malnutrition or severe illness. Much of a person's physical development falls into this category. Other changes are brought about through learning, as individuals interact with their environment. Such changes make up a large part of a person's social development. But what about the development of thinking and personality? Most psychologists agree that in these areas, both maturation and interaction with the environment (or *nature* and *nurture,* as they are sometimes called) are important, but they disagree about the amount of emphasis to place on each.

Although there is disagreement about what is involved in development and about the way it takes place, there are a few general principles almost all theorists would support.

1. *People develop at different rates.* In your own classroom, you will have a whole range of examples of different developmental rates. Some students will be larger, better coordinated, or more mature in their thinking and social relationships. Others will be much slower to ma-

Development Orderly, adaptive changes we go through from conception to death.

Physical Development Changes in body structure and function over time.

Personal Development Changes in personality that take place as one grows.

Social Development Changes over time in the ways we relate to others.

Cognitive Development Gradual, orderly changes by which mental processes become more complex and sophisticated.

Maturation Genetically programmed, naturally occurring changes over time.

ture in these areas. Except in rare cases of very rapid or very slow development, such differences are normal and to be expected in any large group of students.

2. *Development is relatively orderly.* People tend to develop certain abilities before others. In infancy they sit before they walk, babble before they talk, and see the world through their own eyes before they can begin to imagine how others see it. In school, they will master addition before algebra, *Bambi* before Shakespeare, and so on. Theorists may disagree on exactly what comes before what, but they all seem to find a relatively logical progression.

3. *Development takes place gradually.* Very rarely do changes appear overnight. A student who cannot manipulate a pencil or answer a hypothetical question may well develop this ability, but the change is likely to take time.

PIAGET'S THEORY OF COGNITIVE DEVELOPMENT

During the past half century, the Swiss psychologist Jean Piaget devised a model describing how humans go about making sense of their world by gathering and organizing information (Piaget, 1954, 1963, 1970). We will examine Piaget's ideas closely, because they provide an explanation of the development of thinking from infancy to adulthood.

According to Piaget (1954), certain ways of thinking that are quite simple for an adult are not so simple for a child. Sometimes all you need to do to teach a new concept is to give a student a few basic facts as background. At other times, however, all the background facts in the world are useless. The student simply is not ready to learn the concept. With some students, you can discuss the general causes of civil wars and then ask why they think the American Civil War broke out in 1861. But suppose the students respond with "When is 1861?" Obviously their concepts of time are different from your own. They may think, for example, that they will someday catch up to a sibling in age, or they may confuse the past and the future.

Influences on Development

As you can see, cognitive development is much more than the addition of new facts and ideas to an existing store of information. According to Piaget, our thinking processes change radically, though slowly, from birth to maturity. Why do these changes occur? Underlying Piaget's theory is the assumption that we constantly strive to make sense of the world. How do we do this? Piaget identified four factors—biological maturation, activity, social experiences, and equilibration—that interact to influence changes in thinking (Piaget, 1970). Most developmental theories include maturation, activity, and experience. Let's briefly examine these three factors.

One of the most important influences on the way we make sense of the world is *maturation,* the unfolding of the biological changes that are genetically programmed in each human being at conception. Parents and teachers have little impact on this aspect of cognitive development.

Jean Piaget was a Swiss psychologist whose insightful descriptions of children's thinking changed the way we understand cognitive development.

Organization Ongoing process of arranging information and experience into mental systems or categories.

Adaptation Adjustment to the environment.

Schemes Mental systems or categories of perception and experience.

Activity is another influence. With physical maturation comes the increasing ability to act on the environment and learn from it. When a young child's coordination is reasonably developed, for example, the child may discover principles about balance by experimenting with a seesaw. So as we act on the environment—as we explore, test, observe, and eventually organize information—we are likely to alter our thinking processes at the same time.

As we develop, we are also interacting with the people around us. According to Piaget, our cognitive development is influenced by *social transmission,* or learning from others. Without social transmission, we would need to reinvent all the knowledge already offered by our culture. The amount people can learn from social transmission varies according to their stage of cognitive development.

Maturation, activity, and social transmission all work together to influence cognitive development. How do we respond to these influences?

Basic Tendencies in Thinking

As a result of his early research in biology, Piaget concluded that all species inherit two basic tendencies, or "invariant functions." The first of these tendencies is toward **organization**—the combining, arranging, recombining, and rearranging of behaviors and thoughts into coherent systems. The second tendency is toward **adaptation,** or adjusting to the environment.

Organization. Thus, according to Piaget, people are born with a tendency to organize their thinking processes into psychological structures. These psychological structures are our systems for understanding and interacting with the world. Simple structures are continually combined and coordinated to become more sophisticated and thus more effective. Very young infants, for example, can either look at an object or grasp it when it comes in contact with their hands. They cannot coordinate looking and grasping at the same time. As they develop, however, infants organize these two separate behavioral structures into a coordinated higher-level structure of looking at, reaching for, and grasping the object. They can, of course, still use each structure separately (Ginsburg & Opper, 1988).

Piaget gave a special name to these structures. In his theory, they are called **schemes.** Schemes are the basic building blocks of thinking. They are organized systems of actions or thought that allow us to represent mentally or "think about" the objects and events in our world. Schemes may be very small and specific—the sucking-through-a-straw scheme or the recognizing-a-rose scheme, for example. Or they may be larger and more general—the drinking scheme or the categorizing-plants scheme. As a person's thinking processes become more organized and new schemes develop, behavior also becomes more sophisticated and better suited to the environment.

Adaptation. In addition to the tendency to organize their psychological structures, people also inherit the tendency to adapt to their environment. Piaget believed that from the moment of birth, a person begins to look for ways to adapt more satisfactorily. Two basic processes are involved in adaptation: assimilation and accommodation.

Assimilation takes place when people use their existing schemes to make sense of events in their world. Assimilation involves trying to understand something new by fitting it into what we already know. At times we may have to distort the new information to make it fit. For example, the first time many children see a skunk, they call it a "kitty." They try to match the new experience with an existing scheme for identifying animals.

Accommodation occurs when a person must change existing schemes to respond to a new situation. If data cannot be made to fit any existing schemes, then more appropriate structures must be developed. We adjust our thinking to fit the new information, instead of adjusting the information to fit our thinking. Children demonstrate accommodation when they add the scheme for recognizing skunks to their other systems for identifying animals.

People adapt to their increasingly complex environments by using existing schemes whenever these schemes work (assimilation) and by modifying and adding to their schemes when something new is needed (accommodation). In fact, both processes are required most of the time. Even using an established pattern like sucking through a straw may require some accommodation if the straw is of a different size or length than the type you are used to. If you have tried drinking juice from box packages, you know that you have to add a new skill to your sucking scheme—don't squeeze the box or you will shoot juice through the straw, straight up into the air. Whenever new experiences are assimilated into an existing scheme, the scheme is enlarged and changed somewhat, so assimilation involves some accommodation.

There are also times when neither assimilation nor accommodation is used. If people encounter something that is too unfamiliar, they may ignore it. Experience is filtered to fit the kind of thinking a person is doing at a given time. For example, if you overhear a conversation in a foreign language, you probably will not try to make sense of the exchange unless you have some knowledge of the language.

Equilibration. According to Piaget, organizing, assimilating, and accommodating can be seen as a kind of complex balancing act. In his theory, the actual changes in thinking take place through the process of **equilibration**—the act of searching for a balance. Piaget assumed that people continually test the adequacy of their thinking processes in order to achieve that balance.

Briefly, the process of equilibration works like this. If we apply a particular scheme to an event or situation and the scheme works, then equilibrium exists. If the scheme does not produce a satisfying result, then **disequilibrium** exists, and we become uncomfortable. This motivates us to keep searching for a solution through assimilation and accommodation, and thus our thinking changes and moves ahead. In order to maintain a balance between our schemes for understanding the world and the data the world provides, we continually assimilate new information using existing schemes and accommodate our thinking whenever unsuccessful attempts to assimilate produce disequilibrium.

How are assimilation and accommodation involved in using this straw? Can the girl respond to this straw exactly as she does to a conventional one?

Assimilation Fitting new information into existing schemes.

Accommodation Altering existing schemes or creating new ones in response to new information.

Equilibration Search for mental balance between cognitive schemes and information from the environment.

Disequilibrium In Piaget's theory, the "out-of-balance" state that occurs when a person realizes that his or her current ways of thinking are not working to solve a problem or understand a situation.

Four Stages of Cognitive Development

Now we turn to the actual differences that Piaget hypothesized for children as they grow. Piaget's four stages of cognitive development are called sensorimotor, preoperational, concrete operational, and formal operational. Piaget believed that all people pass through the same four stages in exactly the same order. These stages are generally associated with specific ages, as shown in Table 2.1. When you see ages linked to stages, remember that these are only general guidelines and not labels for all children of a certain age. Piaget was interested in the kinds of thinking abilities people are able to use, not in labeling. Often, people can use one level of thinking to solve one kind of problem and a different level to solve another. Piaget noted that individuals may go through long periods of transition between stages; and a person may show characteristics of one stage in one situation but show characteristics of a higher or lower stage in other situations. So knowing a student's age is never a guarantee that you know how the child will think in every situation (Ginsburg & Opper, 1988).

Infancy: The Sensorimotor Stage. The earliest period is called the **sensorimotor** stage because development at this stage is based on information obtained from the senses (sensori) and from the actions or body movements (motor) of the infant.

The infant's greatest developmental conquest is the realization that objects in the environment exist whether the baby perceives them or not. This basic understanding, called **object permanence,** arises from many activities with and observations of objects and people appearing, disappearing, and reappearing. As most parents discover, before infants develop object permanence, it is relatively easy to take something away from them. The trick is to distract them and remove the object while they are not looking—"out of sight, out of mind." The older infant who searches for the ball that has rolled out of sight or cries for the toy sneakily removed by a parent is indicating an understanding that the objects still exist though they can't be seen.

A second major accomplishment in the sensorimotor period is the beginning of logical, **goal-directed actions.** Think of the familiar container toy for babies. It is usually plastic, has a lid, and contains several colorful items that can be dumped out and replaced. A 6-month-old baby is likely to become frustrated trying to get to the toys inside. An older child who has mastered the basics of the sensorimotor stage will probably be able to deal with the toy in an orderly fashion. Through trial and error the child will slowly build a "container toy" scheme: (1) get the lid off; (2) turn the container upside down; (3) shake if the items jam; (4) watch the items fall on the floor. Separate lower-level schemes have been organized into a higher-level scheme.

The child is soon able to reverse this action by refilling the container. Learning to reverse actions is a basic accomplishment of the sensorimotor stage. As we will soon see, however, learning to reverse thinking—that is, learning to imagine the reverse of a sequence of actions—takes much longer.

Sensorimotor Involving the senses and motor activity.

Object Permanence The understanding that objects have a separate, permanent existence.

Goal-Directed Actions Deliberate actions toward a goal.

TABLE 2.1 Piaget's Stages of Cognitive Development

Stage	Approximate Age	Characteristics
Sensorimotor	0–2 years	Begins to make use of imitation, memory, and thought. Begins to recognize that objects do not cease to exist when they are hidden. Moves from reflex actions to goal-directed activity.
Preoperational	2–7 years	Gradually develops use of language and ability to think in symbolic form. Able to think operations through logically in one direction. Has difficulties seeing another person's point of view.
Concrete operational	7–11 years	Able to solve concrete (hands-on) problems in logical fashion. Understands laws of conservation and is able to classify and seriate. Understands reversibility.
Formal operational	11–15 years	Able to solve abstract problems in logical fashion. Becomes more scientific in thinking. Develops concerns about social issues, identity.

Source: Adapted from *Piaget's Theory of Cognitive and Affective Development* by Barry J. Wadsworth, 4th ed. Copyright © 1971, 1979, 1984, 1989 by Longman Publishing Group. Reprinted with permission from Longman Publishing Group.

Early Childhood to the Early Elementary Years: The Preoperational Stage. By the end of the sensorimotor stage, the child can use many action schemes. As long as these schemes remain tied to physical actions, however, they are of no use in recalling the past, keeping track of information, or planning. For this, children need what Piaget called **operations,** or actions that are carried out and reversed mentally rather than physically. The stage after sensorimotor is called **preoperational,** because the child has not yet mastered these mental operations but is moving toward mastery.

According to Piaget, the first step from action to thinking is the *internalization* of action—performing an action mentally rather than physically. The first type of thinking that is separate from action involves making action schemes symbolic. The ability to form and use symbols—words, gestures, signs, images, and so on—is thus a major accomplishment of the preoperational period and moves children closer to mastering the mental operations of the next stage. This ability to work with symbols, such as using the word "bicycle" or a picture of a bicycle to stand for a real bicycle that is not actually present, is called the **semiotic function.**

The child's earliest use of symbols is in pretending or miming. Children who are not yet able to talk will often use action symbols—pretending to drink from an empty cup or touching a comb to their hair, showing that they know what each object is for. This behavior also shows that their schemes are becoming more general and less tied to specific actions. The

Operations Actions a person carries out by thinking them through instead of literally performing the actions.

Preoperational The stage before a child masters logical mental operations.

Semiotic Function The ability to use symbols—language, pictures, signs, gestures, etc.—to represent actions or objects mentally.

Pretend games play an important role in children's cognitive development. Often, when children pretend, they use objects in a symbolic way, to "stand for" other objects. A wooden table can become a stove or a tent, for example.

eating scheme, for example, may be used in playing house. During the preoperational stage we also see the rapid development of that very important symbol system, language. Between the ages of 2 and 4, most children enlarge their vocabulary from about 200 to 2,000 words.

As the child moves through the preoperational stage, the developing ability to think about objects in symbolic form remains somewhat limited to thinking in one direction only or using *one-way logic*. It is very difficult for the child to "think backwards" or imagine how to reverse the steps in a task.

Reversible thinking is involved in many tasks that are difficult for the preoperational child, such as the **conservation** of matter. Conservation is the principle that the amount or number of something remains the same even if the arrangement or appearance is changed, as long as nothing is added and nothing is taken away. You know that if you tear a piece of paper into several pieces, you will still have the same amount of paper. To prove this, you know that you can reverse the process by taping the pieces back together.

A classic example of difficulty with conservation is found in the preoperational child's response to the following Piagetian task. Leah, a 5-year-old, is shown two identical glasses, both short and wide in shape. Both have exactly the same amount of colored water in them. The experimenter asks Leah if each glass has the same amount of water, and she answers, "Yes." The experimenter then pours the water from one of the glasses into a tall, narrow glass and asks Leah again if each glass has the same amount of water. Now she is likely to insist that there is more water in the tall, narrow glass, because the water level is higher. Notice, by the way, that Leah shows a basic understanding of identity (it's the

Reversible Thinking Thinking backward, from the end to the beginning.

Conservation Principle that some characteristics of an object remain the same despite changes in appearance.

Guidelines

Teaching the Preoperational Child

Use concrete props and visual aids whenever possible.

Examples

1. When you discuss concepts such as "part," "whole," or "one-half," use shapes on a felt board or cardboard "pizzas" to demonstrate.
2. Let children add and subtract with sticks, rocks, or colored chips.

Make instructions relatively short, using actions as well as words.

Examples

1. When giving instructions about how to enter the room after recess and prepare for social studies, ask a student to demonstrate the procedure for the rest of the class by walking in quietly, going straight to his or her seat, and placing the text, paper, and a pencil on his or her desk.
2. Explain a game by acting out one of the parts.
3. Show students what their finished papers should look like. Use an overhead projector or display examples where students can see them easily.

Don't expect the students to be able consistently to see the world from someone else's point of view.

Examples

1. Avoid social studies lessons about worlds too far removed from the child's experience.
2. Avoid long lectures on sharing. Be clear about rules for sharing or use of materials, but avoid long explanations of the rationales for the rules.

Be sensitive to the possibility that students may have different meanings for the same word or different words for the same meaning. Students may also expect everyone to understand words they have invented.

Examples

1. If a student protests, *"I won't take a nap. I'll just rest!"* be aware that a nap may mean something like *"changing into pajamas and being in my bed at home."*
2. Ask children to explain the meanings of their invented words.

Give children a great deal of hands-on practice with the skills that serve as building blocks for more complex skills like reading comprehension.

Examples

1. Provide cut-out letters to build words.
2. Supplement paper-and-pencil tasks in arithmetic with activities that require measuring and simple calculations—cooking, building a display area for class work, dividing a batch of popcorn equally.

Provide a wide range of experiences in order to build a foundation for concept learning and language.

Examples

1. Take field trips to zoos, gardens, theaters, and concerts; invite storytellers to the class.
2. Give students words to describe what they are doing, hearing, seeing, touching, tasting, and smelling.

same water) but not an understanding that the *amounts* are identical (Ginsburg & Opper, 1988).

Piaget's explanation for Leah's answer is that she is focusing, or centering, attention on the dimension of height. She has difficulty considering more than one aspect of the situation at a time, or **decentering**. The preoperational child cannot understand that increased diameter compensates for decreased height, since this would require taking two dimensions into account at once. Thus, children at the preoperational stage have trouble freeing themselves from their own perceptions of how the world appears. What looks like more must be more, even if logic says otherwise.

Decentering Focusing on more than one aspect at a time.

Egocentric Assuming that others experience the world the way you do.

Collective Monologue Form of speech in which children in a group talk but do not really interact or communicate.

Concrete Operations Mental tasks tied to concrete objects and situations.

Identity Principle that a person or object remains the same over time.

Compensation The principle that changes in one dimension can be offset by changes in another.

Reversibility A characteristic of Piagetian logical operations—the ability to think through a series of steps, then mentally reverse the steps and return to the starting point; also called reversible thinking.

Classification Grouping objects into categories.

This brings us to another important characteristic of the preoperational stage. Preoperational children, according to Piaget, are very **egocentric;** they tend to see the world and the experiences of others from their own viewpoint. Egocentric, as Piaget intended it, does not mean selfish; it simply means children often assume that everyone else shares their feelings, reactions, and perspectives. For example, if a little boy at this stage sees you are upset, he may offer you his "blankie," because that is the comfort he would want. Very young children center on their own perceptions and on the way the situation appears to them. This is one reason it is difficult for these children to understand that your right hand is not on the same side as theirs when you are facing them.

Egocentrism is also evident in the child's language. You may have seen young children happily talking about what they are doing even though no one is listening. This can happen when the child is alone or, even more often, in a group of children—each child talks enthusiastically, without any real interaction or conversation. Piaget called this the **collective monologue.**

Recent research has shown that young children are not totally egocentric in every situation, however. Children as young as 4 change the way they talk to 2-year-olds by speaking in simpler sentences, and even before age 2 children show toys to adults by turning the front of the toy to face the other person. So young children do seem quite able to take the needs and different perspectives of others into account, at least in certain situations (Gelman, 1979; Gelman & Ebeling, 1989).

Later Elementary to the Middle School Years: The Concrete-Operational Stage. Piaget coined the term **concrete operations** to describe this stage of "hands-on" thinking. The basic characteristics of the stage are (1) the recognition of the logical stability of the physical world, (2) the realization that elements can be changed or transformed and still *conserve* many of their original characteristics, and (3) the understanding that these changes can be reversed.

Figure 2.1 shows examples of the different tasks given to children to assess conservation and the approximate age ranges when most children can solve these problems. According to Piaget, a student's ability to solve conservation problems depends on an understanding of three basic aspects of reasoning: identity, compensation, and reversibility. With a complete mastery of **identity,** the student knows that if nothing is added or taken away, the material remains the same. With an understanding of **compensation,** the student knows that an apparent change in one direction can be compensated for by a change in another direction. That is, if the liquid rises higher in the glass, the glass must be narrower. And with an understanding of **reversibility,** the student can mentally cancel out the change that has been made. Note especially that a grasp of reversibility means the student at this stage has mastered two-way thinking.

Another important operation mastered at this stage is **classification.** Classification depends on a student's abilities to focus on a single characteristic of objects in a set and group the objects according to that characteristic. Given 12 objects of assorted color and shapes, the concrete-operational student can invariably pick out the ones that are round.

FIGURE 2.1 **Some Piagetian Conservation Tasks.**   Other tasks involve the conservation of number, length, weight, and volume. These tasks are all achieved over the concrete-operational period.

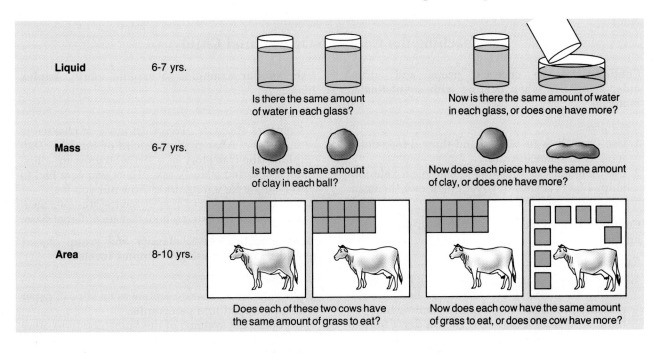

More advanced classification at this stage involves recognizing that one class fits into another. A city can be in a particular state or province and also in a particular country. As children apply this advanced classification to locations, they often become fascinated with "complete" addresses such as Lee Jary, 5116 Forest Hill Drive, Richmond Hill, Ontario, Canada, North America, Northern Hemisphere, Earth, Solar System, Milky Way, Universe.

Classification is also related to reversibility. The ability to reverse a process mentally now allows the concrete-operational student to see that there is more than one way to classify a group of objects. The student understands, for example, that buttons can be classified by color, then reclassified by size or by the number of holes.

Seriation is the process of making an orderly arrangement from large to small or vice versa. This understanding of sequential relationships permits a student to construct a logical series in which $A < B < C$ *(A* is less than *B* is less than *C)* and so on. Unlike the preoperational child, the concrete-operational child can grasp the notion that *B* can be larger than *A* but smaller than *C*.

With the abilities to handle operations like conservation, classification, and seriation, the student at the concrete-operational stage has finally developed a complete and very logical system of thinking. This

Seriation Arranging objects in sequential order according to one aspect, such as size, weight, or volume.

Guidelines

Teaching the Concrete-Operational Child

Continue to use concrete props and visual aids, especially when dealing with sophisticated material.

Examples

1. Use time lines in history and three-dimensional models in science.
2. Use diagrams to illustrate hierarchical relationships like branches of government and the agencies under each branch.

Continue to give students a chance to manipulate and test objects.

Examples

1. Set up simple scientific experiments like the following involving the relationship between fire and oxygen. What happens to a flame when you blow on it from a distance? (If you don't blow it out, the flame gets larger briefly, since it has more oxygen to burn.) What happens when you cover the flame with a jar?
2. Have students make candles by dipping wicks in wax, weave cloth on a simple loom, bake bread, set type by hand, or do other craft work that illustrates the daily occupations of people in the colonial period.

Make sure presentations and readings are brief and well organized.

Examples

1. Assign stories or books with short, logical chapters, moving to longer reading assignments only when students are ready.
2. Break up a presentation with a chance to practice the first steps before introducing the next.

Use familiar examples to explain more complex ideas.

Examples

1. Compare students' lives with those of characters in a story. After reading *Island of the Blue Dolphins* (the true story of a girl who grew up alone on a deserted island), ask, "Have you ever had to stay alone for a long time? How did you feel?"
2. Teach the concept of area by having students measure two rooms in the school that are different sizes.

Give opportunities to classify and group objects and ideas on increasingly complex levels.

Examples

1. Give students separate sentences on slips of paper to be grouped into paragraphs.
2. Compare the systems of the human body to other kinds of systems: the brain to a computer, the heart to a pump. Break down stories into components, from the broad to the specific: author; story; characters, plot, theme; place, time; dialogue, description, actions.

Present problems that require logical, analytical thinking.

Examples

1. Use mind twisters, brain teasers, Master Mind, and riddles.
2. Discuss open-ended questions that stimulate thinking: "Are the brain and the mind the same thing?" "How should the city deal with stray animals?" "What is the largest number?"

system of thinking, however, is still tied to physical reality. The logic is based on concrete situations that can be organized, classified, or manipulated. Thus, children at this stage can imagine several different arrangements for the furniture in their rooms before they act. They do not have to solve the problem strictly through trial and error by actually making the arrangements. But the concrete-operational child is not yet able to reason about hypothetical, abstract problems that involve the coordination of many factors at once. This kind of coordination is part of Piaget's next and final stage of cognitive development.

Being able to manipulate concrete objects helps children understand abstract relationships such as the connection between symbols and quantity.

In any grade you teach, a knowledge of concrete-operational thinking will be helpful. In the early grades the students are moving toward this logical system of thought. In the middle grades it is in full flower, ready to be applied and extended by your teaching. In the high school years it is often used by students whose thinking may not have fully developed to the next stage—the stage of formal operations.

Junior and Senior High: Formal Operations. Some students remain at the concrete-operational stage throughout their school years, even throughout life. However, new experiences, usually those that take place in school, eventually present most students with problems that they cannot solve using concrete operations. It is fine to be able to order items from large to small, but what happens when a number of variables interact, as in a laboratory experiment? Then a mental system for controlling sets of variables and working through a set of possibilities is needed. These are the abilities Piaget called **formal operations.**

At the level of formal operations, all the earlier operations and abilities continue in force; that is, formal thinking is reversible, internal, and organized in a system of interdependent elements. The focus of thinking shifts, however, from what *is* to what *might* be. Situations do not have to be experienced to be imagined. Ask a young child how life would be different if people did not sleep, and the child might say, "People have to sleep!" In contrast, the adolescent who has mastered formal operations can consider contrary-to-fact questions. In answering, the adolescent demonstrates the hallmark of formal operations—**hypothetico-deductive reasoning.** The formal thinker can consider a *hypothetical* situation (people do not sleep) and reason *deductively* (from the general assumption to specific implications, such as longer workdays, more money spent on

Formal Operations Mental tasks involving abstract thinking and coordination of a number of variables.

Hypothetico-Deductive Reasoning A formal-operations problem-solving strategy in which an individual begins by identifying all the factors that might affect a problem and then deduces and systematically evaluates specific solutions.

lighting, or new entertainment industries). Formal operations also include inductive reasoning, or using specific observations to identify general principles. For example, the economist observes many specific changes in the stock market and attempts to identify general principles about economic cycles. Formal-operational thinkers can form hypotheses, set up mental experiments to test them, and isolate or control variables in order to complete a valid test of the hypotheses.

The ability to consider abstract possibilities is critical for much of mathematics and science. After elementary school, most math is concerned with hypotheticals, assumptions, and givens: "Let $x = 10$" or "assume $x^2 + y^2 = z^2$" or "given two sides and an adjacent angle. . . ." Young children cannot reason based on symbols and abstractions, but this kind of reasoning is expected in the later grades (Bjorklund, 1989). Work in social studies and literature requires abstract thinking too; "What did Wilson mean when he called World War I the 'war to end all wars'?" "What are some metaphors for hope and despair in Shakespeare's sonnets?" "What symbols of old age does T. S. Eliot use in *The Waste Land*?" "How do animals symbolize human character traits in Aesop's fables?"

The organized, scientific thinking of formal operations requires that students systematically generate different possibilities for a given situation. The following experiment can help you identify students who apply formal operations. The purpose is to test whether a person can determine, in an organized way, the number of different possibilities that exist within a reasonably limited framework. Ask your students: "How many different outfits can be made with the following clothes: (1) three tops—polo shirt, dress shirt, T-shirt; (2) three pants—jeans, shorts, slacks; and (3) three jackets—bomber, blazer, jeans jacket?" A student capable of formal operations would begin by laying out the possibilities systematically: first each jacket with the polo shirt and jeans, then each jacket with the polo shirt and shorts, then each jacket with the polo shirt and slacks; then on to the jackets with the dress shirt and jeans, then with the dress shirt and shorts, and so forth. A student at the concrete-operational stage, however, would be much less systematic; he or she might start with favorite clothes and continue in the order of preference. It would not be unusual for a student operating at the concrete level to mention only three outfits, using each garment only once. The underlying system of combinations is not yet available.

The ability to think hypothetically, consider alternatives, identify all possible combinations, and analyze one's own thinking has some interesting consequences for adolescents. Since they can think about worlds that do not exist, they often become interested in science fiction. Because they can reason from general principles to specific actions, they often are critical of people whose actions seem to contradict their principles. Adolescents can deduce the set of "best" possibilities and imagine ideal worlds (or ideal parents and teachers, for that matter). This explains why many students at this age develop interests in utopias, political causes, and social issues. They want to design better worlds, and their thinking allows them to do so. Adolescents can also imagine many possible futures for themselves and may try to decide which is best. Feelings about any of these ideals may be strong.

One aspect of formal operations involves taking several variables into account at the same time, as this student must do to coordinate film speed, distance, focus, and light. As one variable changes, the others must change also.

Guidelines

Helping Students to Use Formal Operations

Continue to use concrete-operational teaching strategies and materials.

Examples

1. Use visual aids such as charts and illustrations as well as somewhat more sophisticated graphs and diagrams.
2. Compare the experiences of characters in stories to students' experiences.

Give students the opportunity to explore many hypothetical questions.

Examples

1. Have students write position papers, then exchange these papers with the opposing side and have debates about topical social issues—the environment, the economy, national health insurance.
2. Ask students to write about their personal vision of a utopia; write a description of a universe that has no sex differences; write a description of Earth after humans are extinct.

Give students opportunities to solve problems and reason scientifically.

Examples

1. Set up group discussions in which students design experiments to answer questions.
2. Ask students to justify two different positions on animal rights with logical arguments for each position.

Whenever possible, teach broad concepts, not just facts, using materials and ideas relevant to the students' lives.

Examples

1. When discussing the Civil War, consider other issues that have divided the United States since then.
2. Use lyrics from popular songs to teach poetic devices, to reflect on social problems, and to stimulate discussion on the place of popular music in our culture.

Another characteristic of this stage is **adolescent egocentrism.** Unlike egocentric young children, adolescents do not deny that other people may have different perceptions and beliefs; the adolescents just become very focused on their own ideas. They analyze their own beliefs and attitudes. They reflect on others' thinking as well but often assume that everyone else is as interested as they are in their thoughts, feelings, and behavior. This can lead to what Elkind (1981) calls the sense of an *imaginary audience*—the feeling that everyone is watching. Thus, adolescents believe that others are analyzing them: "Everyone noticed that I wore this shirt twice this week." "The whole class thought my answer was dumb!" "Everybody is going to love my new tape." You can see that social blunders or imperfections in appearance can be devastating if "everybody is watching." Luckily, this feeling of being "on stage" seems to peak in early adolescence by age 14 or 15.

Do We All Reach the Fourth Stage? As we have just seen, most psychologists agree that there is a level of thinking more sophisticated than concrete operations. But the question of how universal formal-operational thinking actually is, even among adults, is a matter of debate. According to Neimark (1975), the first three stages of Piaget's theory are forced on most people by physical realities. Objects really *are* permanent.

Adolescent Egocentrism
Assumption that everyone else shares one's thoughts, feelings, and concerns.

The amount of water *doesn't* change when it is poured into another glass. Formal operations, however, are not so closely tied to the physical environment. They may be the product of experience and of practice in solving hypothetical problems and using formal scientific reasoning. These abilities tend to be valued and taught in literate cultures, particularly in colleges and universities.

Piaget himself (1974) suggested that most adults may be able to use formal-operational thought in only a few areas, areas where they have the greatest experience or interest. So do not expect every student in your junior high or high school class to be able to think hypothetically about all the problems you present. It is important to keep this in mind, since many of the tasks normally presented to high school and even junior high students require a good deal of formal thinking, especially in science and mathematics. Students who have not learned to go beyond the information presented to them are likely to fall by the wayside in these courses. Sometimes students find shortcuts for dealing with problems that are beyond their grasp; they may memorize formulas or lists of steps. These systems may be helpful for passing tests, but real understanding will take place only if students are able to go beyond this superficial use of memorization—only, in other words, if they learn to use formal-operational thinking.

IMPLICATIONS OF PIAGET'S THEORY FOR TEACHERS

Piaget has taught us that we can learn a great deal about how children think by listening carefully—by paying close attention to their ways of solving problems. If we understand children's thinking, we will be better able to match teaching methods to children's abilities.

Understanding Students' Thinking

The students in any class will vary greatly both in their level of cognitive development and in their academic knowledge. As a teacher, how can you determine whether students are having trouble because they lack the necessary thinking abilities or because they simply have not learned the basic facts? To do this, Case (1978a & b, 1985) suggests you observe your students carefully as they try to solve the problems you have presented. What kind of logic do they use? Do they focus on only one aspect of the situation? Are they fooled by appearances? Do they suggest solutions systematically or by guessing and forgetting what they have already tried? Ask your students how they tried to solve the problem. Listen to their strategies. What kind of thinking is behind repeated mistakes or problems? The students are the best sources of information about their own thinking abilities (Confrey, 1990a).

Matching Strategies to Abilities

An important implication of Piaget's theory for teaching is what Hunt years ago (1961) called "the problem of the match." Students must be neither bored by work that is too simple nor left behind by teaching they cannot understand. According to Hunt, disequilibrium must be kept "just right" to encourage growth. Setting up situations that lead to errors can help create an appropriate level of disequilibrium. When students experience some conflict between what they think should happen (a piece of wood should sink because it is big) and what actually happens (it floats!), they may rethink their understanding, and new knowledge may develop.

It is worth pointing out, too, that many materials and lessons can be understood at several levels and can be "just right" for a range of cognitive abilities. Classics such as *Alice in Wonderland,* myths, and fairy tales can be enjoyed at both concrete and symbolic levels. It is also possible for students to be introduced to a topic together, then work individually on follow-up activities matched to their level. Tom Good and Jere Brophy (1991) describe activity cards for three or four ability levels. These cards provide different readings and assignments, but all are directed toward the overall class objectives. One of the cards should be a good "match" for each student.

At every level of cognitive development, you will also want to see that students are actively engaged in the learning process. They must be able to incorporate the information you present into their own schemes. To do this, they must act on the information in some way. Schooling must give the students a chance to experience the world. This active experience, even at the earliest school levels, should not be limited to the physical manipulation of objects. It should also include mental manipulation of ideas that arise out of class projects or experiments (Ginsburg & Opper, 1988). For example, after a social studies lesson on different jobs, a primary-grade teacher might show the students a picture of a woman and ask, "What could this person be?" After answers like "teacher," "doctor," "secretary," "lawyer," "saleswoman," and so on, the teacher could suggest, "How about a daughter?" Answers like "sister," "mother," "aunt," and "granddaughter" may follow. This should help the children switch dimensions in their classification and center on another aspect of the situation. Next the teacher might suggest "American," or "jogger," or "blonde." With older children, hierarchical classification might be involved: it is a picture of a woman, who is a human being; a human being is a primate, which is a mammal, which is an animal, which is a life-form.

Another important part of cognitive development is the ability to apply the principles learned in one situation to new situations. Teachers should constantly be asking students to apply recently learned principles in different situations. For example, the student who has learned how to form plurals by dropping the *y* and adding *-ies* should be asked to form plurals not only of words like *party* and *pony* (where the rule fits) but of words like *donkey* (where the rule does not work). If the principle applies, the student will gain practice in using it. If the principle does not fit, disequilibrium will occur, and new thinking abilities may develop.

All students need to interact with teachers and peers in order to test their thinking, to be challenged, to receive feedback, and to watch how others work out problems. Disequilibrium is often set in motion quite naturally when the teacher or another student suggests a new way of

Can Cognitive Development Be Accelerated?

Ever since Piaget described his stages of cognitive development, some people have asked if progress through the stages could be accelerated. More recently, the question has focused on whether we should accelerate learning for preschoolers and young children at risk of academic failure. Can learning be accelerated and, if so, is this a good idea?

Point: Every child deserves a head start.

Some of the strongest arguments in favor of "speeding up" cognitive development are based on the results of cross-cultural studies of children (studies that compare children growing up in different cultures). These results suggest that certain cognitive abilities are indeed influenced by the environment and education. Children of pottery-making families in one area of Mexico, for example, learn conservation of substance earlier than their peers in families who do not make pottery (Ashton, 1978). Furthermore, children in non-Western cultures appear to acquire conservation operations later than children in Western cultures. It seems likely that factors in the environment contribute to the rate of cognitive development.

But even if cognitive development can be accelerated, is this a good idea? Two of the most vocal (and heavily criticized) advocates of early academic training are Siegfried and Therese Engelmann (1981). In their book, *Give your child a superior mind,* they suggest that children who learn academic skills as preschoolers will be smarter throughout their school years, are less likely to fail, and are more likely to enjoy school. They contend:

Children respond to the environment. Their capacity to learn and what they learn depends on what the environment teaches. . . . Instead of relying on the traditional environment that is rich in learning opportunities for the child, we can take the environment a step further and

thinking about something. As a general rule, students should act, manipulate, observe, and then talk and/or write (to the teacher and each other) about what they have experienced. Concrete experiences provide the raw materials for thinking. Communicating with others makes students use, test, and sometimes change their thinking abilities. Discussions about the implications of Piaget's theory often center on the question of whether cognitive development can be accelerated, as you can see in the **Point/Counterpoint** section above.

Some Limitations of Piaget's Theory

Piaget's influence on developmental psychology and education has been enormous, even though recent research has not supported all his ideas. Although most psychologists agree with Piaget's insightful descriptions of *how* children think, many disagree with his explanations of *why* thinking develops as it does.

The Trouble with Stages. Some psychologists have questioned the existence of four separate stages of thinking, even though they agree that children do go through the changes that Piaget described (Gelman & Baillargeon, 1983). One problem with the stage model is the lack of consistency in children's thinking. Psychologists reason that if there are separate stages, and if the child's thinking at each stage is based on a particular set of operations, then once the child has mastered the operations, he or she should be fairly consistent in solving *all* problems

mold it into a purposeful instrument that teaches and that guarantees your child will have a superior mind. (p. 10)

Counterpoint: Acceleration is ineffective and may be harmful.

The position of Piagetian psychologists who attempt to apply his theory to education is that development should not be speeded up. This traditional view has been well summarized by Wadsworth:

The function of the teacher is not to accelerate the development of the child or speed up the rate of movement from stage to stage. The function of the teacher is to insure that development within each stage is thoroughly integrated and complete. (1978, p. 117)

According to Piaget, cognitive development is based on the self-selected actions and thoughts of the student, not on the teacher's action. If you do try to teach a student something the student is not ready to learn, he or she may learn to give the "correct" answer. But this will not really affect the way the student thinks about this problem. Therefore, why spend a long time teaching something at one stage when students will learn it by themselves much more rapidly and thoroughly at another stage?

Today the pressure is on parents and preschool teachers to create "superkids," three-year-olds who read, write, and speak a second language. David Elkind (1991) asserts that pushing children can be harmful. Elkind believes that preschool children who are given formal instruction in academic subjects often show signs of stress such as headaches. These children may become dependent on adults for guidance. Early focus on "right" and "wrong" answers can lead to competition and loss of self-esteem. Elkind asserts:

The miseducation of young children, so prevalent in the United States today, ignores well-founded and noncontroversial differences between early education and formal education. As educators, our first task is to reassert this difference and insist on its importance. (p. 31)

requiring those operations. In other words, once you can conserve, you ought to know that the number of blocks does not change when they are rearranged (conservation of number) *and* that the weight of a ball of clay does not change when you flatten it (conservation of weight). But it doesn't happen this way. Children can conserve number a year or two before they can conserve weight. Piagetian theorists have tried to deal with these inconsistencies, but not all psychologists are convinced by their explanations (Siegler, 1991).

Some psychologists have pointed to research on the brain to support Piaget's stage model. Epstein observed changes in rates of growth in brain weight and skull size as well as changes in the electrical activity of the brain between infancy and adolescence. These growth spurts occur at about the same time as transitions between the stages described by Piaget (Epstein 1978, 1980). Evidence from animal studies indicates that infant rhesus monkeys show dramatic increases in synaptic (nerve) connections throughout the brain cortex at the same time that they master the kinds of sensorimotor problems described by Piaget (Berk, 1991). This may be true in human infants as well. Transition to the higher cognitive states in humans has also been related to changes in the brain such as production of additional synaptic connections.

Underestimating Children's Abilities. It now appears that Piaget underestimated the cognitive abilities of children, particularly younger ones. The problems he gave young children may have been too difficult and the directions too confusing. His subjects may have understood more than they could show on these problems. For example, work by Gelman and her colleagues (Gelman, Meck, & Merkin, 1986; Miller & Gelman, 1983) shows that preschool children know much more about the concept of number than Piaget thought, even if they sometimes make mistakes or get confused. As long as preschoolers work with only three or four objects at a time, they can tell that the number remains the same, even if the objects are spread far apart or clumped close together. Recent studies of infants show us that they too are much more competent than Piaget thought. Instead of having to learn that objects are permanent, they may just have to learn how to look for them. In other words, we may be born with a greater store of cognitive tools than Piaget suggested. Some basic understandings, like the permanence of objects or the sense of number, may be part of our evolutionary equipment, ready for use in our cognitive development.

Piaget's theory does not explain how even young children can perform at an advanced level in certain areas—areas where they have highly developed knowledge and expertise. An expert 9-year-old chess player may think fairly abstractly about chess moves, while a novice 20-year-old player may have to resort to more concrete strategies to plan and remember moves (Bee, 1989; Siegler, 1991). As John Flavell (1985) noted, "the expert [child] looks very, very smart—very 'cognitively mature'—when functioning in her area of expertise" (p. 83).

Kurt Fischer's skill theory of cognitive development provides one explanation for the fact that children seem to be able to think abstractly about one problem and still have to solve other problems using more concrete approaches. The theory also sheds some light on why movement through stages of cognitive development may appear so slow and gradual.

Fischer's Skill Theory. Like Piaget, Fischer suggests that children pass through a series of developmental stages in their thinking (Fischer, 1980; Fischer & Knight, 1990). Each stage is defined by an upper limit on the child's performance. This upper limit or **optimal level** is the most sophisticated thinking possible at that stage. For example, at about age 14 to 16, children move into a stage defined by the upper limit of *abstract mapping,* or the ability to interrelate several intangible and contradictory concepts. A girl would demonstrate abstract mapping if she could integrate "dishonesty" and "kindness" into the idea of a "social lie"—a kind dishonesty, such as exclaiming that "nobody will ever notice your new braces!" At the previous stage the same child might understand the concepts of "dishonesty" and "kindness" to be opposing values. But to integrate the two concepts into the idea of a "social lie" would be impossible, because a social lie seems to be "good" and "bad" at the same time.

To demonstrate the optimal level of thinking for a given stage, conditions for the child must be ideal—clear instructions, familiar content, activities that are valued by the child's culture, high motivation, good health, tasks that don't overburden the child's memory, and so on. Students at any stage will not demonstrate the optimal-level ability all the time. If they are unfamiliar with the vocabulary of the question or don't understand the instructions or are not particularly motivated, they may fail. The question is not what they do all the time but what they can do

Optimal Level An element of Fischer's skill theory of cognitive development; the highest level of performance that a person can attain under the most supportive conditions.

under the right conditions. This explains why the development of thinking appears so gradual and inconsistent: conditions are seldom ideal when students are asked to demonstrate their thinking. Lack of knowledge or motivation seriously hinders performance.

One of Fischer's experiments demonstrates that rapid movement to higher stages can be seen under ideal conditions, as shown in Figure 2.2. For this study, eight subjects at each grade level from third grade through sophomore year in college were given problems to test their ability to demonstrate abstract mapping in arithmetic. The students were tested under different conditions. The first condition was like a test in school: time pressures, no examples or guidance. Other conditions allowed the

FIGURE 2.2 **Spurts in Cognitive Development.** When students answer abstract math problems under supportive conditions, they show a spurt in ability around ages 14 to 16, in keeping with Fischer's skill theory of development.

Source: Adapted from K. Fischer and C. Knight (1990). Cognitive development in real children: Levels and variations. In R. McClure (Ed.), *Learning and thinking styles: Classroom interaction,* p. 51. Copyright 1990 National Education Association. Reprinted with permission.

subjects to think about the problems for two weeks and also gave examples and explanations. With no support or extra time allowed, performance improved gradually with age. This gradual change gave no evidence of a "leap" in thinking to a new stage. But under supportive conditions, we see a dramatic spurt in abstract mapping thinking abilities right around 14 to 16 years, just as Fischer's theory predicts.

Cognitive Development and Culture. A final criticism of Piaget's theory is that it overlooks the important effects of the child's cultural and social group. Children in Western cultures may master scientific thinking and formal operations because this is the kind of thinking required in Western schools. Even basic concrete operations such as classification may not be so basic to people of other cultures. For example, when African subjects from among the Kpelle people were asked to sort 20 objects, they created groups that made sense to them—a hoe with a potato, a knife with an orange. The experimenter could not get the Kpelle to change their categories; they said this is how a wise man would do it. Finally the experimenter asked in desperation, "Well, how would a fool do it?" The subjects promptly created the four neat classification piles the experimenter had expected—food, tools, and so on (Rogoff & Morelli, 1989).

There is an increasingly influential view of cognitive development that offers an alternative perspective to that of Piaget. Proposed years ago by Lev Vygotsky and recently rediscovered, this theory ties cognitive development to culture.

VYGOTSKY'S ALTERNATIVE TO PIAGET

Many psychologists today believe that the child's culture shapes cognitive development by determining what and how the child will learn about the world. The major spokesperson for this view is a Russian psychologist who died more than 50 years ago. Lev Semenovich Vygotsky was only 38 when he died, but his ideas about language, culture, and cognitive development were very mature. Recent translations of his work show that he provided an alternative to many of Piaget's ideas.

Whereas Piaget described the child as a little scientist, constructing an understanding of the world largely alone, Vygotsky (1978, 1986) suggested that cognitive development depends much more on the people in the child's world. Children's knowledge, ideas, attitudes, and values develop through interactions with others. Vygotsky also believed that language plays a very important role in cognitive development.

The Role of Private Speech

Private Speech Children's self-talk, which guides their thinking and action. Eventually these verbalizations are internalized as silent inner speech.

If you have spent much time around young children, you know that they often talk to themselves as they play. Psychologists today call this phenomenon **private speech.**

Vygotsky's and Piaget's Views Compared. We saw earlier that Piaget called children's self-directed talk "egocentric speech." He assumed that this "egocentric" speech is another indication that young children can't see the world through the eyes of others. They talk about what matters to them without taking into account the needs or interests of their listeners. As they mature, and especially as they have disagreements with peers, Piaget believed, children develop socialized speech. They learn to listen and exchange ideas.

Vygotsky had very different ideas about young children's private speech. Rather than being a sign of cognitive immaturity, Vygotsky suggested that these mutterings play an important role in cognitive development. The children are communicating—they are communicating with themselves to guide their behavior and thinking. In any preschool room you might hear 4- or 5-year-olds saying, "No, it won't fit. Try it here. Turn. Turn. Maybe this one . . ." while they do a puzzle. As these children mature, their self-directed speech goes underground, changing from spoken to whispered speech and then to silent lip movements. Finally, the children just "think" the guiding words. The use of private speech peaks at around 5 to 7 years of age and has generally disappeared by 9 years of age. Brighter children seem to make this transition earlier (Bee, 1989).

Vygotsky identified this transition from audible private speech to silent inner speech as a fundamental process in cognitive development. Through this process the child is using language to accomplish important cognitive activities such as directing attention, solving problems, planning, forming concepts, and gaining self-control. Research supports Vygotsky's ideas (Kohlberg, Yaeger, & Hjertholm, 1969; Berk, 1991). Children tend to use more private speech when they are confused, having difficulties, or making mistakes. Inner speech not only helps us solve problems but also allows us to regulate our behavior. Have you ever thought to yourself something like "Let's see, the first step is . . ." or "As soon as I get home I'm going to . . ." or "If I work to the end of this page, then I can . . ."? You were using inner speech to remind, cue, encourage, or guide yourself. In a really tough situation, you might even find that you return to muttering out loud. Table 2.2 on page 48 contrasts Piaget's and Vygotsky's theories of private speech.

Lev Vygotsky's theories challenge many of Piaget's ideas and highlight the importance of social interaction and support in cognitive development.

Self-Talk and Learning. Because private speech helps students to regulate their thinking, it makes sense to allow and even encourage students to use private speech in school. Insisting on total silence when young students are working on difficult problems may make the work even harder for them. You may notice when mutterings increase—this could be a sign that students need help. One approach, called cognitive self-instruction, teaches students to use self-talk to guide learning. For example, students learn to give themselves reminders to go slowly and carefully. They "talk themselves through" tasks, saying such things as "Okay, what is it I have to do? . . . Copy the picture with the different lines. I have to go slowly and carefully. Okay, draw the line down, down, good; then to the right, that's it; now . . ." (Meichenbaum, 1977, p. 32).

Language and Cognitive Development

In Vygotsky's mind, language is critical for cognitive development. Language in the form of private speech guides cognitive development. Language provides a means for expressing ideas and asking questions and

TABLE 2.2   Differences between Piaget's and Vygotsky's Theories of Egocentric or Private Speech

	PIAGET	VYGOTSKY
Developmental significance	Represents an inability to take the perspective of another and engage in reciprocal communication	Represents externalized thought; its function is to communicate with the self for the purpose of self-guidance and self-direction
Course of development	Declines with age	Increases at younger ages and then gradually loses its audible quality to become internal verbal thought
Relationship to social speech	Negative; least socially and cognitively mature children use more egocentric speech	Positive; private speech develops out of social interaction with others
Relationship to environmental contexts	—	Increases with task difficulty. Private speech serves a helpful self-guiding function in situations where more cognitive effort is needed to reach a solution

Source: Adapted from L. E. Berk & R. A. Garvin, 1984, Development of private speech among low-income Appalachian children. *Developmental Psychology, 20,* 272. Copyright 1984 by the American Psychological Association. Adapted by permission.

it provides the categories and concepts for thinking. When we consider a problem, we generally think in words and partial sentences. Vygotsky placed much more emphasis than Piaget on the role of language in cognitive development. One reason is that he believed cognitive development occurs through the child's interaction with more capable members of the culture—adults or more able peers. These people serve as guides and teachers, providing the information and support necessary for the child to grow intellectually. Most of this guidance is communicated through language. Jerome Bruner called this assistance **scaffolding** (Wood, Bruner, & Ross, 1976). The term aptly suggests that children use this help for support while they build a firm understanding that will eventually allow them to solve the problems on their own.

The Zone of Proximal Development

According to Vygotsky, at any given point in development there are certain problems that a child is on the verge of being able to solve—the child just needs some structure, clues, reminders, help with remembering details or steps, encouragement to keep trying, and so on. Some problems, of course, are beyond the child's capabilities, even if every step is explained clearly. The **zone of proximal development** is the area where the child cannot solve a problem alone but can be successful under adult guidance or in collaboration with a more advanced peer (Wertsch, 1985).

Scaffolding Support for learning and problem solving. The support could be clues, reminders, encouragement, breaking the problem down into steps, providing an example, or anything else that allows the student to grow in independence as a learner.

Zone of Proximal Development Phase at which a child can master a task if given appropriate help and support.

This is the area where instruction can succeed because this is the area where real learning is possible.

For Vygotsky, social interaction was more than a method of teaching—it was the origin of higher mental processes such as problem solving. He assumed that "the notion of mental function can properly be applied to group as well as individual forms of activity" (Wertsch, 1991, p. 27). For example, Vygotsky believed that groups could "remember." Consider this example:

> A six-year-old has lost a toy and asks her father for help. The father asks her where she last saw the toy; the child says "I can't remember." He asks a series of questions—did you have it in your room? Outside? Next door? To each question, the child answers, "no." When he says "in the car?", she says "I think so" and goes to retrieve the toy. (Tharp & Gallimore, 1988, p. 14)

Who remembered? The answer is really neither the father nor the daughter but the two together. The remembering and problem solving was in the interaction, but the child may have internalized strategies to use next time something is lost. At some point the child will be able to function independently to solve this kind of problem. Vygotsky believed that all higher mental functions have their origins in social interactions. Like the above strategy for finding the toy, these higher functions appear first between a child and a "teacher" before they exist within the individual child (Kozulin, 1990).

We can see how Vygotsky's beliefs about the role of private speech in cognitive development fit with the notion of the zone of proximal development. Often, an adult helps a child to solve a problem or accomplish a

Sometimes the best teachers are other students who have just understood a particular concept. These "teachers" may be operating in the zone of proximal development for their fellow students.

task using verbal prompts and structuring. This scaffolding may be gradually reduced as the child takes over the guidance, perhaps first by giving the prompts as private speech and finally as inner speech. If we could move forward to a future day in the life of the girl in the example above and listen to her *thoughts* when she realizes that a schoolbook is missing, they might sound something like this: "Where's my math book? Used it in class. Think I put it in my bag. Fell open on the bus. That dope Larry kicked my stuff so maybe. . . ."

An implication of Vygotsky's zone of proximal development is that students should be put in situations where they have to reach to understand but where support, from other students or from the teacher, is also available. Sometimes the best teacher is another student who has just figured out the problem, because this student probably is operating in the learner's zone of proximal development. Vygotsky's theory suggests that teachers need to do more than just arrange the environment so that students can discover on their own. The students should be guided by explanations, demonstrations, and work with other students—opportunities for cooperative learning. In addition, they should be encouraged to use language to organize their thinking, to talk about what they are trying to accomplish. Having a student work with someone who is just a bit better at the activity would also be a good idea.

Research supports Vygotsky's beliefs about the importance of language in cognitive development. Language both reflects and influences students' mental development. In the next section we examine how language develops and what teachers can do to encourage this development.

THE DEVELOPMENT OF LANGUAGE

The language adults use is just as complicated as their thinking. In fact, if you try diagramming some of the sentences you hear in lecture classes, you may think language is even more complicated than the thoughts it expresses.

There are three aspects of any language: pronunciation, grammar, and meaning. Pronunciation involves the distinctive sounds, or **phonemes,** of a language. These vary from language to language. For example, English has about 40 separate phonemes that make up all the words. If you try to learn a foreign language with different phonemes, you may have trouble pronouncing some of them. In fact, if you are not familiar with the sounds of a foreign language, you will probably have trouble even knowing where one word stops and another begins.

Grammar includes morphemes and syntax. Words are formed with **morphemes.** These are the smallest units in a language that have meaning. Morphemes can be whole words, such as *help,* markers such as *ful* that make nouns function as adjectives (helpful), prefixes such as *un* that change the meaning of words (helpful to unhelpful), and suffixes such as *ed* that change the time of the action of verbs to the past (helped). Help has one morpheme; helpful and helped have two, and unhelpful, three. **Syntax** is the order of words in phrases or sentences. For example, in English the usual order is subject-verb-object. Even very young children know there is something wrong with the sentence "Apples Joan eats."

Phonemes Distinctive sounds of a language.

Morphemes Smallest units in language that have meaning.

Syntax The order of words in phrases or sentences.

Meaning in language is determined by many things. **Semantics** is the meaning of words and combinations of words. Semantics is closely tied to word forms (present or past tense, adjective or adverb, singular or plural) and to the structure or syntax; for example, "Bob hit Sue" means something quite different from "Sue hit Bob." Meaning is also affected by the context, that is, by when something is said, how it is said, and so on. For example, a teacher who says, "This can't be my class!" when noise builds in the room is understood to be calling for a return to order. The same remark made when the class is very quiet might be insulting. **Pragmatics** is the area of language that involves the effects of contexts on meaning and the unstated communication rules, such as when, how, to whom, and about what to speak. Pragmatics also is concerned with how these communication rules shift in different social situations.

By the time they enter school, most children have mastered quite a bit of the pronunciation, grammar, and meaning of their native language. Their knowledge of phonemes, morphemes, syntax, semantics, and even pragmatics is remarkable. As Moskowitz has noted, "Ten linguists working full time for 10 years to analyze the structure of the English language could not program a computer with the ability acquired by an average child in the first 10 or even 5 years of life" (1978, p. 92). As you might expect, there is great disagreement about how people master the complex process of communication.

How Do We Learn Language?

One of the most widely held views of language development assumes that children learn language just as they learn anything else, by repeating those behaviors that lead to some kind of positive result. The child makes a sound, the parent smiles and replies. The child says "Mmm" in the presence of milk, the parent says "Yes, milk, milk" and gives the child a drink. The child learns to say *milk* because it leads to a happy parent and a drink of milk. Children add new words by imitating the sounds they hear and improve their use of language when they are corrected by the adults around them.

Such a theory appears convincing, but research has shown that many of a child's earliest utterances are not imitations but original creations. And they are unlikely to be rewarded, because they are "incorrect," even though they make sense to the people involved. Examples are such phrases as "paper find," "car mosquito," "tooth-guy" (dentist), or "all gone kitty" (Moshman, Glover, & Bruning, 1987). In addition, researchers studying interactions between young children and their parents have discovered that parents rarely correct pronunciation and grammar during the early stages of language development. They are much more likely to respond to the content of a child's remarks (Brown & Hanlon, 1970). In fact, if parents spent all their time correcting a child's language and never "heard" what the child was trying to say, the child might give up trying to master a system as complicated as language.

Adults caring for children seem continually to adapt their language to stay just ahead of the child. Before children begin talking, adults may direct long, complicated sentences to them. But as soon as a child utters identifiable words, adults simplify their language. As the child progresses,

Semantics The meaning of words and combinations of words.

Pragmatics Area of language involving the effects of contexts on meaning.

adults tend to change their language to stay just a bit more advanced than the child's current level of development, thus encouraging new understanding (Bohannon & Warren-Leubecker, 1989). It seems that in order to stretch the child's language development, adults give the kind of support, or scaffolding, that Vygotsky has recommended. Adults, by staying slightly more advanced in their language, may also create disequilibrium and encourage development as a result.

But even this rich learning environment cannot explain how children learn so much language so quickly. Some psychologists explain this amazing accomplishment by assuming that humans are born with a special capacity for language (Chomsky, 1965; Eimas, 1985; Maratsos, 1989). Noam Chomsky is still working on his theory of **transformational grammar,** which endeavors to explain this special capacity. According to this theory, language has a *surface structure,* the actual words and sentences people use, and a *deep structure,* the meaning contained in these words and sentences. Sentences with different surface structures, such as "Logan sent Denzell a letter," and "Denzell was sent a letter by Logan," and "A letter was sent to Denzell by Logan," can all have the same deep structure or underlying meaning. Because humans have a special capacity for language, we have innate *transformational rules* to translate surface structures into meaning, so we understand what is said. We can also translate the deep-structure meaning we want to communicate into surface-structure sentences. These underlying rules, Chomsky believes, are part of our inborn cognitive equipment and do not have to be learned.

It is likely that many factors—biological and experiential—play a role in language development. The important point is that children develop language as they develop other cognitive abilities, by actively trying to make sense of what they hear—by looking for patterns and making up rules to put together the jigsaw puzzle of language. Reward and correction play a role in helping children learn correct language use, but the child's thinking and creativity in putting together the parts of this complicated system are very important. In the process a child makes some very logical "mistakes," as you will see.

Stages in the Process of Language Acquisition

Before they learn to speak, children communicate through crying, smiling, and body movements. By the end of the first year, more or less, most children have spoken their first word. They have entered what psychologists call the one-word stage.

First Words. After the first word, for the next three or four months, children add slowly to their vocabulary until they have about ten words. After this, words are added rapidly. By about 20 months the vocabulary includes approximately 50 words (Nelson, 1981).

Even at this early stage, language is more complex than it might appear. One word can be used to communicate a variety of sophisticated ideas. For example, my daughter's first word was *ite* (translated: light). Said loudly while reaching toward the light switch on the wall, "ITE!" meant "I want to flip the switch on and off (and on and off, and on and off)." When someone else flipped the switch while she was playing on

Transformational Grammar A theory suggesting that humans make sense of language by transforming the surface structure of phrases and sentences into a deep structure of meaning. The ability to make these transformations is assumed to be inborn.

the floor, Elizabeth might remark "Ite," meaning "You turned on the light." When single words are used in this way, they are called **holophrases** because they express whole phrases or complex ideas.

A second, related characteristic of this period is **overextension.** Children may use one word to cover a range of concepts. For example, on a trip to the zoo, the 13-month-old son of a friend pointed excitedly at every animal, including peacocks and elephants, saying "Dug, dug" (translated: dog, dog). This was the only word he had that came close to being adequate. He wisely rejected his other possibilities: "bye-bye," "more," "Mama," and "Dada." He used the language tools available to him to make sense of his world and to communicate. Children sometimes show **underextension** as well; they use words too specifically. For example, Siegler (1991) tells about the child who used the word *bottle* only for her baby bottle and not for soda bottles or water bottles.

First Sentences. At about 18 months many children enter the two-word stage. They begin to string words together in two-word sentences like "Daddy book," "Play car," "Allgone milk," and "More light." This is **telegraphic speech** (R. Brown, 1973). The nonessential details are left out and the words that carry the most meaning are included, as in a telegram. Even though sentences are short, semantics can be complex. Children can express possession ("Daddy book"), recurrence ("More light"), action on an object ("Play car"), and even disappearance or nonexistence ("Allgone milk").

For about one year, children continue to focus on the essential words even as they lengthen their sentences. At a certain point that varies from child to child, new features are added. Children begin to elaborate their simple language by adding morphemes such as plurals, endings for verbs such as *-ed* and *-ing,* and small words like *and, but,* and *in.* In the process of figuring out the rules governing these aspects of language, children make some very interesting mistakes.

Learning Grammar. For a brief time children may use irregular forms of particular words properly, as if they simply are saying what they have heard. Then, as they begin to learn rules, they **overregularize** words by applying the rules to everything. Children who once said "Our car is broken" begin to insist "Our car is broked." Parents often wonder why their child seems to be "regressing." Actually, these "mistakes" show how logical and rational children can be as they try to assimilate new words into existing schemes. Because most languages have many irregular words, accommodation is necessary in mastering language.

Another aspect of overregularizing language involves the order of words in a sentence. Since the usual order in English is subject-verb-object, preschoolers just mastering the rules of language have trouble with sentences in any different order. For example, if they hear a statement in the passive voice, like "The truck was bumped by the car," they usually think the truck did the bumping to the car (Berger, 1986). So in talking with young children, it is generally better to use direct language.

Learning Vocabulary. During the preschool years children learn new words very rapidly, doubling their vocabulary about every six months

Holophrases Single words that express complex ideas.

Overextension Using one word to cover a range of concepts.

Underextension Being too specific in using a word, limiting the word's meaning to a narrow range of possible examples.

Telegraphic Speech Children's speech using only essential words, as in a telegram.

Overregularize Apply a learned rule to all situations, including inappropriate ones.

"WHEN I SAY 'RUNNED', YOU KNOW I
MEAN 'RAN'. LET'S NOT QUIBBLE."

© by Sidney Harris.

between ages 2 and 4, from about 200 to 2,000 words. During this time they may enjoy making up words. Because their thinking is egocentric, they may assume you know exactly what they mean. They also tend to center on one meaning for a word.

Preschool children like to play with language. They enjoy sounds and silliness. The young son of a friend of mine wanted to name his new baby sister Brontosaurus because he "just liked to say it!" Think of all the language games, rhymes, taunts, chants, secret languages (Pig Latin, Obish), and rituals that filled your early days. In my time it was "Sticks and stones may break my bones, but words will never hurt me," and the ever-popular "School's out, school's out. . . ."

Language Development in the School Years

By about age 5 or 6, most children have mastered the basics of their native language. As noted earlier, the language of these children can still be quite egocentric. Preschoolers may have special meanings for words. They may talk to themselves as they work, first clearly, then in a whisper, and finally silently. What remains for the school-age child to accomplish?

Pronunciation. The majority of first graders have mastered most phonemes, but a few may remain unconquered. As you can see from Figure 2.3, the *j, v, th,* and *zh* sounds are the last to develop. About 10 percent of 8-year-olds still have some trouble with *s, z, v, th,* and *zh* (Rathus, 1988). Young children may understand and be able to use many words but prefer to use the words they can pronounce easily.

Intonation or word emphasis may also cause problems for young children. If the meaning of a sentence is ambiguous and intonation makes the difference, then children as old as 8 or 9 may misunderstand. Moshman, Glover, and Bruning (1987) give this example. Consider the sentence, "George gave the book to David and he gave one to Bill." If you emphasize the *he,* then the meaning is "George gave the book to David and David gave another book to Bill." With a different intonation, emphasizing the *and,* for example, the meaning is changed to "George gave the book to David and George also gave one to Bill." Don't expect early elementary-school students to pick up subtle meanings in intonation.

Syntax. Children master the basics of word orders in their native language early. But the more complicated forms, such as the passive voice, take longer to master. By early elementary school, many children can understand the meaning of passive sentences, yet they do not use such constructions in their normal conversations. Other accomplishments during elementary school include first understanding and then using complex grammatical structures such as extra clauses, qualifiers, and conjunctions.

Vocabulary and Semantics. Between the ages of 2 and 6 the average child learns between six and ten words a day. This means the average 6-year-old has a vocabulary of 8,000 to 14,000 words. From ages 9 to 11, about 5,000 new words are added to this repertoire. It seems that the time before puberty, especially the preschool years, is a sensitive period for language growth. Research has shown that we can learn much about lan-

FIGURE 2.3 **Acquisition of the Sounds of Speech.** The solid bar for each sound of speech begins at the age by which 50 percent of children pronounce it properly. The bar ends at the age by which 90 percent of children are pronouncing the sound correctly.

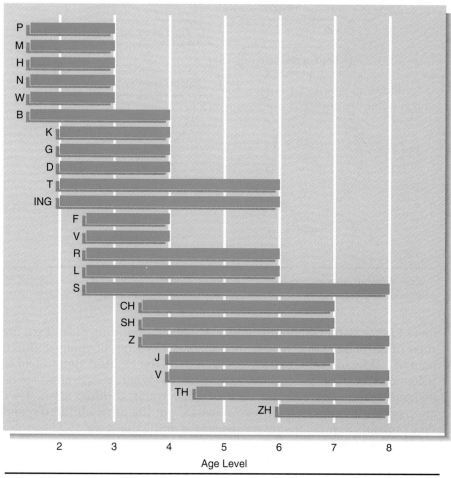

Source: Figure from *Understanding Child Development* by Spencer A. Rathus, copyright © 1988 by Holt, Rinehart and Winston, Inc.; reprinted by permission of the publisher.

guage after puberty, but very positive or very negative conditions during the sensitive period before puberty can greatly help or hinder language development (Berger, 1986; Johnson & Newport, 1989).

In the early elementary years some children may have trouble with abstract words such as *justice* or *economy*. They may also take statements literally and thus misunderstand sarcasm or metaphor. Many children are in their preadolescent years before they are able to distinguish being kidded from being taunted or before they know that a sarcastic remark is not meant to be taken literally (Gardner, 1982b).

Pragmatics. Pragmatics involves the appropriate use of language to communicate. Children show an understanding of pragmatics when they talk in simpler sentences to younger children or command their pets to "Come here!" in louder, deeper voices (Rice, 1984). But there is much

FIGURE 2.4   **Conversational Pragmatics.** Young children know the structure of conversations—how to take turns—even though the "talk" is not always related.

Source: Adapted from Robert Siegler, *Children's Thinking,* © 1986, p. 35. Reprinted by permission of Prentice-Hall, Inc., Englewood Cliffs, New Jersey.

more to successful communicating. For instance, children must learn the rules of turn taking in conversation. The conversations of young children tend to follow the rules of turn taking, even if the children don't seem to listen to each other, as illustrated in Figure 2.4. What seem to adults to be disjointed, unrelated remarks do not bother young children at all. They are paying attention to their own remarks, not the other children's, and they probably assume that everyone else is doing the same.

When children begin to have arguments, you can tell that they have begun to listen to each other. In later elementary school, children's conversations start to seem like conversations. Contributions are usually on the same topic. By adolescence, students become interested in analyzing the feelings and views of others. They want to understand the perspective of the other speakers. You will hear "How did you feel when she did that?" or "Why aren't you sitting with Jonah? Did you have a fight?" (Dorval & Eckerman, 1984).

TEACHING AND LANGUAGE

Around the age of 5, students begin to develop **metalinguistic awareness.** This means their understanding about language and how it works becomes explicit. They have knowledge about language itself. They are ready to study and extend the rules that have been implicit—understood but not consciously expressed. This process continues throughout life, as we all become better able to manipulate and comprehend language in increasingly sophisticated ways. Teachers can develop the language abilities and knowledge of their students in a variety of ways.

Metalinguistic Awareness
Understanding about one's own use of language.

Interactions with Students

Teachers can enrich students' language environment by focusing not just on correct or incorrect usage but on the idea expressed. Probe and extend students' ideas. For example, if a student says, "I writed my name on my picture," the teacher could respond, "You wrote your name above the rocket. Where is your astronaut going?" In this way the teacher maintains the student's interest and at the same time introduces a different grammatical construction that the student can observe and perhaps adopt (Rice, 1989).

Cazden (1988) suggests that word meanings are most easily learned through interactions and conversations with an adult in which the adult introduces new words. For example, when a student complains, "He does that on purpose, just to make me mad!," the teacher might respond, "So you think he is *intentionally* tripping by your desk just to *irritate* you? Why have you reached that conclusion?" Reading aloud is also a potent form of language stimulation. Reading to students often leads to conversations about the pictures or the ideas in the books. The importance of one-to-one interaction with an adult in developing language abilities has been stressed by many psychologists (Rice, 1989). This is in keeping with Vygotsky's theory of cognitive development.

Holistic Language: Learning and Teaching

It is generally agreed that the first key to language development in school is to encourage students to use language by talking, listening, reading, and writing. Yetta and Kenneth Goodman (1990) make this argument:

> Language, written language included, is learned most easily in the context of use. When language is whole, relevant, and functional, learners have real purposes for using language, and through their language use, they develop control over the processes of language. (p. 225)

Within this **whole-language** perspective, teaching and learning are seen as reciprocal and collaborative. The teacher becomes an astute observer of students, noticing what support or resources they need in order to learn. Teacher and students together make decisions about curriculum. When students write, they write for an audience with the goal of communicating effectively. Writing is a relevant and meaningful activity. Vygotsky (1978) recognized the importance of authentic writing tasks: ". . . writing should be incorporated into a task that is necessary and relevant for life. Only then can we be certain that it will develop not as a matter of hand and finger habits but as a really new and complex form of speech" (p. 118). David Pearson (1989) makes a similar point: "[We] should ask students to read and write for real reasons (the kind real people in the real world have) rather than fake reasons we give them in school. School is too school-like" (p. 235).

The advocates of whole language insist that the curriculum should be integrated. There is no reason to work on spelling skills, then listening

Whole Language A philosophical approach to teaching and learning that stresses learning through authentic, real-life tasks. Emphasizes using language to learn, integrating learning across skills and subjects, and respecting the language abilities of both student and teacher.

skills, then writing skills, and then social studies or science. All these abilities can be developed together if students work to solve authentic problems. For example, one teacher capitalized on current affairs to encourage student reading, writing, and social studies problem solving:

> Cathie's elementary class learned about the Alaskan oil spill. She brought a newspaper article to class that sequenced in logbook fashion the events of the oil spill in Prince William Sound. To prepare her students to understand the article, she had her students participate in several background-building experiences. First, they used a world map, an encyclopedia, and library books to gather and share relevant information. Next, she simulated an oil spill by coating an object with oil. By then, the class was eager to read the article. (Espe, Worner, & Hotkevich, 1990, p. 45)

After they read and discussed the newspaper article, the teacher asked the class to imagine how the problem might have been prevented. Students had to explain and support their proposed solutions. The next week the students read another newspaper article about how people in their state were helping with the cleanup efforts in Alaska. The teacher asked if the students wanted to help, and they replied with an enthusiastic yes! The students designed posters and made speeches requesting donations of clean towels to be used to clean the oil-soaked animals in Prince William Sound. The class sent four large bags of towels to Alaska to help in the cleanup. The teacher's and the students' reading, writing,

---

TABLE 2.3   Ten Elements of a Whole-Language Program

1. *Reading to children*—the teacher reads quality literature to children to encourage them to read.
2. *Shared book experience*—a cooperative language activity based on the bedtime story tradition; the teacher reads and rereads appealing rhymes, songs, poems, and stories.
3. *Sustained silent reading*—everyone, including the teacher, reads for an extended period of time.
4. *Guided reading*—the teacher assigns books to groups of eight to ten children for independent reading followed by reading conferences; books are selected to keep the children on the cutting edge of their reading ability.
5. *Individualized reading*—an organized alternative to guided reading; grows out of guided reading; careful monitoring of individual progress is done by both child and teacher.

6. *Language experience*—oral language is recorded by a scribe or on tape and made available to children in written format; firsthand or vicarious experience is translated into written language.
7. *Children's writing*—ConVal uses the writing process of rehearse, draft, revise, edit, publish, and receive responses.
8. *Modeled writing*—the teacher models writing process and behavior; children see and hear an "expert" writer in action.
9. *Opportunities for sharing*—a finished piece is presented to an audience; ConVal uses author's teas and published books as two methods.
10. *Content area reading and writing*—students see demonstrations of each type of text (by subject content) and learn about varying reading speed and looking for content clues.

research, and speaking were directed toward solving a real-life problem (Espe, Worner, & Hotkevich, 1990).

There are many approaches to whole-language learning, but most share an emphasis on authentic tasks and integrated curricula. The Contoocook Valley (CoVal) District in New Hampshire has adopted a whole-language approach with ten elements, listed in Table 2.3 on page 58. Whatever your school's philosophy, you might adopt some of the ideas from the whole-language approach to encourage language and cognitive development in your students.

SUMMARY

A DEFINITION OF DEVELOPMENT

Theorists differ greatly in their approach to the study of development, but all tend to agree that people develop at different rates, that development is an orderly process, and that development takes place gradually. Piaget's theory of cognitive development is based on the assumption that people try to make sense of the world and actively create their knowledge through direct experience with objects, people, and ideas. Maturation, activity, social transmission, and the need for equilibrium all influence the way thinking processes and knowledge develop. In response to these influences, according to Piaget's theory, thinking processes and knowledge develop through adaptation (including the complementary processes of assimilation and accommodation) and changes in the organization of thought (the development of schemes).

PIAGET'S THEORY OF COGNITIVE DEVELOPMENT

Piaget believed that young people pass through four stages as they develop: sensorimotor, preoperational, concrete-operational, and formal-operational. In the sensorimotor stage, infants explore the world through their senses and motor activity and work toward mastering object permanence and performing goal-directed activities. In the preoperational stage, symbolic thinking and logical operations begin. Children in the stage of concrete operations can think logically about tangible situations and can demonstrate conservation, reversibility, classification, and seriation. The ability to perform hypothetico-deductive reasoning, coordinate a set of variables, and imagine other worlds marks the stage of formal operations.

IMPLICATIONS OF PIAGET'S THEORY FOR TEACHERS

Teachers can use Piaget's theory of cognitive development to understand students' thinking, to match instructional strategies to students' abilities, and to directly foster students' cognitive development. Piaget's theory has been criticized because children and adults often think in ways that are inconsistent with the notion of invariant stages. It also appears that Piaget underestimated children's cognitive abilities. Fischer's skill theory accounts for some of the inconsistencies in Piaget's model. In Fischer's theory, overlapping developmental stages are characterized by optimal levels of thinking ability under optimal conditions. Fischer's theory helps explain variations in performance within individuals and age groups. Piaget's work is also criticized for overlooking cultural factors in child development. Critics often point to the work of Vygotsky as an example of a theory of cognitive development that does include the important role of culture.

VYGOTSKY'S ALTERNATIVE TO PIAGET

Vygotsky's view is that cognitive development hinges on social interaction and the development of language. As an example, Vygotsky describes the role of children's self-directed talk in guiding and monitoring thinking and problem solving. Vygotsky proposed the concept of a zone of proximal development in which children in challenging situations can develop their own thinking abilities through timely, appropriate guidance and support from teachers or peers.

The Development of Language

Closely linked to cognitive development are the development of language and metalinguistic awareness. Children try to understand and apply language rules. Chomsky and others suggest that some of these rules are inborn in humans as a kind of transformational grammar. Using their capacity for language, children try to solve the puzzle of the language they hear, moving from holophrasic to telegraphic speech, through overextension, underextension, and overregularization, to a basic

understanding of pronunciation, vocabulary, grammar and syntax, semantics, and pragmatics by around age 5 or 6.

Teaching and Language

Teachers have a significant role in helping children develop language ability and knowledge about language. Teachers can focus on effective communication, meaning, comprehension, and respect for language in the classroom. The proponents of whole language have many ideas for developing language (reading, writing, speaking, and listening) through authentic, real-life tasks and integrated curricula.

KEY TERMS AND CONCEPTS

accommodation, p. 29
adaptation, p. 28
adolescent egocentrism, p. 39
assimilation, p. 29
classification, p. 34
cognitive development, p. 26
collective monologue, p. 34
compensation, p. 34
concrete operations, p. 34
conservation, p. 32
decentering, p. 33
development, p. 26
disequilibrium, p. 29
egocentric, p. 34
equilibration, p. 29
formal operations, p. 37
goal-directed actions, p. 30
holophrases, p. 53

hypothetico-deductive
  reasoning, p. 37
identity, p. 34
maturation, p. 26
metalinguistic awareness, p. 56
morphemes, p. 50
object permanence, p. 30
operations, p. 31
optimal level, p. 44
organization, p. 28
overextension, p. 53
overregularize, p. 53
personal development, p. 26
phonemes, p. 50
physical development, p. 26
pragmatics, p. 51
preoperational, p. 31
private speech, p. 46

reversibility, p. 34
reversible thinking, p. 32
scaffolding, p. 48
schemes, p. 28
semantics, p. 51
semiotic function, p. 31
sensorimotor, p. 30
seriation, p. 35
social development, p. 26
syntax, p. 50
telegraphic speech, p. 53
transformational grammar,
  p. 52
underextension, p. 53
whole language, p. 57
zone of proximal development,
  p. 48

WHAT WOULD YOU DO?

PRESCHOOL AND KINDERGARTEN

A group of vocal parents wants you to introduce workbooks to teach basic arithmetic in your class for 4- and 5-year-olds. They seem to think that that "play" with blocks, water, sand, clay, and so on is "wasted time." How would you respond?

ELEMENTARY AND MIDDLE SCHOOL

The district curriculum guide calls for a unit on poetry, including lessons on symbolism in poems. You are concerned that many of your students may not be ready to understand this abstract concept. How would you approach this unit? What would you do to "listen" to your students' thinking so you could match your teaching to their level of thinking? How would you give them concrete experience with symbolism?

Two very concerned parents want to have a conference with you about their son's "language problems." He is in first grade and has some trouble with pronunciation. How would you prepare for the conference?

JUNIOR HIGH AND HIGH SCHOOL

The students in your class persist in simply memorizing definitions for many of the important

abstract concepts in your class. They insist, "That's what you have to do to make a good grade in this class." Even though they can repeat the definitions precisely, they seem to have no conception of what the terms mean; they can't recognize examples of the concept in problems or give their own examples. It is almost as if they don't believe there is any real hope of understanding the ideas. Pick one important, difficult concept in your field and design a lesson to teach it to students who believe only in memorization.

It seems as if every fourth word from the mouths of your students is "like" or "you know." Also, their understanding of the material in your class is limited because they don't know the meaning of many words that you assumed high school students would certainly understand, such as "former" and "latter." What would you do to encourage language development along with teaching your subject?

COOPERATIVE LEARNING ACTIVITY

Working with four or five other members of your educational psychology class, solve either the "poetry" or the "memorization" problem described above. Then pair up with another group and take turns teaching the lessons you designed.

TEACHERS' CASEBOOK

ENCOURAGING LANGUAGE DEVELOPMENT

One of your students seldom speaks and communicates only in short, incomplete sentences or monosyllables. The student is a middle child in a large family, and you suspect there is little conversation or reading at home. How would you encourage language development for this student?

FOSTER SELF-EXPRESSION

In a situation like this you as a teacher need to provide an outlet for the child to express him- or herself. This can be done by first using written communication, such as daily journals. The student writes down thoughts or events and the teacher responds, also in writing. After you learn more about the student (likes, dislikes, interests), you can engage him or her in brief conversations and build from that. From there, you can go on to sharing books orally and so forth. School may be the most stable and comfortable environment for some students, and we as teachers need to utilize that situation.

Candice J. Gallagher, *Fourth-Grade Teacher*
Fredericktown Intermediate School, Fredericktown, Ohio

TEACHING ABSTRACT CONCEPTS

How would you teach the abstract concept of "justice" to students who think very concretely?

ROLE PLAYS

Justice is such an abstract idea that many students have a difficult time in grasping the concept. One of the best ways to demonstrate the idea of justice in a democratic society is to role play.

I would have the students take the roles of court personnel: judge, jury, defense, prosecutor. The defense would then present the story of *The Three Little Pigs*. The defendant would be the Wolf and the prosecuting witness would be the Third Little Pig.

The prosecution would bring in exhibits: straw, sticks, and so forth. The Third Little Pig could tell his side of the story. The defense could take another approach. The Wolf could tell his side of the story as told in the book *The True Story of the Three Little Pigs* by Jon Scieszka. When the prosecution and defense had finished, the verdict would be left up to the jury and the sentencing up to the judge.

The method of role playing, using a basic story, allows the students to think and interact with an abstract concept. The concept of justice is transformed into a concrete element. The idea of role playing could also be used in illustrating what justice looks like in different cultures.

Julie A. Addison, *Sixth-Grade Teacher*
Roxborough Elementary School, Littleton, Colorado

MOCK COURTROOMS

I would role play "injustice" for the students by arbitrarily dividing the class into two groups and giving one group a special privilege such as fifteen minutes of game time while I asked the other group to complete a boring task like copying all the "a" words in the dictionary. After fifteen minutes I would bring the students back together to discuss how they felt and contrast the injustice they had experienced with the concept of justice. I might set up a mock courtroom and put a familiar character like Goldilocks on trial or read excerpts from books like *Tom Sawyer, Charlotte's Web, The Three Little Pigs,* and *A Cricket in Times Square* and have the class record if they believe a character experienced justice or injustice.

Joanne S. Groseclose, *Virginia 1991 Teacher of the Year*
Marion Intermediate School, Marion, Virginia

I would relate the concept of justice to their world in a sense of fairness with things that happen to them and to their peers. I would even at times lead the students to make decisions as a group when certain events are related to this concept. Even young children, who are at a very concrete state of development, are able to recognize the fairness of events in their world and are able to come to decisions which represent fairness or justice. The problem with students this age is that everything is black or white; there is no gray for them, therefore they cannot see that certain circumstances may dictate a certain response. However, there are times when discussion can help them to see the unusualness or specialness of what is happening, and they can be led to alter a decision to meet the situation. As students reach fifth grade, they are more able to assess situations individually and understand the concept of justice in its full flavor.

Brenda M. Lloyd, *Third- and Fourth-Grade Teacher*
St. Anne's–Belfield, Charlottesville, Virginia

EXPERIENCING OTHERS' POINTS OF VIEW

In childhood and adolescence, children tend to be egocentric and have difficulty seeing the world from another person's point of view. When you notice students experiencing this difficulty, what do you do?

**EACH A PART OF
THE WHOLE**

The first day of school I want the students to realize that each of them is unique and essential to the class. The interdependence and value of everyone's resources enhances all that we do. I glue a large poster onto a piece of tag board, then cut it into thirty odd-shaped puzzle pieces (enough for each student to have one with a few extra pieces left over). The pieces have plenty of notches and grooves for secure assembly. The pieces are in a brown paper bag. At the beginning of the class, I explain how glad I am that each of them is a part of the class, and how everybody had something unique and special to offer to the group. I emphasize that I have as much to learn from them as they do from me. As I talk, I walk around and personally hand each of the students a brightly colored piece of the puzzle. I then pair the students with the person next to them. Student one is directed to talk for one minute without stopping about his piece while student two listens without saying a word. At the end of one minute, student two has to tell student one what he said. (They are always taken off guard and realize that they have not really heard too much.) The exercise is repeated with student two talking for one minute while student one listens and later repeats what was said.

The students realize that no other piece is like theirs, but they still have no idea what the big picture for the puzzle is. We gather around one table, or on the floor, and I share a few words on how important each piece is to the whole picture. They then have to figure out how to put the picture together. I add the extra pieces, and explain how I need the students' pieces just as much as they need mine.

Some very interesting interactions take place, depending on the grade level and the chemistry of the group; but they always manage to get the picture together and experience considerable satisfaction in finding out what the poster is. We then glue it together and hang it in the room for the rest of the year as a reminder that "we are all in this together."

Betty Garner, *Elementary Art Teacher*
Pattonville I.D.E.A.L. Center, Maryland Heights, Missouri

3 PERSONAL, SOCIAL, AND MORAL DEVELOPMENT

$\mathbf{A}$s we all know from experience, schooling involves more than cognitive development. In this chapter we examine emotional, social, and moral development.

We begin with the work of Erik Erikson, whose comprehensive theory provides a framework for studying personal and social development. Next we explore ideas about how we come to understand ourselves and others. What is the meaning of the self-concept, and how is it shaped? How do our views of others change as we grow? What factors determine our views about morality? Do moral actions follow from moral beliefs? What can teachers do to foster such personal qualities as honesty, cooperation, empathy, and self-esteem? We then consider the two major influences on children's personal and social development: families and schools. Families today have gone through many transitions, and these changes affect the roles of teachers.

With an understanding of some important aspects of personal and social development, we can consider a pressing question: "What is a developmentally appropriate education for students?" Several issues are important in the early years—physical development, reactions to preschool experience, and the child's changing relationships with friends. As the child enters adolescence, other issues become important—physical and sexual maturing and health risks such as drugs and AIDS.

By the time you have completed this chapter, you should be able to do the following:

- Describe Erikson's stages of psychosocial development and list several of his theory's implications for teaching.

- Suggest how teachers can foster self-esteem in their students.

- Describe Kohlberg's stages of moral reasoning and give an example of each.

- Evaluate alternatives to Kohlberg's theory.

- Explain the factors that encourage cheating and aggression in classrooms and discuss possible responses to each.

- Take a stand on affective and moral education.

- Describe the child's changing view of friendship.

- List the problems of early and late maturers.

- Suggest ways to help adolescents make responsible decisions about sex and drugs.

THE WORK OF ERIKSON

Like Piaget, Erik Erikson did not start out as a psychologist. In fact, Erikson never graduated from high school. He spent his early adult years studying art and traveling around Europe. A meeting with Sigmund Freud in Vienna led to an invitation from Freud to study psychoanalysis. After completing this training, Erikson emigrated to America to practice his profession and to escape the threat of Hitler.

In his influential *Childhood and Society* (1963), Erikson offered a basic framework for understanding the needs of young people in relation to the society in which they grow, learn, and later make their contributions. His later books, *Identity, Youth, and Crisis* (1968) and *Identity and the Life Cycle* (1980) expanded on his ideas. Although Erikson's approach is not the only explanation of personal and social development, I have chosen it to organize our discussion for several reasons. Erikson emphasizes the emergence of the self, the search for identity, and the individual's relationships with others throughout life. Because children spend many important years in school as their sense of themselves and others is emerging, the school is a major factor in development.

After studying child-rearing practices in several cultures, Erikson concluded that all humans have the same basic needs and that each society must provide in some way for those needs. Emotional changes and their relation to the social environment follow similar patterns in every society. This emphasis on the relationship of culture and the individual led Erikson to propose a **psychosocial** theory of development.

Like Piaget, Erikson saw development as a passage through a series of stages, each with its particular goals, concerns, accomplishments, and dangers. The stages are interdependent: accomplishments at later stages depend on how conflicts are resolved in the earlier years. At each stage, Erikson suggests, the individual faces a **developmental crisis.** Each crisis involves a conflict between a positive alternative and a potentially unhealthy alternative. The way in which the individual resolves each crisis will have a lasting effect on that person's self-image and view of society. An unhealthy resolution of problems in the early stages can have potential negative repercussions throughout life, although sometimes damage can be repaired at later stages. We will look briefly at all eight stages in Erikson's theory—or, as he calls them, the "eight ages of man." Table 3.1 presents the stages in summary form.

Erik Erikson proposed a theory of psychosocial development that describes tasks to be accomplished at different stages of life.

Psychosocial Describing the relation of the individual's emotional needs to the social environment.

Developmental Crisis A specific conflict whose resolution prepares the way for the next stage.

TABLE 3.1	Erikson's Eight Stages of Psychosocial Development	
Stage	**Approximate Age**	**Description**
1. Basic trust vs. basic mistrust	Birth to 12–18 months	The infant must form a first loving, trusting relationship with the caregiver, or develop a sense of mistrust.
2. Autonomy vs. shame/doubt	18 months to 3 years	The child's energies are directed toward the development of physical skills, including walking, grasping, and sphincter control. The child learns control but may develop shame and doubt if not handled well.
3. Initiative vs. guilt	3 to 6 years	The child continues to become more assertive and to take more initiative, but may be too forceful, leading to guilt feelings.
4. Industry vs. inferiority	6 to 12 years	The child must deal with demands to learn new skills or risk a sense of inferiority, failure, and incompetence.
5. Identity vs. role confusion	Adolescence	The teenager must achieve a sense of identity in occupation, sex roles, politics, and religion.
6. Intimacy vs. isolation	Young adulthood	The young adult must develop intimate relationships or suffer feelings of isolation.
7. Generativity vs. stagnation	Middle adulthood	Each adult must find some way to satisfy and support the next generation.
8. Ego integrity vs. despair	Late adulthood	The culmination is a sense of acceptance of oneself as one is and of feeling fulfilled.

Source: Adapted from Lester A. Lefton, *Psychology,* 4th ed., p. 350. Copyright © 1991. Reprinted with permission of Allyn and Bacon.

The Preschool Years: Trust, Autonomy, and Initiative

Erikson identifies *trust versus mistrust* as the basic conflict of infancy. In the first months of life, babies begin to find out whether they can depend on the world around them. According to Erikson, the infant will develop a sense of trust if needs for food and care are met with comforting regularity. Closeness and responsiveness on the part of the parents at this time contribute greatly to this sense of trust (Lamb, 1982; Bretherton & Waters, 1985).

Note that in this first year, infants are in the early part of Piaget's sensorimotor stage. They are just beginning to learn that they are separate

Guidelines

Encouraging Initiative in the Preschool Child

Encourage children to make and to act on choices.

Examples

1. Have a free-choice time when children can select an activity or game.
2. As much as possible, avoid interrupting children who are very involved in what they are doing.
3. When children suggest an activity, try to follow their suggestions or incorporate their ideas into ongoing activities.
4. Offer positive choices: instead of saying, "You can't have the cookies now," ask, "Would you like the cookies after lunch or after naptime?"

Make sure that each child has a chance to experience success.

Examples

1. When introducing a new game or skill, teach it in small steps.
2. Avoid competitive games when the range of abilities in the class is great.

Encourage make-believe with a wide variety of roles.

Examples

1. Have costumes and props that go along with stories the children enjoy. Encourage the children to act out the stories or make up new adventures for favorite characters.
2. Monitor the children's play to be sure no one monopolizes playing "teacher," "Mommy," "Daddy," or other heroes.

Be tolerant of accidents and mistakes, especially when children are attempting to do something on their own.

Examples

1. Use cups and pitchers that make it easy to pour and hard to spill.
2. Recognize the attempt, even if the product is unsatisfactory.

Autonomy   Independence.

Initiative   Willingness to begin new activities and explore new directions.

from the world around them and that other objects and people exist even when they cannot see them. This realization of separateness is part of what makes trust so important: Infants must trust the aspects of their world that are beyond their control (Bretherton & Waters, 1985).

Erikson's second stage, **autonomy** *versus shame and doubt,* marks the beginning of self-control and self-confidence. Young children are capable of doing more and more on their own. They must begin to assume important responsibilities for self-care like feeding, toileting, and dressing. They are striving toward autonomy.

During this period parents must tread a fine line; they must be protective but not overprotective. If parents do not maintain a reassuring, confident attitude and do not reinforce the child's efforts to master basic motor and cognitive skills, children may begin to feel shame; they may learn to doubt their abilities to manage the world on their own terms. Erikson believes that children who experience too much doubt at this stage will lack confidence in their own powers throughout life.

For Erikson, "initiative adds to autonomy the quality of undertaking, planning, and attacking a task for the sake of being active and on the move" (Erikson, 1963, p. 255). But with **initiative** comes the realization that some activities are forbidden. At times children may feel torn between what they want to do and what they should (or should not) do. The challenge of this period is to maintain a zest for activity and at the same time to understand that not every impulse can be acted upon.

It would certainly be faster for this grandfather to fix the bike himself, but by letting his granddaughter join in, he nurtures her sense of initiative.

Young children can imagine themselves playing various adult roles and begin to test their powers at "grown-up" tasks. The 4-year-old passing tools to a parent who is fixing a broken bicycle is involved in important work. Children at this stage imagine what the future might hold for them. Play is an important form of initiative, and pretend games are common.

These children are eager for responsibility. They require confirmation from adults that their initiative is accepted and that their contributions, no matter how small, are truly valued. Again, adults must tread a fine line, this time in providing supervision without interference. If children are not allowed to do things on their own, a sense of guilt may develop; they may come to believe that what they want to do is always "wrong."

Elementary and Middle School Years: Industry versus Inferiority

In the early school years, students are developing what Erikson calls a sense of **industry.** They are beginning to see the relationship between perseverance and the pleasure of a job completed. The crisis at this stage is *industry versus inferiority.* For children in modern societies the school and the neighborhood offer a new set of challenges that must be balanced with those at home. Interaction with peers becomes increasingly important as well. The child's ability to move between these worlds and to cope with academics, group activities, and friends will lead to a growing sense of competence. Difficulty with these challenges can result in feelings of inferiority.

Work by George and Caroline Vaillant (1981) supports Erikson's notion of the importance of industry. These researchers followed 450 males for 35 years, beginning in early childhood. Their conclusion was that the men who had been the most industrious and willing to work as children

Children are more likely to develop trust if their needs for food, care, and comfort are reliably and consistently met in the first year of life.

Industry Eagerness to engage in productive work.

Guidelines

Encouraging Industry

Make sure that students have opportunities to set and work toward realistic goals.

Examples

1. Begin with short assignments, then move on to longer ones. Monitor student progress by setting up progress checkpoints.
2. Teach students to set reasonable goals. Write down goals and have students keep a journal of progress toward goals.

Give students a chance to show their independence and responsibility.

Examples

1. Tolerate honest mistakes.

2. Delegate to students tasks like watering class plants, collecting and distributing materials, monitoring the computer lab, grading homework, keeping records of forms returned, and so on.

Provide support to students who seem discouraged.

Examples

1. Use individual charts and contracts that show student progress.
2. Keep samples of earlier work so students can see their improvements.
3. Have awards for most improved, most helpful, most hardworking.

were the best adjusted, most motivated, and best paid as adults. These men also had the most satisfying personal relationships. The willingness to work hard as a child seemed to be more important for success in later life than intelligence or family background. These are only correlational data. We don't know for sure that being industrious *causes* success in later life. Still, industry is worth encouraging.

Adolescence: The Search for Identity

The central issue for adolescents is the development of an **identity** that will provide a firm basis for adulthood. The individual has of course been developing a sense of self since infancy. But adolescence marks the first time that a conscious effort is made to answer the now-pressing question, "Who am I?" The conflict defining this stage is *identity versus role confusion*.

Erikson notes that the healthy resolution of earlier conflicts can now serve as a foundation for the search for identity. Adolescents who have established a basic sense of *trust* are prepared to find people and ideas worthy of their trust. A firm sense of *autonomy* gives the adolescent courage to insist upon free choice about her or his career and lifestyle. The *initiative* that prompted the young child to play lawyer or painter can help the adolescent take steps toward assuming a real adult role. And out of a strong sense of *industry* can grow a feeling of competence, a belief in one's ability to make meaningful contributions to society.

Exactly what do we mean by identity, and what does the crisis of this adolescent stage involve? Identity refers to the organization of the individual's drives, abilities, beliefs, and history into a consistent image

Identity The complex answer to the question "Who am I?"

For some adolescents, membership in a gang becomes an important influence in the search for identity.

of self. It involves deliberate choices and decisions, particularly about vocation, sexual orientation, and a "philosophy of life" (Marcia, 1987; Waterman, 1985). If adolescents fail to integrate all these aspects and choices, or if they feel unable to choose at all, role confusion threatens.

Elaborating on Erikson's work, James Marcia and his colleagues have suggested that there are four alternatives for adolescents as they confront themselves and their choices (Marcia, 1980; Schiedel & Marcia, 1985). The first is **identity achievement.** This means that after considering the realistic options, the individual has made choices and is pursuing them. It appears that few students achieve this status by the end of high school. Most are not firm in their choices for several more years (Archer, 1982). **Identity foreclosure** describes the situation of adolescents who do not experiment with different identities or consider a range of options but simply commit themselves to the goals, values, and lifestyles of others, usually their parents. **Identity diffusion,** on the other hand, occurs when individuals reach no conclusions about who they are or what they want to do with their lives; they have no firm direction. Adolescents experiencing identity diffusion may have struggled unsuccessfully to make choices, or they may have avoided thinking seriously about the issues at all. Finally, adolescents in the midst of struggling with choices are experiencing what Erikson called a **moratorium.** This is what is really meant when we talk about an identity crisis. Erikson used the term moratorium to describe a *delay* in the adolescent's commitment to personal and occupational choices. This delay is very common, and probably healthy, for modern adolescents. Marcia expands the meaning of moratorium to include the adolescent's *active efforts* to deal with the crisis of shaping an identity. Table 3.2 on page 72 gives examples of the four alternatives in the adolescent's search for identity.

Identity Achievement
Strong sense of commitment to life choices after free considerations of alternatives.

Identity Foreclosure
Acceptance of parental life choices without consideration of options.

Identity Diffusion
Uncenteredness; confusion about who one is and what one wants.

Moratorium Identity crisis; suspension of choices because of struggle.

TABLE 3.2 Marcia's Identity Statuses

James Marcia has suggested that there are four possible statuses for the adolescent identity. Here are examples of the types of responses he received from adolescents in each status to questions like "How willing would you be to give up your current plans for your career if something better came along?"

Identity achievement: "It's hard to imagine anything really better for me. I guess I might consider it, but I've thought about my decision for a long time—it's the right one for me."

Identity foreclosure: "I wouldn't want to change my plans. My family and I have been working toward this ever since I can remember. Actually, I can't even imagine doing anything else; I just wouldn't feel comfortable."

Identity diffusion: "I don't really have any plans, so there must be something better than the last couple of things I've been turning over in my mind. I don't really know what might work for me, anyway, or what I'd be able to do. . . ."

Moratorium: "Certainly, I might be willing to change. But I've been focusing on this one idea for a while, looking at it from all kinds of angles. It's driving me crazy, but I'm almost to the point where I can say it looks like the best idea for me. But I couldn't say I'm sure yet."

Source: Based on ideas found in J. E. Marcia (1980), Identity formation in adolescence. In J. Adelson (Ed.), *Handbook of Adolescent Psychology*. New York, Wiley.

Identity and the Role of the School. Many times the teacher is the most appropriate and available adult to help adolescents in their search for themselves. When college students are asked to list reasons for choosing a particular major, they often mention the importance of a teacher who was effective, demanding, and warm. Teachers can offer students ideas and people to trust. Teachers can support the students' need for free choice of careers. They can encourage aspirations and offer objective feedback on accomplishments in relevant subjects.

But beware. As adolescents attempt to establish their own identities and see themselves as separate from their parents, they may also reject other authority figures, including teachers. Don't take this questioning of authority too personally. It comes with the territory if you work with adolescents. If there are conflicts, avoid the temptation to label an adolescent based on his or her "experimental" or "defiant" identify. A student who tries drugs or shoplifts once or twice is not an addict or a delinquent. Labeling students may convince them that you "just don't understand." Deal with the behavior, but don't assume it is a permanent aspect of the student's identity (Kroger, 1989).

The school years may see only the beginning of identity formation. As with formal operations, identity formation can be an extended process for many people (Manaster, 1989). Many college students move from a mora-

Guidelines

Encouraging Identity Formation

Give students many models for career choices and other adult roles.

Examples

1. Point out models from literature and history. Have a calendar with the birthdays of eminent women, minority leaders, or people who made a little-known contribution to the subject you are teaching. Briefly discuss the person's accomplishments on his or her birthday.
2. Invite guest speakers to describe how and why they chose their professions. Make sure all kinds of work and workers are represented.

Help students find resources for working out personal problems.

Examples

1. Encourage them to talk to school counselors.
2. Discuss potential outside services.

Be tolerant of teenage fads as long as they don't offend others or interfere with learning.

Examples

1. Discuss the fads of earlier eras (neon hair, powdered wigs).
2. Don't impose strict dress or hair codes.

Give students realistic feedback about themselves.

Examples

1. When students misbehave or perform poorly, make sure they understand the consequences of their behavior—the effects on themselves and others.
2. Give students model answers or show them other students' completed projects so they can compare their work to good examples.
3. Since students are "trying on" roles, keep the roles separate from the person. You can criticize behavior without criticizing the student.

torium to an identity-achieved status between freshman and senior years (Adams & Fitch, 1982).

Ethnic Pride and Identity. For all students, pride in family and community is part of the foundation for a stable identify. Because ethnic-minority students are members of both a majority culture and a subculture, it is sometimes difficult for them to establish a clear identity. Values, learning styles, and communication patterns of the students' subculture may be inconsistent with the expectations of the school and the larger society. If the students' first language is not English, the problem may be even greater, especially if the school places little value on the students' language and culture. Special efforts to encourage **ethnic pride** are especially important so these students do not get the message that differences are deficits. For example, differences in skin color, hair length, dress, dialect, or accent are just that—differences, not inferior or superior qualities (Spencer & Markstrom-Adams, 1990).

Beyond the School Years

The crises of Erikson's stages of adulthood all involve the quality of human relations. The first of these stages is *intimacy versus isolation.* Intimacy in this sense refers to a willingness to relate to another person on a deep level, to have a relationship based on more than mutual need.

Ethnic Pride A positive self-concept about one's racial or ethnic heritage.

Someone who has not achieved a sufficiently strong sense of identity tends to fear being overwhelmed or swallowed up by another person and may retreat into isolation.

The conflict at the next stage is *generativity versus stagnation.* **Generativity** extends the ability to care for another person and involves caring and guidance for the next generation and for future generations. While generativity frequently refers to having and nurturing children, it has a broader meaning. Productivity and creativity are essential features.

The last of Erikson's stages is *integrity versus despair* and involves coming to terms with death. Achieving **integrity** (Erikson calls it *ego integrity*) means consolidating one's sense of self and fully accepting that self, its unique and now unalterable history. Those unable to attain a feeling of fulfillment and completeness sink into despair.

UNDERSTANDING OURSELVES AND OTHERS

With Erikson's theory of psychosocial development as a framework, we can now examine several aspects of personal and social development that are issues throughout childhood and adolescence.

What is self-concept? How do we come to understand ourselves and other people? How do we develop a sense of right and wrong—and do these beliefs affect our behavior? You will see that developments in these areas follow patterns similar to those we noted in chapter 2 for cognitive development. Children's understandings of themselves are concrete at first and then become more abstract. Early views of self and friends are based on immediate behaviors and appearances. Children assume that others share their feelings and perceptions. Their thinking about themselves and others is simple, segmented, and rule-bound, not flexible and integrated into organized systems. In time children are able to think abstractly about internal processes—beliefs, intentions, values, motivations. With these developments, knowledge of self, others, and situations can incorporate more abstract qualities (Berk, 1991).

Self-Concept and Self-Esteem

Generativity Sense of concern for future generations.

Integrity Sense of self-acceptance and fulfillment.

Self-Concept Our perceptions about ourselves.

Self-Esteem The value each of us places on our own characteristics, abilities, and behaviors.

Self-concept, like many other psychological terms, is part of our everyday conversation. We talk about people who have a "low" self-concept or individuals whose self-concept is not "strong." In psychology, the term generally refers to "the composite of ideas, feelings, and attitudes people have about themselves" (Hilgard, Atkinson, & Atkinson, 1979, p. 605). We could also consider the self-concept to be our attempt to explain ourselves to ourselves, to build a scheme (in Piaget's terms) that organizes our impressions, feelings, and attitudes about ourselves. But this model or scheme is not permanent, unified, or unchanging. Our self-perceptions vary from situation to situation and from one phase of our lives to another. **Self-esteem** is our evaluation of our own self-concept. If people have positive self-concepts—if they "like what they see" in themselves— we say that they have high self-esteem. The terms often are used interchangeably, even though they have distinct meanings.

How Self-Concept Develops. Young children see themselves in terms of their physical appearance, name, actions, and abilities but do not have a sense of their enduring characteristics or "personality." As they mature, children move from concrete, fragmented views of themselves to more abstract, organized, and objective views that include psychological characteristics. In answer to the question "Who are you?" a 7-year-old might say, "I am a girl. I have long, brown hair. My favorite color is blue and my favorite food is nachos." A 9-year-old or a 10-year-old might answer the same question by listing traits such as, "I'm funny and lazy, but I'm smart in arithmetic. I'm silly sometimes." Older children's self-descriptions include interpersonal characteristics such as friendly, shy, a good team member. As they enter adolescence, children begin to think of themselves in terms of abstract values and attitudes. As Erikson and Marcia noted, conscious decisions about religion, philosophy of life, sexual beliefs, and career choices become part of the self-concept during high school and college, when identity issues are being resolved.

There is another change as students mature. From about fourth grade on, self-esteem tends to increase. One exception is the transition from elementary to junior high school. Until students adjust to the new demands of junior high schedules and workload, they may experience a decrease in self-esteem. With growing competence and independence in adolescence, growth in self-esteem resumes (Powers, Hauser, & Kilner, 1989).

The developing self-concept of the child is influenced by parents and other family members in the early years and by friends, schoolmates, and teachers as the child grows. Before about age 7, children tend to see themselves in global terms—if they have a positive self-concept, they assume that they are good in all areas of performance (Harter, 1990). But as they mature, children's views of themselves become more differentiated; that is, multiple concepts of the self come into play. For example, an 11-year-old girl may see herself simultaneously as a loyal friend, an alienated family member, a strong math student, an uncoordinated athlete, and so on. As part of this differentiation, separate concepts of self as student (academic self-concepts) and self beyond school (nonacademic self-concepts) emerge (Byrne & Shavelson, 1986; Marsh, 1990; Shavelson, Hubner, & Stanton, 1976). One view of the structure of self-concept is shown in Figure 3.1 on page 76.

As you can see, the person's general view of self is made up of other, more specific concepts, including the nonacademic self-concept, self-concept in English, and the view of self in mathematics. (Only English and math have been studied using Shavelson's model. There may be other subject-specific self-concepts, for example in science.) Research has shown that these separate nonacademic, English, and mathematics self-concepts are not highly correlated (Marsh, 1990; Marsh & Holmes, 1990).

The nonacademic, English, and mathematics self-concepts at the second level are themselves made up of more specific, separate conceptions of the self, such as conceptions about physical ability, appearance, relations with peers, and relations with family (particularly parents). These specific self-concepts are based on many experiences and events such as how well we do in sports; how we regard our body, skin, or hair;

FIGURE 3.1   Structure of Self-Concept   Students have many separate but sometimes related concepts of themselves. The overall sense of self appears to be divided into at least three separate, but slightly related, self-concepts—English, mathematics, and nonacademic.

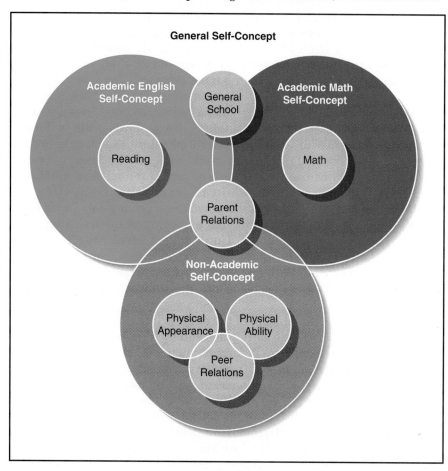

Source: Based on ideas found in H. W. Marsh and R. J. Shavelson, 1985, Self-concept: Its multifaceted, hierarchical structure. *Educational Psychologist, 20.*

our friendships; our artistic abilities; our contributions to community groups, and so on.

The self-concept evolves through constant self-evaluation in different situations (Shavelson & Bolus, 1982). Children and adolescents are continually asking themselves, in effect, "How am I doing?" They compare their performance with their own standards and with the performances of peers. They also gauge the verbal and nonverbal reactions of significant people—parents, best friends, leaders, teachers. The context of school makes a difference too. Students who are strong in math in an average school feel better about their math skills than students of equal ability in high-achieving schools. Marsh (1990) calls this the "Big-Fish-Little-Pond Effect." The way individuals explain their successes or failures also is important. We must attribute our successes to our own actions, not to luck or to special assistance, in order to build self-esteem.

Self-Concept and School Life. For teachers there are at least two important, interrelated questions to ask about self-concept. (1) How does self-concept affect a student's behavior in school? (2) How does life in school affect a student's self-concept?

In answer to the first question, it appears that students with higher self-esteem are somewhat more likely to be successful in school (Marsh, 1990), although the strength of the relationship varies greatly depending on the characteristics of the students and the research methods used (Hansford & Hattie, 1982; Marsh & Holmes, 1990). In addition, higher self-esteem is related to more favorable attitudes toward school, more positive behavior in the classroom, and greater popularity with other students (Cauley & Tyler, 1989; Metcalfe, 1981; Reynolds, 1980). Of course, as we discussed in chapter 1, knowing that two variables are related (correlated) does not tell us that one is causing the other. It may be that high achievement and popularity lead to positive self-concept, or vice versa. In fact, it probably works both ways (Marsh, 1987; Shavelson & Bolus, 1982).

This leads us to the second question of how school affects self-concept. Good and Weinstein (1986) make this observation:

> School is a place where children develop or fail to develop a variety of competencies that come to define self and ability, where friendships with peers are nurtured, and where the role of the community member is played out, all during a highly formative period of development. Thus the building of self-esteem, interpersonal competence, social problem solving, and leadership becomes important in its own right and as a critical underpinning of success in academic learning. (p. 1095)

Is school really so important? A recent study that followed 322 sixth-grade students for two years would say yes. Hoge, Smit, and Hanson (1990) found that students' satisfaction with the school, their sense that classes were interesting and that teachers cared, and teacher feedback and evaluations influenced students' self-esteem. Teacher feedback and grades in particular subjects affected self-concepts in those subjects. In physical education, teachers' opinions were especially powerful in shaping students' conceptions of their athletic abilities. Interestingly, special programs like "Student of the Month," participation in the Science Olympiad or Talent Search, or admission to advanced math classes had little effect on self-esteem. (Relate this to the "Big-Fish-Little-Pond Effect.")

So teachers can make a difference in how students feel about their abilities in particular subjects. Given this responsibility, what can teachers do? The recommendations in Table 3.3 on page 78 are a beginning.

The Self and Others

As we seek our own identity and form images of ourselves in various academic and social situations, we are also seeking and forming ways to

TABLE 3.3 Suggestions for Encouraging Self-Esteem

1. Value and accept all pupils, for their attempts as well as their accomplishments.
2. Create a climate that is physically and psychologically safe for students.
3. Become aware of your own personal biases (everyone has some biases) and expectations.
4. Make sure that your procedures for teaching and grouping students are really necessary, not just a convenient way of handling problem students or avoiding contact with some students.
5. Make standards of evaluation clear; help students learn to evaluate their own accomplishments.
6. Model appropriate methods of self-criticism, perseverance, and self-reward.
7. Avoid destructive comparisons and competition; encourage students to compete with their own prior levels of achievement.

8. Accept a student even when you must reject a particular behavior or outcome. Students should feel confident, for example, that failing a test or being reprimanded in class does not make them "bad" people.
9. Remember that positive self-concept grows from success in operating in the world *and* from being valued by important people in the environment.
10. Encourage students to take responsibility for their reactions to events; show them that they have choices in how to respond.
11. Set up support groups or "study buddies" in school and teach students how to encourage each other.
12. Help students set clear goals and objectives; brainstorm about resources they have for reaching their goals.
13. Highlight the value of different ethnic groups—their cultures and accomplishments.

Sources: Information from J. Canfield (1990), Improving students' self-esteem, *Educational Leadership, 48* (1), pp. 48–50; M. M. Kash & G. Borich (1978), *Teacher behavior and student self-concept* (Menlo Park, CA: Addison-Wesley); H. H. Marshall (1989), The development of self-concept, *Young Children, 44* (5), pp. 44–51.

understand the "significant others" around us. Children learn to see themselves as separate and thus to see others as separate people as well, with *their* own identities. How do we learn to interpret what others are thinking and feeling?

Social Cognition. Psychologists interested in **social cognition** study questions about "how children conceptualize other people and how they come to understand the thoughts, emotions, intentions, and viewpoints of others" (Shantz, 1975, p. 1). Martin Hoffman (1979) describes four stages in the development of a child's concept of other people. During the first year or so, children do not distinguish between themselves and others in their world. Toward the end of the first year, along with object permanence, children develop "person permanence"—the awareness that other people are separate physical beings. But children at this stage still believe that everyone else has thoughts and feelings identical to their own. During the next two years children move toward an understanding that in a particular situation another person can have separate feelings and ideas. But children are 8 to 12 years old before they fully understand that other people have distinct, separate identities, life histories, and futures. You may remember feeling intrigued when you were a young adolescent by the idea that all the people passing you in cars on a busy street led separate lives filled with unique experiences—that they were all "heroes" in their own "movies."

Social Cognition An individual's conceptions of other people.

Empathy. Martin Hoffman (1978, 1983, 1984) has also suggested that **empathy** develops along with the understanding of others' separate identities. Empathy is the ability to feel an emotion as it is experienced by another person—to put yourself in another's shoes. Both adults and children respond emotionally to signs of distress in others. But the emotional reaction of a young child is not based on an understanding of how another feels, since the child cannot yet see the other's emotions as separate. Very young children may respond to seeing another child hurt as if they had been hurt themselves. A little later, children begin to be aware that others' feelings are separate but assume that those feelings must be the same as their own. Hoffman cites the example of a young boy who brought his own mother to comfort his crying friend, even though the friend's mother was available to help. The boy evidently assumed that his friend would want *exactly* the comfort he himself usually wanted in a time of trouble. Children eventually become more and more able to imagine how other people would feel in a given situation.

Empathy plays an important part in our ability to understand and get along with one another (Chapman, Zahn-Waxler, Cooperman, & Iannotti, 1987). Teachers can encourage the development of empathy by allowing students to work together and discuss emotional reactions to various experiences. When disputes arise in the later elementary and the secondary grades, teachers can resist the temptation to quote rules or act as a judge and instead can help the students see one another's point of view.

The ability to empathize with others and respect their views can be learned more readily by working toward common goals than by listening to a lecture from the teacher on the importance of respect. Here these "study buddies" check each other's work.

MORAL DEVELOPMENT

If you have spent time with young children, you know that there is a period when you can say, "Eating in the living room is not allowed!" and get away with it. For young children, rules simply exist. Piaget (1965) called this the state of *moral realism.* At this stage the child of 5 or 6 believes that rules about conduct or rules about how to play a game are absolute and can't be changed. If a rule is broken, the child believes that the punishment should be determined by how much damage is done, not by the intention of the child or by other circumstances. So accidentally breaking three cups is worse than intentionally breaking one, and in the child's eyes, the punishment for the three-cup offense should be greater.

As children interact with others and see that different people have different rules, there is a gradual shift to a *morality of cooperation.* Children come to understand that people make rules and people can change them. When rules are broken, both the damage done and the intention of the offender are taken into account. These developmental changes and others are reflected in Kohlberg's theory of moral development, based in part on Piaget's ideas.

Kohlberg's Stages of Moral Development

Lawrence Kohlberg (1963, 1975, 1981) has proposed a detailed sequence of stages of **moral reasoning,** or judgments about right and wrong, and has led the field in studying their evolution. He has divided moral development into three levels: (1) preconventional, where judgment is

Empathy Ability to feel emotion as experienced by others.

Moral Reasoning The thinking processes involved in judgments about questions of right and wrong.

based solely on a person's own needs and perceptions; (2) conventional, where the expectations of society and law are taken into account; and (3) postconventional, where judgments are based on abstract, more personal principles that are not necessarily defined by society's laws. Each of these three levels is then subdivided into stages, as shown in Table 3.4.

In numerous studies Kohlberg has evaluated the moral reasoning of both children and adults by presenting them with **moral dilemmas,** or hypothetical situations in which people must make difficult decisions.

TABLE 3.4   Kohlberg's Stage Theory of Moral Reasoning

Level 1. Preconventional Moral Reasoning

Judgment is based on personal needs and others' rules.

Stage 1   Punishment-Obedience Orientation
            Rules are obeyed to avoid punishment. A good or bad
            action is determined by its physical consequences.

Stage 2   Personal Reward Orientation
            Personal needs determine right and wrong. Favors are
            returned along the lines of "You scratch my back, I'll
            scratch yours."

Level 2. Conventional Moral Reasoning

Judgment is based on others' approval, family expectations, traditional
  values, the laws of society, and loyalty to country.

Stage 3   Good Boy–Nice Girl Orientation
            Good means "nice." It is determined by what pleases, aids,
            and is approved by others.

Stage 4   Law and Order Orientation
            Laws are absolute. Authority must be respected and the
            social order maintained.

Level 3. Postconventional Moral Reasoning

Stage 5   Social Contract Orientation
            Good is determined by socially agreed-upon standards of
            individual rights. This is a morality similar to that of the
            U.S. Constitution.

Stage 6*   Universal Ethical Principle Orientation
            Good and right are matters of individual conscience and
            involve abstract concepts of justice, human dignity, and
            equality.

*In later work Kohlberg questioned whether Stage 6 exists separately from Stage 5.

Source: Adapted by permission of the *Journal of Philosophy* from L. Kohlberg (1975), The cognitive-developmental approach to moral education, *Phi Delta Kappan,* 56, p. 671.

Moral Dilemmas
Situations in which no choice is clearly and indisputably right.

Subjects are asked what the person caught in the dilemma should do and why. In these situations there is no obvious answer; no action will provide a complete solution.

One of the most commonly used moral dilemmas can be summarized as follows: A man's wife is dying. There is one drug that could save her, but it is very expensive, and the druggist who invented it will not sell it at a price low enough for the man to buy it. Finally, the man becomes desperate and considers stealing the drug for his wife. What should he do, and why?

At level 1 (preconventional), the child's answer might be, "It is wrong to steal because you might get caught." This answer reflects the child's basic egocentrism. The reasoning might be: "What would happen to me if I stole something? I might get caught and punished."

At level 2 (the conventional level), the subject is able to look beyond the immediate personal consequences and consider the views, and especially the *approval,* of others. Laws, religious or civil, are very important and are regarded as absolute and unalterable. One answer stressing adherence to rules is "It is wrong to steal because it is against the law." Another answer, placing high value on loyalty to family and loved ones but still respecting the law, is "It's right to steal because the man means well—he's trying to help his wife. But he will still have to pay the druggist when he can or accept the penalty for breaking the law."

At level 3 (the postconventional level), an answer might be "It is not wrong to steal because human life must be preserved. The worth of a human life is greater than the worth of property." This response considers the underlying individual values that might be involved in the decision. Abstract concepts are no longer rigid; and as the name of this level implies, principles can be separated from conventional values. A person reasoning on this level understands that what is considered right by the majority may not be considered right by an individual in a particular situation. Rational, personal choice is stressed.

Moral reasoning is related to both cognitive and emotional development. Formal operations and empathy in particular play large roles in a progression through Kohlberg's stages and levels. As we have seen, abstract thinking becomes increasingly important in the higher stages of moral development, as children move from decisions based on absolute rules to decisions based on principles such as justice and mercy. Empathy, the ability to see another's perspective and to imagine alternative bases for laws and rules, also enters into judgments at the higher stages.

Alternatives to Kohlberg's Theory

Kohlberg's stage theory has been criticized, first, because the stages do not seem in reality to be separate, sequenced, and consistent. People often give reasons for moral choices that reflect several different stages simultaneously. Or a person's choices in one instance may fit one stage and in a different situation may reflect another stage.

Social Conventions versus Moral Issues. Another criticism is that Kohlberg's theory does not differentiate between social conventions and true moral issues until the higher stages of moral reasoning. Social con-

Point/Counterpoint

Are There Sex Differences in Moral Reasoning?

The highest stage in Kohlberg's theory of moral development involves decisions based on universal principles of justice and fairness. Reasoning based on caring for others and maintaining relationships is scored at a lower level in Kohlberg's theory. Because women traditionally are seen as more concerned about people and relationships and men as more concerned about principles of justice and fairness, some psychologists have claimed that Kohlberg's theory is biased against women. One of the most vocal critics has been Carol Gilligan (1982). Gilligan suggests not only that Kohlberg's theory is biased, but also that it overlooks an important aspect of morality, the "ethic of care." Are there differences in the ways men and women reason about moral issues?

Point: Women care more about other people.

Many of Kohlberg's early studies of moral reasoning found that most men progressed to stages 4 and 5 by adulthood, while most women "stayed" at stage 3. This makes it appear as if women are moral midgets. Because the stage theory was based on a longitudinal study of men only, it is very possible that the moral reasoning of women and the stages of women's development are not adequately represented. Because Kohlberg assumed that reasoning about justice represents the highest level of morality, his theory can describe only how this narrow kind of moral reasoning develops. Carol

ventions are the social rules and expectations of a particular group or society—for example, "It is rude to eat with your hands" or "Men don't wear dresses." These rules are somewhat arbitrary. There is nothing inherently right or wrong about the actions. The behaviors would not be inappropriate if there were no social convention prohibiting them. True moral issues, on the other hand, involve the rights of individuals, the general welfare of the group, or the avoidance of harm. "Stealing" would be wrong, even if there were no "rule" against it. Larry Nucci (1987) has found that children as young as 3 can distinguish between social conventions and moral issues. They know, for example, that being noisy in school would be fine if there were no rule requiring quiet, but that it would not be right to hit another child, even if there were no rule against it. So even very young children can reason based on moral principles that are not tied to social conventions and rules.

The Morality of Caring. One of the most hotly debated criticisms of Kohlberg's theory is that the stages are biased in favor of males and do not represent the way moral reasoning develops in women (Gilligan, 1982; Gilligan & Attanucci, 1988). The **Point/Counterpoint** section above examines this issue.

Another criticism of Kohlberg's stage theory is that stages 5 and 6 in moral reasoning are biased in favor of Western, male values that emphasize individualism. In cultures that are more family centered or group oriented, the highest moral value might involve putting the opinions of the group before decisions based on individual conscience. There has been much disagreement over the "highest" moral stage. In fact, Kohlberg

Gilligan has proposed a different sequence of moral development—a morality of care. Gilligan suggests that individuals move from a focus on self-interests to moral reasoning based on commitment to specific individuals and relationships, and then to the highest level of morality, based on the principles of responsibility and care for all people.

Counterpoint: Both males and females are caring.

Recent studies find few significant differences between men and women in their level of moral reasoning as measured by Kohlberg's procedures. Lawrence Walker and B. de Vries (1985) examined the results of 80 studies that involved over 10,000 subjects and found differences based on sex in only a few of the investigations.

Another review of 56 samples and over 6,000 subjects found a small advantage for women (Thoma, 1986). In order to study moral reasoning as it actually happens in real life and to get an idea about the basis for decisions, Walker and his colleagues (Walker, de Vries, & Trevethan, 1987; Walker, 1989) asked children, adolescents, and adults to describe a personal moral problem and to analyze a traditional moral dilemma. For both types of problems, males and females revealed both a morality of caring and a concern with justice. So both justice and caring seem to be important bases for moral reasoning for both men and women. While Gilligan has not demonstrated that there are sex differences in moral reasoning, her criticisms and ideas have broadened the view of what constitutes morality.

himself has questioned the applicability of stage 6. Very few people other than trained philosophers reason naturally or easily at this level. Kohlberg (1984) suggested that stages 5 and 6 might be combined for all practical purposes.

There is some question about whether ability to reason at a particular level has much to do with actual reasoning in real situations or with actual behavior. What encourages the development of moral behavior?

Moral Behavior

As people move toward higher stages of moral reasoning, they also evidence more sharing, helping, and defending of victims of injustice. This relationship between moral reasoning and moral behavior is not very strong, however (Berk, 1991). Many other factors besides reasoning affect behavior. Two important influences on moral behavior are internalization and modeling.

Most theories of moral behavior assume that young children's moral behavior is first controlled by others through direct instruction, supervision, rewards and punishments, and correction. But in time children *internalize* the moral rules and principles of the authority figures who have guided them; that is, children adopt the external standards as their own. If children are given reasons when they are corrected or instructed about their actions, then they are more likely to internalize moral principles (Berk, 1991). They can then behave morally even when "no one is watching."

A second important influence on the development of moral behavior is *modeling.* Children who have been consistently exposed to caring, generous adult models will tend to be more concerned for the rights and feelings of others (Lipscomb, MacAllister, & Bregman, 1985). Let's consider several moral issues that arise in classrooms. What can teachers actually do to deal with such moral issues as cheating, bullying, or the destruction of school property?

Cheating. Early research indicates that cheating seems to have more to do with the particular situation than with the general honesty or dishonesty of the individual (R. Burton, 1963). A student who cheats in math class is probably more likely to cheat in other classes but may never consider lying to a friend or taking candy from the local grocery store. Most students will cheat if the pressure to perform well is great and the chances of being caught are slim. When asked why students cheat, the 1,100 high school subjects in a study by Schab (1980) listed three reasons: (1) being too lazy to study, (2) fear of failure, and (3) parental pressure for good grades. The students in this study were very pessimistic about the incidence of cheating. Both boys and girls in the survey believed that over 97 percent of their peers had cheated at one time or another. However,

Young people today witness violence on television, in films, and—too often—in their own neighborhoods.

Aggression   Bold, direct action that is intended to hurt someone else or take property; unprovoked attack.

this estimate may have been high; figures depend partly on how cheating is defined.

The implications for teachers are fairly straightforward. To prevent cheating, try to avoid putting students in high-pressure situations. Make sure they are well prepared for tests, projects, and assignments so they can do reasonably well without cheating. Make extra help available for those who need it. Be clear about your policies in regard to cheating, and enforce them consistently. Help students resist temptation by monitoring carefully during testing.

Aggression. **Aggression** is not to be confused with assertiveness, which means affirming or maintaining a legitimate right. Helen Bee (1981) gives this example of the difference between the two types of behavior: "A child who says, 'That's my toy!' is showing assertiveness. If he bashes his playmate over the head to reclaim it, he has shown aggression" (p. 350).

Modeling plays an important role in the expression of aggression (Bandura, Ross, & Ross, 1963). One very real source of aggressive models is found in almost every home in America—television. Most children spend more time watching television than they do in any other activity except sleep (Timmer, Eccles, & O'Brien, 1988). Anyone who has watched television knows that violence is common on many programs. How does all this violence affect children who are watching such programs? One conclusion of the National Institute of Mental Health's 1982 review of research on television viewing was that watching violence on television encourages aggressive behavior in children. Some studies have found, for example, that the more television children watch, the more violent they are in their play (Huessmann, Lagarspetz, & Eron, 1984).

You can reduce the negative effects of TV violence by stressing three points with your students: (1) Most people do not behave in the aggressive ways shown on television; (2) the violent acts on TV are not real but are created by special effects and stunts; and (3) there are better ways to resolve conflicts, and these are the ways most real people use to solve their problems (Huessmann, Eron, Klein, Brice, & Fischer, 1983).

Television is not the only source of violent models in modern society. Many popular films are filled with graphic depictions of violence, sometimes performed by the "hero." Students growing up in the inner cities see street gangs and drug deals. Newspapers, magazines, and the radio are filled with stories of murder, rapes, and robberies. In some preschools the children don't play "Mommy" and "Daddy"; they pretend to sell "nickel bags" of heroin to their playmates. This description appeared in the *Washington Post* (June 2, 1988):

> As children huddle, drug games begin. From one child's pocket comes chalk, crushed to resemble cocaine, inside plastic sandwich bags smuggled from home. Soon another child passes cash—thick knots of Monopoly money, or notebook paper, wrapped with rubber bands and dubbed "bankroll."

There are many ways that you, the teacher, can discourage aggression. The Guidelines on page 86 list several possibilities.

Guidelines

Encouraging Positive Social Behavior

Present yourself as a nonaggressive model.

Examples

1. Do not use threats of aggression to win obedience.
2. When problems arise, model nonviolent conflict-resolution strategies.

Ensure that your classroom has enough space and appropriate materials for every student.

Examples

1. Prevent overcrowding.
2. Make sure prized toys or resources are plentiful.
3. Remove or confiscate materials that encourage personal aggression, such as toy guns.

Make sure students do not profit from aggressive behaviors.

Examples

1. Comfort the victim of aggression and ignore the aggressor.

2. Use reasonable punishment, especially with older students.

Teach directly about positive social behaviors.

Examples

1. Incorporate lessons on social ethics/morality through reading selections and discussions.
2. Discuss the effects of antisocial actions such as stealing, bullying, and spreading rumors.

Provide opportunities for learning tolerance and cooperation.

Examples

1. Emphasize the similarities among people rather than the differences.
2. Set up group projects that encourage cooperation.

SOCIALIZATION: THE HOME AND THE SCHOOL

Socialization is the process by which the mature members of a society, such as parents and teachers, shape the behaviors of children, enabling them to fully participate in and contribute to the society. In this section we will consider two of the most important influences on the development and socialization of children—the family and the school.

American Families Today

Socialization The ways in which members of a society encourage positive development for the immature individuals of the group.

Blended Families Parents, children, and stepchildren merged into families through remarriages.

The most appropriate expectation to have about your students' families is no expectation at all. The idea of two parents, 2.2 children, Dad with the only job, and Mom in the kitchen is no longer the norm. In fact, this pattern held true for only 7 percent of American families in the mid-1980s, down from 60 percent in the 1950s (Hodgkinson, 1985).

The size of the American family is decreasing. More students today will have only one or no sibling—or they may be part of **blended families,** with stepbrothers or stepsisters who move in and out of their lives. Some of your students may live with an aunt, with grandparents, with one parent, in foster or adoptive homes, or with an older brother or sister. So the best advice is to drop the phrases "Your parents" and "your mother and father" and speak of "your family" when talking to students.

Many middle-class couples are waiting longer to have children and are providing more material advantages. Children in these homes may have more "things" but may also have less time with their parents. Of course, not all students are middle-class. About one-quarter of all children under 18 live with one parent, usually their mother, and almost half of these families have incomes below the poverty level (U.S. Bureau of the Census, 1990). Your students are likely to be alone or unsupervised much of the day. The growing number of these *latchkey children* has prompted many schools to offer before and after school programs.

Growing Up Too Fast. Joan Isenberg (1991) summarizes the situation confronting children this way:

© 1989 M. Twohy—*Phi Delta Kappan.*

> Today's youth live in a fast-paced, changing world characterized by social pressures that push them to grow up too fast. They are pressured to adapt to changing family patterns, to achieve academically at early ages, and to participate and compete in sports and specialized skills. Moreover, they are pressured to cope with adult information in the media before they have mastered the problems of childhood. Such pressure places increased responsibility and stress on children while simultaneously redefining the essence of childhood itself. (p. 38)

David Elkind (1986) talks about the "hurried child," and other psychologists note the "adultification" of children's television and literature. An article in *Newsweek* (1991) on "The End of Innocence" began with this story:

> A 16-year-old Houston girl was babysitting for two boys, 6 and 9 years old. The kids were glued to the George Michael "I Want Your Sex" video on MTV. Singing along, the boys came to the words "sex with you alone." The younger one looked a little puzzled. "What's that thing when it isn't alone, when lots of people do it?" he asked. "A *borney*?" "No," his older brother shot back contemptuously. "You're so dumb. It's an *orgy*." (p. 62)

No matter what their grade-level assignment, the student teachers in my classes are amazed at the seeming sophistication of their young students. Every night on the news, these children hear about drugs, sex, AIDS, and other "adult" subjects. But don't assume because your students know the vocabulary that they really understand these subjects or that they are emotionally ready to deal with them.

Children of Divorce. Many of your students, ready or not, *have* to deal with one adult issue—divorce. It is now estimated that 50 percent of current marriages of young adults will end in divorce. Almost 60 percent of the children born in 1983 will spend some time living in a single-parent household (Brough, 1990). In any given year, about 1 million children are living in families going through a divorce (Craig, 1986). By the year 2020 about 20 million children *will not* be living with both parents (Pallas, Natriello, & McDill, 1989).

New elementary teachers are often dismayed to learn how many of their students return to empty houses. What sort of support do these students need? How might this affect homework? Perhaps students should have homework hotlines and phone pals.

As many of us know from experiences in our own families, separation and divorce are stressful events for all participants, even under the best circumstances. The actual separation of the parents may have been preceded by years of conflict in the home or may come as a shock to all, including friends and children. Before they break up permanently, about one-half of divorcing couples separate and reconcile at least once. During the divorce itself, conflict may increase as property and custody rights are being decided. Children may have to cope with angry, tired, anxious parents.

After the divorce more changes may disrupt the children's lives. The parent who has custody (today, as in the past, usually the mother) may have to move to a less expensive home, find new sources of income, go to work for the first time, or work longer hours. For the child this can mean leaving behind important friendships in the old neighborhood or school, just when support is needed the most. It may mean having just one parent, who has less time than ever to be with the children.

The economic hardships of divorce seem particularly great for women who take over as heads of their households. Only 1 in 19 two-parent families lives below the poverty level, but almost 1 in 2 female single-parent families is in this category (Hetherington, 1989; Moshman, Glover, & Bruning, 1987). Money shortages lead to fewer toys and trips and less recreation in general. Children may also be asked to accept their parents' new lovers or even new stepparents. In some divorces there are few conflicts, ample resources, and the continuing support of friends and extended family. But divorce is never easy for anyone.

Just as no two divorces are the same, the effects of divorce on children vary from one situation to the next. The first two years after the divorce seem to be the most difficult period for both boys and girls. During this

Guidelines

Helping Children of Divorce

Take note of any sudden changes in behavior that might indicate problems at home.

Examples

1. Be alert to physical symptoms like repeated headaches or stomach pains, rapid weight gain or loss, fatigue or excess energy.
2. Be aware of signs of emotional distress, like moodiness, temper tantrums, difficulty in paying attention or concentrating.
3. Let parents know about the students' signs of stress.

Talk individually to students about their attitude or behavior changes. This gives you a chance to find out about unusual stress such as divorce.

Examples

1. Be a good listener. Students may have no other adult willing to hear their concerns.
2. Let students know you are available to talk and let the student set the agenda.

Watch your language to make sure you avoid stereotypes about "happy" (two-parent) homes.

Examples

1. Simply say "your families" instead of "your mothers and fathers" when addressing the class.
2. Avoid statements such as "We need volunteers for room mother" or "Your father can help you."

Help students maintain self-esteem.

Examples

1. Recognize a job well done.
2. Make sure the student understands the assignment and can handle the workload. This is not the time to pile on new and very difficult work.
3. The student may be angry at his or her parents but may direct the anger at teachers. Don't take the student's anger personally.

Find out what resources are available at your school.

Examples

1. Talk to the school psychologist, guidance counselor, social worker, or principal about students who seem to need outside help.
2. Consider establishing a discussion group, led by a trained adult, for students going through a divorce.

Be sensitive to both parents' rights to information.

Examples

1. When parents have joint custody, both are entitled to receive information and attend parent-teacher conferences.
2. The noncustodial parent may still be concerned about the child's school progress. Check with your principal about state laws regarding the noncustodial parent's rights.

time children may have problems in school, lose or gain an unusual amount of weight, develop difficulties sleeping, and so on. They may blame themselves for the breakup of their family or hold unrealistic hopes for a reconciliation (Hetherington, 1989; Pfeffer, 1981). Long-term adjustment is also affected. Boys tend to show a higher rate of behavioral and interpersonal problems at home and in school than girls in general or boys from intact families. Girls may have trouble in their dealings with males. They may become more sexually active or have difficulties trusting males (Wallerstein & Blakeslee, 1989). But living with one fairly content, if harried, parent may be better than living in a conflict-filled situation with two unhappy parents.

Judith Wallerstein suggests that all children of divorce must face several tasks. They must separate real changes brought by the divorce from fantasy fears of abandonment or losing their parents. They must separate themselves from their parents' pain and get on with their own lives. Parents often make this very difficult by inflicting their own anger and loneliness on their children. Students experiencing divorce must deal with the very real loss of their family unit and usually lose the company of one parent as well. Feelings of anger and guilt are unavoidable, and students must handle these appropriately. Ultimately, students have to accept that the divorce is permanent, that their family system is forever changed, and still be willing to take a chance on loving in this uncertain world of relationships.

Child Abuse. All teachers must be alert to another situation that develops in many families—child abuse. Accurate information about the number of abused children in the United States is difficult to find; estimates range from 1.5 to 2 million children per year (Straus, Gelles, & Steinmetz, 1980), but most experts agree that an enormous number of cases go unreported. About half of all abusive parents could change their destructive behavior patterns if they received help. But without assistance probably only about 5 percent of abusing parents improve (Starr, 1979). Of course, parents are not the only people who abuse children. Siblings, other relatives, and even teachers have been responsible for the physical and sexual abuse of children.

As a teacher, you must alert your principal, school psychologist, or school social worker if you suspect abuse. In all 50 states of the United States, the District of Columbia, and the U.S. territories, the law *requires* certain professionals, often including teachers, to report suspected cases of child abuse. The legal definition of abuse has been broadened in many states to include neglect and failure to provide proper care and supervision. Most laws also protect teachers who report suspected neglect in good faith (Beezer, 1985). Be sure to understand the laws in your state or province on this important issue—as well as your own moral responsibility. Approximately 2,000 children die of abuse or neglect each year in the United States, in many cases because no one would "get involved."

New Roles for Teachers

When we consider the high rates of divorce and child abuse, we see that teachers today are dealing with issues that once stayed outside the walls of the school. The first and most important task of the teacher is to educate, but student learning suffers when there are problems with personal and social development. What do teachers think about their responsibilities for **affective education**—for encouraging personal and social growth in school?

What Do Teachers Think about Affective Education? A study by Richard Prawat and his colleagues asked this question (Prawat, Anderson, Diamond, McKeague, & Whitmer, 1981). The researchers interviewed 40 elementary-school teachers from 24 schools to determine what teachers really believed about encouraging personal and social development in schools and how their thinking influenced their behavior. By asking the teachers a series of indirect and probing questions and then analyzing the 3,600 pages of interview transcripts, Prawat reached the

Affective Education
Education focusing on emotional growth.

Guidelines

Affective Education Programs

Help students examine the kinds of dilemmas they are currently facing or will face in the near future.

Examples

1. In elementary school, discuss sibling rivalries, teasing, stealing, prejudice, treatment of new students in the class, behavior toward handicapped classmates.
2. In high school, discuss cheating, letting friends drive when they are intoxicated, conforming to be more popular, protecting a friend who has broken a rule.

Help students see the perspectives of others.

Examples

1. Ask a student to describe his or her understanding of the views of another, then have the other person confirm or correct the perception.
2. Have students exchange roles and try to "become" the other person in a discussion.

Help students make connections between expressed values and actions.

Examples

1. Follow a discussion of "What should be done?" with "How would you act? What would be your first step? What problems might arise?"

2. Help students see inconsistencies between their values and their own actions. Ask them to identify inconsistencies, first in others, then in themselves.

Safeguard the privacy of all participants.

Examples

1. Remind students that in a discussion they can "pass" and not answer questions.
2. Intervene if peer pressure is forcing a student to say more than he or she wants to.
3. Don't reinforce a pattern of telling "secrets."

Make sure students are really listening to each other.

Examples

1. Keep groups small.
2. Be a good listener yourself.
3. Recognize students who pay careful attention to each other.

Make sure that as much as possible your class reflects concern for moral issues and values.

Examples

1. Make clear distinctions between rules based on administrative convenience (keeping the room orderly) and rules based on moral issues.
2. Enforce standards uniformly. Be careful about showing favoritism.

Source: Adapted with permission from J. W. Eiseman (1981), What criteria should public school moral education programs meet? *The Review of Education, 7,* pp. 226–227.

following conclusions. First, over twice as many teachers emphasized affective as opposed to cognitive goals. Affective goals included interpersonal skills, independence, self-discipline, responsibility, self-worth, self-understanding, enthusiasm for learning, and "manners." Second, most teachers judged the success of a school day based upon affective accomplishments, such as getting everyone to cooperate and participate enthusiastically in activities. Third, when teachers described their ideal student, they stressed personal qualities like eagerness, self-motivation, high standards, and pleasant, well-mannered (but not conforming) behavior as much as they emphasized academic abilities. Fourth, the teachers' views about the importance of personal and social development were related to their own behavior. Teachers who emphasized independence, for example, had fewer class rules about when and how to move around the room; teachers most concerned about self-worth had fewer quietness rules.

How Do Teachers Encourage Personal Growth? Teachers are sometimes the best source of help for students facing emotional or interpersonal problems. When students have chaotic and unpredictable home lives, they need warm, firm structure in school. They need teachers who set clear limits, are consistent, enforce rules firmly but not punitively, and show genuine concern. As a teacher, you need not (and cannot) solve the students' problems, but you can create a predictable, stable world where they can succeed and learn. You can help students understand the effects of their behavior on others. You can be available to talk about personal problems, while never requiring that your students do so. One of my student teachers gave a boy in her class a journal entitled "Very Hard Thoughts" so that he could write about his parents' divorce. Sometimes he talked to her about the journal entries, but at other times he just recorded his feelings. The student teacher was very careful to respect the boy's privacy about his writings.

Now that we have a framework for analyzing development, let's put these ideas together and look at the students. For the remainder of this chapter we consider the needs of children at different grade levels.

THE PRESCHOOL YEARS

In the next few pages we examine three important issues: physical development during the preschool years, the effects of day care on children, and the need for developmentally appropriate preschools.

Physical Development

Preschool children are very active. Their **gross-motor skills,** which involve control of the large muscles, improve greatly over the years from ages 2 to 5, as you can see in Table 3.5. Between ages 2 and about 4 or 5, preschoolers' muscles grow stronger, their balance improves, and their center of gravity moves lower, so they are able to run, jump, climb, and hop. Most of these movements develop naturally if the child has normal physical abilities and the opportunity to play. Children with physical problems, however, may need special training to develop these skills. For young children, physical activity can be an end in itself. It is fun just to improve. But preschoolers may literally run till they drop. They need periods of rest scheduled after physical exertion.

Gross-Motor Skills
Voluntary body movements that involve the large muscles.

Fine-Motor Skills
Voluntary body movements that involve the small muscles.

Fine-motor skills such as tying shoes or fastening buttons, which require the coordination of small movements, also improve greatly during the preschool years, as shown in Table 3.5. Children need to work with large paintbrushes, fat pencils and crayons, large pieces of drawing paper, and soft clay or playdough to accommodate their developing skills. During this time children will begin to show a preference for their right or left hand. Most students, about 85 percent during this time, will

TABLE 3.5 Motor Skills Improve throughout the Preschool Years		
Approximate Age	Gross-Motor Skills	Fine-Motor Skills
Birth to 3 years	sits and crawls; walks; begins to run	picks up, grasps, stacks, and releases objects
3 to 4.5 years	walks up and down stairs; jumps with both feet; throws ball	holds crayon; uses utensils; buttons; copies shapes
4.5 to 6 years	skips; rides two-wheel bicycle; catches ball; plays sports	uses pencil, makes representational drawings; cuts with scissors, prints letters

prefer their right hand, but those who prefer their left should not be forced to change. This means that there must be a good supply of left-handed scissors for preschool classes.

The Impact of Day Care

Half of the infants in the United States have mothers who work outside the home (Clarke-Stewart, 1989). With increases in two-career families and single-parent households, more and more children are spending part of their daily lives in group settings outside the family. What are the effects of day-care arrangements on the millions of children involved? Researchers have examined this question since the 1960s. Almost all the studies have focused on children in formal day-care or preschool programs, so information on children cared for in private homes is very limited. This is true in part because data on private care arrangements are difficult to collect.

During the 1960s and 1970s, research on the effects of preschool experiences generally focused on compensatory programs—programs for children from low-income families, like Operation Head Start. Initial results showed that these programs raised intelligence and achievement test scores at first but that gains seemed to fade after a few years in elementary school. Recent evaluations, however, have painted a more optimistic picture. When we look at criteria of success other than test scores and follow the graduates of high-quality programs through high school, we see definite differences. For example, recent studies of 12 experimental preschool programs for economically disadvantaged children compared program participants to children of similar age and background who did not attend special preschools (Berrueta-Clement, Schweinhart, Barnett, Epstein, & Weikart, 1984; Haskins, 1989). Children who attended the preschool programs had to repeat fewer grades, were assigned less often to special education classes and were classified less often as mentally retarded, were arrested less frequently, had fewer illegitimate children, graduated from high school and went on to advanced schooling more often, depended less on welfare, and worked more.

So good preschool programs can benefit children from low-income families. But what about other children? Here the answer is not clear. One study found that children who were placed in day care before they were 2 years old did not do as well intellectually as children the same age who were cared for in their own or a sitter's home. But children who started day care at 3 or 4 did better than children that age who remained at home (Schwartz, Scarr, & McCartney, 1983). In the first two years, children benefit from frequent one-to-one interactions with adults. It is possible that very young children in day-care situations do not get enough of this kind of intensive interaction. After age 3 or 4, however, the stimulation of other children, teachers, and new environments may become important. At least it seems clear that day care for older children does not harm intellectual development and that it may help (Harvard University, 1985).

Good day-care and preschool programs have generally positive effects on social development as well. Children in these programs are more assertive, self-confident, socially mature, and outgoing. But children who attend preschool programs tend to interact more with their peers in negative as well as in positive ways. Some results indicate that these children may be more aggressive. Apparently, most children in preschools will not learn to solve conflicts peacefully unless special efforts are made to teach them how. The effect of this aggression in later years has not yet been determined (Clarke-Stewart, 1989).

Findings about the potential positive effects of preschool have led some educators to favor more formal academic schooling for young children. Is this a good idea? Some psychologists answer with a loud *no*.

Developmentally Appropriate Preschools

David Elkind (1989, 1991) has been one of the most vocal critics of formal education for preschool children. He suggests that before 1960 there were few preschools as we know them today. But changing family styles and pressure on education to improve sinking test scores led to an emphasis on teaching children *more, sooner.* Middle-class working parents paid for preschool experiences that promised to make up for time lost with Mom and Dad. Elkind (1989) believes that "teaching young children in a didactic way, as if they were miniature second or third graders, can have lasting negative effects on their academic careers and their successful adaptation to the larger society" (p. 47).

These negative effects include stress reactions such as headaches, stomachaches, and behavior problems. In addition, children who are given too much teacher direction at a time when they need to follow their own direction may develop a sense of guilt rather than initiative (in Erikson's terms), diminished self-confidence, and decreased motivation for academic learning later in life. They may learn to wait to be told what to learn and how to learn it. Furthermore, after a few years of elementary

Developmentally appropriate materials such as blocks, paints, and big books allow students to play on many different levels. One student might simply look at the pictures in a book while another listens as the teacher reads and still another uses the book to play school.

school, they will be no farther ahead than children who spent their preschool years playing instead of "studying."

What is a **developmentally appropriate education** for preschoolers—an education that fits their physical, social, emotional and cognitive needs? Many suggestions echo the ideas we examined in the Guidelines in chapter 2 for teaching preoperational children and in this chapter for encouraging initiative. Because young children are so variable in their development at this time, Elkind suggests grouping several ages together so that slower 5-year-olds can play and interact with more advanced 4-year-olds, and so on. If children must be grouped by age, then activities and materials must take into account the wide range of development. Materials should be *nongraded,* that is, appropriate for a range of ages. You have seen these before: blocks, water, sand, dolls, pretend props, a range of books, animals, cars, and playdough. A 2-year-old can stack three blocks and improve motor development. A 4-year-old can use the same blocks with a friend to develop some basic idea about counting and cooperating. The teacher is a matchmaker between child and materials, understanding what children are ready to learn and providing situations that support that learning (Bredekemp, 1986).

THE ELEMENTARY-SCHOOL YEARS

As children move out of their families and into school, new challenges greet them. This can be a happy time for many children. They are growing physically, becoming more and more skillful. They are learning to read, write, solve problems, and understand their world. They are developing

Developmentally Appropriate Education Educational programs and activities designed to meet the cognitive, emotional, social, and physical needs of students.

good friends. But failures in these areas can be devastating. The child who continually fails in school or who is rejected by other children can be a very unhappy person.

Physical Development

During the elementary-school years, physical development is fairly steady for most children. They become taller, leaner, and stronger, so they are better able to master sports and games. There is tremendous variation, however. A particular child can be much larger or smaller than average and still be perfectly healthy. Since children at this age are very aware of physical differences but are not the most tactful people, you may hear comments like "You're too little to be in fifth grade. What's wrong with you?" or "How come you're so fat?"

Unfortunately, children who are very different physically can have trouble making and keeping friends. This can be a particular problem for children who are obese, a category that includes about 10 percent of American children (Walker & Shaw, 1988). In the past 20 years the number of children in this category has increased by almost 50 percent (*Science,* 1986). Obese children tend to have fewer friends and more negative feelings about themselves. Since they are often ostracized from games and sports, they miss opportunities for the exercise they need so much. And when they do play, they have to put up with all the taunts.

Throughout elementary school, many of the girls are likely to be as large as or larger than the boys in their classes. Between the ages of 11 and 14, girls are, on the average, taller and heavier than boys of the same age (Tanner, 1970). The size discrepancy can give the girls an advantage in physical activities, though some girls may feel conflict over this and, as a result, downplay their physical abilities.

Friendships in Childhood

During their early school years, children move rather freely in and out of three overlapping worlds: the home, the school, and the neighborhood. Parents remain important, but children spend increasing amounts of time with other youngsters. Psychologists have found that as children mature, the meaning of friendship changes for them (Damon, 1977; Selman, 1981; Youniss, 1980).

Damon has described three levels of friendship. At the first level, friends are the other children a child plays with often. Friends share food or toys and act "nice" toward each other. But friendships can begin and end quickly based on acts of kindness or "meanness." There is little sense that friends have stable characteristics, so moment-to-moment actions define the friendship (Berndt & Perry, 1986). Teachers working with young children should be aware that these rapidly changing allegiances are a normal part of development. Note, too, that a child's view of friends at this level may be related to the level of cognitive development: young children have difficulty seeing beyond the immediate situation.

Friendships at the next level are defined by a willingness to help when help is needed. Friends are playmates and companions. Children begin to base their choices for friends on fairly concrete but stable personal qualities in another child, such as, "She always shares her lunch with me," or "He takes my side when people are mean to me." This level of friendship may be linked to concrete operational cognitive abilities.

At the highest level, as children move into adolescence, friends are seen as people who share common interests and values, faithfully keep one's most private revelations a secret, and provide psychological support when necessary. The personal qualities of a friend—loyalty, similar philosophy of life—are more abstract and less tied to behaviors (Furman & Bierman, 1984). The cognitive abilities to understand abstract concepts and to base judgments upon them may come into play here. Friendship is now a long-term proposition and usually cannot be destroyed by one or even several incidents. At this stage friendships can be very intense, especially for girls. At every stage, girls are more likely than boys to have one "best" friend and are more reluctant than boys to admit new members to a tight group of friends (Lever, 1978).

At every level, friendships play a very significant role in healthy personal and social development. There is strong evidence that adults who had close friends as children have higher self-esteem and are more capable of maintaining intimate relationships than adults who spent lonely childhoods. Adults who were rejected as children tend to have more problems, such as dropping out of school or committing crimes (Hartup, 1989; Kupersmidt, Coie, & Dodge, 1990). Teachers sometimes forget just how central friendships are to their students' lives. When a student is having a problem with a friend, when there has been a falling-out or an argument, when one child is not invited to a sleep-over, when rumors are started and pacts are made to ostracize someone, the results can be devastating to the children involved. Even when students begin to mature and know intellectually that rifts will soon be healed, they may still be emotionally crushed by temporary trouble in the friendship.

A teacher should also be aware of how each student gets along with the group. Are there outcasts? Do some students play the bully role? Careful adult intervention can often correct such problems, especially at the middle elementary-school level. In these years one of the teacher's jobs is to balance students' need to learn the curriculum with their need to establish healthy peer relationships.

ISSUES AFFECTING ADOLESCENTS

As students enter adolescence, they undergo dramatic changes. Differences in rates of physical and sexual development have important repercussions for personal/social development. In addition, adolescents today face risks that were much less prevalent a few generations ago—pregnancy, depression, drugs, and AIDS. We will turn our attention first to the effects of individual differences in the rate of physical and sexual development.

Early and Late Maturers

Puberty marks the beginning of sexual maturity. It is not a single event, but a series of changes involving almost every part of the body. The final outcome of the changes is the ability to reproduce. The sex differences in

Puberty The period in early adolescence when individuals begin to reach physical and sexual maturity.

physical development we saw during the later elementary years become even more pronounced at the beginning of puberty. Generally, girls begin puberty about two years ahead of boys and reach their final height by age 16; most boys continue growing until about age 18. For the typical girl, the adolescent growth spurt begins with breast development between the ages of 10 and 11 and continues for about three years. While this is the average time frame for girls, the actual range is from 9 to 16 years. Eighty percent of American girls have their first menstrual period between the ages of 11 1/2 and 14 1/2. For the typical boy, the growth spurt begins between the ages of 12 and 13. In general, boys are more variable than girls when it comes to the physical changes of adolescence. The length of time that is required for all the changes of puberty to occur varies more with boys, and the range of differences in height and weight at the end of puberty is greater for boys than for girls (Rogers, 1985).

The physical changes of adolescence have significant effects on the individual's identity. Psychologists have been particularly interested in the academic, social, and emotional differences they have found between adolescents who mature early and those who mature later. Remember, though, that the trends described below are based on averages. What is true for a group in general will not be true for every individual in the group.

First, there seems to be an academic advantage in early maturation. On the average, students who are physically mature tend to score higher on most tests of mental ability than less mature students of the same age (Fein, 1978). Second, early maturation seems to have certain special advantages for boys. Early-maturing boys are more likely to enjoy high social status; they tend to be popular and to be leaders. Many of these advantages are sustained in later life. On the other hand, boys who mature late have an especially difficult time. Since girls mature well ahead of boys, even late-maturing girls have developed by the time the late-maturing boy finally has his chance. The last to leave childhood, he may have been surrounded by mature peers for years. These late- maturing boys tend to be less popular, more talkative, and hungrier for attention (Kaplan, 1984). However, some studies show that in adulthood, males who matured early are less flexible and less creative in their thinking, whereas males who matured later tend to be more creative, tolerant, and perceptive. Perhaps the trials and anxieties of maturing late teach some boys to be better problem solvers (Seifert & Hoffnung, 1991).

For girls, early physical maturity seems to be less important in determining social status. But maturing way ahead of classmates can be a definite disadvantage. Being larger than everyone else in the class is not a valued characteristic for girls in our culture. A girl who begins to mature early probably will be the first in her peer group to start the changes of puberty. This can be very upsetting to some girls, especially if they have not been prepared for the changes or if friends tease them. Later-maturing girls seem to have fewer problems, but they may worry that something is wrong with them. All students can benefit from knowing that the range of normal differences in rates of maturation is great and that there are advantages for both early and late maturers.

There is a period of time when girls' physical development, on the average, is ahead of boys', but there is tremendous individual variation as well.

Adolescents at Risk

It has always been difficult to navigate the adolescent years, but today the waters seem more dangerous than ever. Many challenges confront junior and senior high school students today. We will touch on only a few.

Teenage Sexuality and Pregnancy. Probably the most important aspect of development during these years is sexual maturation. Sexually mature adolescents are physically and hormonally equipped for sexual relationships, but modern cultures require them to go through an extended period of education or other training before society considers them ready for marriage. As their bodies become sexually mature, adolescents must make psychological and emotional adjustments. Their views of what it means to be male or female have been developing for years, probably since infancy. But now they must begin to solidify their sexual identity and feel comfortable with it. In the process, some problems can arise.

Today about 80 percent of American men and 70 percent of American women have had sexual intercourse by age 19 (Guttmacher Institute, 1984). *Newsweek* (1991) reported that 50 percent of 15-year-old girls have had intercourse. The emotional impact of these early sexual experiences may have repercussions in the school, both for the students involved and for fellow students who hear about the experiences. Even more troubling, today one consequence of this early sexual activity seems to be unexpected and unwanted pregnancy. Each year about 1 million teenage girls become pregnant—30,000 of them are younger than 15 years old. The number of babies born to unmarried teenagers doubled between 1960 and 1980 (Scarr, Weinberg, & Levine, 1986).

A remarkable number of American adolescents have little information or indeed the wrong information about birth control. For example, over a third of the adolescent girls who become pregnant do so in their first three months of sexual activity; often they haven't decided yet what to do about birth control, partly because they don't expect anything to happen so quickly. It can! In fact many teenage girls don't know when in their menstrual cycle they can become pregnant. Some adults fear that giving adolescents accurate information about sex will encourage them to experiment. Results of research indicate that this is not a danger, however. The main effect of providing the facts appears to be fewer unwanted pregnancies (Brooks-Gunn & Furstenberg, 1989; Gordon 1986).

Teachers are likely to have in almost every class students who vary greatly in size, maturity, and sexual sophistication. The Guidelines on page 100 offer ideas for helping students deal with these differences.

Eating Disorders. Adolescents going through the changes of puberty are very concerned about their bodies. This has always been true, but today the emphasis on fitness and appearance makes adolescents even more likely to worry about how their bodies "measure up." For some, the concern becomes excessive. One consequence is eating disorders such as **bulimia** (binge eating) and **anorexia nervosa** (self-starvation), both of which are much more common in females than in males. Bulimics often binge, eating an entire gallon of ice cream or a whole cake. Then, to avoid

Bulimia Eating disorder characterized by overeating, then getting rid of the food by self-induced vomiting or laxatives.

Anorexia Nervosa Eating disorder characterized by very limited food intake.

Guidelines

Dealing with Differences in Growth and Development

Do not call unnecessary attention to physical differences among students.

Examples

1. Avoid seating arrangements that are obviously based on height, but try to seat smaller students so they can see and participate in class activities.
2. Avoid games that call attention to differences in height, size, or strength.
3. Don't use or allow students to use nicknames based on physical traits.

Help students obtain factual information on differences in physical development.

Examples

1. Set up science projects on sex differences in growth rates.
2. Have readings and discussions that focus on differences between early and late maturers. Make sure that you present the positives and the negatives of each.
3. Find out the school policy on sex education and on informal guidance for students. Some schools, for example, encourage teachers to talk to girls who are upset about their first menstrual period, while other schools expect teachers to send the girls to talk to the school nurse.
4. Give students models in literature or in their community of high-achieving individuals who do not fit the ideal physical stereotypes.

Accept that concerns about appearance and the opposite sex will occupy much time and energy for adolescents.

Examples

1. Allow students a few moments at the end of class to socialize.
2. Deal with some of these issues in curriculum-related materials.

gaining weight, they force themselves to vomit or use strong laxatives, to purge themselves of the extra calories. Bulimics tend to maintain a normal weight, but their digestive systems can be permanently damaged. Anorexia is an even more dangerous disorder, for anorexics refuse to eat or eat practically nothing. In the process they may lose 20 to 25 percent of their body weight, and some (about 20 percent) literally starve themselves to death. These eating disorders often begin in adolescence and require professional help (Siegel, 1983).

Drug Abuse. Modern society makes growing up a very confusing process. Notice the messages from films and billboards. "Beautiful," popular people drink alcohol and smoke cigarettes with little concern for their health. We have over-the-counter drugs for almost every common ailment. Coffee wakes us up and a pill helps us sleep. And then we tell students to "Just say no!" to drugs.

For many reasons, not just these contradictory messages, drug use has become a problem for students. Accurate statistics are hard to find, but estimates from the National Center for Education Statistics indicate that 92 percent of high school seniors report some experience with alcohol—66 percent using it in the past month. Five percent are daily drinkers and 38 percent have had at least one episode of heavy drinking (five or more drinks in a row). About 20 percent of seniors are daily smokers, and 30 percent have tried at least one illegal drug. If we consider how many people will be affected, the greatest short-term drug dangers for most teens are from drinking and driving. Over the long term, the greatest health hazard is a lifetime of cigarette smoking. Of course, drugs like cocaine and crack can be instantly fatal.

What can be done about drug use among our students? First, we should distinguish between experimentation and abuse. Many students try something at a party but do not become regular users. The best way to help students who may want to say no but have trouble saying it appears to be through peer programs that teach *how* to say no assertively. The successful programs also teach general social skills and build self-esteem (Newcomb & Bentler, 1989). Also, the older students are when they experiment with drugs, the more likely they are to make responsible choices, so helping younger students say no is a clear benefit.

For students caught in the grip of real drug abuse, most educational programs appear to be ineffective at best. Some programs even encourage experimentation. These students need to be given real alternatives to drug use—tutoring, job training, community activities, physical skills development, and sometimes hospitalization and therapy.

This girl is getting the facts about AIDS, but will she act on this information? One problem with teenagers is that they feel somewhat "invulnerable," and assume that nothing bad will happen to them, only to someone else.

FIGURE 3.2 Increasing Suicide Rates among Adolescents From 1960 through 1987 the number of suicides per 100,000 adolescents has steadily increased for all groups except nonwhite females. The increase for white males has been the greatest.

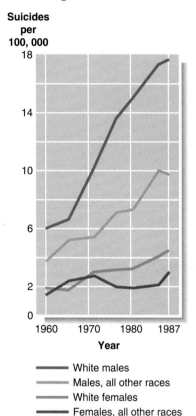

Source: U.S. Department of Health and Human Services, as reported in *Newsweek Special Issue, Education: A Consumer's Handbook* (Fall-Winter 1990–91), p. 15.

AIDS. A growing health risk for everyone, but especially for adolescents, is the spread of AIDS (acquired immune deficiency syndrome). As of 1992, only about 3 percent of all AIDS cases are individuals under the age of 21, and many of these are young children. But the frightening fact is that this percentage is growing rapidly, especially among adolescents. In most cases, adolescents contract AIDS through intimate sexual contact or intravenous drug use. For the virus to be transmitted, people have to exchange bodily fluids without the fluids coming into contact with the air first. Obviously, this can happen a number of ways, but contact has to be more than casual. Many students do not understand that the AIDS virus is unable to survive in air or water, so AIDS cannot be transmitted by casual day-to-day touching, hugging, or sharing food—or even by being spit on (Seifert & Hoffnung, 1991). The Task Force on Pediatric AIDS of the American Psychological Association (1989) recommends education about AIDS for students, beginning in the early years and continuing through high school. In this area, education can be life-saving and does not appear to encourage experimentation.

Suicide. For young people ages 15 to 24, the suicide rate has tripled in the past 30 years. Suicide is now the third most common cause of death in this age group (Pfeffer, 1986). Figure 3.2 shows a steady climb in the number of suicides among all males and among white females.

Suicide often comes as a response to life problems—problems that parents and teachers sometimes dismiss. There are a number of warning signs that trouble is brewing. Watch for *changes* in eating or sleeping habits, weight, grades, disposition, activity level, or interest in friends.

TABLE 3.6 Myths and Facts about Suicide

Myth: People who talk about suicide don't kill themselves.

Fact: Eight out of ten people who commit suicide tell someone that they're thinking about hurting themselves before they actually do it.

Myth: Only certain types of people commit suicide.

Fact: All types of people commit suicide—male and female, young and old, rich and poor, country people and city people. It happens in every racial, ethnic, and religious group.

Myth: When a person talks about suicide, you should change the subject to get his or her mind off it.

Fact: You should take them seriously. Listen carefully to what they are saying. Give them a chance to express their feelings. Let them know you are concerned. And help them get help.

Myth: Most people who kill themselves really want to die.

Fact: Most people who kill themselves are confused about whether they want to die. Suicide is often intended as a cry for help.

Source: From R. Bell (1980), *Changing bodies, changing lives: A book for teens on sex and relationships.* New York: Random House, p. 142.

Students at risk sometimes suddenly give away prize possessions such as stereos, CDs, clothing, or pets. They may seem depressed or hyperactive. It is especially dangerous if the student not only talks about suicide and but has a plan for acting. If you suspect that there is a problem, talk to the student directly. One feeling shared by many people who attempt suicide is that no one really takes them seriously (Frymier, 1988). Table 3.6 lists some common myths and facts about suicide.

This has been a brief and selective look at the needs of children. As we saw earlier, educators and psychologists are concerned about providing a developmentally appropriate education for preschool students. The term *developmentally appropriate education* could be applied more broadly. All students, whatever their age, require an education that fits their physical, cognitive, personal, and social levels of development.

SUMMARY

THE WORK OF ERIKSON

According to Erik Erikson's theory of emotional development, people go through eight life stages between infancy and old age, each of which involves a central crisis. Adequate resolution of each crisis leads to greater personal and social competence and a stronger foundation for solving future crises. In the first two stages an infant must develop a sense of trust over mistrust and a sense of autonomy over shame and doubt. In early childhood the focus of the third stage is on developing initiative and avoiding feelings of guilt. In the child's elementary-school years, the fourth stage involves achieving a sense of industry and avoiding feelings of inferiority.

In Erikson's fifth stage, identity versus role confusion, adolescents consciously attempt to solidify their identity. According to James Marcia, these efforts may lead to identity achievement, foreclosure, diffusion, or moratorium. Pride in family, community, and ethnicity is an important part of a strong and stable identity. Erikson's three stages of adulthood involve struggles to achieve intimacy, generativity, and integrity.

UNDERSTANDING OURSELVES AND OTHERS

Our self-concept and self-esteem—our definition and evaluation of ourselves—become increasingly complex, differentiated, and abstract as we mature. Self-concept evolves through constant self-evaluation, social interaction, and experiences in and out of school. Teachers can have a profound effect on students' self-concept and self-esteem. Social cognition—our conception of other people—also changes as we mature. Young children believe that everyone has the same thoughts and feelings they do. Later they learn that others have separate identities and therefore separate feelings. This aids in the development of empathy—the ability to feel emotions as experienced by others.

MORAL DEVELOPMENT

Lawrence Kohlberg's theory of moral development includes three levels: (1) a preconventional level, where judgments are based on self-interest; (2) a conventional level, where judgments are based on traditional family values and social expectations; and (3) a postconventional level, where judgments are based on more abstract and personal ethical principles. Critics suggest that Kohlberg's view does not account for possible sex differences in moral reasoning or differences between moral reasoning and moral behavior. Cheating and aggression are two common behavior problems in the schools that involve moral issues.

SOCIALIZATION: THE HOME AND THE SCHOOL

Changes in family structures, parenting styles, childhood stress, divorce, and child abuse profoundly affect development. In light of social challenges, teachers are faced with new roles, including supporting the affective development of their students.

THE PRESCHOOL YEARS

Quality day-care and preschool programs generally have positive effects on emotional, intellectual, and social development, as well as on the development of motor skills. Developmentally appropriate education and opportunities to forge friendships during childhood are important.

THE ELEMENTARY-SCHOOL YEARS

Friendships progress from play relationships based on immediate situations, through companionship based on a growing understanding of sta-

ble personal qualities, to close and psychologically supportive relationships that can be long-lasting and are tied to abstract values.

ISSUES AFFECTING ADOLESCENTS

With adolescence come puberty and emotional struggles to cope with all the related changes. Females mature about two years ahead of males. Early maturation is generally beneficial, though it is not without its disadvantages, especially for girls. Adolescents face many risks today, including pregnancy, eating disorders, drug abuse, AIDS, and suicide.

At all stages of development, teachers must address students' needs for education that is appropriate to their physical, cognitive, personal, and social levels of development.

KEY TERMS AND CONCEPTS

affective education, p. 90
aggression, p. 84
anorexia nervosa, p. 99
autonomy, p. 68
blended families, p. 86
bulimia, p. 99
developmental crisis, p. 66
developmentally appropriate
  education, p. 95
empathy, p. 79

ethnic pride, p. 73
fine-motor skills, p. 92
generativity, p. 74
gross-motor skills, p. 92
identity, p. 70
identity achievement, p. 71
identity diffusion, p. 71
identity foreclosure, p. 71
industry, p. 69
initiative, p. 68

integrity, p. 74
moral dilemmas, p. 80
moral reasoning, p. 79
moratorium, p. 71
psychosocial, p. 66
puberty, p. 97
self-concept, p. 74
self-esteem, p. 74
social cognition, p. 78
socialization, p. 86

WHAT WOULD YOU DO?

PRESCHOOL

Two students in your 4-year-old group will soon have a new baby in their families. As the time draws nearer, the students become more and more disruptive. What would you do?

ELEMENTARY AND MIDDLE SCHOOL

One of the girls in your class is desperate for friends but can't keep them. She gives special gifts, tries to be helpful, but always seems to be the one exploited or hurt. How would you help this student form some genuine relationships?

You notice a fairly dramatic change in one of your students. This boy seems very tired and anxious, and he is not doing his homework. How would you approach this problem?

JUNIOR HIGH AND HIGH SCHOOL

You hear from one of your students that a group of seniors has a small "business" selling college applications essays. What would you do?

Several of your junior high school students are afraid to go to gym class because a gang of students has been extorting money and personal possessions. What steps would you take to end this situation?

COOPERATIVE LEARNING ACTIVITY

With four or five other members of your class, select a moral issue and develop a plan for integrating discussion of that issue into a lesson for the age level you will teach. How would you assess the effectiveness of your lesson?

TEACHERS' CASEBOOK

FOSTERING SOCIAL DEVELOPMENT

One of your students is painfully shy and seems to have no friends. The student eats lunch alone, walks to classes alone, and is never chosen by other students for group projects. This student seems immature and is easily upset. What would you do to help?

POSITIVE SELF-CONCEPTS

Each child is unique and behaves in the manner that he or she believes is best. People change their behavior as they change their perceptions of themselves. A person who feels worthy and wanted is open to change. This child not only needs to learn how to have friends, but also needs to learn how to be a friend. To help this child develop a more positive self-concept I would do positive action units every day in my classroom. I would try to elicit from the group ideas about friendship (ways to get friends, and ways to be a friend). Role playing could be done, as well as reflective writing about friendship. As the class learns to value differences, each student will develop his or her own uniqueness. Group cohesiveness will be developed through the interaction of individuals. In addition to this I would allow this particular child to be in charge of something, where the child could learn leadership roles too.

Roseanne O. Newell, *Third-Grade Teacher*
Twin Peaks Elementary School, Salt Lake City, Utah

HANDLING AGGRESSION

You have heard from several parents that a student in your class is threatening their children and extorting money, articles of clothing, and other possessions. The student's parents seem unable to exercise control. How would you deal with this student's aggression?

FACING THE CONSEQUENCES

When threatening situations interrupt a student's environment, teachers and administrators need to be involved, and all strategies should be utilized. If a rapport exists between the teacher and the extortionist, a discussion outlining logical consequences is the first intervention. The consequences must be unpleasant, requiring an inventory analysis of the student by the teacher to learn what consequences are most uncomfortable for the student. If extortion is the case and is proven, the student must compensate the victim by returning the goods or items taken. Suspension in or out of school may be in order. There should be good documentation of the evidence and a contingency plan for future incidents. Proving that the incident occurred is difficult. Students who extort will lie, so witnesses are valuable. Questioned well and in the proper setting, other students are willing collaborators in the search for truth.

Marc Gray, *Science Teacher*
Highland Middle School, Louisville, Kentucky

MODELING VALUES

If the parents are unable to control the child, I would assume that values toward possession of property have not been instilled in the child early on. It then becomes the teacher's responsibility to convey respect for the rights of others. I would begin communication with the child about basic societal interactions and teach what is acceptable or unacceptable in various situations, giving the child the opportunity to relate successfully to other people. If the child cannot achieve self-control, the teacher can be externally "visible" to establish control until the child is able to attain it independently. It may even be possible to employ the child so the child can earn the things he or she wants badly enough to extort.

Jan Reynolds, *Fifth-Grade Teacher*
Fredericktown Intermediate School, Fredericktown, Ohio

DIRECT INTERVENTION

Dealing with a child's aggression toward his/her classmates is a particularly difficult situation, especially because the aggressive behavior usually occurs out of the teacher's sight. This requires the teacher to rely on so-called hearsay evidence, making it difficult to confront the child directly with irrefutable proof of the behavior. Thus, I would take a number of steps to circumvent extortion and other negative behaviors. First, I would try to exercise more direct supervision over the child during recess or other more unstructured activities, when the child is more likely to be practicing extortion. If necessary, I would enlist the assistance of other teachers. I would also discuss the matter with the entire class, without specifically naming the guilty student. Developmental guidance activities focused on building positive peer relationships, creating a sense of honesty and trust in the group, and respecting other people's property would be good for all the students, not just the offender. Other instructional concepts, such as developing self-esteem and learning decision-making skills, would also assist the students in resisting the aggressive behavior of the student offender.

Jane C. Dusell, *English Teacher*
Medford Area Senior High School, Medford, Wisconsin

HELPING STUDENTS COPE

The parents of one of your students are going through a nasty divorce. The student is often upset, distracted, tired, or withdrawn and is not doing well in schoolwork or homework. The parents seem too concerned with their own problems to notice the effects they are having on their child. Can you do anything to help?

SUPPORT GROUPS

Our guidance department runs a series of specialized support groups to help students deal with intense, immediate problems such as this. These support groups have provided effective help in the past, so I would contact them to work with the student. If a school does not have such an ad hoc student support group system, but could have, I would encourage its implementation.

James D. Kraft, *Social Studies Teacher*
Wausau West High School, Wausau, Wisconsin

CHILD ADVOCACY

Children need to feel and believe that their teachers care about their welfare. Children who are experiencing the heartbreak of divorce may need their teachers to become advocates for them.

A teacher who recognizes behaviors that are the result of family strain and tensions should attempt to meet with the parents of the student. Parents who are embroiled in a divorce may be completely unaware of the impact on their children. A conference explaining the effects that the family pressures are having on the student may be enough to make the parents more sensitive to the child.

Parents who are still unresponsive after attempts by the teacher may be experiencing too many of their own problems to be able to react to a child's problems. When this is the case, the teacher must realize that a friendly word, smile, and an offer to help with tutoring will show the student that the teacher is there for support and guidance. Sometimes we can do little more than stand by our students and let them know we care. They understand we sometimes can't make certain situations better, but they can be strengthened by our support.

Darlene A. Walsh, *Rhode Island 1991 Teacher of the Year*
Greenbush Elementary School, West Warwick, Rhode Island

4 LEARNING ABILITIES AND EXCEPTIONALITIES

So far we have talked little about individuals. We have discussed principles of development that apply to everyone—stages, processes, conflicts, and tasks. Our development as human beings is similar in many ways—but not in every way. Even among members of the same family, there are marked contrasts in appearance, interests, abilities, and temperament. Some people learn very quickly in school. Others learn slowly or do not seem at all interested in learning. Many students have special needs.

We will begin our discussion of exceptional learners with a look at the names and labels that have been applied to them. Then we turn to an extended examination of intellectual abilities, which vary so greatly from individual to individual and have proved so difficult to define and measure. How can teachers work with such a wide range of abilities? Is ability grouping a good answer? What are the special needs of the gifted and the retarded? How do individual cognitive styles and learning preferences affect learning?

The next section covers the kinds of learning problems students may have. As we discuss each problem area, we will consider how a teacher might recognize problems, seek help from school and community resources, and plan instruction based on individuals' needs. Recent changes in federal legislation mean that you probably will have at least one exceptional student in your class, whatever grade you teach. We will discuss the laws and how to cope with their effects.

When you complete this chapter, you should be able to do the following:

- Discuss the potential problems in categorizing and labeling students.

- Begin to develop a personal concept of intelligence to aid you in your teaching.

- Discuss how you might recognize and teach students who are mildly retarded or who are gifted.

- Adapt lessons to make them appropriate for students with varying learning styles.

- List indicators of hearing, vision, language, and behavior problems, as well as indicators of specific learning disabilities.

- Adapt teaching methods to meet the needs of exceptional students.

- Discuss the implications of Public Laws 94-142 and 99-457 for your teaching.

WHAT DO YOU THINK?

Have you ever had the experience of being the only one in a group who had trouble doing something? The first time you tried to skate, throw a football, play tennis, or bowl, perhaps you were the only one who didn't know how. How would you feel if every day in school you faced the same kind of difficulty, while everyone else seemed to find the work easier than you? What kind of support and teaching would you need to keep trying?

WHAT DOES IT MEAN TO BE EXCEPTIONAL?

Every child is a distinctive collection of talents, abilities, and limitations. In that sense we all are "exceptional." But some students are called *exceptional* because they have learning abilities or problems and require special education or other services to reach their potential. **Exceptional students** may be mentally retarded, gifted, physically challenged, emotionally disturbed/behaviorally disordered, learning disabled, communication disordered, visually impaired, or hearing impaired. Even though we will use these terms throughout the chapter, a caution is in order: labeling students is a controversial issue.

No child is born "mildly retarded," "gifted," or "learning disabled" in the same way that a child is born female or with blood type O. The decision that an individual is retarded is a judgment based on the way the individual performs certain tasks. For many years the purpose of labels was diagnostic. Assigning labels was a way of determining eligibility for special services in the school or community. The model for this procedure was basically the disease model used by physicians; and the assumption of the disease model is that each disease has a particular treatment, which usually is effective.

Unfortunately, few specific "treatments" automatically follow from a diagnosis such as mental retardation. Many different teaching strategies and materials are appropriate for students labeled retarded. Similarly, a student who is visually impaired may benefit from the same techniques used to teach students whose sight is perfect but who have great difficulty remembering what they see. Critics of labeling claim the categories have no educational relevance, because a label does not tell the teacher which methods or materials to use with individual students. They believe, furthermore, that the labels can become self-fulfilling prophecies. Everyone—teachers, parents, classmates, and even the students themselves—may see a label as a permanent problem, a stigma that cannot be changed.

On the other hand, some educators argue that for younger students, at least, being labeled as special helps protect the child. For example, if classmates know a student is retarded, they will adjust their standards and be more willing to accept his or her limitations. And when a child is classified, parents and teachers have some guidelines in seeking information on particular problems. Of course, labels still open doors to some special programs or financial assistance.

Exceptional Students
Students who have abilities or problems so significant that the students require special education or other services to reach their potential.

Labels probably both stigmatize and help students (Heward & Orlansky, 1984; MacMillan, 1982). But until we are able to make diagnoses with greater accuracy, we should be very cautious about describing a whole human being with one word.

This caution also applies to many of the common descriptions heard in schools every day. Today some people object to labels such as "the mentally retarded" or "at-risk students" because describing a complex person with one or two words is perceived as implying that the condition labeled is the most important aspect of the person. An alternative is to speak of "students with mental retardation" or "students placed at risk." Here the emphasis is on the students first, not on the special challenges they face. In this chapter I use the two methods of description interchangeably to maintain the readability of the material.

In the next section we consider a concept that has provided the basis for many labels—intelligence.

INDIVIDUAL DIFFERENCES IN INTELLIGENCE

Because the concept of **intelligence** is so important in education, so controversial, and so often misunderstood, we will spend quite a few pages discussing it. Let us begin with a basic question.

What Does Intelligence Mean?

The idea that people vary in what we call intelligence has been with us for a long time. Plato discussed similar variations over 2,000 years ago. Most early theories about the basic nature of intelligence involved one or more of the following three themes: (1) the capacity to learn, (2) the total knowledge a person has acquired, and (3) the ability to adapt successfully to new situations and to the environment in general.

In this century there has been considerable controversy over the meaning of intelligence. In 1921, 14 psychologists offered 14 different views about the nature of intelligence in a symposium on the subject, reported in the *Journal of Educational Psychology* (Neisser, 1979). Sternberg and Detterman repeated this process in 1986, asking 24 experts for their definitions of intelligence. Again, opinion was divided. One point of disagreement in 1921 and today is whether intelligence is a single ability or many separate abilities.

Intelligence: One Ability or Many? Some theorists believe intelligence is a basic ability that affects performance on all cognitively oriented tasks. An "intelligent" person will do well in computing mathematical problems, analyzing poetry, taking history essay examinations, and solving riddles. Evidence for this position comes from correlational evaluations of intelligence tests. In study after study, moderate to high positive correlations are found among all the different tests that are designed to measure separate intellectual abilities (Lohman, 1989; McNemar, 1964). But the correlations are not perfect. What could explain these results?

Charles Spearman (1927) suggested there is one factor or mental attribute, which he called *g* or *general intelligence,* that is used to perform any mental test, but that each test also requires some specific abilities in

Intelligence Ability or abilities to acquire and use knowledge for solving problems and adapting to the world.

addition to *g*. For example, performance on a test of memory for numbers probably involves both *g* and some specific ability for immediate recall of what is heard. Spearman assumed that individuals vary in both general intelligence and specific abilities and that together these factors determine performance on mental tasks.

Critics of Spearman's position insisted that there are several "primary mental abilities," not just one. Thurstone (1938) listed verbal comprehension, memory, reasoning, ability to visualize spatial relationships, numerical ability, word fluency, and perceptual speed as the major mental abilities underlying intellectual tasks. But tests of these "separate" factors showed that ability in one area was correlated with ability in the others.

Multiple Intelligences. J. P. Guilford (1988) and Howard Gardner (1983) are the most prominent modern proponents of the concept of multiple cognitive abilities. Guilford suggests that there are three basic categories, or **faces of intellect:** *mental operations,* or the processes of thinking; *contents,* or what we think about; and *products,* or the end results of our thinking. In this model, mental operations are divided into six subcategories: cognition (recognizing old information and discovering new), convergent thinking (where there is only one answer or solution), divergent thinking (used when many answers may be appropriate), evaluation (decisions about how good, accurate, or suitable something is), memory recording (immediate memory), and memory retention (memory over several days). The contents on which people operate are divided into five subcategories: visual content, auditory content, word meanings, symbols, and behaviors. The different products that may result are: units, classes, relations, systems, transformations, and implications. Figure 4.1 shows the elements of Guilford's model.

According to this view, carrying out a cognitive task is essentially performing a mental operation on some specific content to achieve a product. For example, listing the next number in the sequence 3, 6, 12, 24, . . . requires a *convergent operation* (there is only one right answer) with *symbolic content* (numbers) to achieve a *relationship product* (each number is double the one before). Painting an abstract conception of a still life requires a *divergent thinking operation* (many possible "answers") about *visual content* to create a *transformational product* (the actual objects are transformed into the artist's view). There are 180 combinations of operations, contents, and products—$6 \times 5 \times 6$.

Guilford's model of intelligence has several advantages as well as one major drawback. The model broadens our view of the nature of intelligence by adding such factors as social judgment (the evaluation of others' behavior) and creativity (divergent thinking) (Gleitman, 1987). On the other hand, even though human mental abilities are complex, Guilford's model may be *too* complex to serve as a guide for predicting behavior in real situations or for planning instruction. In addition, when people are tested on these different abilities, the abilities prove to be related. The problem of explaining the positive correlations among all these supposed separate mental abilities remains unsolved.

Howard Gardner (1983) has proposed a "theory of **multiple intelligences.**" According to Gardner there are at least seven separate kinds of intelligence: linguistic (verbal), musical, spatial, logical-mathematical, bodily, knowledge of self, and understanding of others (see Table 4.1 on

Faces of Intellect In Guilford's theory, the three basic categories of thinking—operations, contents, and products.

Multiple Intelligences In Gardner's theory of intelligence, a person's seven separate abilities: logical-mathematical, verbal, musical, spatial, bodily-kinesthetic, interpersonal, intrapersonal.

FIGURE 4.1 Faces of Intellect Guilford's theory of the three faces of intellect suggests that people use six *mental operations,* which can be applied to five kinds of *content* to achieve six types of *products.*

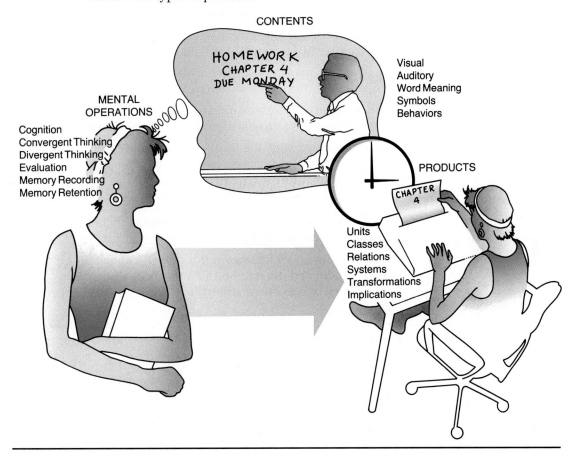

CONTENTS

HOMEWORK
CHAPTER 4
DUE MONDAY

Visual
Auditory
Word Meaning
Symbols
Behaviors

MENTAL
OPERATIONS

Cognition
Convergent Thinking
Divergent Thinking
Evaluation
Memory Recording
Memory Retention

PRODUCTS

CHAPTER
4

Units
Classes
Relations
Systems
Transformations
Implications

page 114). Gardner has based his notion of separate abilities in part on evidence that brain damage (from a stroke, for example) often interferes with functioning in one area, such as language, but does not affect functioning in other areas. Gardner has also noted that individuals often excel in one of these seven areas but have no remarkable abilities in the other six.

Intelligence as a Process. As you can see, the theories of Spearman, Thurstone, Guilford, and Gardner tend to describe how individuals *differ* in the *content* of intelligence—the different abilities underlying intelligent behavior. Recent work in cognitive psychology has emphasized instead the thinking *processes* that may be *common* to all people. How do humans gather and use information to solve problems and behave intelligently? New views of intelligence are growing out of this work.

Robert Sternberg's (1985, 1990) **triarchic theory of intelligence** is an example of a cognitive process approach to understanding intelligence. As you might guess from the name, this theory has three parts.

The first describes the mental processes of the individual that lead to more or less intelligent behavior. These processes are defined in terms of **components.** A component is "an elementary information process that

Triarchic Theory of Intelligence Three-part description of mental abilities (thinking processes, coping with new experiences, and adapting to context) that lead to more or less intelligent behavior.

Components In an information-processing view, basic problem-solving processes underlying intelligence.

TABLE 4.1 Gardner's Seven Intelligences

Intelligence	End States	Core Components
Logical-mathematical	Scientist Mathematician	Sensitivity to, and capacity to discern, logical or numerical patterns; ability to handle long chains of reasoning.
Linguistic	Poet Journalist	Sensitivity to the sounds, rhythms, and meanings of words; sensitivity to the different functions of language.
Musical	Composer Violinist	Abilities to produce and appreciate rhythm, pitch, and timbre; appreciation of the forms of musical expressiveness.
Spatial	Navigator Sculptor	Capacities to perceive the visual-spatial world accurately and to perform transformations on one's initial perceptions.
Bodily-kinesthetic	Dancer Athlete	Abilities to control one's body movements and to handle objects skillfully.
Interpersonal	Therapist Salesman	Capacities to discern and respond appropriately to the moods, temperaments, motivations, and desires of other people.
Intrapersonal	Person with detailed, accurate self-knowledge	Access to one's own feelings and the ability to discriminate among them and draw upon them to guide behavior; knowledge of one's own strengths, weaknesses, desires, and intelligence.

Source: H. Gardner and T. Hatch (1989), Multiple intelligences go to school. *Educational Researcher, 18* (8), p. 6. Copyright 1989 by the American Educational Research Association. Reprinted by permission of publisher.

operates upon internal representations of objects or symbols" (Sternberg, 1985, p. 97). Components are classified by the functions they serve and by how general they are. There are at least three different functions served. The first function—higher-order planning, strategy selection, and monitoring—is performed by *metacomponents.* Examples of meta-components are identifying the problem, allocating attention, and monitoring how well a strategy is working. A second function served by components—executing the strategies selected—is handled by *performance components.* One performance component allows us to perceive and store new information. The third function—gaining new knowledge—is performed by *knowledge-acquisition components,* such as separating relevant from irrelevant information as you try to understand a new concept (Sternberg, 1985).

Some components are specific; that is, they are necessary for only one kind of task, such as solving analogies. Other components are very general and may be necessary in almost every cognitive task. For example, metacomponents are always operating to select strategies and keep track of progress. This may help to explain the persistent correlations among all types of mental tests. People who are effective in selecting good problem-solving strategies, monitoring progress, and moving to a new approach when the first one fails are more likely to be successful on all types of tests. Metacomponents may be the modern-day version of Spearman's *g.*

FIGURE 4.2 Sternberg's Triarchic Theory of Intelligence Sternberg's triarchic theory suggests that intelligent behavior is the product of applying thinking strategies, handling new problems creatively and quickly, and adapting to contexts by selecting and reshaping our environment.

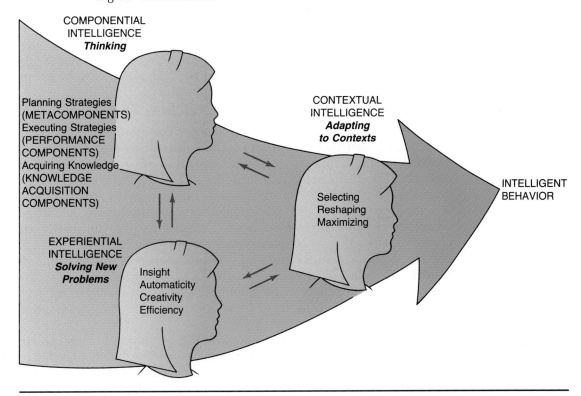

The second part of Sternberg's triarchic theory involves coping with new experiences. Intelligent behavior is marked by two characteristics: (1) the ability to deal effectively with novel situations and (2) the ability to become efficient and automatic in thinking and problem solving. So intelligence involves creative thinking in solving new problems and **automaticity**—quickly turning new solutions into routine processes that can be applied without much cognitive effort.

The third part of Sternberg's theory highlights the importance of choosing an environment in which a person can succeed and adapting to that environment or reshaping it if necessary. Here, culture is a major factor in defining successful choice, adaptation, and shaping. What works in one cultural group will not work in another. For example, abilities that make a person successful in a rural farm community may be useless in the inner city or at a country club in the suburbs. People who are successful often seek situations in which their abilities will be valuable, then work hard to capitalize on those abilities and compensate for any weaknesses. Thus intelligence in this third sense involves practical matters such as career choice or social skills. Figure 4.2 summarizes the elements of Sternberg's triarchic theory of intelligence and shows how they may relate mental abilities to one another and to the thinking processes underlying these abilities.

Automaticity The result of learning to perform a behavior or thinking process so thoroughly that the performance is automatic and does not require effort.

How Is Intelligence Measured?

Because cognitive process approaches like Sternberg's are relatively new, they have not produced any widely used tests of intelligence. The tests of intelligence used in schools are based almost entirely on the definition of intelligence as content—specific and general abilities. Even though psychologists do not agree about what intelligence is, they do agree that intelligence, as measured by these standard tests, is related to learning in school. Why is this so? It has to do in part with the way intelligence tests were first developed.

Binet's Dilemma. In 1904 Alfred Binet was confronted with the following problem by the minister of public instruction in Paris: How can students who will need special teaching and extra help be identified early in their school careers, before they fail in regular classes? At the time many of these students, who are now called mentally retarded, were likely to spend several years in regular classes, falling farther and farther behind, when they might have been in classes designed to meet their needs. Binet's task was to devise some way to identify these students. Binet was also a political activist, very concerned with the rights of children. He believed that having an objective measure of learning ability could protect students from poor families who might be forced to leave school because they were the victims of discrimination and assumed to be slow learners.

Binet and his collaborator Theophile Simon wanted to measure not merely school achievement but the intellectual skills students needed to do well in school. They searched first for test items that could discriminate between students who were doing well and students of the same age who were doing poorly. They tested students in regular schools and students of the same age in institutions for the retarded and then compared the results. After trying many different texts and eliminating items that did not discriminate between successful and unsuccessful students, Binet and Simon finally identified 58 tests, several for each age group from 3 to 13. Binet's tests allowed the examiner to determine a **mental age** for a child. A child who succeeded on the items passed by most 6-year-olds, for example, was considered to have a mental age of 6, whether the child was actually 5, 6, or 7 years old. Some sample items from Binet's test are shown in Table 4.2.

The concept of **intelligence quotient** or **IQ** was added after the test was brought to the United States and revised at Stanford University to give us the Stanford-Binet test. An IQ score was computed by comparing the mental-age score to the person's actual chronological age. The formula was

$$\text{intelligence quotient} = \frac{\text{mental age}}{\text{chronological age}} \times 100$$

The early Stanford-Binet has been revised four times, most recently in 1986 (Thorndike, Hagen, & Sattler, 1986). The practice of computing a mental age proved problematic. As children grow older, the range and

Alfred Binet developed a systematic procedure for assessing learning aptitudes. His goal was to understand intelligence and use this knowledge to help children.

Mental Age In intelligence testing, a score based on average abilities for that age group.

Intelligence Quotient (IQ) Score comparing mental and chronological ages.

TABLE 4.2 Intelligence Test Items at Three Different Age Levels of Binet's Test, 1911 Version		
Year 3	**Year 7**	**Year 15**
1. Point to eyes, nose, and mouth 2. Repeat 2 digits 3. Identify objects in a picture 4. Repeat a sentence of 6 syllables	1. Show right hand and left ear 2. Describe a picture 3. Carry out 3 commands given simultaneously 4. Count the value of 6 coins	1. Repeat 7 digits 2. Find 3 rhymes for a given word in 1 minute 3. Repeat a sentence of 26 syllables 4. Interpret a set of given facts

Source: J. Darley, S. Glucksberg, and R. Kinchla (1988), *Psychology,* 5th ed., © 1991, p. 298. Reprinted by permission of Prentice-Hall, Englewood Cliffs, New Jersey.

variability of mental ages increase. By age 13 or 14, the variability of mental ages in a large sample of students is much greater than it was when the same children were 3 or 4. For this reason, IQ scores calculated on the basis of mental age do not have the same meaning at every age. To cope with this problem, the concept of **deviation IQ** was introduced. The deviation IQ score is a number that tells exactly how much above or below the average a person scored on the test, compared to others in the same age group.

Group versus Individual IQ Tests. The Stanford-Binet is an individual intelligence test. It has to be administered to one student at a time by a trained psychologist and takes about two hours. Psychologists also have developed group tests that can be given to whole classes or schools. A group test is much less likely to yield an accurate picture of any one person's abilities. When students take tests in a group, they may do poorly because they do not understand the instructions, because their pencils break, because they are distracted by other students, or because they do not shine on paper-and-pencil tests. On an individual test, by contrast, most of the questions are asked orally and do not require reading or writing. A student can usually pay closer attention and be more motivated to do well when working directly with an adult. As a teacher, you should be very wary of IQ scores based on group tests.

What Does an IQ Score Mean?

Most intelligence tests are designed so that they have certain statistical characteristics. Like college entrance examinations, intelligence tests have a standard average score. For IQ tests, the average score is 100. Fifty percent of the people from the general population who take the tests will score 100 or above, and 50 percent will score below 100. About 68 percent of the general population will earn IQ scores between 85 and 115. Only about 16 percent of the population will receive scores below 85, and only 16 percent will score above 115. Note, however, that these figures

Deviation IQ Score based on statistical comparison of individual's performance with the average performance of others in that age group.

Point/Counterpoint

Are Intelligence Tests Biased against Minority-Group Students?

Because the average IQ test score for many ethnic groups is below the average for native-born Anglo-European Americans, some educators and psychologists believe that the tests are biased against minority-group students. Should the use of intelligence tests be banned for minority-group students?

Point: The tests are biased and should be banned.

Critics of intelligence testing with minority-group students make six main arguments against testing (Hallahan & Kauffman, 1991; Sattler, 1988):

1. Intelligence tests are biased in favor of white, Anglo-European, middle-class students. The tests' language better fits the experiences of these students. For example, one question asks the function of the stomach. Students familiar

with the vocabulary of "stomach" and "digestion" earn points for a correct answer.
2. The national norms used to determine scores on the tests are inappropriate for gauging minority-group students' performance, because the norm groups are made up almost entirely of white middle-class students.
3. Students from ethnic cultures may do poorly on intelligence tests because their values and beliefs do not encourage competition and personal achievement, but rather cooperation and team achievement.
4. Most examiners are white, and this may make minority-group children uncomfortable. The adult may even misunderstand the child's answer or assume the child does not know the answer.
5. The lower test scores for minority-group children lead to placement in inferior tracks or

hold true for white native-born Americans whose first language is standard English. As you can see in the **Point/Counterpoint** section above, whether IQ tests should even be used with ethnic minority-group students is hotly debated.

Intelligence and Achievement. People often wonder what IQ scores mean in terms of future achievement. Intelligence test scores predict achievement in schools quite well, at least for large groups. For example, the correlation is about .65 between school achievement and scores on a popular individual intelligence test, the revised Wechsler Intelligence Scale for Children (WISC-III) (Sattler, 1988). This isn't surprising, because the tests were designed to predict school achievement. Remember, Binet threw out test items that did not discriminate between good and poor students.

But do people who score high on IQ tests achieve more in life? Here the answer is less clear. People with higher intelligence-test scores tend to complete more years of school and to have higher-status jobs. But when the number of years of education is held constant, IQ scores and school achievement are not highly correlated with income and success in later life. If you complete college, your chances of doing well in your career in comparison to your classmates cannot be predicted accurately from your scores on IQ tests (McClelland, 1973). Within a given type of job, success does not seem to be related to measured intelligence (Jencks et al., 1972). Other factors like motivation, social

special education classes. Students experience an inferior education and therefore learn less.

6. Using an intelligence test as the only assessment procedure puts all the responsibility for difficulties on the student.

Counterpoint: The tests are not biased and provide valuable information.

Supporters of intelligence testing with minority group students counter the above six arguments with these assertions:

1. There is no evidence that the language of IQ tests causes problems for minority-group students. These students do no worse than whites on test items that have "middle-class" words.

2. The norm groups for all the major individual intelligence tests include minority-group students in the same proportion as they are in the general population. To have separate norms for each ethnic group would be very discriminatory and misleading.

3. Cultural differences in test-taking skills and difficulties in communication between the test examiner and the student *are* potential sources of bias against minority-group students. These problems should be kept in mind by everyone.

4. In fact, most students are placed in special education classes on the basis of poor performance in regular classes and teacher recommendations. A full individual intelligence test is seldom given, but when it is, it may identify students who do not belong in classes for the retarded but instead have other kinds of learning problems.

Supporters of intelligence testing believe that these tests do a good, objective job of capturing students' current learning abilities. To ignore this information, the advocates say, is like refusing to determine the blood pressure of a particular African-American child because African-Americans as a group have higher blood pressure than many other ethnic groups. If testing is denied to minority-group students, they may also be denied admission to special remediation, enrichment, and acceleration programs.

skills, and luck may make the difference. There are individuals with higher and lower IQ scores in every kind of job (Sattler, 1988).

Intelligence: Heredity or Environment? Nowhere, perhaps, has the nature-versus-nurture debate raged so hard as in the area of intelligence. The main topic of controversy is whether intelligence should be seen as a potential, limited by our genetic makeup, that once fulfilled cannot be exceeded. Or does intelligence simply refer to an individual's current level of intellectual functioning, as fed and influenced by experience and education? In fact, it is almost impossible to separate intelligence "in the genes" from intelligence "due to experience." Today most psychologists believe that differences in intelligence are due to both heredity and environment, probably in about equal proportions. "Genes do not fix behavior. Rather they establish a range of possible reactions to the range of possible experiences that the environment can provide" (Weinberg, 1989, p. 101).

So what can we conclude about intellectual abilities? Abilities as measured by standard IQ tests seem to be strongly influenced by heredity, but what people do with these abilities, their level of achievement, seems very much influenced by environment. And environmental influences can range from the health of a child's mother during pregnancy to the quality of teaching a child receives. As a teacher, it is especially important for you to realize that cognitive skills, like any other skills, are always improvable. Intelligence is a current state of affairs, affected by

This girl is trying to arrange the red and white blocks so that they match the pattern in the booklet. Her performance is timed. This subtest of the Wechsler Intelligence Scale for Children assesses spatial ability.

Guidelines

Interpreting IQ Scores

Check to see if the score is based on an individual or a group test. Be wary of group test scores.

Examples

1. Individual tests include the Wechsler Scales (WPPSI, WISC-III, WAIS-R), the Stanford-Binet, the McCarthy Scales of Children's Abilities, the Woodcock-Johnson Psycho-Educational Battery, and the Kaufman Assessment Battery for Children.
2. Group tests include the Lorge-Thorndike Intelligence Tests, the Analysis of Learning Potential, the Kuhlman-Anderson Intelligence Tests, the Otis-Lennon Mental Abilities Tests, and the School and College Ability Tests (SCAT).

Remember that IQ tests are only estimates of general aptitude for learning.

Examples

1. Ignore small differences in scores among students.
2. Bear in mind that even an individual student's scores may change over time for many reasons, including measurement error.

3. Be aware that a total score is usually an average of scores on several kinds of questions. A score in the middle or average range may mean that the student performed at the average on every kind of question, or that the student did quite well in some areas (for example, on verbal tasks) and rather poorly in other areas (for example, on quantitative tasks).

Remember that IQ scores reflect a student's past experiences and learning.

Examples

1. Consider these scores as predictors of school abilities, not measures of innate intellectual abilities.
2. If a student is doing well in your class, do not change your opinion or lower your expectations just because one score seems low.
3. Be wary of IQ scores for minority students and for students whose first language was not English. Even scores on "culture-free" tests are lower for disadvantaged students.

past experiences and open to future changes—probably within limits, but limits that are not yet fully understood. Even if intelligence is a limited potential, the potential is still quite large; and that potential is a challenge to all teachers.

ABILITY DIFFERENCES AND TEACHING

In this section we consider how you might handle differences in academic ability in your classes. First we examine a commonly used approach—ability grouping. Is this a solution to the challenge of ability differences? If so, when and for whom? Then we turn our attention to students who represent the extremes in ability, the retarded and the gifted. Both groups need teachers who understand their particular needs.

Ability Grouping

The expressed goal of ability grouping is to make teaching more appropriate for students. As we will see, this does not always happen. There are two main ways to group students by ability. The first is to assign

Every individual is a product of both heredity and environment, interacting in complex and ever-changing ways. Although cultural influences create commonalities, there may still be differences among people of the same culture.

students to classes or tracks based on their ability. The second is to form small groups within a given class based on ability.

The first method, **between-class ability grouping,** involves forming whole classes based on ability. It is a common practice in secondary schools and can be found in many elementary schools as well. Most high schools have "college prep" courses and "general" courses or, for example, high-, middle-, and low-ability classes in a particular subject. Although this seems on the surface to be an efficient way to teach, research has consistently shown that segregation by ability does not improve learning and may cause problems for low-ability students (Good & Marshall, 1984; Slavin, 1987, 1990a).

There are several problems with between-class grouping. Low-ability classes seem to receive lower-quality instruction in general. Teachers tend to focus on lower-level objectives and routine procedures. There are more management problems. Teacher enthusiasm and enjoyment are less in the low-ability classes. These differences in instruction and the teachers' negative attitudes may mean that low expectations are communicated to the students. Student self-esteem suffers almost as soon as the assignment to "dummy" English or math is made. Attendance may drop along with self-esteem. Often the lower tracks have a disproportionate number of minority-group and economically disadvantaged students, so ability grouping, in effect, becomes resegregation in school. Possibilities for friendships become limited to students in the same ability range. Often, assignments to classes are made on the basis of group IQ tests instead of tests in the subject area itself. Yet group IQ tests are not good guides for what someone is ready to learn in a particular subject area (Corno & Snow, 1986; Good & Brophy, 1984; Kulik & Kulik, 1982; Slavin, 1987, 1990a; Slavin & Karweit, 1985).

Between-Class Ability Grouping System of grouping in which students are assigned to classes based on their measured ability or achievements.

There are two exceptions to the general finding that between-class ability grouping leads to lower achievement. The first is found in honors or gifted classes, where high-ability students tend to perform better than comparable students in regular classes. The second exception is the Joplin Plan. In this arrangement, students are grouped by ability in reading, regardless of their age or grade. A reading class might thus have students from several grades, all working on the same level on reading. This cross-grade grouping seems to be effective for students of all abilities (Slavin, 1987).

The second method, **within-class ability grouping,** clustering students by ability within the same class, is another story. Almost all elementary-school classes are grouped for reading, and many are grouped for math. The results are generally positive for students at all ability levels, if the following conditions are met (Good & Brophy, 1991; Slavin, 1987).

1. The groups should be formed and reformed on the basis of students' current performance in the subject being taught. This means students are grouped on the basis of current reading level for reading instruction and on the basis of current math achievement for math instruction. This also means frequent changes in group placement when students' achievement changes.

2. The teacher should discourage comparisons between groups and encourage students to develop a whole-class spirit. Group by ability for one or, at the most, two subjects. Make sure there are many lessons and projects that mix members from the groups. Experiment with learning strategies in which cooperation is stressed (described in chapter 10).

3. The number of groups should be kept small (two or three at most) so that the teacher can provide as much direct teaching as possible. When we discuss effective teaching in chapter 13, you will see that leaving students alone for too long leads to less learning.

4. Make sure teachers, methods, and pace are adjusted to fit the needs of the group. Just putting similar-ability students together will not be effective unless the teaching is appropriate for the students' level of understanding.

What should teachers do when they face more extreme differences in student ability? We turn to this question next.

Mental Retardation

Before the 1970s, **mental retardation** was often defined simply as a score below a particular cutoff point on an intelligence test. Since one school district might use a cutoff of, say, 75 and another a cutoff of 67, a student could be labeled mentally retarded in one district but not in another. Using an IQ score alone is *never* an appropriate way to classify a student. Almost every definition of mental retardation includes the idea that mentally retarded individuals cannot adapt adequately to their environment.

Definition and Prevalence. According to the American Association on Mental Deficiency (AAMD), there are three key factors in mental retardation.

Within-Class Ability Grouping System of grouping in which students in a class are divided into two or three groups based on ability in an attempt to accommodate student differences.

Mental Retardation Significantly below-average intellectual and adaptive social behavior, evident before age 18.

1. Intellectual function must be significantly below average. (This is usually defined as a score lower than two standard deviations below the mean on an individual intelligence test—for example, a score below 70 on the WISC-III.)

2. Adaptive behavior must also be so deficient that the individuals do not meet the standards of personal independence and social responsibility expected of people their age in their own cultural group.

3. Finally, these deficiencies of intellectual functioning and adaptive behavior must have appeared before age 18. Problems occurring after that are assumed to be due to other factors, such as brain damage or emotional disturbance.

Of the three factors, "the test of social adequacy is the most basic indicator of retarded mental development. If a person is socially and economically self-sufficient, low test scores are relatively meaningless" (Smith & Neisworth, 1975, p. 307). This caution is especially important when interpreting the scores of students from different cultures. Defining retardation based on test scores alone can create what some critics call "6-hour retardates"—students who are seen as retarded only for the part of the day they attend school.

Only about 1 to 2 percent of the population fit the AAMD's definition of retarded in both intellectual functioning and adaptive behavior (Hallahan & Kauffman, 1991). Of this group, most—about 75 percent—are mildly retarded. Only 20 percent of all retarded individuals are moderately retarded, and only 5 percent are severely or profoundly affected. Table 4.3 on page 124 describes typical behaviors for mildly, moderately, severely, and profoundly retarded people at preschool- and school-age levels.

Causes of Retardation. We know of organic (physical) causes of retardation for only about 10 to 25 percent of the individuals involved. One is **Down syndrome,** a condition caused by the presence of an extra chromosome (though the extra chromosome does not appear to be inherited). Children with Down syndrome range in intelligence from very severely retarded to almost normal.

Other causes of mental retardation include maternal infections such as rubella (German measles), syphilis, or herpes simplex during pregnancy; blood-type incompatibility between the mother and the unborn baby; maternal alcohol or drug use during pregnancy; premature birth; lead poisoning in young children; or the inherited diseases phenylketonuria (PKU) or Tay-Sachs (Hardman, Drew, Egan, & Wolf, 1990).

Teaching Retarded Learners. As a regular teacher, you may have limited contact with severely or moderately retarded children, but you probably will work with mildly retarded children. In the early grades these students may simply learn more slowly than their peers. By the third or fourth grade, they will probably have fallen far behind.

Learning goals for mildly retarded students between the ages of 9 and 13 include basic reading, writing, arithmetic, learning about the local environment, social behavior, and personal interests. In junior and senior high school, the emphasis is on vocational and domestic skills; literacy for living

Down Syndrome
Retardation caused by presence of extra chromosome.

TABLE 4.3   Developmental Characteristics of Mentally Retarded Individuals

Degree of Retardation and IQ Range	Preschool Years (0–5)	School Years (6–20)
Mild 50–55 to approx. 70	Capable of developing social and communication skills Minimal sensorimotor retardation Retardation may not be obvious at this age	By late teens, can attain about sixth-grade academic level Social conformity and acceptance with guidance "Educable"
Moderate 35–40 to 50–55	Can talk or communicate Poor social awareness Fair motor development Moderate supervision necessary Training in self-help useful	Progress beyond second-grade academic level unlikely Training in social and occupational skills beneficial Can learn to get around alone in familiar places
Severe 20–25 to 35–40	Minimal speech; few or no communication skills Poor motor development Self-help training generally unprofitable	Can talk or learn to communicate Systematic training in basic hygiene and other self-care habits beneficial
Profound Below 20–25	Minimal sensorimotor functioning capacities Nursing care required	Some motor development Limited self-help training may be useful

Sources: Adapted from Samuel Kirk and James Gallagher, *Educating Exceptional Children,* Third Edition, p. 142. Copyright © 1979 by Houghton Mifflin Company. Used by permission. Originally from the President's Committee on Mental Retardation, 1975. Also adapted by permission from H. G. Grossman (Ed.) (1983), *Classification in Mental Retardation.* Washington D.C.: American Association on Mental Deficiency, p. 13.

(using the telephone book; reading signs, labels, and newspaper ads; completing a job application); job-related behaviors like courteousness and punctuality; health self-care; and citizenship skills. Today there is a growing emphasis on **transition programming**—preparing the retarded student to live and work in the community. As you will see later in the chapter, the law requires that schools design an IEP, or individualized educational program, for every disabled child. An ITP, or individualized transition plan, may be part of the retarded student's IEP (Hallahan & Kauffman, 1991).

The Guidelines list suggestions for teaching students with below-average general intelligence.

Transition Programming
Gradual preparation of exceptional students to move from high school into further education or training, employment, or community involvement.

Gifted and Talented

There is another group of students with special educational needs who are often overlooked by the schools: the gifted and talented. In the past, providing an enriched education for extremely bright or talented students was seen as undemocratic and elitist. Why use extra resources for students who already have so much ability when disabled students need the

Guidelines

Teaching Retarded Students

1. Determine readiness: however little a child may know, he or she is ready to learn a next step.
2. State and present objectives simply.
3. Base specific learning objectives on an analysis of the child's learning strengths and weaknesses.
4. Present material in small, logical steps. Practice extensively before going on to the next step.
5. Work on practical skills and concepts based on the demands of adult life.
6. Do not skip steps. Students with average intelligence can form conceptual bridges from one step to the next, but retarded children need every step and bridge made explicit. Make connections for the student. Do not expect him or her to "see" the connections.
7. Be prepared to present the same idea in many different ways.
8. Go back to a simpler level if you see the student is not following.
9. Be especially careful to motivate the student and maintain attention.
10. Find materials that do not insult the student. A junior high boy may need the low vocabulary of "See Spot run" but will be insulted by the age of the characters and the content of the story.
11. Focus on a few target behaviors or skills so you and the student have a chance to experience success. Everyone needs positive reinforcement.
12. Be aware that retarded students must overlearn, repeat, and practice more than children of average intelligence. They must be taught how to study, and they must frequently review and practice their newly acquired skills in different settings.
13. Pay close attention to social relations. Simply including retarded students in a regular class will not guarantee that they will be accepted or that they will make and keep friends.

resources so desperately? But there is a growing recognition that gifted students are being poorly served by most public schools. A recent national survey found that more than one-half of all gifted students do not achieve in school at a level equal to their ability (Tomlinson-Keasey, 1990). It is a tragedy whenever students are prevented from fulfilling their potential, whether they are retarded or gifted.

Who Are the Gifted? There is no agreement about what constitutes a **gifted student.** Individuals can have many different gifts. Remember that Gardner (1983) identified 7 separate kinds of "intelligence," and Guilford (1988) claims there are 180. J. S. Renzulli (1982) suggests that we distinguish between academic giftedness and "creative/productive" giftedness. The academically gifted learn lessons very easily and quickly and generally score well on tests of intelligence. These indicators do not, however, necessarily predict success in later life. The creatively gifted tend to excel in situations that require the application of information to solve problems in new and effective ways. These characteristics are more likely to be associated with success in adulthood.

Using these ideas, Renzulli has defined giftedness as a combination of three basic characteristics: above-average general ability, a high level of task commitment or motivation to achieve in certain areas, and a high level of creativity. Renzulli believes that truly gifted children are not the students who simply learn quickly with little effort. The work of gifted students is original, extremely advanced for their age, and potentially of lasting importance.

Gifted Student A very bright, creative, and talented student.

What do we know about these remarkable individuals—whom former U.S. Commissioner of Education Sidney P. Marland has called "our most neglected students"? A classic study of the characteristics of the gifted was started decades ago by Lewis Terman and colleagues (1925, 1947, 1959). This huge project is following the lives of 1,528 gifted males and females and will continue until the year 2010. The subjects all have IQ scores in the top 1 percent of the population (140 or above on the Stanford-Binet individual test of intelligence). They were identified on the basis of teacher recommendations and IQ tests, so they probably fall into Renzulli's academically gifted category.

Terman and colleagues found that these gifted children were larger, stronger, and healthier than the norm. They often walked sooner and were more athletic. They were more emotionally stable than their peers and became better-adjusted adults than the average. They had lower rates of delinquency, emotional difficulties, divorces, drug problems, and so on. Of course, the teachers in Terman's study who made the nominations may have selected students who were better adjusted initially.

What Problems Do the Gifted Face? In spite of Terman's findings, it would be incorrect to say that every gifted student is superior in adjustment and emotional health. Many problems confront a gifted child, including boredom and frustration in school as well as isolation (sometimes even ridicule) from peers because of seemingly unbridgeable differences in interests and concerns. For example, schoolmates may be consumed with a passion for baseball or worried about failing math, while the gifted child is fascinated with Mozart or Rembrandt, focused on an abstract moral issue, or totally absorbed in computers, drama, or geology. Gifted children may also find it difficult to accept their own emotions, since the mismatch between mind and emotion can be great. They may be impatient with friends, parents, and even teachers who do not share their interests or abilities.

A recent follow-up of Terman subjects 60 years later reached some surprising conclusions about the relationship between popularity as a student and intellectual accomplishment as an adult. Terman's subjects who were popular and outgoing as children were less likely to maintain serious intellectual interests as adults. The authors of the study speculate that gifted students who became more accomplished as adults may have preferred adult company as children or may have been comfortable being alone. And it is possible that an active social life diverts interest away from intellectual pursuits (Tomlinson-Keasey & Little, 1990). Each path has its benefits and its liabilities for the individual.

Recognizing Students' Special Abilities. It may seem to you that identifying a gifted child would be simple. This is not always the case. Many parents provide early educational experiences for their children. A preschool or primary student coming to your class may read above grade level, play an instrument quite well, or whiz through every assignment. But even very advanced reading in the early grades does not guarantee that students will still be outstanding readers years later (Mills & Jackson, 1990). How do you separate gifted students from hardworking or parentally pressured students? In junior high and high school some very able students deliberately make lower grades, so their abilities are even harder to recognize. And, because many talents and abilities are involved, there is no single straightforward way to recognize gifted students.

Teachers are successful only about 10 to 50 percent of the time in picking out the gifted children in their classes (Fox, 1981). These seven questions, taken from an early study of gifted students, are still good guides today (Walton, 1961):

Who learns easily and rapidly?

Who uses a lot of common sense and practical knowledge?

Who retains easily what he or she has heard?

Who knows about many things that the other children don't?

Who uses a large number of words easily and accurately?

Who recognizes relations and comprehends meanings?

Who is alert and keenly observant and responds quickly?

Giftedness and Formal Testing. The best single predictor of *academic* giftedness is still the individual IQ test. Many schools identify the academically gifted as those who score in the top 3 percent for their ethnic or cultural group (an IQ of about 130 for white, native-born Americans). But an individual intelligence test is costly and time-consuming—and far from perfect.

Group achievement and intelligence tests tend to underestimate the IQs of very bright children. Group tests may be appropriate for screening but are not appropriate for making placement decisions. Many psychologists recommend a case study approach to identifying gifted students. This means gathering many kinds of information, test scores, grades, examples of work, projects and portfolios, letters or ratings from teachers, self-ratings, and so on (Sisk, 1988). Especially for recognizing artistic talent, experts in the field can be called in to judge the merits of a child's creations. Science projects, exhibitions, performances, auditions, and interviews are all possibilities. Creativity tests may identify some children not picked up by other measures, particularly minority students who may be at a disadvantage on the other types of tests (Maker, 1987).

"I COULD HAVE DONE BETTER, BUT I DIDN'T WANT TO DEPART TOO FAR FROM THE ACCEPTED NORM."

© W. A. Vanselow—*Phi Delta Kappan.*

Teaching Gifted Students. There are at least two issues in making educational plans for gifted students. One is how students should be grouped and paced. The other is what teaching methods are most effective.

Educators disagree about grouping and pacing. Some educators believe that gifted students should be *accelerated*—moved quickly through the grades or through particular subjects. Other educators prefer *enrichment*—giving the students additional, more sophisticated, and more thought-provoking work but keeping them with their age-mates in school. Actually, both may be appropriate (Torrance, 1986).

Many people object to acceleration, but most careful studies indicate that truly gifted students who begin primary, elementary, junior high, high school, college, or even graduate school early do as well as and usually better than nongifted students who are progressing at the normal pace. Social and emotional adjustment does not appear to be impaired.

Gifted students tend to prefer the company of older playmates and may be miserably bored if kept with children of their own age. Skipping grades may not be the best solution for a particular student, but it does not deserve the bad name it has received (Kulik & Kulik, 1984; Richardson & Benbow, 1990). An alternative to skipping grades is to accelerate students in one or two particular subjects but keep them with peers for most classes (Reynolds & Birch, 1988).

Teaching methods for gifted students should encourage abstract thinking (formal-operational thought), creativity, and independence, not simply the learning of greater quantities of facts. In working with gifted and talented students, a teacher must be imaginative, flexible, and unthreatened by the capabilities of these students. The teacher must ask, What does this child need most? What is she or he ready to learn? Who can help me to help? Answers might come from faculty members at nearby colleges, retired professionals, books, museums, or older students. Strategies might be as simple as letting the child do math with the next grade or as complicated as helping the parents find an appropriate residential school or an interesting, challenging after-school or summer program. Increasingly, more flexible programs are being devised for gifted students. Summer institutes; courses at nearby colleges; classes with local artists, musicians, or dancers; independent research projects; selected classes in high school for younger students; honors classes; and special-interest clubs are all options for offering gifted students appropriate learning experiences (Mitchell, 1984).

We have spent quite a bit of time considering differences in cognitive ability. But there are many more differences among students that have implications for teachers. We turn to these next.

COGNITIVE AND LEARNING STYLES

In this section we examine individual differences that have very little to do with intelligence but can influence students' learning in school. These differences have been called *cognitive styles* or *learning styles.* Be aware that you may hear these terms used interchangeably. In general, educators prefer the term "learning styles" and include many kinds of differences in this broad category. Psychologists tend to prefer the term "cognitive styles" and to limit their discussion to differences in the ways people process information (Bjorklund, 1989). We will examine both cognitive styles as traditionally defined by psychologists and two more controversial differences in **learning styles**—learning modality preferences and right-brain/left-brain thinking. We examine the latter two because you will encounter these ideas in the schools and you should be able to judge their merits for yourself.

Cognitive Styles

The notion of **cognitive styles** is fairly new. It grew out of research on how people perceive and organize information from the world around them. Results from these studies suggest that individuals differ in how they approach a task, but these variations do not reflect levels of intelligence

Learning Styles Individual differences that affect classroom learning.

Cognitive Styles Different ways of perceiving and organizing information.

or patterns of special abilities. Instead, they have to do with "preferred ways that different individuals have for processing and organizing information and for responding to environmental stimuli" (Shuell, 1981a, p. 46). For example, certain individuals respond very quickly in most situations. Others are more reflective and slower to respond, even though both types of people may be equally knowledgeable about the task at hand.

Cognitive styles are often described as falling on the borderline between mental abilities and personality traits (Shuell, 1981a). They are styles of "thinking" and thus are probably influenced by and in turn influence cognitive abilities (Brodzinsky, 1982). But these preferred ways of dealing with the world also affect social relationships and personal qualities.

Field Dependence and Field Independence. In the early 1940s Herman Witkin became intrigued by the observation that certain airline pilots would fly into a bank of clouds and fly out upside down, without realizing that they had changed position. His interest led to a great deal of research on how people separate one factor from the total visual field. Based on his research, Witkin identified the cognitive styles of **field dependence** and **field independence** (Witkin, Moore, & Goodenough, 1977). People who are *field dependent* tend to perceive a pattern as a whole, not separating one element—for example, true upright position— from the total visual field. Like the upside-down pilots, field-dependent individuals have difficulty focusing on one aspect of a situation, picking out details, or analyzing a pattern into different parts. *Field-independent* people are more likely to perceive separate parts of a total pattern and be able to analyze a pattern according to its components. Look at Figure 4.3 on page 130. Can you find a different single figure from the first row embedded in each of the complex figures in the second row? This is part of the Hidden Figures Test to assess field dependence/independence. If you quickly found the hidden figures, you probably are more field independent. If you had as much trouble as I did, you may be more field dependent.

Although you will not necessarily be able to determine all the variations in your students' cognitive styles, you should be aware that students approach problems in different ways. Some may need help learning to pick out important features and to ignore irrelevant details. They may seem lost in less-structured situations and need clear, step-by-step instructions. Other students may be great at organizing but less sensitive to the feelings of others and not as effective in social situations. Table 4.4 on page 131 presents some of the other learning characteristics of field-dependent and field-independent individuals. Teachers also have their own cognitive styles, which affect their approaches to teaching, also noted in Table 4.4 (Garger & Guild, 1984).

Impulsive and Reflective Cognitive Styles. Another aspect of cognitive style is impulsivity versus reflectiveness. An **impulsive** student works very quickly but makes many mistakes. The more **reflective** student, on the other hand, works slowly and makes few errors.

As with field dependence/independence, impulsive and reflective cognitive styles are not highly related to intelligence within the normal

Field Dependence Cognitive style in which patterns are perceived as wholes.

Field Independence Cognitive style in which separate parts of a pattern are perceived and analyzed.

Impulsive Characterized by cognitive style of responding quickly but often inaccurately.

Reflective Characterized by cognitive style of responding slowly, carefully, and accurately.

FIGURE 4.3   **Measure of Flexibility of Closure**   *Instructions:* This is a test of your ability to tell which one of five simple figures (A–E) can be found in a more complex pattern. There is only one of these figures in each pattern, and this figure will always be right side up and exactly the same size as one of the five lettered figures.

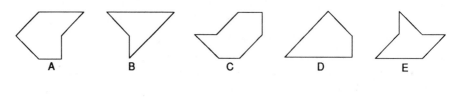

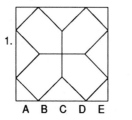
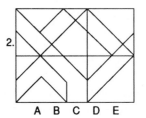
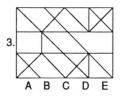

Source: Adapted from Hidden Figures Test (Cf–1), Kit of Factor-Referenced Tests. © 1962 by Educational Testing Service: Figure 4.1. Reprinted by permission of Educational Testing Service, the copyright owner.

range. However, as children grow older, they generally become more reflective, and for school-age children being more reflective does seem to improve performance on school tasks such as reading (Kogan, 1983; Smith & Caplan, 1988).

Students can learn to be more reflective, however, if they are taught specific strategies. One that has proved successful in many situations is **self-instruction,** described in chapter 2. This approach capitalizes on the beneficial use of private speech described by Vygotsky (Meichenbaum, 1986). Another possibility is learning scanning strategies. For example, students taking multiple-choice tests might be encouraged to cross off each alternative as they consider it, so that no possibilities will be ignored. They might work in pairs and talk about why each possibility is right or wrong. In math classes, impulsive children need to be given specific strategies for checking their work. Just slowing down is not enough. These students must be taught effective strategies for solving the problem at hand by considering each reasonable alternative.

I have also encountered several bright students who seem *too* reflective. They turn 30 minutes of homework into an all-night project. These children may be afraid of failure, or they may be bored with the assignment. They need help in learning to work steadily through a project and in being selective about when to analyze each alternative carefully and when to move quickly to a few reasonable choices.

Self-Instruction Talking oneself through the steps of a task.

TABLE **4.4** **Learning and Teaching Styles of Field-Dependent and Field-Independent Individuals**

LEARNING STYLES

Field-Dependent	Field-Independent
Perceives globally	Perceives analytically
Makes broad general distinctions among concepts	Makes specific concept distinctions
Has social orientation	Has impersonal orientation
Learns material with social content best	Learns social material only as an intentional task
Requires externally defined goals and reinforcements	Has self-defined goals
Needs organization provided	Can self-structure situations
Is more affected by criticism	Is less affected by criticism
Uses spectator approach for concept attainment	Uses hypothesis testing to attain concepts
Is best motivated through: verbal praise, helping the teacher, external rewards and seeing the task's value to other people	Is best motivated through: grades. competition, choice of activities, and seeing how the task is useful personally

TEACHING STYLES

Field-Dependent	Field-Independent
Prefers teaching situations that allow interaction and discussion with students	Prefers impersonal teaching situations such as lectures; emphasizes cognitive aspect
Uses student-centered activities	Uses a teacher-organized learning situation
Is viewed by students as one who teaches facts	Is viewed as helping students apply principles
Provides less feedback; avoids negative evaluation	Gives corrective feedback; uses negative evaluation
Establishing a warm, personal classroom	Strong in organizing and guiding student learning

Source: Reprinted by permission from S. Garger and P. Guild (1984), Learning styles, The crucial differences, *Curriculum Review, 23.*

Learning Style Preferences

Since the late 1970s a great deal has been written about differences in students' learning style preferences (Dunn, 1987; Dunn & Dunn, 1978, 1987; Gregorc, 1982; Keefe, 1982). Workshops and in-service training sessions around the country focus on this topic. Learning preferences are usually called *learning styles* in these workshops, but I believe *preferences* is a more accurate label. **Learning style preferences** are individual preferences for particular learning environments. They could be preferences for where, when, with whom, or with what lighting, food, or music you like to study. They could be tendencies to learn better from visual as opposed to verbal materials. Think for a minute about how you learn best. I like to study and write during large blocks of time, late at night. I usually make some kind of commitment or deadline every week so that I have to work under pressure in long stretches to finish the work before that deadline. Then I take a day off. When I plan or think, I have to make brief notes or outlines to organize my thoughts—I have to *see* my thinking. I

Learning Style Preferences
Preferred ways of studying and learning, such as using pictures instead of text, working with other people versus alone, learning in structured or in unstructured situations, and so on.

People have different preferences for how and where they like to learn. Students who are very distracted by noise may work better in a quiet space, even if that place is on the floor in the hall.

have a colleague who draws diagrams of relationships when she takes notes or plans a paper. You may be similar or very different, even though we all work fairly effectively.

There are a number of instruments for assessing students' learning preferences. *The Learning Style Inventory* by Renzulli and Smith (1978) asks students to indicate preferences for different types of instruction, such as lecture, discussion, projects, games, and so on. The *Learning Style Inventory* by Dunn, Dunn, and Price (1984) measures preferences for 23 elements of the instructional program, including the immediate environment (temperature, noise level, etc.); emotional involvement (motivational strategies, structure, etc.); social support (working alone or with others, etc.); physical characteristics (time of day, visual versus auditory materials, etc.); and psychological inclinations (impulsive or reflective, global or analytic, etc.). *The Learning Style Profile* (Keefe & Monk, 1986) is a 126-item test based on a broad definition of learning style that includes cognitive, affective, and physiological differences.

Tests of learning style have been criticized for lacking evidence of reliability and validity. This led Snider (1990) to conclude, "People are different, and it is good practice to recognize and accommodate individual differences. It is also good practice to present information in a variety of ways through more than one modality, but it is not wise to categorize learners and prescribe methods solely on the basis of tests with questionable technical qualities. . . . The idea of learning styles is appealing, but a critical examination of this approach should cause educators to be skeptical" (p. 53).

It may be too much to expect the teacher to provide every student with his or her preferred setting and support for learning. But the teacher can make options available. Having quiet, private corners as well as large tables for working; comfortable cushions as well as straight chairs; brightly lighted desks along with darker areas; headphones for listening to music as well as earplugs; structured as well as open-ended assignments; information available from films and tapes as well as in books—all these options will allow students to work and learn in their preferred mode at least some of the time. If you do decide to provide some alternatives for your students, however, be sure that teaching and learning time is not lost as students move in and out of these arrangements.

Will making these alterations lead to greater learning? Here the answer is not clear. Results of some research indicate that students learn more when they study in their preferred setting and manner (Dunn, Beaudry, & Klavas, 1989; Dunn & Dunn, 1987). There is some evidence that very bright students need less structure and prefer quiet, solitary learning (Torrance, 1986). But before you try to accommodate all your students' learning styles, remember that students, especially younger ones, may not be the best judges of how they should learn. Preference for a particular style may not always guarantee that using the style will be effective. Sometimes students, particularly poorer students, prefer what is easy and comfortable. But real learning can be hard and uncomfortable. Sometimes students prefer to learn in a certain way because they have no alternatives; it is the only way they know how to approach the task. These students may benefit from developing new—and perhaps more effective—ways to learn (Weinstein, 1991).

Right-Brain/Left-Brain Processing

We turn now to consider a very controversial source of differences in learning and cognitive style, **hemispheric specialization,** or a person's preference for right-brain versus left-brain processing. According to some educators, many students have problems learning because they tend to process information using the right hemisphere of their brain, whereas the tasks of school require mostly left-hemisphere processing. Is this true?

Let's look first at the evidence for differences in the functions of the two halves of the brain or hemispheres. We know that each half of the brain controls the opposite side of the body. Damage to the right side of the brain will affect movement of the left side of the body and vice versa. In addition, certain areas of the brain affect particular behaviors. For most of us, the left hemisphere of the brain is the major factor in language processing, and the right hemisphere has the most to do with handling spatial-visual information and emotions (nonverbal information). For some left-handed people, the relationship may be reversed, but for most left-handers there is simply less hemispheric specialization altogether (Berk, 1991).

Unfortunately, results of research on hemispheric specialization were popularized and oversimplified by the media. Figure 4.4 on page 134 is an example taken from *Newsweek*. Based on exaggerated views of the

Hemispheric Specialization A property of the human brain—the right and left halves or hemispheres of the brain are involved with different functions, so that control of certain behaviors tends to be dominated by the right or by the left side, depending on the function.

FIGURE 4.4   **Beware of Simplified Views of the Brain**   There is some evidence that certain abilities are located in certain areas of the brain, but this simplified view is misleading.

HOW THE BRAIN DIVIDES ITS WORK

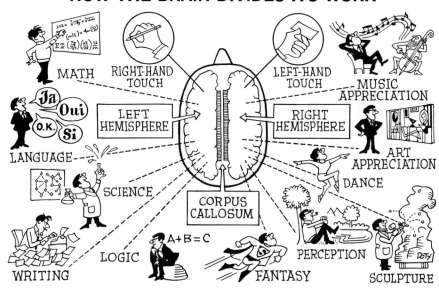

Source: Newsweek—Roy Doty.

separation of abilities in the brain, some educators developed explanations for learning problems as well as suggestions for improving creativity. Two basic assumptions underlying these ideas are that different abilities are completely controlled by one side of the brain or the other, and that individuals favor one hemisphere over the other in processing information. In other words, they are "right-brained" or "left-brained."

There is little evidence for either of these assumptions. For people who have normal intact brains, both hemispheres are involved in all learning tasks, even if one side may be more or less involved at any given moment (Bjorklund, 1989). Poets write in words but paint images and patterns with their verse. Sculptors often plan analytically, think logically, and perform calculations as they sculpt (Caine & Caine, 1991). It is possible that researchers will trace certain learning problems to aspects of hemispheric specialization, but the evidence is not yet conclusive. In fact, some preliminary research indicates that the front-to-back functioning of the brain may be as important as left/right functioning in understanding learning disabilities (Jordan & Goldsmith-Phillips, in press).

STUDENTS WITH LEARNING CHALLENGES

Thus far we have focused mostly on teachers' responses to the varying abilities and styles of students. For the rest of the chapter we will consider several kinds of problems or disabilities that can interfere with learning. Before we continue, though, let's analyze the difference between a *disability* and a *handicap.* A **disability** is just what the word implies—an inability to do something specific such as see or walk. A **handicap** is a disadvantage in certain situations. Some disabilities lead to handicaps. For example, being blind (a visual disability) is a handicap if you are doing work that requires sight. But this disability is not a handicap when you are doing work that requires other skills, such as composing music, finding your way around in complete darkness, or talking on the telephone. Not all disabilities are handicaps in every situation. And not all handicaps are due to disabilities; they may be caused by lack of experience or training. Hallahan and Kauffman (1991) remind us that "when working and living with individuals who have disabilities, we must constantly strive to separate the disability from the handicap. That is, our goal should be to confine their handicap to those characteristics that cannot be changed and to make sure that we impose no further handicap by our attitudes or our unwillingness to accommodate their disability" (p. 6).

Students with Physical Challenges

Some students must have special **orthopedic devices** such as braces, special shoes, crutches, or wheelchairs to participate in a normal school program. Accidents, disease, or birth defects can lead to conditions that require these devices. If the school has the necessary architectural features, such as ramps, elevators, and accessible rest rooms, and if teachers allow for the physical limitations of students, little needs to be done to alter the usual educational program.

Epilepsy. Many of us tend to have more misinformation than information about **epilepsy.** Its exact causes are unknown, but the seizures that accompany some forms of epilepsy result from uncontrolled, spontaneous firings of neurons in the brain. Not all seizures are the result of epilepsy; temporary conditions such as high fevers or infections can also trigger seizures.

There are two major types of epilepsy you may encounter in the classroom. A *partial seizure* involves only a small part of the brain. It is characterized by a brief loss of contact with the outside world. The student may stare, fail to respond to questions, drop objects, and miss what has been happening for 1 to 30 seconds. A *generalized seizure* involves a large portion of the brain and is characterized by uncontrolled jerking movements that ordinarily last 2 to 5 minutes, followed by a deep sleep or coma. Upon regaining consciousness the student may be very weary, confused, and in need of extra sleep.

Since partial seizures are not dramatic, the condition can easily go undetected. If a child in your class appears to daydream frequently, does not seem to know what is going on at times, or cannot remember what has just happened when you ask, you should consult the school psychologist or nurse. The major problem for students with partial seizures is that they miss the continuity of the class interaction. If their seizures are frequent, they will find the lessons confusing. As a teacher, you should question these students to be sure they are understanding and following the lesson. Be prepared to repeat yourself periodically.

Disability The inability to do something specific such as walk or hear.

Handicap A disadvantage in a particular situation, sometimes caused by a disability.

Orthopedic Devices Devices such as braces and wheelchairs that aid the physically handicapped.

Epilepsy Disorder marked by seizures and caused by abnormal electrical discharges in the brain.

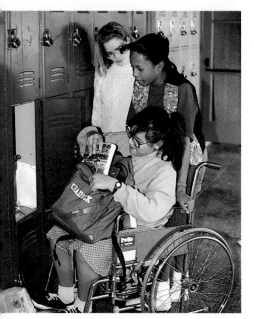

Students with physical disabilities may need some assistance to participate fully in regular classes and other students are often the best sources of help.

Cerebral Palsy Condition involving a range of motor or coordination difficulties due to brain damage.

Spasticity Overly tight or tense muscles, characteristic of some forms of cerebral palsy.

A generalized seizure requires a reaction from the teacher. The major danger to a student having a generalized seizure is getting hurt by striking a hard surface during the violent jerking. But do not try to restrain the child's movements. Lower the child gently to the floor, away from furniture or walls. Move hard objects away. Turn the child's head gently to the side and loosen any tight clothing. Some experts advise gently placing a soft material like a handkerchief between the back teeth. Never use anything hard; you might injure the student. Find out from the student's parents how the seizure is usually dealt with. If one seizure follows another and the student does not regain consciousness in between, get medical help right away (Hallahan & Kauffman, 1991).

During a seizure the student may perspire heavily, foam at the mouth, or lose bladder or bowel control. As a teacher, your calm and sympathetic response is very important. The other students in the class will be upset if you are upset. If you seem fearful or disgusted, they will learn to respond in similar ways. A student who has just come through a seizure should not be greeted by a classroom of staring children. It is also your responsibility to prepare the class for the possibility of further seizures occurring during school. Some students may believe that epilepsy is contagious; this and any other mistaken notions should be corrected.

Cerebral Palsy. Damage to the brain before or during birth or during infancy can cause a child to have difficulty moving and coordinating his or her body. The problem may be very mild, so the child simply appears a bit clumsy, or so severe that voluntary movement is practically impossible. The most common form of **cerebral palsy** is characterized by **spasticity** (overly tight or tense muscles). The damage to the brain may be such that only movement is affected. Children with this form of cerebral palsy may wear a brace or use a wheelchair and need no special educational program. But many children with cerebral palsy have secondary handicaps (Bigge & Sirvis, 1982). In the classroom, these secondary handicaps are the greatest concern—and these are generally what the regular teacher can help with most. For example, many children with cerebral palsy also have hearing impairments, speech problems, or mild mental retardation. The strategies described in this chapter should prove helpful in such situations.

Hearing Impairment. Students with severe hearing or vision losses, especially younger students who have not yet learned how to function in regular classrooms, spend most of their school time in special classes. But students with mild impairments and students with more severe problems who have had special training are frequently placed in regular classrooms for most or all of their instruction.

Hearing losses may be caused by genetic factors, maternal infections such as rubella during pregnancy, complications during birth, or early childhood diseases such as mumps or measles. Many children today are protected from hearing loss by vaccinations against such infections.

Signs of hearing problems are turning one ear toward the speaker, favoring one ear in conversation, or misunderstanding conversation when the speaker's face cannot be seen. Other indications include not following directions, seeming distracted or confused at times, frequently asking people to repeat what they have said, mispronouncing new words or names, and being reluctant to participate in class discussions. Take note particularly of students who have frequent earaches, sinus infections, or allergies.

In the past, educators have debated whether oral or manual approaches are better for children with hearing impairments. Oral approaches involve **speech reading** (also called lip reading) as well as training students to use whatever limited hearing they may have. Manual approaches include **sign language** and **finger spelling.** Research indicates that children who learn some manual method of communicating perform better in academic subjects and are more socially mature than students who are exposed only to oral methods. Today the trend is to combine both approaches (Hallahan & Kauffman, 1991)

Vision Impairment. Mild vision problems can be overcome with corrective lenses. Only about .1 percent of the students in this country have visual impairments so serious that special educational services are needed. Most of this group needing special services is classified as having **low vision.** This means they can read with the aid of a magnifying glass or large-print books. A small group of students, about 1 in every 2,500, are **educationally blind.** These students must have Braille materials (Kirk & Gallagher, 1982).

Special materials and equipment that help visually handicapped students to function in regular classrooms include large-print typewriters; variable-speed tape recorders (allowing teachers to make time-compressed tape recordings, which speed up the rate of speech without changing the voice pitch); special calculators; the abacus; three-dimensional maps, charts, and models; and special measuring devices. For students with visual problems, the quality of the print is often more important than the size, so watch out for hard-to-read handouts and ditto sheets. You can buy ditto masters that print in black, red, or green. These may be easier to read than the standard purple we all know and love. The Instructional Materials Reference Center of the American Printing House for the Blind (1839 Frankfort Avenue, Louisville, KY 40206) has catalogs of instructional materials for visually impaired students.

Students who have difficulty seeing often hold books very close to or very far from their eyes. They may squint, rub their eyes frequently, or complain that their eyes burn or itch. The eyes may actually be swollen, red, or encrusted. Students with vision problems may misread material on the chalkboard, describe their vision as being blurred, be very sensitive to light, or hold their heads at an odd angle (DeMott, 1982). Any of these signs should be reported to a qualified school professional.

Communication Disorders

Language is a complex learned behavior. Language disorders may arise from many sources, since so many different aspects of the individual are involved in learning language. A child with a hearing impairment will not learn to speak normally. A child who hears inadequate language at home will learn inadequate language. Children who are not listened to or whose perception of the world is distorted by emotional problems will

Speech Reading Using visual cues to understand language.

Sign Language Communication system of hand movements that symbolize words and concepts.

Finger Spelling Communication system that "spells out" each letter with a hand position.

Low Vision Vision limited to close objects.

Educationally Blind Needing Braille materials in order to learn.

reflect these problems in their language development. Since speaking involves movements, any impairment of the motor functions involved with speech can cause language disorders. And because language development and thinking are so interwoven, any problems in cognitive functioning can affect ability to use language.

Speech Impairments. Students who cannot produce sounds effectively for speaking are considered to have a **speech impairment.** About 5 percent of school-age children have some form of speech impairment. Articulation problems and stuttering are the two most common problems.

Articulation disorders include substituting one sound for another ("I *t*ought I *t*aw a pu*dd*y *t*at"), distorting a sound (*shoup* for *soup*), adding a sound (*ideer* for *idea*), or omitting sounds (*po-y* for *pony*) (Cartwright, Cartwright, & Ward, 1981). But keep in mind that most children are 6 to 8 years old before they can successfully pronounce all English sounds in normal conversation. The sounds of the consonants *l, r, y, s,* and *z* and the consonant blends *sh, ch, zh,* and *th* are the last to be mastered.

Stuttering generally appears between the ages of 3 and 4. It is not yet clear what causes stuttering; stuttering, though, can cause embarrassment and anxiety for the sufferer. In about 50 percent of cases, stuttering disappears during early adolescence (Wiig, 1982).

Voicing problems, a third type of speech impairment, include speaking with an inappropriate pitch, quality, or loudness or in a monotone (Wiig, 1982). A student with any of these problems should be referred to a speech therapist. Recognizing the problem is the first step. Be alert for students whose pronunciation, loudness, voice quality, speech fluency, expressive range, or rate is very different from that of their peers. Pay attention also to students who seldom speak. Are they simply shy, or do they have difficulties with language?

Oral Language Disorders. There are four kinds of language disorders, summarized in Table 4.5. Language differences are not necessarily language disorders. Students with language disorders are those who are markedly deficient compared with other students of their own age and cultural group. Students who seldom speak, who use few words or very short sentences, or who rely only on gestures to communicate should be referred to a qualified school professional for observation or testing.

Emotional/Behavioral Disorders

Students with emotional and behavioral disorders can be among the most difficult to teach in a regular class. Behavior becomes a problem when it deviates so much from appropriate behaviors for the child's age group that it significantly interferes with (1) the child's own growth and development and/or (2) the lives of others. Clearly, deviation implies a difference from some standard, and standards of behavior differ from one situation, age group, culture, and historical period to another. Thus, what passes for team spirit in the football bleachers might be seen as disturbed behavior in a bank or restaurant.

Six Dimensions of Emotional/Behavioral Disorders. Quay and Peterson (1987) describe six dimensions of emotional/behavioral disor-

Speech Impairment
Inability to produce sounds effectively for speaking.

Articulation Disorders
Any of a variety of pronunciation difficulties, such as the substitution, distortion, or omission of sounds.

Stuttering Repetitions, prolongations, and hesitations that block flow of speech.

Voicing Problems
Inappropriate pitch, quality, loudness, or intonation.

TABLE 4.5 Types of Language Disorders	
Type	**Commonly Suspected Causative Factors or Related Conditions**
No Verbal Language	
Child does not show indications of understanding or spontaneously using language by age 3.	Congenital or early acquired deafness Gross brain damage or severe mental retardation Childhood psychosis
Qualitatively Different Language	
Child's language is different from that of nonhandicapped children at any stage of development— meaning and usefulness for communication are greatly lessened or lost.	Inability to understand auditory stimuli Childhood psychosis Learning disability Mental retardation Hearing loss
Delayed Language Development	
Language follows normal course of development but lags seriously behind that of most children who are the same chronological age.	Mental retardation Experiential deprivation Lack of language stimulation Hearing loss
Interrupted Language Development	
Normal language development begins but is interrupted by illness, accident, or other trauma; language disorder is acquired.	Acquired hearing loss Brain injury due to oxygen deprivation, physical trauma, or infection

Sources: Adapted from D. Hallahan and J. Kauffman, *Exceptional children: Introduction to special education,* 5th ed., p. 239. Copyright © 1991. Reprinted with permission of Allyn and Bacon. Also adapted by permission from D. Shriberg and J. H. Saxman (Eds.), *Introduction to Communication Disorders* (Englewood Cliffs, N.J.: Prentice-Hall, 1980).

ders. Children who have *conduct disorders* are aggressive, destructive, disobedient, uncooperative, distractible, disruptive, and persistent. They have been corrected and punished for the same misbehavior countless times. Many of these children are disliked by the adults and even the other children in their lives. The most successful strategies for helping these children are the behavior management approaches described in chapter 6. These students need very clear rules and consequences, consistently enforced. The future is not promising for students who never learn to control their behavior and who also fail academically. Waiting for the students to "outgrow" their problems is seldom effective (O'Leary & Wilson, 1987).

Children who are extremely anxious, withdrawn, shy, depressed, and hypersensitive, who cry easily and have little confidence, are said to have an *anxiety–withdrawal disorder.* These children have few social skills and consequently very few friends. The most successful approaches with them appear to involve the direct teaching of social skills (Gresham, 1981).

The third category is *attentional problems–immaturity.* Characteristics include a short attention span, frequent daydreaming, little initiative, messiness, and poor coordination. If an immature student is not too far behind others in the class, she or he may respond to the behavior management strategies described in chapter 6. But if these approaches fail or if the problem is severe, you should consult the school psychologist, guidance counselor, or another mental health professional. Related to this dimension is the category of *motor excess.* These students are restless and tense; they seem unable to sit still or stop talking.

The fifth category of behavior disorders is *socialized aggression.* Students in this group are often members of gangs. They may steal or vandalize because their peer culture expects it.

Finally, some students exhibit *psychotic behavior.* You are not likely to work with many of these students. Their behavior may be bizarre, and they may express very far-fetched ideas. These six categories are very general. Let's look at one common problem in more detail.

Hyperactivity and Attention Disorders. You have probably heard and may even have used the term **hyperactivity.** The notion is a modern one; there were no children considered hyperactive 30 to 40 years ago. Today, if anything, the term is applied too often and too widely. Hyperactivity is not one particular condition; it is "a set of behaviors—such as excessive restlessness and short attention span—that are quantitatively and qualitatively different from those of children of the same sex, mental age, and SES [socioeconomic status]" (O'Leary, 1980, p. 195).

Today most psychologists agree that the main problem for children labeled "hyperactive" is directing and maintaining attention, not simply controlling their restlessness and physical activity. The American Psychiatric Association has established a diagnostic category called **attention deficit–hyperactive disorder** to identify children with this problem.

Hyperactive children not only are more physically active and inattentive than other children; they also have difficulty responding appropriately and working steadily toward goals (even their own goals), and they may not be able to control their behavior on command, even for a brief period. The problem behaviors are generally evident in all situations and with every teacher. It is difficult to know how many children should be classified as hyperactive. The most common estimate is 5 percent of the elementary-school population (O'Leary, 1980). More boys than girls are identified as hyperactive. Adolescents are rarely classified in this category (Haring & McCormick, 1986).

There is great disagreement about the cause or causes of attention disorders and hyperactivity. The list includes subtle damage to the brain, often called minimal brain damage (MBD); slower than normal neurological development; chemical imbalances in the body; genetic factors; food allergies; lead poisoning; maternal drinking or smoking during pregnancy; and inappropriate learning (O'Leary & Wilson, 1987). The underlying problem may not be the same for each child.

As a teacher or parent, you are more concerned with cures than causes. Unfortunately, there are no completely effective approaches. Many children, about 750,000 in fact, receive stimulant medication, usually Dexedrine or Ritalin. These stimulants in particular dosages tend to have paradoxical effects on these children: short-term effects include

Hyperactivity Behavior disorder marked by atypical, excessive restlessness and inattentiveness.

Attention Deficit– Hyperactive Disorder Current term for disruptive behavior disorders marked by overactivity, excessive difficulty sustaining attention, or impulsiveness.

possible improvements in social behaviors such as cooperation, attention, and compliance. Research suggests that about 70 percent of hyperactive children are more manageable when on medication. But for many there are negative side effects such as increased heart rate and blood pressure, interference with growth rate, insomnia, weight loss, nausea (Pelham & Murphy, 1986; Walden & Thompson, 1981). In addition, little is known about the long-term effects of drug therapy. There also is no evidence of improvement in academic learning or peer relationships—two areas where hyperactive children have great problems. Since students appear to improve dramatically in their behavior, parents and teachers, relieved to see change, may assume the problem has been cured. It hasn't. The students still need special help in learning.

The methods that have proved most successful in helping students with attention deficits are based on the behavioral principles described in chapter 6. One promising approach combines instruction in learning and memory strategies with motivational training. The goal is to give students the "skill and will" (Paris, 1988) to improve their achievement. Students learn how and when to apply learning strategies and study skills. They are also encouraged to be persistent and to see themselves as "in control" (Reid & Borkowski, 1987). These methods should be thoroughly tested with the student before drugs are used. Even if students in your class are on medication, it is critical that they also learn the academic and social skills they will need to survive. Again, this will not happen by itself, even if behavior improves with medication (Kneedler, 1984).

Specific Learning Disabilities

How do you explain what is wrong with a student who is not mentally retarded, emotionally disturbed, educationally deprived, or culturally different, who has normal vision, hearing, and language capabilities, and who still cannot learn to read, write, or compute? One explanation is that the student has a **specific learning disability.** This is a relatively new category of exceptional students. The category is controversial, partly because professionals cannot agree on who belongs in it. The federal government gives this classic definition:

> "Specific learning disability" means a disorder in one or more of the basic psychological processes involved in understanding or using language, spoken or written, which may manifest itself in an imperfect ability to listen, think, speak, read, write, spell, or to do mathematical calculations. The term includes such conditions as perceptual handicaps, brain injury, minimal brain dysfunction, dyslexia, and developmental aphasia. (*Federal Register,* August 23, 1977)

The definition goes on to say that these disorders of listening, thinking, and so on are *not* due primarily to other conditions, such as mental retardation, emotional disturbance, or educational disadvantages.

Learning Disabled Students. As with any of the groups of handicapped students described thus far, students with learning disabilities are

Specific Learning Disability Problem with acquisition and use of language; may show up as difficulty with reading, writing, reasoning, or math.

not all alike. Many different characteristics have been attributed to learning disabled students. The most common are specific difficulties in one or more academic areas; poor coordination; problems paying attention; hyperactivity and impulsivity; problems organizing and interpreting visual and auditory information; disorders of thinking, memory, speech, and hearing; and sharp emotional ups and downs (Hallahan & Kauffman, 1991). As you can see, many students with other handicaps (such as hyperactivity), and many normal students may have some of the same characteristics. To complicate the situation even more, not all students with learning disabilities will have these problems, and few will have *all* of the problems.

There is no agreement about the causes of learning disabilities. Explanations include lack of dominance of one side of the brain, mild or slight physical damage to the brain, chemical imbalances in the body due to allergies to foods or additives, poor early nutrition, genetic factors, immaturity of the central nervous system, underdeveloped perceptual motor skills, poor teaching, lack of motivation, and inadequate structure in the educational program (Mercer, 1982). You can see that some explanations refer to factors within the child and others refer to environmental factors.

Early diagnosis is important so that learning disabled students do not become terribly frustrated and discouraged. The students themselves do not understand why they are having such trouble, and they may become victims of **learned helplessness.** This condition was first identified in learning experiments with animals. The animals were put in situations where they received punishment (electric shocks) that they could not control. Later, when the situation was changed and they could have escaped the shocks or turned them off, the animals didn't even bother trying (Seligman, 1975). They had learned to be helpless victims. Learning disabled students may also come to believe that they cannot control or improve their own learning. This is a powerful belief. The students never exert the effort to discover that they can make a difference in their own learning, so they remain helpless.

Learning disabled students may also try to compensate for their problems and develop bad learning habits in the process, or they may begin avoiding certain subjects out of fear of not being able to handle the work. To prevent these things from happening, the teacher should refer the students to the appropriate professionals in the school.

Teaching Learning Disabled Students. There is also controversy over how best to help these students. Many programs have been developed to "train" the underlying learning processes. In general, attempts to train perceptual processes directly have not been very successful in improving academic performance (Reid, Hresko, & Swanson, 1991). A more promising approach seems to be to emphasize study skills and methods for processing information in a given subject like reading or math. Many of the principles of cognitive learning from chapters 7 and 8 can be applied to help all students improve their attention, memory, and problem-solving abilities. The Kansas Learning Strategies Curriculum is one example of this approach (Deshler & Schumaker, 1986). No set of teaching techniques will be effective for every learning disabled child. You should work with the special education teachers in your school to design appropriate instruction for individual students.

Learned Helplessness The expectation, based on previous experiences with a lack of control, that all one's efforts will lead to failure.

Finally, many people believe the learning disability label is overused and abused. The number of children classified as learning disabled increased 119 percent between 1977 and 1985. Some researchers have suggested that half or more of the students called learning disabled are really slow learners in average schools, average learners in high-achieving schools, students with second-language problems, or class "troublemakers"; or that they may simply be behind in their work because they are absent frequently or have to change schools often (Gartner & Lipsky, 1987).

MAINSTREAMING

We have been discussing in detail the many special problems of exceptional students because, no matter what grade or subject you teach, you will encounter these students in your classroom. The movement to educate exceptional students in regular classrooms sometimes is called **mainstreaming,** because the exceptional students are educated in the mainstream of American education.

Public Laws 94-142, 99-457, and 101-476

In 1975 the Education for All Handicapped Children Act (Public Law 94-142) was passed, requiring states to provide "a free, appropriate public education for every child between the ages of 3 and 21 (unless state law does not provide free public education to children 3 to 5 or 18 to 21 years of age) regardless or how, or how seriously, he may be handicapped." In 1986 PL 99-457 extended the requirement for a free, appropriate education to all handicapped children ages 3 to 5, even in states that do not

Mentally retarded students may not automatically become part of classroom social groups, but with the teacher's support and sensitivity, friendships can develop.

Mainstreaming Teaching disabled children in regular classes for part or all of their school day.

have public schooling for children this age. Also in the mid-1980s, some special educators and educational policy makers suggested that regular and special education should be merged so that regular teachers would have to take even more responsibility for the education of exceptional students. This movement is called the **regular education initiative.**

In 1990 PL 94-142 was amended by the Individuals with Disabilities Education Act (PL 101-476). This legislation replaced the word "handicapped" with "disabled" and expanded the services for disabled students. Let's examine the legal requirements that affect you as a teacher. The legislation has three major points of interest to teachers: the concept of "least restrictive placement"; the individualized education program (IEP); and the protection of the rights of disabled students and their parents.

Least Restrictive Placement. The law requires states to develop procedures for educating each child in the **least restrictive placement.** This means a setting that is as normal and as much in the mainstream of education as possible. Some disabled students may spend most of the day in a special class but attend one or two regular classes in physical education and art. In most schools severely disabled students are not integrated into regular classes; but in some districts there is a movement toward **total inclusion**—integrating all students, even those with severe disabilities, into regular classes. Advocates of total inclusion believe that disabled students can benefit from involvement with their nonhandicapped peers and should be educated with them, even if doing so calls for special aids, services, and training or consultation for the regular teaching staff.

Individual Education Program. The drafters of PL 94-142 and the laws that came after recognized that each student is unique and may need a specially tailored program to make progress. The **individualized education program,** or **IEP,** is written by a team that includes the student's teacher or teachers, a qualified school psychologist or special education supervisor, the parent(s) or guardian(s), and (when possible) the student. The program must be updated each year and must state in writing:

1. The student's present level of achievement.
2. Goals for the year and short-term measurable instructional objectives leading to those goals.
3. A list of specific services to be provided to the student and details of when those services will be initiated.
4. A description of how fully the student will participate in the regular school program.
5. A schedule telling how the student's progress toward the objectives will be evaluated and approximately how long the services described in the plan will be needed.
6. Beginning at age 16, a statement of needed transitional services to move the student toward further education or work in adult life.

The Rights of Students and Parents. Several stipulations in these laws protect the rights of parents and students. Schools must have proce-

Regular Education Initiative An educational movement that advocates giving regular education teachers, not special education teachers, responsibility for teaching mildly (and sometimes moderately) handicapped students.

Least Restrictive Placement Placement of each child in as normal an educational setting as possible.

Total Inclusion A philosophy of education that assumes that all disabled students, no matter how handicapped, should be in the regular classroom, learning alongside their nonhandicapped peers.

Individualized Education Program (IEP) Annually revised program for an exceptional student, detailing present achievement level, goals, and strategies, drawn up by teachers, parents, specialists, and (if possible) student.

dures for maintaining the confidentiality of school records. Testing practices must not discriminate against students from different cultural backgrounds. Parents have the right to see all records relating to the testing, placement, and teaching of their child. If they wish, parents may obtain an independent evaluation of their child. Parents may bring an advocate or representative to the meeting at which the IEP is developed. Students whose parents are unavailable must be assigned a surrogate parent to participate in the planning. Parents must receive written notice (in their native language) before any evaluation or change in placement is made. Finally, parents have the right to challenge the program developed for their child and are protected by due process of law.

Today, about 11 to 12 percent of the schoolchildren in the United States participate in special education programs. Many are in regular classes for at least part of the day. As you can see in Figure 4.5, some

FIGURE 4.5 Where Are Disabled Children Taught? Percentage of disabled children (ages 3 to 21) served in six educational environments by disabling condition, school year 1987–1988.

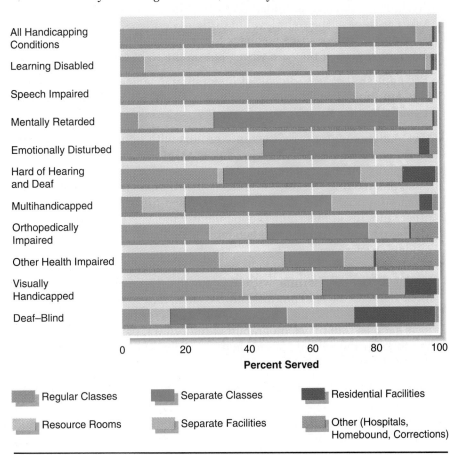

Source: Eleventh Annual Report to Congress on the Implementation of the Education of the Handicapped Act (Washington, D.C.: U.S. Department of Education, 1989).

categories of disabled students are more likely than others to be in regular classes.

Effective Teaching in Mainstreamed Classrooms

When you think about working with disabled students, what are your concerns? Do you have enough training? Will you get the support you need from school administrators or specialists? Will working with the disabled students take time away from your other responsibilities? These are common questions. Sometimes concerns are justified, but effective teaching for mainstreamed students is not a unique set of skills. It is a combination of good teaching practices and sensitivity to all your students. Disabled students need to learn the academic material, and they need to be full participants in the day-to-day life of the classroom.

To accomplish the first goal, Larrivee (1985) concluded that effective teachers of mainstreamed students do the following:

1. Use time efficiently by having smooth management routines, avoiding discipline problems, and planning carefully.
2. Ask questions at the right level of difficulty.
3. Give supportive, positive feedback to students, helping them figure out the right answer if they are wrong but on the right track.

To accomplish the second goal, of integrating disabled students into the day-to-day life of the classroom, Ferguson, Ferguson, and Bogdan (1987) give the following guidelines:

1. Mix students with disabilities into groups with nondisabled students. Avoid resegregating the disabled students into separate groups.
2. Instead of sending students out for special services like speech therapy, remedial reading, or individualized instruction, try to integrate the special help into the class setting, perhaps during a time when the other students are working independently too.
3. Make sure your language and behavior with disabled students is a good model for everyone.
4. Teach about differences among people as part of the curriculum. Let students become familiar with aids for the disabled such as hearing aids, sign language, communication boards, and so on.
5. Have students work together in cooperative groups or on special projects such as role plays, biographical interviews, or lab assignments.
6. Try to keep the schedules and activity patterns of disabled and nondisabled students similar.

Resource Rooms and Helping Teachers. Many schools provide additional help for classroom teachers working with disabled students. A **resource room** is a classroom with special materials and equipment and a specially trained teacher. Students may come to the resource room each day for several minutes to several hours to receive instruction individually or in small groups. The rest of the day the students are in regular classes.

Resource Room Classroom with special materials and a specially trained teacher.

TABLE 4.6 Making a Referral

1. Contact the student's parents. It is very important that you discuss the student's problems with the parents *before* you refer.
2. Before making a referral, check *all* the student's school records. Has the student ever:

   - had a psychological evaluation?
   - qualified for special services?
   - been included in other special programs (e.g., for disadvantaged children; speech or language therapy)?
   - scored far below average on standardized tests?
   - been retained?

   Do the records indicate:

   - good progress in some areas, poor progress in others?
   - any physical or medical problem?
   - that the student is taking medication?

3. Talk to the student's other teachers and professional support personnel about your concern for the student. Have other teachers also had difficulty with the student? Have they found ways of dealing successfully with the student? Document the strategies that you have used in your class to meet the student's educational needs. Your documentation will be useful as evidence that will be helpful to or required by the committee of professionals who will evaluate the student. Demonstrate your concern by keeping written records. Your notes should include items such as:

   - exactly what you are concerned about
   - why you are concerned about it
   - dates, places, and times you have observed the problem
   - precisely what you have done to try to resolve the problem
   - who, if anyone, helped you devise the plans or strategies you have used
   - evidence that the strategies have been successful or unsuccessful

Remember that you should refer a student only if you can make a convincing case that the student may have a handicapping condition and probably cannot be served appropriately without special education. Referral for special education begins a time-consuming, costly, and stressful process that is potentially damaging to the student and has many legal ramifications.

Source: Reprinted by permission of the publisher from Patricia L. Pullen and James M. Kauffman, *What should I know about special education? Answers for classroom teachers* (Austin, Texas: Pro-Ed, 1987).

The resource room can also be used as a crisis center. Individual students may spend an hour, a day, or a week there during a crisis, when their regular teacher is unable to give them the necessary attention and guidance. Besides working with students directly, a resource teacher may also work with them indirectly by giving the regular teacher ideas, materials, or actual demonstrations of teaching techniques.

Making a Referral. If you want to refer a student for evaluation, how would you begin? Table 4.6 guides you through the referral process.

Computers and Exceptional Students

Computers have improved the education of exceptional children in countless ways. Given the record keeping and program planning needed to meet federal regulations, teachers can use computers to manage instruction. For students who require small steps and many repetitions to

Computers and other technology can support learning for disabled students so that disabilities are less handicapping.

learn a new concept, computers are the perfect patient tutors, repeating steps and lessons as many times as necessary. A well-designed computer instructional program is engaging and interactive—two important qualities for students with problems paying attention or with a history of failure that has eroded motivation. For example, a math or spelling program might use images, sounds, and gamelike features to maintain the attention of a student with an attention-deficit disorder. Many programs do not involve sound, so hearing-impaired students can get the full benefit from the lessons. Students who have trouble reading can use programs that will "speak" a word for them if they touch the unknown word with a light pen or with the cursor. With this immediate access to help, the students are much more likely to get the reading practice they need to prevent falling farther and farther behind. And for the learning disabled student whose writing can't be read, word processors produce perfect penmanship so the ideas can finally get on paper. Once the ideas are on paper, the student can reorganize and improve the writing without the agony of rewriting by hand (Hallahan & Kauffman, 1991; Hardman, Drew, Egan, & Wolf, 1990; Reynolds & Birch, 1988).

For gifted students, computers can be a connection with data bases and computers in universities, museums, and research labs. Computer networks allow students to work on projects and share information with others across the country. It is also possible to have gifted students write programs for students and teachers. Quite a few principals around the country rely on their students to make the technology in the school work. These are just a few examples of what technology can do. Check with the resource teachers in your district to find out what is available in your school.

SUMMARY

What Does It Mean to Be Exceptional?

Exceptional learners have learning abilities or problems that require special education. In the past, education for children with learning problems or physical handicaps followed a medical disease model and often meant segregating children in separate classes or programs.

Labels and diagnostic classifications of exceptional students can easily become both stigmas and self-fulfilling prophecies, but can also open doors to special programs and help teachers develop appropriate instructional strategies.

Individual Differences in Intelligence

Psychologists disagree on what intelligence is—a collection of discrete abilities; a general mental ability to learn new information and cope with the world; abilities for problem solving; or an array of multiple intelligences that include, for example, social judgment and creativity. The models of Spearman, Guilford, and Gardner describe the content of intelligence, while Sternberg's triarchic theory views intelligence as a process.

IQ, as it is measured today through individually administered tests such as the Stanford-Binet and the Wechsler Scales, is closely related to success in school, but not necessarily to success in life. In the past, IQ compared mental age with chronological age, but today these tests compare the individual's performance with average scores for the same age group. IQ scores must be interpreted with caution, because many factors other than intelligence influence scores. Both heredity and environment play a role in intelligence, which is never fixed but is continually open to change.

Ability Differences and Teaching

Academic ability groupings can have both disadvantages and advantages for students and teachers. For low-ability students, however, between-class ability grouping generally has a negative effect on achievement, social adjustment, and self-esteem. Within-class ability grouping, if handled sensitively and flexibly, can have more positive effects.

Mentally retarded students have significantly below-average intellectual skills and difficulty adapting adequately to social norms. Transition programming prepares retarded students to live and work in the community. Gifted students—those who are exceptionally bright, creative, or talented—also may have social adjustment problems and are often unable to fulfill their potential in public schools. Acceleration, enrichment, or out-of-school programs can help meet the needs of exceptionally able students.

Cognitive and Learning Styles

Individuals have characteristic differences in personality, in the way they organize and process information, and in the conditions in which they learn best. Field dependence versus field independence and impulsive versus reflective cognitive styles are examples of these differences. While cognitive styles and learning preferences are not related to intelligence or effort, they do affect school performance. Applied with caution, learning style inventories can be used to modify instructional strategies and the classroom environment to take advantage of individual differences that help students learn. Some proposed differences, such as left-brain/right-brain dominance, while popular, are oversimplifications of the complex structure and function of the human brain.

Students with Learning Challenges

A disability and a handicap are not the same, and teachers must avoid imposing handicaps on disabled learners. Physically challenged students may rely on orthopedic devices, may have health problems such as epilepsy or cerebral palsy, or may be hearing impaired or vision impaired to varying degrees. Communication disorders include speech impairments (articulation disorders, stuttering, and voicing problems) and oral language disorders. Behavioral and emotional problems include conduct disorders, anxiety–withdrawal, attentional problems/immaturity, motor excess, socialized aggression, psychotic behavior, and attention deficit–hyperactive disorder.

Specific learning disabilities often involve physical, behavioral, and emotional challenges. Learning disabled students may become victims of learned helplessness when they come to believe that they cannot control or improve their own learning and therefore cannot succeed.

MAINSTREAMING

Public Law 94-142 (1975) requires that each exceptional learner or special needs student be educated in the least restrictive environment according to an individualized education program. The law also protects the rights of special needs students and their parents. Public Law 99-457 extends the mainstreaming law to preschool-age children, and PL 101-476 extends services to include transition programming for exceptional learners 16 years old and older. The regular education initiative calls for regular classroom teachers to receive training in teaching exceptional learners. Well-developed instructional strategies and technologies exist for helping exceptional students to learn.

KEY TERMS AND CONCEPTS

articulation disorders, p. 138
attention deficit–hyperactive
  disorder, p. 140
automaticity, p. 115
between-class ability grouping,
  p. 121
cerebral palsy, p. 136
cognitive styles, p. 128
components, p. 113
deviation IQ, p. 117
disability, p. 135
Down syndrome, p. 123
educationally blind, p. 137
epilepsy, p. 135
exceptional students, p. 110
faces of intellect, p. 112
field dependence, p. 129
field independence, p. 129
finger spelling, p. 137

gifted student, p. 125
handicap, p. 135
hemispheric specialization, p. 133
hyperactivity, p. 140
impulsive, p. 129
individualized education
  program (IEP), p. 144
intelligence, p. 111
intelligence quotient (IQ), p. 116
learned helplessness, p. 142
learning style preferences, p. 131
learning styles, p. 128
least restrictive placement, p. 144
low vision, p. 137
mainstreaming, p. 143
mental age, p. 116
mental retardation, p. 122
multiple intelligences, p. 112
orthopedic devices, p. 135

reflective, p. 129
regular education initiative,
  p. 144
resource room, p. 146
self-instruction, p. 130
sign language, p. 137
spasticity, p. 136
specific learning disability,
  p. 141
speech impairment, p. 138
speech reading, p. 137
stuttering, p. 138
total inclusion, p. 144
transition programming, p. 124
triarchic theory of intelligence,
  p. 113
voicing problems, p. 138
within-class ability grouping,
  p. 122

WHAT WOULD YOU DO?

PRESCHOOL AND KINDERGARTEN

A little girl in your kindergarten class seldom speaks. When she does, she usually says only a word or two. She seems to understand when others talk, but almost never responds verbally. How would you approach this situation?

ELEMENTARY AND MIDDLE SCHOOL

The school psychologist tells you that one of your students is going to start taking medication designed to "calm him down." What would you want to know? How would you respond?

The principal tells you that she is assigning two more students to your class because you are "new and have more training in mainstreaming than the older teachers." One student is mildly retarded and has problems making friends. The other is blind. How would you prepare your class and modify your teaching for these students?

JUNIOR HIGH AND HIGH SCHOOL

A student in your fifth-period class is failing. When you look at your grade book, you see that it is the written work that is giving the student trouble. Multiple-choice test scores and class participation are fine. How would you identify the source of the problem?

Your school has just received the results of the fall testing, including scores for all your students on a group test of intelligence. What would you do with the results?

How would you adapt your teaching to accommodate a hearing-impaired student in your biology lab class?

COOPERATIVE LEARNING ACTIVITY

Assume the faculty at your school has decided to reconsider how students are assigned to classes. The traditional way in the school has been between-class ability grouping, because your school serves a very wide range of students. Work with four or five members of your educational psychology class to design a system, then present your recommendations to the entire class. Be prepared to justify your recommendations and explain how you would implement them.

MANAGING DISRUPTIVE STUDENTS

You have a student in your class who seems unable to sit still, responds impulsively, and continually interrupts other students. How would you deal with these symptoms of "attention-deficit disorder" in your classroom?

A BEHAVIOR MANAGEMENT PROGRAM

The first thing you should analyze is the reason for the interruptions. If it is to receive your attention, moving the child closer to you may help. If the reason is to be a "class clown" and perform for the others, moving the child to the back of the room may help the situation. In the back of the room the rest of the class can't see the child and will usually ignore the antics. If the child is interrupting out of habit or impulse, a behavior management program might help.

For the program to be most effective, parental involvement is desirable. If the parent or parents will support your efforts and those of the child, changing behavior is quicker and easier. But even if the teacher has no parental support, the program can still be effective. The teacher makes a grid showing the different activities of the day or time period. If the behavior is favorable, a token or sticker can be given to the child. If the behavior is not satisfactory, no reward is given. When a preset limit is reached, a reward is given, such as a reward letter, a small trinket, time at the computer or listening center, or extra time at the media center. The reward should be something that the child will strive to reach. The teacher must be sure that the child will succeed right away, or discouragement will dissolve the program. After the child has achieved success for a while, the limits and restrictions can be increased before an award is earned. Eventually the program can be tapered off entirely.

Many teachers are reluctant to use this system because they feel it shows favoritism to one student. However, the other students know that the behavior being addressed is not allowed, and they want everyone to follow the rules. The class will be supportive and encouraging to the child.

Ida Pofahl, *Second-Grade Teacher*
Denison Elementary School, Denison, Iowa

HAVE A "TINGLE" DAY

Roger, a fifth-grade student, described in detail how he got a "tingle" from making other students laugh or go "Ooooh, look what Roger did!" He had such a reputation for being disruptive and "bad" in school that no one (teachers or students) wanted to be around him. When I undertood where he was coming from, I made every effort to help him get a "tingle" from being successful, receiving attention for doing positive things, and building on his strengths. I specifically noticed that Roger acted out his attention deficit when new material was introduced, when he did not understand old material, and when he was stuck (mentally disengaged). I began to watch for early signs of confusion—such as putting off doing the work, saying he had done it when he had not. Roger was very bright and enjoyed doing what he was good at doing. When he was mentally engaged in figuring things out, he was successful and there was little evidence of attention deficit. I saw the need to focus on the causes of inattention rather than trying to control the symptoms. This meant I had to change some of the things I was doing. Material is now presented in a much more experiential way, so that the students can be actively involved in the creation of meaning. I design projects that have divergent outcomes, use cooperative learning, integrate content areas, encourage reflective thinking, and stimulate active participation. It is exciting to get a "tingle" with the students as we learn together. We all need a "tingle a day"!

Betty Garner, *Art Teacher*
Pattonville I.D.E.A.L. Center, Maryland Heights, Missouri

Mainstreaming Concerns

A new student has just been assigned to your class from a special education class. You don't believe the student is ready for full-time particiapation in your class, but the administration disagrees. What would you do?

Record Keeping

First I would discuss the child with the administration to find out their reason for wanting the child in the regular classroom. I would also voice my concerns. Then I would suggest placing the child in the classroom for partial days for about three weeks. During this time I would keep notes on the child's adjustment. It would be helpful to videotape the child on several occasions. I would also request the administration to make several observations. Thus if the child were not ready for full-time participation in the classroom, the administration should realize this from the documentation presented.

Kathryn Daniels, *Second-Grade Teacher*
Fredericktown Elementary School, Fredericktown, Ohio

Ability Groupings

Do you use ability groupings in your classes? If so, why and for what subjects? Which type of ability grouping do you use? If not, why not?

Flexibility and Creativity

The "cluster model" for grouping of gifted/talented (G/T) students has been successfully incorporated with the "inclusive model" for special services students. Within this framework, identified G/T students are clustered together in homerooms. This allows these students to interact throughout the day with three to four others that share common strengths and needs. Clustering four to five students together in a homeroom also ensures that enrichment activities will be provided to this "visible" group. The classroom teacher can group by interest, by learning style, or by another heterogeneous grouping pattern. The "inclusive model" allows special service teachers to come into the classroom and adapt or provide alternative teaching strategies on the spot. This allows learning-disabled and other special service students the opportunity to work with their peers as often as possible.

There are times when grouping ability is still necessary for exceptional learners determined on a case by case analysis. There will be times when special service students will need to be put in a resource setting for individual or small-group instruction. Time, space, and availability of resources and money dictate this as well as the need of the child. Educators tend to overreact to current trends, and I believe this is the case with the area of ability grouping for exceptional learners. We, as educators, need to be flexible and creative when determining the most appropriate grouping for each activity or lesson. Ability grouping should be included as a possible form of alternative grouping strategies.

Lawrence Leebens, *Curriculum Resource Coordinator*
Forest Hills Elementary School, Eden Prairie, Minnesota

It Depends on the Subject

Ability grouping is a strategy that can be helpful in certain subject areas and a hindrance in others. Where skills mastery is essential prior to learning the next skill, such as in reading and math, it is better to have a homogeneous class. In those classes the students will be working on the same level and the teacher can spend as long as the group needs on that skill. In classes such as science and social studies, where the emphasis is more on oral discussion and student participation, I think that the low-achieving students gain a great deal from what they hear their peers say.

Dori Hoffman-Latter, *Special Education Teacher*
Walker Middle School, Charlottesville, Virginia

5 THE IMPACT OF CULTURE AND COMMUNITY

The face of American classrooms is changing. In this chapter we examine the many cultures that form the fabric of our society. We begin by tracing the schools' responses to different ethnic and cultural groups and consider the concept of multicultural education. With a broad conception of culture as a basis, we then examine three important dimensions of every student's identity: social class, ethnicity, and gender. For each dimension, we will explore the experiences of the various groups in the schools, possible differences in achievement and learning styles, and explanations for the lower achievement of some groups. Then we turn to a consideration of language and bilingual education. The last section of the chapter presents three general principles for teaching every student.

By the time you complete this chapter you should be able to do the following:

- Compare the old notion of the melting pot with current views about multicultural education.

- Define culture and list the various groups that make up your own cultural identity.

- Explain why the school achievement of low-income students often falls below that of middle- and upper-income students.

- Give examples of conflicts and compatibilities between home and school cultures.

- Describe the school's role in the development of gender differences.

- Summarize the arguments for and against bilingual education.

- Incorporate multicultural concepts into your teaching.

TODAY'S MULTICULTURAL CLASSROOMS

Who are the students in American classrooms today? Here are a few statistics:

- 1 in 5 Americans under the age of 18 lives in poverty. For children under age 3, the number is 1 in 3.
- Nearly 50 percent of all black children are poor.
- 1 in 3 children lives with a single parent, usually a working mother.
- 12 percent of all students are in bilingual classes.
- 15 percent of the children entering school in 1986 were immigrants who spoke little or no English; 10 percent had poorly educated or illiterate parents.
- 3 in 10 students probably will not finish high school; many of these will be members of minority groups (3 in 10 blacks, 4 in 10 Hispanics, 4 in 10 Native Americans, 1 in 10 whites).
- By the year 2010, 38 percent of all students will be members of minority groups. (Grant & Sleeter, 1989; *Teacher Magazine,* April 1991)

How should the schools respond to these challenges? First, we consider the approaches of earlier times, when educators assumed all students—rich and poor, minority-group or majority, male or female—should adapt to the expectations of traditional schools.

Old Views: The Students Must Adapt

Since the beginning of the twentieth century, a flow of immigrants has entered the United Kingdom, Western Europe, Canada, Australia, the United States, and many other developed countries. As these new immigrants arrived in most areas, they were expected to be assimilated—that is, to enter the cultural **melting pot** and become like those who had arrived earlier. For years the goal of American schools was to be the fire under the melting pot. Immigrant children who spoke different languages and had different religious and cultural heritages were supposed to come to the schools and learn to become mainstream Americans. They were

Melting Pot A metaphor for the absorption and assimilation of immigrants into the mainstream of society so that ethnic differences vanish.

expected to master standard English, adopt the beliefs and behaviors of the middle class, and leave their ethnic heritage behind.

In the 1960s and 1970s, some educators suggested that minority-group and poor students had problems in school because they had not fully assimilated into mainstream American life; they had not adopted the "right" values and skills. The students were described as "culturally disadvantaged" or "culturally handicapped." The assumption of this **cultural deficit model** was that the students' home culture was inferior because it had not prepared them to fit into the schools. Today most people reject the idea of cultural deficits. They believe that no culture is deficient but rather that there may be incompatibilities between the student's home culture and the cultural expectations of the school.

What are the expectations of schools? Many reformers have noted that American schools typically reflect the white, Anglo-Saxon, Protestant, middle-class, male-dominated values that have characterized mainstream America. Schedules are tight and planned months in advance (I just got my daughter's college vacation and exam schedule for the next four years!). Students are expected to be on time and to do one activity at a time. The future is primary. Students are told to do well so they will get good grades, graduate from high school, get into college, and then (finally) find a good job. Competition is encouraged, and the phrase "Do your own work!" is repeated daily. Unless it is part of the teacher's lesson plan, "cooperation" is seen as cheating. Words, ideas, and knowledge are more important than feelings. Individuals are to work hard and achieve; they are responsible for their own destinies. Generally, the teacher talks more than the students and students are expected to respect the teacher's authority. Teachers ask and initiate; students answer and react—one at a time. Spontaneous student talk, and several students talking at once, is discouraged. Working fast and being neat are valued (Banks, 1991; Bennett, 1990; Boykin, 1986).

But these values and expectations are not shared by all people. Some groups, as you will see later in this chapter, teach people to put the good of the group ahead of the needs of the individual. Cooperation is valued, not individualism and competition. Particularly when resources are scarce, people are taught to rely on family and friends (Harrison, Wilson, Pine, & Buriel, 1990). There is a growing recognition that the schools have a responsibility to adapt to some extent to the values and skills of students instead of expecting every student to adapt to all the traditional expectations of the school.

New Views: Multicultural Education

Multicultural education, according to James Banks (1991), is an idea, an educational reform movement, and a process.

The *idea* of multicultural education is that all students—male, female, disabled, rich, poor, from different racial and ethnic groups, or speaking different languages—*all students* should have a full and equal opportunity to learn in school and to be respected. To make this statement more than just a slogan, teachers must understand the barriers some students face in attaining an education. Why is it that girls and boys

Cultural Deficit Model A model that explains the school achievement problems of ethnic-minority students by assuming that their culture is inadequate and does not prepare them to succeed in school.

Multicultural Education Education that teaches the value of cultural diversity.

Point/Counterpoint

Should Multicultural Education Emphasize Similarities or Differences?

"In principle, virtually all of the experts who have studied, advocated, and criticized the various forms of multicultural education now taking shape in the United States agree on one point: Such education should provide students with a fuller, more balanced truth about their own history and culture than they have had up to now" (Viadero, 1990, p. 14). The question is how. Should education emphasize the similarities or the differences among people?

Point: Emphasize what is common among all students (traditional approaches).

Richard Rodriguez (1987), a well-known contemporary writer and editor, made a case for emphasizing what is common to all citizens in his criticism of a report by the Study Commission on Global Education:

> Few words issue from the commission's 52-page report with more frequency or less preci-

sion than does the word, "diversity." The dilemma of our national diversity becomes, with a little choke on logic, the solution: American educators "must understand diversity." "Appreciate diversity." "Deal constructively with diversity." Pay "greater attention to . . . diversity . . . around the world and within the United States. . . ." Diversity is a liquid noun. Diversity admits everything, stands for nothing. . . .

I do not agree that the primary purpose of early education is to teach diversity. I believe something closer to the reverse—that education's primary purpose, its distinguishing obligation, is to foster communality. It is in the classroom that the child comes to learn a public identity. The child learns the skills of numbers and words crucial to public survival, and learns to put on a public self, apart from family or ethnic community.

achieve equally in science and math during the early grades, but that beyond elementary school the performance of girls drops off? By the time they reach college, even in the top schools, women often have less to say in class and doubt their abilities more than men (Sadker, Sadker, & Klein, 1991). A similar pattern occurs for African-American, Hispanic-American, and Native-American students. The longer they stay in school, the more their achievement lags behind that of white students (Banks, 1991).

As an *educational reform movement,* multicultural education seeks to change the effects described above. Exactly how to do this is the topic of heated debate. Some reformers urge schools to focus on improving human relations so that students will learn to respect all people. Other educators press for in-depth studies of various racial and ethnic groups as part of the curriculum. But critics believe this is not enough. They want to infuse the entire curriculum with material written by and about minority group members. Still another approach to multicultural education is to transform the entire educational system so that students learn to be politically effective in reshaping society (Grant & Sleeter, 1989). An examination of the alternative approaches to multicultural education is beyond the scope of an educational psychology text, but be aware that there is no general agreement about the "best" approach, as you can see in the **Point/Counterpoint** section above.

As a *process,* multicultural education is ongoing. Schools cannot just institute a program or hire a consultant to "solve" the problem. Teachers

I submit that America is not a tale for sentimentalists. I read writings of 18th-century white men who powdered their wigs and kept slaves, because they were the men who shaped the country that shapes my life. I am brown and of Mexican ancestry, one generation into this country. I claim Thomas Jefferson as a cultural forefather.

Counterpoint: Emphasize diversity (ethnocentric approaches).

In response to Rodriguez's position, Alba Rosenman (1987) believes:

> Education that values cultural diversity does not say that "diversity admits everything and stands for nothing," as Mr. Rodriguez puts it, but rather that a culture is not wrong because it is different. Knowledge of other societies and customs gives students choices that may be more meaningful to them than those offered in our society. It is possible that there are other and better ways to live than those we have grown to know and love. We might yet learn something from that imprecise mass called American "diversity." . . . A multicultural curriculum tries, while valuing differences, to teach a fair curriculum to students with diverse backgrounds. There is no threat to society here, simply a relevant education.

Rosenman agrees with Rodriguez that "the primary purpose of an early education should not be to 'teach diversity.' Its primary purposes are to teach students that in school they will learn how to survive in our society and to solidify their feelings of worth."

Sources: Reprinted with permission from "What Is an American Education?" by Richard Rodriguez. Copyright © 1987 by Richard Rodriguez. First published in *Education Week, 7* (September 9). Reprinted with permission from Alba A. Rosenman (1987), "The Value of Multicultural Curricula," *Education Week, 7* (10), November 11.

have to reach out to all children every day and keep trying. Multicultural education rejects the idea of the melting pot. According to the multicultural ideal, America should be transformed into a society that values diversity (Casanova, 1987; Grant & Sleeter, 1989). Let's take a closer look at the differences that make up the mosaic of cultural diversity.

American Cultural Diversity

In this text we take a broad interpretation of culture and multicultural education; so we will examine social class, race, ethnicity, and gender as aspects of diversity. We begin with a look at the meaning of culture. Many people associate this concept with the "cultural events" section of the newspaper—art galleries, museums, Shakespeare, classical music, and so on. Culture has a much broader meaning; it has to do with the whole way of life of a group of people.

Culture and Group Membership. There are many definitions of **culture.** Most include the knowledge, rules, traditions, attitudes, and values that guide behavior in a particular group of people. "The total history of a group, combined with its present modes of living, coalesces to form its culture" (Garcia, 1991, p. 68). The group creates a culture—a program for living—and communicates the culture to members. Thus people are members of groups, they are not members of cultures. Groups can be defined along regional, ethnic, religious, racial, gender, social

Culture The knowledge, values, attitudes, and traditions that guide the behavior of a group of people and allow them to solve the problems of living in their environment.

159

class, or other lines. Each of us is a member of many groups, as depicted in Figure 5.1, so we all are influenced by many different cultures. Sometimes the influences are incompatible or even contradictory. For example, if you are a feminist but also a Roman Catholic, you may have trouble reconciling the two different cultures' beliefs about the ordination of women as priests. Your personal belief on the issue will be based, in part, on how strongly you identify with each group (Banks, 1991).

There are many different cultures, of course, in every modern country. In the United States, students growing up in a small rural town in the Deep South are part of a cultural group different from that of students in a large urban center or students in a West Coast suburb. In Canada, students living in the suburbs of Toronto certainly differ in a number of ways from students growing up in a Montreal high-rise apartment or on a

FIGURE 5.1   Individuals Belong to Many Different Groups   Each of us is a member of many different groups and each group brings a different set of influences. The memberships shown here are not the only ones, but they are our major influences.

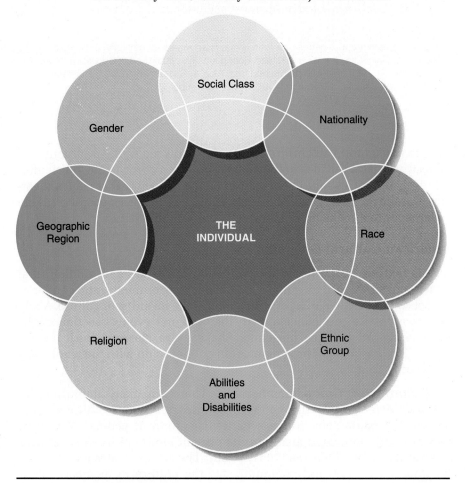

Source: Adapted with permission of the author from J. A. Banks, *Multiethnic education: Theory and practice,* 2d ed. (Boston: Allyn & Bacon, 1988), p. 79.

farm in Quebec. Within those small towns in the Deep South or in Quebec, the child of a gas station attendant grows up in a different culture than the child of the town doctor or dentist. Individuals of African, Asian, Hispanic, Native-American, or European descent have distinctive histories and traditions. The experiences of males and females are different in most ethnic and economic groups. Everyone living within a particular country shares many common experiences and values, especially because of the influence of the mass media. But other aspects of their lives are shaped by differing cultural backgrounds.

Cautions in Interpreting Cultural Differences. Before we examine the bases for cultural differences, two cautions are necessary. First, we will consider social class, ethnicity, and gender separately because much of the available research focuses on only one of these variables. Of course, real children are not just African-American, or middle-class or female—they are complex beings and members of many groups.

The second caution comes from James Banks (1989), who has written several books on multicultural education:

> Although membership in a gender, racial, ethnic, social-class, or religious group can provide us with important clues about an individual's behavior, it cannot enable us to predict behavior. . . . *Membership in a particular group does not determine behavior but makes certain types of behavior more probable.* (p. 13)

Keep this in mind as you read about characteristics of economically disadvantaged students or Asian Americans or males. The information we will examine reflects tendencies and probabilities. It does not tell you about a specific person. Remember that you will be teaching individual students, not cultural groups. Each child is a unique product of many influences—a member of many groups. For example, if a minority-group student in your class consistently arrives late, you should not assume that the student's behavior reflects a cultural difference in beliefs about punctuality. It may be that the student has a job before school or must walk a long distance, or even that he or she hates school.

One of the greatest challenges for many Americans is to maintain strong and authentic connections with both their ethnic heritage and the wider culture.

SOCIAL CLASS DIFFERENCES

The term used by sociologists for variations in wealth, power, and prestige is **socioeconomic status,** or **SES.** In modern societies, levels of wealth, power, and prestige are not always consistent. Some people—like university professors—are members of professions that are fairly prestigious, but provide little wealth or power. Other people have political power, though they are not wealthy. No single variable, not even income, is an effective measure of SES. In spite of these inconsistencies, most researchers identify four general levels of SES—upper, middle, working, and lower. The main characteristics of these four levels are summarized in Table 5.1 on page 162.

Social class is a powerful dimension of cultural differences, often overpowering other differences such as ethnicity or gender. For example,

Socioeconomic Status (SES) Relative standing in the society based on income, power, background, and prestige.

TABLE 5.1 Selected Characteristics of Different Social Classes				
	Upper Class	**Middle Class**	**Working Class**	**Lower Class**
Income	$100,000+	$40,000–$100,00 (⅓) $25,000–$39,999 (⅔)	$12,000–$40,000	Below $12,000
Occupation	Corporate, professional, family money	White-collar, skilled blue-collar	Blue-collar	Minimum-wage unskilled labor
Education	Prestigious colleges and professional schools	High school, college, or professional school	High school	High school or less
Home ownership	At least one home	Usually own home	About half own a home	No
Health coverage	Full	Usually	Limited	No
Access to community resources	All	Many	Some	Few
Neighborhoods	Exclusive or comfortable	Comfortable	Modest	Deteriorating
Ability to send children to college	Easily	Depends on income and number of children	Seldom	No
Political power	National, state, or local	State or local	Limited	No

Source: Information from J. J. Macionis (1991), *Sociology,* 3rd ed. (Englewood Cliffs, N.J.: Prentice-Hall), pp. 262–264.

upper-class Anglo-Europeans, African Americans, and Hispanic Americans typically find that they have more in common with each other than they have with lower-class individuals from their own ethnic groups.

Who Are the Poor?

Over one in five Americans under the age of 18 lives in poverty, defined as an income below $12,092 for a family of four living in an urban area (Macionis, 1991). By 2020 this number will be one in four. But these percentages don't tell the whole story. As you can see in Figure 5.2, the absolute number of poor children will increase substantially. By 2020, schools will have to teach 5.4 million more poor students than they taught in 1984. The United States has the highest rate of poverty for children of all developed nations, as much as three times higher than most other industrialized countries. And these children are not concentrated in the inner cities. Twice as many poor children live outside as within large urban areas (Reed & Sautter, 1990).

FIGURE 5.2 **Projected Number of Children in Poverty** The number of children who live in poverty in the United States grows each year and is projected to reach 20 million by the year 2020.

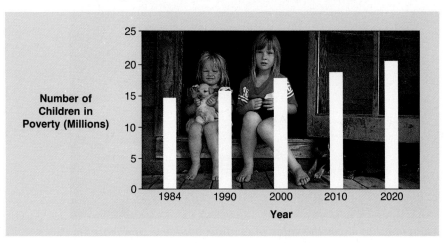

Source: Aaron M. Pallas, Gary Natriello, and Edward L. McDill, The changing nature of the disadvantaged population: Current dimensions and future trends. *Educational Researcher, 18* (June–July 1989), p. 19. Copyright 1989 by the American Educational Research Association. Reprinted by permission of the publisher.

The majority of these poor children, about 65 percent, are white, because the total number of poor white families is greater than any other ethnic group. But even though the total number of poor African-American and Hispanic-American children is smaller than the number of poor white children, the percentages are higher. About 38 percent of all Hispanic-American children and 44 percent of all African-American children live in poverty. Compare this to an overall poverty rate of 20 percent for all children in the United States (Macionis, 1991).

SES and Achievement

There are many relationships between SES and school performance. For example, it is well documented that high-SES students of all ethnic groups show higher average levels of achievement on test scores, receive better grades, and stay in school longer than low-SES students (Alwin & Thornton, 1984; Goleman, 1988; White, 1982). When SES is measured solely in terms of parents' education, income, or occupation, the relationship between SES and achievement is weaker. But when SES is measured in terms that include family atmosphere variables such as parents' attitudes toward education, their aspirations for their children, or the intellectual activities of the family, then the correlation is stronger (Laosa, 1984; White, 1982). This is an encouraging result. It indicates that lack of income may not be as important for school achievement as the actual attitudes and behaviors of the child's family life.

What are the effects of low socioeconomic status that might explain the lower school achievement of these low-SES students? Many factors

When families stress the value of reading, studying, and learning, their children are usually at an advantage in school.

maintain a cycle of poverty. Poor health care for mother and child, limited resources, family stress, interruptions in schooling, discrimination, and other factors lead to school failures, low-paying jobs—and another generation born in poverty. Garcia (1991), while cautioning that research on this question is meager, lists five other possible explanations. Let's take a closer look at each of them.

Low Expectations—Low Self-Esteem. Because low-SES students may wear old clothes, speak ungrammatically, or be less familiar with books and school activities, teachers and other students may assume that these students are not bright. The teacher may avoid calling on them to protect them from the embarrassment of giving wrong answers or because they make the teachers uncomfortable. The children come to believe that they aren't very good at schoolwork. The following true story shows how powerful this effect on self-esteem can be. Terrence Quinn, principal of an elementary school in New York, spends his mornings serving coffee and doughnuts in a welfare hotel six blocks from his school—trying to convince parents to send their children to school.

> Last spring, Jacqueline, a sixth-grader who had lived at the hotel, was selected as the school's valedictorian. One month before the official announcement, she entered Quinn's office and asked to speak to him in private.
> "Can someone on welfare actually be the valedictorian?" she asked.
> Quinn reassured Jacqueline, a youngster who has overcome many obstacles. . . . Why should a child such as Jacqueline feel so humiliated and ashamed of her predicament? (Reed and Sautter, 1990, p. K2)

Learned Helplessness. Low-SES children may be the victims of learned helplessness, described in the previous chapter. That is, low-SES students (or any students who fail continually) may come to believe that doing well in school is hopeless. Many of their friends and relatives never finished school, so it seems normal to quit. In fact, about one-fourth of children from poor families drop out of school (Bennett, 1990). Without a high school diploma, these students find few rewards awaiting them in the work world. Many available jobs barely pay a living wage. If the head of a family of three works full time at the minimum wage, the family's income will still be $2,500 *below* the poverty line (Reed & Sautter, 1990). Low-SES children, particularly those who also encounter racial discrimination, "become convinced that it is difficult if not impossible for them to advance in the mainstream by doing well in school" (Goleman, 1988).

Resistance Cultures. Some researchers have suggested that low-SES students may become part of a **resistance culture.** To members of this culture, making it in school means selling out and trying to act "middle-class." In order to maintain their identity and their status within the group, low-SES students must reject the behaviors that would make them successful in school—studying, cooperating with teachers, even coming to class (Bennett, 1990; Ogbu, 1987). John Ogbu linked identification in a resistance culture to poor Hispanic-American, Native-American, and African-American groups, but similar reactions have been noted for poor white students both in the United States and in England (Willis, 1977).

Tracking. Another explanation for the lower achievement of many low-SES students is that these students experience a different **academic socialization;** that is, they are actually taught differently. If they are tracked into "low ability" or "general" classes, they may be taught to memorize and be passive. Their classes may be low-level and teacher-dominated. Middle-class students are more likely to be encouraged to think and create in their classes (Anyon, 1980). When low-SES students receive an inferior education, their academic skills are inferior.

Childrearing Styles. The oldest explanation for the academic problems of low-SES children is that their home environment does not give them the head start in school provided by middle- and upper-class homes. Adjustment to school may be more difficult for these children, since schools tend to value and expect the behaviors more often taught in middle-class homes. Differences in the childrearing styles of low-SES and high-SES parents may put low-SES children at a disadvantage when they try to master the verbal skills so necessary for success in school. Let's take a closer look at this last explanation.

Studies have shown that middle-class mothers talk more; give more verbal guidance; help their children understand the causes of events, make plans, and anticipate consequences; direct their children's attention to the relevant details of a problem; and, rather than impose solutions, encourage children to solve problems themselves (Hess & Shipman, 1965; L. Hoffman, 1984; Willerman, 1979). By assisting their children in these ways, mothers are actually following Vygotsky's advice

Resistance Culture Group values and beliefs about refusing to adopt the behaviors and attitudes of the majority culture.

Academic Socialization The ways that children are taught how to be students, the value of learning, and their own role in schooling.

to provide intellectual support, or scaffolding, in the children's zone of proximal development, as we discussed in chapter 2. Contrast these two interactions as a mother works with a child on a puzzle:

> "What shape is that piece? Can you find a spot that is straight like the piece? Yes, that's straight, but look at the color. Does the color match? No? Look again for a straight, *red* piece. Yes—try that one. Good for you! You finished the corner."

> "No, that piece goes here!"

You can see how the first approach is more likely to encourage learning concepts (straight, shape, color, corner, match) and problem solving. Hess and McDevitt (1984) studied mothers and children over an eight-year period and found evidence that this "teaching as opposed to telling" style, often used by middle-class mothers, is related to higher achievement test scores for children aged 4 through 12. These differences in parental interaction styles may account for some of the differences among children from various SES groups.

You should be wary, however, of prejudging families based on their socioeconomic status. Many low-income families provide a rich learning environment for their children. When parents of any SES level support and encourage their children—by reading to them, providing books and educational toys, taking the children to the library, making time and space for learning—the children tend to become better, more enthusiastic readers (Morrow, 1983; Shields, Gordon, & Dupree, 1983). Remember, White (1982) found that the actual behaviors of the parents were more predictive of their children's school achievement than income level or parents' occupation.

ETHNIC AND RACIAL DIFFERENCES

Ethnicity A cultural heritage shared by a group of people.

Race A group of people who share common biological traits that are seen as self-defining by the people of the group.

Minority Group A group of people who have been socially disadvantaged— not always a minority in actual numbers.

Ethnicity is "a cultural heritage shared by a category of people" (Macionis, 1991, p. 309). This shared sense of identity may be based on geography, religion, race, or language. We all have some ethnic heritage, whether our background is Italian, Jewish, Ukrainian, Hmong, Vietnamese, Chinese, Japanese, Korean, Navajo, Hawaiian, Puerto Rican, Cuban, Eskimo, German, African, or Irish—to name only a few. **Race,** on the other hand, is defined as "a category composed of men and women who share biologically transmitted traits that are defined as socially significant" such as skin color or hair texture (Macionis, 1991, p. 308). Depending on the traits you measure and the theory you follow, there are between 3 and 300 races. In effect, race is a label people apply to themselves and to others based on appearances. There are no biologically pure races.

Sociologists sometimes use the term **minority group** to label a group of people which receives unequal or discriminatory treatment. Strictly speaking, however, the term refers to a numerical minority compared to the total population. Referring to particular racial or ethnic groups as "minorities" is technically incorrect in some situations, because in certain places the "minority" group is actually the majority—for example, blacks in Chicago or Mississippi. The practice of referring to people as "minorities" because of their racial or ethnic heritage has been criticized for this reason.

The Changing Demographics

Between 1981 and 1990 the number of immigrants entering the United States was the largest ever. Results of the 1990 census in Table 5.2 show that the number of ethnic Americans has increased substantially. By the year 2020, almost half of the population of the country will be from African-American, Asian, Hispanic, or other ethnic groups.

What do these numbers mean for teaching? First, let's consider the ways that different ethnic cultures influence their members.

Cultural Differences

Ricardo Garcia (1991) compares culture to an iceberg. One-third of the iceberg is visible; the rest is hidden and unknown. The visible signs of culture, such as costumes and marriage traditions, represent only a small portion of the differences among cultures. Many of the differences are "below the surface." They are implicit, unstated, even unconscious biases and beliefs. Each cultural group teaches its members certain "lessons" about living (Casanova, 1987; Kagan, 1983; Maehr, 1974).

Cultures differ in rules for conducting interpersonal relationships, for example. In some groups listeners give a slight affirmative nod of the head and perhaps an occasional "uh huh" to indicate they are paying attention and understand what the speaker is saying. But members of other cultures listen without giving acknowledgment or with eyes downcast, as a sign of respect. In some cultures high-status individuals initiate conversations and ask the questions, and low-status individuals only respond. In other cultures, the pattern is reversed.

Cultural influences are widespread and pervasive. Some psychologists even suggest that culture defines intelligence. For example, physical grace is essential in Balinese social life, so the ability to master physical movements is a mark of intelligence in that culture. Manipulating words and numbers is important in Western societies, so in these cultures such skills are indicators of intelligence (Gardner, 1983).

TABLE 5.2 Results of the 1990 Census for Selected Ethnic Groups		
Group	**Total Number**	**Increase Since 1980**
African American	30.0 million	13.2%
Asian	7.3 million	107.8%
Native American	2.0 million	37.9%
Hispanic	22.4 million	53.0%
Other	9.8 million	

Source: U.S. Bureau of the Census, 1990.

Cultural Conflicts. The above are just a few areas where cultures may teach different lessons about living. The differences may be very obvious, such as holiday customs; or they may be very subtle, such as how to get your turn in conversations. The more subtle and unconscious the difference, the more difficult it is to change or even recognize (Casanova, 1987). Cultural conflicts are usually about below-the-surface differences, because when subtle cultural differences meet, misunderstandings are common. Thus, the members of a different culture may be misperceived as rude, slow, or disrespectful.

For example, Erickson and Shultz (1982) studied school counselors working with students from the same and from different cultures. They found that the culturally different students did not nod and say "uh huh" as they listened to the counselors. Not having received this expected feedback, the counselors assumed that the culturally different students had not understood, and so the counselors repeated their remarks in simpler form. Again no nod, so they simplified and repeated once more. When the students were interviewed afterwards, many said that the counselors had made them feel stupid. In fact, the counselors had decided that these students were not very bright. Neither participant realized that a subtle cultural difference in how to listen was probably to blame for the impressions. In contrast, when students and counselors shared the same background, discussions proceeded smoothly, without the cycles of simplifying and repeating. The students knew the counselors' tacit rules for listening (or at least appearing to listen), because both counselor and student had learned from the same teacher—their common culture.

Cultural Compatibility. Not all cultural differences lead to clashes, however. In the Vietnamese culture, for example, children learn to value self-improvement and accept the directions of legitimate authorities like parents, employers, or teachers. These values fit the demands of American schools, so Vietnamese children often do well.

In the Chinese tradition, achievement is seen as dependent more on concentration, effort, and persistence than on talent. Centuries ago Xu Gan, a revered Chinese scholar, said, "Will is the teacher of study and talent is the follower of study. If a person has no talent, [achievement] is possible. But if a person has no will, it is not worth talking about study" (Hess, Chih-Mei, & McDevitt, 1987, p. 180).

A recent study comparing mothers in the People's Republic of China, Chinese-American mothers, and Caucasian-American mothers found dramatic differences in beliefs about motivation and the value of education that are consistent with this philosophy (Hess, Chih-Mei, & McDevitt, 1987). For example, the Chinese mothers attributed school failure to lack of effort more often than the Caucasian-American mothers. The Chinese-American mothers were in the middle, attributing failure to lack of effort more than the Caucasian-American mothers but less than the Chinese mothers.

This does not mean that all Vietnamese- or Chinese-American children are perfectly equipped for the American school, however. Children may perform well on tests and assignments but feel uncomfortable in social situations, where subtle rules for interacting are not second nature to them (Casanova, 1987). Later in this chapter we will explore ways to make classrooms compatible with the home cultures of students. First, however, we need to see some of the effects of cultural conflicts and discrimination on student achievement.

Ethnic and Racial Differences in School Achievement

A major concern in schools is that some ethnic groups consistently achieve below the average for all students. Table 5.3 gives examples. This pattern of results tends to hold for all standardized achievement tests.

Although there are consistent differences among ethnic groups on tests of cognitive abilities, most researchers agree that these differences are mainly the legacy of discrimination, the product of cultural mismatches, or a result of growing up in a low-SES environment. Because many minority-group students are also economically disadvantaged, it is important to separate the effects of these two sets of influences on school achievement. When we compare students from different ethnic and racial groups who are all at the same SES level, then their achievement differences diminish (Gleitman, 1991; Scarr & Carter-Saltzman, 1982).

TABLE 5.3 National Assessment of Educational Progess, by Subject and by Ethnic Group*

Reading, 1987–88	9-year-olds	13-year-olds	17-year-olds
National average	211.8	257.5	290.1
White	217.7	261.3	294.7
Black	188.5	242.9	274.4
Hispanic	193.7	240.1	270.8

Writing, 1988	4th graders	8th graders	11th graders
National average	173.3	208.2	220.7
White	180.0	213.1	225.3
Black	150.7	190.1	206.9
Hispanic	162.2	197.2	202.0

Mathematics, 1985–86	9-year-olds	13-year-olds	17-year-olds
National average	222.0	269.0	302.0
White	227.0	274.0	308.0
Black	202.0	249.0	279.0
Hispanic	205.0	254.0	283.0

*National Assessment of Educational Progress scales in reading, writing, and mathematics range from 0 to 500.

Source: National Center for Education Statistics, *Digest of education statistics,* 1990 (Washington, D.C.: National Center for Education Statistics, U.S.Department of Education, 1991), pp. 113, 116, 118, 120, 121.

The Legacy of Discrimination

When we considered explanations for why low-SES students have trouble in school, we listed the low expectations and biases of teachers and fellow students. This has been the experience of many ethnic minority students as well. Imagine that the child described below is your own. What would you do?

> Almost forty years ago, in the city of Topeka, Kansas, a minister walked hand in hand with his seven-year-old daughter to an elementary school four blocks from their home. Linda Brown wanted to enroll in the second grade, but the school refused to admit her. Instead, public school officials required her to attend another school two miles away. This meant that she had to walk six blocks to a bus stop, where she sometimes waited half an hour for the bus. In bad weather, Linda Brown would be soaking wet by the time the bus came; one day she became so cold at the bus stop that she walked back home. Why, she asked her parents, could she not attend the school only four blocks away? (Macionis, 1991, p. 307)

9-year-old Linda Brown, the plaintiff in Brown vs. the Board of Education of Topeka.

Her parents' answer to this question, with the help of other concerned families, was to file a suit challenging the school policy. You know the outcome of *Brown* v. *the Board of Education of Topeka*. "Separate but equal" schools for black children were declared inherently unequal. Even though segregation in schools became illegal in 1954, about two-thirds of all African-American students still attend schools where members of minority groups make up at least 50 percent of the student body. For about one-third of all black students, this figure is over 90 percent (Schofield, 1991). This is because segregation in housing and neighborhoods persists and because not every district has fully complied with Supreme Court decisions on desegregation (Calmore, 1986).

Years of research on the effects of desegregation have mostly shown that legally mandated integration is not a quick solution to the detrimental effects of centures of racial inequality. Too often, minority-group students are resegregated in low ability tracks even in integrated schools. Simply putting people in the same building does not mean that they will come to respect each other or even that they will experience the same quality of education (Schofield, 1991).

What is the legacy of unequal treatment and discrimination? Part of the testimony during the *Brown* v. *Board of Education* case in the 1950s was that when black children in a study were asked to pick the more attractive or smarter doll, they usually chose a white doll and rejected a black one. This test was repeated in 1990 with the same results (Pine & Hilliard, 1990).

Continuing Prejudice. The wounds of discrimination are deep. A 1991 survey by the National Opinion Research Center found that even though racial attitudes had improved somewhat since 1970, most of the groups surveyed felt at least some prejudice against all the other groups. For example, 78 percent of non-Hispanic Americans (whites, blacks, and Asian Americans) agreed with the statement that Hispanic Americans prefer to live off welfare, and 55 percent believed that Hispanic Americans are less intelligent.

The results were virtually the same when whites were asked their opinions of African Americans. The United States is a racist society, and this racism is not confined to one group. Tom Smith, a survey director for the National Opinion Research Center, noted that education is one of the strongest influences counteracting prejudice. If schools emphasize acceptance and teach about the history and contributions of all ethnic groups, then attitudes may change (Armstrong, 1991).

Continuing Discrimination. Clearly, ethnic Americans face prejudice and discrimination in subtle or blatant ways every day. One of the most discouraging findings I encountered while writing this chapter is that only 4 percent of the scientists, engineers, and mathematicians and only 6.8 percent of the teachers in the United States are either African-American or Hispanic-American—whereas more than 20 percent of the total population is from one of these groups. Even though their attitudes toward science and math are more favorable than the attitudes of white students, black and Hispanic students begin to lose out in science and math as early as elementary school. They are chosen less often for gifted classes and acceleration or enrichment programs. They are more likely to be tracked into "basic skills" classes. As they progress through junior high, high school, and college, their paths take them farther and farther out of the pipeline that produces our scientists. If they do persist and become scientists or engineers, they, along with women, will still be paid less than whites for the same work (National Science Foundation, 1988; Oakes, 1990).

WOMEN AND MEN: SEX DIFFERENCES IN THE CLASSROOM

While I was proofreading this very page today, riding cross-country on a train, the conductor stopped to take my ticket. He said, "I'm sorry, dear, for interrupting your homework, but do you have a ticket?" I had to smile at his (I'm sure unintended) sexism. I doubt that he made the same comment to the man across the aisle writing on his legal pad. Like racial discrimination, messages of sexism can be subtle. In this section we will examine how men and women are socialized and the role of teachers in providing an equitable education for both sexes.

Sex Role Development

Beliefs about what it means to be male or female are strongly influenced by culture. Two important sources of influence in modern cultures are parents and schools.

We all may learn very early what it means to be male or female through the actions of our parents in the first years of our lives. Both parents play more roughly and vigorously with sons than they do with daughters. Parents tend to touch male infants more at first; later, they keep male toddlers at a greater distance than females. Parents also seem to spend more time interacting with sons, trying to get the babies to laugh or smile (Jacklin, DiPietro, & Maccoby, 1984). Even today, when white middle-class parents are asked about what they value in their children, they list achievement, competitiveness, and emotional control for their sons and warmth and "ladylike" behavior for their daughters (Block, 1983; McGuire, 1988).

Sex-Role Stereotyping in the Preschool Years. Different treatment of the sexes and **sex role stereotyping** continue in early childhood. Boys are encouraged to be more physically active; girls are encouraged to be affectionate and tender. Researchers have found that boys are given more freedom to roam the neighborhood and are not protected for as long a time as girls from potentially dangerous activities like playing with sharp scissors or crossing the street alone. Parents quickly come to the aid of their daughters but are more likely to insist that their sons handle problems themselves (Block, 1983; Fagot, Hagan, Leinbach, & Kronsberg, 1985). Thus, independence and initiative seem to be encouraged more in boys than in girls. Lois Hoffman (1977) has suggested that girls are not so much trained in dependency as they are deprived of independence training.

For an eye-opening experience, visit a large toy store. In buying a birthday gift for my 2-year-old nephew lately, I could choose between two sets of sandbox toys. The boys' set featured drills and hammers; the girls got muffin pans and dishes. Had my nephew been a niece, I could have chosen the box of lavender and pink plastic construction blocks!

Many of my student teachers are surprised when they hear young children talk about sex roles. Even in this era of great progress toward equal opportunity of the sexes, a preschool girl is more likely to tell you she wants to become a secretary than to say she wants to be an engineer. A colleague of mine brought her young daughter to her college class after she had given a lecture on the dangers of sex stereotyping in schools. The students asked the little girl, "What do you want to be when you grow up?" The child immediately replied, "A doctor," and her professor/mother beamed with pride. Then the girl whispered to the students in the front row, "I really want to be a nurse, but my Mommy won't let me." Actually, this is a common reaction for young children. Preschoolers tend to have more stereotyped notions of sex roles than older children, and all ages seem to have more rigid and traditional ideas about male occupations than about what females do.

Gender Bias in the Curriculum. During the elementary-school years, children continue to learn about what it means to be male or female. Unfortunately, schools often foster these **gender biases** in a number of ways. Most of the textbooks produced for the early grades before 1970 portrayed both males and females in sexually stereotyped roles. Materials for the later grades often omitted women altogether from illustrations and text. In a study of 2,760 stories in 134 books from 16 publishers, a group called Women on Words and Images (1975) found the total number of stories dealing with males or male animals to be four times greater than the number of stories dealing with females or female animals. They also found that females tended to be shown in the home, behaving passively and expressing fear or incompetence. Males usually were more dominant and adventurous; they often rescued the females.

Sex Role Stereotyping Rigid beliefs about characteristics and behaviors associated with one sex as opposed to the other.

Gender Biases Different views of males and females, often favoring one gender over the other.

In recent years textbook publishers have recognized these problems to some extent and established guidelines to prevent them. It still makes sense to check your teaching materials for such stereotypes, however. When Purcell and Stewart (1990) used the same design as Women on Words and Images to analyze 62 elementary readers, they found that the numbers of male and female characters were about equal and that girls were shown in a wide range of activities; but girls were still portrayed as more helpless than boys.

And don't assume that books for older children are free of sexual stereotypes. Biases can be subtle. Jacklin and Maccoby (1972) examined word problems in math textbooks and found differences in the ways males and females were presented. In one set of problems, for example, boys were described building things or earning money while girls were involved in cooking and sewing. Despite new publishers' guidelines, problems have not disappeared entirely (Powell, Garcia, & Denton, 1985).

The teacher's own attitude toward sex differences may be influential as well. One reason there have been more children's books and stories with male characters is the belief held by many teachers that boys like to read stories about boys and girls don't mind reading stories about boys— so why not assign stories about boys? It will help the boys be motivated to read and it won't hurt the girls. Publishers seem to agree with this logic. When Scott O'Dell was looking for a publisher for his *Island of the Blue Dolphins,* he was told by several editors that he needed to make a small change—turn this story of a girl's courageous fight for survival into a story about a boy. O'Dell refused, and the book went on to win a Newbery Award for children's literature (Sadker, Sadker, & Klein, 1991).

The truth about reading preferences is not so simple. It appears that boys do like to read about male characters, but girls appear to prefer female characters; and both sexes find stories about nontraditional females to be at least as interesting as stories about traditional male characters (Sadker, Sadker, & Klein, 1991).

Sex Discrimination in Classrooms. There has been quite a bit of research on teachers' treatment of male and female students. One of the best documented findings of the past 20 years is that teachers interact more with boys than with girls. This is true from preschool to college. Teachers ask more questions of males; give males more feedback (praise, criticism, and correction); and give more specific and valuable comments to boys. As girls move through the grades, they have less and less to say. By the time students reach college, men are twice as likely to initiate comments as women (Sadker & Sadker, 1985, 1986b; Serbin & O'Leary, 1975; Wingate, 1986). The effect of these differences is that from preschool through college girls, on the average, receive 1,800 fewer hours of attention and instruction than boys (Sadker, Sadker, & Klein, 1991). Of course, these differences are not evenly distributed. Some boys, generally high-achieving white students, receive more than their share. Minority-group boys, like girls, tend to receive much less attention from the teacher.

Teachers can perpetuate stereotypes in many ways, some obvious, some subtle. When boxes must be carried to the basement, the teachers may ask for male volunteers. When refreshments are needed or flowers must be arranged, the teacher may again fall victim to stereotyped images and ask for female volunteers. When student teams are formed and the groups all choose boys as the leaders and girls as the secretaries, the teacher may accept these decisions. Guidance counselors, parents, and teachers often do not protest at all when a bright girl says she doesn't want to take any more math or science courses; but when a boy of the same ability wants to forget about math or science, they will object. In these subtle ways, students' stereotyped expectations for themselves can be reinforced (Sadker & Sadker, 1985).

Gender and Mental Abilities

From infancy through the preschool years, most studies find few differences between boys and girls in overall mental and motor development or in specific abilities. During the school years and beyond, psychologists find no differences in general intelligence on the standard measures; but these tests have been designed and standardized to minimize sex differences. Usually these tests omit items that favor one sex or balance them by adding an equal number of items that favor the other sex. Even though the overall IQ scores of males and females are not significantly different on the average, however, scores on several subtests show sex differences.

Studies conducted before 1974 showed that males performed significantly better than females on tests of spatial ability. Since 1974 the differences have virtually disappeared, except on tests that require mental rotation of a figure in space. Here males are faster, though not more accurate. This quickness in mental rotation of objects has been related to male participation in athletics (Linn & Hyde, 1989; Newcombe &

Gender bias in the classroom can be very subtle. Do males in math class get criticized for not solving a difficult problem while females are praised for correct answers to easy problems? Do males get more explanation of complex concepts and girls get more "help"? These actions can communicate to students that males can succeed if they try and females don't have the basic capacity for difficult work.

Baenninger, 1990). Males' extensive experiences with video and arcade games may play a role as well.

Gender and Mathematics. In studies conducted before 1974, males outperformed females in mathematics. Again, in recent studies the differences are disappearing, though males still maintain a slight edge overall (Linn & Hyde, 1989). On the SAT quantitative tests, however, the highest scores still go to males. For example, for the 1988–89 administrations of the SAT math section, 89 percent of the students who earned a score of 750 or higher were males (National Center for Education Statistics, 1990). There is some evidence that male superiority on this test is related to their ability to work quickly and to estimate answers (Linn & Hyde, 1989). Why this may be so is not fully understood.

It is important to realize that when differences are found between the average scores of boys and girls on tests of spatial and mathematical ability, the differences are rather small (Linn & Hyde, 1989). Some researchers have found that girls are better than boys on some kinds of problems—for example, on computational problems and logical, abstract problems— while boys do better than girls on other kinds of problems—for example, story problems and spatial relations problems (Hyde, Fennema, & Lamon, 1990; Marshall, 1984).

One controversial question is whether boys are better in mathematics because they take more math courses than girls. There appear to be few or no differences between boys and girls in math achievement at the beginning of high school. But during high school girls take fewer math courses (Pallas & Alexander, 1983). As soon as mathematics courses become optional, many girls avoid them, as you can see in Table 5.4. There is mounting evidence that the differences between boys and girls in math achievement decrease substantially or disappear altogether when the actual number of previous math courses taken by each student is consid-

---

TABLE 5.4 Who Finishes What Courses?

A government survey revealed the following data on the percentages of males and females who enrolled in and then completed high school courses in several areas.

Courses	Percent Males Completing	Percent Females Completing
Algebra	81.6	76.8
Trigonometry or geometry	60.1	50.3
Chemistry or physics	54.2	42.3
English, 3 years or more	92.8	94.1
Foreign language, 2 years or more	39.1	48.1

Source: National Center for Education Statistics, *Digest of Education Statistics, 1990* (Washington, D.C.: National Center for Education Statistics, U.S. Department of Education, 1991), p. 130.

ered (Fennema & Sherman, 1977; Oakes, 1990; Pallas & Alexander, 1983). But other researchers have reported that high-ability boys are superior to high-ability girls in mathematics reasoning, even when participation in previous math courses is taken into account (Benbow & Minor, 1986; Benbow & Stanley, 1980, 1983a&b; Kolata, 1980).

When Oakes (1990) analyzed the reasons why only 15 percent of the scientists, engineers, and mathematicians in the United States are women, she concluded, "Precollege course taking is key to the participation discrepancies for both minorities and women. However, for women, choices appear to be the critical factor . . . girls who are academically qualified more often choose not to take more advanced mathematics and science course offerings" (p. 189). Thus, girls tend not to develop their abilities in this area. In the process they limit their college and career choices, since colleges require applicants to possess some proficiency in mathematics and many jobs demand abilities in this area as well.

Another controversial question is whether teachers are responsible, in part, for the lower participation of girls in math and science studies. There is some evidence that teachers treat girls and boys differently in mathematics classes. For example, some elementary-school teachers spend more academic time with boys in math and with girls in reading. In one study, high school geometry teachers directed most of their questions to boys, even though the girls asked questions and volunteered answers more often. Several researchers have found that some teachers

Guidelines

Avoiding Sexism in Teaching

Check to see if textbooks and other materials you are using present an honest view of the options open to both males and females.

Examples

1. Are both males and females portrayed in traditional and nontraditional roles at work, at leisure, and at home?
2. Discuss your analyses with students, and ask them to help you find sex role biases in other materials—magazine advertising, TV programs, news reporting, for example.

Watch for any unintended biases in your own classroom practices.

Examples

1. Do you group students by sex for certain activities? Is the grouping appropriate?
2. Do you call on one sex or the other for certain

answers—boys for math and girls for poetry, for example?

Look for ways in which your school may be limiting the options open to male or female students.

Examples

1. What advice is given by guidance counselors to students in course and career decisions?
2. Is there a good sports program for both girls and boys?

Use gender-free language as much as possible.

Examples

1. Do you speak of "law-enforcement officer" and "mail carrier" instead of "policeman" and "mailman"?
2. Do you name a committee "head" instead of a "chairman"?

tend to accept wrong answers from girls, saying, in effect, "Well, at least you tried." But when boys give the wrong answer, the teachers are more likely to say, "Try harder! You can figure this out." These messages, repeated time and again, can convince girls that they just aren't cut out for mathematics (Harvard University, 1986). If you are like a few of the student teachers I have supervised who "really hate math," please don't pass this attitude on to your students. You may have been the victim of sex discrimination yourself.

Eliminating Gender Bias. We don't know what the situation would be like if all students, boys and girls, received appropriate instruction and encouragement in math. For example, Patricia Casserly of the Educational Testing Service studied 20 high schools where no sex differences in mathematics performance were found. Even though the schools were not alike in all ways, they shared several common features. The teachers had strong backgrounds in mathematics, engineering, or science, not just in general education. They were enthusiastic about mathematics. The brightest students, male and female, were grouped together for instruction in math, and there was heavy emphasis on reasoning in the classes (Kolata, 1980). The activities used to teach math may make a difference as well. Elementary-age girls may do better in math if they learn in cooperative as opposed to competitive activities. Certainly it makes sense to balance both cooperative and competitive approaches so that students who learn better each way have equal opportunities (Fennema & Peterson, 1988). The Guidelines on page 176 provide additional ideas for how to avoid sexism in your teaching.

LANGUAGE DIFFERENCES IN THE CLASSROOM

In the classroom, quite a bit happens through language. Teachers explain and question. Students answer and ask. Communication is at the heart of teaching; but as we have seen in this chapter, culture affects communication. In this section we will examine two kinds of language differences—dialect differences and bilingualism.

Dialects

A **dialect** is a language variation spoken by a particular ethnic, social, or regional group. The rules for a language define how words should be pronounced, how meaning should be expressed, and the ways the basic parts of speech should be put together to form sentences. Dialects appear to differ in their rules in these areas, but it is important to remember that these differences are not errors. Each dialect within a language is just as logical, complex, and rule governed as the standard form of the language (often called standard speech).

An example of this is the use of the double negative. In Standard English the redundancy of the double negative is not allowed. But in many nonstandard dialects, like "black English," just as in many other languages (for instance, Russian, French, Spanish, and Hungarian), the double negative is required by the grammatical rules. To say "I don't want

Dialect Rule-governed variation of a language spoken by a particular group.

anything" in Spanish, you must literally say, "I don't want nothing," or *No quiero nada.* Haitian dialects differ from "black English" because French is the primary language, and some Hispanic-English dialects reflect the influence of Spanish and Creole language variations.

Dialects and Language Skills. Another area in which nonstandard dialects differ from Standard English is pronunciation, which can lead to spelling problems. In "black English" and in Southern dialects, for instance, there is less attention paid to pronouncing the ends of words than in standard English. A lack of attention to final consonants, such as *s,* can lead to failure to indicate possession, third-person singular verbs, and plurals in the standard way. So *John's book* might be *John book,* and words such as *thinks, wasps,* and *lists* may be difficult to pronounce. When endings are not pronounced, there are more homonyms (words that sound alike but have different meanings) in the student's language than the unknowing teacher may expect; *spent* and *spend* might sound alike, for example. Even without the confusions caused by dialect differences, there are many homonyms in English. Usually special attention is given to words such as these when they come up in the spelling lesson. If the teacher is aware of the special homonyms in student dialects, direct teaching of these spelling differences is also possible.

Dialects and Teaching. Now we turn to a very important issue. While the various dialects of a language may be equally logical, complex, and rule governed, should teachers make learning easier for children by teaching in the dialect of the majority of students? To do this would show respect for the children's language. But the children would be robbed of the opportunity to learn the standard speech of the dominant culture. Being able to communicate effectively in standard speech allows adults to take advantage of many social and occupational opportunities.

The best teaching approach seems to be to focus on understanding the children and to accept their dialect as a valid and correct language system, but to teach as an alternative the standard form of English (or whatever the dominant language is in your country). Learning the standard speech is fairly easy for most children whose original language is a dialect, as long as they have good models.

What does all this mean for teachers? How can they cope with linguistic diversity in the classroom? First, they can be sensitive to their own possible negative stereotypes about children who speak a different dialect. Taylor (1983) found that teachers who held negative attitudes toward "black English" gave lower ratings for reading comprehension to students using that dialect, even when the accuracy of the students' performance was the same as that of standard English speakers. Second, teachers can ensure comprehension by repeating instructions using different words and by asking students to paraphrase instructions or give examples. The Guidelines give more ideas taken from Bennett (1990).

Bilingualism

Bilingualism Speaking two languages fluently.

Bilingualism is a topic that sparks heated debates and touches many emotions. One reason is the changing demographics discussed earlier in this chapter. In the United States in the late 1980s, 2.5 million school-age

Guidelines

Teaching Dialect-Dominant Students

1. Become familiar with features of the students' dialect. This will allow you to understand students better and to distinguish a reading miscue (a noncomprehension feature) from a comprehension error. Students should not be interrupted during the oral reading process. Correction of comprehension features is best done after the reading segment.

2. Allow students to listen to a passage or story first. This can be done in two ways: (a) finish the story and then ask comprehension questions or (b) interrupt the story at key comprehension segments and ask students to predict the outcome.

3. Use predictable stories, which can be familiar episodes in literature, music, or history. They can be original works or experiential readers.

4. Use visual aids to enhance comprehension. Visual images, whether pictures or words, will aid word recognition and comprehension.

5. Use "cloze procedure" deletions to focus on vocabulary and meaning. Cloze procedures are simply selected deletions of words from a passage in order to focus on a specific text feature. *Examples:* (a) The little red hen found an ear of corn. The little red _____ said, "Who will dry the ear of _____?" (vocabulary focus) (b) Today I feel like a (*noun*). (grammar focus) (c) There was a (*pain*) in the pit of his stomach. (semantic focus).

6. Allow students to retell the story or passage in various speech styles. Have students select different people to whom they would like to retell the story (family member, principal, friend) and assist them in selecting synonyms most appropriate to each audience. This allows both teacher and student to become language authorities.

7. Integrate reading, speaking, and writing skills whenever possible.

8. Use the microcomputer (if available) as a time-on-task exercise. The microcomputer can effectively assist in teaching the reading techniques of skimming (general idea), scanning (focused reference), reading for comprehension (mastery of total message), and critical reading (inference and evaluation).

Source: Christine I. Bennett, *Comprehensive multicultural education*, pp. 234–235. Copyright © 1990. Reprinted with permission of Allyn and Bacon.

children were not native English speakers. This number is expected to double by the year 2000. As you can see in Figure 5.3 on page 180, in some states almost one-fourth of all students speak a first language other than English—usually Spanish. Two terms that you will see associated with bilingualism are **English as a second language (ESL),** describing classes for students whose primary language is not English, and **limited English proficiency (LEP),** referring to students whose English skills are limited.

What Does Bilingualism Mean? There are disagreements about the meaning of bilingualism. Some definitions focus exclusively on a language-based meaning: bilingual people, or bilinguals, speak two languages. But this limited definition minimizes the significant problems that bilingual students face. Consider the words of these two students:

A ninth-grade boy, who recently arrived in California from Mexico: "There is so much discrimination and hate. Even from other kids from Mexico who have been here longer. They don't treat us like brothers. They hate even more. It makes them feel more like natives. They want to be American. They don't want to speak Spanish to us,

English as a Second Language (ESL) Designation for programs and classes to teach English to students who are not native speakers of English.

Limited English Proficiency (LEP) Descriptive term for students who have limited mastery of English.

FIGURE 5.3 **Number of Persons with Non-English Mother Tongues by State**
Many states in the United States have over 100,000 people whose first language is not English. The statistics represented in this map have changed dramatically between the 1980 and the 1990 censuses. According to the 1990 census, for example, Florida now has more than two million people who speak a language other than English while Connecticut now has fewer than 500,000 who do so. These changes reflect shifts in population and migration statistics.

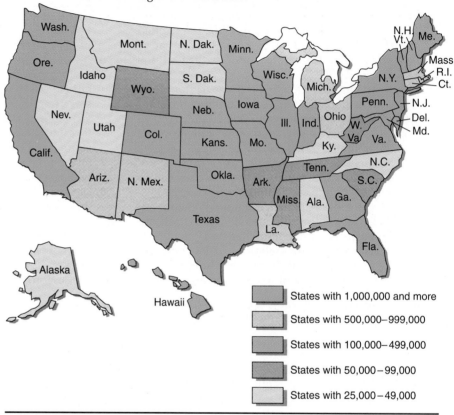

States with 1,000,000 and more
States with 500,000–999,000
States with 100,000–499,000
States with 50,000–99,000
States with 25,000–49,000

Source: Reprinted with permission of The Free Press, a Division of Macmillan, Inc., from *A Host of Tongues* by Nancy Faires Conklin and Margaret A. Lourie. Copyright © 1983 by The Free Press.

they already know English and how to act. If they are with us, other people will treat them more like wetbacks, so they try to avoid us." (Olsen, 1988, p. 36)

A tenth-grade Chinese-American girl who had been in America for several years: "I don't know who I am. Am I the good Chinese daughter? Am I an American teenager? I always feel I am letting my parents down when I am with my friends because I act so American, but I also feel that I will never really be an American. I never feel really comfortable with myself anymore." (Olsen, 1988, p. 30)

The experiences of these two students show that there is more to being bilingual than just speaking two languages. You must also be able to move back and forth between two cultures while still maintaining a sense of your own identity (Hakuta & Garcia, 1989). Being bilingual and bicultural means mastering the knowledge necessary to communicate in two cultures as well as dealing with potential discrimination. As a teacher, you will have to help your students learn all these skills.

Becoming Bilingual. Early research on bilingualism concluded that speaking two languages was so taxing on the mental development of the child that cognitive abilities suffered. Thus the child should learn English as quickly as possible. Better-designed studies today show that the opposite is true. Higher degrees of bilingualism are correlated with increased cognitive abilities in such areas as concept formation, creativity, knowledge of the workings of language, and cognitive flexibility. These findings seem to hold as long as there is no stigma attached to being bilingual and as long as students are not expected to abandon their first language to learn English (Dias, 1983; Galambos & Goldin-Meadow, 1990; Hakuta & Garcia, 1989).

Psychologists studying **second-language acquisition** now believe that people learn a second language in much the same way as they learned the first—by making sense of the language puzzle, building schemes, and understanding meaning. Learning the second language does not interfere with understanding in the first language. In fact, the more proficient the speaker is in the first language, the faster she or he will master a second language (Cummins, 1984). If children learn two languages simultaneously as toddlers, there is a period between ages 2 and 3 when they progress more slowly because they have not yet figured out that they are learning two different languages. They may mix up the grammar of the two. But researchers believe that by age 4, if they have enough exposure to both languages, they get things straight and speak as well as native **monolinguals** (Reich, 1986).

Proficiency in a second language has two separate aspects: face-to-face communication (known as "contextualized language skills") and academic uses of language like reading and doing grammar exercises ("decontextualized language skills") (Snow, 1987). It takes students about 2 years in a good-quality program to be able to communicate face-to-face in a second language, but mastering decontextualized, academic language skills in the new language takes 5 to 7 years. So students who seem in conversation to "know" a second language may still have great difficulty with complex schoolwork in that language (Ovando, 1989).

Bilingual Education. Virtually everyone agrees that all citizens should learn the official language of their country. But when and how should instruction in that language begin? Is it better to teach non-English-speaking and limited-English-proficiency students to read first in their native language or to begin reading instruction in English? Do these children need some oral lessons in English before reading instruction can be effective? Should other subjects, such as mathematics and social studies, be taught in the primary (home) language until the children are fluent in English? On these questions there are two basic positions, which have given rise to two contrasting teaching approaches.

Second-Language Acquisition The process of learning a second language, very similar to the process of first-language learning.

Monolinguals Individuals who speak only one language.

Proponents of the first approach believe that English ought to be introduced as early as possible; they argue that valuable learning time is lost if students are taught in their native language. Most bilingual programs today follow this line of thinking. Critics, however, raise three important issues. First, children who are forced to try to learn math or science in an unfamiliar language are bound to have trouble. Think of how you would have done with math if you had been forced to learn fractions or algebra in a second language that you had studied for only a semester. Some psychologists believe students taught by this approach may become **semilingual** or inadequate speakers of both languages. Second, students may get the message that their home languages (and therefore, their families and cultures) are second class. You saw the seeds of these feelings in the stories of the two students at the beginning of this section.

Third, ironically, by the time students have mastered academic English and let their home language deteriorate, they reach secondary school and are encouraged to learn a second language. Had both the home language and English been developed all along, they would already be fluent in two languages without taking French I or Introductory Spanish. Kenji Hakuta (1986) expresses this hope:

> Perhaps the rosiest future for bilingual education in the United States can be attained by dissolving the paradoxical attitude of admiration and pride for school-attained bilingualism on the one hand and scorn and shame for home-brewed immigrant bilingualism on the other. The goals of the educational system could be seen as the development of all students as functional bilinguals, including monolingual English speakers. (p. 229)

In many bilingual classrooms, English is featured prominently along with the students' first language. But even in this second-grade class where Spanish seems to be the students' native language, there may be students whose first language is neither English nor Spanish.

Semilingual Not proficient in any language; speaking one or more languages inadequately.

The second approach to teaching advocates using the child's native language for some subject teaching while simultaneously developing English proficiency. Supporters of this approach believe that children have a right to be proficient speakers of their native language *and* to become fully competent speakers of the dominant language of their country. One new approach to reaching this goal is to create classes that mix students who are learning a second language with students who are native speakers. The goal is for both groups to become fluent in both languages (Snow, 1986). My daughter spent a summer in such a program in Quebec and has been ahead in every French class ever since. For truly effective bilingual education, we will need many bilingual teachers. If you have a competence in another language, you might want to develop it fully for your teaching.

We have dealt with a wide range of differences in this chapter. How can teachers provide an appropriate education for all their students? One response is to make the classroom compatible with the students' cultural heritage. Such a classroom is described as being *culturally compatible.*

One goal of creating culturally compatible classrooms is to encourage mutual acceptance and respect among students from all backgrounds.

CREATING CULTURALLY COMPATIBLE CLASSROOMS

The goal of creating **culturally compatible classrooms** is to eliminate racism, sexism, and ethnic prejudice while providing equal educational opportunities for all students. Roland Tharp (1989) states that "two decades of data on cultural issues in classroom interactions and school outcomes have accumulated. When schools are changed, children's experiences and achievement also change" (p. 349). Tharp outlines several dimensions of classrooms that can be tailored to fit the needs of students. Three dimensions are social organization, learning style, and sociolinguistics.

Social Organization

Tharp states that "a central task of educational design is to make the organization of teaching, learning, and performance compatible with the social structures in which students are most productive, engaged, and likely to learn" (p. 350). Social structure or *social organization* in this context means the ways people interact to accomplish a particular goal. For example, the social organization of Hawaiian society depends heavily on collaboration and cooperation. Children play together in groups of friends and siblings, with older children often caring for the younger ones. When cooperative work groups of four or five boys and girls were established in Hawaiian classrooms, student learning and participation improved. The teacher worked intensively with one group while the children in the remaining groups helped each other. But when the same structure was tried in a Navajo classroom, students would not work together. These students are socialized to be more solitary and not to play with the opposite sex. By setting up same-sex working groups of only two or three Navajo students, teachers encouraged them to help each other.

Culturally Compatible Classrooms Classrooms in which procedures, rules, grouping strategies, attitudes, and teaching methods do not cause conflicts with the students' culturally influenced ways of learning and interacting.

Learning Styles

Some psychologists have found ethnic-group differences in students' cognitive styles. You may remember from the previous chapter that cognitive styles are the ways that individuals typically process information. The following are a few examples.

Hispanic Americans. Results of some research suggest that Mexican Americans tend to be *field dependent,* preferring holistic, concrete, social approaches to learning. Because being field independent is related to achievement in mathematics, the tendency to be field dependent may interfere with performance in mathematics if it is taught in the usual abstract, analytical way (Buenning & Tollefson, 1987). Other researchers have suggested that Hispanic-American students are more oriented toward family and group loyalty and less individualistic. This may mean that Hispanic-American students prefer cooperative activities and dislike being made to compete with fellow students (Vasquez, 1990).

African Americans. Bennett (1990) summarizes research that suggests the learning styles of African Americans may be inconsistent with teaching approaches in most schools. Some of the characteristics of this learning style are a visual/global rather than a verbal/analytic approach; a preference for reasoning by inference rather than formal logic; a focus on people and relationships; a preference for energetic involvement in several activities simultaneously rather than routine, step-by-step learning; and a greater dependence on nonverbal communication. To capitalize on these learning styles, Hale-Benson (1986) recommends the following strategies with young African-American children:

  use appropriate nonverbal cues, gestures, and eye contact
  allow equal "talking time" for teacher and students
  emphasize small-group learning and hands-on contact with the teacher
  use a variety of learning activities that include movement, games, poetry, and music

Native Americans. Native Americans also appear to have a more global and visual style of learning. For example, Navajo students prefer hearing a story all the way through to the end before discussing parts of the story. Teachers who stop to ask questions seem odd to these students and interrupt the learning process (Tharp, 1989). Also, these students sometimes show strong preferences for learning privately, through trial and error, rather than having their mistakes made public (Vasquez, 1990).

Asian Americans. There has been little research on the learning styles of Asian Americans, perhaps because they are seen as "successful minorities." As we discussed earlier, many of the values and attitudes taught by some Asian cultures, such as respect for teachers, hard work, and persistent effort, can support academic achievement. One recent study of among refugee students found that they tended to be field dependent and global in their approach to problem solving. They tended to be more passive and learned best in cooperative settings with good support from peers and the teacher. Of course, strong support may be helpful for any group trying to cope with a new and very different culture.

There are dangers when teachers stereotype Asian Americans as hardworking and passive. This practice

> tends to reinforce conformity and stifle creativity. Asian and Pacific American students, therefore, frequently do not develop the ability to assert and express themselves verbally and are channeled in dispro-portionate numbers into the technical/scientific fields. As a result, many Asian and Pacific American students undergo traumatic fam-ily/school discontinuities, suffer from low self-esteem, are overly conforming, and have their academic and social development nar-rowly circumscribed. (Suzuki, 1983, p. 9)

Suzuki's cautions are echoed by many critics of the research on ethnic differences in learning styles.

Criticisms of Learning-Styles Research. In considering this research on learning styles, you should keep two points in mind. First, the validity of some of the learning-styles research has been strongly questioned, as we saw in the previous chapter. Second, there is an *extremely* heated debate today about whether identifying ethnic-group differences in learn-ing styles and preferences is a dangerous, racist, sexist exercise. As Edmund Gordon (1991) commented, "In a society where racist and sexist attitudes are ubiquitous, it is difficult to engage in a dispassionate discus-sion of manifest differences among groups of human beings who also differ in their assigned status" (p. 103). In our society we are quick to move from the notion of "difference" to the idea of "deficit." I have included the information about learning-style differences because I be-lieve with Gordon that, used sensibly, this information can help you better understand your students.

It is dangerous and incorrect, however, to assume that every individ-ual in a group shares the same learning style. Also, information about the "typical" learning styles of a given ethnic group can become just one more basis for stereotyping, as mentioned above (Gordon, 1991; O'Neil, 1990a). The best advice for teachers is to be sensitive to individ-ual differences in *all* your students and to make available alternative paths to learning. Never prejudge how a student will learn best on the basis of assumptions about the student's ethnicity or race. Get to know the individual.

Sociolinguistics

Sociolinguistics is the study of "the courtesies and conventions of con-versation across cultures" (Tharp, 1989, p. 351). A knowledge of sociolin-guistics will help you understand why communication sometimes breaks down in classrooms. The classroom is a special setting for communicat-ing; it has its own set of rules for when, how, to whom, about what subject, and in what manner to use language. Sometimes the sociolinguis-tic skills of students do not fit the expectations of teachers.

Sociolinguistics The study of the formal and informal rules for how, when, about what, to whom, and how long to speak in conversations within cultural groups.

Participation Structures. In order to be successful, students must know the communication rules; that is, they must understand the pragmatics of the classroom—when, where, and how to communicate. (See chapter 2 for a discussion of pragmatics.) This is not such an easy task. As class activities change, rules change. Sometimes you have to raise your hand (during the teacher's presentation), but sometimes you don't (during storytime on the rug). Sometimes it is good to ask a question (during discussion), but other times it isn't so good (when the teacher is scolding you). The differing activity rules are called **participation structures.** These structures define appropriate participation for each class activity. Most classrooms have many different participation structures.

To be competent communicators in the classroom, students sometimes have to read very subtle, nonverbal cues telling them which participation structures are currently in effect. For example, in one classroom, when the teacher stood in a particular area of the room, put her hands on her hips, and leaned forward at the waist, the children in the class were signaled to "stop and freeze," look at the teacher, and anticipate an announcement (Shultz & Florio, 1979).

Sources of Misunderstandings. Some children are simply better than others at reading the classroom situation because the participation structures of the school match the structures they have learned at home. The communication rules for most school situations are similar to those in middle-class homes, so children from these homes often *appear* to be more competent communicators. They know the unwritten rules. Students from different cultural backgrounds may have learned participation structures that conflict with the behaviors expected in school. For example, one study found that the home conversation style of Hawaiian children is to chime in with contributions to a story. In school, however, this overlapping style is seen as "interrupting." But when the teachers in one school learned about these differences and made their reading groups more like their students' home conversation groups, the young Hawaiian children in their classes improved in reading (Au, 1980; Tharp, 1989).

The source of misunderstanding can be a subtle sociolinguistic difference, such as how long the teacher waits to react to a student's response. White and Tharp (1988) found that when Navajo students in one class paused in giving a response, their Anglo teacher seemed to think that they were finished speaking. As a result, the teacher often unintentionally interrupted students. In another study, researchers found that Pueblo Indian students participated twice as much in classes where teachers waited longer to react.

So it seems that even students who speak the same language as their teachers may still have trouble communicating, and thus learning school subjects, if their knowledge of pragmatics does not fit the school situation. What can teachers do? Especially in the early grades, you should make communication rules for activities clear and explicit. Do not assume students know what to do. Use cues to signal students when changes occur. Explain and demonstrate appropriate behavior. I have seen teachers show young children how to "talk in your inside voice" or "whisper so you won't disturb others." One teacher said and then demonstrated, "If you have to interrupt me while I'm working with other chil-

Participation Structures
The formal and informal rules for how to take part in a given activity.

Guidelines

Creating Culturally Compatible Classrooms

Experiment with different grouping arrangements to encourage social harmony and cooperation.

Examples

1. Try "study buddies" and pairs.
2. Organize heterogeneous groups of four or five.
3. Establish larger teams for older students.

Provide a range of ways to learn material to accommodate a range of learning styles.

Examples

1. Give students verbal materials at different reading levels.
2. Offer visual materials—charts, diagrams, models.
3. Provide tapes for listening and viewing.
4. Set up activities and projects.

Teach classroom procedures directly, even ways of doing things that you thought everyone would know.

Examples

1. Tell students how to get the teacher's attention.
2. Explain when and how to interrupt the teacher if students need help.
3. Show which materials students can take and which require permission.
4. Demonstrate acceptable ways to disagree with or challenge another student.

Learn the meaning of different behaviors for your students.

Examples

1. Ask students how they feel when you correct or praise them. What gives them this message?

2. Talk to family and community members and other teachers to discover the meaning of expressions, gestures, or other responses that are unfamiliar to you.

Emphasize meaning in teaching.

Examples

1. Make sure students understand what they read.
2. Try storytelling and other modes that don't require written materials.
3. Use examples that relate abstract concepts to everyday experiences; for instance, relate negative numbers to being overdrawn in your checkbook.

Get to know the customs, traditions, and values of your students.

Examples

1. Use holidays as a chance to discuss the origins and meaning of traditions.
2. Analyze different traditions for common themes.
3. Attend community fairs and festivals.

Help students detect racist and sexist messages.

Examples

1. Analyze curriculum materials for biases.
2. Make students "bias detectives," reporting comments from the media.
3. Discuss the ways that students communicate biased messages about each other and what should be done when this happens.
4. Discuss expressions of prejudice such as anti-Semitism.

dren, stand quietly beside me until I can help you." Be consistent in responding to students. If students are supposed to raise their hands, don't call on those who break the rules.

Bringing It All Together: Teaching Every Student

The goal of this chapter is to give you a sense of the diversity in today's and tomorrow's schools and to help you meet the challenges of teaching in a multicultural classroom. How will you understand and build on all the cultures of your students? How will you deal with many different languages? Here are three general teaching principles to guide you in finding answers to these questions.

Know Your Students. Nothing you read in a chapter on cultural differences will teach you enough to understand the lives of all your students. If you can take other courses in college or read about other cultures, I encourage you to do it. But reading and studying are not enough. You should get to know your students' families and communities. Try to spend time with students and parents on projects outside school. Ask parents to help in class or to speak to your students about their job, their hobby, or the history and heritage of their ethnic group. In the elementary grades, don't wait until a student is in trouble to have the first meeting with a family member. Watch and listen to the ways that your students interact in large and small groups. Have students write to you and write back to them. Eat lunch with one or two students. Spend some nonteaching time with them.

Respect Your Students. From knowledge ought to come respect for your students' learning strengths—for the struggles they face and the obstacles they overcome. For a child, genuine acceptance is a necessary condition for developing self-esteem. Self-esteem and pride are important accomplishments of the school years. Sometimes the self-image and occupational aspirations of minority children actually decline in their early years in public school, probably because of the emphasis on majority culture values, accomplishments, and history. By presenting the accomplishments of particular members of an ethnic group or by bringing that group's culture into the classroom (in the form of, say, literature, art, or music), teachers can help students maintain a sense of pride in their cultural group. This integration of culture must be more than the "tokenism" of sampling ethnic foods or wearing costumes. Students should learn about the socially and intellectually important contributions of the various groups.

Tiedt and Tiedt (1990) have provided a great many useful suggestions for multicultural teaching. Here are just a few:

Ask students to draw a picture or bring in a photograph of themselves. Have each student list all her or his group memberships on a page with this picture. For example, Sue Wong is a female, a daughter, a Chinese American, a Methodist, a Camp Fire Girl. . . . Display the pages around the room or bind them into a book.

Study in depth one cultural group, such as Cherokees, Puerto Ricans, Chicanos, Haitians, or Vietnamese Americans.

Create a learning center based on a particular culture. Use maps, postcards, books, encyclopedias, recordings of the native language, posters, flags, biographies, art.

Have students draw maps, calculate distances, convert money, act out historical events or important holiday traditions, write their own "encyclopedia" articles or travelogues, or write for more information to the appropriate public or private agencies within that country.

Introduce lessons based on a multicultural calendar. Tiedt and Tiedt provide a calendar for each school month showing the important holidays of various cultures and the contributions of these groups to American society.

Teach Your Students. The most important thing you can do for your students is teach them to read, write, speak, compute, think, and create. Too often, goals for low-SES or minority-group students have focused exclusively on basic skills. Students are taught words and sounds, but the meaning of the story is supposed to come later. Knapp, Turnbull, and Shields (1990, p. 5) make these suggestions:

Focus on meaning and understanding from beginning to end—for example, by orienting instruction toward comprehending reading passages, communicating important ideas in written text, or understanding the concepts underlying number facts.

Balance routine skill learning with novel and complex tasks from the earliest stages of learning.

Provide context for skill learning that establishes clear reasons for needing to learn the skills.

Influence attitudes and beliefs about the academic content areas as well as skills and knowledge.

Eliminate unnecessary redundancy in the curriculum (e.g., repeating instruction in the same mathematics skills year after year).

And finally, teach students directly about how to be students. In the early grades this could mean directly teaching the courtesies and conventions of the classroom: how to get a turn to speak, how and when to interrupt the teacher, how to whisper, how to get help in a small group, how to give an explanation that is helpful. In the later grades it may mean teaching the study skills that fit your subject. You can ask students to learn "how we do it in school" without violating principle number two above—respect your students. Ways of asking questions around the kitchen table at home may be different from ways of asking questions in school, but students can learn both ways, without deciding that either way is superior.

SUMMARY

TODAY'S MULTICULTURAL CLASSROOMS

Statistics point to increasing cultural diversity in American society. Old views—that minority-group members and immigrants should lose their cultural distinctiveness in the American "melting pot" or be regarded as culturally deficient—are being replaced by new emphases on multicultural education, equal educational opportunity, and the celebration of cultural diversity.

Everyone is a member of many cultural groups, defined in terms of geographic region, nationality, ethnicity, race, gender, social class, and religion.

Membership in a particular group does not determine behavior or values but makes certain values and kinds of behavior more likely. Wide variations exist within each group.

SOCIAL CLASS DIFFERENCES

Socioeconomic status (SES) is determined by several factors—not just income—and often overpowers other cultural differences. Disproportionate numbers of low-SES families are African American and Hispanic American.

Socioeconomic status and academic achievement are closely related. Low-SES students may suffer from teachers' lowered expectations of them, low self-esteem, learned helplessness, participation in resistance cultures, school tracking, and understimulating childrearing styles.

ETHNIC AND RACIAL DIFFERENCES

Ethnicity (culturally transmitted behavior) and race (biologically transmitted physical traits) are socially significant categories people use to describe themselves and others. Minority groups, whether viewed as numerically in the minority or historically unempowered, are rapidly increasing in population.

Conflicts between groups can arise from differences in culture-based beliefs, values, and expectations. Differences among ethnic groups in cognitive and academic abilities are largely the legacy of racial segregation and continuing prejudice and discrimination.

WOMEN AND MEN: SEX DIFFERENCES IN THE CLASSROOM

Educational equity for females and males is also an issue. Research shows that sex-role stereotyping begins in the preschool years and continues through gender bias in the school curriculum and sex discrimination in the classroom. Teachers often unintentionally perpetuate these problems.

Some measures on IQ and SAT tests have shown small sex-linked differences, especially in spatial abilities and mathematics. Research on the causes of these differences has been inconclusive, except to indicate that academic socialization and teachers' treatment of male and female students in mathematics classes do play a role. Teachers can use many strategies for reducing gender bias.

LANGUAGE DIFFERENCES IN THE CLASSROOM

Language differences among students include dialects, bilingualism, and culture-based communication styles. Dialects are not inferior languages and should be respected, but Standard English should be taught for academic contexts.

Bilingual students speak a first language other than English, learn English as a second language, may have some degree of limitation in English proficiency, and also must often struggle with social adjustment problems relating to biculturalism. While there is much debate over the best way to help bilingual students master English, studies show it is best if they are not forced to abandon their first language. The more proficient students are in their first language, the faster they will master the second. Mastering academic language skills in any new language takes 5 to 7 years.

CREATING CULTURALLY COMPATIBLE CLASSROOMS

Culturally compatible classrooms are free of racism, sexism, and ethnic prejudice and provide equal educational opportunities for all students. Dimensions of classroom life that can be modified to that end are social organization, learning-style formats, and participation structures. Teachers, however, must avoid stereotypes of culture-based learning styles and must not assume that every individual in a group shares the same style.

Communication may break down in classrooms because of differences in sociolinguistic styles and skills. Teachers can directly teach appropriate participation structures and be sensitive to culture-based communication rules. To help create compatible multicultural classrooms, teachers must know and respect all their students, have high expectations of them, and teach them what they need to know to succeed.

KEY TERMS AND CONCEPTS

academic socialization, p. 165
bilingualism, p. 178
cultural deficit model, p. 157
culturally compatible
  classrooms, p. 183

culture, p. 159
dialect, p. 177
English as a second language
  (ESL), p. 179
ethnicity, p. 166

gender biases, p. 172
limited English proficiency
  (LEP), p. 179
melting pot, p. 156
minority group, p. 166

WHAT WOULD YOU DO?

PRESCHOOL

You overhear children arguing in the block area. Two boys are saying to a girl, "You can't play here. These toys are for boys and you're a girl. Girls can't build space stations!" What would you do?

ELEMENTARY AND MIDDLE SCHOOL

Several of your students are from a public housing project in the district and clearly have fewer advantages than the other students in your class. You are concerned that the "project" students never seem to work or play with the others in the class. What would you do?

Every year the number of non-English-speaking students in your class increases. This year there are four different language groups represented—and you know only about five words in each language., The school's resources are very limited. Pick one topic and tell how you would teach it to accommodate the limited English proficiency of your students.

JUNIOR HIGH AND HIGH SCHOOL

One day you notice that the males are doing most of the talking in your classes, particularly the advanced classes. Just out of curiosity, you start to note each day how many girls and boys make contributions and ask questions. You are really surprised to see that your first impression was correct. What would you do to encourage more participation on the part of your female students?

For some reason, this year there have been several racial incidents in your school. Each incident seems a bit nastier and more dangerous than the one before. What would you do in your classes to improve the situation?

COOPERATIVE LEARNING ACTIVITY

Your school has received a $30,000 grant from a private foundation to "improve cross-cultural communications in the school."

Suggestions for accomplishing this include assessing the learning styles of all the students, hiring a consultant, buying new curriculum materials, sending teachers to multicultural workshops, and hiring more teachers' aides. With four or five other members of your educational psychology class, prepare a set of recommendations for spending the money so that the greatest benefit is achieved.

TEACHERS' CASEBOOK

TEACHER-STUDENT DIFFERENCES

Suppose you have a student in your class who is different from you racially, culturally, and temperamentally, and who has a different background and values from your own. You notice that you tend to avoid this student and that other students follow your example. How could you establish a relationship and reverse the trend toward estrangement and isolation?

AWARENESS FIRST

Students who are different racially, culturally, and with a different background are often intimidating to a teacher. Particularly in this age of "political correctness," teachers often revert to the technique of least resistance—we tend to avoid any confrontation between values by ignoring the student. *Noticing* that one tends to avoid a relationship with such a student is clearly the first, and perhaps most important, step. A second step is deliberately to engage that student on a one-to-one basis. Using the content of the class is a "values neutral" method of doing so. A debate with a student of any race or ethnic background on the subject of Rome's downfall or the steps to a geometry proof will reveal the commonality of human logic as greater than the differences in background. I have often found that once such a dialogue is established, the relationship can proceed to a less formal one, which invariably reveals that young adults of all backgrounds have common fears and aspirations. Finally, enough trust is established that we can venture into areas in which variation in cultural values may, in fact, lead to a different interpretation of data or conflicting conclusions. By this time, however, the differences can be accepted or even debated within an accepting relationship. Awareness and perseverance, however, are required.

Karen B. Kreider, *Pennsylvania 1991 Teacher of the Year*
Central High School, Philadelphia, Pennsylvania

EXTRA EFFORT PAYOFF

In teaching a child with a different cultural background, value system, or temperament, a teacher must first acknowledge the student's right to be respected and treated with consideration in the classroom. The teacher must also recognize his or her responsibility as a role model for the other students. Students will learn to accept individual differences only if the teacher demonstrates compassion and understanding toward all students.

When I feel tension between myself and a student, it is usually due to a lack of mutual understanding. If I am confused by a child's behavior or attitude, I attempt to learn more about the student and the student's background. I may examine the child's school records to obtain further information. I will visit with the child and get to know him or her personally. Conversely, I also want the student to acquire a better, personal understanding of me.

Often, I can better understand a student if I meet the student's family and, perhaps, visit the home. In the secure and sterile environment of the school, it is easy to ignore the poverty and broken homes that many students must endure. Furthermore, I may talk to other persons with similar cultural backgrounds or read about the student's culture in order to gain more insight.

Kathy Andrews, *Special Education Teacher*
Lane Center School for Exceptional Children, Houston, Texas

SEX ROLE STEREOTYPES

Students often have stereotypical ideas about occupational and social roles for males and females. What, if anything, do you do in your classroom to help students broaden their conceptions about sex roles?

MODEL BROAD-MINDEDNESS

As a junior high teacher of math, science, health, study skills, and art, I model a broad-minded approach to sex role conceptualization. By modeling attitudes of acceptance and open-mindedness, I encourage students to pursue their personal vision of self-actualization. I encourage and facilitate math/science aspirations for both males and females. I display bulletin boards, posters, and newspaper clippings depicting men and women in a variety of occupations that transcend possible preconceived stereotypes. Although my students graduate from elementary school and move on to high school, I provide individual tutoring as needed to facilitate their progress in advanced math courses. Aspirations and success break the bondage of stereotypes. As a teacher, my charge is to provide aspirations and maximize each student's opportunity for success.

Stephen C. Ellwood IV, *Maine 1991 Teacher of the Year*
St. Francis Elementary School, St. Francis, Maine

IMPROVING CLASSROOM SOCIAL RELATIONS

In your class are students from four main cultural groups, speaking a first language other than English. The groups are becoming cliquish and disrespectful of one another. What would you do to improve social relations in your class?

TEACH HONOR AND RESPECT

I believe that in any class it's important to teach honor and respect for individual differences, whether they be cultural, physically limiting, or academic. Beyond modeling respect for each student or cultural group, I would want to teach the entire class about the gifts of each of the cultures and the gift of diversity. I would create units to study each culture represented, making the learning fun and exciting. I would introduce students to foods, beliefs, music, literature, language, and ways of life from each one. Throughout, I would initiate discussions focusing on how rich and full our world and our lives are because of the diversity that is found in every part of life—cultures, aniamls, plant life, even snowflakes—and how boring our lives would be without that diversity.

Sarah Gustafson, *Florida 1991 Teacher of the Year*
The Okeechobee Center, Okeechobee, Florida

FOSTER COOPERATIVE LEARNING

Educators must create learning environments that enhance the self-worth and mutual respect of each and every child. It is imperative to teach and to demonstrate valuing of different cultures and ideologies. Students working together in teams of cooperative learning models learn to rely upon the collective input and combined skills of their partners for a common goal or purpose. Role playing of hypothetical conflicts, situations, and dilemmas allows students to examine their own values and beliefs. Switching roles provides personal insight on feelings from a different perspective and point of view. Classroom climate can be enhanced by celebrations of multicultural days and events. Develop activities that are rich in cultural tradition and ethnicity. Invite community participation and provide cultural role models for each group.

Bruce D. Fisher, *California 1991 Teacher of the Year*
Fortuna Elementary School, Fortuna, California

6 BEHAVIORAL LEARNING THEORIES

If you were asked to give 10 to 20 different examples of learning, what would your response be? You might begin by listing academic subjects or certain activities you had set about mastering at some point in your life. You might also list different emotional reactions or insights you have had. But unless you've already had a few courses in psychology, it is likely that the examples you chose would cover only a few of the aspects included in the psychological definition of learning. We will spend the next three chapters looking at learning and its applications.

We begin this chapter with a general definition of learning that takes into account the opposing views of different theoretical groups. We will then highlight one of these groups, the behavioral theorists, in this chapter and the other major group, the cognitive theorists, in chapters 7 and 8.

Our discussion in this chapter will focus on four behavioral learning processes: contiguity, classical conditioning, operant conditioning, and observational learning, with the greatest emphasis on the last two processes. After examining the implications of applied behavior analysis for teaching, we look at three recent directions in behavioral approaches to learning—social learning theory, self-management, and cognitive behavior modification.

By the time you have completed this chapter, you should be able to do the following:

- Define learning.
- Compare contiguity, classical conditioning, and operant conditioning, giving examples of each.
- Give examples of four different kinds of consequences that may follow any behavior and the effect each is likely to have on future behavior.
- Select a common academic or behavior problem and design an intervention based on applied behavior analysis.
- Describe situations in which a teacher may wish to use modeling.
- Compare self-management and cognitive behavior modification.
- Discuss potential dangers and ethical issues involved in the use of any behavior change technique.

WHAT DO YOU THINK?

Should students be rewarded with prizes or privileges for doing well in school? Did your parents give you money when your grades were good? Did they praise you or give you special privileges? Think of a time when you worked really hard in a class. Why did you work so hard? What did you hope to gain?

UNDERSTANDING LEARNING

When we hear the word "learning," most of us think of studying and school. We think about subjects or skills we intend to master, such as algebra, Spanish, chemistry, or karate. But learning is not limited to school. We learn every day of our lives. Babies learn to kick their legs to make the mobile above their cribs move, teenagers learn the lyrics to all their favorite songs, middle-aged people like me learn to change their diet and exercise patterns, and every few years we all learn to find a new style of dress attractive while the old styles (the styles we once loved) become odd-looking. This last example shows that learning is not always intentional. We don't try to like new styles and dislike old; it just seems to happen that way. We don't intend to become nervous when we see the dentist fill a syringe with Novocain or when we step onto a stage, yet many of us do. So what is this powerful phenomenon called *learning*?

Learning: A Definition

In the broadest sense, **learning** occurs when experience causes a relatively permanent change in an individual's knowledge or behavior. The change may be deliberate or unintentional, for better or for worse. To qualify as learning, this change must be brought about by experience—by the interaction of a person with his or her environment. Changes due simply to maturation, such as growing taller or turning gray, do not qualify as learning. Temporary changes due to illness, fatigue, or hunger are also excluded from a general definition of learning. A person who has gone without food for two days does not *learn* to be hungry, and a person who is ill does not *learn* to run more slowly. Of course, learning plays a part in how we *respond* to hunger or illness.

Our definition specifies that the changes resulting from learning are in the individual's *knowledge* or *behavior*. While most psychologists would agree with this statement, some tend to emphasize the change in knowledge, others the change in behavior. Cognitive psychologists, who focus on changes in knowledge, believe learning is an *internal* mental activity that cannot be observed directly. As you will see in the next chapter, cognitive psychologists studying learning are interested in unobservable mental activities such as thinking, remembering, creating, and solving problems (Schwartz & Reisberg, 1991).

The psychologists discussed in this chapter, on the other hand, favor **behavioral learning theories.** The behavioral view generally assumes that

Learning Process through which experience causes permanent change in knowledge or behavior.

Behavioral Learning Theories Explanations of learning that focus on external events as the cause of changes in observable behaviors.

time you are in that situation you will tend to do the same thing again" (Hill, 1990, p. 42).

We all learned many basic facts in school through the repetitive pairing of a stimulus and a correct response. Doing spelling drills, reciting states and capitals, and memorizing vocabulary words in foreign-language classes are examples of contiguity—learning by association. Some results of contiguous learning were evident in Elizabeth's class. When she said "South," students associated the words "Carolina" and "Dakota." They had heard these words together many times.

Contiguity also plays a major role in another, more complex learning process best known as classical conditioning.

CLASSICAL CONDITIONING: PAIRING AUTOMATIC RESPONSES WITH NEW STIMULI

Through the process of **classical conditioning,** humans and animals can learn to respond automatically to a stimulus that previously had no effect or a very different effect on them. The learned response may be an emotional reaction, such as fear or pleasure, or a physiological response, such as muscle tension. Classical conditioning was discovered by Ivan Pavlov, a Russian physiologist, in the 1920s.

Pavlov's Dilemma and Discovery

In his laboratory Pavlov was plagued by a series of setbacks. He was trying to answer questions about the digestive system of dogs, including how long it took a dog to secrete digestive juices after it had been fed. But the intervals of time kept changing. At first the dogs salivated in the expected manner while they were being fed. Then the dogs began to salivate as soon as they saw the food. Finally they salivated as soon as they saw the scientist enter the room. Pavlov decided to make a detour from his original experiments and examine these unexpected interferences in his work.

In one of his first experiments, Pavlov began by sounding a tuning fork and recording a dog's response. As expected, there was no salivation. Then he fed the dog. The response was salivation. The food in this case was an **unconditioned stimulus,** since it brought forth an automatic response of salivation. The salivation was an **unconditioned response,** again because it occurred automatically. No prior learning or "conditioning" was needed to establish the natural connection between food and salivation. The sound of the tuning fork, on the other hand, was at this point a neutral stimulus because it brought forth no response.

Using these three elements—the food, the salivation, and the tuning fork—Pavlov demonstrated that a dog could be conditioned to salivate after hearing the tuning fork. He did this by contiguous pairing of the sound with food. At the beginning of the experiment, he sounded the fork and then quickly fed the dog. After Pavlov repeated this several times, the dog began to salivate after hearing the sound but before receiving the food. Now the sound had become a **conditioned stimulus** that could bring

Classical Conditioning Association of automatic responses with new stimuli.

Unconditioned Stimulus (US) Stimulus that automatically produces an emotional or physiological response.

Unconditioned Response (UR) Naturally occurring emotional or physiological response.

Conditioned Stimulus (CS) Stimulus that evokes an emotional or physiological response after conditioning.

FIGURE 6.1   **Pavlov's Experiment** In a classical conditioning experiment, an animal comes to respond to a stimulus that once prompted no response. The process is as follows: Before conditioning, the unconditioned stimulus (meat, in this case) prompts an unconditioned response (salivation), but the conditioned stimulus (a tone) prompts no response. During conditioning the conditioned stimulus (tone) is presented, immediately followed by the unconditioned stimulus (meat). After several such pairings, the conditioned stimulus (tone) prompts the conditioned response (salivation) by itself.

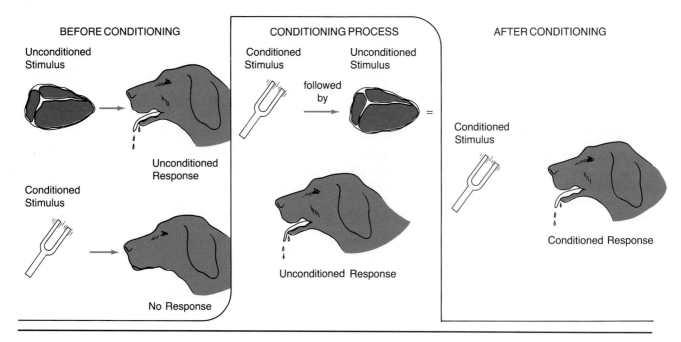

forth salivation by itself. The response of salivating after the tone was now a **conditioned response**. Figure 6.1 is a schematic diagram of what happened in Pavlov's laboratory.

Generalization, Discrimination, and Extinction

Pavlov's work also identified three other processes in classical conditioning: generalization, discrimination, and extinction. After the dogs learned to salivate in response to hearing one particular sound, they would also salivate after hearing other higher or lower tones. This process is called **generalization** because the conditioned response of salivating *generalized* or spread to similar situations. Pavlov could also teach his dogs **discrimination**—different responses to similar stimuli—by making sure that food always followed only one tone, not any others. Learning to discriminate depends on another process, called extinction. **Extinction** occurs when a conditioned stimulus (a particular tone) is presented repeatedly but is not followed by the unconditioned stimulus (food). The conditioned response (salivating) gradually fades away and finally is "extinguished"—it disappears altogether.

Pavlov's findings and those of others who have studied classical conditioning have implications for teachers. It is possible that many of our emotional reactions to various situations are learned in part through

Conditioned Response (CR) Learned response to a previously neutral stimulus.

Generalization Responding in the same way to similar stimuli.

Discrimination Responding differently to similar, but not identical stimuli.

Extinction Gradual disappearance of a learned response.

Guidelines

Using Principles of Classical Conditioning

Associate positive, pleasant events with learning tasks.

Examples

1. Emphasize group competition and cooperation over individual competition. Many students have negative emotional responses to individual competition that may generalize to other learning.
2. Make division drills fun by having students decide how to divide refreshments equally, then letting them eat the results.
3. Make voluntary reading appealing by creating a comfortable reading corner with pillows, colorful displays of books, and reading props such as puppets (see Morrow & Weinstein, 1986, for more ideas).

Help students to risk anxiety-producing situations voluntarily and successfully.

Examples

1. Assign a shy student the responsibility of teaching two other students how to distribute materials for map study.

2. Devise small steps toward a larger goal; for example, give ungraded practice tests daily, and then weekly, to students who "freeze" in test situations.
3. If a student is afraid of speaking before the class, let the student read a report to a small group while seated, then read it while standing, then give the report from notes instead of reading it verbatim. Next move in stages toward having the student give a report to the whole class.

Help students recognize differences and similarities among situations so they can discriminate and generalize appropriately.

Examples

1. Explain that it is appropriate to avoid strangers who offer gifts or rides but safe to accept favors from adults when parents are present.
2. Assure students who are anxious about taking college entrance exams that this test is like all the other achievement tests they have taken.

classical conditioning. For example, Elizabeth's anxious response when she saw her college supervisor might be traced to previous unpleasant experiences with him. Now his mere presence makes her nervous. Or perhaps she was embarrassed during past evaluations of her performance, and now just being observed causes anxiety. Remember that emotions and attitudes as well as facts and ideas are learned in classrooms. This emotional learning can sometimes interfere with academic learning. By the same token, procedures based on classical conditioning can be used to help people learn more adaptive emotional responses, as the Guidelines suggest.

OPERANT CONDITIONING: TRYING NEW RESPONSES

So far we have concentrated on the automatic conditioning of involuntary responses such as salivation and fear. These involuntary actions are often called **respondents.** Clearly, not all human learning is so automatic and unintentional. Learners are consciously involved in their own learning. People actively "operate" on their environment to reach certain goals or to achieve particular effects. These deliberate, goal-directed actions are

Respondents Responses (generally automatic or involuntary) elicited by specific stimuli.

called **operants.** The learning process involved in changing operant behavior is called **operant conditioning.**

Behavior, like *response* or *action,* is simply a word for what a person does in a particular situation. Conceptually, we may think of a behavior as sandwiched between two sets of environmental influences: those that precede it (its **antecedents**) and those that follow it (its **consequences**) (Mahoney & Thoresen, 1974). This relationship can be shown very simply as antecedent → behavior → consequence, or $A \rightarrow B \rightarrow C$. As behavior is ongoing, a given consequence becomes an antecedent for the next *ABC* sequence. For example, when I drive my regular route to work, the antecedent of being at the end of my driveway is followed by the behavior of turning right. The consequence is that I soon reach a stop sign. This consequence then becomes an antecedent for my behavior of turning left, leading to the new consequence of reaching a traffic light, and so on.

Research in operant conditioning shows that behavior can be altered by changes in the antecedents, the consequences, or both. Early work focused on consequences.

The Work of Thorndike and Skinner

Edward Thorndike and B. F. Skinner both played major roles in developing knowledge of operant conditioning. Thorndike's (1913) early work was with cats he placed in problem boxes. To escape from the box and reach food outside, the cats had to pull out a bolt or perform some other task. They had to act on their environment. During the frenzied movements that followed the closing of the box, the cats eventually made the correct movement to escape, usually by accident. After repeating the process several times, the cats learned to make the correct response almost immediately. Thorndike decided, on the basis of these experiments, that one important law of learning was the **law of effect:** Any act that produces a satisfying effect in a given situation will tend to be repeated in that situation. Because pulling out a bolt produced satisfaction (access to food), cats repeated that movement when they found themselves in the box again.

Thorndike thus established the basis for operant conditioning, but the person generally thought to be responsible for developing the concept is B. F. Skinner (1953). Skinner began with the belief that the principles of classical conditioning account for only a small portion of learned behaviors. Classical conditioning describes only how existing behaviors might be paired with new stimuli but does not explain how new behaviors are acquired. Many human behaviors are operants, not respondents. According to Skinner, these operants are affected by what happens after them—their consequences. Thus, he believed, operant learning involves controlling the consequences of behavior.

To study the effects of consequences on behavior under carefully controlled conditions, Skinner designed a special cagelike apparatus. The subjects of Skinner's studies were usually rats or pigeons placed in the cages, which soon came to be called Skinner boxes. A typical Skinner box is a small enclosure containing only a food tray and a lever or bar (for rats) or a disk (for pigeons). The lever or disk is connected to a food

B. F. Skinner's work on operant conditioning changed the way we think about consequences and learning.

Operants Voluntary (and generally goal-directed) behaviors emitted by a person or an animal.

Operant Conditioning Learning in which voluntary behavior is strengthened or weakened by consequences or antecedents.

Antecedents Events that precede an action.

Consequences Events that follow an action.

Law of Effect Law stating that any action producing a satisfying effect will be repeated in similar situations.

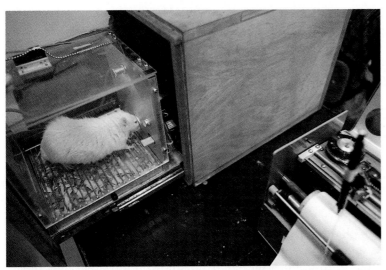

The Skinner box is a controlled environment for observing the effects of positive and negative consequences on behavior. This rat has learned to press the lever to receive food.

hopper. Modifications of this basic box include lights close to the lever or disk and electrified floors used to give mild shocks to the animals.

You can probably imagine how such a box might be used to study the effects of positive consequences (food) or unpleasant consequences (shocks). A hungry pigeon is placed in the box and proceeds to explore it. Since pigeons tend to peck, the animal will eventually get around to pecking the disk. At that point, a small food pellet will drop into the food tray. The hungry animal eats the pellet, moves around the box, and soon pecks the disk again. There is more food, and before long the pigeon is pecking and eating continuously. The next time the pigeon is placed in the box, it will go directly to the disk and begin pecking.

Using this approach, Skinner studied many questions about the effects of consequences on behavior. For example, how is the rate of pecking affected if the pigeons do not get food every time they peck? How long will the pigeons continue to peck if no food follows at all? How does the negative effect of a shock compare with the positive effect of food?

Controlling the Consequences

According to the behavioral view, because the consequences brought about by a particular behavior can be pleasant, unpleasant, or neutral for the person or animal involved, consequences determine to a great extent whether a person will repeat the behavior. The type and timing of consequences, in other words, can strengthen or weaken behaviors. We will look first at consequences that strengthen behavior.

Reinforcement. While reinforcement is commonly understood to mean "reward," this term has a particular meaning in psychology. A **reinforcer** is any *consequence* that strengthens the behavior it follows.

Reinforcer Any event that follows a behavior and increases the chances that the behavior will occur again.

That is, behaviors followed by reinforcers are likely to be repeated in the future. **Reinforcement** is the *process* of using reinforcers to strengthen behavior. Whenever you see a behavior persisting or increasing over time, you can assume the effects of that behavior are reinforcing for the individual involved. The reinforcement process can be diagrammed as follows:

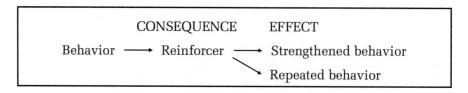

Individuals vary greatly in their perceptions of events as pleasant or desirable. Whether the consequences of any action are reinforcing probably depends on the individual's perception of the event and the meaning it holds for her or him. For example, students who repeatedly get themselves sent to the principal's office for misbehavior may be indicating that the consequence is reinforcing for them, even if it hardly seems desirable to you. *Reinforcers are identified by their effect of strengthening behavior.* Another way of defining reinforcer is to say that a reinforcer is anything a person will work to attain.

There are two types of reinforcement. The first, called **positive reinforcement,** occurs when a (usually pleasant) stimulus is *presented* following a particular behavior. Examples include the money or praise that students may receive when they bring home *As* on report cards or the cheers and laughter of fellow students following the class clown's latest remark. Notice that positive reinforcement can occur even when the behavior being reinforced (silly remarks) is not "positive" from the teacher's point of view.

Positive reinforcement of inappropriate behaviors occurs unintentionally in many classrooms. Teachers help maintain problem behaviors by inadvertently reinforcing them. For example, Elizabeth unintentionally reinforced problem behavior in her class by laughing the first time the boy answered, "Clark Gable."

Whereas positive reinforcement involves the *presentation* of a desired stimulus, the second kind of reinforcement, called **negative reinforcement,** involves the *removal* of (or *escape* from) an aversive (unpleasant) stimulus. A stimulus is aversive if you would work to escape or avoid it. If a particular action causes an aversive stimulus to go away or allows you to escape or avoid something unpleasant, you are likely to repeat the action when you are faced with a similar situation. Consider the students who are repeatedly sent to the principal's office. Their rule breaking is probably being reinforced in some way because they continue to do it. The misbehavior may be getting them out of "bad" situations such as a test or a class that causes anxiety. If so, the misbehavior is being maintained through negative reinforcement.

Negative reinforcement operates in many everyday situations. One example is a policy allowing cars with more than one passenger to bypass the toll at the Oakland Bay Bridge in San Francisco. Here the behavior of

Reinforcement Use of consequences to strengthen behavior.

Positive Reinforcement Strengthening behavior by presenting a desired stimulus after the behavior.

Negative Reinforcement Strengthening behavior by removing an aversive stimulus.

carpooling is strengthened, so the process is reinforcement. The reinforcing consequence in this case is the *avoidance of an aversive situation*—waiting in line and having to pay—so the reinforcement is negative (Baldwin & Baldwin, 1986). This example shows that the "negative" in negative reinforcement does not imply that the behavior being reinforced is necessarily negative. The meaning is closer to that of "negative" numbers—something is subtracted. Associate positive and negative reinforcement with *adding* or *subtracting* something following a behavior.

Punishment. Negative reinforcement is often confused with punishment. The process of reinforcement (positive or negative) always involves strengthening behavior. **Punishment,** on the other hand, involves decreasing or suppressing behavior. A behavior followed by a "punisher" is *less* likely to be repeated in similar situations in the future. Again, it is the effect that defines a consequence as punishment, and different people have different perceptions of what is punishing. One student may find suspension from school punishing while another student wouldn't mind at all. The process of punishment is diagrammed as follows:

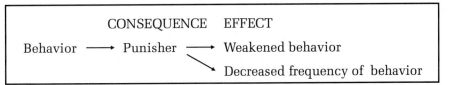

Like reinforcement, punishment may take one of two forms. The first type has been called Type I punishment, but this name isn't very informative, so I use the term **presentation punishment.** It occurs when the *appearance* of a stimulus following the behavior suppresses or decreases the behavior. When teachers assign demerits, extra work, running laps, and so on, they are using presentation punishment. The other type of punishment (Type II punishment) I call **removal punishment,** because it involves removing a stimulus. When teachers or parents take away privileges after a young person has behaved inappropriately, they are applying removal punishment. With both types, the effect is to decrease the behavior that led to the punishment. Figure 6.2 on page 206 summarizes the processes of reinforcement and punishment we have just discussed.

Reinforcement Schedules

When people are learning a new behavior, they will learn it faster if they are reinforced for every correct response. This is a **continuous reinforcement schedule.** Then, when the new behavior has been mastered, they will maintain it best if they are reinforced intermittently rather than every time. An **intermittent reinforcement schedule** helps students to maintain skills without expecting constant reinforcement.

There are two basic types of intermittent reinforcement schedules. One—called an interval schedule—is based on the amount of time that passes between reinforcers. The other—a ratio schedule—is based on the number of responses learners give between reinforcers. Interval and ratio

Punishment Process that weakens or suppresses behavior.

Presentation Punishment Decreasing the chances that a behavior will occur again by presenting an aversive stimulus following the behavior; also called Type I punishment.

Removal Punishment Decreasing the chances that a behavior will occur again by removing a pleasant stimulus following the behavior; also called Type II punishment.

Continuous Reinforcement Schedule Presenting a reinforcer after every appropriate response.

Intermittent Reinforcement Schedule Presenting a reinforcer after some but not all responses.

FIGURE 6.2   **Kinds of Reinforcement and Punishment**   Negative reinforcement and punishment are often confused. It may help you to remember that negative reinforcement is always associated with increases in behavior and punishment always involves decreasing or suppressing behavior.

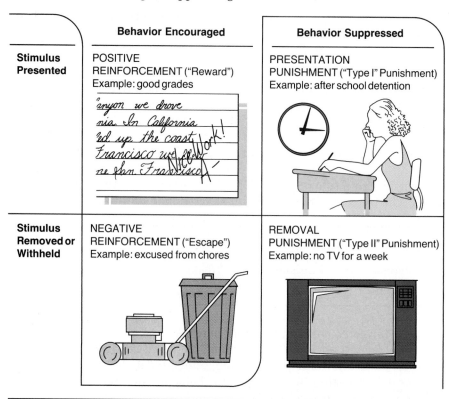

schedules may be either fixed (predictable) or variable (unpredictable). Table 6.1 summarizes the five possible reinforcement schedules (the continuous schedule and the four kinds of intermittent schedules).

Fixed-Interval Schedules. A **fixed-interval reinforcement schedule** (every 5 minutes, for example) is predictable. A reinforcer will always be given for the first correct response that occurs after a certain time period has lapsed. Because the reinforcement is so predictable, the individual responds more rapidly as the expected time for reinforcement approaches, and then pauses briefly right after the reinforcer is given. Assume, for example, that students know the teacher will stop by the library every 15 minutes and note who is working. As the time approaches, they may begin to focus on their reading so the teacher will not catch them talking. After the teacher completes a visit, they may relax and take a break, knowing that their chances for reinforcement (or punishment) will not come again for several minutes. If the teacher missed a few 15-minute visits, the students might stop reading altogether.

Variable-Interval Schedules. Under a **variable-interval reinforcement schedule,** however, the pattern of responding is quite different. If

Fixed-Interval Reinforcement Schedule Reinforcing a behavior after a predictable, fixed amount of time.

Variable-Interval Reinforcement Schedule Reinforcing a behavior after varying amounts of time.

Schedule	Definition	Example	Response Pattern	Reaction When Reinforcement Stops
Continuous	Reinforcement after every response	Turning on the television	Rapid learning of response	Very little persistence; rapid disappearance of response
Fixed-interval	Reinforcement after a set period of time	Weekly quiz	Response rate increases as time for reinforcement approaches, then drops after reinforcement	Little persistence; rapid drop in response rate when time for reinforcement passes and no reinforcer appears
Variable-interval	Reinforcement after varying lengths of time	Pop quizzes	Slow, steady rate of responding; very little pause after reinforcement	Greater persistence; slow decline in response rate
Fixed-ratio	Reinforcement after a set number of responses	Piece work Bake sale	Rapid response rate; pause after reinforcement	Little persistence; rapid drop in response rate when expected number of responses are given and no reinforcer appears
Variable-ratio	Reinforcement after a varying number of responses	Slot machines	Very high response rate; little pause after reinforcement	Greatest persistence; response rate stays high and gradually drops off

the teacher described above stopped by the library at highly unpredictable intervals, students would work more steadily and pause less after each teacher visit. A teacher who wanted some serious studying to take place would be happier with a variable-interval schedule. Also, if the teacher missed several visits, students might persist in reading, not noticing the change. Unpredictable reinforcement encourages persistence.

Fixed-Ratio Schedules. An everyday example of a **fixed-ratio reinforcement schedule** is piece work. If you take a summer job processing credit card applications for a local mall and you are paid a certain amount for every 50 completed applications (another fixed-ratio schedule), you will likely stop working temporarily after reaching your quota. You might even be tempted to take the rest of the day off. Also, if your boss occasionally neglects to pay you after you complete the specified number, you may not persist at the task.

Variable-Ratio Schedules. If your job involved contacting potential customers and your pay was based on the number of people you convinced to complete a credit card application, however, you would be on a

Fixed-Ratio Reinforcement Schedule Reinforcing a behavior after a fixed number of responses.

variable-ratio reinforcement schedule. That is, your pay (reinforcer) would depend on how many people you approached; but this number would vary. One day you might have to talk to 48 people to get 10 applications; the next day you might get 10 applications after talking to only 17. Under a variable-ratio schedule, you are more likely to work quickly and steadily. And because the chances for reinforcement are unpredictable, you are likely to keep working persistently, even if you occasionally encounter a long string of refusals.

So the reinforcement schedule influences how persistently we will respond when reinforcement is withheld. What happens when reinforcement is completely withdrawn?

Extinction. In classical conditioning, we saw that the conditioned response was extinguished (stopped) when the conditioned stimulus appeared but the unconditioned stimulus did not follow (tone but no food). In operant conditioning, a person or an animal will not persist in a certain behavior if the usual reinforcer does not follow. The behavior will eventually be extinguished (stop). For example, if you go for a week without selling even one magazine door-to-door, you may give up. Removal of reinforcement altogether leads to extinction. The process may take a while, however, as you know if you have tried to extinguish a child's tantrums by withholding your attention. Often the child wins and instead of extinction, intermittent reinforcement occurs. This, of course, may encourage even more persistent tantrums in the future.

Summarizing the Effects of Reinforcement Schedules. Persistence in performance depends on predictability. Continuous reinforcement and both kinds of fixed reinforcement (ratio and interval) are quite predictable. We come to expect reinforcement at certain points and generally are quick to give up when the reinforcement does not meet our expectations. To encourage persistence of response, variable schedules are most appropriate. In fact, if the schedule is gradually changed until it becomes very "lean"—meaning that reinforcement occurs only after many responses or a long time interval—then people can learn to work for extended periods without any reinforcement at all. Just watch gamblers playing slot machines to see how powerful a lean reinforcement schedule can be.

Speed of performance depends on control. If reinforcement is based on the number of responses you give, then you have more control over the reinforcement: the faster you accumulate the correct number of responses, the faster the reinforcement will come. Therefore, people work faster on ratio than on interval schedules. A teacher who says, "As soon as you complete these ten problems correctly, you may go to the student lounge," can expect higher rates of performance than a teacher who says, "Work on these ten problems for the next 20 minutes. Then I will check your papers and those with ten correct may go to the lounge."

Variable-Ratio Reinforcement Schedule Reinforcing a behavior after varying numbers of responses.

Controlling the Antecedents

In operant conditioning, antecedents—the events preceding behaviors—provide information about which behaviors will lead to positive consequences and which to negative. Skinner's pigeons learned to peck for food when a light was on, but not to bother when the light was off, because no food followed pecking when the light was off. In other words, they learned to use the antecedent light as a cue to **discriminate** the likely consequence of pecking. The pigeons' pecking was under *stimulus control,* controlled by the discriminative stimulus of the light. You can see that this idea is related to discrimination in classical conditioning, but here we are talking about voluntary behaviors like pecking, not reflexes like salivating.

We all learn to discriminate—to read situations. When should you ask to borrow your roommate's car: after a major disagreement or after you both have had a great time at a party? The antecedent cue of a school principal standing in the hall helps students discriminate the probable consequences of running or attempting to break into a locker. We often respond to such antecedent cues without fully realizing that they are influencing our behavior. But teachers can use cues deliberately in the classroom.

Cueing. By definition, **cueing** is the act of providing an antecedent stimulus just before a particular behavior is to take place. Cueing is particularly useful in setting the stage for behaviors that must occur at a specific time but are easily forgotten. In working with young people, teachers often find themselves correcting behaviors after the fact. For example, they may ask students, "When are you going to start remembering to . . . ?" Such reminders often lead to irritation. The mistake is already made, and the young person is left with only two choices, to promise to try harder or to say, "Why don't you leave me alone?" Neither response is very satisfying. Presenting a nonjudgmental cue can help prevent these negative confrontations. When a student performs the appropriate behavior after a cue, the teacher can reinforce the student's accomplishment instead of punishing the student's failure.

Prompting. Sometimes students need help in learning to respond to a cue in an appropriate way so the cue becomes a discriminative stimulus. One approach is to provide an additional cue, called a **prompt,** following the first cue. There are two principles for using a cue and a prompt to teach a new behavior (Becker, Engelmann, & Thomas, 1975). First, make sure the environmental stimulus that you want to become a cue occurs immediately before the prompt you are using, so students will learn to respond to the cue and not rely only on the prompt. Second, fade the prompt as soon as possible so students do not become dependent on it.

An example of cueing and prompting is providing students with a checklist or reminder sheet. Figure 6.3 on page 210 is a checklist for the steps in peer tutoring. Working in pairs is the cue; the checklist is the prompt. As students learn the procedures, the teacher may stop using the checklist, but may remind the students of the steps. When no written or oral prompts are necessary, the students have learned to respond appropriately to the environmental cue of working in pairs—they have learned how to behave in tutoring situations. But the teacher should continue to monitor the process, recognize good work, and correct mistakes.

Discriminate Make a different voluntary response to similar stimuli.

Cueing Providing a stimulus that "sets up" a desired behavior.

Prompt A reminder that follows a cue to make sure the person reacts to the cue.

FIGURE 6.3   Written Prompts: A Peer-Tutoring Checklist By using this checklist, students are reminded how to be effective tutors. As they become more proficient, the checklist may be less necessary.

Remember to...

_____ 1. Have the lesson ready.

_____ 2. Talk clearly.

_____ 3. Be friendly.

_____ 4. Tell the student when he is right.

_____ 5. Correct mistakes. STOP! Give the right answer. Have the student do it.

_____ 6. Praise good work!

_____ 7. Make the lesson fun.

_____ 8. Do not give TOO MUCH help.

_____ 9. Fill out the daily sheet.

_____ 10. Can you add a suggestion?

Source: Figure from *Achieving educational excellence using behavioral strategies* by Beth Sulzer-Azaroff and G. Roy Mayer, copyright © 1986 by Holt, Rinehart and Winston, Inc.; reprinted by permission of the publisher.

APPLIED BEHAVIOR ANALYSIS

Applied behavior analysis is the application of behavioral learning principles to change behavior. The method is sometimes called **behavior modification,** but this term has negative connotations for many people and is often misunderstood (Alberto & Troutman, 1990; Kaplan, 1991).

Ideally, applied behavior analysis requires clear specification of the behavior to be changed, careful measurement of the behavior, analysis of the reinforcers that might be maintaining inappropriate or undesirable behaviors, interventions based on behavioral principles to change the behavior, and careful measurement of changes. In research on applied behavior analysis, an ABAB design is common. That is, researchers take a baseline measurement of the behavior (A), then apply the intervention (B), then stop the intervention to see if the behavior goes back to the baseline level (A), and then reintroduce the intervention (B).

In classrooms, teachers usually cannot follow all the ABAB steps, but they can do the following:

Applied Behavior Analysis
The application of behavioral learning principles to understand and change behavior.

Behavior Modification
Systematic application of antecedents and consequences to change behavior.

1. Clearly specify the behavior to be changed and note the current level. For example, if a student is "careless," does this mean 2, 3, 4, or more computation errors for every 10 problems?
2. Plan a specific intervention using antecedents, consequences, or both. For example, offer the student 1 extra minute of computer time for every problem completed with no errors.
3. Keep track of the results, and modify the plan if necessary.

Let's consider some specific methods for accomplishing step 2—the intervention.

Methods for Encouraging Behaviors

As we discussed earlier, to encourage behavior is to reinforce it. There are a number of specific ways to use positive and negative reinforcement to encourage existing behaviors or teach new ones. These include praise, the Premack principle, shaping, and positive practice.

Reinforcing with Teacher Attention. Based on early work such as that of Madsen, Becker, and Thomas (1968) demonstrating that teachers can improve student behavior by praising students who are following rules and ignoring rule-breakers, many psychologists advised teachers to "accentuate the positive"—liberally praise students for good behavior while ignoring mistakes and misbehavior. This praise-and-ignore approach can be helpful, but we should not expect it to solve all management problems. Several studies have shown that disruptive behaviors persist when teachers use positive consequences (mostly praise) as their only classroom management strategy (Pfiffner, Rosen, & O'Leary, 1985; Rosen, O'Leary, Joyce, Conway, & Pfiffner, 1984).

The praise-and-ignore approach should be considered a method for dealing with minor misbehaviors or an option to accompany other strategies. There is a second consideration in using praise. The positive results found in research occur when teachers carefully and systematically praise their students. Unfortunately, praise is not always given appropriately and effectively. Simply "handing out compliments" will not improve behavior. To be effective, praise must (1) be contingent on the behavior to be reinforced, (2) specify clearly the behavior being reinforced, and (3) be believable (O'Leary & O'Leary, 1977). In other words, the praise should be sincere recognition of a well-defined behavior, so students understand what they did to warrant the recognition. Teachers who have not received special training often violate these conditions (Brophy, 1981). Ideas for using praise effectively, based on Brophy's extensive review of the subject, are presented in the Guidelines on page 210.

Some psychologists have suggested that teachers' use of praise tends to focus students on learning to win approval rather than on learning for its own sake. Perhaps the best advice is to be aware of the potential dangers of the overuse or misuse of praise and to navigate accordingly.

Selecting Reinforcers: The Premack Principle. In most classrooms, there are many readily available reinforcers other than teacher attention,

This student looks a bit tentative about reaching into the hamster's cage. If students fear particular situations but you are sure they are not in danger, encourage them to take small steps to approach the things they fear.

Guidelines

Using Praise Appropriately

Be clear and systematic in giving praise.

Examples

1. Make sure praise is tied directly to appropriate behavior.
2. Make sure the student understands the specific action or accomplishment that is being praised. Say, "You returned this poster on time and in good condition." not, "You were very responsible."

Recognize genuine accomplishments.

Examples

1. Reward the attainment of specified goals, not just participation.
2. Do not reward uninvolved students just for being quiet and not disrupting the class.
3. Tie praise to students' improving competence or to the value of their accomplishment. Say, "I noticed that you double-checked all your problems. Your score reflects your careful work."

Set standards for praise based on individual abilities and limitations.

Examples

1. Praise progress or accomplishment in relation to the individual student's past efforts.

2. Focus the student's attention on his or her own progress, not on comparisons with others.

Attribute the student's success to effort and ability, so the student will gain confidence that success is possible again.

Examples

1. Don't imply that the success may be based on luck, extra help, or easy material.
2. Ask students to describe the problems they encountered and how they solved them.

Make praise really reinforcing.

Examples

1. Avoid singling out students for praise in an attempt to influence the rest of the class. This tactic often backfires, since students know what's really going on. In addition, you risk embarrassing the student.
2. Don't give undeserved praise to students simply to balance failures. It is seldom consoling and calls attention to the student's inability to earn genuine recognition.

Premack Principle
Principle stating that a more-preferred activity can serve as reinforcer for a less-preferred activity.

such as the chance to talk to other students or feed the class animals. But teachers tend to offer these rewards in a rather haphazard way. Just as with praise, by making privileges and rewards directly contingent upon learning and positive behavior, the teacher may greatly increase both learning and desired behavior.

A helpful guide for choosing the most effective reinforcers is the **Premack principle,** named for David Premack (1965). According to the Premack principle, a high-frequency behavior (a preferred activity) can be an effective reinforcer for a low-frequency behavior (a less-preferred activity). This is sometimes referred to as "Grandma's rule": First do what I want you to do, then you may do what you want to do. Elizabeth used this principle in her class when she told them they could work together on their Civil War news program after they quietly completed the first section of the worksheet on their own.

If students didn't have to study, what would they do? The answers to this question may suggest many possible reinforcers. For most students, talking, moving around the room, sitting near a friend, being exempt from assignments or tests, reading magazines, or playing games are preferred activities. The best way to determine appropriate reinforcers for your students may be to watch what they do in their free time. If you find yourself saying to a student, "Stop doing that and pay attention!" or "Please put that away until the end of class!" you have probably found a perfect reinforcer for the student.

For the Premack principle to be effective, the low-frequency (less-preferred) behavior must happen first. In the following dialogue, notice how the teacher loses a perfect opportunity to use the Premack principle:

"Hey, wait a minute! You're cleaning erasers as a punishment? I'm cleaning erasers as a reward!"

© 1991 Tony Saltzman.

Students: Oh, no! Do we have to diagram sentences again today? The other classes got to discuss the film we saw in the auditorium this morning.

Teacher: But the other classes finished the lesson on sentences yesterday. We're almost finished too. If we don't finish the lesson, I'm afraid you'll forget the rules we reviewed yesterday.

Students: Why don't we finish the sentences at the end of the period and talk about the film now?

Teacher: Okay, if you promise to complete the sentences later.

Discussing the film could have served as a reinforcer for completing the lesson. As it is, the class may well spend the entire period discussing the film. Just as the discussion becomes fascinating, the teacher will have to end it and insist that the class return to diagramming sentences.

Some teachers use questionnaires like the one in Table 6.2 to identify effective reinforcers for their students. Remember, what works for one student may not be right for another. And students can get "too much of a good thing"—reinforcers can lose their potency if they are overused.

TABLE 6.2 What Do You Like? Reinforcement Ideas from Students

Name _____ Grade _____ Date _____

Please answer all the questions as completely as you can.

1. The school subjects I like best are:
2. Three things I like most to do in school are:
3. If I had 30 minutes' free time at school each day to do what I really liked, it would be:
4. My two favorite snacks are:
5. At recess I like most to (three things):
6. If I had $1 to spend on anything, I would buy:
7. Three jobs I would enjoy in the class are:
8. The two people I most like to work with in school are:
9. At home I really enjoy (three things):

Source: Adapted from G. Blackham & A. Silberman (1979), *Modification of child and adolescent behavior* (3rd ed.). Belmont, CA: Wadsworth, pp. 281–283. © 1979 by Wadsworth Publishing Co., Inc. Reprinted by permission of publisher.

Shaping. What happens when students continually fail to gain reinforcement because they simply cannot perform a skill or behavior in the first place? Consider these examples:

A fourth-grade student looks at the results of the latest mathematics test. "No credit on almost half of the problems again because I made one dumb mistake in each problem. I hate math!"

A 10th-grade student tries each day to find some excuse for avoiding the softball game in gym class. The student cannot catch a ball and now refuses to try.

In both situations the students are receiving no reinforcement for their work because the end product of their efforts is not good enough. A safe prediction is that the students will soon learn to hate the class, the subject, and perhaps the teacher and school in general. One way to prevent this problem is the strategy of **shaping,** also called successive approximations. Shaping involves reinforcing progress instead of waiting for perfection. In order to use shaping, the teacher must break down the final complex behavior the student is expected to master into a number of small steps. Krumboltz and Krumboltz (1972) have described the following four methods of shaping.

1. **Reinforce each subskill.** A research paper, for example, can be broken down into outlining, using indexes and tables of contents, summarizing information from several sources, drawing conclusions, writing footnotes, and so on.

2. **Reinforce improvements in accuracy.** A French teacher, for example, might first reinforce a vague approximation of the correct pronunciation of *monsieur,* then continue to raise standards gradually until pronunciation is close to that of a native.

3. **Reinforce longer and longer periods of performance.** Students often can perform in a desirable fashion, but only for a few minutes at a time. As you learned in the section on reinforcement schedules, students can be encouraged to persist at a task if they are reinforced at longer and longer intervals.

4. **Reinforce longer and longer periods of participation.** Students are sometimes reluctant to participate because they have been embarrassed in the past. In this case, a teacher could begin by reinforcing, in a matter-of-fact way, even the smallest contributions of a student who seldom participates in class.

Shaping Reinforcing each small step of progress toward a desired goal or behavior.

Positive Practice Practicing correct responses immediately after errors.

Many behaviors can be improved through shaping, especially skills that involve persistence, endurance, increased accuracy, greater speed, or extensive practice to master. Because shaping is a time-consuming process, however, it should not be used if success can be attained through simpler methods like cueing.

Positive Practice. A strategy for helping students replace one behavior with another is **positive practice.** This approach is especially appropriate for dealing with academic errors. When students make a mistake, they must correct it as soon as possible and practice the correct response (Gibbs & Luyben, 1985; Kazdin, 1984). The same principle could be applied when students break classroom rules. Instead of being punished, the student might be required to practice the correct alternative action.

Coping with Undesirable Behavior

No matter how successful you are at accentuating the positive, there are times when you must cope with undesirable behavior, either because other methods do not seem sufficient or because the behavior itself is dangerous or calls for direct action. For this purpose, negative reinforcement, satiation, and punishment all offer possible solutions.

Negative Reinforcement. Recall the basic principle of negative reinforcement: If an action stops or avoids something unpleasant, then the action is likely to occur again in similar situations. An example is the use of seat-belt buzzers in cars. Fastening the seat belt stops the buzzer. After fastening the seat belt for several weeks, you may continue to do so (for a while at least) even if your buzzer breaks down. Negative reinforcement was operating in Elizabeth's classroom. When she gave in to the moans and complaints of her class and canceled the test, her behavior was being negatively reinforced. She escaped the unpleasant student comments by changing her assignment.

Negative reinforcement may also be used to enhance learning. To do this, you place students in mildly unpleasant situations so they can "escape" when their behavior improves. Consider these examples:

Teacher to a third-grade class: "When the supplies are put back in the cabinet and each of you is sitting quietly, we will go outside. Until then, we will miss our recess."

High school teacher to a student who seldom finishes in-class assignments: "As soon as you complete the assignment, you may join the class in the auditorium. But until you finish, you must work in the study hall."

You may wonder why these examples are not considered punishment. Surely staying in during recess or not accompanying the class to a special program is punishing. But the focus in each case is on strengthening specific behaviors (putting away supplies or finishing assignments). The teacher strengthens (reinforces) the behaviors by removing something aversive as soon as the desired behaviors occur. Since the consequence involves removing or "subtracting" a stimulus, the reinforcement is negative.

Negative reinforcement also gives students a chance to exercise control. Missing recess and staying behind in study hall are unpleasant situations, but in each case the students retain control. As soon as they perform the appropriate behavior, the unpleasant situation ends. In contrast, punishment occurs after the fact, and a student cannot so easily control or terminate it.

Guidelines

Using Positive Reinforcement

Make sure you recognize positive behavior in ways that students value.

Examples

1. When presenting class rules, set up positive consequences for following rules as well as negative consequences for breaking rules.
2. Recognize honest admissions of mistakes by giving a second chance: "Because you admitted that you copied your paper from a book, I'm giving you a chance to rewrite it."
3. Offer desired rewards for academic efforts, such as extra recess time, exemptions from homework or tests, extra credit on major projects.

When students are tackling new material or trying new skills, give plenty of reinforcement.

Examples

1. Find and comment on something right in every student's first life drawing.
2. Reinforce students for encouraging each other. "French pronunciation is difficult and awkward at first. Let's help each other by eliminating all giggles when someone is brave enough to attempt a new word."

After new behaviors are established, give reinforcement on an unpredictable schedule to encourage persistence.

Examples

1. Offer surprise rewards for good participation in class.
2. Start classes with a short, written extra-credit question. Students don't have to answer, but a good answer will add points to their total for the semester.
3. Make sure the good students get compliments for their work from time to time. Don't take them for granted.

Use cueing to help establish new behaviors.

Examples

1. Put up humorous signs in the classroom to remind students of rules.
2. At the beginning of the year, as students enter class, call their attention to a list on the board of the materials they should have with them when they come to class.

Make sure all students, even those who often cause problems, receive some praise, privileges, or other rewards when they do something well.

Examples

1. Review your class list occasionally to make sure all students are receiving some reinforcement.
2. Set standards for reinforcement so that all students will have a chance to be rewarded.

Establish a variety of reinforcers.

Examples

1. Let students suggest their own reinforcers or choose from a "menu" of reinforcers with "weekly specials."
2. Talk to other teachers or parents about ideas for reinforcers.

Use the Premack principle to identify effective reinforcers.

Examples

1. Watch what students do with their free time.
2. Notice which students like to work together. The chance to work with friends is often a good reinforcer.

Krumboltz and Krumboltz (1972) offer several rules for negative reinforcement: (1) Describe the desired change in a positive way. (2) Don't bluff. Make sure you can enforce your unpleasant situation. (3) Follow through despite complaints. (4) Insist on action, not promises. If the unpleasant situation terminates when students promise to be better next time, you have reinforced making promises, not making changes.

Satiation. Another way to stop problem behavior is to insist that students continue the behavior until they are tired of doing it. This

Guidelines

Using Punishment

Try to structure the situation so you can use negative reinforcement rather than punishment.

Examples

1. Allow students to escape unpleasant situations (completing additional workbook assignments, weekly tests of math facts) when they reach a level of competence.
2. Insist on actions, not promises. Don't let students convince you to change terms of the agreement.

Be consistent in your application of punishment.

Examples

1. Avoid inadvertently reinforcing the behavior you are trying to punish. Keep confrontations private, so that students don't become heroes for standing up to the teacher in a public showdown.
2. Let students know in advance the consequences of breaking the rules by posting major class rules for younger students or outlining rules and consequences in a course syllabus for older students.
3. Tell students they will receive only one warning before punishment is given. Give the warning in a calm way, then follow through.
4. Make punishment as unavoidable and immediate as is reasonably possible.

Focus on the students' actions, not on the students' personal qualities.

Examples

1. Reprimand in a calm but firm voice.
2. Avoid vindictive or sarcastic words or tones of voice. You might hear your own angry words later when students imitate your sarcasm.
3. Stress the need to end the problem behavior instead of expressing any dislike you might feel for the student.

Adapt the punishment to the infraction.

Examples

1. Ignore minor misbehaviors that do not disrupt the class, or stop these misbehaviors with a disapproving glance or a move toward the student.
2. Don't use homework as a punishment for misbehaviors like talking in class.
3. When a student misbehaves to gain peer acceptance, removal from the group of friends can be effective, since this is really time out from a reinforcing situation.
4. If the problem behaviors continue, analyze the situation and try a new approach. Your punishment may not be very punishing, or you may be inadvertently reinforcing the misbehavior.

procedure, called **satiation,** should be applied with care. Forcing students to continue some behaviors may be physically or emotionally harmful or even dangerous.

An example of an appropriate use of satiation is related by Krumboltz and Krumboltz (1972). In the middle of a ninth-grade algebra class, the teacher suddenly noticed four students making all sorts of unusual motions. In response to persistent teacher questioning, the students finally admitted they were bouncing imaginary balls. The teacher pretended to greet this idea with enthusiasm and suggested the whole class do it. At first, there was a great deal of laughing and joking. After a minute this stopped, and one student even quit. The teacher, however, insisted that all the students continue. After 5 minutes and a number of exhausted sighs, the teacher allowed the students to stop. No one bounced an imaginary ball in that class again.

Teachers also may allow students to continue some action until they stop by themselves, if the behavior is not interfering with the rest of the class. A teacher can do this by simply ignoring the behavior. Remember that responding to an ignorable behavior may actually reinforce it.

Satiation Requiring a person to repeat a problem behavior past the point of interest or motivation.

Should Punishment Be Used in Schools?

Most educators and psychologists agree, in theory at least, that punishment may be necessary when negative behaviors are extreme or dangerous. But what about using punishment for more common discipline problems? Is this good practice?

Point: Punishment is not good practice.

Critics stress that punishment can have several negative side effects. Most of us have strong emotional reactions to being punished. The people or situations involved in the punishment tend to become associated with these negative feelings. And we all tend to avoid people and situations associated with pain or unpleasantness. Students may learn to fear or hate teachers, subjects, and events that have been punishing, especially if the students have received little reinforcement in those situations to offset the punishment. The students may also become hardened to the punishment, so that it is no longer effective. In addi-

tion, changes in behavior may be temporary. The students may behave appropriately only when the teacher is looking. But from the teacher's perspective the punishment seems to "work," because the behavior stops, at least for the moment. The teacher may be "reinforced" for using punishment and thus may continue to apply this short-term solution. If the punishing consequences of failing are too severe, students may learn to lie, cry, or cheat to avoid failure. If the consequences of attending school are too unpleasant, students may cut class or drop out altogether (Jenson, Sloane, & Young, 1988; Kaplan, 1991; Martin & Pear, 1992).

Time out and corporal punishment are two procedures that cause great controversy. Critics say that these methods are cruel and unnecessary. Time out deprives students of the chance to learn by removing them from the classroom. Using corporal punishment puts teachers in the awkward

In using satiation, a teacher must take care not to give in before the students do. It is also important that the repeated behavior be the one you are trying to end. If the algebra teacher above had insisted that the students write, "I will never bounce imaginary balls in class again" 500 times, the students would have become satiated with writing rather than with bouncing balls.

Reprimands. In an issue of the *Junction Journal,* my daughter's elementary-school newspaper, I read the following lines in a story called "Why I Like School," written by a fourth grader: "I also like my teacher. She helps me understand and learn. She is nice to everyone. . . . I like it when she gets mad at somebody, but she doesn't yell at them in front of the class, but speaks to them privately."

A study by Dan O'Leary and his associates examined the effectiveness of soft, private **reprimands** versus loud, public reprimands in decreasing disruptive behavior (O'Leary, Kaufman, Kass, & Drabman, 1970). Reprimanding a problem student quietly so that only the student can hear seems to be much more effective. When the teacher in the study spoke to offenders loudly enough for the entire class to hear, the disruptions increased or continued at a constant level. Some students enjoy public recognition for misbehavior. Perhaps public condemnation encourages a student to save face by having the last word. At any rate, the extra time and effort required to use private reprimands seems to be a good investment in making lasting improvements. If reprimands are not used too

Reprimands Criticisms for misbehavior; rebukes.

position of hurting students while claiming that it is wrong for the students to hurt others. An adult's response to the misbehavior of a student can become a model for dealing with problems. If you listen to the conversations or watch the play of children, you often see conflicts solved through aggression. Children may learn to punish others because they were routinely punished themselves (Martin & Pear,1992).

Counterpoint: Punishment is sometimes necessary.

Despite the potentially harmful side effects of negative control, supporters believe that punishment may sometimes be necessary. If a student consistently misbehaves, rarely acts in any positive way that can be reinforced, and shows no desire to change, the problem behavior must be stopped or at least reduced in frequency so that other responses can occur and be reinforced. And remember, we saw earlier that disruptive behav-iors may persist when teachers use positive consequences as their only classroom management strategies (Pfiffner, Rosen, & O'Leary, 1985). In addition, actions that are genuinely dangerous to the student, to others, or to school property must also be punished. Garry Martin and Joseph Pear (1992) make this argument:

> Although [several] authors provide many good examples of alternatives that should be tried before resorting to aversive methods, it is not clear that the methods they propose can effectively replace aversive methods in all cases. What is clear is that the decision to use or not use aversive methods in a particular case requires considerable professional training and expertise and should not be made by unqualified individuals. (p. 175)

Clearly, effective punishment requires hard work and careful management.

often, and if the classroom is generally a positive, warm environment, then students usually respond quickly (Van Houten & Doleys, 1983).

Response Cost. The concept of **response cost** is familiar to anyone who has ever paid a fine. For certain infractions of the rules, people must lose some reinforcer (money, time, privileges, pleasures). In a class, the concept of response cost may be applied in a number of ways. The first time a student breaks a class rule, the teacher gives a warning. The second time, the teacher makes a mark beside the student's name in the grade book. The student loses 2 minutes of recess for each mark accumulated. For older students, a certain number of marks might mean losing the privilege of working in a group or going on a class trip.

Social Isolation. One of the most controversial behavioral methods for decreasing undesirable behavior is the strategy of **social isolation,** often called **time out** from reinforcement. The process involves removing a highly disruptive student from the classroom for 5 to 10 minutes. The student is placed in an empty, uninteresting room alone. It seems likely that the factor that actually decreases behavior is the punishment of brief isolation from other people (O'Leary & O'Leary, 1976a). A trip to the principal's office or confinement to a chair in the corner of the regular classroom does not have the same effect as sitting alone in an empty room. See the **Point/Counterpoint** section above for a discussion of this approach.

Response Cost Punishment through loss of reinforcers.

Social Isolation Removal of a disruptive student for 5 to 10 minutes.

Time Out Technically, the removal of all reinforcement. In practice, isolation of a student from the rest of the class for a brief time.

Some Cautions. Punishment does not, in and of itself, lead to any positive behavior. Thus, whenever you consider the use of punishment, you should make it part of a two-pronged attack. The first goal is to carry out the punishment and suppress the undesirable behavior. The second goal is to make clear what the student should be doing instead and to provide reinforcement for those desirable actions. Thus, while the problem behaviors are being suppressed, positive alternative responses are being strengthened.

SOCIAL LEARNING THEORY

In recent years most behavioral psychologists have found that operant conditioning offers too limited an explanation of learning. Many have expanded their view of learning to include the study of cognitive processes that cannot be directly observed, such as expectations, thoughts, and beliefs. A prime example of this expanded view is Albert Bandura's (1986) **social cognitive theory.** Bandura believes that the traditional behavioral views of learning, while accurate, are incomplete. They give only part of the explanation of learning and overlook important aspects of the situation, particularly the important social influences on learning.

Bandura distinguishes between the acquisition of knowledge (learning) and the observable performance based on that knowledge (behavior). In other words, Bandura suggests that we all may know more than we show. Students may have learned how to simplify fractions but may perform badly on a test because they are anxious or ill or have misread the problem. While learning may have occurred, it may not be demonstrated until the situation is right. In social cognitive theory, therefore, both internal and external factors are important. Environmental events, personal factors (such as thinking and motivation), and behavior are seen as interacting, each influencing the others in the process of learning. Bandura calls this interaction of forces **reciprocal determinism.**

One factor overlooked by traditional behavioral theories is the powerful effect that modeling and imitation can have on learning. People and animals can learn merely by observing another person or animal learn, and this fact challenges the behaviorist idea that cognitive factors are unnecessary in an explanation of learning. If people can learn by watching, they must be focusing their attention, constructing images, remembering, analyzing, and making decisions that affect learning.

Learning by Observing Others

When Elizabeth laughed at the "Clark Gable" comment in class, she communicated that laughing was appropriate in this situation. Soon all the students were laughing along with her, and she did not try to stop them until it was too late. They were learning through **modeling** or observation, even though this was not the type of learning Elizabeth had intended. Elizabeth, through her behavior, provided a model for her students to imitate.

There are two main modes of **observational learning** First, learning through observation can take place through vicarious conditioning. This happens when we see others being rewarded or punished for particular

Social Cognitive Theory Theory that emphasizes learning through observation of others.

Reciprocal Determinism An explanation of behavior that emphasizes the mutual effects of the individual and the environment on each other.

Modeling Changes in behavior, thinking, or emotions that occur through observing another person—a model.

Observational Learning Learning by observation and imitation of others.

actions and then modify our behavior as if we had received the consequences ourselves. For example, if you compliment two students on the attractive illustrations in their lab reports, several other students who observe your compliments may turn in illustrated lab reports next time. This demonstrates **vicarious reinforcement.** Punishment can also be vicarious: you may slow down on a stretch of highway after seeing several people get speeding tickets there.

In the second kind of observational learning, the observer imitates the behavior of a model even though the model receives no reinforcement or punishment while the observer is watching. Often the model is demonstrating something the observer wants to learn and expects to be reinforced for mastering; for example, the proper way to position hands while playing a piano or the correct way to assemble laboratory equipment. But imitation can also occur when the observer simply wants to become more like an admired or high-status model. Models need not be real people. We may also use fictional characters or stereotypical images as models and try to behave as we imagine the model would (Hill, 1990).

Observation can be a very efficient learning process. The first time children hold hairbrushes, cups, tennis rackets, or steering wheels, they usually brush, drink, swing, or steer as well as they can, given their current muscle development and coordination. Through modeling we learn not only how to perform a behavior but also what will happen to us in specific situations if we do perform it. For example, you may be more careful about reading the newspaper in certain classes because you have seen what happens to other students in those classes who were caught doing so. Let's take a closer look at how observational learning occurs.

Elements of Observational Learning

Bandura (1986) notes that there are four important elements to be considered in observational learning. They are paying attention, retaining information or impressions, producing behaviors, and being motivated to repeat the behaviors.

Attention. In order to learn through observation, we have to pay attention. We typically pay attention to people who are attractive, popular, competent, or admired (Sulzer-Azaroff & Mayer, 1986). For younger children this could mean parents, older brothers or sisters, or teachers. For older students, it may mean popular peers, rock stars, or TV idols.

In teaching, you will have to ensure students' attention to the critical features of the lesson by making clear presentations and highlighting important points. In demonstrating a skill (for example, threading a sewing machine or operating a lathe), you may need to have students look over your shoulder as you work. Seeing your hands from the same perspective as they see their own directs attention to the right features of the situation and makes observational learning easier.

Retention. In order to imitate the behavior of a model, you have to remember it. This involves mentally representing the model's actions in some way, probably as verbal steps ("Hwa-Rang, the eighth form in Tae Kwan Do karate, is a palm-heel block, then a middle riding stance punch, then . . ."), or as visual images, or both. Retention can be improved by

Vicarious Reinforcement
Increasing the chances that you will repeat a behavior by observing another person being reinforced for that behavior.

mental rehearsal (imagining imitating the behavior) or by actual practice. In the retention phase of observational learning, practice helps us remember the elements of the desired behavior, such as the sequence of steps.

Production. Once we "know" how a behavior should look and remember the elements or steps, we still may not perform it smoothly. Sometimes we need a great deal of practice, feedback, and coaching about subtle points before we can reproduce the behavior of the model. In the production phase, practice makes the behaviors smoother and more expert. A sense of **self-efficacy,** the belief that we are capable of performing the behavior, is important at this phase and influences our motivation to perform.

Motivation and Reinforcement. As mentioned earlier, social cognitive theory distinguishes between acquisition and performance. We may acquire a new skill or behavior through observation, but we may not perform that behavior until there is some motivation or incentive to do so. Reinforcement can play several roles in observational learning. If we anticipate being reinforced for imitating the actions of a model, we may be more motivated to pay attention, remember, and reproduce the behaviors. In addition, reinforcement is important in maintaining learning. A person who tries a new behavior is unlikely to persist without reinforcement (Barton, 1981; Ollendick, Dailey, & Shapiro, 1983). For example, if an unpopular student adopted the dress of the ingroup but was greeted with teasing and ridicule, it is unlikely that the imitation would continue.

Bandura identifies three forms of reinforcement that can encourage observational learning. First, of course, the observer may reproduce the behaviors of the model and receive *direct reinforcement,* as when a gymnast successfully executes a front flip/round-off combination and the coach/model says, "Excellent!" But the reinforcement need not be direct—it may be *vicarious reinforcement* as well. As mentioned earlier, the observer may simply see others reinforced for a particular behavior and then increase his or her production of that behavior. Most TV ads hope for this kind of effect. People in commercials become deliriously happy when they drive a particular car or drink a specific juice, and the viewer is supposed to do the same; the viewer's behavior is reinforced vicariously by the actors' obvious pleasure. The final form of reinforcement is **self-reinforcement** or controlling your own reinforcers. This sort of reinforcement is important—for students and teachers. We want our students to improve not because it leads to external rewards but because the students value and enjoy their growing competence. And as a teacher, at times self-reinforcement is all that keeps you going.

Observational Learning in Teaching

There are five possible effects of observational learning: teaching new behaviors and attitudes, encouraging existing behaviors, changing inhibitions, directing attention, and arousing emotions. Let's look at each of these outcomes as they occur in classrooms.

Teaching New Behaviors. Modeling has long been used, of course, to teach dance, sports, and crafts, as well as skills in subjects such as home

Self-Efficacy A person's sense of being able to deal effectively with a particular task.

Self-Reinforcement Providing yourself with positive consequences, contingent on accomplishing a particular behavior.

economics, chemistry, and shop. Modeling can also be applied deliberately in the classroom to teach mental skills and to broaden horizons—to teach new ways of thinking. Teachers serve as models for a tremendous range of behaviors, from pronouncing vocabulary words, to reacting to the seizure of an epileptic student, to being enthusiastic about learning. For example, a teacher might model sound critical thinking skills by thinking "out loud" about a student's question. Or a high school teacher concerned about girls who seem to have stereotyped ideas about careers might invite women with nontraditional jobs to speak to the class.

Modeling, when applied deliberately, can be an effective and efficient means of teaching new behavior (Bandura, 1986; Schunk, 1987). Studies indicate that modeling can be most effective when the teacher makes use of all the elements of observational learning described in the previous section, especially reinforcement and practice.

Models who are the same age as the students may be particularly effective. For example, Schunk and Hanson (1985) compared two methods for teaching subtraction to second graders who had difficulties learning this skill. One group of students observed other second graders learning the procedures, then participated in an instructional program on subtraction. Another group of students watched a teacher's demonstration, then participated in the same instructional program. Of the two groups, the students who observed peer models learning not only scored higher on tests of subtraction after instruction but also gained more confidence in their own ability to learn. For students who doubt their own abilities, a good model is a low-achieving student who keeps trying and finally masters the material (Schunk, 1987).

Encouraging Already-Learned Behaviors. All of us have had the experience of looking for cues from other people when we find ourselves in unfamiliar situations. Observing the behavior of others tells us which of our already-learned behaviors to use: the proper fork for eating the salad, when to leave a gathering, what kind of language is appropriate, and so on. Adopting the dress and grooming styles of TV idols is another example of this kind of effect.

Strengthening or Weakening Inhibitions. If class members witness one student breaking a class rule and getting away with it, they may learn that undesirable consequences do not always follow rule-breaking. The class may be less inhibited in the future about breaking this rule. If the rule-breaker is a well-liked, high-status class leader, the effect of the modeling may be even more pronounced. One psychologist has called this phenomenon the **ripple effect** (Kounin, 1970). The ripple effect can work for the teacher's benefit. When the teacher deals effectively with a rule-breaker, especially a class leader, the idea of breaking this rule may be suppressed in the other students viewing the interaction. This does not mean that teachers must reprimand each student who breaks a rule; but once a teacher has called for a particular action, following through is an important part of capitalizing on the ripple effect.

Directing Attention. By observing others, we not only learn about actions, we also notice the objects involved in the actions. For example, in a preschool class, when one child plays enthusiastically with a toy that

Ripple Effect "Contagious" spreading of behaviors through imitation.

Guidelines

Using Observational Learning

Model behaviors and attitudes you want your students to learn.

Examples

1. Show enthusiasm for the subject you teach.
2. Be willing to demonstrate both the mental and the physical tasks you expect the students to perform. I once saw a teacher sit down in the sandbox while her 4-year-old students watched her demonstrate the difference between "playing with sand" and "throwing sand."
3. When reading to students, model good problem solving. Stop and say, "Now let me see if I remember what happened so far" or "That was a hard sentence. I'm going to read it again."

Use peers as models.

Examples

1. In group work, pair students who do well with those who are having difficulties.
2. Ask students to demonstrate the difference between "whispering" and "silence—no talking."

Make sure students see that positive behaviors lead to reinforcement for others.

Examples

1. Point out the connections between positive behavior and positive consequences in stories.
2. Be fair in giving reinforcement. The same rules for rewards should apply to the problem students as to the good students.

Enlist the help of class leaders in modeling behaviors for the entire class.

Examples

1. Ask a well-liked student to be friendly to an isolated, fearful student.
2. Let high-status students lead an activity when you need class cooperation or when students are likely to be reluctant at first. Popular students can model dialogues in foreign-language classes or be the first to tackle dissection procedures in biology.

---

has been ignored for days, many other children may want to have the toy, even if they play with it in different ways or simply carry it around. This happens, in part, because the children's attention has been drawn to that particular toy.

Arousing Emotion. Finally, through observational learning, people may develop emotional reactions to situations they themselves have never experienced, such as flying or driving. A child who watches a friend fall from a swing and break an arm may become fearful of swings. Students may be anxious when they are assigned to a certain teacher just because they've heard frightening stories about how "mean" that teacher is. Note that hearing and reading about a situation are also forms of observation. The Guidelines will give you some ideas about using observational learning in the classroom.

Self-Management Use of behavioral learning principles to change your own behavior.

SELF-REGULATION AND COGNITIVE BEHAVIOR MODIFICATION

The most recent application of behavioral views of learning emphasizes **self-management**—helping students gain control of their own learning. As you will see throughout this book, the role of students in their own learning is a major concern of psychologists and educators today. This concern is not restricted to any one group or theory. Different areas of research and theory all converge on one important idea—that responsibility and the ability to learn rest within the student. No one can learn for someone else (Manning, 1991; Zimmerman, 1990; Zimmerman & Schunk, 1989).

One reason that behavioral psychologists became interested in self-management is that students taught with classic behavioral methods seldom generalized their learning to new situations. For example, in my dissertation research I found that inattentive students could learn to pay excellent attention to lessons when they were systematically reinforced in a small group. But when they returned to the regular classroom, they did not take their new skill back with them (Woolfolk & Woolfolk, 1974). Many behavioral psychologists decided that generalization would be encouraged if students became partners in the behavior change procedures. About this same time, Donald Meichenbaum (1977) was having success teaching impulsive students to "talk themselves through" tasks, so there was evidence that students could benefit from what Meichenbaum termed cognitive behavior modification (Manning, 1991).

Self-Management

If one goal of education is to produce people capable of educating themselves, students must learn to manage their own lives, set their own goals, and provide their own reinforcement. In adult life, rewards are sometimes vague and goals often take a long time to reach. Think how many small steps are required to complete an education and find your first job. Life is filled with tasks that call for this sort of self-management (Kanfer & Gaelick, 1986).

Students may be involved in any or all of the steps in implementing a basic behavior change program. They may help set goals, observe their own work, keep records of it, and evaluate their own performance. Finally, they can select and deliver reinforcement. This kind of involvement can help students learn to perform all the steps on their own in the future (Kaplan, 1991).

Goal Setting. It appears that the goal-setting phase is very important in self-management. In fact, some research suggests that setting specific goals and making them public may be the critical elements of self-management programs. For example, S. C. Hayes and his colleagues identified college students who had serious problems with studying and taught them how to set specific study goals. Students who set goals and announced them to the experimenters performed significantly better on tests covering the material they were studying than students who set goals privately and never revealed them to anyone (Hayes, Rosenfarb, Wulfert, Munt, Korn, & Zettle, 1985).

Higher standards tend to lead to higher performance (McLaughlin & Gnagey, 1981). Unfortunately, student-set goals have a tendency to become lower and lower. Teachers can help students maintain high standards by monitoring the goals set and reinforcing high standards. In one study, a teacher helped first-grade students raise the number of math problems they set for themselves to work on each day by praising them whenever they increased their objective by 10 percent. The students maintained their new, higher work standards, and the improvements even generalized to other subjects (Price & O'Leary, 1974).

Recording and Evaluating Progress. Students may also participate in the recording and evaluation phases of a behavior change program. Some examples of behaviors that are appropriate for self-recording are the number of assignments completed, time spent practicing a skill, number of books read, and number of times out of seat without permission. Tasks that must be accomplished without teacher supervision, like homework or private study, are also good candidates for self-monitoring. Students keep a chart, diary, or checklist recording the frequency or duration of the behaviors in question. Many examples of self-recording forms are available in E. Workman's *Teaching Behavioral Self-Control to Students* (1982).

A progress record card can help older students break assignments down into small steps, determine the best sequence for completing the steps, and keep track of daily progress by setting goals for each day. The record card itself serves as a prompt that can be gradually faded (Jenson, Sloane, & Young, 1988). Because cheating on records is a potential problem, especially when students are rewarded for improvements, intermittent checking by the teacher plus bonus points for accurate recording may be helpful (Hundert & Bucher, 1978).

Self-evaluation is somewhat more difficult than simple self-recording, because it involves making a judgment about quality. Very few studies have been conducted in this area, but it appears that students can learn to evaluate their behavior with reasonable accuracy (Rhode, Morgan, & Young, 1983). One key seems to be periodically checking students' self-evaluations and giving reinforcement for accurate judgments. Older students may learn accurate self-evaluation more readily than younger students. Again, bonus points can be awarded when the teachers' and students' evaluations match (Kaplan, 1991).

A study conducted by Mark Morgan (1985) combined goal setting, self-recording, and self-evaluation. Morgan taught self-monitoring strategies to all the education students in the required educational psychology course at his college. The students who set specific short-term objectives for each study unit and monitored their progress toward the objectives outperformed the students who simply monitored study time, even though the students who monitored their time actually spent more hours studying!

Self-Reinforcement. The last step in self-management is self-reinforcement. There is some disagreement, however, as to whether this step is actually necessary. Some psychologists believe that setting goals and monitoring progress alone are sufficient and that self-reinforcement adds nothing to the effects (Hayes et al., 1985). Others believe that rewarding yourself for a job well done can lead to higher levels of performance than simply setting goals and keeping track of progress (Bandura, 1986). If you are willing to be tough and really deny yourself something you want until your goals are reached, then perhaps the

Guidelines

Instituting Self-Management Programs

Introduce the system in a positive way.

Examples

1. Emphasize the system in a positive way.
2. Consider starting the program just with volunteers.
3. Describe how you use self-management programs yourself.

Help students learn to set appropriate goals.

Examples

1. Monitor goals frequently at first, and praise reasonably high standards.
2. Make goals public by having students tell you or members of their work group what they want to accomplish.

Provide a way for students to record and evaluate their progress.

Examples

1. Divide the work into easily measured steps.

2. Provide models of good work where judgments are more difficult, such as in creative writing.
3. Give students a record form or checklist to keep track of progress.

Check the accuracy of student records from time to time, and encourage students to develop forms of self-reinforcement.

Examples

1. Have many checkups when students are first learning, fewer later.
2. Have students check one another's records.
3. Where appropriate, test the skills that students are supposed to be developing and reward students whose self-evaluations match their test performances.
4. Have students brainstorm ideas for rewarding themselves for jobs well done.

promise of the reward can provide extra incentive for work. With that in mind, you may want to think of some way to reinforce yourself when you finish reading this chapter. A similar approach helped me write the chapter in the first place.

Sometimes teaching students self-management can solve a problem for teachers and provide fringe benefits as well. For example, the coaches of a competitive swim team with members aged 9 to 16 were having difficulty persuading swimmers to maintain high work rates. Then the coaches drew up four charts indicating the training program to be followed by each member and posted the charts near the pool. The swimmers were given the responsibility of recording their numbers of laps and completion of each training unit. Because the recording was public, swimmers could see their own progress and that of others, give and receive congratulations, and keep accurate track of the work units completed. Work output increased by 27 percent. The coaches also liked the system because swimmers could begin to work immediately without waiting for instructions (McKenzie & Rushall, 1974).

Cognitive Behavior Modification

Self-management generally means getting students involved in the basic steps of a behavior change program. **Cognitive behavior modification** adds an emphasis on thinking and self-talk to the package. For this

Cognitive Behavior Modification Procedures based on both behavioral and cognitive learning principles for changing your own behavior by using self-talk and self-instruction.

reason, many psychologists consider cognitive behavior modification more a *cognitive* than a *behavioral* approach. I present it here because it serves as a bridge to the coming chapters on cognitive learning.

As noted in chapter 2, there is a stage in cognitive development when young children seem to guide themselves through a task using private speech. They talk to themselves, often repeating the words of a parent or teacher. In cognitive behavior modification, students are taught directly how to use self-instruction. Meichenbaum (1977) outlined the steps:

1. An adult model performs a task while talking to self out loud (cognitive modeling);
2. The child performs the same task under the direction of the model's instructions (overt, external guidance);
3. The child performs the task while instructing self aloud (overt, self-guidance);
4. The child whispers the instructions to self as he/she goes through the task (faded, overt self-guidance);
5. The child performs the task while guiding his/her performance via private speech (covert self-instruction). (p. 32)

Actually, cognitive behavior modification as it is practiced by Meichenbaum and others has many more components than just teaching students to use covert self-instruction. Meichenbaum's methods, for example, also include dialogue and interaction between teacher and student, modeling, guided discovery, motivational strategies, feedback, careful matching of the task with the student's developmental level, and other principles of good teaching. The student is even involved in designing the program (Harris, 1990; Harris & Pressley, in press). Given all this, it is no surprise that students do seem to generalize to new learning situations the skills developed with cognitive behavior modification (Harris, Graham, & Pressley, in press).

Poor readers have been taught a set of self-instructions to guide reading. They learn to ask themselves questions about the content as they go along, outline each passage in their heads, relate the ideas in the reading to other information, and so on (Bornstein, 1985; Dush, Hirt, & Schroeder, 1983; Meichenbaum, 1977). One important aspect of the self-instructional approach is to give students something concrete to do that focuses their attention. This task must fit the goals of the particular situation. Asking questions as you read, for example, not only helps maintain attention but also helps you understand what you are reading. Some other system, like imagining painful punishment every time your mind wanders, might keep you focused on the words in the book, but it probably would not improve comprehension. Of course, students must also be capable of the tasks they are instructing themselves to do. Self-instructional support for reading will do little good if the passage is too difficult for the student (Harris, 1990).

PROBLEMS AND ISSUES

The preceding sections provide an overview of several strategies for changing classroom behavior. However, you should be aware that these strategies are tools that may be used responsibly or irresponsibly. What, then, are some issues you should keep in mind?

Ethical Issues

The ethical questions related to the use of the strategies described in this chapter are similar to those raised by any process that seeks to influence people. What are the goals? How do these goals fit in with those of the school as a whole? Might students be rewarded for the "wrong" thing, though it seems "right" at first? By what criteria should strategies be chosen? What effect will a strategy have on the individuals involved? Is too much control being given to the teacher, or to a majority?

Goals. The strategies described in this chapter could be applied exclusively to teach students to sit still, raise their hands before speaking, and remain silent at all other times (Winett & Winkler, 1972). This certainly would be an unethical use of the techniques. It is true that a teacher may need to establish some organization and order, but stopping with improvements in conduct will not ensure academic learning. On the other hand, in some situations, reinforcing academic skills may lead to improvements in conduct. Emphasis should be placed, whenever possible, on academic behaviors. Academic improvements generalize to other situations more successfully than do changes in classroom conduct.

Strategies. As noted earlier, punishment can have negative side effects; it can serve as a model for aggressive responses, and it can encourage negative emotional reactions. Punishment is unnecessary and even unethical when positive approaches, which have fewer potential dangers, might work as well. A set of guidelines originally prepared to select programs for retarded students offers a logical progression of strategies that may be applied in any classroom setting (American Psychological Association, 1976). When simpler, less-restrictive procedures fail, then more complicated procedures should be tried. Table 6.3 shows a general hierarchy based on these guidelines.

A second consideration in the selection of a strategy is the impact of the strategy on the individual student. For example, some teachers arrange for students to be rewarded at home with a gift or activities based

---

TABLE 6.3 Choosing Strategies for Classroom Management

First try:	Praising positive behaviors and ignoring undesirable behaviors.
If that doesn't work, try:	Praise-and-ignore techniques with prompting and cueing, soft reprimands, modeling, or shaping.
If that doesn't work, try:	Praise-and-ignore techniques with negative reinforcement, satiation, response cost, or social isolation.

on good work in school. But if a student has a history of being severely punished at home for bad reports from school, a home-based reinforcement program might be very harmful to that student. Reports of unsatisfactory progress at school could lead to increased abuse at home.

Criticisms of Behavioral Methods

Properly used, the strategies in this chapter can be effective tools to help students learn academically and grow in self-sufficiency. Effective tools, however, do not automatically produce excellent work. The indiscriminate use of even the best tools can lead to difficulties. Critics of behavioral methods point to two basic problems that may arise.

Decreased Interest in Learning. Some psychologists fear that rewarding students for all learning will cause the students to lose interest in learning for its own sake (Deci, 1975; Deci & Ryan, 1985; Lepper & Greene, 1978). Studies have suggested that using reward programs with students who are already interested in the subject matter may, in fact, cause students to be less interested in the subject when the reward program ends.

Impact on Other Students. Just as you must take into account the effects of a reward system on the individual, you must also consider the impact on other students. Using a reward program or giving one student increased attention may have a detrimental effect on the other students in the classroom. Is it possible that other students will learn to be "bad" in order to be included in the reward program? Most of the evidence on this question suggests that reward programs do not have any adverse effects

Guidelines

Making Ethical Use of Behavioral Methods

1. Use behavioral methods in appropriate contexts to reinforce positive academic and social learning behaviors, not merely to enforce rules of conduct.
2. Encourage student awareness of and cooperation in behavioral change programs. So far as possible, make sure changes in behavior occur for reasons students themselves understand and accept.
3. Know your students. Fit behavioral strategies to the special needs of each one, carefully considering all possible consequences. This includes carefully selecting reinforcers and fitting rewards to the individual. Consult with parents and school professionals to ensure that a reinforcement program is appropriate for, and will not harm, the student. At the same time, consider the needs of other students and of the whole group when implementing reinforcement programs that target particular individuals.
4. Use reinforcement selectively, and only when needed. Try the simplest, most positive, least restrictive, and least intrusive procedures first. Leave as much responsibility for learning as possible in the hands of students.
5. Encourage reliance on intrinsic rewards and incentives first and whenever possible. Make sure extrinsic rewards are understood as symbols of task mastery and not as ends in themselves. Phase out reward systems as student motivation and success improve.

on students who are not participating in the program if the teacher believes in the program and explains the reasons for using it to the nonparticipating students (Christy, 1975). If the conduct of some students does seem to deteriorate when their peers are involved in special programs, many of the same procedures discussed in this chapter should help them return to previous levels of appropriate behavior.

SUMMARY

UNDERSTANDING LEARNING

Although theorists disagree about the definition of learning, most would agree that learning occurs when experience causes a change in a person's knowledge or behavior. Behavioral theorists emphasize the role of environmental stimuli in learning and focus on observable responses. Behavioral learning processes include contiguity learning, classical conditioning, operant conditioning, and observational learning.

CONTIGUITY: LEARNING THROUGH SIMPLE ASSOCIATIONS

In contiguity learning, two events that repeatedly occur together become associated in the learner's mind. Later, in the presence of one event the learner remembers the other.

CLASSICAL CONDITIONING: PAIRING AUTOMATIC RESPONSES WITH NEW STIMULI

In classical conditioning, discovered by Pavlov, a previously neutral stimulus is repeatedly paired with a stimulus that evokes an emotional or physiological response. Later, the previously neutral stimulus alone evokes the response—that is, the conditioned stimulus brings forth a conditioned response. Conditioned responses are subject to the processes of generalization, discrimination, and extinction.

OPERANT CONDITIONING: TRYING NEW RESPONSES

In operant conditioning, studied by Thorndike and Skinner, people learn through the effects of their deliberate responses to their environment. Operant conditioning is most applicable to classroom learning. For an individual, the effects of consequences following an action may serve as reinforcement or punishment. Positive and negative reinforcements strengthen a response, while punishment decreases or suppresses the behavior. In addition, the scheduling of reinforcement influences the rate and persistence of responses. Ratio schedules encourage higher rates of response and variable schedules encourage persistence of responses. In addition to controlling consequences of behavior, teachers can also control the antecedents of behavior through cueing and prompting.

APPLIED BEHAVIOR ANALYSIS

Applied behavior analysis provides teachers with methods for encouraging positive behaviors and coping with undesirable ones. Teachers can reinforce positive, appropriate student behavior through attention, recognition, praise, and the judicious use of reinforcers. The Premack principle, that a more-preferred activity can be used as a reinforcer for a less-preferred one, can help teachers choose effective reinforcers for both individuals and groups. Teachers can use shaping and positive practice to help students develop new responses. Negative reinforcement, satiation, and forms of punishment—such as reprimands, response cost, and social isolation—can also help change behavior but must be used with caution.

SOCIAL LEARNING THEORY

Social learning theorists, such as Bandura, emphasize the role of observation in learning and in nonobservable cognitive processes, such as thinking and knowing. Observational learning occurs through vicarious conditioning and imitation of high-status models and involves paying attention, retaining information or impressions, producing behaviors, and repeating behaviors through reinforcement or motivation. Teachers can use observational learning to teach new behaviors—providing peer models, for example—and also to encourage already-learned behaviors, strengthen or weaken inhibitions, or arouse emotions.

Self-Regulation and Cognitive Behavior Modification

Cognitive psychologists have influenced behavioral views, pointing, for example, to the importance of self-regulation in learning. Students can apply behavior analysis on their own to manage their own behavior. Teachers can encourage the development of self-management skills by allowing students to participate in setting goals, keeping track of progress, evaluating accomplishments, and selecting and giving their own reinforcements. Teachers can also use cognitive behavior modification, a behavior change program described by Meichenbaum in which students are directly taught how to use self-instruction.

Problems and Issues

The misuse or abuse of behavioral learning methods is unethical. Critics of behavioral methods also point out the danger that reinforcement could decrease interest in learning by overemphasizing rewards and could have a negative impact on other students. Guidelines do exist, however, for helping teachers use behavioral learning principles appropriately and ethically.

KEY TERMS AND CONCEPTS

antecedents, p. 202
applied behavior analysis, p. 210
behavioral learning theories, p. 196
behavior modification, p. 210
classical conditioning, p. 199
cognitive behavior modification, p. 227
conditioned response (CR), p. 200
conditioned stimulus (CS), p. 198
consequences, p. 202
contiguity, p. 198
continuous reinforcement schedule, p. 205
cueing, p. 209
discriminate, p. 209
discrimination, p. 200
extinction, p. 200
fixed-interval reinforcement schedule, p. 206
fixed-ratio reinforcement schedule, p. 207

generalization, p. 200
intermittent reinforcement schedule, p. 205
law of effect, p. 202
learning, p. 196
modeling, p. 220
negative reinforcement, p. 204
observational learning, p. 220
operant conditioning, p. 202
operants, p. 202
positive practice, p. 214
positive reinforcement, p. 204
Premack principle, p. 212
presentation punishment, p. 205
prompt, p. 209
punishment, p. 205
reciprocal determinism, p. 220
reinforcement, p. 204
reinforcer, p. 203
removal punishment, p. 205
reprimands, p. 218
respondents, p. 201

response, p. 198
response cost, p. 219
ripple effect, p. 223
satiation, p. 217
self-efficacy, p. 222
self-management, p. 224
self-reinforcement, p. 222
shaping, p. 214
social cognitive theory, p. 220
social isolation, p. 219
stimulus, p. 198
time out, p. 219
unconditioned response (UR), p. 199
unconditioned stimulus (US), p. 199
variable-interval reinforcement schedule, p. 206
variable-ratio reinforcement schedule, p. 208
vicarious reinforcement, p. 221

WHAT WOULD YOU DO?

PRESCHOOL AND KINDERGARTEN

A student in your class is terrified of the class pet guinea pigs. The child won't get close to the cages and wants you to "give them away." How would you help this child overcome this fear?

ELEMENTARY AND MIDDLE SCHOOL

You were hired in January to take over the class of a teacher who moved away. The class is a nightmare! Evidently the teacher had no control over the students. They get up and walk around while you are reading to the class, interrupt you when you are working with a group, and seldom finish their classwork or homework. How would you approach the situation?

You want your students to improve their time management and self-management abilities so they will be prepared for the increased demands of high school next year. What would you do?

JUNIOR HIGH AND HIGH SCHOOL

You have been assigned an emotionally disturbed student. She seemed fine at first, but now you notice that when she encounters difficult work, she often interrupts or teases other students. How would you work with this student and the class to improve the situation?

It takes you 10 minutes to get your class settled down after the bell rings. Analyze this situation. What could be maintaining this problem? What would you do?

COOPERATIVE LEARNING ACTIVITY

Work with two or three other members of your educational psychology class to develop a plan using applied behavior analysis for tackling one of the following problems:

- Three students who "hang out" together in your class persist in saying insulting and disrespectful things to you, often in front of the entire class.
- Your class has gotten into the habit of ignoring due dates.
- One of the students in your class continues to attack other students verbally and physically.

DEALING WITH INAPPROPRIATE BEHAVIOR

The boys in your class perennially imitate the latest action heroes. Years ago it was Star Wars heroes wielding "the force"; then it was karate-chopping Ninja Turtles. What do you do about this kind of behavior during class?

RULES FOR IN-SCHOOL PLAY

Knowing that the average child spends 20 hours or better each week in front of a television set compounds this problem. When we're having behavior problems, I take some time and talk to the students about what is appropriate and inappropriate behavior for school. We talk about what is after-school play and in-school play. From this basis, I lay down some ground rules of what will happen if they choose to use inappropriate school behavior (lose a set amount of recess time or special time), and then I always follow through with it.

Candice J. Gallagher, *Fourth-Grade Teacher*
Fredericktown Intermediate School, Fredericktown, Ohio

BEHAVIOR MANAGEMENT PROGRAMS

Have you ever used a systematic reward and/or punishment program with your students, such as marbles in a jar for good behavior, demerits for rule violations, or some other system? Why did you establish the program, and how did it work?

GRAB-BAG POINTS

I have used a point system to motivate students to stay on task and to do their best. Before beginning the reward program, I surveyed the students to discover the type of items they found rewarding. When a student accumulated 20 points, he or she could choose from a grab bag filled with items such as free homework passes, pencils, markers, Hot Wheels, jewelry, stickers, books, game time cards, opportunity to be the teacher for an instructional period cards, bookmarks, and even one class pizza party certificate. The element of surprise created by the grab bags proved to be the most motivating. I found the system to be very effective, but some expense of time and money was involved for the teacher.

Joanne S. Groseclose, *Virginia 1991 Teacher of the Year*
Marion Intermediate School, Marion, Virginia

SIGNATURE CARDS

Systematic rewards for positive and negative behaviors work only if the students have a say in the process.

I have used a system called Signature Cards. The Signature Card, a note card, is placed either on an individual's desk or at a group table. When the individual or group is not behaving according to set standards (set by the class), the student(s) get my signature on the card. Each signature, or lack thereof, has positive and negative consequences. The type of consequence is a difficult problem. If the students do not "buy in," the most elaborate system is useless. Recently, I tried a consensus-building activity using a "fishbowl" to arrive at class consequences. The process is as follows:

1. Each student generates a list of positive and negative consequences for their appropriate actions. They are limited to six.
2. Each student then gets a partner and together they compromise on a list of six consequences, using each of their lists as a starting place.
3. Each pair joins another pair; this group of four then compromises on a set of six consequences.
4. Each group of four picks a spokesperson to support and defend the group's ideas.
5. All the spokespersons make a small circle in the middle of the room, while the other members make a large circle encompassing them.

6. The inner circle discusses and decides, by consensus, on six consequences for the class. The outer circle is to listen carefully.
7. If anyone in the room has a question or concern they call a time out. As in a football game, when one team calls a time out, the other teams consult also.
8. The teacher's role is to facilitate and record.
9. At the end of the process, six consequences for inappropriate behavior are generated by a consensus model and the students have "bought in" to the system.

Julie A. Addison, *Sixth-Grade Teacher*
Roxborough Elementary School, Littleton, Colorado

CATCH THE CHILD BEING GOOD

According to one of the principles of operant conditioning, if you want to increase a child's desirable behavior, positively reinforce that behavior when it occurs. Teachers are told, "Catch the child being good." In the course of a busy school day, however, it is often difficult, especially for beginning teachers, to act on this advice and to feel natural and comfortable about it. How did you get yourself into the habit of noticing desirable behaviors?

REWARDS FOR PERSEVERANCE

As a first-year teacher, I quickly realized that I could "catch more flies with honey than vinegar." When I accentuated attention on the appropriate behavior displayed by students, discipline problems were substantially reduced and a healthy classroom environment was established. By constantly giving my attention to minor infractions, I was encouraging misbehavior and defiance of the school rules! I discovered that most of the same students who misbehaved for negative attention just as readily behaved for positive reinforcement.

Praise must be sincere to be effective. Children quickly recognize insincerity. They do not trust authority figures who are less than honest. In addition, desciptive praise is the most productive. A teacher should reinforce specific behavior. "Johnny, I like the way you blended the paints to make such an interesting blue sky," is a more descriptive and personal form of praise than "Johnny, that's a pretty picture."

Kathy Andrews, *Special Education Teacher*
Lane Center for Exceptional Children, Houston, Texas

KEEP THEM GUESSING

Studies of operant conditioning indicate that there are advantages to variable reinforcement schedules—reinforcing at unpredictable intervals or at unpredictable stages in a task. How do you go about making rewards unpredictable? Have you found that unpredictable rewards work in your classroom?

ON OUR TOES

Children, like adults, like to receive "strokes" when deserved. The element of surprise is often effective. I will sometimes give children a sticker, star, or a verbal compliment on the spur of the moment. This tends to keep children "on their toes," since they don't know when I will do this. Also, it gives me a chance to recognize the child who seldom gets a reward (verbal or otherwise) in the rare moment that she or he truly deserves the positive recognition. That child needs this too—perhaps more than anyone else in the classroom! But the praise must be honest and earned.

Carolyn R. Cook, *Kingergarten Teacher*
Ramona Elementary School, Ramona, California

7 COGNITIVE LEARNING THEORIES

In this chapter we turn from behavioral theories of learning to a different perspective, the cognitive orientation. Essentially, this means a shift from "viewing the learners and their behaviors as products of incoming environmental stimuli" to seeing the learners as "sources of plans, intentions, goals, ideas, memories, and emotions actively used to attend to, select, and construct meaning from stimuli and knowledge from experience" (Wittrock, 1982, pp. 1–2). We will begin with a discussion of the general cognitive approach to learning and memory and the importance of knowledge in learning. Then we will introduce a widely accepted cognitive model—information processing. This model suggests that information moves through three different storage systems. We will examine each storage system by describing the capacity, duration, contents, processes for storing and retrieving information, and causes of forgetting. Next we will explore a promising new field of study—metacognition—that may provide insights into individual and developmental differences in learning. Of course, all these facets of human learning and memory have implications for teaching. By the time you have completed this chapter, you should have a number of new ideas about how learning takes place and how you can improve your own learning. More specifically, you should be able to do the following:

- Discuss the role of knowledge in learning.
- Describe a cognitive model of human learning—information processing.
- Give examples of the roles of perception and attention in learning.
- Explain how schemata and scripts influence learning and remembering.
- Discuss individual differences in short- and long-term memory.
- Use memory strategies and study skills derived from cognitive theory to prepare for the test you may have to take on this chapter.
- Develop a plan for teaching learning strategies and study skills to your students.

> ## WHAT DO YOU THINK?
>
> *What makes a lesson easy to learn and remember? Think about the classes you are taking this semester. What information that you studied in the last two or three days do you expect to remember next week? Next year? What is different about the information you expect to remember as opposed to the information you probably will forget? What is different about the way you learned the information you expect to remember?*

ELEMENTS OF THE COGNITIVE PERSPECTIVE

From the late 1800s, when the scientific study of learning began, until about 30 years ago, almost all of the research on learning was in the behavioral tradition. But research on the development of complex human skills during World War II, the computer revolution, and breakthroughs in understanding language development all stimulated the growth of cognitive research. In the 1960s and early 1970s, evidence accumulated indicating that people do more than simply respond to reinforcement and punishment. For example, we plan our responses, use systems to help us remember, and organize the material we are learning in our own unique ways (Miller, Galanter, & Pribram, 1960; Shuell, 1986). With the growing realization that learning is an active mental process, educational psychologists became interested in how people learn concepts and solve problems.

Interest in concept learning and problem solving soon gave way, however, to interest in how knowledge is represented in the mind and, particularly, how it is remembered. Remembering and forgetting became major topics for investigation in cognitive psychology.

Today many cognitive theorists have a renewed interest in learning, but they have not yet developed a unified theory. The **cognitive view of learning** can best be described as a generally agreed-upon philosophical orientation. This means that cognitive theorists share basic notions about learning and memory. Cognitive theorists believe, for example, that learning is the result of our attempts to make sense of the world. To do this, we use all the mental tools at our disposal. The ways we think about situations, along with our knowledge, expectations, and feelings, influence how and what we learn.

Cognitive View of Learning A general approach that views learning as an active mental process of acquiring, remembering, and using knowledge.

Comparing Cognitive and Behavioral Views

The cognitive and behavioral views differ in their assumptions about what is learned. In the cognitive view, knowledge is learned and changes in knowledge make changes in behavior possible. In the behavioral view, the new behaviors themselves are learned (Shuell, 1986). Both behavioral and cognitive theorists believe reinforcement is important in learning, but for different reasons. The strict behaviorist maintains that reinforcement strengthens responses; cognitive theorists see reinforcement as a source of feedback. This feedback provides information about what is likely to happen if behaviors are repeated. In the cognitive view, reinforcement serves to reduce uncertainty and thus leads to a sense of understanding and mastery. For example, the *A* you receive after studying hard for a test tells you that you know how to handle the material in that particular class, so you are more certain about how to proceed and you feel more competent.

The cognitive view of learning sees people as active processors of information who initiate experiences that lead to learning, seek out information to solve problems, and reorganize what they already know to achieve new learning. Instead of being passively influenced by environmental events, people actively choose, practice, pay attention, ignore, and make many other responses as they pursue goals.

Differences between behavioral and cognitive views also are apparent in the methods each group has used to study learning. Much of the work on behavioral learning principles has been with animals in controlled laboratory settings. The goal is to identify a few general laws of learning that apply to all higher organisms (including humans, regardless of age, intelligence, or other individual differences). The behaviorists believe that these laws may predict and control changes in the behavior of any organism.

Cognitive psychologists, on the other hand, study a wide range of learning situations. Because of their focus on individual and developmental differences in cognition, they have not sought general laws of learning that apply to both animals and humans in all situations. This is one of the reasons that there is no single cognitive model or theory of learning representative of the entire field.

Knowledge and the Cognitive View

Knowledge is the outcome of learning. When we learn a fact, a name, the rules of tennis, how to use the word processor's spelling checker, when to ask a friend for a favor, or the causes of the Persian Gulf war, we know something new. And knowledge is more than the end product of previous learning; it also guides new learning. The cognitive approach suggests that one of the most important elements in the learning process is what the individual brings to the learning situation. What we already know determines to a great extent what we will learn, remember, and forget (Peeck, van den Bosch, & Kreupeling, 1982; Resnick, 1981; Shuell, 1986). "Knowledge creates our perceptions, focuses our attention, and is the 'stuff' of our memories" (Glover, Ronning, & Bruning, 1990, p. 13).

The Importance of Knowledge in Learning. A study by Recht and Leslie (1988) shows the importance of knowledge in understanding and remembering new information. These psychologists identified junior high students who were very good or very poor readers. Then they tested the students on their knowledge of baseball and found that knowledge of baseball was not related to reading ability. So the researchers were able to identify four groups of students: good readers/high baseball knowledge, good readers/low baseball knowledge, poor readers/high baseball knowledge, and poor readers/low baseball knowledge. All the subjects read a passage describing a baseball game and then were tested in a number of ways to see if they understood and remembered what they had read.

The results demonstrated the power of knowledge. Poor readers who knew baseball remembered more than good readers with little baseball knowledge and almost as much as good readers who knew baseball. Poor readers who knew little about baseball remembered the least of what they had read. So a good basis of knowledge can be more important than good learning strategies in understanding and remembering.

Kinds of Knowledge. Cognitive psychologists make several distinctions about kinds of knowledge. Some knowledge is general—it applies to many different situations. For example, **general knowledge** about how to read or spell or use a word processor is useful in and out of school. **Domain-specific knowledge,** on the other hand, pertains to a particular task or subject. For example, knowing that the shortstop plays between second and third base is specific to the domain of baseball. Of course, there is no absolute line between general and domain-specific knowledge. When you were first learning to read, you may have learned specific facts about the sounds of letters. At that time, knowledge about letter sounds was specific to the domain of reading class. But now you can use both knowledge about sounds and the ability to read in more general ways (Schunk, 1991a).

Another way of categorizing knowledge is as declarative, procedural, or conditional (Paris, Lipson, & Wixson, 1983). **Declarative knowledge** is "knowing that" something is the case. The common sense use of the term *knowledge* usually refers to declarative knowledge—facts, beliefs, theories, opinions, poems or passages or song lyrics, rules, names, and so on. Robert Gagné (1985) calls this category *verbal information*. The range of declarative knowledge is tremendous. You can know very specific facts (the atomic weight of gold is 196.967) or generalities (leaves of some trees change color in autumn) or personal preferences (I don't like lima beans) or personal events (I went to my brother's wedding last January) or rules (to divide fractions, invert the divisor and multiply). Small units of declarative knowledge can be organized into larger units; for example, principles of reinforcement and punishment can be organized in your thinking into a theory of behavioral learning (E. Gagné, 1985).

Procedural knowledge is "knowing how" to do something such as divide fractions or clean a carburetor. Notice that repeating the rule "to divide fractions, invert the divisor and multiply" shows declarative knowledge—the student can state the rule. But to show procedural knowledge, the student must act. When faced with a fraction to divide, the student must divide correctly (E. Gagné, 1985). Robert Gagné (1985) calls this kind of knowledge *intellectual skills*. Students demonstrate procedural knowledge when they translate a passage into Spanish or correctly categorize a geometric shape or diagram a sentence.

Conditional knowledge is "knowing when and why" to apply your declarative and procedural knowledge. Given many kinds of math

General Knowledge
Information that is useful in many different kinds of tasks; information that applies to many situations.

Domain-Specific Knowledge Information that is useful in a particular situation or that applies only to one specific topic.

Declarative Knowledge Verbal information; facts; "knowing that" something is the case.

Procedural Knowledge Knowledge that is demonstrated when we perform a task; "knowing how."

Conditional Knowledge "Knowing when and why" to use declarative and procedural knowledge.

TABLE 7.1 Kinds of Knowledge		
	General Knowledge	**Domain-Specific Knowledge**
Declarative	Hours the library is open Rules of grammar	The definition of "hypotenuse" The lines of the poem "The Raven"
Procedural	How to use your word processor How to drive	How to solve an oxidation-reduction equation How to throw a pot on a potter's wheel
Conditional	When to give up and try another approach When to skim and when to read carefully	When to use the formula for calculating volume When to rush the net in tennis

problems, it takes conditional knowledge to know when to apply one procedure and when to apply another to solve each problem. It takes conditional knowledge to know when to read every word in a text and when to just skim. For many students, conditional knowledge is a stumbling block. They have the facts and can do the procedures, but they don't seem to apply what they know at the appropriate time. Robert Gagné (1985) calls this kind of knowledge *cognitive strategies.*

You can see in Table 7.1 that we can combine our two systems for describing knowledge. Declarative, procedural, and conditional knowledge can be either general or domain-specific.

We have spent several paragraphs discussing kinds of knowledge because different kinds of knowledge require different learning and teaching approaches. As a framework for presenting some of the major findings from cognitive research, we will use the most influential and thoroughly studied model—information processing.

The Information Processing Model of Learning

The **information processing** approach relies on the computer as a model for human learning. Like the computer, the human mind takes in information, performs operations on it to change its form and content, stores the information, retrieves it when needed, and generates responses to it. Thus, processing involves gathering and representing information, or *encoding;* holding information, or *storage;* and getting at the information when needed, or *retrieval.* The whole process is controlled by "programs" that determine how and when information will flow through the system, as shown in Figure 7.1 on page 242.

For some cognitive psychologists, the computer model is only a metaphor for human mental activity. But other cognitive scientists, particularly those studying **artificial intelligence,** try to design and program computers to "think" and solve problems like human beings (Schunk, 1991). Some theorists suggest that the operation of the brain resembles a large number of very slow computers, all operating in parallel (at the

Information Processing Human mind's activity of taking in, storing, and using information.

Artificial Intelligence The capability of a computer or computer system to simulate human thinking and problem solving.

FIGURE 7.1   Computers as an Analogy for Human Information Processing
Many people compare the human information processing system to the components of a computer. Information is encoded or entered, stored temporarily in a "workspace," and saved in long-term storage. Once saved, the information can be recalled into the workspace to be used to solve problems.

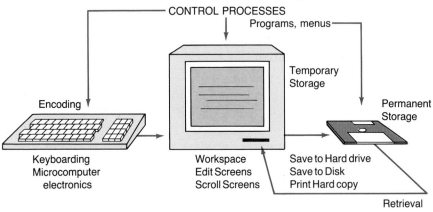

same time), with each computer dedicated to a different and fairly specific task (Martindale, 1991).

Information processing theorists approach learning primarily through a study of memory. Figure 7.2 is a schematic representation of a typical information processing model of memory, derived from the ideas of several theorists (Atkinson & Shiffrin, 1968; R. Gagné, 1985). Other models have been suggested, but all of the models, despite their variations, resemble the flow charts used to represent computer programs.

In Figure 7.2, the three circles depict knowledge structures where information may be held and transformed. The arrows indicate the flow of information. The box at the top of the figure represents control processes that affect the flow of information throughout the system. In order to understand this model, let's first look at the whole system in operation, then examine each element in depth.

The first step in the information processing model begins when one or more of our senses (hearing, vision, etc.) receives stimuli from the outside world. These sensations are held very briefly in the *sensory register* where they are recognized or perceived—we *see* a dog or *hear* our name, for example.

The sensations that we pay attention to and recognize are then transferred to *short-term memory,* a storage area with very limited capacity. Short-term memory also serves as our working memory. *Working memory* holds what we are thinking about at any given time—the information that is *activated.*

With some mental work, information can be transferred to *long-term memory.* The capacity of long-term memory is remarkable. Some psychologists believe that information is never really lost from long-term memory—even though it may be "misplaced." When we need to use information from long-term memory, we search for it. Sometimes the search is conscious, as when you see a friend approaching and search for

FIGURE 7.2 **The Information Processing System** The three stages of the information processing system are the sensory register, short-term memory, and long-term memory. Information is encoded in the sensory register where perception determines what will be held in short-term memory for further use. Thoroughly processed information becomes part of long-term memory and can be activated at any time to return to working memory.

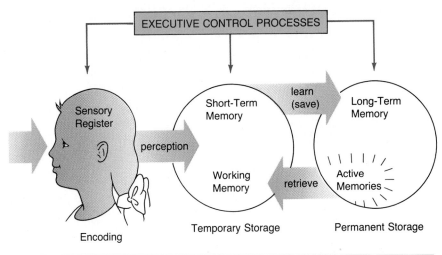

her name. At other times the location and use of information from long-term memory is automatic, as when you dial a telephone or solve a math problem without having to search for each step in the process. The information in long-term memory often is brought into working memory and combined with new, incoming information to help us make sense of the current situation. So, for example, when you read above that the information processing model is like a computer, you probably had to retrieve what you know about computers from your long-term memory to understand the sentence.

You can think of long-term memory as a huge shelf full of tools and supplies ready to be brought to the workbench of working memory to accomplish a task, as shown in Figure 7.3 on page 244. The shelf (long-term memory) stores an incredible amount, but it may be hard to find quickly what you are looking for. The workbench (working memory) is small, but anything on it is immediately available. Because it is small, however, supplies (bits of information) sometimes are lost when the workbench overflows (E. Gagné, 1985).

The last element in the model is *executive control*. This system monitors and guides the whole process—from focusing attention right now to finding information learned long ago. Returning to our workroom analogy, these control processes focus your attention on new information on the working-memory workbench, decide what you need from the long-term-memory storage shelves to solve the current problem on the workbench, guide your search for the necessary information, and so on.

Let's look at this model more carefully—first, the sensory register.

FIGURE 7.3   **Working Memory**   Working memory serves as a "workbench" in the human information processing system.

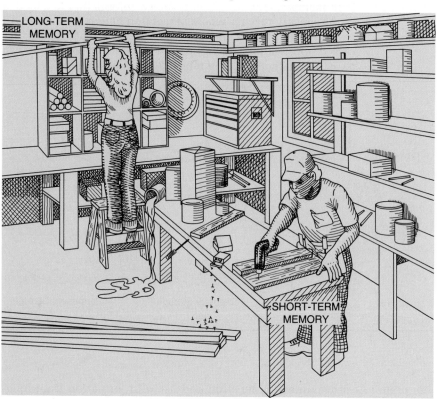

Source: Based on R. Klatzky (1975), *Human Memory: Structures and Processes* (San Francisco: W. H. Freeman).

THE SENSORY REGISTER

Stimuli from the environment (sights, sounds, smells, and so on) constantly bombard our receptors. **Receptors** are the body's mechanisms for seeing, hearing, tasting, smelling, and feeling. The whole system of receptors is called the **sensory register** or, simply, *sensory memory.*

Capacity, Duration, and Contents of Sensory Memory

The *capacity* of the sensory register is very large. More information than we can possibly handle at once gets into the sensory register. Because the sensory register holds everything briefly, however, we have a chance to make sense of it—to organize it (Lindsay & Norman, 1977). Organization is necessary because there is much more information available in the sensory register than can possibly enter the next system—short-term memory.

This vast amount of sensory information is fragile in *duration.* It lasts only between one and three seconds. You can experience this brief holding of sensory information in your own sensory register. Tap your

Receptors   Parts of the human body that receive sensory information.

Sensory Register   System of receptors holding sensory information very briefly.

fingers against your arm. Feel the immediate sensations. Then stop tapping and note how the sensations fade away. At first you retain the actual feeling of the tapping but soon you only recollect that your arm was tapped. Wave a pencil (or your finger) back and forth before your eyes while you stare straight ahead. See the shadowy image that trails behind the object? In each of these cases, the sensory input remains very briefly after the stimulus has left. You can feel a trace of the tap and see a trace of the pencil after the actual stimulus has been removed (Lindsay & Norman, 1977).

The *content* of the sensory register resembles the sensations from the original stimulus. Visual sensations are coded briefly by the sensory register as images, almost like photographs. Auditory sensations are coded as sound patterns. It may be that the other senses also have their own codes. Thus, for a second or so, a wealth of data from sensory experience remains intact. In these moments, we have a chance to select information for further processing. Instead of perceiving everything, we pay attention to certain features of the total content in the sensory register and look for patterns. The processes of perception and attention are critical at this stage.

The Influence of Perception

The meaning we attach to the information received through our senses is called **perception.** This meaning is constructed partly from objective reality and partly from the way we organize the information based on our existing knowledge. For example, consider these marks: ß . If asked what the letter is, you would say "B." If asked what the number is, you would say "13." The actual marks remain the same; the perception of them—their meaning—changes in keeping with your expectation to recognize a number or a letter. To a child without appropriate knowledge to perceive either a number or a letter, the marks would probably be meaningless (Smith, 1975).

Some of our present-day understanding of perception is based on studies conducted early in this century in Germany (and later in the United States) by psychologists called Gestalt theorists. **Gestalt,** which means something like *pattern* or *configuration* in German, refers to people's tendency to organize sensory information into patterns or relationships. Instead of perceiving bits and pieces of unrelated information, "the human brain transforms objective reality into mental events organized as meaningful wholes" (Schunk, 1991, p. 129). Figure 7.4 on page 246 presents a few Gestalt principles. The Gestalt principles are valid explanations of certain aspects of perception, but they are not the whole story. For example, you would not have seen the marks above as the letter *B* if you had no knowledge of the Roman alphabet. So what you know also affects what you are able to perceive.

There are two current explanations for how we recognize patterns and give meaning to sensory events. The first is called *feature analysis,* or **bottom-up processing.** This explanation suggests that we search a new stimulus for defining elements or features. For example, a capital letter *A* consists of two relatively straight lines joined at a 45-degree angle (∧) and a horizontal line (–) through the middle. Whenever we see these features,

Perception Interpretation of sensory information.

Gestalt German for pattern or whole; Gestalt theorists hold that people organize their perceptions into coherent wholes.

Bottom-Up Processing Perceiving based on noticing separate defining features and assembling them into a recognizable pattern.

FIGURE 7.4 Examples of Gestalt Principles Gestalt principles of perception explain how we "see" patterns in the world around us.

a. *Figure-ground*
What do you see? Faces or a vase? Make one figure–the other ground.

b. *Proximity*
You see these lines as 3 groups because of the proximity of lines.

c. *Similarity*
You see these lines as an alternating pattern because of the similarity in height of lines.

d. *Proximity*
outweighing similarity
You see these lines as proximal groups instead similar heights.

e. *Common direction*
You perceive a continuous line going up and down.

f. *Simplicity*
You perceive two whole shapes instead of five separate shapes.

g. *Closure*
You perceive a circle instead of dotted curved lines.

Source: Adapted with the permission of Merrill, an imprint of Macmillan Publishing Company, from *Learning theories: An educational perspective* by Dale H. Schunk, p. 131. Copyright © 1991 by Macmillan Publishing Company.

or anything close enough, we recognize an *A.* Thus A, **A**, *A*, *A*, A, and **A** may all be perceived as *A*'s (Anderson, 1990). This explains how we are able to read words written in other people's handwriting. Feature analysis is often called bottom-up processing because the stimulus must be analyzed into specific features or building blocks and assembled into a meaningful pattern "from the bottom up."

If all perception relied on feature analysis, learning would be very slow. Luckily, humans are capable of another type of perception, based on knowledge and context, often called **top-down processing.** We do not need to analyze every feature in a particular stimulus to make sense of it. Much of the information is redundant anyway. To recognize patterns rapidly, in addition to noting features, we use the context of the situation—what we know about words or pictures or the way the world generally operates. If you catch only a fleeting glimpse of a medium-sized, four-legged animal being led down a city street on a leash, you are likely to perceive a dog, based on the context and what you know about the situation. Of course you may be wrong, but not very often.

The patterns people perceive are based on their prior knowledge, what they expect to see, the concepts they understand, specific features of the situation, and many other factors. Sometimes the different factors give confusing signals. For example, a neighbor had never seen me in my college office and was used to seeing me only in our community. When the young woman decided to take some courses at the college and encountered me in my office, she had a difficult time placing my face. She finally remarked, "Oh, Mrs. Woolfolk, what are you doing here?" Her

Top-Down Processing
Perceiving based on the context and the patterns you expect to occur in that situation.

expectations and the context of the situation had interfered with her ability to use feature analysis to identify a familiar face.

The Role of Attention

Our senses are bombarded with sights and sounds every second. If every variation in color, movement, sound, smell, temperature, and so on had to be perceived, life would be impossible. By paying attention to certain stimuli and ignoring others, we select from all the possibilities what will be processed. But **attention** is a very limited resource. We can never pay attention to all the separate sensations available in the sensory register.

There was a time while my daughter was learning to drive when she couldn't listen to the radio and drive at the same time. After some practice, she could listen but had to turn the radio off when traffic was heavy. Unless you are very accomplished at two demanding tasks, you probably cannot do both at once. Like Liz, when you were learning to drive, knit, or type, you probably had to concentrate. However, if you are now accomplished at any of these tasks, you may be able to talk, listen to music, or compose a letter as you drive, knit, or type. This is because many processes that initially require attention and concentration become automatic with practice. Actually, **automaticity** probably is a matter of degree—we are not completely automatic, but rather more or less automatic in our performances depending on how much practice we have had (Anderson, 1990).

Attention and Teaching

The first step in learning is paying attention. Students cannot process something that they do not recognize or perceive. Many factors in the classroom influence student attention. Eye-catching or startling displays or actions can draw attention at the beginning of a lesson. A teacher might begin a science lesson on air pressure by blowing up a balloon until it pops. Bright colors, unusual placement of words, underlining, highlighting of written or spoken words, surprise events, and changes in voice level, lighting, or pacing can all be used to gain attention. There is some evidence that students learn more when the teacher is animated in delivering a lecture and uses nonverbal material along with the verbal (Kaufman, 1976). Table 7.2 on page 248 offers additional ideas for capturing students' attention.

In summary, how do people make sense of the vast amount of sensory stimuli around them? They do so by using a variety of strategies that include paying attention to certain aspects of the situation and by using Gestalt principles, feature detection, the context of the situation, and prior knowledge about similar situations to recognize patterns. The next step in processing information is moving it to short-term memory.

SHORT-TERM MEMORY

Once transformed into patterns of images or sounds (or perhaps other types of sensory codes), the information in the sensory register can enter the **short-term memory** system.

Ways of directing and supporting students' attention must fit the developmental needs of students. These young children are engrossed in the discussion, in part because they are paying attention to the puppet.

Attention Focus on a stimulus.

Automaticity The ability to perform thoroughly learned tasks without much mental effort.

Short-Term Memory Working memory, holding a limited amount of information briefly.

TABLE 7.2 Suggestions for Focusing Attention

1. Tell students the purpose of the lesson. Indicate how learning the material will be useful or important to them.

2. Ask students why they think learning the material will be important.

3. Arouse curiosity with questions such as "What would happen if . . . ?"

4. Create shock by staging an unexpected event such as a loud argument just before a lesson on communication.

5. Alter the physical environment by changing the arrangement of the room or moving to a different setting.

6. Shift sensory channels by giving a lesson that requires students to touch, smell, or taste.

7. Use movements, gestures, and voice inflection—walk around the room, point, speak softly and then more emphatically.

8. Avoid distracting behaviors such as tapping a pencil.

Source: Adapted from E. Emmer & G. Millett (1970), *Improving teaching through experimentation: A laboratory approach.* Adapted by permission of Allyn and Bacon.

Capacity, Duration, and Contents of Short-Term Memory

Short-term memory *capacity* is limited by the number of "bits" of information that can be held at one time. In experimental situations, it appears that only about five to nine separate new items can be held in short-term memory at one time (Miller, 1956). This limitation holds true to some degree in everyday life. It is quite common to remember a new phone number after looking it up, as you walk across the room to make the call. But what if you have two phone calls to make in succession? Two phone numbers (14 digits) probably cannot be stored simultaneously. In any event, by the time you finish the first conversation, you probably will have forgotten the second number.

Remember—put in your short-term memory—that we are discussing the recall of *new* information. In daily life we certainly can hold more than five to nine units of information in our short-term memories at once. While you are dialing that seven-digit phone number you just looked up, you are bound to have other things "on your mind"—in your memory—such as how to use a telephone, whom you are calling, and why. You don't have to pay attention to these things; they are not new knowledge. Some of the processes, such as dialing the phone, have become automatic. However, because of the short-term memory's limitations, if you were in a foreign country and were attempting to use an unfamiliar telephone system, you might very well have trouble remembering the phone number because you were trying to figure out the phone system at the same time.

The *duration* of information in short-term memory, as in the sensory register, is short, about 20 to 30 seconds at the most. Information can be held for a longer period of time only if you keep it *activated,* that is, only if you keep working with it in some way. It may seem to you that a memory system with a 20-second time limit is not very useful. But without this system you already would have forgotten what you read in the first part of this sentence before you came to these last few words. This would clearly make understanding sentences very difficult.

The short-term memory is sometimes known as **working memory,** because its *content* is activated information—what you are thinking about at the moment. This activated information may be knowledge from long-term memory that you are currently thinking about or something new you have just encountered (Anderson, 1990). For this reason, some psychologists consider the working memory to be synonymous with "consciousness." The information in short-term memory may be in the form of images that resemble the perceptions in the sensory register, or the information may be structured more abstractly, based on meaning. So you might hold pictures, words, associations, or ideas in short-term memory.

Processing Information in Short-Term Memory

Because information in short-term memory is fragile and easily lost, it must be kept activated to be retained. Activation is high as long as you are focusing on information, but it decays or fades quickly when attention shifts away (Anderson, 1990). When activation fades, forgetting follows, as shown in Figure 7.5 on page 250.

Retaining Information. To keep information activated in short-term memory for longer than 20 seconds, most people rehearse the information mentally. There are two types of rehearsal (Craik & Lockhart, 1972). **Maintenance rehearsal** involves repeating the information in your mind. As long as you repeat the information, it can be maintained in short-term memory indefinitely. Maintenance rehearsal is useful for retaining something you plan to use and then forget, like a phone number.

Elaborative rehearsal involves associating the information you are trying to remember with something you already know—with information from long-term memory. For example, if you meet someone at a party whose name is the same as your brother's, you don't have to repeat the name to keep it in memory, you just have to make the association. This kind of rehearsal not only retains information in working memory, but helps move information from short-term to long-term memory. Rehearsal is thus an "executive control process" that affects the flow of information through the information processing system.

The limited capacity of short-term memory can also be somewhat circumvented by the control process of **chunking.** Because the number of bits of information, not the size of each bit, is the limitation for short-term memory, you can retain more information if you can group individual bits of information. For example, if you have to remember the six digits 3, 5, 4, 8, 7, and 0, it is easier to put them together into three chunks of two digits each (35, 48, 70) or two chunks of three digits each (354, 870). With these changes, there are only two or three bits of information rather than six to hold at one time. Chunking helps you remember a telephone number or a social security number.

Working Memory The information that you are focusing on at a given moment.

Maintenance Rehearsal Keeping information in working memory by repeating it to yourself.

Elaborative Rehearsal Keeping information in working memory by associating it with something else you already know.

Chunking Grouping individual bits of data into meaningful larger units.

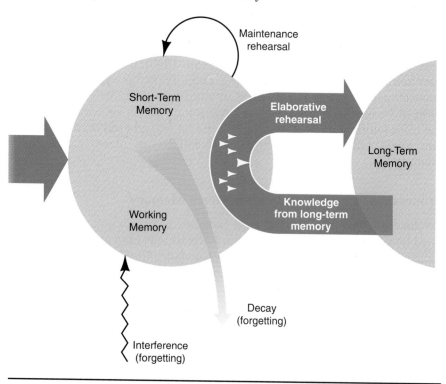

FIGURE 7.5   Short-Term Memory Information in short-term memory can be kept activated through maintenance rehearsal or transferred into long-term memory by being connected with information in long-term memory (elaborative rehearsal). Forgetting is caused by interference and time decay.

Forgetting. Information may be lost from short-term memory through interference or decay. **Interference** is fairly straightforward: remembering new information interferes with or gets in the way of remembering old information. The new thought replaces the old one. As new thoughts accumulate, old information is lost from short-term memory. Information is also lost from short-term memory by time **decay.** If you don't continue to pay attention to information, the activation level decays (weakens) and finally drops so low that the information cannot be reactivated—it disappears altogether.

Forgetting is very useful. Without forgetting, people would quickly overload their short-term memories and learning would cease. Also, it would be a problem if you remembered permanently every sentence you ever read. Finding a particular bit of information in all that sea of knowledge would be impossible. It is helpful to have a system that provides temporary storage.

LONG-TERM MEMORY

Short-term memory holds the information that is currently activated, such as a new telephone number you have just located and are about to

Interference The process that occurs when remembering certain information is hampered by the presence of other information.

Decay The weakening and fading of memories with the passage of time.

TABLE 7.3 **Short-Term and Long-Term Memory**

Type of Memory	Input	Capacity	Duration	Contents	Retrieval
Short-term	Very fast	Limited	Very brief: 20–30 sec.	Words, images, ideas, sentences	Immediate
Long-term	Relatively slow	Practically unlimited	Practically unlimited	Propositional networks, schemata, productions, episodes, perhaps images	Depends on representation and organization

Source: Adapted by permission of the author from F. Smith (1975), *Comprehension and learning: A conceptual framework for teachers,* published by Holt, Rinehart and Winston.

dial. **Long-term memory** holds the information that is well learned, such as all the other telephone numbers you know. Well-learned information is said to be high in **memory strength** or *durability* (Anderson, 1990).

Capacity and Duration of Long-Term Memory

There are a number of differences between short-term and long-term memory, as you can see in Table 7.3. Information enters short-term memory very quickly. To move information into long-term storage requires more time and a bit of effort. Whereas the capacity of short-term memory is limited, the capacity of long-term memory appears to be unlimited for all practical purposes. In addition, once information is securely stored in long-term memory, it can remain there permanently. Theoretically, we should be able to remember as much as we want for as long as we want. Of course, the problem is to find the right information when it is needed. Our access to information in short-term memory is immediate, because information in short-term memory is what we are thinking about at that very moment. But access to information in long-term memory requires time and effort.

Contents of Long-Term Memory: Networks and Schemata

Allan Paivio (1971, 1986; Clark & Paivio, 1991) suggests that information is stored in long-term memory as either visual images or verbal units, or both. Psychologists who agree with this point of view believe that information coded both visually and verbally is easiest to remember. (This may be one reason why explaining an idea with words and representing it visually in a figure, as we do in textbooks, has proved helpful to students.) Paivio's ideas have some support, but critics contend that the capacity of the brain is not large enough to store all the images we can imagine. They suggest that the images are actually stored as verbal codes and then translated into visual information when an image is needed (Schunk, 1991). Most cognitive psychologists distinguish three categories of memory: semantic, episodic, and procedural.

Long-Term Memory Permanent store of knowledge.

Memory Strength The durability of a memory; if information is well learned, it is more durable.

FIGURE 7.6
A Propositional Network

The sentence "Ida borrowed the antique tablecloth" has two propositions: (1) Ida borrowed the tablecloth [in the past] and (2) The tablecloth is an antique.

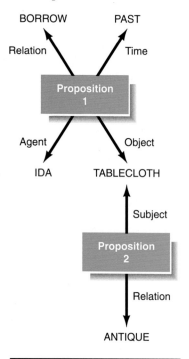

Source: Developed from material in J. Anderson (1985), *Cognitive psychology and its implications* (2nd ed.). San Francisco: W. H. Freeman; and D. Gentner (1975), Evidence for the psychological reality of semantic components: The verbs of possession. In D. Norman and D. Rumelhart (Eds.), *Explorations in cognition.* San Francisco: W. H. Freeman.

Semantic Memory
Memory for meaning.

Propositional Network Set of interconnected concepts and relationships in which long-term knowledge is held.

Schemata (singular, **Schema**) Basic structures for organizing information; concepts.

Semantic Memory. Memory for meaning is called **semantic memory.** Semantic memories are stored in propositions, networks, and schemata. Because these are very important concepts for teaching, we will spend some extra time on them.

A *proposition* is the smallest unit of information that can be judged true or false. The statement *Ida borrowed the antique tablecloth* has two propositions:

1. Ida borrowed the tablecloth.
2. The tablecloth is an antique.

A **propositional network** is an interconnected set of bits of information. Different cognitive psychologists have slightly different methods for diagramming propositional networks. Figure 7.6 is a common way of representing the relationships in the sentence "Ida (the *agent*) borrowed the antique tablecloth (the *object*)." Since the verb is in the past tense, the *time* of action is in the past. The same propositional network would apply to these sentences: *The antique tablecloth was borrowed by Ida,* or *Ida borrowed the tablecloth, which was an antique.* The meaning is the same, and it is this meaning that is stored in memory.

It is possible that all or most information is stored and represented in propositional networks. When we want to recall a bit of information, we may translate its meaning (as represented in the propositional network) into familiar phrases and sentences, or mental pictures. Also, because of the network, recall of one bit of information can trigger recall of another. We are not aware of these networks, for they are not part of our conscious memory (Anderson, 1990). In much the same way, we are not aware of underlying grammatical structure when we form a sentence in our own language; we don't have to diagram a sentence in order to say it.

As John Anderson (1985) has noted, "Propositions are fine for representing small units of meaning, but they fail when it comes to representing the larger sets of organized information that we know about particular concepts" (p. 124). For this larger, more complex task we need data structures that organize vast amounts of information. These data structures are called **schemata.** A **schema** (the singular form) is a pattern or guide for understanding an event, a concept, or a skill. Figure 7.7 is a representation of a partial schema for the category of "antique."

The schema tells you what features are typical of a category, what to expect. The schema is like a prototype or representative case, specifying the "standard" relationships and sequence of events involved with an object or situation (Rumelhart & Ortony, 1977). You encountered the very similar concept of *scheme* in the discussion of Piaget's theory of cognitive development in chapter 2.

When you hear the sentence *Ida borrowed the antique tablecloth,* you know even more about it than the propositions in Figure 7.6. This is because you have schemata about borrowing, tablecloths, antiques, and maybe even Ida herself. You know without being told, for example, that the lender does not have the tablecloth now, because it is in Ida's possession; and that Ida has an obligation to return the tablecloth to the lender (Gentner, 1975). None of this information is explicitly stated, but it is part of our schema for understanding the meaning of *borrow.* Other schemata

FIGURE 7.7 **A Schema for "Antique"** The concept of "antique" falls under the general category of "collectible object." It is related to other concepts, such as "hobby" and "traveling to flea markets," depending on the individual's experience with antiques.

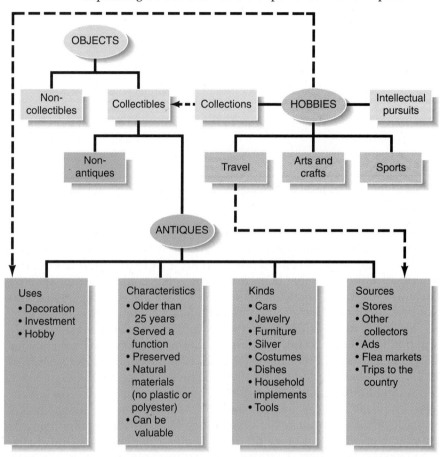

allow you to infer that the cloth is not plastic (if it is a real antique) and that Ida has probably invited guests for a meal. Your schema about Ida may even allow you to predict how promptly the cloth will be returned and in what condition.

Many cognitive psychologists believe schemata are the "key units of the comprehension process" (Rumelhart & Ortony, 1977, p. 111). To comprehend a story, we select a schema that seems appropriate. Then we use this framework to decide which details are important, what information to seek, and what to remember. It is as though the schema is a theory about what should occur in the story. The schema guides us in "interrogating" the text, filling in the specific information we expect to find so that the story makes sense (Resnick, 1981). Without the appropriate schema, trying to understand a story, textbook, or classroom lesson is a very slow and difficult process, something like finding your way through a new town without a map.

One type of schema, called a **story grammar,** helps students to understand and remember stories (Rumelhart, 1977). A story grammar could be

Story Grammar Typical structure or organization for a category of stories.

FIGURE 7.8 **"Lunchtime at the Day Care Center" Script**   This script is typical of ones generated by children of 5 or 6 years of age. Younger children give scripts that are less detailed and that contain fewer main acts.

First you play outside for awhile.

Then, when the teacher calls your name, you go in.

You get your lunchbox and sit down.

Then you eat.

Then you throw away your trash.

You get ready for your nap.

Source: From L. E. Berk, *Child Development,* 2nd ed., p. 282. Copyright © 1991. Reprinted with permission of Allyn and Bacon.

something like this: Murder discovered, search for clues, murderer's fatal mistake identified, trap set to trick suspect into confessing, murderer takes bait—mystery solved! In other words, a story grammar is a typical general structure—a schema or stereotype—that could fit many specific stories. If you know what to expect next as you are reading a story, you will probably find it easier to understand and remember the story.

A schema representing the typical sequence of events in an everyday situation is called a **script.** Children as young as 3 have basic scripts for the familiar events in their lives (Nelson, 1986). A kindergartener's script for "lunch" might be something like the one in Figure 7.8.

Storing knowledge of the world in schemata and scripts has advantages and disadvantages. Having a well-developed schema about Ida lets you recognize her (even as her appearance changes), remember many of her characteristics, and make predictions about her behavior. But it also allows you to be wrong. You may have incorporated incorrect or biased information into your schema of Ida. For example, if Ida is a member of an ethnic group different from yours and if you believe that group is dishonest, you may assume that Ida will keep the tablecloth. In this way, racial and ethnic stereotypes can function as schemata for misunderstanding individuals and for racial discrimination.

Episodic Memory. Memory for information tied to a particular place and time, especially information about the events of your own life, is called **episodic memory.** Episodic memory keeps track of the order of things, so it is also a good place to store jokes, gossip, or plots from films. Martindale (1991) distinguishes between semantic and episodic memory as follows:

Semantic memory contains the basic elements of knowledge, and episodic memory is made up from these elements. Semantic memory is like a dictionary containing the meanings of all of the words and images you know. Episodic memory is like a novel or movie that puts these concepts together in particular ways. (p. 181)

Script   Schema or expected plan for the sequence of steps in a common event such as buying groceries or ordering take-out pizza.

Episodic Memory   Long-term memory for information tied to a particular time and place, especially memory of the events in a person's life.

How would you answer these questions: What did you do on your 18th birthday? What did you have for dinner last Saturday night? Where were you on New Year's Eve, 1991? Most people answer these questions by imagining themselves in the situations and trying to "see" what was happening. Episodic memories probably are stored like semantic memories—in associated networks and schemata—but are often retrieved with the help of images. These memories can be strong and may be learned without effort. I did not work at remembering the dress I wore to the ninth-grade prom, but I can tell you *all* about it. Ask me what I wore any of the other days of the ninth grade and I would have to work hard to retrieve even one outfit. Ordinary episodic memories—like what you had for dinner every day last week—are not very strong, because we repeat most events many times and the memories tend to get muddled together.

Procedural Memory. Memory for how to do things is called **procedural memory.** It may take a long time to create a procedural memory—such as how to ski, serve a tennis ball, or factor an equation—but once learned, these memories tend to remain strong. Procedural memories are stored as *condition-action rules,* sometimes called **productions.** Productions specify what to do under certain conditions—*if A* occurs, *then do B.* A production might be something like "if you want to ski faster, lean back slightly" or "if your goal is to increase student attention, and a student has been paying attention a bit longer than usual, then praise the student." People can't necessarily state all their condition-action rules, but they act on them nevertheless. The more practiced the procedure, the more automatic the action (E. Gagné, 1985).

Storing Information in Long-Term Memory

Just what is done to "save" information permanently—to create semantic, episodic, or procedural memories? How can we make the most effective use of our practically unlimited capacity to learn and remember? Even though our long-term memory system is theoretically unlimited in capacity and duration, you probably know from experience that successful recall is no simple matter. The way you learn information in the first place—the way you process it at the outset—seems to affect its recall later. One important requirement is that you integrate new material with information already stored in long-term memory. Here elaboration, organization, and context play a role.

Elaboration. When confronted with the sentence about Ida and the tablecloth, we tend to "fill in," or elaborate, the new information with what we already know. **Elaboration** is the addition of meaning to new information through its connection with already existing knowledge. In other words, we apply our schemata and draw on already-existing knowledge to make sense of new information. We often elaborate automatically. Much as with Ida's sentence, a paragraph we read about a historic figure in the seventeenth century tends to activate our already-existing knowledge about that period; we use the old knowledge to understand the new.

Material that is elaborated when first learned will be easier to recall later. First, as we saw earlier, elaboration is a form of rehearsal. It keeps

Procedural learning may go slowly at first, but once these students "master the moves" in basketball, they will remember them automatically for a long time.

Procedural Memory
Long-term memory for how to do things.

Productions The contents of procedural memory; rules about what actions to take, given certain conditions.

Elaboration Adding and extending meaning by connecting new information to existing knowledge.

the information activated in working memory long enough to have a chance for permanent storage in long-term memory. Second, elaboration builds extra links to existing knowledge. The more one bit of information or knowledge is associated with other bits, the more routes there are to follow to get to the original bit. To put it another way, you have several "handles," or retrieval cues, by which you can recognize or "pick up" the information you might be seeking (Schunk, 1991). Psychologists have also found that the more precise and sensible the elaborations, the easier recall will be (Bransford, Stein, Vyell Franks, Auble, Mezynski, & Perfetto, 1982; Stein, Littlefield, Bransford, & Persampieri, 1984).

Organization. A second element of processing that improves retrieval, particularly of complex or large amounts of information, is **organization.** Material that is well organized is easier to learn and to remember than bits and pieces of information. Placing a concept in a structure will help you learn and remember either general definitions or specific examples. The structure serves as a guide back to the information when you need it. For example, Table 7.1 on page 241 organizes information about types of knowledge; Table 7.3 on page 251 gives an organized view of the capacity, duration, contents, and retrieval of information from short- and long-term memory, and Figure 7.7 on page 253 organizes my (limited) knowledge about antiques.

Context. A third element of processing that influences retrieval is **context.** Aspects of physical and emotional context—places, rooms, how we are feeling on a particular day, who is with us—are learned along with other information. Later, if you try to remember the information, it will be easier if the current context is similar to the original one. This has been demonstrated in the laboratory. Students who learned material in one type of room performed better on tests taken in a similar room than on tests taken in a very different-looking room (Smith, Glenberg, & Bjork, 1978). So studying for a test under "testlike" conditions may result in improved performance. Taking a psychology exam in the same room where the course is held will also improve your chances of remembering the material. Of course, you can't always go back to the same or to a similar place in order to recall something. But you can picture the setting, the time of day, and your companions, and you may eventually reach the information you seek.

Retrieving Information from Long-Term Memory

Organization Ordered and logical network of relations.

Context The physical or emotional backdrop associated with an event.

Retrieval Process of searching for and finding information in long-term memory.

In long-term memory the information is still available, even when it is not activated—when you are not thinking about it at the moment. **Retrieval,** or recall, is the challenge. Successful retrieval is really a problem-solving process that makes use of logic, cues, and other knowledge to reconstruct information and fill in any missing parts.

Sometimes reconstructed recollections are incorrect. For example, in 1932, F. C. Bartlett conducted a series of famous studies on remembering stories. He read a complex, unfamiliar Native-American tale to students at England's Cambridge University and then asked the students to recall the story after various lengths of time. The students' recalled stories were generally shorter than the original and were translated into the concepts and language of the Cambridge student culture. The story told of a seal hunt, for instance, but many students remembered a "fishing trip," an activity closer to their experiences. Instead of remembering the exact words of the story, the students remembered the meaning, but the meaning they remembered was altered slightly to fit their cultural expectations and stereotypes—in other words, their schemata.

Another example of **reconstruction** occurs when we retrieve information that is only partially correct. You probably have had an experience like this: You are looking for a book and saying, "I know it's blue with white letters on the cover." When you finally find the book, it does have white letters, but the cover is really green. Maybe you had not paid attention to the color; maybe the color of the object was encoded incorrectly in the first place; maybe you confused it with another book you were reading at the time (you forgot because of interference); or perhaps you encoded the right color, but it never reached your long-term memory (it was not elaborated enough). You did, however, retrieve part of the information. The parts you couldn't remember, you reconstructed.

Sometimes we attempt to retrieve information from our long-term memory and feel as if we're "about to remember" but cannot quite grasp what we're looking for. You may run into an acquaintance whose name seems to be "on the tip of your tongue"; you may even recall the sound of the name or the first letter. This near-retrieval is known, not surprisingly,

FIGURE 7.9 **Long-Term Memory** We activate information from long-term memory to help us understand new information in short-term memory. With mental work and processing (elaboration, organization, context) the new information can be stored permanently in long-term memory. Forgetting is caused by interference and time decay.

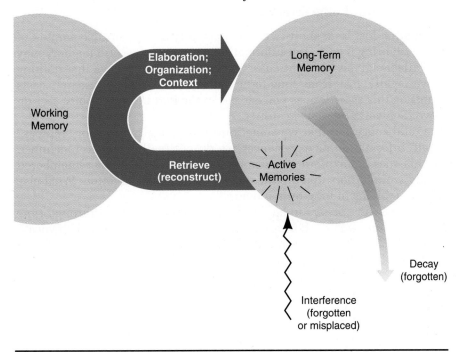

Reconstruction Recreating information by using memories, expectations, logic, and existing knowledge.

Do We Really Know How Memory Works?

Over the years, a number of principles of memory have been identified, only to be questioned later and rejected. You may have encountered some of these principles in the popular psychology press. Does research on memory point to clear laws of human functioning?

Point: Research supports some definite conclusions about memory.

Years ago Wilder Penfield, a neurosurgeon, was operating on the brain of an epilepsy patient. This surgery was performed under local anesthesia so that Penfield could stimulate specific areas of the brain with weak electrical current and the patient could report reactions. The patient's reactions guided the surgery. The surprising reaction of the patient to the stimulation suggested to Penfield that all memories are stored somewhere in the brain, even events that have been long "forgot-

ten." As the electrode touched a spot on the brain cortex, the patient reported a vivid recollection of a distant event. When the electrode was removed, the memory stopped. This "stimulated recall" occurred with several patients, and many of the memories seemed accurate (Houston, 1991; Penfield, 1969). It appears that memory is complete and detailed—it's all there somewhere (Schwartz & Reisberg, 1991).

In another series of classic experiments, Hermann Ebbinghaus (1913) established a principle of forgetting that seemed to stand the test of time. He demonstrated that forgetting is not steady and linear, but more like a curve. If we study and learn something but then stop practicing or paying attention to it, we forget quite a bit of the information right away. But then the amount we forget decreases each day, until we remember about the same amount for quite a while.

as the **tip-of-the-tongue phenomenon** (Brown & McNeill, 1966). The learning and retrieving processes of long-term memory are diagrammed in Figure 7.9 on page 257.

Forgetting and Long-Term Memory

Information lost from short-term memory truly disappears. No amount of effort will bring it back. But information stored in long-term memory may be available, given the right cues. Some researchers believe that nothing is ever really lost from long-term memory; but recent research casts doubts on this assertion, as you can see in the **Point/Counterpoint** section above (Schwartz & Reisberg, 1991).

Freud suggested that we sometimes intentionally forget or "repress" certain information or experiences we do not really want to remember. But this does not explain why some painful experiences are remembered vividly while others that are pleasant or neutral are forgotten. What else causes problems in long-term memory?

Information appears to be lost from long-term memory through *time decay* and *interference*. For example, memory for Spanish-English vocabulary decreases for about three years after a person's last course in Spanish, then stays level for about 25 years, then drops again for the next 25 years. One explanation for this decline is that neural connections, like muscles, grow weak without use. After 25 years, it may be that the memories are still somewhere in the brain but are too weak to be reactivated (Anderson, 1990).

Tip-of-the-Tongue Phenomenon Sense of being about to recall something.

Counterpoint: There's more to memory than we think we know.

While Penfield's reports caused quite a stir for many years, recently they have come under close scrutiny. It turns out that only a few of his patients—less than 10 percent—reported such vivid memories. There is no way to determine whether the reports were accurate memories or just very plausible *reconstructions* of what might have happened. The "memories" could have been real-seeming hallucinations or dreamlike sensations of some kind. Penfield did not provide independent evidence that the reported events actually occurred. And even if some memories are stored permanently in the brain, this does not prove that *all* memories are "in there somewhere."

And what about Ebbinghaus's classic *forgetting curve*? Does this really describe the pattern of losing information over time? Alan Baddeley (1990) reviewed the research on forgetting of different kinds of material and concluded:

Some types of material appear to show virtually no forgetting as in the case of continuous motor skills [like riding a bicycle]; other material such as languages appears to show rapid initial forgetting, followed by further excellent retention, while yet other skills such as those involved in cardiac resuscitation appear to show a relatively steep rate of forgetting, unless they are repeatedly practised. It is hard to escape the suspicion that the 'classic' forgetting curve of Ebbinghaus that is shown in all the introductory psychology texts may be rather less universal than we tend to assume. There are, of course, many differences between the various experiments I have cited, but they reinforce a conclusion that keeps cropping up in discussing the psychology of forgetting, namely that we know surprisingly little about this fundamental aspect of human memory. (pp. 242–243)

The idea that interference causes forgetting in long-term as well as in short-term memory seems to be supported by evidence from research. Newer memories may interfere with or obscure older memories. When new verbal associations make it difficult for a person to remember older information, the interference is called **retroactive interference.** If older associations make it difficult to remember new information, the interference is called **proactive interference** (Crouse, 1971). It seems that interference occurs when the same schema or script is used on several different occasions and elements of the different situations get confused (Schunk, 1991b).

The Guidelines on page 260 summarize several applications of information processing for teaching.

Another View of Memory

Not all cognitive psychologists believe that human memory can be completely explained by the three-store (sensory register, short-term, long-term) model. Craik and Lockhart (1972) first proposed their **levels of processing theory** as an alternative to three-store models. They suggested that what determines how long information is remembered is not where it is stored but how completely the information is analyzed and connected with other information. The more completely information is processed, the better our chances of remembering it. For example, according to the levels of processing theory, if I ask you to sort pictures of dogs based on the color of their coats, you might not remember many of the

Retroactive Interference New information interfering with old.

Proactive Interference Old information interfering with new.

Levels of Processing Theory Theory that recall of information is based on how deeply it is processed.

Guidelines

Using Information Processing Ideas in the Classroom

Make sure you have the students' attention.

Examples

1. Develop a signal that tells students to stop what they are doing and focus on you. Some teachers move to a particular spot in the room, flick the lights, or play a chord on the class piano.
2. Move around the room, use gestures, avoid speaking in a monotone.
3. Begin a lesson by asking a question that stimulates interest in the topic.
4. Regain the attention of individual students by walking closer to them, using their names, or asking them a question.

Help students separate essential from nonessential details and focus on the most important information.

Examples

1. Summarize instructional objectives to indicate what students should be learning. Relate the material you are presenting to the objectives as you teach: "Now I'm going to explain exactly how you can find the information you need to meet Objective One on the board—determining the tone of the story."
2. When you make an important point, pause, repeat, ask a student to paraphrase, note the information on the board in colored chalk, or tell students to highlight the point in their notes or readings.

Help students make connections between new information and what they already know.

Examples

1. Review prerequisites to help students bring to mind the information they will need to understand new material: "Who can tell us the definition of a quadrilateral? Now, what is a rhombus? Is a square a quadrilateral? Is a square a rhombus? What did we say yesterday about how you can

tell? Today we are going to look at some other quadrilaterals."
2. Use an outline or diagram to show how new information fits with the framework you have been developing. For example, "Now that you know the duties of the FBI, where would you expect to find it in this diagram of the branches of the U.S. government?"
3. Give an assignment that specifically calls for the use of new information along with information already learned.

Provide for repetition and review of information.

Examples

1. Begin the class with a quick review of the homework assignment.
2. Give frequent, short tests.
3. Build practice and repetition into games, or have students work with partners to quiz each other.

Present material in a clear, organized way.

Examples

1. Make the purpose of the lesson very clear.
2. Give students a brief outline to follow. Put the same outline on an overhead so you can keep yourself on track. When students ask questions or make comments, relate these to the appropriate section of the outline.
3. Use summaries in the middle and at the end of the lesson.

Focus on meaning, not memorization.

Examples

1. In teaching new words, help students associate the new word to a related word they already understand: "*Enmity* is from the same base as *enemy*. . . ."
2. In teaching about remainders, have students group 12 objects into sets of 2, 3, 4, 5, 6, and 7. Ask them to count the "leftovers" in each case.

pictures later. But if I ask you to rate each dog on how likely it is to chase you as you jog, you probably would remember more of the pictures. To rate the dogs you must pay attention to details in the pictures, relate features of the dogs to characteristics associated with danger, and so on. This rating procedure requires "deeper" processing and more focus on the meaning of the features in the photos.

Craik (1979) suggested that the three-store model and the levels of processing view are not entirely incompatible. There may be different structural components or memory stores similar to the sensory register, short-term, and long-term distinctions, as well as different strategies or levels of processing that "move" information from one stage to the next (Reed, 1992).

One problem with the levels of processing theory is that it has proved very difficult to define "processing depth." Is deep processing focusing on meaning, or is it forming a rich network of associations? Or both? Even though most researchers have turned away from a levels of processing approach, Schwartz and Reisberg (1991) argue that "there is an important and correct insight at the heart of the levels view: Finding meaningful connections between what you know and what you learn is very important. Conversely, thinking about what you learn in superficial ways tends not to promote learning" (p. 285). We turn now to examine what directs and monitors the powerful human information processing system.

METACOGNITION, SELF-REGULATION, AND INDIVIDUAL DIFFERENCES

One question that intrigues many cognitive psychologists is why some people learn and remember more than others. Part of the answer lies in the **executive control processes** shown in Figure 7.2 (page 243). Executive control processes guide the flow of information through the information processing system. They are like the software or programs of the computer. We have already discussed a number of control processes, including selective attention, maintenance rehearsal, elaborative rehearsal, organization, and elaboration. These executive control processes are sometimes called *metacognitive skills.* **Metacognition** literally means knowledge about cognition. Donald Meichenbaum and his colleagues describe metacognition as people's "awareness of their own cognitive machinery and how the machinery works" (Meichenbaum, Burland, Gruson, & Cameron, 1985, p. 5). Because people differ in their metacognitive knowledge and skills, they differ in how well and how quickly they learn.

Some of the differences in metacognitive abilities are due to development. As children grow older they are more able to exercise executive control and use strategies. For example, as children grow older, they are more able to determine if they have understood instructions (Markman, 1977, 1979) or if they have studied enough to remember a set of items (Flavell, Friedrichs, & Hoyt, 1970). Older children automatically use more efficient techniques than younger children for memorizing information (Flavell, 1985; Pressley, 1982). Metacognitive abilities begin to develop around ages 5 to 7 and improve throughout school. Most children go through a transitional period during which they can apply a particular strategy if reminded but will not apply it on their own (Garner, 1990).

Not all differences in metacognitive abilities have to do with age or maturation. There is great variability even among students of the same developmental level. Some individual differences in metacognitive abilities probably are caused by biological differences or by variations in learning experiences.

Executive Control Processes Processes such as selective attention, rehearsal, elaboration, and organization that influence encoding, storage, and retrieval of information in memory.

Metacognition Knowledge about our own thinking processes.

Using computer "menus" is analogous to the use of metacognitive skills in information processing. In both cases, the individual decides what procedure is needed next, selects procedures from several choices, monitors the effect of making the choice, and returns to the menu if the results are unsatisfactory or if a new procedure is needed.

Metacognition involves at least two separate components: (1) declarative and procedural knowledge of the skills, strategies, and resources needed to perform a task effectively—knowing *what* to do and *how* to do it; and (2) conditional knowledge to ensure the successful completion of the task—knowing *when* to do it. The strategies in the first component—knowing what to do—include rehearsing information, forming associations and images, using memory strategies, organizing new material to make it easier to remember, identifying the main idea while reading, applying test-taking techniques, outlining, and note taking. The second component—knowing when—includes checking to see if you understand, predicting outcomes, evaluating the effectiveness of an attempt at a task, planning the next move, deciding how to apportion time and effort, and revising or switching to other strategies to overcome any difficulties encountered (Baker & Brown, 1984a). The use of these regulatory or metacognitive abilities is known as **cognitive monitoring** (Flavell, 1985).

Let's examine some of the individual differences in metacognitive abilities that affect the three stages of information processing: sensory register, short-term memory, and long-term memory.

Individual Differences and Sensory Memory

John Flavell (1985) has described four aspects of attention that seem to develop as children mature.

1. *Controlling Attention.* As children grow older, they are more able to control their attention. They not only have longer attention spans; they also focus more accurately on what is important while ignoring irrele-

Cognitive Monitoring
Monitoring of our thinking and learning strategies.

vant details. In addition, they can simultaneously pay attention to more than one dimension of a situation. These improved abilities lead to better performance on conservation tasks.

2. *Fitting Attention to the Task.* As children develop, they become better at fitting their attention to the task. Older children, for example, know that they should focus their attention on the items they keep missing when they are trying to learn a list of words or pictures (Berk, 1991).

3. *Planning.* Children improve in their ability to plan how to direct their attention. They look for clues to tell them what is important and are ready to pay attention to those things. For example, older children who can tell from the teacher's gestures and tone of voice that the next part of the lesson is important will prepare themselves to pay full and concentrated attention.

4. *Monitoring.* Children improve their abilities to monitor their attention, to decide if they are using the right strategy, and to change approaches when necessary to follow a complicated series of events. For example, when students have been doodling in their notebooks while trying to listen, but realize they are having trouble understanding the teacher, they can stop doodling and focus only on what the teacher is saying.

Many differences in attention and perception relate to factors other than age and maturation. Students can vary greatly in their ability to attend selectively to information in their environment. In fact, many students diagnosed as learning disabled actually have attention disorders (Hallahan & Kauffman, 1991), particularly with long tasks (Pelham, 1981). Attention and perception are also influenced by the individual and cultural differences we examined in chapters 4 and 5, such as learning abilities and preferences, cognitive styles, and cultural background. Students who are field dependent, for example, have difficulty perceiving elements in a pattern and tend to focus on the whole.

Individual Differences and Working Memory

As you might expect, there are both developmental and individual differences in short-term memory. Research indicates that young children have very limited working memories but that memory span improves with age, as shown in Figure 7.10 on page 264 (Siegler, 1991). It is not clear whether these differences are due to changes in memory *capacity* or improvements in *strategy use.* Case (1985a & b) suggests that the total amount of "space" available for processing information is the same at each age; but young children must use quite a bit of this space to remember how to execute basic operations, like reaching for a toy, finding the right word for an object, or counting. Using a new operation takes up quite a bit of the child's working memory. Once an operation is mastered, however, there is more working memory available for short-term storage of new information. Biology may play a role too. As the brain and neurological system of the child mature, processing may became more efficient so that more working-memory space is available.

FIGURE 7.10   **Improvement with Age in Memory Span for Numbers and Letters**   As children mature, their memory for a sequence of letters or numbers gradually improves. By age 12, they can remember an average of 6 to 7 numbers and 5 to 6 letters.

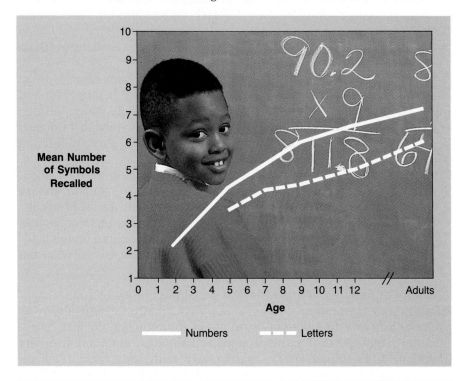

Sources: Adapted by permission from Robert S. Siegler, *Children's thinking,* 2nd ed., © 1991, p. 179. Prentice-Hall, Englewood Cliffs, New Jersey. Also adapted from F. N. Dempster (1981). Memory span: Sources of individual and developmental differences. *Psychological Bulletin, 89,* 63–100. Copyright 1981 by the American Psychological Association. Reprinted by permission.

As children grow older, they develop more effective strategies for remembering information. Most children spontaneously discover rehearsal around age 5 or 6. Siegler (1991) describes a 9-year old boy who witnessed a robbery, then mentally repeated the license number of the getaway car until he could give the number to the police. Younger children can be taught to rehearse and will use the strategy effectively as long as they are reminded. But they will not apply the strategy spontaneously. Children are 10 to 11 years old before they have adultlike working memories.

According to Case (1985a & b), young children often use reasonable but incorrect strategies for solving problems because of their limited memories. They try to simplify the task by ignoring important information or skipping steps to reach a correct solution. This puts less strain on memory. For example, when comparing quantities young children may consider only the height of the water in a glass, not the diameter of the glass, because this approach demands less of their memory. According to

Case, this explains young children's inability to solve the classic Piagetian conservation problem.

Besides developmental differences, there are other individual variations in short-term memory. Some people seem to have more efficient short-term memories than others (Dempster, 1981), and differences in working memory may be associated with giftedness in math and verbal areas. For example, subjects in one research study were asked to remember lists of numbers, the locations of marks on a page, letters, and words (Dark & Benbow, 1991). Subjects who excelled in mathematics remembered numbers and locations significantly better than subjects talented in verbal areas. The verbally talented subjects, on the other hand, had better memories for words. Based on these results, Dark and Benbow believe that basic differences in information processing abilities play a role in the development of mathematical and verbal talent.

Because working memory is limited, students—particularly younger and less able students—often try to simplify new information by ignoring some elements. This can lead to errors. Case (1985b) suggests the following procedures for dealing with young children or with any students whose working-memory capacity is limited. First, observe the students who are failing at a particular task and determine if they are trying to oversimplify the task. Second, find some way to point out what they are ignoring and why their oversimplified approach won't work. Then demonstrate a better strategy. Finally, have the students practice the new approach. Throughout this process, try to minimize the amount of information the students have to remember by reducing the number of items involved, using familiar terms, emphasizing what is really important, keeping the steps small, and giving lots of practice so that each step becomes as automatic as possible.

Individual Differences and Long-Term Memory

There are several developmental differences in how students use organization, elaboration, and knowledge to process information in long-term memory. Most children discover the value of using *organizational strategies* around age 6, and by 9 or 10 they use these strategies spontaneously. So, given the following words to learn:

> couch, orange, rat, lamp, pear, sheep, banana, rug, pineapple, horse, table, dog,

an older child or an adult might organize the words into three short lists of furniture, fruit, and animals. Younger children can be taught to use organization to improve memory, but they probably won't apply the strategy unless they are reminded. Children also become more able to use *elaboration* as they mature, but this strategy is developed late in childhood. Creating images or stories to remember ideas is more likely for older elementary-school students and adolescents (Siegler, 1991).

The major individual difference that affects long-term memory is knowledge. When students have more *domain-specific declarative* and *procedural knowledge,* they are better at learning and remembering material in that domain. Think what it is like for you to read a very technical textbook in an area you know little about. Every line is difficult. You have to stop and look up words or turn back to read about concepts you don't understand. It is hard to remember what you are reading, because you are trying to understand and remember at the same time. But with a good basis of knowledge, learning and remembering become easier; the more you know, the easier it is to know more. This is true in part because having knowledge improves strategy use.

Some students are better than others at using knowledge to help them learn and remember. They have the *conditional knowledge* to know when and how to apply information. For example, Bransford and his colleagues (1981) asked high- and low-achieving students to memorize the characteristics of two kinds of robots. *Extendable* robots wash windows on two-story houses; they are made of heavy steel and have spiked feet that hold them in the ground. *Unextendable* robots wash windows in high-rise buildings; they are made of light material, and have suction-cup feet and a parachute that opens if they fall. Successful students used their knowledge of each robot's function to understand why the characteristics were important (spiked feet to keep the on-the-ground robot steady, suction-cup feet to let the high-rise robot climb). Their recall of robot characteristics was excellent. Unsuccessful students just tried to memorize the characteristics without connecting characteristics to function. They remembered much less. Not using existing knowledge kept the poor students from learning more, so they did not develop their knowledge base.

Now that we have an understanding of the whole information processing system and the ways that individual students differ, let's turn to the really important question: How can teachers help students learn and remember better?

HELPING STUDENTS BECOME STRATEGIC LEARNERS

As you have seen, people learn best when they have a good base of knowledge in the area they are studying. With many well-elaborated schemata and scripts to guide them, new material makes more sense and there are many possible networks for connecting new information with old. But students don't always have a good base of knowledge. In the early phases of learning, students of any age must grope around the landscape a bit, searching for landmarks and direction. Even experts in an area must use some learning strategies when they encounter unfamiliar material or new problems (Garner, 1990; Perkins & Salomon, 1989; Shuell, 1990).

First we will discuss *rote memorization* strategies for helping students remember information that has little inherent meaning but may provide the basic building blocks for other learning—the populations of the 10 largest cities in the world, for example. Next we will examine *mnemonic* strategies that *build in* meaning by connecting what is to be learned with established words or images. Then we explore approaches that *build on* the inherent meaning of the information to be learned.

Rote Memorization

Some things need to be learned by rote, but not very many. We all probably learned the names of the numbers 1 to 10 by rote memorization. After 10, the whole procedure became easier because prior knowledge of the first 10 numbers helped us crack the system.

Let's look at another example of **rote memorization.** How might a student go about memorizing all the states and their capitals by rote in a single weekend? One possibility is to break the list into a number of separate lists and practice each one intermittently throughout the weekend. The student might also ask a friend to hear recitations of the short lists and later ask the friend to pick some states at random and give a test.

Breaking the list into segments is an example of **part learning.** Moving information into long-term memory takes effort; only a few items can move into long-term memory at any given time. So it makes sense to concentrate on a limited number of items. The immediate success of learning each partial list can encourage the student to continue.

If you have tried to memorize a list of items that are all similar to one another, you may have found that you tended to remember items at the beginning and at the end of the list but forgot those in the middle. This is called the **serial-position effect.** Part learning can help prevent this effect, because breaking a list into several short lists means there will be fewer middle items to forget.

Another strategy for memorizing a long list is the use of **distributed practice.** A student who studies the states and their capitals intermittently throughout the weekend will probably do much better than a student who tries to memorize the entire list on Sunday night. Studying for an extended period, rather than for briefer periods with rest time in between, is called **massed practice.** There are several reasons why distributed practice is more effective. Too long a study session leads to fatigue, and motivation lags. In addition, forgetting begins promptly at the end of the learning session. If several sessions are used, what is forgotten from one session can be relearned in the next. The **relearning** will be faster than starting from scratch because forgetting is only partial, and some items will be familiar.

Mnemonics

Mnemonics are systematic procedures for improving one's memory. Since the 1970s there has been a surge of interest in examining how mnemonic aids actually work in classroom contexts. Mnemonic techniques have been demonstrated to be effective for students of all ages, from preschool to college (Levin, 1985; McCormick & Levin, 1987). Many of these mnemonic strategies use imagery.

Peg-Type Mnemonics. To use **peg-type mnemonics** you first memorize a standard list of places or words. Then, whenever you want to learn a list of items, you associate the new information with the "pegs" already in memory. One peg-type approach, the **loci method,** derives its name from the plural of the Latin word *locus,* meaning "place."

To use the loci method, you must first imagine a very familiar place, such as your own house or apartment, and pick out particular locations

Rote Memorization
Remembering information by repetition without necessarily understanding the meaning of the information.

Part Learning Breaking a list of rote items into shorter lists.

Serial-Position Effect The tendency to remember the beginning and the end but not the middle of a list.

Distributed Practice Practice in brief periods with rest intervals.

Massed Practice Practice for a single extended period.

Relearning Filling in the gaps and encoding more completely material that is not totally unfamiliar.

Mnemonics Techniques for remembering; also, the art of memory.

Peg-Type Mnemonics Systems of associating items with cue words.

Loci Method Technique of associating items with specific places.

that you might notice in a walk through that place. Whenever you have a list to remember, simply place each item from the list in one of these locations in the house. For instance, let's say you want to remember to buy milk, bread, butter, and cereal at the store. Imagine a giant bottle of milk blocking the entry hall, a lazy loaf of bread sleeping on the living-room couch, someone sliding on a stick of butter and knocking over the dining-room table, and dry cereal covering the entire kitchen floor. When you want to remember the items, all you have to do is take an imaginary walk and see what is in the entry hall, the living room, the dining room, and the kitchen. The same locations serve as pegs every time you have a list to remember.

Other types of peg approaches work better if you need to remember information for long periods of time. One common type is the **acronym**—a word formed from the first letters of the words of a phrase. Examples include NATO (North Atlantic Treaty Organization), scuba (self-contained underwater breathing apparatus), and laser (light amplification by stimulated emission of radiation). An acronym is a kind of abbreviation. Another method involves forming phrases or sentences out of the first letters of each word or item in a list. You may be familiar with a sentence known by all young music students—Every Good Boy Does Fine. The first letter of each word stands for the name of a line of the G clef—*E, G, B, D, F.* The first letter of each word in the sentence provides the peg. Since the words must make sense as a sentence, this approach also has some characteristics of the chain methods described next.

Chain Mnemonics. Methods that connect the first item to be memorized with the second, the second item with the third, and so on are called **chain mnemonics** (or linking mnemonics). In one type of chain method, each item on a list is linked to the next through some visual association. If you have to stop at the cleaners, the bank, the post office, and the supermarket, you might begin by imagining the cleaner pressing the money that is going to be sent to the bank. Then you might imagine the money stuffed in envelopes. Finally, you might imagine these envelopes in a shopping cart. In each case, one visual cue leads you to the next.

Another chain-type approach is to incorporate all the items to be memorized into a jingle with rhymes, like "*i* before *e* except after *c*" or "Thirty days hath September." These approaches do stick in our memories. Most of us still repeat the "Thirty days" rhyme to determine the length of a given month.

The Keyword Method. The mnemonic system that has been most extensively applied in teaching is the **keyword method.** Although the idea has a long history, research by Atkinson and his colleagues in the mid-1970s sparked serious interest, especially in foreign-language teaching (Atkinson, 1975; Atkinson & Raugh, 1975).

The approach has two stages. To remember a foreign word, you first choose an English word, preferably a concrete noun, that sounds like the foreign word or a part of it. Next, you associate the meaning of the foreign word with the English word through an image or sentence. For example, the Spanish word *carta* (meaning "letter") sounds like the English word

"HOW MANY TIMES MUST I TELL YOU—IT'S 'CAT' BEFORE 'TEMPLE' EXCEPT AFTER 'SLAVE.'"

By permission of Bo Brown.

Acronym Technique for remembering names, phrases, or steps by using the first letter of each word to form a new, memorable word.

Chain Mnemonics Memory strategies that associate one element in a series with the next element.

Keyword Method System of associating new words or concepts with similar-sounding cue words.

"cart." Cart becomes the keyword: you imagine a shopping cart filled with letters on its way to the post office, or you make up a sentence such as "The cart full of letters tipped over" (Pressley, Levin, & Delaney, 1982). Figure 7.11 offers another example of this method, this time used to learn English vocabulary.

The keyword method has also been used successfully with poor readers and learning disabled students (Goin, Peters, & Levin, 1986; Peters & Levin, 1986; Scruggs, Mastropieri, McLoone, Levin, & Morrison, 1985). One problem, however, is that the method does not work well if it is difficult to identify a keyword for a particular item. Many words and ideas that students need to remember do not lend themselves to associations with keywords (Hall, 1991; Pressley, 1991).

FIGURE 7.11   Using the Keyword Method to Learn English Vocabulary
Here the keyword is "purse." It is a concrete noun that sounds like "persuade" (the vocabulary word to be learned). The keyword, definition, and vocabulary word are linked in an image.

Source: J. R. Levin, C. B. McCormick, G. E. Miller, J. K. Berry, and M. Pressley (1982). Mnemonic versus nonmnemonic vocabulary—learning strategies for children. *American Educational Research Journal, 19,* 121–136. Copyright 1982 by the American Educational Research Association. Reprinted by permission of the publisher and author.

In general, the techniques that require self-generated imagery are more appropriate for students in the later elementary and secondary grades. Younger students have some difficulty forming their own images. For them, memory aids that rely on auditory cues—rhymes like "*i* before *e* except after *c*," and "Thirty days hath September" seem to work better. If you want to use aids requiring imagery with younger or less-able students, you will probably need to help them find appropriate images or keywords (Pressley, 1991; Pressley, Levin, & Delaney, 1982).

Until a student has some knowledge to guide learning, it may help to use rote memorization and mnemonic approaches to build vocabulary and facts. But as knowledge grows, other learning strategies are more helpful.

Making It Meaningful

Perhaps the best single method for helping students learn is to make each lesson as meaningful as possible. Meaningful lessons are presented in vocabulary that makes sense to the students. New terms are clarified through associations with more familiar words and ideas. Meaningful lessons are also well organized, with clear connections between the different elements of the lesson. Finally, meaningful lessons make natural use of old information to help students understand new information through examples or analogies.

The importance of meaningful lessons is emphasized in an example presented by Smith (1975). Consider the three lines below:

1. KBVODUWGPJMSQTXNOGMCTRSO
2. READ JUMP WHEAT POOR BUT SEEK
3. KNIGHTS RODE HORSES INTO WAR

Begin by covering all but the first line. Look at it for a second, close the book, and write down all the letters you remember. Then repeat this procedure with the second and third lines. Each line has the same number of letters, but the chances are great that you remembered all the letters in the third line, a good number of letters in the second line, and very few in the first line.

The first line makes no sense. There is no way to organize it in a brief glance. The second line is more meaningful. You do not have to see each letter because you bring prior knowledge of spelling rules and vocabulary to the task. The third line is the most meaningful. Just a glance and you can probably remember all of it because you bring to this task prior knowledge not only of spelling and vocabulary but also of rules about syntax and probably some historical information about knights (they didn't ride in tanks). This sentence is meaningful because you have existing schemata for assimilating it. It is fairly easy to associate the words and meaning with other information already in long-term memory.

The challenge for teachers is to make lessons less like learning the first line and more like learning the third line. Although this may seem obvious, think about the times when you yourself have read a sentence in a text or heard an explanation from a professor that might just as well have been KBVODUWGPJMSQTXNOGMCTRSO.

Teaching Learning Strategies and Study Skills

Meaningful teaching is important—but it is not enough. Research on learning reveals one undeniable fact—students must be engaged in order to learn. They must actively process information. The emphasis today is on helping students develop effective learning strategies and tactics.

Learning Strategies and Tactics. **Learning strategies** are plans for accomplishing learning goals; a learning strategy is a kind of overall plan of attack. **Learning tactics** are the specific techniques that make up the plan (Derry, 1989). Your *strategy* for learning the material in this chapter, for example, might include the *tactics* of using mnemonics to remember key terms, skimming the chapter first to identify the organization, and writing sample answers to possible essay questions. Your use of strategies and tactics reflects your metacognitive knowledge.

One goal of education, according to many experts, should be to help students learn to use effective learning strategies. Such help is rarely given. For example, one study found that elementary-school teachers made suggestions to their students about using memory and learning strategies only around 3 percent of the time (Moely, Hart, Santulli, Leal, Johnson, Rao, & Burney, 1986). Fortunately, studying how to teach these executive control skills has become a high priority in education, and several important principles have been identified.

1. Students must be exposed to a number of different strategies: not only general learning strategies but very specific tactics, such as the mnemonic techniques described earlier in this chapter.

2. Teach conditional knowledge about when, where, and why to use various strategies (Pressley, 1986). Although this may seem obvious, teachers often neglect this step, either because they do not realize its significance or because they assume students will make inferences on their own. A strategy is more likely to be maintained and employed if students know when, where, and why to use it.

3. Students may know when and how to use a strategy, but unless they also develop the desire to employ these skills, general learning ability will not improve. Those who use strategies effectively believe that they can successfully affect their own performance; other students must also be given the opportunity to develop these feelings of effectiveness. Several learning strategy programs (Borkowski, Johnston, & Reid, 1986; Dansereau, 1985) include a motivational training component. In chapters 9 and 10 we will look more closely at this important issue of motivation.

4. Direct instruction in schematic knowledge is often an important component of strategy training. In order to identify main ideas—a critical skill for a number of learning strategies—you must have an appropriate schema for making sense of the material. The effectiveness of specific schema training has been repeatedly demonstrated. Table 7.4 on page 272 is a summary of several learning tactics for learning declarative (verbal) and procedural information (Derry, 1989).

Study Skills. Do you underline or highlight key phrases in textbooks? Are my words turning yellow or pink at this very moment? What about

Learning Strategies General plans for approaching learning tasks.

Learning Tactics Specific techniques for learning, such as using mnemonics or outlining a passage.

TABLE 7.4 Examples of Learning Tactics

	Examples	Use When?
Tactics for Learning Verbal Information	**1.** Attention Focusing ■ Making outlines, underlining	With easy, structured materials; for good readers
	■ Looking for headings and topic sentences	For poorer readers; with more difficult materials
	2. Schema Building ■ Story grammars ■ Theory schemata ■ Networking and mapping	With poor text structure, goal is to encourage active comprehension
	3. Idea Elaboration ■ Self-questioning ■ Imagery ■ PQ4R	To understand and remember specific ideas
Tactics for Learning Procedural Information	**1.** Pattern Learning ■ Hypothesizing ■ Identifying reasons for actions	To learn attributes of concepts To match procedures to situations
	2. Self-instruction ■ Comparing own performance to expert model	To tune, improve complex skills
	3. Practice ■ Part practice	When few specific aspects of a performance need attention
	■ Whole practice	To maintain and improve skill

Source: Based on S. Derry (1989), Putting learning strategies to work, *Educational Leadership,* January, pp. 5–6.

outlining or taking notes? Underlining and note taking are probably two of the most commonly used strategies among college students. Yet few students have ever received any direct instruction in the best ways to underline and take notes. So it is not surprising that many students use ineffective strategies.

One common problem is that students underline or highlight too much. It is better to be selective. In studies that limit how much students can underline—for example, only one sentence per paragraph—learning has improved (Snowman, 1984). In addition to being selective, you also should actively transform the information into your own words as you underline or take notes. Don't rely on the words of the book or lecturer. Note connections between what you are hearing or reading and other things you already know. Draw diagrams to illustrate relationships. Finally, look for organizational patterns in the material and use them to guide your underlining or note taking (Irwin, 1986; Kiewra, 1988).

If you want to improve your study skills, there are study-strategy books that provide excellent guidelines. The suggestions in the *Study Guide* for this text are taken from one of these books, *How to Study in*

Guidelines

Using Study Skills and Learning Strategies

Make sure you have the necessary declarative knowledge (facts, concepts, ideas) to understand new information.

Examples

1. Keep definitions of key vocabulary available as you study.
2. Review required facts and concepts before attempting new material.

Find out what type of test the teacher will give (essay, short answer), and study the material with that in mind.

Examples

1. For a test with detailed questions, practice writing answers to possible questions.
2. For a multiple-choice test, use mnemonics to remember definitions of key terms.

Make sure you are familiar with the organization of the materials to be learned.

Examples

1. Preview the headings, introductions, topic sentences, and summaries of the text.
2. Be alert for words and phrases that signal relationships, such as *on the other hand, because, first, second, however, since.*

Know your own cognitive skills and use them deliberately.

Examples

1. Use examples and analogies to relate new material to something you care about and understand well, such as sports, hobbies, or films.
2. If one study technique is not working, try another—the goal is to stay involved, not to use any particular strategy.

Study the right information in the right way.

Examples

1. Be sure you know exactly what topics and readings you will be expected to master.
2. Spend your time on the important, difficult, and unfamiliar material that will be required for the test or assignment.
3. Keep a list of the parts of the text that give you trouble and spend more time on those pages.
4. Process the important information thoroughly by using mnemonics, forming images, creating examples, answering questions, making notes in your own words, and elaborating on the text. Do not try to memorize the author's words—use your own.

Monitor your own comprehension.

Examples

1. Use questioning to check your understanding.
2. When reading speed slows down, decide if the information in the passage is important. If it is, note the problem so you can reread or get help to understand. If it is not important, ignore it.
3. Check your understanding by working with a friend and quizzing one another.

College by Walter Pauk (1989). Your college may have a study-skills center that can provide extra help.

Effective use of underlining and note taking depends on an understanding of the organization of the text. Some study strategies have been developed to help students with this key element. Armbruster and Anderson (1981) taught students specific techniques for diagramming rela-

FIGURE 7.12   **Mapping a Social Studies Chapter**   This student has mapped information related to the concept of "Puritan values" by relating ideas about history, literature, work, and education.

Map A

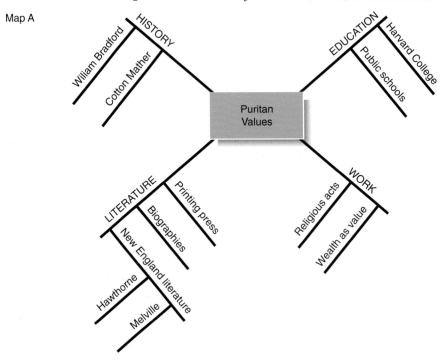

Source: From Judith Westphal Irwin (1986), *Teaching reading comprehension processes.* © 1986, p. 55. Reprinted by permission of Allyn and Bacon.

tionships among ideas presented in a text. "Mapping" these relationships by noting causal connections, comparison/contrast connections, and examples improved recall. Davidson (1982) suggested that students compare one another's "maps" and discuss the differences. As you can see, the map in Figure 7.12 uses a main idea/detail structure to organize information about the Puritans. There are usually many different ways to map the ideas in a passage.

AN APPLICATION TO READING INSTRUCTION

To discover the practical significance of metacognition and learning strategies, let's focus on a common element of schoolwork—reading comprehension. Clearly, much of the knowledge available to students in schools is packaged in the form of written materials. Reading comprehension is important in all school subjects—it is general procedural knowledge.

If you were asked to describe what you did as you were reading the previous paragraph, you'd probably say, "What do you mean, what did I do? I just read the words." But reading comprehension is a much more complicated process than just "reading the words." Comprehension is the result of an interaction between the text itself and the cognitive structures

Students who can study effectively, matching their approach to the demands of the material, are at an advantage as courses become harder and the work load increases in high school and college.

(story grammars, other schemata, propositional networks, strategies) that the reader draws on and applies during the reading process. To get a feel for this interaction, we can examine differences in metacognitive skills between expert (older or better) readers and novice or unskilled (younger or poorer) readers.

Expert and Novice Readers

Younger and poorer readers treat reading as a decoding process (they try to understand each separate word) rather than as a meaning-getting process (understanding what the text as a whole means) (Garner & Kraus, 1982). Decoding is the translation of the printed word to speech. Children are taught to read by decoding, so for young readers decoding is generally

TABLE 7.5 Comprehension Failures and Remedies

Possible Comprehension Failures

1. Failure to understand a word
   a. Novel word
   b. Known word that doesn't make sense in context
2. Failure to understand a sentence
   a. Can find no interpretation
   b. Can find only vague, abstract interpretation
   c. Can find several possible interpretations (ambiguous sentence)
   d. Interpretation conflicts with prior knowledge
3. Failure to understand how one sentence relates to another
   a. Interpretation of one sentence conflicts with another
   b. Can find no connection between the sentences
   c. Can find several possible connections between the sentences
4. Failure to understand how the whole text fits together
   a. Can find no point to whole or part of the text
   b. Cannot understand why certain episodes or sections occurred
   c. Cannot understand the motivations of certain characters

Possible Remedies

1. *Ignore and read on,* because this information is relatively unimportant.
2. *Suspend judgment,* because it is likely to be cleared up later.
3. *Form a tentative hypothesis* to be tested as reading continues.
4. *Reread the current sentence(s)* or look for a tentative hypothesis.
5. *Reread the previous context* to resolve the contradiction.
6. *Go to an expert source,* because it simply doesn't make any sense.

Source: Adapted by permission from A. Collins and E. Smith (1980), *Teaching the process of reading comprehension* (Technical report no. 182). Urbana-Champaign: Center for the Study for Reading, University of Illinois.

the only activity involved in reading. The reading rate of both younger and poorer readers tends to be unvarying, whatever their purpose in reading is (Forrest & Waller, 1980). In other words, it doesn't matter whether they are reading to study, for fun, or to skim, these readers make no adjustment in the way they read. They also have difficulty selecting the important ideas in the text (Brown & Smiley, 1977) and detecting gross violations of logical structure in a text (Danner, 1976). For example, if two sentences in the same paragraph contradict each other, a less-able reader might not notice the contradiction. Moreover, poorer and younger readers have difficulties bringing to mind related knowledge and using the context to help them interpret what they are reading (Winograd & Johnston, 1982). In fact, these readers lack the awareness that they should even do these things. Finally, younger and poorer readers have few strategies at their disposal for dealing with any failures to understand the text, even if they become aware of problems (Baker & Brown, 1984b).

The first part of Table 7.5 on page 275 lists the difficulties younger or less-able students may have as they try to comprehend written material. As you can see, students can fail to understand a word, a sentence, a group of sentences, or the whole passage. The second part of the table offers some remedies that students might use to resolve these failures (Collins & Smith, 1980). Notice that these remedies are presented from the least disruptive to the most disruptive and should probably be tried in this order. For instance, ignoring and reading on is less disruptive than rereading the material.

Tools for Reading and Studying

Over the years there have been many suggestions for understanding and remembering what you read. One of the most enduring systems is the SQ3R (Survey, Question, Read, Recite, Review) approach developed by F. P. Robinson (1961). You may have been exposed to this study strategy at some point during your academic career. A more recent variation is called **PQ4R** (Thomas & Robinson, 1972). In this system the extra *R* is for *reflection,* and the *P* stands for *preview;* so the acronym means Preview, Question, Read, Reflect, Recite, and Review.

Applying PQ4R. Here is how you would apply the PQ4R method to study this text.

1. *Preview.* Introduce yourself to the chapter you are about to read by surveying the major topics and sections. Read the overview, the objectives, the section headings and subheadings, the summary, and perhaps the initial sentences of the major sections. All of these procedures will help activate schemata so you can interpret and remember the text that follows. Previewing also allows you to formulate your own general purpose for reading each section, whether it is to identify the main idea or to note the general biases of the author.

2. *Question.* For each major section, generate questions that are related to your reading purposes. One way is to turn the headings and subheadings into questions. For example, in this chapter you might ask: "How can I help students comprehend what they read?" and "Why is

PQ4R A method for studying text that involves six steps: Preview, Question, Read, Reflect, Recite, Review.

knowledge important in learning?" If you are beginning to use this method of reading, it often is helpful to write down brief questions as they come to mind.

3. *Read.* At last! The questions you have formulated can be answered through reading. You should pay attention to the main ideas, supporting details, and other data in keeping with your purposes. You may have to adjust your reading speed to suit the difficulty of the material and your purpose in reading.

4. *Reflect.* While you are reading, try to think of examples or create images of the material. Elaborate and try to make connections between what you are reading and what you already know.

5. *Recite.* After reading each section, sit back and think about your initial purposes and questions. Can you answer the questions without looking at the book? In doing this, you give your mind a second chance to connect what you have read with what you already know. If your mind is blank after reading the section, it may have been too difficult to read comfortably, or you may have been daydreaming. Reciting helps you to monitor your understanding and tells you when to reread before moving on to the next section. Reciting should take place after each headed section but may be required more often when you are reading difficult material.

6. *Review.* Effective review incorporates new material more thoroughly into your long-term memory. As study progresses, review should be cumulative, including the sections and chapters you read previously. Rereading is one form of review, but trying to answer key questions without referring to the book is the best way. Wrong answers can direct you to areas that need more study, especially before an exam.

Effectiveness of the PQ4R Method. In a study by Adams, Carnine, and Gersten (1982), fifth-grade students given systematic instruction in the PQ4R technique recalled more information than other students on both immediate and delayed tests. Why might this be so? Anderson (1990) suggests several reasons for PQ4R's effectiveness. First, following the steps makes students more aware of the organization of a given chapter. How often have you skipped reading headings entirely and thus missed major clues to the way the information was organized? Readers who use the author's organization to organize their own memory of material actually recall more than those who do not follow the text's organization (Meyer, Brandt, & Bluth, 1980). Next, these steps require the student to study the chapter in sections instead of trying to learn all the information at once. This makes use of distributed practice. Creating and answering questions about the material force the student to process the information more deeply and with greater elaboration. Student-generated questions, as well as questions in the text, have been shown to improve retention of information (Doctorow, Wittrock, & Marks, 1978; Hamilton, 1985). Reviewing with questions in mind encourages more connections to be made between new and old information. In general, using the PQ4R method means investing greater time and effort in studying.

As you may have guessed, the PQ4R method is most appropriate for older children. Very little is known about teaching study skills to students before about fifth grade. The effective application of study skills probably requires metacognitive development beyond the range of most very young children. And of course, young children are still focusing much of their attention on learning the basics of word recognition and decoding.

Reciprocal Teaching

Collins and Smith (1982) have demonstrated the effectiveness of modeling as a technique for teaching reading comprehension strategies. One successful method is called **reciprocal teaching** (Palincsar, 1986; Palincsar & Brown, 1984). This approach teaches students four strategies: summarizing the content of a passage, asking a question about the central point, clarifying the difficult parts of the material, and predicting what will come next. First the teacher and group of students read a short passage silently. Then the teacher provides a model by summarizing, questioning, clarifying, and predicting based on the reading. Next, everyone reads another passage, and the students begin to assume the teacher's role. Often the students' first attempts are halting and incorrect. But the teacher gives clues, guidance, and encouragement (what Vygotsky might call scaffolding) to help the students master these strategies.

An Example of Reciprocal Teaching. Let's look at some examples of reciprocal teaching in action. The first example is an early lesson. Here the teacher is guiding a student as he tries to formulate a question about the central point in a passage on spiders (Harvard University, March 1986, p. 6):

These students must be at an advanced stage of reciprocal teaching—they have completely taken over the role of the teacher.

Reciprocal Teaching A method, based on modeling, to teach reading comprehension strategies.

Text: Spinner's mate is much smaller than she, and his body is dull brown. He spends most of his time sitting at one side of her web.

Charles: (No question)

Teacher: What's this paragraph about?

Charles: Spinner's mate. How do spinner's mate. . . .

Teacher: That's good. Keep going.

Charles: How do spinner's mate is smaller than. . . . How am I going to say that?

Teacher: Take your time with it. You want to ask a question about spinner's mate and what he does, beginning with the word "how."

Charles: How do they spend most of his time sitting?

Teacher: You're very close. The question would be, "How does spinner's mate spend most of his time?" Now, you ask it.

Charles: How does spinner's mate spend most of his time?

After a while, students are usually able to take more and more responsibility for the teaching. In the following example, Laura shows how much progress she has made after about 12 lessons (Harvard University, March 1986, p. 6):

Text: The second oldest form of salt production is mining. Unlike early methods that made the work extremely dangerous and difficult, today's methods use special machinery, and salt mining is easier and safer. The old expression "back to the salt mine" no longer applies.

Laura: Name two words that often describe mining salt in the old days.

Kim: Back to the salt mines?

Laura: No. Angela?

Angela: Dangerous and difficult.

Laura: Correct. This paragraph is all about comparing the old mining of salt and today's mining of salt.

Teacher: Beautiful!

Laura: I have a prediction to make.

Teacher: Good.

Laura: I think it might tell when salt was first discovered . . . well, it might tell what salt is made of and how it's made.

Teacher: O.K. Can we have another teacher?

Applying Reciprocal Teaching. Research on reciprocal teaching has shown some dramatic results. Most of the work has been done with young adolescents who can read aloud fairly accurately but are far below average in reading comprehension. After 20 hours of practice with this approach, many students who were in the bottom quarter of their class moved up to the average level or above on tests of reading comprehension. Based on the results of several studies, Palincsar has identified three guidelines for effective reciprocal teaching (Harvard University, March 1986; Palincsar & Brown, 1984):

1. *Shift gradually.* The shift from teacher control to student responsibility must be gradual.
2. *Match demands to abilities.* The difficulty of the task and the responsibility must match the abilities of each student and grow as these abilities develop.
3. *Diagnose thinking.* Teachers should carefully observe the "teaching" of each student for clues about how the student is thinking and what kind of instruction the student needs.

SUMMARY

ELEMENTS OF THE COGNITIVE PERSPECTIVE

Cognitive learning theorists focus on the human mind's active attempts to make sense of the world. The ways we think about situations—along with our beliefs, expectations, and feelings—influence what and how we learn. Cognitivists view knowledge as the outcome of learning and the power of knowledge as the driving element in learning. Knowledge can be general or domain-specific and can be classified as declarative, procedural, and conditional. Different kinds of knowledge require different teaching approaches.

One widely used cognitive model of the structure and processes of learning is the information processing model, based on the analogy between the mind and the computer. This model includes storage systems such as the sensory register, short-term memory, and long-term memory. Information processing involves encoding, retention, retrieval, and other processes.

THE SENSORY REGISTER

In the information processing model, the sensory register takes in sensory stimuli and briefly holds the information. Attention and perception—the meaning and importance we attach to data received through our senses—affect the contents of the sensory register. Our understanding of perception, such as bottom-up processing (recognizing familiar elements) and top-down processing (using previous knowledge to fill in incomplete patterns), began with the work of the Gestalt psychologists in the early twentieth century.

SHORT-TERM MEMORY

Short-term memory, or working memory, contains five to nine bits of information at a time for 20 to 30 seconds. The duration of short-term memory can be extended through maintenance rehearsal, elaboration rehearsal, and chunking. Forgetting in short-term memory results from interference and from time decay.

LONG-TERM MEMORY

Long-term memory seems to hold an unlimited amount of information permanently. Information may be coded verbally or both verbally and visually as part of our semantic, episodic, or procedural memory. In long-term memory, bits of information may be stored and interrelated in terms of propositional networks and schemata (such as story grammars and scripts)—data structures that allow us to represent large amounts of complex information, make inferences, and understand new information. As in short-term memory, forgetting in long-term memory occurs through interference and decay.

Remembering is a reconstruction process leading to accurate, partly accurate, or inaccurate recall. A sense of almost remembering—the tip-of-the-tongue phenomenon—also occurs. Accurate retrieval depends on the extent to which information is elaborated, organized, and embedded in a context.

A view of memory that does not depend on the information processing model is the levels of processing theory, in which recall of information is determined by how completely it is processed.

METACOGNITION, SELF-REGULATION, AND INDIVIDUAL DIFFERENCES

Metacognition—knowledge about thinking—and monitoring are powerful executive controls in the information processing system. Metacognition involves an awareness of what thinking strategies to use and when, how, and why to apply them. Teachers can teach metacognitive skills to help students become strategic learners.

HELPING STUDENTS BECOME STRATEGIC LEARNERS

Rote memorization can best be improved by part learning and distributed practice. Mnemonics as memorization aids include peg-type approaches, such as the loci method; acronyms; chain mnemonics; and the keyword method. Making the information to be remembered meaningful is important and often the greatest challenge for teachers.

Teachers also need to teach learning strategies (plans) and learning tactics (techniques), including study skills. Examples of study skills that aid both memory and comprehension are underlining, note taking, concept mapping, and PQ4R. A successful technique for teaching reading comprehension strategies is called reciprocal teaching.

KEY TERMS AND CONCEPTS

acronym, p. 268
artificial intelligence, p. 241
attention, p. 247
automaticity, p. 247
bottom-up processing, p. 245

chain mnemonics, p. 268
chunking, p. 249
cognitive monitoring, p. 262
cognitive view of learning,
  p. 238

conditional knowledge, p. 240
context, p. 256
decay, p. 250
declarative knowledge, p. 240
distributed practice, p. 267

WHAT WOULD YOU DO?

PRESCHOOL AND KINDERGARTEN

The first-grade teachers believe that the kindergarten teachers could do a better job of preparing their students to "pay attention" in class. As a kindergarten teacher, what would you do? How would you justify your plans to the first-grade teachers?

ELEMENTARY AND MIDDLE SCHOOL

The principal and curriculum coordinator in your school have decided that study skills will be a high priority this year. How would you approach teaching study skills to your third-grade class? To your sixth-grade class?

Several students in your class are recent immigrants and have limited knowledge of the kinds of experiences described in your basal reader series (county fairs, zoos, trips to the beach, shopping malls, etc.). The students speak and read English but still have difficulty understanding and remembering what they read. What would you do?

JUNIOR HIGH AND HIGH SCHOOL

You have reached a very complicated chapter in your text—one that is difficult for students every year. How would you make the highly abstract concepts (such as sovereignty and jurisprudence) understandable for your students?

The students in your classes seem to equate understanding with memorizing. They prepare for each unit test by memorizing the exact words of the textbook definitions. How would you help them understand that comprehension is the goal?

COOPERATIVE LEARNING ACTIVITY

You just learned that next week the school must begin emergency construction right outside your classroom window. With four or five other members of your class, develop a plan for the week of the construction that will keep your students' attention on the lessons and away from the forklift.

TEACHERS' CASEBOOK

MAKING IT MEANINGFUL

Research shows that we remember best the information that is most meaningful to us: information that makes sense in terms of what we already know and that is clear, organized, and personally relevant. What strategies do you use in your classes to make lessons meaningful and relevant to students?

CURRICULUM INTEGRATION

Integrating the elementary curriculum helps students see that all learning is interrelated. I teach using a hands-on, investigative approach to learning. Instead of teaching math and language separately, lessons often incorporate these two subjects. We keep math journals with daily entries. Using the newspaper is an excellent way to incorporate all subjects. We use many manipulatives, and I encourage students to use manipulatives at home as well as at school.

Integration takes a lot of teacher preparation. You need to know where you're going with the idea and how you'll end the idea, and you must acquire the needed materials. It's well worth the effort, as my students think learning is fun.

Kathy A. Minniear, *Third-Grade Teacher*
LaVeta Bauer Elementary School, Dayton, Ohio

PERSONALIZED KNOWLEDGE

Kahlil Gibran once wrote, "For thought is a bird of flight that in a cage of words may indeed unfold its wings, but cannot fly." My students say the same thing when they say, "I know what I want to say, but can't put it into words." Students must constantly be encouraged to "put it into words" in both their writing and their class discussions. To accomplish this, we constantly work on a process I call the "personalization of knowledge." It involves (1) defining concepts in one's own words without destroying the meaning, (2) providing one's own examples, (3) cross-referencing items with other experiences and situations, and (4) reviewing repeatedly from varied perspectives. (I have found that one of the best ways to review is to have students convert key phrases into topic sentences, then support them with evidence.)

To make the personalization of knowledge process effective, students must know about it and consciously and consistently practice it. In addition, knowledge must be seen as cumulative. If you are not using ideas from the beginning of the year in new and varied ways at the end of the year, you are doing something wrong.

James D. Kraft, *Social Studies Teacher*
Wausau West High School, Wausau, Wisconsin

STUDENT PROJECTS

Obviously the best way to make something meaningful is to apply it to one's own set of circumstances. One of my favorite classroom projects comes after the lesson on operant conditioning. Each student designs his or her own behavior modification project, establishing a baseline, determines reinforcers and contingencies, and starts to work on the selected behavior. After three weeks of modification, the students outline their projects and discuss the outcomes. I find that each student winds up displaying a thorough understanding of the material.

Linda Stahl, *Psychology Teacher*
Ponca City Senior High School, Ponca City, Oklahoma

HELPING THEM REMEMBER WHAT YOU TEACH

How do you help students with those basic skills, retaining and retrieving information? Do you have special techniques for preventing boredom in the unavoidable rote memorization tasks? What about teaching vocabulary, facts, or concepts?

MAKE IT FUN

One method I have found helpful in memorizing and retaining information is to have a catchy sentence. For example, to help my students memorize the names of the planets, I give them the following sentence: My Very Efficient Mother, Jean, Serves Unusually Nice Pies.

For my poetry lessons, I read one line at a time leaving out one word. The children fill it in. Next we follow the same procedure leaving out two or more words. I have found this technique very successful and enjoyable for all.

Marie Vachon, *Eighth-Grade Teacher*
St. Paul School, Ramsey, New Jersey

ACT IT OUT

I use mnemonic devices and spelling tricks to help students do rote memory work. Also, acting out situations can help students personalize and thus retain information. An example: Laurie is the sun, Steve is the earth, and Susie is the moon. Steve is the one who needs to understand what the earth does. Laurie stands in the center, Steve rotates around her, Susie revolves around Steve. After repeating this a few time on subsequent days, Steve will understand.

Bonnie Hettman, *High School Teacher*
Lima Central Catholic High School, Lima, Ohio

ACTIVE AND CREATIVE PARTICIPATION

There are a variety of methods I have found helpful. Here are some examples.

- Role playing: "If you were a medieval laborer after the Black Death had reduced the population by 40 percent, would your labor be worth more or less than previously?"
- Reading aloud from literature: "Here, you look like a good Falstaff. Read these outrageous lines with a yawn every 10 seconds."
- Blackboard: Tactile use of pen on paper to copy. Arrangement of ideas in space on blackboard.
- "Everybody Participates": "John here has this view on these poems. Who agrees? Who disagrees? Looks like the vote is 10 to 5. Who would like to speak for the majority? Who would like to refute?"

Don Knies, *Head and English Teacher*
Brooklyn Friends School, Brooklyn, New York

READING COMPREHENSION

Many students do not seem to realize they have not fully understood what they have read. How do you help them learn to monitor their own reading comprehension and get the most out of their reading?

BRING THE TEXTS TO LIFE

There are several ways to deepen students' reading and self-monitoring abilities—and to develop a greater appreciation of reading in the process. Students can pick out the three main points of a text or themes of a story and do three drawings to illustrate each. They can make up their own tests based on the text to give to one another. Sometimes checklists of who, what, where, and when are useful for younger students to refer to as they read. Older students often enjoy reversals—let them pick out three minor details or characters and rewrite the text using these as the main points or characters. Set up a talk show around several texts: some students play the authors and are interviewed by student-hosts about their work. Or have a trial based on a novel or play, with the main action as the crime and each character interrogated about his role. Students not taking active roles can be journalists covering the trial.

Simone Wharton, *English Teacher*
New York, New York

8 APPLICATIONS OF COGNITIVE LEARNING THEORIES

$\mathbf{A}$s you saw in the previous chapter, the cognitive approach to learning emphasizes how people perceive, understand, and remember information. The focus of this chapter is on instructional approaches that have evolved from the cognitive orientation. We will be concerned with the implications of cognitive theories for the day-to-day practice of teaching.

Since the cognitive perspective is a philosophical orientation and not a unified theoretical model, teaching methods derived from it are varied. In this chapter, we will first examine four important areas in which cognitive theorists have made suggestions for learning and teaching: concept learning, problem solving, creativity, and thinking skills. Next, we will explore the question of how to encourage the transfer of learning from one situation to another to make learning more useful. In the final section we will discuss the instructional theories of three cognitive psychologists—Jerome Bruner's discovery learning, David Ausubel's expository teaching, and Robert Gagné's instructional events.

By the time you finish this chapter, you should be able to do the following:

- Design a lesson for teaching a key concept in your subject area.
- Describe the steps in solving complex problems and explain the role of problem representation.
- List three ways you might encourage creativity in your students.
- Discuss the implications of cognitive theories for teaching critical thinking.
- List three ways a teacher might encourage positive transfer of learning.
- Develop lessons using Bruner's, Ausubel's, and Gagné's approaches.

WHAT DO YOU THINK?

List three skills you learned in junior high or high school that you use regularly. These could be procedures, learning strategies, or just useful information. Why do you remember and apply this knowledge? How was it taught?

TEACHING AND LEARNING ABOUT CONCEPTS

The word *concept* has appeared repeatedly throughout this text. It is common in everyday conversation as well. In fact, most of what we know about the world involves concepts and relations among concepts (Schwartz & Reisberg, 1991). But what exactly is the concept of *concept*? Do you have to understand it before you can define it?

Understanding the World

A **concept** is a category used to group similar events, ideas, objects, or people. When we talk about a particular concept like *student,* we refer to a category of people who are similar to one another. The concept *student* refers to all people who study a subject. The people may be old or young, in school or not; they may be studying baseball or Bach, but they can all be categorized as students. Concepts are abstractions. They do not exist in the real world. Only individual examples of concepts exist.

Concepts help us organize vast amounts of information into manageable units. For instance, there are about 7.5 million distinguishable differences in colors. By categorizing these colors into some dozen or so groups, we manage to deal with this diversity fairly well (Bruner, 1973). Without the ability to form concepts, we would find life a confusing series of unrelated experiences. There would be no way of grouping things together, no symbols or shorthand for talking and thinking about similar objects and events. Nothing would be like anything else, and communication would be impossible (Reed, 1992).

Views of Concept Learning

Traditionally, psychologists have assumed that members of a category share a set of **defining attributes,** or distinctive features. Students all study; books all contain pages of printed, drawn, or photographed materials that are bound together in some way. You can see the similarity between the *defining attributes* notion of concepts and the *feature analysis* (bottom-up processing) involved in perception. Like feature analysis, the defining attributes theory of concepts suggests that we recognize specific examples by noting key features.

Since about 1970, however, these long-popular views about the nature of concepts and category systems have been challenged (Benjafield, 1992). While some concepts, such as *equilateral triangle,* have clear-cut

Concept General category of ideas, objects, people, or experiences whose members share certain properties.

Defining Attributes Distinctive features shared by members of a category.

defining attributes, most concepts do not. Take the concept of *party*. What are the defining attributes? You might have difficulty listing these attributes, but you probably recognize a party when you see (or hear) one. What about the concept of bird? Your first thought might be that birds are animals that fly. But is an ostrich a bird? What about a penguin?

Prototypes and Exemplars. According to critics of the traditional view of concept learning, we have in our minds a prototype of a party and a bird—an image that captures the essence of each concept. A **prototype** is the best representative of its category. For instance, the best representative of the "birds" category for many Americans might be a robin (Rosch, 1973). Other members of the category may be very similar to the prototype (sparrow) or similar in some ways but different in others (chicken, ostrich). At the boundaries of a category, it may be difficult to determine if a particular instance really belongs. For example, is a telephone a piece of "furniture"? Is an elevator a "vehicle"? Is an olive a "fruit"? Whether something fits into a category is a matter of degree. Thus, categories have fuzzy boundaries and **graded membership** (Schwartz & Reisberg, 1991). Some events, objects, or ideas are simply better examples of a concept than others, as you can see in Table 8.1 (Rosch, 1975).

Another explanation of concept learning suggests that we identify members of a category by referring to exemplars. **Exemplars** are actual memories of specific birds, parties, furniture, and so on that we use to

TABLE 8.1 Typical and Unusual Members of Categories

Category		
Furniture	**Vehicle**	**Fruit**
Chair	Car	Orange
Sofa	Truck	Apple
Table	Bus	Banana
Dresser	Motorcycle	Peach
Desk	Train	Pear
Bed	Trolley car	Apricot
Bookcase	Bicycle	Plum
Piano	Tractor	Grapefruit
Mirror	Wheelchair	Blueberry
Stove	Sled	Honeydew
Clock	Horse	Pomegranate
Closet	Skates	Coconut
Vase	Wheelbarrow	Tomato
Telephone	Elevator	Olive

The lists are based on subjects' ratings of the typicality of items in these three categories. Items are listed from most to least typical.

Source: From "Family Resemblance: Studies in the Internal Structure of Categories," by E. Rosch and C. B. Mervis, 1975, *Cognitive Psychology, 7*, pp. 573–605. Copyright 1975 by Academic Press, Inc. Reprinted by permission.

Prototype Best representative of a category.

Graded Membership The extent to which something belongs to a category.

Exemplar A specific example of a given category that is used to classify an item.

compare with an item in question to see if that item belongs in the same category as our exemplar. For example, if you see a strange steel and stone bench in a public park, you may compare it to the chair in your living room to decide if the uncomfortable-looking creation is still a chair, or if it has crossed a fuzzy boundary into "sculpture."

Prototypes probably are built from experiences with many exemplars. This happens naturally because episodic memories of particular events tend to blur together over time, creating an average or typical chair prototype from all the chair exemplars you have experienced (Schwartz & Reisberg, 1991).

Concepts and Schemata. In addition to prototypes and exemplars, there is a third element involved when we recognize a concept—our *schematic knowledge* related to the concept. How do we know that counterfeit money is not "real" money, even though it perfectly fits our "money" prototype and exemplars? We know because of its history. It was printed by the "wrong" people. So our understanding of the concept of *money* is connected with concepts of crime, forgery, the federal treasury, and many others. Our knowledge about particular concepts is embedded in schemata so we can be flexible in recognizing concepts without being fooled by appearances. A prototype can be considered the "default" schema—the average or typical version of a concept. Your prototype for a *kitchen,* for example, probably includes a kitchen table—that's part of your default schema for kitchen. But you have no trouble recognizing a kitchen without a table; you just fill the "table" slot in your kitchen schema with the information "not in this particular kitchen."

Strategies for Teaching Concepts

Most of the current approaches to teaching concepts still rely heavily on the traditional analysis of defining attributes. Interest is growing, however, in the prototypes view of concept learning, partly because children first learn many concepts in the real world from best examples or prototypes pointed out by adults (Tennyson, 1981). The teaching of concepts can combine both distinctive features and prototypes, and new approaches that do so are promising (Tennyson & Cocchiarella, 1986).

Lesson Components. Whatever strategy you use for teaching concepts, you will need to have four components in any lesson: (1) the name of the concept, (2) a definition, (3) relevant and irrelevant attributes, and (4) examples and nonexamples (Joyce & Weil, 1986). In addition, visual aids such as pictures, models, graphs, diagrams, or maps will improve learning of many concepts (Anderson & Smith, 1987).

The name of the concept is important for communicating but is somewhat arbitrary. The verbal label that identifies the concept is not the same as the concept itself. Simply learning a label does not mean the person understands the concept, although the label is necessary for the understanding.

A definition makes the nature of the concept clear. A good definition has two elements: a reference to any more *general category* that the new concept falls under, and a statement of the new concept's *defining attri-*

butes (Klausmeier, 1976). For example, an equilateral triangle is defined as a plane, simple, closed figure (general category), with three equal sides and three equal angles (defining attributes). This kind of definition helps place the concept in a schema of related knowledge.

The identification of relevant and irrelevant attributes is another aspect of teaching concepts. The ability to fly, as we've seen, is not a relevant attribute for classifying animals as birds. Even though many birds fly, some birds do not (ostrich, penguin), and some nonbirds do (bats, flying squirrels). The ability to fly would have to be included in a discussion of the bird concept, but students should understand that flying does not mark an animal as a bird.

Examples are essential in teaching concepts. More examples are needed in teaching complicated concepts and in working with younger or less-able students. Both examples and nonexamples (sometimes called *positive* and *negative instances*) are necessary to make the boundaries of the category clear. So a discussion of why a bat (nonexample) is not a bird will help students define the boundaries of the bird concept.

In teaching some concepts "a picture is worth a thousand words"—or at least a few hundred. Seeing and handling specific examples or pictures of examples help young children learn concepts. For students of all ages, the complex concepts in history, science, and mathematics can often be illustrated in diagrams or graphs. For example, Anderson and Smith (1983) found that only 20 percent of the students they taught could understand the role of reflected light in our ability to see objects when the students just read about the concept. But when the students worked with diagrams such as the one in Figure 8.1 on page 290, almost 80 percent understood the concept.

Lesson Structure. Start your concept lesson with prototypes, or best examples, to help the students establish the category. For instance, if you were teaching the concept of *liquid*, you might start with examples such as *water* or *juice.* Then move to more difficult, less obvious examples such as *cake batter, shampoo,* or *honey.* These examples show the wide range of possibilities the category includes and the variety of irrelevant attributes within a category. This information helps students avoid focusing on an irrelevant attribute as a defining feature. The *cake batter* example tells students that liquids can be thick and opaque as well as thin and clear. The *shampoo* example indicates that liquids do not have to be edible. Including liquids that are thick and thin, clear and opaque, and edible and inedible will prevent **undergeneralization,** or the exclusion of some substances from their rightful place in the category *liquid.*

Nonexamples should be very close to the concept but miss by one or just a few critical attributes. For instance, sand is not an example of liquid, even though it shares one of the characteristics of liquids. You can pour it. Including nonexamples will prevent **overgeneralization,** or the inclusion of substances that are not liquids.

Once students have a good sense of a concept, they should use it. This might mean doing exercises, solving problems, writing, reading, explaining, or any other activity that requires them to apply their new understanding. This will connect the concept into the students' web of related schematic knowledge. One new approach that you may see in

Undergeneralization
Exclusion of some true members from a category; limiting a concept.

Overgeneralization
Inclusion of nonmembers in a category; overextending a concept.

FIGURE 8.1 **Understanding Complex Concepts** Words alone may not be enough. Illustration can help students grasp a difficult concept.

Q. When sunlight strikes the tree it helps the girl to see the tree. How does it do this?

Q. When sunlight strikes the tree it helps the girl to see the tree. How does it do this?

A. Some of the light bounces (is reflected) off the tree and goes to the girl's eyes.

Source: From *The Educator's Handbook,* edited by Virginia Richardson-Koehler. Copyright © 1987 by Longman Publishing Group. Reprinted with permission from Longman Publishing Group.

some texts and workbooks is **concept mapping** (Novak & Musonda, 1991). Students "diagram" their understanding of the concept, as Amy has in Figure 8.2 on page 291. Amy's map shows a reasonable understanding of the concept of *molecule* but also indicates that Amy holds one misconception. She thinks that there is no space between the molecules in solids.

PROBLEM SOLVING

"Educational programs," Gagné has written, "have the important ultimate purpose of teaching students to solve problems— mathematical and physical problems, health problems, social problems, and problems of personal adjustment" (1977, p. 177). A **problem** is "a situation in which you are trying to reach some goal and must find a means for getting there"

Concept Mapping Student's diagram of his or her understanding of a concept.

Problem Any situation in which you are trying to reach some goal and must find a means to do so.

FIGURE 8.2 **Amy's Molecule** Amy, an eighth grader, has drawn a map to represent her understanding of the concept of "molecule." Her concept includes one misconception—that there is no space between molecules in solids.

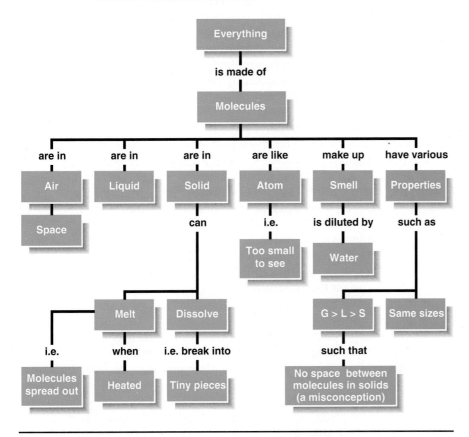

Source: J. D. Novak and D. Musonda, A twelve-year longitudinal study of science concept learning. *American Educational Resource Journal, 28,* 137. Copyright 1991 by the American Educational Research Association. Reprinted by permission of the publisher.

(Chi & Glaser, 1985, p. 229). Problems have an *initial state*—the current situation—and a *goal*—the desired outcome. Problem solvers often have to set and reach *subgoals* as they move toward the final solution (Schunk, 1991a). **Problem solving** is usually defined as formulating new answers, going beyond the simple application of previously learned rules to create a solution. Problem solving is what happens when routine or automatic responses do not fit the current situation.

Problem Solving—General or Domain-Specific?

There is an interesting debate about problem solving. Some psychologists believe that effective problem-solving strategies are specific to the problem area. That is, the problem-solving strategies in mathematics are unique to math, the strategies in art are unique to art, and so on. Becoming an expert problem solver in an area requires that you master the

Problem Solving Creating new solutions for problems.

strategies of the area. The other side of the debate claims that there are some general problem-solving strategies that can be useful in many areas.

There is evidence for both sides of the argument. In fact, it appears that people move between general and specific approaches, depending on the situation and their level of expertise. Early on, when we know little about a problem area or domain, we may rely on general learning and problem-solving strategies to make sense of the situation. As we gain more domain-specific knowledge (particularly procedural knowledge about how to do things in the domain), we need the general strategies less and less. But if we encounter a problem outside our current knowledge, we may return to relying on general strategies to attack the problem (Perkins & Salomon, 1989; Shuell, 1990). Perhaps the best approach for teachers is to give students both general and specific strategies.

Think of a general problem-solving strategy as a beginning point, a broad outline. Such strategies usually have five stages (Derry, 1991; Derry & Murphy, 1986; Gallini, 1991; Gick, 1986). John Bransford and Barry Stein (1984) use the acronym IDEAL to identify the five steps:

I   Identify the problem.
D   Define and represent the problem.
E   Explore possible strategies.
A   Act on the strategies.
L   Look back and evaluate the effects of your activities.

The first step, identifying that a problem exists, begins the process. This is not always straightforward. For example, there is a story describing tenants who were angry about the slow elevators in their building.

In order to solve a problem, students must first have an accurate representation of the situation. Often it helps to use visual representations—diagrams, models, drawings, etc.—to "see" the problem more clearly.

Consultants hired to "fix the problem" reported that the elevators were no worse than average and that improvements would be very expensive. Then one day, as the building supervisor watched people waiting impatiently for an elevator, he realized that the problem was not slow elevators but the fact that people were bored; they had nothing to do while they waited. When the boredom problem was identified, the simple solution of installing a mirror on each floor eliminated complaints.

Assuming a solvable problem is identified, what next? We will examine steps 2 through 5 in some detail, because these are the heart of the problem-solving process.

Defining and Representing the Problem

Defining and representing a problem often requires finding the relevant information and ignoring the irrelevant details. In other words, we must use our information processing skill of selective attention. For example, consider the following problem adapted from Sternberg & Davidson (1982):

> If you have black socks and white socks in your drawer, mixed in the ratio of four to five, how many socks will you have to take out to make sure of having a pair the same color?

What information is relevant to solving this problem? Did you realize that the information about the four-to-five ratio of black socks to white socks is irrelevant? As long as you have only two different colors of socks in the drawer, you will have to remove only three socks before two of them are bound to match.

In addition to identifying the relevant information in a problem, you must develop an accurate representation of the situation involved. This may require knowledge that is specific to the problem area. Let's assume we are dealing with story problems—problems that are stated orally or written out, like the socks problem above. To represent these problems successfully, you must (1) understand the *words* and *sentences,* and (2) activate the right *schema* to understand the whole problem (Mayer, 1983a & b, 1992).

Understanding the Elements. The first task in representing a story problem is **linguistic comprehension,** or understanding the meaning of each sentence. Take, for example, the following sentence from an algebra story problem:

> The riverboat's rate in still water is 12 miles per hour more than the rate of the river current.

This is a *relational proposition.* It describes the relationship between two rates, that of the riverboat and that of the current. Here is another sentence from a story problem:

> The cost of the candy is $2.75 per pound.

Linguistic Comprehension
Understanding of the meaning of sentences.

This is an *assignment proposition.* It simply assigns a value to something, in this case, the cost of one unit of candy.

To solve a problem containing either of these two sentences, you must understand the proposition. But some propositions are more difficult than others to figure out. Research shows that relational propositions are harder to understand and remember than assignment propositions. In one study, when students had to recall relational and assignment propositions like those above, the error rate for recalling relational propositions was about three times higher than the error rate for assignment propositions. Some students even turned relational propositions into assignment propositions, remembering, for example, "The riverboat's rate in still water is 12 miles per hour more than the rate of the current" simply as "The riverboat's speed in still water is 12 miles per hour" (Mayer, 1982). If you misunderstand the meaning of individual statements in a problem, you will have a hard time representing the whole problem correctly.

The main stumbling block in representing many word problems is the students' understanding of *part-whole relations* (Riley & Greeno, 1991). Students have trouble figuring out what is part of what, as evident in this dialogue between a teacher and a first grader:

Teacher: Pete has three apples; Ann also has some apples; Pete and Ann have nine apples altogether; how many apples does Ann have?

Student: Nine.

Teacher: Why?

Student: Because you just said so.

Teacher: Can you retell the story?

Student: Pete had three apples; Ann also had some apples; Ann had nine apples; Pete also has nine apples. (adapted from De Corte & Verchaffel, 1985, p. 19)

The student seems to interpret "altogether" (the whole) as "each" (the parts).

Understanding the Whole Problem. The second task in representing a problem is to assemble all the sentences into an accurate understanding or *translation* of the total problem. Even if you understand every sentence, you may still misunderstand the problem as a whole. Consider this example, diagrammed in Figure 8.3:

Two train stations are 50 miles apart. At 2 P.M. one Saturday afternoon two trains start toward each other, one from each station. Just as the trains pull out of the stations, a bird springs into the air in front of the first train and flies ahead to the front of the second train. When the bird reaches the second train it turns back and flies toward the first train. The bird continues to do this until the trains meet. If both trains travel at the rate of 25 miles per hour and the bird flies at 100 miles per hour, how many miles will the bird have flown before the trains meet? (Posner, 1973)

Your interpretation of the problem is called a translation because you translate the problem into a schema that you understand. If you translate

FIGURE 8.3 **Representing a Problem** If the bird travels back and forth between the two oncoming trains, how many miles will it have flown when the two trains meet?

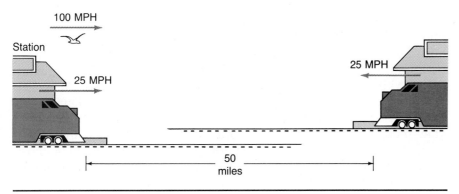

this as a *distance* problem ("I have to figure out how far the bird travels before it meets the oncoming train and turns around, then how far it travels before it has to turn again, and finally add up all the trips back and forth . . ."), then you have a very difficult problem on your hands. But there is a better way to structure the problem. You can represent it as a question of *time* and focus on the time the bird is in the air. If you know how long the bird is in the air, then you can easily determine the distance it will cover, since you know exactly how fast it flies. The solution could be stated like this:

> Since the stations are 50 miles apart and the trains are moving toward each other at the same speed, the trains will meet in the middle—25 miles from each station. Because they are traveling 25 mph, it will take the trains one hour to reach the meeting point. In the one hour it takes the trains to meet, the bird will cover 100 miles because it is flying at 100 miles per hour. Easy!

Research shows that students can be too quick to decide what a problem is asking. The subjects in one study made their decisions about how to categorize standard algebra problems after reading only the first few sentences of a problem (Hinsley, Hayes, & Simon, 1977). Once a problem is categorized —"Aha, it's a distance problem!"—a particular schema is activated. The schema directs attention to relevant information and sets up expectations for what the right answer should look like (Hayes, Waterman, & Robinson, 1977; Robinson & Hayes, 1978).

When students do not have the necessary schemata to represent problems, they often rely on surface features of the situation and represent the problem incorrectly—like the student who wrote "15 + 24 = 39" as the answer to the question, *"Joan has 15 bonus points and Louise has 24. How many more does Louise have?"* This student saw two numbers and the word "more," so he applied the *"add to get more"* procedure. When students use the wrong schema, they overlook critical information, use irrelevant information, and may even misread or misremember critical information so that it fits the schema. Errors in representing the problem and difficulties in solving it are the results. But when students use the proper schema for representing a problem, they are less likely to be confused by irrelevant information or tricky wording, like *more* in a problem that really requires *subtraction* (Resnick, 1981).

Translation and Schema Training. How can students improve translation and schema selection? To answer this question, we often have to move from general to area-specific problem-solving strategies. In mathematics, for example, it appears that students benefit from seeing many different kinds of example problems worked out correctly for them. The common practice of showing students a few examples, then having students work many problems on their own, is less effective. Especially when problems are unfamiliar or difficult, worked examples are helpful (Cooper & Sweller, 1987). The most effective examples seem to be those that *do not* require students to integrate several sources of information, such as a diagram *and* a set of statements about the problem. This kind of attention splitting may put too much strain on the working memory. When students are learning, worked examples should deal with one source of information (Ward & Sweller, 1990). Ask students to compare examples. What is the same about each solution? What is different? Why? The same procedures may be effective in areas other than mathematics.

How else might students develop the schemata they will need to represent problems in a particular subject area? Mayer (1983b) has recommended giving students practice in the following:

1. Recognizing and categorizing a variety of problem types;
2. Representing problems—either concretely, in pictures, symbols, or graphs, or in words;
3. Selecting relevant and irrelevant information in problems.

The Results of Problem Representation. You may have noticed that there are two main outcomes of the problem representation stage of problem solving, as shown in Figure 8.4. If your representation of the

FIGURE 8.4 **Diagram of the Problem-Solving Process**   There are two paths to a solution. In the first, the correct schema for solving the problems activated and the solution is apparent. But if no schema is available, searching and testing may become the path to a solution.

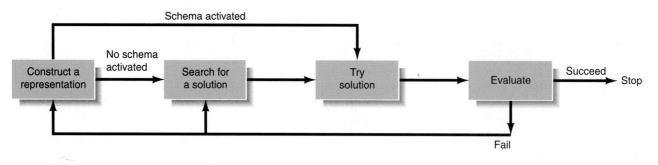

Source: Adapted by permission of the publisher and author from M. L. Gick (1986), Problem-solving strategies. *Educational Psychologist, 21,* p. 101.

problem suggests an immediate solution, your task is done. In the language of the cognitive scientist, you have activated the right schema and the solution is apparent because it is part of the schema. In one sense, you haven't really solved a new problem, you have simply recognized the new problem as a "disguised" version of an old problem that you already knew how to solve. This has been called **schema-driven problem solving,** a kind of matching between the situation and your store of systems for dealing with different problems (Gick, 1986). In terms of Figure 8.4, you have taken the *schema-activated* route and have proceeded directly to a solution. But what if you have no existing way of solving the problem or if your activated schema fails? Time to search for a solution!

Exploring Possible Solution Strategies

If you do not have existing schemata that suggest an immediate solution, then you must take the *search-based* route indicated in Figure 8.4. Obviously, this path is not as efficient as activating the right schema, but sometimes it is the only way. In conducting your search for a solution, you have available two general kinds of procedures, algorithmic and heuristic.

Algorithms. An **algorithm** is a step-by-step prescription for achieving a goal. It usually is domain-specific; that is, tied to a particular subject area. In solving a problem, if you choose an appropriate algorithm and implement it properly, a right answer is guaranteed. Unfortunately, students often apply algorithms haphazardly. They try first this, then that. They may even happen upon the right answer, but not really understand (or remember) how they found it.

In math classes you probably experienced some success applying algorithms. As long as you were careful in your computations, you were able to solve even such complicated problems as $.17[43(90 + \frac{15}{78})]-[\frac{5}{9}(\frac{12356}{2})]$. Later, if you were given geometry proofs to verify or equations to differentiate, you soon discovered that there were no algorithms guaranteeing a solution. At that point, if you did not learn some *heuristics,* you probably bailed out of math classes as soon as possible.

Heuristics. A **heuristic** is a general strategy that might lead to the right answer. Since many of life's problems are fuzzy, with ill-defined problem statements and no apparent algorithms, the discovery or development of effective heuristics is important. Let's examine a few.

In **means-ends analysis,** the problem is divided into a number of *subgoals* and then a means of solving each is figured out. For example, writing a 20-page term paper can loom as an insurmountable problem for some students. They would be better off breaking this task down into several subgoals, such as selecting a topic, locating sources of information, reading and organizing the information, making an outline, and so on. Keep in mind that psychologists have yet to discover an effective heuristic for students who are just starting their term paper the night before it is due.

Schema-Driven Problem Solving Recognizing a problem as a "disguised" version of an old problem for which one already has a solution.

Algorithm Step-by-step procedure for solving a problem; prescription for solutions.

Heuristic General strategy used in attempting to solve problems.

Means-Ends Analysis Heuristic in which goal is divided into subgoals.

Some problems lend themselves to a **working-backward strategy,** in which you begin at the goal and move back to the unsolved initial problem. Working backward is sometimes an effective heuristic for solving geometry proofs. It can also be a good way to set intermediate deadlines ("Let's see, if I have to submit this chapter in three weeks, then it has to be in the mail by the 28th, so I should have a first draft by the 11th . . .").

Another useful heuristic is **analogical thinking** (Copi, 1961), which limits your search for solutions to situations that have something in common with the one you currently face. When submarines were first designed, for example, engineers had to figure out how battleships could determine the presence and location of vessels hidden in the depths of the sea. Studying how bats solve an analogous problem of navigating in the dark led to the invention of sonar.

Research shows, however, that people often fail to use analogies in solving problems, even when they have the analogy that they need (Reed, 1992; Schunk, 1991a). For example, adults were asked to solve a problem about how to use radiation to destroy a tumor. Rays that are strong enough to destroy the tumor also destroy all the healthy tissue they pass through on the way to the tumor. The solution is to direct many low-intensity rays along different paths through the body, converging at the site of the tumor. Then the tissue around the tumor is undamaged because the radiation is strong enough to destroy tissue only at the spot where all the low-intensity rays meet. Very few subjects were able to solve this problem. When they were given a story about soldiers converging on a fortress from many sides at once, destroying the fortress, *and* they were prompted to use the military analogy to solve the tumor problem, most of the subjects succeeded. Without the prompt, however, few subjects used analogical thinking and thus, few solved the problem (Gick & Holyoak, 1983).

Putting your problem-solving plan into words and giving reasons for selecting it can lead to successful problem solving (Cooper & Sweller, 1987). You may have discovered the effectiveness of this **verbalization** process accidentally when a solution popped into your head as you were explaining a problem to someone else. Gagné and Smith (1962) found that when ninth-grade and tenth-grade students were instructed to state a reason for each step they were taking, they were much more successful in solving the problem than students who did not state reasons.

Acting on the Strategies and Looking Back

After representing the problem and selecting the approach, the next step is to execute the plan. If the plan primarily involves the use of algorithms, it is important to keep in mind that systematic "bugs," or erroneous algorithms, may have developed in the procedures. Brown and Burton (1979) developed computer programs that located bugs used by students in solving subtraction problems. Their research indicated that children's algorithms contain many more bugs than teachers realize. One buggy algorithm they found, for example, was the consistent subtraction of the smaller from the larger number, regardless of which one was on top. Once teachers discover a bug, they can give specific tips for reworking prob-

Working-Backward Strategy Heuristic in which one starts with the goal and moves backward to solve the problem.

Analogical Thinking Heuristic in which one limits the search for solutions to situations that are similar to the one at hand.

Verbalization Putting your problem-solving plan and its logic into words.

lems. This corrective feedback is much more helpful than merely advising the child to try again and be more careful.

After you choose a solution strategy and implement it, you should evaluate the results. This involves checking for evidence that confirms or contradicts your solution. Many people tend to stop working before reaching the best solution and simply accept an answer that works in some cases. I once tested a high school student with the following problem:

Find the value of x and y that will solve both these equations:
$$8x + 4y = 28$$
$$4x - 2y = 10$$

The student quickly wrote: $x = 2$, $y = 3$. This solution works for the first equation, but not for the second. The student found evidence to confirm the solution but did not keep checking to see if the solution fit all aspects of the problem.

In other mathematical problems, evaluating the answer also might mean applying a checking routine such as adding to check the result of a subtraction problem or, in a long addition problem, adding the column from bottom to top instead of top to bottom. Another possibility is estimating the answer. For example, if the computation was 11×21, the answer should be around 200, since 10×20 is 200. A student who reaches an answer of 2,311 or 23 or 562 should quickly realize these cannot be correct. Estimating an answer is particularly important when students rely on calculators, since they cannot go back and spot an error in the figures.

Factors That Hinder Problem Solving

Consider the following situation:

> You enter a room. There are two ropes suspended from the ceiling. You are asked by the experimenter to tie the two ends of the ropes together and assured that the task is possible. On a nearby table are a few tools, including a hammer and pliers. You grab the end of one of the ropes and walk toward the other rope. You immediately realize that you cannot possibly reach the end of the other rope. You try to extend your reach using the pliers but still cannot grasp the other rope. What can you do? (Maier, 1933)

Functional Fixedness. This problem can be solved by using an object in an unconventional way. If you tie the hammer or the pliers to the end of one rope and start swinging it like a pendulum, you will be able to catch it while you are standing across the room holding the other rope, as shown in Figure 8.5 on page 300. You can use the weight of the tool to make the rope come to you instead of trying to stretch the rope. People often fail to solve this problem, because they seldom consider unconventional uses for materials that have a specific function. This difficulty is called **functional fixedness** (Duncker, 1945). Problem solving requires seeing things in new ways. In your everyday life, you may often exhibit functional fixed-

Functional Fixedness
Inability to use objects or tools in a new way.

FIGURE 8.5   Overcoming Functional Fixedness In the two-string problem the subject must set one string in motion in order to tie both strings together.

ness. Suppose a screw on a dresser-drawer handle is loose. Will you spend 10 minutes searching for a screwdriver? Or will you think to use another object not necessarily designed for this function, like a knife or a dime?

Response set can be another block to effective problem solving. Consider the following:

> In each of the four matchstick arrangements below, move only one stick to change the equation so that it represents a true equality such as V = V.

$$\lor = \lor || \qquad \lor | = \times | \qquad \times || = \lor || \qquad \lor | = ||$$

You probably figured out how to solve the first example quite quickly. You simply move one matchstick from the right side over to the left to make $\lor|=\lor|$. Examples two and three can also be solved without too much difficulty by moving one stick to change the $\lor$ to an $\times$ or vice versa. But the fourth example (taken from Raudsepp & Haugh, 1977) probably has you stumped. To solve this problem you must change your response set, or switch schemata, because what has worked for the first three problems will not work this time. The answer here lies in changing from Roman numerals to Arabic numbers and using the concept of square root. By overcoming response set, you can move one matchstick from the right to the left to form the symbol for square root; the solution reads $\sqrt{}=|$, which is simply the symbolic way of saying that the square root of 1 equals 1.

Response Set Rigidity; tendency to respond in the most familiar way.

The Importance of Flexibility. Functional fixedness and response set point to the importance of flexibility in understanding problems. If you get started with an inaccurate or inefficient representation of the true problem, it will be difficult or at least very time-consuming to reach a solution (Wessells, 1982). Sometimes it is helpful to "play" with the problem. Ask yourself: "What do I know? What do I need to know to answer this question? Can I look at this problem in other ways?" Try to think conditionally rather than rigidly and divergently rather than convergently. Ask, "What could this be?" instead of "What is it?" (Benjafield, 1992).

If you open your mind to multiple possibilities, you may have what the Gestalt psychologists called an insight. **Insight** is the sudden reorganization or reconceptualization of a problem that clarifies the problem and suggests a feasible solution. The supervisor described earlier, who suddenly realized that the problem in his building was not slow elevators but impatient, bored tenants, had an insight that allowed him to reach the solution of installing mirrors by the elevators.

EFFECTIVE PROBLEM SOLVING: WHAT DO THE EXPERTS DO?

Most psychologists agree that effective problem solving is based on an ample store of knowledge about the problem area. In order to solve the matchstick problem, for example, you had to understand Roman and Arabic numbers as well as the concept of square root. You also had to know that the square root of 1 is 1. Experts in any given field have a good supply of knowledge, facts, concepts, and procedures. This rich store of knowledge is elaborated and organized so that it is easy to retrieve from long-term memory when needed.

Experts not only have a wealth of *declarative knowledge*—facts and verbal information; they also have at their command considerable *procedural knowledge*—an understanding of how to perform various cognitive activities. And they know when and why to apply their understandings; that is, they have *conditional knowledge* so they can readily manipulate their declarative and procedural knowledge to solve problems. Not surprisingly, the processes experts apply to solve problems seem to be quite different from those of beginners.

Expert Pattern Recognition

The modern study of expertise began with investigations of chess masters (Simon & Chase, 1973). Results indicated that masters can quickly recognize about 50,000 different arrangements of chess pieces. They can look at one of these patterns for a few seconds and remember where every piece on the board was placed. It is as though they have a "vocabulary" of 50,000 patterns. For the masters, patterns of pieces are like words. If you were shown any word from your vocabulary store for just a few seconds, you would be able to remember every letter in the word in the right order (assuming you could spell the word).

But a series of letters arranged randomly is hard to remember, as you saw in chapter 7. An analogous situation holds for chess masters. When

Insight Sudden realization of a solution.

Experts in a domain have a great deal of knowledge and a store of experiences to draw on for solutions to problems. The importance of knowledge in expertise was documented in early studies of chess. Even young children can solve abstract problems in chess if they are very knowledgeable and experienced.

chess pieces are placed on a board randomly, masters are no better than average players at remembering the positions of the pieces. The master's memory is for patterns that make sense or could occur in a game. Thus, "high level competence in this case does not appear to reside in conscious analytical thinking processes. The chess master is a superior recognizer rather than a deep thinker" (Glaser, 1981, p. 931).

A similar phenomenon occurs in other fields. There may be an intuition about how to solve a problem based on recognizing patterns and knowing the "right moves" for those patterns. Experts in physics, for example, organize their knowledge around central principles, whereas beginners organize their smaller amounts of physics knowledge around the specific details stated in the problems. The experts can find the patterns needed to solve a particular problem very quickly without straining. They use less feature-by-feature processing of details. So experts literally don't have to think as hard (Glaser, 1981).

In addition to representing a problem very quickly, experts know what to do next. They have a large store of *productions* or *condition-action schemata* about what action to take in various situations. So the steps of understanding the problem and choosing a solution happen simultaneously and fairly automatically (Norman, 1982). The experts are more likely to take the short cut—the schema-activated path illustrated in Figure 8.4 on page 294. Of course, this means that they must have many, many schemata available. A large part of becoming an expert is simply acquiring a great store of knowledge about a particular field. To do this, you must encounter many different kinds of problems in that field, see problems solved by others, and practice solving many yourself.

Novice Knowledge

Studies of the differences between experts and novices in particular areas have revealed some surprising things about how novices understand and misunderstand a subject. Physics again provides many examples. Most beginners approach physics with a great deal of misinformation, partly because many of their intuitive ideas about the physical world are wrong. For example, most elementary-school children believe that light helps us see by brightening the area around objects. They do not realize that we see an object because the light is reflected off the object to our eyes. This concept does not fit with the everyday experience of turning on a light and "brightening" the dark area. Researchers from the Elementary Science Project at Michigan State University found that even after completing a unit on light in which materials explicitly stated the idea of reflected light and vision, most fifth-grade students—about 78 percent—continued to cling to their intuitive notions. But when new materials were designed that directly confronted the students' misconceptions, only about 20 percent of the students failed to understand (Eaton, Anderson, & Smith, 1984).

It seems quite important for science teachers to understand their students' intuitive models of basic concepts. If the students' intuitive model includes misconceptions and inaccuracies, then the students are likely to develop inadequate or misleading representations of a problem. In order to learn new information and solve problems, students must sometimes "unlearn" commonsense ideas (Joshua & Dupin, 1987).

Helping Novices Become Experts: An Example

When people have little knowledge in a particular area, they usually have difficulties solving problems. They often reach an impasse in the early stages of problem solving, particularly at the problem-representation stage. Three factors seem to improve problem solving in a particular area (Delclos & Harrington, 1991).

1. Present the needed facts as well as several examples of how to use the facts in solving the problem at hand.
2. Let students practice using the facts in several actual problem-solving situations.
3. Provide some way for students to monitor their use of problem-solving strategies as they work.

Victor Delclos and Christine Harrington (1991) tested these steps with 30 fifth- and sixth-grade students learning to solve logic problems using the computer game "Rocky's Boots." Ten students received the problem-solving guidelines listed in Table 8.2 on page 304. Another ten received the guidelines *and* were also taught to monitor their problem solving by answering the self-monitoring questions in Table 8.2. The last ten students served as a control group; they received no special guidance. The

TABLE 8.2   Helping Students Learn to Solve Logic Problems

Problem-Solving Guidelines

Students were working with a computer logic game called "Rocky's Boots." The point of the game is to build the correct logic "machine" to solve each set of problems.

Before solving a problem:

1. You must have a problem to solve.
2. You must have an adequate background for solving the problem.
3. You must have the right attitude.

When solving the problem:

1. Ask yourself, "What is causing the problem?"
2. Look for clues to help you solve the problem.

3. You may need to redefine or clarify the problem.
4. You may want to break the problem into smaller parts.
5. Look at problems that are similar. How did you solve them?
6. Look for alternative solutions.
7. Use available debugging tools.

After solving the problem:

1. Check your solution.
2. If your solution is incorrect, use debugging tools to find your mistake.

Contents of Monitored Problem-Solving Booklets

All monitored-problem-solving students wrote answers to all of the following questions as part of their practice session.

Before starting each game:

1. What is the title of the game you are about to play?
2. Are you determined that you can win this game?
3. Have you looked at the problem carefully and thought about how to solve it?
4. Do you have an adequate background to build this machine? If not, where can you obtain it?

After building the machine, but before running it:

Draw your machine.

1. Did you look for clues that would help you solve this problem? If so, check those used: (a) title of the game, (b) point values of the targets, (c) other (specify).
2. Did you redefine or clarify the problem? If so, how?

3. Did you break the problem into smaller parts? If so, what did you do?
4. Did you look at a similar problem to help you with the solution? If so, which one?

Run your machine.

After running the machine:

1. How many points did your machine score?
2. Have you looked for causes of bugs in your machine? (Please do so now.) What caused the bug(s)? (a) use of the wrong gate(s), (b) a glitch, (c) other.
3. Did you use available debugging tools to find the sources of bugs? If so, which ones did you use? (a) title of the game, (b) point values of the targets, (c) other.

Rebuild your machine.

Source: V. R. Delclos and C. Harrington (1991), Effects of strategy monitoring and proactive instruction on children's problem-solving performance. *Journal of Educational Psychology, 83,* p. 42. Copyright 1991 by the American Psychological Association. Reprinted by permission.

study showed the importance of self-monitoring. The monitored problem-solving group solved more complex problems and took less time to do so than either of the other two groups. So it appears that students need to be taught not only how to solve problems but also how to regulate their own problem solving. Other Guidelines follow for helping students learn efficient and useful problem-solving strategies for any subject area.

Guidelines

Problem Solving

Ask students if they are sure they understand the problem.

Examples

1. Can they separate relevant from irrelevant information?
2. Are they aware of the assumptions they are making?
3. Encourage them to visualize the problem by diagramming or drawing it.
4. Ask them to explain the problem to someone else. What would a good solution look like?

Encourage attempts to see the problem from different angles.

Examples

1. Suggest several different possibilities yourself and then ask students to offer some.
2. Give students practice in taking and defending different points of view on an issue.

Help students develop systematic ways of considering alternatives.

Examples

1. Think out loud as you solve problems.

2. Ask, "What would happen if . . . ?"
3. Keep a list of suggestions.

Teach heuristics.

Examples

1. Ask students to explain the steps they take as they solve problems.
2. Use analogies to solve the problem of limited parking in the downtown area. How are other "storage" problems solved?
3. Use working backward to plan a party.

Let students do the thinking; don't simply provide solutions.

Examples

1. Offer individual problems as well as group problems, so that each student has the chance to practice.
2. Give partial credit if students have good reasons for "wrong" solutions to problems.
3. If students are stuck, resist the temptation to give too many clues. Let them think about the problem overnight.

CREATIVITY AND CREATIVE PROBLEM SOLVING

To some psychologists, **creativity** is a personal quality or trait. We often talk about creative people. Other psychologists suggest that creativity is not a personality trait but a skill or process that produces a "creative" product, such as a painting, invention, computer program, or solution to a personal problem. At the heart of all concepts of creativity we find the notion of newness. Creativity results in new, original, independent, and imaginative ways of thinking about or doing something. Although we frequently associate the arts with creativity, any subject can be approached in a creative manner.

Creativity and Cognition

Robert Sternberg (1985) suggests that creativity comes from using the *knowledge-acquisition* components (one of the three aspects of intelligence described in chapter 4) in an insightful way. Having a rich store of knowledge in an area is the basis for creativity, but something more is needed. For many problems, that "something more" is the ability to break set—**restructuring** the problem to see things in a new way, which leads to

Creativity Imaginative, original thinking or problem solving.

Restructuring Conceiving of a problem in a new or different way.

a sudden insight. Often this happens when a person has struggled with a problem or project, then sets it aside for a while. The story of Archimedes and the king's crown is a famous example.

> The Greek scientist Archimedes (287–212 B.C.) tried to determine whether the king's crown was made of solid gold or had been adulterated with silver. Archimedes knew the weight of gold and silver per unit volume but he did not know how to measure the volume of a complicated object such as a crown. One day, in his bath, he noticed how the water level rose as he immersed his body. Here was the solution: the crown's volume is determined by the water it displaces. Carried away by this sudden insight, he jumped out of his bath and ran naked through the streets of Syracuse shouting "Eureka! I have found it!" (Gleitman, 1991, p. 305)

Some psychologists have attributed these sudden solutions to the process of **incubation,** a kind of unconscious working through the problem while you are away from it. But it is more likely that leaving the problem for a time interrupts rigid ways of thinking, such as functional fixedness and response set, so you can restructure it (Gleitman, 1991).

Howard Gardner's (1982a) description of Charles Darwin's creativity downplays sudden, dramatic insight but still highlights the role of knowledge restructuring.

> Darwin experienced no sudden epiphany of inspiration, no wholly novel thoughts or theories. Instead, Darwin marshalled endless lists of thoughts, images, questions, dreams, sketches, comments, arguments, and notes to himself, all of which he continually organized and reorganized. . . . Pivotal insights were anticipated in earlier scribbles, and occasionally discovered twice. (p. 353)

So it seems that creativity requires extensive knowledge, flexibility, and the continual reorganizing of ideas. Darwin's work also shows that motivation and persistence play important roles in creative problem solving.

Assessing Creativity

Psychologists and educators confront all the usual research problems when they attempt to study creativity. "How shall we define creativity?" becomes "How shall we measure creativity?" Several answers have been proposed. One answer has been to equate creativity with **divergent thinking.** As we saw when we discussed Guilford's faces of intellect (p. 112), divergent thinking is the ability to propose many different ideas or answers. **Convergent thinking** is the more common ability to identify only one answer.

Paper-and-Pencil Tests of Creativity. E. P. Torrance has developed two types of creativity tests, verbal and graphic (Torrance, 1972; Torrance & Hall, 1980). In the verbal test, you might be instructed to think up as many uses as possible for a tin can or asked how a particular toy might be

Incubation Unconscious work toward a solution while one is away from the problem.

Divergent Thinking Coming up with many possible solutions.

Convergent Thinking Narrowing possibilities to the single answer.

changed to make it more fun to play with. On the graphic test, you might be given 30 pairs of parallel vertical lines and asked to create 30 different drawings, each drawing including one pair of lines (Sattler, 1988).

Responses to all these tasks are scored for originality, fluency, and flexibility, three aspects of divergent thinking. Originality is usually determined statistically. To be original, a response must be given by fewer than 5 or 10 people out of every 100 who take the test. Fluency is simply the number of different responses. Flexibility is generally measured by the number of different categories of responses. For instance, if you listed 100 uses for a tin can but each use was as some type of container, your fluency score might be high, but your flexibility score would be quite low. But of the three measures, fluency—the number of responses—is the best predictor of divergent thinking (Bjorklund, 1989).

Do measures of divergent thinking really assess creativity? David Bjorklund (1989) says,

> The answer would seem to be that they do, but far from perfectly. There are individual differences in divergent thinking among children. There is only moderate stability of patterns of divergent thinking over childhood, and divergent thinking is marginally related to some aspects of real-life creative activity. Creativity is an elusive concept and one not easily measured by paper-and-pencil tests. (p. 279)

Have you ever visited a science fair? If you have, you probably noticed that projects varied widely in their creativity and inventiveness. You probably also noticed that sometimes the creativity displayed was not the child's, but the parents'. Too much emphasis on competition can squelch students' creativity and turn such activities into contests among parents.

Teachers' Judgments of Creativity. If test scores are not reliable indicators of creativity, what about teachers' opinions? Teachers are not always the best judges of creativity. In fact, Torrance (1972) reports data from a 12-year follow-up study indicating *no* relationship between teachers' judgments of their students' creative abilities and the actual creativity these students revealed in their adult lives. Some psychologists suggest that the best way to identify creative students is through their achievements. Jerome Sattler (1988) recommends the rating scale in Table

TABLE 8.3 Rating Scale

Rating Scale: 1 Not present   4 Moderately present
                 2 Minimally present   5 Strongly present
                 3 Somewhat present

Trait	Rating (circle one number)	Trait	Rating (circle one number)
1. Ability to concentrate	1 2 3 4 5	**19.** Internal locus of control and evaluation	1 2 3 4 5
2. Ability to defer judgment	1 2 3 4 5	**20.** Inventiveness	1 2 3 4 5
3. Above-average IQ	1 2 3 4 5	**21.** Lack of tolerance for boredom	1 2 3 4 5
4. Adaptability	1 2 3 4 5	**22.** Need for supportive climate	1 2 3 4 5
5. Aesthetic appreciation	1 2 3 4 5	**23.** Nonconformism	1 2 3 4 5
6. Attraction to the complex and mysterious	1 2 3 4 5	**24.** Openness to experience	1 2 3 4 5
7. Curiosity	1 2 3 4 5	**25.** Playfulness	1 2 3 4 5
8. Delight in beauty of theory	1 2 3 4 5	**26.** Willingness to take risks	1 2 3 4 5
9. Delight in invention for its own sake	1 2 3 4 5	**27.** Self-confidence	1 2 3 4 5
10. Desire to share products and ideas	1 2 3 4 5	**28.** Sense of identity as originator	1 2 3 4 5
11. Eagerness to resolve disorder	1 2 3 4 5	**29.** Sense of mission	1 2 3 4 5
12. Extensive knowledge background	1 2 3 4 5	**30.** Sensitivity	1 2 3 4 5
13. Flexibility	1 2 3 4 5	**31.** Ability to see that solutions generate new problems	1 2 3 4 5
14. Good memory, attention to detail	1 2 3 4 5	**32.** Spontaneity	1 2 3 4 5
15. High energy level, enthusiasm	1 2 3 4 5	**33.** Commitment to task	1 2 3 4 5
16. Humor (perhaps bizarre)	1 2 3 4 5	**34.** Tolerance for ambiguity and conflict	1 2 3 4 5
17. Imagination, insight	1 2 3 4 5	**35.** Willingness to face social ostracism	1 2 3 4 5
18. Independence	1 2 3 4 5	**36.** Willingness to daydream and fantasize	1 2 3 4 5

Some of the possible characteristics of creative students are listed on this form.

Source: Reprinted by permission from J. Sattler (1988), *Assessment of children* (3rd ed.) (San Diego: Jerome M. Sattler Publisher), p. 682.

8.3 to identify creative students. As you can see, many of the traits of creative individuals can make them a challenge in the classroom.

Creativity in the Classroom

Even though creative students may be difficult to identify (and sometimes difficult to handle), creativity is worth fostering. Certainly the many social, environmental, and economic problems facing our society will require creative solutions. How can teachers promote creative thinking?

Perhaps the most important step teachers can take to encourage creativity is to make sure students know that their creativity will be appreciated. All too often, in the crush of day-to-day classroom life, teachers stifle creative ideas without realizing what they are doing. Teachers are in an excellent position to encourage or discourage creativity through their acceptance or rejection of the unusual and imaginative. Rejection may be fatal to creativity.

The Brainstorming Strategy. In addition to encouraging creativity through everyday interactions with students, teachers can try **brainstorming.** The basic tenet of brainstorming is to separate the process of creating ideas from the process of evaluating them because evaluation often inhibits creativity and problem solving (Osborn, 1963). In discussions such as the following, for example, the attempt to have creative ideas about solving a problem often turns into a debate about the merits of one idea:

> We have to decide on a senior project.
>
> How about cleaning up the river by the park?
>
> No, that won't work. Someone's bound to get hurt.
>
> Not necessarily. Five years ago the senior class did it and everything went fine.
>
> Yes, but. . . .

Many participants in such discussions become bored and tune out.

The goal of brainstorming is to generate as many ideas as possible, no matter how impractical they seem at first. Evaluation, discussion, and criticism are postponed until all possible suggestions have been made. In this way, one idea inspires others and people do not withhold potentially creative solutions out of fear of criticism. After all the ideas are expressed, they can be evaluated, modified, or combined to produce a creative solution.

Individuals as well as groups may benefit from brainstorming. In writing this book, for example, I have sometimes found it helpful simply to list all the different topics that could be covered in a chapter, then leave the list and return to it later to evaluate the ideas.

Take Your Time—and Play! There is some evidence that preschool children who spend more time in fantasy and pretend play are more creative. In fact, playing before taking a creativity test resulted in higher

Brainstorming Generating ideas without stopping to evaluate them.

Guidelines

Encouraging Creativity

Accept and encourage divergent thinking.

Examples

1. During class discussion, ask: "Can anyone suggest a different way of looking at this question?"
2. Reinforce attempts at unusual solutions to problems, even if the final product is not perfect.

Tolerate dissent.

Examples

1. Ask students to support dissenting opinions.
2. Make sure nonconforming students receive an equal share of classroom privileges and rewards.

Encourage students to trust their own judgment.

Examples

1. When students ask questions you think they can answer, rephrase or clarify the questions and direct them back to the students.
2. Give ungraded assignments from time to time.

Emphasize that everyone is capable of creativity in some form.

Examples

1. Avoid describing the feats of great artists or inventors as if they were superhuman accomplishments.
2. Recognize creative efforts in each student's work. Have a separate grade for originality on some assignments.

Be a stimulus for creative thinking.

Examples

1. Use a class brainstorming session whenever possible.
2. Model creative problem solving by suggesting unusual solutions for class problems.
3. Encourage students to delay judging a particular suggestion for solving a problem until all the possibilities have been considered.

scores on the test for the young students in one study (Bjorklund, 1989). Teachers can encourage students of all ages to be more reflective—to take time for ideas to grow, develop, and be restructured. Recent evidence suggests that working in Logo computer environments can enhance both visual and verbal creativity in young children (Clements, 1991). The Guidelines above, adapted from Frederiksen (1984) and Sattler (1988), describe other possibilities for encouraging creativity.

TEACHING CRITICAL THINKING SKILLS

Even if we are successful in teaching reading and the other basics, can we be sure that our students will be able to analyze and evaluate what they read? Will they be able to go beyond the information given to apply their knowledge, make judgments, and generate new ideas? In other words, will they be able to think (Prawat, 1991)? Answering this question has become a national issue.

Many educational psychologists believe that thinking skills can and should be developed in school. The opening sentence of the 1989 yearbook of the Association for Supervision and Curriculum Development is, "As we enter the 1990s, thoughtful educators everywhere are calling attention to the importance of developing students' thinking skills through their experiences in school" (Resnick & Klopfer, 1989, p. 1). But clearly, the teaching of thinking entails much more than the standard classroom practices of completing worksheets, answering "thought" questions at the end of the chapter, and participating in teacher-led discussions. What else is needed? There are two main approaches to the development of thinking skills: stand-alone programs that teach skills directly and indirect methods that embed development of thinking in the regular curriculum.

Stand-Alone and Embedded Programs for Developing Thinking

There are many different programs that teach thinking skills directly. A resource book for educators (Costa, 1985) lists over 15 different programs, including de Bono's CORT system; Odyssey: A Curriculum for Thinking; Winocur's Project Impact; Lipman's Philosophy for Children; and Meeker's SOI. In these programs students learn skills such as comparing, ordering, classifying, and making inferences. The advantage of these **stand-alone thinking skills programs** is that students do not need extensive subject matter knowledge to master the skills. So students who have had trouble with the traditional curriculum may achieve success—and perhaps an enhanced sense of self-esteem—through these programs. The disadvantage is that the general skills often are not used outside the program unless teachers make a concerted effort to show students how to apply the skills in specific subjects. As you will see shortly when we discuss *transfer,* encouraging students to apply knowledge and skills to new situations is a challenge for all teachers (Prawat, 1991).

Another way to develop students' thinking skills is to embed them in the regular lessons of the curriculum. David Perkins (1987) proposes two kinds of "thinking frames" that can be embedded in lessons. The first, *executive control frames,* relates to thinking processes. We discussed many of these frames in the previous chapter when we examined metacognition and learning strategies. A few examples are using headings to guide reading; outlining; self-questioning; mapping key relationships; and the *prewrite, write, rewrite* formula used by many instructors to guide students' writing. Another example is the reciprocal teaching strategy for guiding reading comprehension. These frames help guide students' thinking in a particular subject.

The second kind of thinking frame that can be embedded in regular lessons, **critical thinking,** focuses on the products of thinking. These frames give students a way of evaluating their own ideas or the ideas of others. Because this is an important skill, we will look at it in some depth.

Critical Thinking

Critical thinking skills are useful in almost every life situation—even in evaluating the media ads that constantly bombard us. To evaluate the claim that 99 out of 100 dentists prefer a particular brand of toothpaste, you must consider such questions as: Which dentists were polled? How were they chosen? Was the toothpaste company involved in the polling

Stand-Alone Thinking Skills Programs Programs that teach thinking skills directly without need for extensive subject matter.

Critical Thinking Evaluating conclusions by logically and systematically examining the problem, the evidence, and the solution.

process? If so, how could this bias the results of the poll? Or when you see a group of gorgeous people extolling the virtues of a particular brand of orange juice as they frolic in skimpy bathing suits, you must decide if sex appeal is a relevant factor in choosing a fruit drink.

Psychologists have not been able to agree on the skills that constitute critical thinking. Perkins (1986) emphasizes the capacities to identify the problem, to detect and avoid bias in reasoning, and to see knowledge as an invention of people for a particular purpose, not as information that is set or unchanging. Other psychologists have different ideas. Table 8.4, taken from Kneedler (1985), provides a representative list of critical thinking skills.

How might you incorporate critical thinking frames into your regular lessons? Let's assume you teach history and have decided to focus on detecting bias, a skill many experts list as an important component of critical thinking. Exactly how would you go about it? Beyer (1985) describes one approach involving the steps of *introduction, experimentation, reflection, application,* and *review.*

First, the teacher gives a brief and general *introduction,* stating the purpose of the lesson (to learn how to detect bias in historical documents) and perhaps giving a definition and a few examples of bias in written

---

TABLE 8.4   Examples of Critical Thinking Skills

Defining and Clarifying the Problem

1. Identify central issues or problems.
2. Compare similarities and differences.
3. Determine which information is relevant.
4. Formulate appropriate questions.

Judging Information Related to the Problem

5. Distinguish among fact, opinion, and reasoned judgment.
6. Check consistency.
7. Identify unstated assumptions.
8. Recognize stereotypes and clichés.
9. Recognize bias, emotional factors, propaganda, and semantic slanting.
10. Recognize different value systems and ideologies.

Solving Problems/Drawing Conclusions

11. Recognize the adequacy of data.
12. Predict probable consequences.

Source: Adapted from P. Kneedler (1985), California assesses critical thinking. In A. Costa (Ed.), *Developing minds: A resource book for teaching thinking.* Alexandria, VA: Association for Supervision and Curriculum Development, p. 277. Reprinted with permission of the Association for Supervision and Curriculum Development and the author. Copyright 1985 by the Association for Supervision and Curriculum Development. All rights reserved.

materials. Without any other explanation, the students are given the following passage so they can *experiment:*

Excerpt A

Some of these lords of the loom . . . employ thousands of miserable creatures . . . [who are] kept, fourteen hours in each day, locked up, summer and winter, in a heat of from eighty to eighty-four degrees. What then must be the situation of these poor creatures who are doomed to toil day after day . . . ? Can any man, with a heart in his body . . . refrain from cursing a system that produces such slavery and cruelty? [These] poor creatures have no cool room to retreat to . . . [and] are not allowed to send for water to drink; . . . even the rain water is locked up, by the masters' order. . . . [A]ny spinner found with his window open . . . is to pay a fine. (Cobbett, 1824)

Experimenting simply means attempting to identify bias in the passage as best you can. Students might work alone, in pairs, or in small groups.

Next, students *reflect* on what they have just read. Is the passage biased? Most students will answer a resounding "Yes!" As evidence of bias they may list emotionally charged words and phrases like "miserable creatures" or "doomed to toil." They may notice overgeneralization ("Any spinner") or rhetorical questions ("Can any man, with a heart"). After identifying a number of examples, the student can begin to notice similarities. What could we call phrases like "miserable creatures" or "doomed to toil"? The general category of "emotionally charged language" should emerge from this discussion.

At this stage in Beyer's approach, the students are ready to *apply* the categories they have just identified to a new passage. They are given the following passage:

Excerpt B

I have visited many factories . . . and I never saw . . . children in ill humor. They seemed to be always cheerful and alert, taking pleasure in the light play of their muscles—enjoying the mobility natural to their age. The scene of industry . . . was exhilarating. It was delightful to observe the nimbleness with which they pieced the broken ends as the mule carriage began to recede from the fixed roller-beam and to see them at leisure after a few seconds' exercise of their tiny fingers, to amuse themselves in any attitude they chose. . . . The work of these lively elves seemed to resemble a sport. . . . [T]hey evidenced no trace of exhaustion on emerging from the mill in the evening; for they . . . skip about any neighborhood playground. (Ure, 1861)

The last step is to *review* what has been learned. What kinds of clues do you look for in detecting bias? What general procedures should you follow?

Whether you use Beyer's approach or another, it is important to follow up with additional guided practice. One lesson is not enough.

Analyzing other written historical documents, contemporary advertisements, or news stories will give needed practice. Until thinking skills become overlearned and relatively automatic, they are not likely to be transferred to new situations. Instead, students will generally use these skills only to complete the lesson in social studies, not to evaluate the claims made by friends, politicians, toy manufacturers, or diet plans. The need to teach so that new skills transfer to other situations is a significant concern in educational psychology.

TEACHING FOR TRANSFER

Think back for a moment to a class in one of your high school subjects you did not go on to study in college. Imagine the teacher, the room, the textbook. If you can do all of this, you are using your information processing strategies for search and retrieval very well. Now remember what you actually studied in class. If it was a science class, what were some of the formulas you learned? How about chemical reactions? Oxidation reduction? If you are like most of us, you may remember *that* you learned these things, but you will not be quite sure exactly *what* you learned. Were those hours wasted? These questions are about the transfer of learning.

Defining Transfer

Whenever something previously learned influences current learning, **transfer** has occurred. If students learn a mathematical principle in first period and use it to solve a physics problem in fifth period, then *positive transfer* has taken place. Even more rewarding for teachers is the positive transfer that takes place when a math principle learned in October is applied to a physics problem in March.

Drawing by Ziegler; © 1983 The New Yorker Magazine, Inc.

Transfer Influence of previously learned material on new material.

Real-life tasks such as producing a school newspaper can encourage transfer by calling on previously learned math, writing, reading, communication, and social skills.

However, the effect of past learning on present learning is not always positive. Both proactive interference (old learning interferes with new) and retroactive interference (new learning wipes out old) are examples of *negative transfer.* So are functional fixedness and response set, since they involve the attempt to apply familiar but inappropriate strategies to a new situation.

Specific transfer occurs when a rule, fact, or skill learned in one situation is applied in another very similar situation; for example, applying rules of punctuation to write a job application letter or using knowledge of the alphabet to find a word in the dictionary. *General transfer* involves applying to new problems principles and attitudes learned in other, often dissimilar situations. Thus, general transfer might mean using problem-solving heuristics to solve issues in your personal life—for example, applying working backward to decide when to call for an appointment to have a dentist check a sore tooth in time to get any necessary work done before you leave for spring break.

Early Research on Mental Discipline. Studies of transfer undertaken early in the twentieth century may have had more impact on education than any other research conducted by psychologists (Travers, 1977). Before that, it was assumed that learning certain subjects, such as Latin and mathematics, provided students with powers of thinking and mental discipline that could be applied to all subjects. Thorndike and his colleagues conducted research to determine if studying Latin, Greek, and mathematics actually did lead to increased intellectual achievement in other subjects (Brolyer, Thorndike, & Woodyard, 1927). They found no general transfer to other areas. Learning Latin, for example, seemed to

TABLE 8.5 Kinds of Transfer

	Low-Road Transfer	High-Road Transfer
Definition	Automatic transfer of highly practiced skill	Conscious application of abstract knowledge to a new situation
Key Conditions	Extensive practice Variety of settings and conditions Overlearning to automaticity	Mindful focus on abstracting a principle, main idea, procedure that can be used in many situations
Examples	Driving many different cars Finding your gate in an airport	Applying PQ4R in reading texts Applying procedures from math in designing a page layout for the school newspaper

transfer primarily to learning more Latin (and perhaps to learning some English vocabulary). In other words, transfer was specific, not general.

Once the findings of Thorndike's research were publicized, the notion of mental discipline began to fade, and curricula and graduation requirements were altered. Partly because of educational psychology, and for better or for worse, students do not have to study Greek and Latin throughout their school years.

A Contemporary View of Transfer. Gavriel Salomon and David Perkins (1989) describe two kinds of transfer, termed low-road and high-road transfer. **Low-road transfer** "involves the spontaneous, automatic transfer of highly practiced skills, with little need for reflective thinking" (p. 118). For example, you probably have little trouble driving a friend's car, even though it is different from your car, because you have practiced the skill of driving until it is automatic. You might have trouble, of course, if your friend's car has a standard transmission and you haven't driven a stick shift in years, because you lack recent practice with this kind of car. The key to low-road transfer is practicing a skill often and in a *variety* of situations until your performance becomes *automatic.* So if you worked one summer for a temporary secretarial service and were sent to many different offices to work on all kinds of typewriters and word processors, by the end of the summer you probably would be able to handle most machines easily. Your practice with many machines would let you transfer your skill automatically to a new situation.

High-road transfer, on the other hand, involves consciously applying abstract knowledge learned in one situation to a different situation. This can happen in one of two ways. You may learn a principle or a strategy, intending to use it in the future. For example, if you plan to apply what you learn in anatomy class this semester to work in a life-drawing course you will take next semester, you may search for principles about human proportions, muscle definition, and so on. This is called *forward-reaching transfer,* because you are looking forward to applying the knowledge gained. *Backward-reaching transfer* occurs when you are faced with a

Low-Road Transfer
Spontaneous and automatic transfer of highly practiced skills.

High-Road Transfer
Application of abstract knowledge learned in one situation to a different situation.

problem and look back on what you have learned in other situations to help you in this new one. Analogical thinking is an example of this kind of transfer. You search for other related situations that might provide clues to the current problem. The key to high-road transfer is *mindful abstraction*, or the deliberate identification of a principle, main idea, strategy, or procedure that is not tied to one specific problem or situation but could apply to many. Such an abstraction becomes part of your metacognitive knowledge, available to guide future learning and problem solving. Table 8.5 on page 316 summarizes the types of transfer.

Teaching for Positive Transfer

Years of research and experience show that teachers cannot expect students automatically to transfer what they learn to new situations. We have seen repeatedly in this book that students will master new knowledge, problem-solving procedures, and learning strategies, but not use them unless prompted or guided. How can you make sure your students will use what they learn?

What Is Worth Learning? First you must answer the question "What is worth learning?" The learning of basic skills like reading, writing, computing, and speaking will definitely transfer to other situations, because these skills are necessary for later work both in and out of school—writing job applications, reading government forms, calculating insurance needs, figuring income tax, locating and evaluating needed services, among others. All later learning depends on positive transfer of these basics to new situations.

Teachers must also be aware of what the future is likely to hold for their students, both as a group and as individuals. What will society require of them as adults? What will their careers require of them? As a child growing up in Texas in the 1950s and 1960s, I studied nothing about computers, even though my father was a computer systems analyst; yet now I spend a great deal of time at this word processor. Computer programming and word processing were not part of my high school curriculum. But learning to use a slide rule was taught. Now calculators and computers have made this skill obsolete. Undoubtedly changes as extreme and unpredictable as these await the students you will teach. For this reason, the general transfer of principles, attitudes, critical thinking ability, and problem-solving strategies will be just as important to these students as the specific transfer of basic skills.

How Can Teachers Help? To have something to transfer, students must first learn and understand. Thorough understanding involves incorporating new information into existing schemata, elaborating it, and organizing it as much as possible—in other words, encoding it for storage in long-term memory in easily retrievable form. Making learning meaningful really implies teaching for transfer— teaching for deep processing, permanent storage, and easy retrieval.

Students will be more likely to transfer information to new situations if they have been actively involved in the learning process. They must be encouraged to form abstractions that they will apply later. For example, Salomon and Perkins (1989) give this advice for teaching history:

> [The] history teacher can introduce direct discussion of contemporary events. To provoke forward-reaching transfer, the teacher can select an episode in history and encourage students to seek contemporary analogs. To provoke backward-reaching transfer, the teacher can choose a current phenomenon . . . and urge students to reach into their historical repertoires for analogies and disanalogies. (p. 136)

Newly mastered concepts, principles, and strategies must be practiced in a wide variety of situations. Positive transfer is encouraged when skills are practiced under conditions similar to those that will exist when the skills are needed later. Some of these applications should involve complex, unstructured problems, since many of the problems to be faced in later life, in school and out, will not come to students complete with instructions.

Greater transfer can also be ensured by **overlearning** or practicing a skill past the point of mastery. Many of the basic facts students learn in elementary school, such as the multiplication tables, are traditionally overlearned. Overlearning helps students retrieve the information quickly and automatically when it is needed.

The cognitive perspective on learning is the foundation for much of the information presented in this chapter on concepts, problem solving, creativity, thinking, and transfer of learning. In addition, cognitive theorists have developed several models of instruction that apply many of the principles of concept learning, problem solving, and transfer that we have discussed in the preceding pages. In the next section we examine three of these models.

Jerome Bruner's writings about education have influenced teaching for several decades.

Overlearning Practicing a task past the point of mastery to combat forgetting and improve transfer.

COGNITIVE MODELS OF TEACHING

Many instructional models are consistent with cognitive theories of learning. We will consider Jerome Bruner's discovery learning, David Ausubel's expository teaching, and Robert Gagné's instructional events model.

Discovery Learning

Jerome Bruner's early research on thinking (Bruner, Goodnow, & Austin, 1956) stirred his interest in educational approaches that encourage the development of thinking. This interest led Bruner to write several books on teaching and learning, including *The Process of Education* (1960), *Toward a Theory of Instruction* (1966), and *The Relevance of Education* (1971). In these books Bruner emphasizes the importance of understanding the structure of a subject being studied, the need for active learning to make personal discoveries as the basis for true understanding, and the value of inductive reasoning in learning.

This field trip might be the first step in discovery learning. Students collect samples of different plants, then return to class to create categories and share ideas about their groupings.

Structure and Discovery. **Subject structure** refers to the fundamental ideas, relationships, or patterns of the field—that is, the essential information. Because structure does not include specific facts or details about the subject, the essential structure of an idea can be represented simply as a diagram, set of principles, or formula. Many of the tables and figures in this text attempt to communicate the structure of key ideas in educational psychology; for example, the different kinds of reinforcement schedules (Table 6.1, 207) or the processes of learning and forgetting in long-term memory (Figure 7.2, p. 243). According to Bruner, learning will be more meaningful, useful, and memorable for students if they focus on understanding the structure of the subject being studied. For example, if you learned the concepts *figure, plane, simple, closed, quadrilateral, isosceles, scalene, equilateral,* and *right,* you would be on your way to understanding one aspect of geometry. But how do these terms relate to one another? If you can place the terms into a coding system such as the one in Figure 8.6 on page 320, you will have a better understanding of the basic structure of this part of geometry.

A **coding system** is a hierarchy of related concepts. At the top of the coding system is the most general concept, in this case *plane, simple, closed figure.* More specific concepts are arranged under the general concept.

In order to grasp the structure of information, Bruner believes, students must be active—they must identify key principles for themselves rather than simply accepting teachers' explanations. He believes that teachers should provide problem situations stimulating students to question, explore, and experiment. This process has been called discovery learning. In **discovery learning,** the teacher presents examples and the students work with the examples until they discover the interrelationships—the subject's structure. Thus, Bruner believes that classroom

Subject Structure
According to Bruner, the fundamental framework of ideas.

Coding System A hierarchy of ideas or concepts.

Discovery Learning
Bruner's approach, in which students work on their own to discover basic principles.

FIGURE 8.6   A Coding System for Triangles   Place the concept in a hierarchy so you know what concepts are above and possibly below.

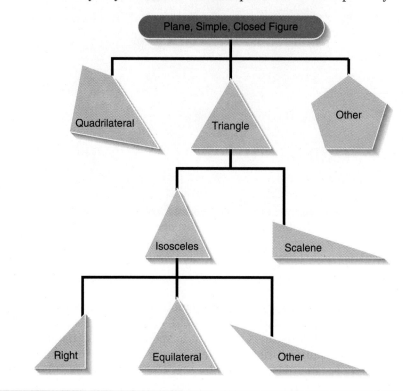

learning should take place through **inductive reasoning;** that is, by using specific examples to formulate a general principle. For instance, if students are presented with enough examples of triangles and nontriangles, they will eventually discover what the basic properties of any triangle must be. Encouraging inductive thinking in this way is sometimes called the **eg-rule method,** from the Latin *e.g.,* meaning "for example."

Discovery in Action. An inductive approach requires **intuitive thinking** on the part of students. Bruner suggests that teachers can nurture this intuitive thinking by encouraging students to make guesses based on incomplete evidence and then to confirm or disprove the guesses systematically (Bruner, 1960). After learning about ocean currents and the shipping industry, for example, students might be shown old maps of three harbors and asked to guess which one became a major port. Then students could check their guesses through systematic research. Unfortunately, educational practices often discourage intuitive thinking by punishing wrong guesses and rewarding safe but uncreative answers.

Notice that in Bruner's discovery learning, a teacher organizes the class so that the students learn through their own active involvement. A distinction is usually made between discovery learning, in which the students work on their own to a very great extent, and **guided discovery,** in which the teacher provides some direction. Unguided discovery is

Inductive Reasoning Formulating general principles based on knowledge of examples and details.

Eg-Rule Method Teaching or learning by moving from specific examples to general rules.

Intuitive Thinking Making imaginative leaps to correct perceptions or workable solutions.

Guided Discovery An adaptation of discovery learning, in which the teacher provides some direction.

Guidelines

Applying Bruner's Ideas in the Classroom

Present both examples and nonexamples of the concepts you are teaching.

Examples

1. In teaching about mammals, include people, kangaroos, whales, cats, dolphins, and camels as examples and chickens, fish, alligators, frogs, and penguins as nonexamples.
2. Ask students for additional examples and nonexamples.

Help students see connections among concepts.

Examples

1. Ask questions such as these: What else could you call this apple? (Fruit.) What do we do with fruit? (Eat.) What do we call things we eat? (Food.)
2. Use diagrams, outlines, and summaries to point out connections.

Pose a question and let students try to find the answer.

Examples

1. How could the human hand be improved?
2. What is the relation between the area of one tile and the area of the whole floor?

Encourage students to make intuitive guesses.

Examples

1. Instead of giving a word's definition, say, "Let's guess what it might mean by looking at the words around it."
2. Give students a map of ancient Greece and ask where they think the major cities were.
3. Don't comment after the first few guesses. Wait for several ideas before giving the answer.
4. Use guiding questions to focus students when their discovery has led them too far astray.

appropriate for preschool children, but in a typical elementary or secondary classroom, unguided activities usually prove unmanageable and unproductive, so for these situations, guided discovery is preferable. Students are presented with intriguing questions, baffling situations, or interesting problems: Why does the flame go out when we cover it with a jar? Why does this pencil seem to bend when you put it in water? What is the rule for grouping these words together? Instead of explaining how to solve the problem, the teacher provides the appropriate materials and encourages students to make observations, form hypotheses, and test solutions.

For example, to answer the question about the flame, students might note the size of the jar, how long it takes for the flame to go out, and what happens if the jar has holes or if someone blows into the jar with a straw. To solve the problem, students must use both intuitive and analytical thinking. The teacher guides the discovery by asking leading questions: Does a candle burn longer in a larger or a smaller jar? (Larger.) What is there more of in a large, empty jar than in a small, empty jar? (Air.) What happens when you cover a fire with dirt? (It goes out.) Why? (No air.) The teacher also provides feedback about the direction activities take. Feedback must be given at the optimal moment, when students can either use it to revise their approach or take it as encouragement to continue in the direction they've chosen. The Guidelines above should help you apply Bruner's suggestions to various classroom situations.

Is Discovery Learning Effective?

Most psychologists and educators agree that students must make sense of information in order to learn and remember it. Simply memorizing lists and facts leads to superficial understanding and rapid forgetting. When students struggle with perplexing problems, test possible solutions, and finally discover for themselves the fundamental structure of a key concept, then the students are more likely to understand and remember the information. But critics of discovery learning raise some important questions. Is discovery learning an effective method?

Point: Discovery learning matches cognitive development.

Educators favoring discovery learning note that this approach is consistent with the ways that people learn and develop. For example, Jerome Bruner (1966, 1971) identified three stages of cognitive growth, similar to the stages identified by Piaget. Bruner believes that children move from an *enactive* stage to an *iconic* stage and finally to a *symbolic*

stage. In the enactive stage (similar to Piaget's sensorimotor stage), the child represents and understands the world through actions—to understand something is to manipulate it, taste it, throw it, break it, and so on. At the iconic stage, the child represents the world in images—appearances dominate. This stage corresponds to Piaget's preoperational thinking, in which the higher the water level, the more water there must be in the glass, because that's what *appears* to be true. At the final level, the child is able to use abstract ideas, symbols, language, and logic to understand and represent the world. Actions and images can still be used in thinking, but they do not dominate.

Discovery learning allows students to move through these three stages as they encounter new information. First the students manipulate and act on materials, then they form images as they note specific features and make observations, then they abstract general ideas and principles from these experiences and observations. Because they have experienced each stage of representation,

Discovery learning appears to have many advantages, but even Bruner believes that it is not appropriate in every situation. The **Point/ Counterpoint** section above examines the pros and cons of this approach.

Reception Learning

David Ausubel's (1963, 1977) view of learning offers an interesting contrast to that of Bruner. According to Ausubel, people acquire knowledge primarily through reception rather than through discovery. Concepts, principles, and ideas are presented to them and received by them, not discovered by them. The more organized and focused the presentation, the more thoroughly the person will learn, as you saw in the previous chapter.

Ausubel stresses what is known as **meaningful verbal learning**—verbal information, ideas, and relationships among ideas, taken together. Rote memorization is not considered meaningful learning, since material learned by rote is not connected with existing knowledge. Unfortunately, despite the ineffectiveness of rote learning, many lessons seem to rely on little else (Ausubel, 1977). Ausubel has proposed his **expository teaching**

Meaningful Verbal Learning Focused and organized relationships among ideas and verbal information.

Expository Teaching Ausubel's method— teachers present material in complete, organized form, moving from broadest to more specific concepts.

Bruner believes, the students will have a better understanding of the topic. When students are motivated and really participate in the discovery project, discovery learning leads to superior learning (Strike, 1975).

Counterpoint: Discovery learning is impractical.

In theory, discovery learning seems ideal, but in practice there are problems. To be successful, discovery projects often require special materials and extensive preparations. And these preparations can't guarantee success. For example, a discovery lesson on the effects of light on plants takes many hours and often falls flat because the plants grown in darkness and those grown in light don't always behave as they should—many factors other than light affect growth (Anderson & Smith, 1987).

In order to benefit from a discovery situation, students must have basic knowledge about the problem and must know how to apply problem-solving strategies. Without this knowledge and skill, they will flounder and grow frustrated. In-stead of learning from the materials, they may simply play with them. The brightest students may make some discoveries, while the others lose interest or just wait passively for someone else to complete the project. Instead of benefiting from a teacher's organized explanation, these "non-discovering" students may get an inadequate explanation from a fellow student who can't quite communicate his or her discoveries. Everyone may grow frustrated as the teacher seems to withhold the solutions and explanations needed.

Critics believe that discovery learning is so inefficient and so difficult to organize successfully that other methods are preferable. This seems especially true for lower-ability students. Discovery methods may make too many demands on these students, because they lack the background knowledge and problem-solving skills needed to benefit. Some research has shown that discovery methods are ineffective and even detrimental for lower-ability students (Corno & Snow, 1986; Slavin, Karweit, & Madden, 1989).

model to encourage meaningful rather than rote reception learning. (Exposition means explanation, or the setting forth of facts and ideas.) In this approach, teachers present materials in a carefully organized, sequenced, and somewhat finished form, and students thus receive the most usable material in the most efficient way. Ausubel does agree with Bruner that people learn by organizing new information into hierarchies or coding systems. Ausubel calls the general concept at the top of the system the *subsumer,* because all other concepts are subsumed under it, as in Figure 8.6 on page 320. Ausubel believes that learning should progress, not inductively as Bruner recommends, but deductively: from the general to the specific, or from the rule or principle to examples. The **deductive reasoning** approach is sometimes called the **rule-eg method.**

Ausubel's expository teaching model has four major characteristics. First, it calls for a great deal of interaction between teacher and students. Although the teacher makes the initial presentation, students' ideas and responses are solicited throughout each lesson. Second, expository teaching makes great use of examples. Although the stress is on verbal learning, examples may include drawings, diagrams, or pictures. Third, expository teaching is deductive, as you've seen. The most general and

Deductive Reasoning
Drawing conclusions by applying rules or principles; logically moving from a general rule or principle to a specific solution.

Rule-Eg Method Teaching or learning by moving from general principles to specific examples.

inclusive concepts are presented first, and the more specific concepts are derived from them. Finally, it is sequential. Certain steps must be followed, beginning with an advance organizer.

Advance Organizers. Optimal learning generally occurs when there is a potential fit between the student's schemata and the material to be learned. To make this fit more likely, a lesson following Ausubel's strategy always begins with an **advance organizer.** This is an introductory statement of a relationship or a high-level concept broad enough to encompass all the information that will follow.

The function of advance organizers is to provide *scaffolding* or *support* for the new information. You can also see the advance organizer as a kind of conceptual bridge between new material and students' current knowledge (Faw & Waller, 1976). Textbooks often contain such advance organizers—the chapter overviews and "What Do You Think?" questions in this book are examples. The organizers can serve three purposes: They can direct your attention to what is important in the coming material; they can highlight relationships among ideas that will be presented; and they can remind you of relevant information you already have. In teaching a lesson on the caste system in India, for example, the organizer might deal with the concepts of social classes and social stratification in societies (Joyce & Weil, 1986). A teacher introducing a unit on poetry might ask, "What is poetry?" and provide a poetic quote defining poetry, as well as examples of rhymed, unrhymed, and free verse.

In general, advance organizers fall into one of two categories, *comparative* and *expository* (Mayer, 1979, 1984). Each fulfills an important function. Comparative organizers *activate* (bring into working memory) already existing schemata. They remind you of what you already know but may not realize is relevant. A comparative advance organizer for long division, for example, might point out the differences and similarities between division and multiplication (Joyce & Weil, 1986). You might begin a history lesson on revolutions with a statement that contrasts military uprisings with the physical and social changes involved in the Industrial Revolution; you could also compare the common aspects of the French, English, Mexican, Russian, Iranian, and American revolutions (Salomon & Perkins, 1989).

In contrast, expository organizers provide *new* knowledge that students will need to understand the upcoming information. An expository organizer is thus a statement of a subsumer, a definition of a general concept. In an English class, for example, you might begin a large thematic unit on rites of passage in literature with a very broad statement of the theme and why it has been so central in literature— something like, "A central character coming of age must learn to know himself or herself, often makes some kind of journey of self-discovery, and must decide what in the society is to be accepted, what rejected. . . ."

The general conclusion of research on advance organizers is that they *do* help students learn, especially when the material is quite unfamiliar, complex, or difficult (Mayer, 1984; Shuell, 1981b). Of course, the effects of advance organizers depend on how good they are and how students

Advance Organizer
Statement of inclusive concepts to introduce and sum up material that follows.

actually use them. First, to be effective, the organizer must be processed and understood by the students. This was demonstrated dramatically in a study by Dinnel and Glover (1985). They found that instructing students to paraphrase an advance organizer—which, of course, requires them to understand its meaning—increased the effectiveness of the organizer. Second, the organizer must really be an organizer—it must encompass all the material that will follow and must indicate relations among the basic concepts and terms that will be used. In other words, a true organizer isn't just a statement of historical or background information. No amount of student processing can make a bad organizer more effective. Concrete models, diagrams, or analogies seem to be especially good organizers (Mayer 1983a, 1984).

Steps in an Expository Lesson. After presenting an advance organizer, the next step in a lesson using Ausubel's approach is to present content in terms of basic similarities and differences, using specific examples. If you began with a comparative organizer, now you can expand on these comparisons. Ausubel's emphasis on both similarities and differences reflects one of his basic ideas, the importance of the *schemata-fit* notion. To learn any new material, students must see not only the similarities between the material presented and what they already know; they must also see the differences so that interference—the confusion of old and new material—can be avoided.

It is often helpful in an expository lesson to ask students to supply similarities and differences themselves. In a grammar lesson, you might ask, "What are the differences between the way commas and semicolons are used?" Or suppose in teaching the coming-of-age theme in literature, you choose *The Diary of Anne Frank* and *The Adventures of Huckleberry Finn* as the basic material for the unit. As the students read the first book, you might ask them to compare the central character's growth, state of mind, and position in society with characters from other novels, plays, and films. When the class moves on to the second book, you can start by asking students to compare Anne Frank's inner journey with Huck Finn's trip down the Mississippi. As comparisons are made, whether within a single class lesson or during an entire unit, it is useful to underscore the goal of the lesson and occasionally to repeat the advance organizer, with amendments and elaborations.

Along with the comparisons, *specific* examples must come into play. You can see that the best way to point out similarities and differences is with examples. There must be specific examples of comma and semicolon usage; the specific elements of Huck Finn's and Anne Frank's dilemmas must be clear. Finally, when all the material has been presented, ask students to discuss how the examples can be used to expand on the original advance organizer.

Making the Most of Expository Teaching. As with any teaching approach, expository teaching works better in some situations than in others. First, this approach is most appropriate when you want to teach about the relationships among several concepts. Students must have

Guidelines

Applying Ausubel's Ideas in the Classroom

Use advance organizers.

Examples

1. English: Shakespeare used the social ideas of his time as a framework for his plays—*Julius Caesar, Hamlet,* and *Macbeth* dealt with concepts of natural order, a nation as the human body, etc.
2. Social studies: Geography dictates economy in preindustrialized regions or nations.
3. History: Important concepts during the Renaissance were symmetry, admiration of the classical world, the centrality of the human mind.

Use a number of examples.

Examples

1. In mathematics class, ask students to point out all the examples of right angles that they can find in the room.
2. In teaching about islands and peninsulas, use maps, slides, models, postcards.

Focus on both similarities and differences.

Examples

1. In a history class, ask students to list the ways in which the North and South were alike and different before the Civil War.
2. In a biology class, ask students how they would transform spiders into insects or an amphibian into a reptile.

some knowledge of the actual concepts first. What if students in a history class had never heard of the French Revolution or the Industrial Revolution? How could they compare these specific events to get a better understanding of elements that characterize different kinds of revolutions? They might resort to memorizing definitions and lists, such as "the five characteristics of a revolution are. . . ." Even in a lesson on what poetry is, students who don't have a basic understanding of the concept of literature—why people write and why they read—will be at a loss.

Another consideration with expository teaching is the age of the students. This approach requires students to manipulate ideas mentally, even if the ideas are fairly simple and based on physical realities such as rocks and minerals. This means that expository teaching is generally more developmentally appropriate for students at or above later elementary school—around the fifth or sixth grade (Luiten, Ames, & Ackerson, 1980). The Guidelines above should help you follow the main steps in expository teaching.

The Instructional Events Model

Robert Gagné (1977; Gagné & Driscoll, 1988) has proposed a well-developed theory of instruction based on the information processing model of learning described in chapter 7. He is less concerned about whether students learn by discovery or by reception and more interested in the quality, permanence, and usefulness of their learning. Figure 8.7 shows

FIGURE 8.7 **Gagné's Phases of Learning** This figure illustrates the elements of instruction that support learning at each phase in Gagné's model of learning.

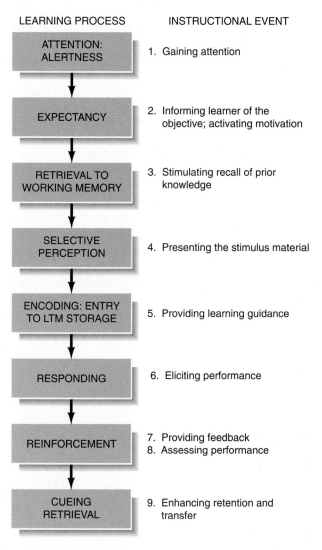

LEARNING PROCESS	INSTRUCTIONAL EVENT
ATTENTION: ALERTNESS	1. Gaining attention
EXPECTANCY	2. Informing learner of the objective; activating motivation
RETRIEVAL TO WORKING MEMORY	3. Stimulating recall of prior knowledge
SELECTIVE PERCEPTION	4. Presenting the stimulus material
ENCODING: ENTRY TO LTM STORAGE	5. Providing learning guidance
RESPONDING	6. Eliciting performance
REINFORCEMENT	7. Providing feedback 8. Assessing performance
CUEING RETRIEVAL	9. Enhancing retention and transfer

Source: From R. Gagné and M. Driscoll (1988). *Essentials of learning for instruction* (2nd ed.). Copyright © 1988. Reprinted with permission of Allyn and Bacon.

Gagné's phases of learning and the "instructional events" associated with each phase.

As you can see, in the **instructional events model** the first step in learning, and the first challenge for the teacher, is to gain the students' attention. The next step is to set an expectancy for learning by letting the students know the goals of the lesson and perhaps arousing their curios-

Instructional Events Model A theory of learning that relates phases of instruction to stages of information processing.

ity or providing other motivation for learning (more about this in the next two chapters). When the students are paying attention and have the right expectations, they need to be reminded of what they already know that is related to the material to be learned. With this prior knowledge in their working memories, they are ready to make connections between new and old information. Now it is time to present the new material, highlighting the important aspects or key features. At this point the students should have the new material in their short-term or working memories, so they are ready to process the information and move it to long-term memory. The teacher's role now is to provide learning guidance, such as explanations and examples, or a guided-discovery exercise to a film.

But learning does not stop here. In Gagné's model, students have to demonstrate, to the teacher and to themselves, that they really understand the material. The students must respond in some way. These responses allow the teacher to check the students' understanding and provide reinforcement or corrections or both. Finally, to ensure that they can retrieve and apply their new knowledge readily, students should practice in a variety of situations. Reviews at the end of the lesson, week, and unit encourage transfer by extending practice over time.

This chapter has covered quite a bit of territory, partly because the cognitive perspective has so many implications for instruction. Although they are varied, you can see that most of the cognitive ideas for teaching concepts, problem-solving skills, and thinking emphasize the role of the student's prior knowledge in learning and the need for active, mindful information processing.

SUMMARY

Teaching and Learning about Concepts

Concepts are categories used to group similar events, ideas, people, or objects. We probably learn concepts from prototypes or exemplars of the category, understood in terms of our schematic knowledge, and then refine concepts through our additional experience of relevant and irrelevant features. Lessons about concepts include four basic components: concept name, definition, attributes, and examples.

Problem Solving

Problem solving is both general and domain-specific. The five stages of problem solving are identifying the problem, understanding the problem through representation, exploring possible solutions, selecting a strategy or executing a plan, and evaluating the results. A critical element in solving problems in school is representing the problem accurately, showing understanding of both the whole problem and its discrete elements. Translation and schema training may improve this ability.

Effective Problem Solving: What Do the Experts Do?

The application of algorithms and of heuristics—such as means-ends analysis, analogical thinking, working backward, and verbalization—may help students solve problems. Factors that hinder problem solving include functional fixedness or rigidity (response set) that disallow the flexibility needed to represent problems accurately and to have insight into solutions. Expert problem solvers have a rich store of declarative, procedural, and conditional knowledge. They organize this knowledge around general principles or patterns that apply to large classes of problems.

Creativity and Creative Problem Solving

Creativity is a process that involves independently restructuring problems to see things in new, imaginative ways. Creativity is difficult to measure, but tests of divergent thinking can assess originality, fluency, and flexibility. Teachers can encourage creativity by providing opportunities for play, using brainstorming techniques, and accepting divergent ideas.

Teaching Critical Thinking Skills

Two approaches to teaching thinking skills are to use stand-alone programs or to embed programs in the regular curriculum. Embedded programs tap executive control thinking processes and promote critical thinking skills. According to some psychologists, experimentation, reflection, and application are part of the critical thinking process.

Teaching for Transfer

The transfer of learning from one situation to another may be positive or negative and general or specific. Transfer involving spontaneity and automaticity in familiar situations has been called low-road transfer. High-road transfer involves reflection and conscious application of abstract knowledge to new situations. Teachers can promote thinking and learning skills by teaching for mastery, and for the positive, general transfer of knowledge.

Cognitive Models of Teaching

According to Jerome Bruner's discovery model of teaching, students learn best when they themselves discover the structure of a subject through inductive reasoning (the eg-rule method) and intuitive thinking. In guided discovery, the teachers ask leading questions and give directive feedback. According to David Ausubel's reception model, learning should be primarily deductive (the rule-eg method) and based on meaningful verbal learning. In expository teaching, teachers present material that is fully organized and sequenced from the general (subsumers and advance organizers) to the specific. In Robert Gagné's instructional events model, which is based on the information processing model of learning, teachers match their instructional strategies to the phases of their students' learning process.

KEY TERMS AND CONCEPTS

advance organizer, p. 324
algorithm, p. 297
analogical thinking, p. 298
brainstorming, p. 309
coding system, p. 319
concept, p. 286
concept mapping, p. 290
convergent thinking, p. 306
creativity, p. 305
critical thinking, p. 311
deductive reasoning, p. 323
defining attributes, p. 286
discovery learning, p. 319
divergent thinking, p. 306
eg-rule method, p. 320
exemplar, p. 287
expository teaching, p. 322

functional fixedness, p. 299
graded membership, p. 287
guided discovery, p. 320
heuristic, p. 297
high-road transfer, p. 316
incubation, p. 306
inductive reasoning, p. 320
insight, p. 301
instructional events model,
 p. 327
intuitive thinking, p. 320
linguistic comprehension, p. 293
low-road transfer, p. 316
meaningful verbal learning,
 p. 322
means-ends analysis, p. 297
overgeneralization, p. 289

overlearning, p. 318
problem, p. 290
problem solving, p. 291
prototype, p. 287
response set, p. 300
restructuring, p. 305
rule-eg method, p. 323
schema-driven problem solving,
 p. 297
stand-alone thinking skills
 programs, p. 311
subject structure, p. 319
transfer, p. 314
undergeneralization, p. 289
verbalization, p. 298
working-backward strategy,
 p. 298

WHAT WOULD YOU DO?

PRESCHOOL AND KINDERGARTEN

Several students in your class still have trouble discriminating among simple shapes. What would you do to help them understand?

ELEMENTARY AND MIDDLE SCHOOL

Students in your class are having a really hard time with the concepts of heat and energy. What would you do?

Your students' first attempt at writing an essay comparing two short poems is a disaster. They write a few lines giving superficial descriptions of each poem and then tell which one they liked best. There is no critical thinking or analysis. Where would you go from here?

JUNIOR HIGH AND HIGH SCHOOL

Students in your math class can solve problems for homework but get confused on tests that cover several chapters. They don't seem to know when to apply one procedure and when to apply another. How would you help them?

You decide to give an essay test that requires creativity and critical thinking. Your students perform very badly and protest loudly that the test is "unfair." They want to use the definitions and facts they have so carefully memorized. What would you do?

COOPERATIVE LEARNING ACTIVITY

With four or five other members of your class, design a lesson or series of lessons that teach important content and thinking skills at the same time. How would you introduce the lessons, and how would you evaluate students' learning?

EFFECTIVE PROBLEM SOLVING

How do you help students in your class to become effective problem solvers, particularly when they are dealing with the complex, often ambiguous, problems of daily life?

TEACH COGNITIVE SKILLS

Students become effective problem solvers by developing the mental structures needed to gather, organize, and evaluate information. I encourage students to (1) "notice" details and suspend judgment until all relevant information is gathered; (2) use reflective thinking to find patterns and relationships with previous knowledge and experience; (3) create meaning within a personal context; and (4) organize information for output according to accepted conventions of language and expression. I ask questions in such a way that they cannot be answered with yes/no or one-word responses. Students must explain why and how they arrived at a particular answer so that they see a need for logical justification rather than memorized statements or guesses about what the teacher wants to hear. I try to challenge students to use comparative thinking and explain how the material is alike or different from other contexts and contents. When students are invited to do hypothetical ("what if") thinking, they utilize their creative capabilities to come up with unexpected solutions and then use reflective thinking to manipulate the variables mentally and evaluate the possible outcomes.

When students are dealing with complex personal problems, I encourage them to write down what they perceive the problems to be. The students may also draw how they feel about the situation. Once the students have reflected enough to give "form" to their problems, they are more able to talk about cause/effect relationships, alternative solutions, and why they feel the way the do. My role is to empower the students through the systematic collection and analysis of data so that they can solve their own problems.

Betty Garner, *Art Teacher*
Pattonville I.D.E.A.L. Center, Maryland Heights, Missouri

LET STUDENTS MAKE DECISIONS

In order for students to learn to solve problems, they must be allowed to make decisions and to learn the consequences of inappropriate choices. Start with simple choices such as listing two assignments and letting them choose the one they want to do first. Then increase the choices and let them choose which ones to do and which ones to ignore. Gradually give them the power to make other decisions that affect the whole class. Plan a class walk, and let the children decide what they should be seeing and the route they should take. Have them draw out a map and show the most direct or the most enlightening way. The class should vote for the preferred route, and that route should be the one taken.

Another method would be to make up simulation exercises in which different decisions will affect the outcome. Discussing the pros and cons of the decisions will give the students useful insights on managing their choices. Empowering the students with decision making is going to give them the confidence to make complex decisions in the future.

Ida Pofahl, *Second-Grade Teacher*
Denison Elementary School, Denison, Iowa

AIDING TRANSFER

What kinds of in-class activities have you found aid students' transfer of learning? How do you make connections between lessons and the "real life" beyond the school walls?

BRING OUTSIDE WORLD INSIDE

I feel students transfer learning best if they actually get involved in their work. In math, we have a week of following the stock market. We keep a chart in the room to see if we make money. We also write checks and balance a family budget for a month. In spelling, we play games like the Great American Giveaway, which reinforces learning so students can retain and transfer it. If students spell three unit words correctly, they can choose one of two doors. Behind each door is a picture from a magazine of something the children enjoy or want—for example, Oreo-cookie ice cream. The child who opens that door wins an imaginary month's supply of the ice cream.

Sharon Klotz, *Sixth-Grade Teacher*
Kiel Middle School, Kiel, Wisconsin

USE NEIGHBORHOOD RESOURCES

To make learning more applicable to life outside the classroom, I have days when students bring in calculators for math. I also try to utilize the resource people of the neighborhood—artists or nurses, for example—who speak to the class about relevant topics. For each of the seven social studies units, we have a guest speaker who has lived or traveled in the area being studied. I think children want to feel connected to the outside world. They appreciate knowing that classroom lessons are not restricted to teachers and students, that the broader community also uses the same knowledge.

Louise Harrold Melucci, *Fourth-Grade Teacher*
Greenwood School, Warwick, Rhode Island

DISCOVERING LEARNING

Describe a "discovery learning" lesson that really seemed to work well with your students. Why do you think it was so successful?

HANDS-ON EXPERIENCES

In second grade we do a unit on magnets. At the beginning of the unit, the children (in small groups) go to five various centers to make their own discoveries. At each center is a card that tells the children to do various things with the magnet. For example, they try to pull a paper fish (with a paper clip underneath) through water with a magnet. Then they write down their discovery. In this instance they find that magnets do work through water. The children work together to make their discoveries. This is much more effective and enjoyable than a lecture on magnets.

Kathryn Daniels, *Second-Grade Teacher*
Fredericktown Elementary School, Fredericktown, Ohio

CHANNELING ENERGY

It's difficult to restrain children who are overflowing with energy and ideas. They can take over a classroom if you let them. What can teachers do? We can talk to the whole class about respecting the rights of all and giving everyone an opportunity to respond. Perhaps we can allow the advanced children to lead the discussions, at least in part, after we have modeled this behavior. Another thing to do is encourage all the children to come up with many different ideas, avoid acknowledging any correct response, and have each child back up his or her answers. We can also have children draw pictures or write out their discoveries before verbalizing them. Some discovery activities have no right or wrong answers, and these can be used to encourage all children to respond without feeling threatened.

Carolyn R. Cook, *Kindergarten Teacher*
Ramona Elementary School, Ramona, California

9 MOTIVATION AND THE INDIVIDUAL LEARNER

"Why don't the students pay attention?" "Kids today don't seem to care about school." "The trouble is these kids have no motivation!" If you have spent much time in schools, you have heard these laments before. Is lack of motivation really at the heart of school failure? Or are students motivated, but not necessarily to do what their teachers want? Whatever the answers, most educators agree that motivating students toward appropriate goals is one of the critical tasks of teaching.

We begin with the question "What is motivation?" and continue by sketching many of the answers that have been proposed. This leads to a discussion of intrinsic and extrinsic motivation and four general theories of motivation: behavioral, humanistic, cognitive, and social learning.

The remainder of the chapter examines more closely several personal factors that frequently appear in discussions of motivation: arousal, interests, curiosity, anxiety, goals, needs for self-actualization and for achievement, beliefs about the causes of success and failure in school, and notions about ability and self-worth. In chapter 10 we will complete the picture with an examination of the external factors that can affect motivation.

By the time you finish this chapter, you should be able to do the following:

- Give examples of intrinsic and extrinsic motivation.

- Define the concept of motivation from the behavioral, humanistic, cognitive, and social learning points of view.

- Describe the roles of arousal, interest, curiosity, and anxiety motivation.

- Set motivating goals for yourself and your students.

- List Maslow's seven levels of needs and give a classroom example of each.

- Explain how to encourage the need for achievement in your class.

- Discuss the possible motivational effects of success and failure and how these effects relate to beliefs about ability.

- Describe the characteristics of mastery-oriented, failure-avoiding, and failure-accepting students.

WHAT DO YOU THINK?

Take a minute to list all the things you did in the past 24 hours. Beside each entry, write what motivated you to do that particular activity at that time. Was your motivation based more on intrinsic interest in the activity or on possible rewards or punishments? Were the activities related to any of your short-term or long-term goals? How did accomplishing the activities influence your sense of confidence and self-esteem?

WHAT IS MOTIVATION?

Motivation is usually defined as an internal state that arouses, directs, and maintains behavior. Psychologists studying motivation have focused on three basic questions. First, what is it that originally causes a person to initiate some action? Second, what causes a person to move toward a particular goal? And third, what causes a person to persist in attempts to reach that goal?

Traits and States

We all know how it feels to be motivated, to move energetically toward a goal. We also know what it is like to work hard, even if we are not fascinated by the task. Why are you reading this chapter? Are you interested in the topic of motivation? Maybe you enjoy learning about something new, deepening your understanding of yourself and others. Or is there a quiz coming up? Do you need this course to earn a teaching certificate or to graduate? Maybe you want a good grade because you like making an *A* or because you need it to save a sinking grade-point average. Maybe you believe that you have a good chance to do well in this class, and that belief keeps you working. Perhaps it is some combination of these.

Explanations of motivation include all of these factors and others as well. Answers to the question "What energizes and directs behavior?" include descriptions of instincts, drives, needs, incentives, fears, goals, social pressure, self-confidence, interests, curiosity, attributions for success and failure, beliefs, values, and more. Some psychologists have explained motivation in terms of personal *traits* or individual characteristics. Certain people, so the theory goes, have a strong need to achieve, a fear of tests, or an enduring interest in art, so they behave accordingly. They work hard to achieve, avoid tests, or spend hours in art galleries. Other psychologists see motivation more as a *state,* a temporary situation. If, for example, you are reading this paragraph because you have a test tomorrow, you are motivated (at least for now) by the situation. Of course, the motivation we experience at any given time usually is a combination of

Motivation Internal state that arouses, directs, and maintains behavior.

trait and state. You may be studying because you are curious about the topic of motivation *and* because your instructor often gives pop quizzes.

Intrinsic and Extrinsic Motivation

As you can see, some explanations of motivation rely on personal factors such as needs, interests, curiosity, and enjoyment. Other explanations point to external, environmental factors—rewards, social pressure, punishment, and so on. Motivation that stems from factors such as interest or curiosity is called **intrinsic motivation.** When we are intrinsically motivated, we do not need incentives or punishments to make us work, because the activity itself is rewarding. We enjoy the task or the sense of accomplishment that it brings. In contrast, when we do something in order to earn a reward, avoid punishment, please the teacher, or for some other reason that has very little to do with the task itself, we experience **extrinsic motivation.** We are not really interested in the activity for its own sake; we care only about what it will gain us.

In schools, both intrinsic and extrinsic motivation are important. Many activities are, or could be, interesting to students. Teaching can create intrinsic motivation by stimulating the students' curiosity and making them feel more competent as they learn. But you know this won't work all the time. Did you find long division or grammar inherently interesting? Was your curiosity piqued by the states and their capitals? If teachers count on intrinsic motivation to energize all their students all of the time, they will be disappointed. There are situations when incentives and external supports are necessary. Teachers must encourage and nurture intrinsic motivation while making sure that the level of extrinsic motivation is right (Brophy, 1988). To do this, they need to know about the personal and environmental factors that influence motivation.

Theories of Motivation

Motivation is a vast and complicated subject with many, many theories. Some theories were developed through work with animals in laboratories. Others are based on research with humans in situations that used games or puzzles. Some theories grow out of the work done in clinical or industrial psychology. Our examination of the field will be selective; otherwise we will never finish the topic. Before we turn to specifics, let's set the stage by outlining four general approaches to motivation: behavioral, humanistic, cognitive, and social learning.

Behavioral Approaches to Motivation. As we saw in chapter 6, behavioral psychologists have developed concepts such as contiguity, reinforcement, punishment, and modeling to explain learning. Those principles also explain motivation: within the strict behavioral framework, to motivate students is really to apply the principle described in chapter 6 for strengthening, maintaining, or suppressing behaviors. Behaviorists such as B. F. Skinner assume that we have basic physiological needs that motivate—hunger, thirst, sex, and so on. These needs are met by **primary reinforcers** such as food. When these needs are met, certain

Intrinsic Motivation
Motivation associated with activities that are their own reward.

Extrinsic Motivation
Motivation created by external factors like rewards and punishments.

Primary Reinforcers
Stimuli with reinforcing properties built into the organism itself.

Point/Counterpoint

What Should Schools Do to Encourage Students' Self-Esteem?

James Beane (1991) begins his article "Sorting Out the Self-Esteem Controversy" with this statement: "In the '90s, the question is not whether schools should enhance students' self-esteem, but how they propose to do so" (p. 25). Attempts to improve students' self-esteem have taken three main forms: personal development activities such as sensitivity training; self-esteem programs where the curriculum focuses directly on improving self-esteem; and structural changes in schools that place greater emphasis on cooperation, student participation, community involvement, and ethnic pride.

Point: The self-esteem movement has problems.

Attempts to encourage self-esteem directly through sensitivity training or self-esteem courses have not proven very successful. As Beane notes, "Saying 'I like myself and others' in front of a group is not the same as actually feeling that way, especially if I am only doing it because I am supposed to. Being nice has a place in enhancing self-esteem, but it is not enough" (p. 26). Many of the self-esteem courses are commercial packages—costly for schools but without solid evidence that they make a difference for students (Crisci, 1986; Leming, 1981).

Sensitivity training and self-esteem courses share a common conceptual problem. They assume that we encourage self-esteem by changing the individual's beliefs, making the young person work harder against the odds. But what if the student's environment is truly unsafe, debilitating, and unsupportive? Some people have overcome tremendous problems, but to expect everyone to do so "ignores the fact that having positive self-esteem is almost impossible for many young people, given the deplorable conditions under

events and experiences are associated with the primary reinforcers, probably through classical conditioning. These associated events become **secondary reinforcers.** For example, affection becomes associated with food as we are fed and nurtured by our parents. You may remember that one definition of a reinforcer given in chapter 6 is something you will work to attain. Thus, according to the behavioral view, we are motivated to behave as we do to gain primary and secondary reinforcers and avoid punishment.

If we are consistently reinforced for certain behaviors, we may develop habits or tendencies to act in certain ways. For example, if a student is repeatedly rewarded with affection, money, praise, or privileges for earning letters in baseball but receives little recognition for studying, the student will probably work longer and harder on perfecting her fastball than on understanding geometry. Of course, in any individual case, many other factors affect how a person will behave. The emphasis in behavioral theories is on extrinsic reinforcement. Providing grades, points, stars, and other rewards for learning is an attempt to motivate students by extrinsic means.

Humanistic Approaches to Motivation. The **humanistic view** is sometimes referred to as "third-force" psychology, because it developed in the 1940s as a reaction against the two forces then dominant: behaviorism and Freudian psychoanalysis. Proponents of humanistic psychology

Secondary Reinforcers
Stimuli that acquire their reinforcing properties through learning.

Humanistic View
Approach to motivation that emphasizes personal freedom, choice, self-determination, and striving for personal growth.

338

which they are forced to live by the inequities in our society" (Beane, 1991, p. 27).

Because many attempts to encourage self-esteem have been superficial, commercial, and filled with "pop psychology," the self-esteem movement has become an easy target for critics in magazine articles such as "Education: Doing Bad and Feeling Good" (*Time,* February 5, 1990) and "The Trouble with Self-Esteem" (*U.S. News and World Report,* April 2, 1990).

Counterpoint: The self-esteem movement has promise.

Beyond the "feel-good psychology" of some aspects of the self-esteem movement is a basic truth: "Self-esteem is a central feature of human dignity and thus an inalienable human entitlement. As such, schools and other agencies have a moral obligation to help build it and avoid debilitating it" (Beane, 1991, p. 28). If we view self-esteem accurately as a product of our thinking and our actions—our values, ideas, and beliefs as well as

our interactions with others—then we see a significant role for the school. Practices that allow authentic participation, cooperation, problem solving, and accomplishment should replace policies that damage self-esteem such as tracking and competitive grading.

Beane suggests four principles to guide educators:

First, being nice is surely a part of this effort, but it is not enough. Second, there is a place for some direct instruction regarding affective matters, but this is not enough either. Self-esteem and affect are not simply another school subject to be placed in set-aside time slots. Third, the negative affect of "get tough" policies is not a promising route to self-esteem and efficacy. This simply blames young people for problems that are largely not of their own making. Fourth, since self-perceptions are powerfully informed by culture, comparing self-esteem across cultures without clarifying cultural differences is distracting and unproductive. (pp. 29–30)

such as Abraham Maslow and Carl Rogers felt that neither behavioral nor Freudian psychology adequately explained why people act as they do.

Humanistic interpretations of motivation emphasize personal freedom, choice, self-determination, and striving for personal growth, or as Maslow called it, *self-actualization.* Humanistic psychologists stress the importance of intrinsic motivation. In many humanistic theories, the role of needs (such as the need for self-esteem or for self-actualization) is central. One current reflection of the humanistic perspective is the "self-esteem movement," a controversial approach to meeting students' needs for dignity and self-esteem. The **Point/Counterpoint** section above explores this issue.

When we examine the role of needs in motivation, we will see another example of a humanistic approach to motivation, Maslow's theory of the hierarchy of needs.

Cognitive Approaches to Motivation. In many ways, cognitive theories of motivation also developed as a reaction to the behavioral views. One of the central assumptions in cognitive approaches is that people respond not to external events or physical conditions like hunger, but rather to their interpretations of these events. You may have had the experience of being so interested and involved in a project that you missed a meal, not realizing you were hungry until you noticed the time. Food deprivation did not automatically motivate you to seek food. Cogni-

Respect for ethnic heritage in the classroom supports the developing self-esteem of students.

tive theorists believe that behavior is determined by our thinking (beliefs, expectations, goals, values, etc.), not simply by whether we have been rewarded or punished for the behavior in the past (Schunk, 1991a; Stipek, 1988).

Some cognitive theories assume that humans have a basic need to understand their environment and to be competent, self-directed, and active in coping with the world (Deci & Ryan, 1985; Deci, Vallerand, Pelletier, & Ryan, 1991; White, 1959). This assumption is similar to Piaget's notion of equilibration, the search for mental balance. Equilibration is based on the need to assimilate new information and make it fit cognitive schemes—in other words, the need to understand. So in cognitive theories, people are seen as active and curious, searching for information to solve personally relevant problems. People work hard because they enjoy the work and because they want to understand. Thus, cognitive theorists emphasize intrinsic motivation. We will see examples of cognitive theories of motivation when we examine Bernard Weiner's attribution theory and Martin Covington's self-worth theory.

Social Learning Approaches to Motivation. Social learning theories of motivation are integrations of behavioral and cognitive approaches: they take into account both the behaviorists' concern with the effects of outcomes of behavior and the cognitivists' interest in the impact of individual beliefs. Many influential social learning explanations of motivation could be characterized as **expectancy × value theories.** This means that motivation is seen as the product of two main forces: the individual's expectation of reaching a goal and the value of that goal to him or her. In other words, the important questions are, "If I try hard, can I succeed?" and "If I succeed, will the outcome be valuable or reinforcing to me?" Motivation is a product of these two forces, because if either factor is zero, there is no motivation to work toward the goal. For example, if I

Expectancy × Value Theories Explanations of motivation that emphasize individuals' expectations for success combined with their valuing of the goal.

believe I have a good chance of making the basketball team (high expectation) and if making the team is very important to me (high value), then my motivation should be strong. But if either factor is zero (I believe I haven't a prayer of making the team, or I could care less about playing basketball), then my motivation will be zero too.

Bandura's *social cognitive theory* is an example of an expectancy × value approach to motivation. Bandura (1977, 1986) suggests several basic sources of motivation. One source consists of thoughts and projections about possible outcomes of behavior: "Will I succeed or fail? Will I be liked or laughed at?" We imagine future consequences based on past experiences, the consequences of those experiences, and our observations of others. These projections are also affected by our sense of **self-efficacy.** This concept, an important aspect of Bandura's theory, refers to our beliefs about our personal competence in a given area. Clearly, our expectations for succeeding or failing at a particular task will be influenced by our sense of self-efficacy in that area.

According to Bandura, another source of motivation is the active setting of goals. The goals we set become our standards for evaluating performance. As we work toward our goals, we imagine the possible positive outcomes of succeeding and the negative outcomes of failing. We tend to persist in our efforts until we meet the standards we have set. Upon reaching our goals, we may be satisfied for a short time but then tend to raise our standards and set new goals. Our sense of self-efficacy comes into play here as well, influencing the goals we will attempt to reach. Dale Schunk notes that "people who have a low sense of efficacy for accomplishing a task may avoid it: those who feel efficacious are hypothesized to work harder and persist longer when they encounter difficulties than those who doubt their capabilities" (1991b, p. 208).

Much of my own recent research has focused on a particular kind of self-efficacy—sense of efficacy in teaching (Hoy & Woolfolk, 1990, in press; Woolfolk & Hoy, 1990; Woolfolk, Rosoff, & Hoy, 1990). **Teaching efficacy** is a teacher's belief that he or she can reach even difficult students to help them learn. This sense of efficacy has two dimensions: the belief that teachers in general can be powerful influences on students and the belief that you as an individual teacher can be effective with your students. Teachers' sense of efficacy appears to be one of the few personal characteristics of teachers that is correlated with student achievement (Ashton & Webb, 1986). Self-efficacy theory predicts that teachers with a high sense of efficacy work harder and persist longer, even when students are difficult to teach, in part because these teachers believe in themselves and in their students.

We have found that prospective teachers tend to increase in their personal sense of efficacy as a consequence of completing student teaching. It also appears that the climate of the school affects teachers' sense of efficacy. Teachers' sense of personal efficacy is higher in schools where the other teachers and administrators have high expectations for students and where teachers receive help from their principals in solving instructional and management problems (Hoy & Woolfolk, in press). Another important conclusion from our research is that efficacy grows from real success with students, not just from the moral support or cheerleading of

Self-Efficacy Beliefs about personal competence in a particular situation.

Teaching Efficacy A teacher's belief that he or she can reach even the most difficult students and help them learn.

TABLE 9.1 Four Views of Motivation

	Behavioral	Humanistic	Cognitive	Social Learning
Source of Motivation	Extrinsic reinforcement	Intrinsic reinforcement	Intrinsic reinforcement	Extrinsic and intrinsic reinforcement
Important Influences	Primary and secondary reinforcers and punishers	Need for self-esteem and self-fulfillment	Beliefs, attributions for success and failure, expectations	Value of goals, expectation of reaching goals, self-efficacy
Key Theorists	Skinner	Maslow	Weiner	Bandura

your professors and colleagues. Any experience or training that helps you succeed in the day-to-day tasks of teaching will give you a foundation for developing a sense of efficacy in your career.

The behavioral, humanistic, cognitive, and social learning approaches to motivation are summarized in Table 9.1. These theories differ in their answers to the question "What is motivation?" but several factors—arousal, goals, needs, and beliefs—are common in many of these explanations for why we behave as we do. Let's examine these four important personal factors influencing motivation.

AROUSAL AND MOTIVATION

Just as we all know how it feels to be motivated, we all know what it is like to be aroused. **Arousal** involves both physical and psychological reactions. When we are aroused, there are changes in brain wave patterns, heart rate, blood pressure, and breathing rate. We are alert, attentive, wide awake, or even excited. To understand how the level of arousal is important in motivation, think of two extreme situations. The first is late at night. You are trying for the third time to understand a section in an assigned reading, but you are so sleepy. You just cannot keep your attention on the material. You seem to have no energy and, even though there is a test coming up, your motivation is weak. You decide to go on to bed and get up early the next morning to study (a plan you know seldom works). At the other extreme, imagine a situation in which you must do complicated mental calculations while under tremendous time pressure. Also, your first mistake will cost you $5,000. In both situations you want to do well but arousal interferes with performance. In the first instance arousal is too low; in the second it is too high.

Research suggests that there is an optimum level of arousal for most activities, as shown in Figure 9.1 (Morris, 1988). Generally speaking, a higher level of arousal is helpful on simple tasks like sorting buttons by color or reciting a poem that you know very well, but lower levels of arousal are better for complex tasks like composing an original essay or taking the GREs. Teachers have to raise and lower arousal levels in their classes, depending on the students' needs. Consider first how to increase

Arousal Physical and psychological reactions causing a person to be alert, attentive, wide awake.

FIGURE 9.1 **Arousal and Quality of Performance** On a simple or well-practiced task, the best performance occurs when arousal is moderately high. But ona complex task, lower arousal leads to better performance—as long as the arousal isn't *too* low.

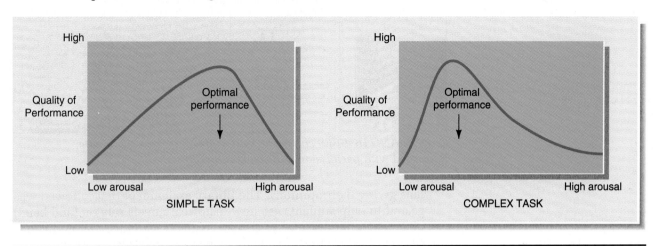

Source: Adapted from Charles G. Morris, *Psychology: An Introduction* (6th ed.), © 1988, p. 439. Adapted by permission of Prentice-Hall, Inc., Englewood Cliffs, New Jersey.

low arousal by incorporating students' interests and "arousing" their curiosity.

Tapping Interests and Arousing Curiosity

It seems logical that learning experiences should be related to the interests of the students. But this is not always an easy or even a desirable strategy; there are times when students must master basic skills that hold no intrinsic interest for them. Nevertheless, if a teacher knows what students' interests are, these can be part of many teaching strategies. Sylvia Ashton-Warner (1963), for example, has described a system for teaching reading by using students' own stories about topics of interest to them. This system is also used in basic reading classes for adults.

There are a number of ways to determine students' interests. The most direct is to ask the students themselves, either in a discussion or through a questionnaire. You can also observe students during free time. How do they spend it? Attentiveness during classroom lessons is another clue. Once you have an understanding of your students' interests, you can apply this knowledge in your teaching. Three examples should show some of the many ways student interests can encourage classroom motivation.

One high school teacher used students' interest in popular music to make the science laboratory a more pleasant place to work.

A music teacher encouraged an interest in Bach by helping students see how certain popular music used a similar style.

A history teacher discovered that some students were interested in historical novels. "What was the truth about Anne Boleyn?" one student asked. A brief argument ensued, with the other historical-novel

Calvin and Hobbes

by Bill Watterson

CALVIN AND HOBBES copyright 1991 Universal Press Syndicate. *Reprinted with permission. All rights reserved.*

fans giving their opinions. The library assignment that followed was geared to help students see how historical novels rely on (and bend) history. The students were also given a chance to learn about historical documents and to debate the questions about Anne Boleyn.

In this last example, the teacher is also modeling an inquiring approach, a willingness to follow the threads of student interest.

Curiosity is another important aspect of motivation that teachers can stimulate and encourage. How? The old saying "Variety is the spice of life" holds true for school. The classroom should be an interesting, provocative (though safe) place.

Displays or activities designed to arouse curiosity can be built into the lesson or unit. These should be matched to the cognitive abilities of the students. For younger students, the chance to manipulate and explore objects relevant to what is being studied may be the most effective way to keep curiosity stimulated. For older students, well-constructed questions or abstract, logical puzzles designed as part of the lesson can have the same effect. Another possibility is to present problems involving paradoxes and contradictions. An example: Ranchers in an area killed the wolves on their land. The following spring they noticed that the deer population was much smaller. How could this be, since wolves hunt the deer and fewer wolves should mean more deer? In searching for a solution, students will learn about ecology and the balance of nature. Without wolves to eliminate the weaker and sicker deer, the deer population expanded so much that the winter food supply could not sustain the deer herds. Many deer died of starvation.

As we discussed earlier, sometimes student arousal is too high, not too low. Because students are evaluated and graded, for example, anxiety can become a factor in their motivation.

Anxiety in the Classroom

Anxiety General uneasiness, a feeling of tension.

Students who are very aroused because they are worried that they will not be able to complete a task satisfactorily often end up with a feeling of **anxiety,** or "an experience of general uneasiness, a sense of foreboding, a feeling of tension" (Hansen, 1977, p. 91). These feelings may be more or less intense, but they do seem to have significant effects on behavior. Like most kinds of arousal, anxiety appears to improve performance on simple tasks or on skills that have been heavily practiced but to interfere with the accomplishment of more complex tasks or skills that are not thoroughly practiced. Perhaps simple, practiced tasks are boring, and a bit of anxiety keeps us alert and eager to finish. But if a task is difficult or new, we need to focus our attention, and anxiety is distracting.

The effects of anxiety on school achievement are clear. "From the time of the earliest work on this problem, starting with the pioneering work of Yerkes and Dodson (1908), to the present day, researchers have consistently reported a negative correlation between virtually every aspect of school achievement and a wide range of anxiety measures" (Covington & Omelich, 1987, p. 393). Estimates are that about 10 million elementary and secondary students suffer serious anxiety in school (Stipek, 1988). Anxiety can be both a cause and an effect of school failure—students do poorly because they are anxious, and their poor performance increases their anxiety.

What Causes Anxiety in School? In the classroom, the conditions surrounding a test can influence the performance of highly anxious individuals. For example, Hill and Eaton (1977) found that very anxious fifth and sixth graders worked as quickly and accurately as their less-anxious classmates when there was no time limit for solving arithmetic problems. With a time limit, however, the very anxious students made three times as many errors as their classmates, spent about twice as much time on each problem, and cheated twice as often as the less-anxious group. Williams (1976) found that very anxious students outperformed all other groups when they did not have to put their names on test papers, which seemed to remove some of the personal cost of failing. Whenever there are pressures to perform, severe consequences for failure, and competitive comparisons among students, anxiety may be encouraged (Wigfield & Eccles, 1989).

Sigmund Tobias (1979, 1985) suggests a model to explain how anxiety interferes with learning and test performance at three points in the learning and performance cycle. When students are learning new material, they must pay attention to it. Highly anxious students evidently divide their attention between the new material and their preoccupation with how nervous they are feeling. So instead of concentrating on a lecture or on what they are reading, they keep noticing the tight feelings in their chest, thinking, "I'm so tense, I'll never understand this stuff!" Much of their attention is taken up with negative thoughts about performing poorly, being criticized, and feeling embarrassed. From the beginning, anxious students may miss much of the information they are supposed to learn because their thoughts are focused on their own worries (Hill & Wigfield, 1984; Paulman & Kennelly, 1984).

But the problems do not end here. Even if they are paying attention, many anxious students have trouble learning material that is somewhat disorganized and difficult—material that requires them to rely on their memory. Unfortunately, much material in school could be described this way. Anxious students may be more easily distracted by irrelevant or incidental aspects of the task at hand. They seem to have trouble focusing on the significant details (Hill & Wigfield, 1984). In addition, many highly anxious students have poor study habits. Simply learning to be more relaxed will not automatically improve these students' performance unless their learning strategies and study skills are improved as well (Naveh-Benjamin, 1991).

Finally, anxious students often know more than they can demonstrate on a test. They may lack critical test-taking skills, or they may have learned the materials but "freeze and forget" on tests. So anxiety can interfere at one or all three points—attention, learning, and testing (Naveh-Benjamin, McKeachie, & Lin, 1987).

Helping Anxious Students. Teachers should help highly anxious students to set realistic goals, since these individuals often have difficulty making wise choices. They tend to select either extremely difficult or extremely easy tasks. In the first case, they are likely to fail, which will

Guidelines

Dealing with Anxiety

Use competition carefully.

Examples

1. Monitor activities to make sure no students are being put under undue pressure.
2. During competitive games, make sure all students involved have a reasonable chance of succeeding.
3. Experiment with cooperative learning activities.

Avoid situations in which highly anxious students will have to perform in front of large groups.

Examples

1. Ask anxious students questions that can be answered with a simple yes or no, or some other brief reply.
2. Give anxious students practice in speaking before smaller groups.

Make sure all instructions are clear.

Examples

1. Write test instructions on the board or on the test itself instead of giving them orally.
2. Check with students to make sure they understand. Ask several students how they would do the first question of an exercise or the sample question on a test. Correct any misconceptions.

3. If you are using a new format or starting a new type of task, give students examples or models to show how it is done.

Avoid unnecessary time pressures.

Examples

1. Give occasional take-home tests.
2. Make sure all students can complete classroom tests within the period given.

Remove some of the pressures from major tests and exams.

Examples

1. Teach test-taking skills; give practice tests; provide study guides.
2. Avoid basing most of a report-card grade on one test.
3. Make extra-credit work available to add points to course grades.
4. Use different types of items in testing, since some students have difficulty with certain types.

Develop alternatives to written tests.

Examples

1. Try oral, open-book, or group tests.
2. Have students do projects, organize portfolios of their work, make oral presentations, or create a finished product.

increase their sense of hopelessness and feelings of foreboding associated with school. In the second case, they probably will succeed, but they will miss the sense of satisfaction that could encourage greater effort, ease their fears about schoolwork, and nurture a sense of self-efficacy. Anxious students may need a good deal of guidance in choosing both short-term and long-term goals. They may also need help working at a moderate pace, especially when taking tests. Often these students either work too quickly and make many careless errors or work too slowly and are never able to finish the task. If possible, consider eliminating time limits for students on important tests. Since anxiety appears to interfere with both attention and retention (Wittrock, 1978), highly anxious students (at least those of average or high ability) benefit most from instruction that is very structured and allows for repetition of parts of the lesson that are missed or forgotten (Seiber, O'Neil, & Tobias, 1977; Wigfield & Eccles, 1989).

Arousal: Lessons for Teachers

You need to work at keeping the level of arousal right for the task at hand. If students are going to sleep, energize them by introducing variety, whetting their curiosity, surprising them, or giving them a brief chance to be physically active. If arousal is too great, follow the Guidelines for dealing with anxiety.

GOALS AND MOTIVATION

You may recall that Bandura's social cognitive theory of motivation emphasizes the importance of setting and working toward goals (Bandura, 1986). This approach is usually effective for me. I often set goals for each day (in addition to the routine tasks, like eating lunch, that will happen without much attention). For example, today I intend to finish this chapter, run, and buy a birthday present for my father. Having decided this, I will feel uncomfortable if I don't complete the list.

Types of Goals

Evidently the types of goals we set influence the amount of motivation we have to reach them. Goals that are specific, moderately difficult, and likely to be reached in the near future tend to enhance motivation and persistence (Schunk, 1991a & b). Specific goals provide clear standards for judging performance. If performance falls short, we keep going. For example, I have decided to "finish this chapter" instead of deciding to "work on the book." Since it is clear when I am finished (the chapter is in the mail), I know when I have met the goal. Anything short of having the chapter in the mail means "Keep working." Moderate difficulty provides a challenge, but not an unreasonable one. I can finish this chapter if I stay with it. Finally, goals that can be reached fairly soon are not likely to be abandoned or pushed aside by the day-to-day business of coping. But good intentions for distant goals are often overshadowed by more immediate concerns. Groups like Alcoholics Anonymous show they are aware of the motivating value of short-term goals when they encourage their members to stop drinking "one day at a time."

There is a second distinction in kinds of goals that is important for learning. In classrooms there are two main categories of goals—performance and learning. When the goal is a **performance goal,** students are focused on how they are judged by others. They want to "look smart" and avoid seeming incompetent. The evaluation of their performance, not what they learn or how hard they try, is what matters. The second kind of goal is a **learning goal.** Here the point is to improve, to learn, no matter how many mistakes you make or how awkward you appear. People who set learning goals tend to seek challenges and persist when they encounter difficulties. People who set performance goals tend to avoid risks and challenges and to give up when they fail (Dweck, 1986). As we will see later in this chapter, students' beliefs about ability and effort affect the kinds of goals they set.

Goals: Lessons for Teachers

Students are more likely to work toward learning goals that are clear, specific, reasonable, moderately challenging, and attainable within a relatively short period of time. A focus on performing and achieving may undermine the students' ability to set such goals. Students may not be expert yet at setting their own goals or keeping the goal in mind, so an award may help spur students to set achievable goals. If you use such a system, however, be sure the goal set is to learn and improve in some area, not just to perform well or "look smart."

NEEDS AND MOTIVATION

A *need* can be defined as "a biological or psychological requirement; a state of deprivation that motivates a person to take action toward a goal" (Darley, Glucksberg, & Kinchla, 1990, p. 743). Our needs are seldom satisfied completely and perfectly; improvement is always possible. People are thus motivated by their needs, or by the tensions the needs create. Their behavior can be seen as movement toward goals they believe will help satisfy their needs. Let's look at one very influential humanistic theory of motivation that deals with this central concept.

Maslow's Hierarchy

Abraham Maslow has had a great impact on psychology in general and on the psychology of motivation in particular. Maslow (1970) suggested that humans have a **hierarchy of needs.** Lower-level needs for survival and safety are the most essential. We all require food, air, water, and shelter; we all seek freedom from danger. These needs determine our behavior until they are met. But once we are physically comfortable and secure, we are stimulated to fulfill needs on the next level—social needs for belonging and love and needs for self-esteem. And when these needs are more or less satisfied, we turn to the higher-level needs for intellectual achievement,

The hours of practice required to master a musical instrument surely involves a large measure of intrinsic motivation, but extrinsic motivation, in the form of praise and rewards, may be helpful, especially in the early stages of learning.

Performance Goal A personal intention to seem competent or perform well in the eyes of others.

Learning Goal A personal intention to improve abilities and understand, no matter how performance suffers.

Hierarchy of Needs Maslow's model of seven levels of human needs, from basic physiological requirements to the need for self-actualization.

aesthetic appreciation, and finally self-actualization. **Self-actualization** is Maslow's term for self-fulfillment, the realization of personal potential. Figure 9.2 is a diagram of Maslow's model.

Maslow (1968) has called the four lower-level needs—for survival, safety, belonging, and self-esteem—**deficiency needs.** When these needs are not met, motivation increases to find ways of satisfying them. When they are satisfied, the motivation for fulfilling them decreases. Maslow has labeled the three higher-level needs—intellectual achievement, aesthetic appreciation, and self-actualization—**being needs.** When they are met, a person's motivation does not cease; instead, it increases to seek further fulfillment. For example, the more successful you are in your efforts to know and understand, the harder you are likely to strive for even greater knowledge and understanding. So unlike the deficiency needs, these being needs can never be completely filled. The motivation to achieve them is endlessly renewed.

Maslow's theory has been criticized for the very obvious reason that people do not always appear to behave as the theory would predict. Most of us move back and forth among different types of needs and may even be motivated by many different needs at the same time. Some people

FIGURE 9.2 Maslow's Hierarchy of Needs The four lower-level needs in Maslow's hierarchy are called deficiency needs because when they are met, the motivation to satisfy them decreases. But when the being needs are met, motivation to seek further fulfilment of these needs increases.

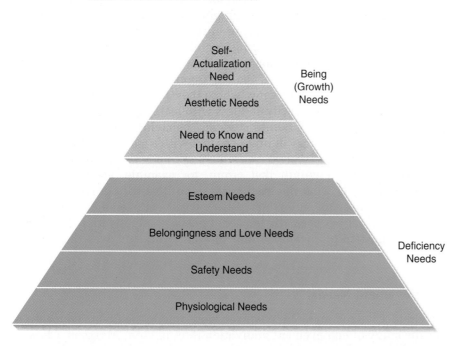

Self-Actualization
Fulfilling one's potential.

Deficiency Needs
Maslow's four lower-level needs, which must be satisfied first.

Being Needs Maslow's three higher-level needs, sometimes called growth needs.

Source: Data (for diagram) based on Hierarchy of Needs in "A Theory of Human Motivation" in *Motivation and Personality,* 2d ed., by Abraham Maslow. Copyright © 1970 by Abraham H. Maslow. Reprinted by permission of Harper & Row, Publishers, Inc.

It's difficult to be motivated to learn when you are hungry. In many schools, students' basic needs for physiological safety are met through breakfast programs.

deny themselves safety or friendship in order to achieve knowledge, understanding, or greater self-esteem.

Criticisms aside, Maslow's theory does give us a way of looking at the whole person, whose physical, emotional, and intellectual needs are all interrelated. This has important implications for education. Students who come to school hungry, sick, or hurt are unlikely to be motivated to seek knowledge and understanding. A child whose feelings of safety and sense of belonging are threatened by divorce may have little interest in learning to divide fractions. If the classroom is a fearful, unpredictable place and students seldom know where they stand, they are likely to be more concerned with security and less with learning. Maslow's hierarchy can provide other insights into students' behavior. Students' desires to fill lower-level needs may at times conflict with a teacher's desire to have them achieve higher-level goals. Belonging to a social group and maintaining self-esteem within that group, for example, are important to students. If doing what the teacher says conflicts with group rules, students may choose to ignore the teacher's wishes or even defy the teacher.

A great deal has been written about needs and motivation. For teaching, the most fully developed and relevant work involves the need to achieve.

Achievement Needs

Achievement Motivation
Desire to excel; impetus to strive for excellence and success.

David McClelland and John Atkinson were among the first to concentrate on the study of **achievement motivation** (McClelland, Atkinson, Clark, & Lowell, 1953). People who strive for excellence in a field for the sake of achieving and not for some reward are considered to have a high need for achievement.

The origins of high achievement motivation are assumed to be in the family and cultural group of the child. If achievement, initiative, and competitiveness are encouraged and reinforced in the home, and if parents let children solve problems on their own without becoming irritated by the children's initial failures, children are more likely to develop a high need for achievement (McClelland & Pilon, 1983). Children who see that their actions can have an impact on their environment and who are taught how to recognize a good performance are more likely to grow up with the desire to excel (Lefton, 1991; Schunk, 1991a).

Atkinson (1964) added a new consideration to the theory of achievement need when he noted that all people have a need to avoid failure as well as a need to achieve. If our need to achieve in a particular situation is greater than the need to avoid failure, the overall tendency, or **resultant motivation,** will be to take the risk and try to achieve. On the other hand, if the need to avoid failure is greater, the risk will be threatening rather than challenging and the resultant motivation will be to avoid the situation. An extended example should help clarify Atkinson's views.

A coach wants the school team to try a new routine at the gymnastic meet coming up in two months. The routine involves several new and very difficult movements. If the movements are executed well, the team is certain to win the meet. If the team tries but fails, it is sure to lose.

Jennifer is one of the best gymnasts on the team and could probably master the movements with ease. But she insists on perfecting the old routine instead of learning a new one. She is immobilized by her fear of embarrassing herself in front of so many people. For Jennifer, the fear of failure is greater than the need for achievement in this particular situation.

Another member of the team, Kelly, is very eager to try the new routine. While she and Jennifer are similar in ability, Kelly is less afraid of embarrassment and is willing to work at mastering the new movements. She is generally the last to leave every practice session and seems to look forward to new challenges. Kelly's need for achievement overcomes any fear of failure.

If students' motivation to achieve is greater than their motivation to avoid failure, a moderate amount of failure can often enhance their desire to pursue a problem. They are determined to achieve, so they try again. If Kelly, for example, were to fall off the balance beam, she would be likely to try even harder to master the balance beam movements. On the other hand, success gained too easily can actually decrease motivation for those with high achievement needs. Kelly probably realizes this. Just relying on the old routine is not particularly motivating for her.

In contrast, students motivated by the need to avoid failure are usually discouraged by failure and encouraged by success. Jennifer, for example, might quit the team if she were embarrassed publicly by her mistakes. If the old routine won the meet, however, she probably would experience unqualified pleasure as well as relief.

Resultant Motivation
Whichever is the stronger tendency—the need to achieve or the need to avoid failure.

Needs and Motivation: Lessons for Teachers

All people need to feel safe, secure, accepted, competent, and effective. Some people may have developed a particularly strong need to achieve. Most people are more motivated when they are involved with tasks that give them a sense of achievement or at least of progress toward achievement. No one enjoys failure, and for some people it is crushing. We are unlikely to stick with tasks or respond well to people who make us feel insecure or incompetent and cause us to fail.

Maslow's theory can suggest ways to plan activities that meet students' needs and increase motivation. Remember that lower-level needs must be met before higher-level needs can become motivating. To make students feel safer and more secure with difficult material, you might organize extra tutoring sessions (Wlodkowski, 1981). You can also create a psychologically safer class environment: wrong answers and mistakes can become occasions for learning, for probing the thinking behind the answers, instead of simply occasions for criticism (Fetterman & Rohrkemper, 1986; Clifford, 1990, 1991). Needs for belonging and self-esteem might be met in part by allowing students to work in teams. We will discuss this possibility more fully in the next chapter.

Since needs for achievement vary from one student to another, and from one situation to another, it may help in planning activities to know where students stand—which students, for instance, have high achieve-

---

TABLE 9.2 Achievement Motivation: Restructuring a High School Physical Education Class

First day
Individual goal setting: Students do self-evaluations of physical fitness, competence, interests; set yearly goals for themselves.

Weekly
Concrete feedback: Students carry out weekly self-tests in flexibility, strength, and posture and record individual scores in team notebook.

Three times a week
Practicing skills: Student set their own specific schedules to practice three times a week; practices recorded on individual cards.

End of first grading period
Checking for realistic goals: Based on scores from self-tests, students set final exam goals for themselves, compare goals to original yearly goals. Variety of ways available to reach each type of goal; for aerobic goals, students can jog, walk, jump rope. Instructor meets with each student to discuss goals.

After final exam
Self-evaluation: Students evaluate what they have learned.

Source: Adapted from M. Alderman and M. Cohen, Eds. (1985). *Motivation theory and practice for preservice teachers.* Washington, DC: Eric Clearinghouse on Teacher Education, pp. 50–51.

ment needs, which are low in achievement needs, and which seem primarily motivated by a need to avoid failure. Those who are more highly motivated to achieve are likely to respond well to challenging assignments, strict grading, corrective feedback, new or unusual problems, and the chance to try again. But for those students who are eager to avoid failure, less challenging assignments, ample reinforcement for success, small steps for each task, lenient grading, and protection from embarrassment are probably more successful strategies. An example of a high school girls' physical education class designed to develop achievement motivation is shown in Table 9.2.

ATTRIBUTIONS, BELIEFS, AND MOTIVATION

We have talked thus far about arousal, goals, and needs, but there is another factor that must be considered in explaining motivation. *Arousal* will not necessarily interfere with motivation unless it is accompanied by worry and anxiety. Worry and anxiety often are caused by a low sense of self-efficacy and a belief that you are likely to fail. *Goals* are not difficult or easy in some absolute sense, but only in relation to your beliefs about your own ability. Meeting *needs* for achievement will not encourage motivation if you believe the success was due to "dumb luck" and probably won't happen again. Failure is not threatening unless you believe that it implies something is "wrong" with you. In other words, our *beliefs and attributions* about what is happening and why—about why we succeed and why we fail—affect motivation.

Attribution Theory

Cognitive explanations of motivation called **attribution theories** begin with the assumption that we all ask "Why?" in our attempts to understand our successes and failures. Students may ask themselves, Why did I flunk my midterm? What's wrong with my essay? Why did I do so well this grading period? They attempt to explain why things happened as they did, to make attributions about causes. Students may attempt to explain their successes and failures by focusing on ability, effort, mood, knowledge, luck, help, interest, clarity of instructions, the interference of others, unfair policies, and so on. Attribution theories of motivation describe how the individual's explanations, justifications, and excuses influence motivation.

Bernard Weiner is one of the main educational psychologists responsible for relating attribution theory to school learning (Weiner, 1979; 1990; Weiner & Graham, 1989). According to Weiner, most of the causes to which students attribute their successes or failures can be characterized in terms of three dimensions: *locus* (location of the cause internal or external to the person), *stability* (whether the cause stays the same or can change), and *responsibility* (whether the person can control the cause). Table 9.3 on page 354 shows the various combinations of these causes. For example, the typical amount of help the student usually seeks from the teacher can be considered an *external, stable,* and *controllable* cause, but the specific help sought on a particular task is *external, unstable,* and *controllable*.

Attribution Theories
Descriptions of how individuals' explanations, justifications, and excuses influence their motivation and behavior.

TABLE 9.3   Weiner's Model of Causal Attribution

| | Internal | | External | |
	Stable	Unstable	Stable	Unstable
Controllable	Typical effort— how hard I usually work	Immediate effort— how hard I work on this particular task	Typical help from the teacher	Help from others on a particular task
Uncontrollable	Ability	Mood; health	Task difficulty	Luck

Source: Adapted from "A theory of motivation for some classroom experiences" by B. Weiner, 1979, *Journal of Educational Psychology, 71,* pp. 3–25. Copyright 1979 by the American Psychological Association. Adapted by permission.

Weiner (1979, 1984) believes that locus, stability, and responsibility have important implications for motivation. The internal/external locus, for example, seems to be closely related to feelings of self-esteem (Weiner, 1980). If success or failure is attributed to internal factors, success will lead to pride and increased motivation, whereas failure will diminish self-esteem.

The stability dimension seems to be closely related to expectations about the future. If, for example, students attribute their success (or failure) to stable factors such as the difficulty of a test, they will expect to succeed (or fail) on difficult tests in the future. But if they attribute the outcome to unstable factors such as mood or luck, they will expect (or hope for) changes in the future when confronted with similar tasks.

The responsibility dimension is related to emotions such as anger, pity, gratitude, or shame. If we fail at something that we believe is controllable, we may feel shame or guilt; whereas if we succeed, we may feel proud. Failing at an uncontrollable task may lead to anger toward the person or institution in control, while succeeding leads to feeling lucky or grateful.

Weiner's locus and responsibility dimensions are closely related to Rotter's (1954) idea of **locus of control.** Rotter suggested that some people have an internal locus of control. They believe they are responsible for their own fate and like to work in situations where skill and effort can lead to success. Other people tend to have an external locus of control, generally believing that people and forces outside themselves control their lives. These individuals prefer to work in situations where luck determines the outcome (Lefcourt, 1966). Locus of control can be influenced by the behavior of others. Continuing discrimination against women, minority-group members, and individuals with special needs can affect these individuals' perceptions of their own ability to control their lives (Beane, 1991).

Locus of Control "Where" people locate responsibility for success and failures— inside or outside themselves.

Attributions and Student Motivation. Most students try to explain their failures to themselves. When usually successful students fail, they often make *internal, controllable* attributions: they misunderstood the directions, lacked the necessary knowledge, or simply did not study hard enough, for example. When students see themselves as capable and attribute failure to lack of effort or insufficient knowledge—controllable causes—they usually focus on strategies for succeeding next time. This is an adaptive, mastery-oriented response, one that often leads to achievement, pride, a greater feeling of control, and a sense of self-efficacy (Ames, 1985).

The greatest motivational problems arise when students attribute failures to *stable, uncontrollable* causes. Such students may seem resigned to failure, depressed, helpless—what we generally call "unmotivated" (Weiner, Russell, & Lerman, 1978). These students respond to failure by focusing even more on their own inadequacy; their attitudes toward schoolwork may deteriorate even further (Ames, 1985). Apathy is a logical reaction to failure if students believe the causes are stable and unlikely to change and are beyond their control anyway. In addition, students who view their failures in this light are less likely to seek help—they believe nothing and no one can help (Ames & Lau, 1982). They may even develop *learned helplessness,* the sense that nothing they do matters, that they are doomed to fail. As we saw in chapters 4 and 5, learned helplessness is a particular danger for students with learning disabilities and students who are the victims of discrimination.

Cues about Causes. How do students determine the causes of their successes and failures? Sandra Graham (1991) gives some surprising answers. The teacher's behaviors can be influential. There is evidence that when teachers respond to students' mistakes with pity, praise, or unsolicited help, the students are more likely to attribute their failure to an uncontrollable cause—usually lack of ability. The logic seems to be, if the student *could* control the situation, then he or she should be held responsible for failure. In this case, a critical, corrective response from the teacher would be appropriate. But if failure results from factors outside the student's control, then the student deserves pity. The same is true for praise and for unsolicited help. When teachers praise students for a "good try" or offer help before the students ask, the students receiving the praise or help (and others watching) attribute the students' failures to low ability rather than to lack of effort or insufficient knowledge.

For example, Graham and Barker (1990) asked subjects of various ages to rate the effort and ability of two boys on a videotape. On the tape was a teacher circulating around the class while students worked. The teacher stopped to look at the two boys' papers, did not comment to the first boy, but said to the second, "Let me give you a hint. Don't forget to carry your tens." The second boy had not asked for help and did not appear to be stumped by the problem. All the age groups watching the tapes, even the youngest, perceived the helped boy as *lower* in ability than the boy who did not get help. It is as if the subjects read the teacher's behavior to say, "You poor child, you just don't have the ability to do this hard work, so I will help."

Does this mean that teachers should be critical and withhold help? Of course not! But it is a reminder that "praise as a consolation prize" for failing (Brophy, 1985) or oversolicitous help can give unintended messages. Graham (1991) suggests that many minority-group students could be the victims of well-meaning pity from teachers. Seeing the very real

FIGURE 9.3 **The Attributional Approach to Explaining Achievement Motivation** There are many factors influencing achievement motivation. Experiencing success or failure and receiving feedback from adults that highlights either effort or ability affects children's attributions to mastery or helplessness. Attributions shape academic self-esteem, and self-esteem influences expectations for future success and sense of efficacy for future related tasks. Expectancies and sense of efficacy together affect achievement motivation. The cycle begins again as motivation influences whether a child succeeds or fails.

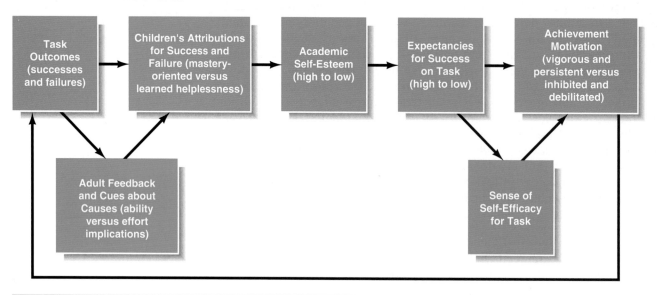

Source: From L. E. Berk, *Child Development*, 2d ed., p. 443. Copyright © 1991. Adapted with permission of Allyn and Bacon.

problems that the students face, teachers may "ease up" on requirements so the students will "experience success" and "feel good about themselves." But a subtle communication may accompany the pity, praise, and extra help: "You don't have the ability to do this, so I will overlook your failure." Graham says, "The . . . pertinent question for blacks is whether their own history of academic failure makes them more likely to be the targets of sympathetic feedback from teachers and thus the recipients of low-ability cues" (1991, p. 28). This kind of sympathetic feedback, even if well-intended, can be a subtle form of racial discrimination.

When students attribute failure to something they cannot control, they have little motivation to try. The cycle of attributions, motivations, and outcomes is depicted in Figure 9.3.

Beliefs about Ability

As you can see, some of the most powerful attributions affecting motivation in school are beliefs about *ability*. By examining these beliefs and how they affect motivation, we will understand why some people set inappropriate, unmotivating goals; why some students adopt self-defeating strategies; and why some students seem to give up altogether.

Adults use two basic concepts of ability. An **entity view of ability** assumes that ability is a *stable, uncontrollable* trait—a characteristic of the individual that cannot be changed. According to this view, some

Entity View of Ability
Belief that ability is a fixed characteristic that cannot be changed.

people have more ability than others, but the amount each person has is set. An **incremental view of ability,** on the other hand, suggests that ability is *unstable* and *controllable*—"an ever-expanding repertoire of skills and knowledge" (Dweck & Bempechat, 1983, p. 144). By hard work, study, or practice, knowledge can be increased and thus ability can be improved. Table 9.4 shows how these two conceptions of ability would fit into Weiner's model of causal attribution (Table 9.3). The entity view of ability is an internal, stable, uncontrollable attribution; the incremental view is an internal, unstable, controllable attribution. You may tend to hold one or the other of these beliefs about ability, or your beliefs may change with the situation. Most of us think of our own ability as improvable (*incremental*), but we may explain other people's performance in terms of set abilities (*entity*). Or we may believe that intellectual ability is fixed but that physical abilities, such as skiing, are improvable.

Young children, on the other hand, tend to hold an exclusively incremental view of ability (Nicholls & Miller, 1984). Through the early elementary grades, most students believe that effort is the same as intelligence. Smart people try hard and trying hard makes you smart. If you fail, you aren't smart and you didn't try hard; if you succeed, you must be a smart, hard worker (Stipek, 1988). Children are age 11 or 12 before they can differentiate among effort, ability, and performance. About this time, they come to believe that someone who succeeds without working at all must be *really smart.* This is when beliefs about ability begin to influence motivation.

Students who hold an entity view of intelligence tend to set *performance goals* and seek situations where they can "look smart." Looking smart means succeeding without too much effort. Entity theorists who lack confidence tend to set goals that are either so easy there is no risk of failure or so hard that no one, not even a very smart person, could succeed. Of course, this is a no-win situation, since succeeding on easy tasks doesn't show you are smart and failing on difficult tasks is still

TABLE 9.4 A Revised View of the Internal Attribution Model with Two Kinds of Ability

	Internal Attribution	
	Stable	**Unstable**
Controllable	Typical effort—how hard I usually work	Immediate effort—how hard I work on this particular task
		Incremental ability
Uncontrollable	Entity ability	Mood; health

Source: Adapted from "A theory of motivation for some classroom experiences" by B. Weiner, 1979, *Journal of Educational Psychology, 71,* pp. 3–25. Copyright 1979 by the American Psychological Association. Adapted by permission.

Incremental View of Ability Belief that ability is a set of skills that can be changed.

failing. Even if entity theorists are confident about their abilities, they often "play it safe" and take only minimal risks. Like Jennifer on the gymnastics team, they keep doing what they can do well without expending too much effort or risking failure, since either one—having to work hard or failing—indicates (to them) low ability. And to work hard but still fail would be a devastating blow to their sense of competence.

If you hold performance goals, another strategy to protect self-esteem is to make a point of not trying at all. If you don't try and fail, no one can accuse you of being dumb. Just before a test a student might say, "I didn't study at all!" or "All I want to do is pass." Then, any grade above passing is a success. Procrastination is another self-protective strategy. Low grades do not imply low ability if the student can claim, "I did okay considering I didn't start the term paper until last night." Some evidence suggests that blaming anxiety for poor test performance can also be a self-protective strategy (Covington & Omelich, 1987). Of course, even though these strategies may help students avoid the negative implications of failure, very little learning is going on.

Incremental theorists, in contrast, tend to set *learning goals* and seek situations in which they can improve their skills, since improvement means getting smarter. Failure is not devastating; it simply indicates more work is needed. Ability is not threatened. Incremental theorists tend to set moderately difficult goals, the kind we have seen are the most motivating.

Attributions, Achievement Motivation, and Self-Worth

What are the connections between our need for achievement, attributions for success and failure, beliefs about ability, and self-worth? Covington and his colleagues suggest that these factors come together in three kinds

Sense of self-efficacy is an important component of motivation. For many young women, a diminished sense of efficacy in math and science has undermined their motivation and achievement. All students should be encouraged to tackle courses that provide challenges and build a sense of efficacy.

TABLE 9.5 Mastery-Oriented, Failure-Avoiding, and Failure-Accepting Students

	Need for Achievement	Goals Set	Attributions	View of Ability	Strategies
Mastery-oriented	High need for achievement; low fear of failure	Learning goals: moderately difficult and challenging	Effort, use of right strategy, sufficient knowledge is cause of success	Incremental; improvable	Adaptive strategies: e.g., try another way, seek help, practice/study more
Failure-avoiding	High fear of failure	Performance goals; very hard or very easy	Lack of ability is cause of failure	Entity; set	Self-defeating strategies: e.g., make a feeble effort, pretend not to care
Failure-accepting	Expectation of failure; depression	Performance goals or no goals	Lack of ability is cause of failure	Entity; set	Learned helplessness; likely to give up

of motivational sets: *mastery-oriented, failure-avoiding,* and *failure-accepting,* as shown in Table 9.5 (Covington, 1984; Covington & Omelich, 1984, 1987).

Mastery-oriented students tend to value achievement and see ability as improvable, so they focus on learning goals in order to increase their skills and abilities. And they are not fearful of failure, since failing does not threaten their sense of competence and self-worth. This allows them to set moderately difficult goals, take risks, and cope with failure constructively. They generally attribute success to their own effort, and so they assume responsibility for learning. They perform best in competitive situations, learn fast, have more self-confidence and energy, are more aroused, welcome concrete feedback (it does not threaten them), and are eager to learn "the rules of the game" so that they can succeed. Taken together, these factors make for persistent, successful learning (Alderman, 1985; McClelland, 1985; Morris, 1991).

Failure-avoiding students tend to hold an entity view of ability, so they set performance goals. They lack a strong sense of their own competence and self-worth separate from their performance. In other words, they feel only as smart as their last test grade. In order to feel competent, they must protect themselves (and their self-images) from failure. If they have been generally successful, they may avoid failure simply by taking few risks and "sticking with what they know." If, on the other hand, they have experienced some successes but also a good bit of failure, they may adopt the strategies we discussed earlier—procrastination, feeble efforts, setting very low or ridiculously high goals, or claiming not to care.

Mastery-Oriented Students Students who focus on learning goals because they value achievement and see ability as improvable.

Failure-Avoiding Students Students who avoid failure by sticking to what they know, by not taking risks, or by claiming not to care about their performance.

Guidelines

Encouraging Students' Self-Worth

Emphasize students' progress in a particular area.

Examples

1. Return to earlier material in reviews and show how "easy" it is now.
2. Encourage students to redo and improve projects when they have learned more.
3. Keep examples of particularly good work in portfolios.

Make specific suggestions for improvement, and revise grades when improvements are made.

Examples

1. Return work with comments noting what the students did right, what they did wrong, and why they might have made the mistakes.
2. Experiment with peer editing.
3. Show students how their revised, higher grade reflects greater competence and raises their class average.

Stress connections between past efforts and past accomplishments.

Examples

1. Have individual goal-setting and goal-review conferences with students, in which you ask students to reflect on how they solved difficult problems.
2. Confront self-defeating, failure-avoiding strategies directly.

Set learning goals for your students, and model a mastery orientation for them.

Examples

1. Recognize progress and improvement.
2. Share examples of how you have developed your abilities in a given area.
3. Read stories about students who overcame physical, mental, or economic challenges.
4. Don't excuse failure because a student has problems outside school. Help the student succeed inside school.

Unfortunately, as we have seen, failure-avoiding strategies are self-defeating, generally leading to the very failure the students were trying to avoid. If failures continue and excuses wear thin, the students may finally decide that they are incompetent. This is what they feared in the first place, but they come to accept it. Their sense of self-worth deteriorates. They give up and thus become **failure-accepting students.** They are convinced that their problems are due to low ability and that there is little hope for change. They can no longer protect themselves from this conclusion. As we saw earlier, students who attribute failure to low ability are likely to become depressed, apathetic, and helpless.

Teachers may be able to prevent some failure-avoiding students from becoming failure-accepting by helping them to find new and more realistic goals. Also, some students may need support in aspiring to higher levels in the face of sexual or ethnic stereotypes about what they "should" want or what they "should not" be able to do well. This kind of support could make all the difference. Instead of pitying or excusing these students, teachers can teach them how to learn and hold them accountable.

Failure-Accepting Students Students who believe their failures are due to low ability and there is little they can do about it.

Attributions and Beliefs: Lessons for Teachers

At the heart of attribution theory is the notion of individual perception. If students believe they lack the ability to deal with higher mathematics,

Depression, apathy, and a sense of helplessness plague many young people, especially those who have little hope of "making it" in the mainstream.

they probably will act on this belief even if their actual abilities are well above average. These students are likely to have little motivation to tackle trigonometry or calculus, since they expect to do poorly in these areas. If students believe that failing means they are stupid, they are likely to adopt many self-protective but also self-defeating strategies.

Just telling students to "try harder" is not particularly effective. The students need real evidence that effort will pay off, that setting a higher goal will not lead to failure, that they can improve, and that abilities can be changed. The Guidelines provide ideas for encouraging self-worth.

SUMMARY

WHAT IS MOTIVATION?

The study of motivation is essentially a study of how and why people initiate actions directed toward specific goals and persist in their attempts to reach these goals. Explanations of motivation include both personal and environmental factors as well as intrinsic and extrinsic sources of motivation.

Behaviorists tend to emphasize extrinsic motivation caused by incentives, rewards, and punishment. Primary and secondary reinforcers play a large role. Humanistic views stress the intrinsic motivation created by the need for personal growth and fulfillment. Cognitive psychologists stress a person's active search for meaning, understanding, and competence and the power of the individual's beliefs and interpretations. Social learning views suggest that motivation to reach a goal is the product of our expectations for success and the value of the goal to us. If either is zero, our motivation is zero also. This general approach is called the expectancy × value theory of motivation.

AROUSAL AND MOTIVATION

Most activities have an optimal level of arousal. If arousal is too low in classrooms, teachers can energize students by tapping their interests and arousing curiosity. Severe anxiety is an example of arousal that is too high for optimal learning. Anxiety can be the cause or the result of poor performance and can interfere with attention to, learning of, and retrieval of information. Many anxious students need help in developing effective test-taking and study skills.

GOALS AND MOTIVATION

Many theories of motivation feature a prominent role for goals. Goals increase motivation if they are specific, moderately difficult, and able to be reached in the near future. An important distinction is between performance goals (the intention to appear smart or capable in the eyes of others) and learning goals (the intention to gain knowledge and master skills).

NEEDS AND MOTIVATION

Needs are also an important component of many theories of motivation. Maslow has suggested that people are motivated by a hierarchy of needs, beginning with basic physiological requirements and moving up to the need for self-fulfillment. Lower-level needs must be met before higher-level needs can influence motivation. The need for achieve-ment is balanced by the need to avoid failure. Together these are strong motivating forces.

ATTRIBUTIONS, BELIEFS, AND MOTIVATION

The attribution theory of motivation suggests that the explanations people give for behavior, particularly their own successes and failures, have strong influences on future plans and performance. One of the important features of an attribution is whether it is internal and within a person's control or external and beyond control. Teachers may cue attributions by the way they respond to students' work. Surprisingly, praise, sympathy, and unsolicited help can communicate to students that they lack the ability to do the work.

When people believe that ability is fixed, they tend to set performance goals and strive to protect themselves from failure. When they believe ability is improvable, however, they tend to set learning goals and handle failure constructively. A low sense of self-worth seems to be linked with failure-avoiding and failure-accepting strategies intended to protect the individual from the consequences of failure. These strategies may seem to help in the short term but are damaging to motivation and self-esteem in the long run.

KEY TERMS AND CONCEPTS

achievement motivation, p. 350
anxiety, p. 344
arousal, p. 342
attribution theories, p. 353
being needs, p. 349
deficiency needs, p. 349
entity view of ability, p. 356
expectancy × value theories, p. 340
extrinsic motivation, p. 337

failure-accepting students, p. 360
failure-avoiding students, p. 359
hierarchy of needs, p. 348
humanistic view, p. 338
incremental view of ability, p. 357
intrinsic motivation, p. 337
learning goal, p. 348
locus of control, p. 354

mastery-oriented students, p. 359
motivation, p. 336
performance goal, p. 348
primary reinforcers, p. 337
resultant motivation, p. 351
secondary reinforcers, p. 338
self-actualization, p. 349
self-efficacy, p. 341
teaching efficacy, p. 341

WHAT WOULD YOU DO?

PRESCHOOL AND KINDERGARTEN

Brainstorm ways to nurture curiosity and a zest for learning in your preschool or kindergarten classroom. How could you help students build a foundation for self-efficacy in school?

ELEMENTARY AND MIDDLE SCHOOL

Your district has no money for new math materials, and the only resources are the workbooks. How would you arouse student curiosity and interest about the material in the workbooks?

Several of your students seem to have given up in science. They almost expect to fail. This is especially troubling because a number of the students are girls who believe that "girls are no good in science." What would you do?

JUNIOR HIGH AND HIGH SCHOOL

You are the faculty advisor for the student newspaper. Your students have grand ideas for stories and features, but they seem to run out of steam and never quite finish. The production of the paper is always last-minute and rush, rush. How would you help the students stay motivated and work steadily?

As the time to take the PSAT nears, a few of your students are becoming so anxious that you wonder if they will make it through the test. What can you do to help them?

COOPERATIVE LEARNING ACTIVITY

With four or five other members of your class, identify ways that you can respond to student mistakes without communicating to students that their mistakes are due to low ability. You also want to avoid being unrealistic about what they can do or implying that the material is "easy."

TEACHERS' CASEBOOK

BUILDING CONFIDENCE

One of your students seems to lack self-confidence. As if expecting to fail, the student just doesn't try. Poor performance then compounds the problem. You think this student is capable of doing better. What would you do to help?

BREAK THE CYCLE

If children feel badly about themselves and their skills (or lack of skills), it becomes very difficult for them to think positively about school and learning. We usually have a class discussion at the beginning of the year about our strengths and weaknesses, similarities and differences, and so on. I guide the children into discovering that we are all good at something. Some of us read well. Others can do math or write well. Some of us color or play well or are good friends. But we are *all* good at something.

If a child is still unable to break out of this cycle, I will sometimes review materials with that child and find out what he or she knows and feels comfortable doing. With that as our starting point, we play games with this information until the child knows it quite well. I gradually add on to this until the child begins to feel more confident giving encouragement each step of the way.

> Carolyn R. Cook, *Kindergarten Teacher*
> *Ramona Elementary School, Ramona, California*

CROSS-AGE TUTORING

A student who lacks confidence in his/her ability sometimes needs more than verbal praise for a "job well done." I have found that by actively involving this student in the subject matter, in this case math, I can help the student develop confidence in a meaningful way. I begin by having the student tutor a younger student who is having difficulty. This gives the tutor a feeling of importance because he/she is responsible for helping another learn. As the tutor develops confidence, I change the tutoring situation to an older student and gradually move up until the student has the confidence to tutor someone in his/her own class. Nothing makes students feel more important than helping others.

For subject areas that do not readily lend themselves to a tutor/tutee situation, a student can build confidence by being actively involved in a project that is significant to him/her. Special projects that are pertinent to the student allow the use of learned skills in meaningful ways and can change negative attitudes into positive ones.

> Malcolm Jarrell, *Remedial Mathematics and Reading Teacher*
> *Jackson-Via Elementary School, Charlottesville, Virginia*

MOTIVATING LEARNERS

Students are better motivated in school when they attribute their successes and failures to personally controllable causes, such as their own efforts. Suppose you have a student who gives up easily and tends to blame poor performance on assignments, on you, or on presumed lack of ability. What can you do to help this student?

PERSONAL GOALS

Goal setting is an important source of personal motivation. My students and I write personal goals at the beginning of each ranking period. We discuss the whole-person model of a balanced life. Specifically, we write two goals in each of four main categories: mental, social, emotional (feelings), and physical. The students write their individual goals on an index card and place the card in a private place (usually in their desk). The goals are personal, and no one is required to discuss their goals. Each morning while I'm taking attendance and completing the school lunch form, the students silently read their goals. At the end of each quarter, we evaluate our progress. Those students who wish to discuss their goals openly do so at this time. We applaud each other's progress and write new goals (or continue past goals) for the next ranking period. As the goals become internalized, motivation naturally develops.

Stephen C. Ellwood IV, *Maine 1991 Teacher of the Year*
St. Francis Elementary School, St. Francis, Maine

TEACHING FOR RELEVANCE

Your students complain that the lessons you are teaching are not relevant to their lives. How do you motivate them to learn, understand, and relate to your lessons?

USE STUDENTS' REALITIES

Perhaps it is not so much that I must "motivate them to learn, understand, and relate to my lessons" as it is incumbent upon me to make my lessons relevant to the students. Learning has to take place within their universe and in their words. If I cannot figure out why something is relevant to my students, perhaps it isn't. In that case, I need to change what I am teaching. This is not as simple as it sounds. I am in no way suggesting that students have to "like" everything they study or that learning has to be dressed up in a "rap mode" in order to entice students in the way that popular entertainment does. Rather, I am promoting the idea that students' learning must be in student words and concepts, must involve student evaluation and require student judgments. Intellectually important ideas will demand this kind of involvement; tasks requiring rote memorization will not.

Karen B. Kreider, *Pennsylvania 1991 Teacher of the Year*
Central High School, Philadelphia, Pennsylvania

TAP STUDENTS' SENSE OF OWNERSHIP

At the beginning of the school year I photograph my students individually with black and white film. Once the pictures are developed, I cut each youngster's face out and glue it on paper which I've ruled into one-inch boxes. Each child's picture is on this one paper, which I then photocopy. I usually make 30 to 40 copies of my original picture paper. The next task is to cut out each child's set of pictures of himself/herself and put these 30 to 40 pictures into an envelope with the youngster's name on it. These pictures are used for many different activities and give the children a sense of ownership in lessons.

At Halloween children come to school in costumes. They stand on an enormous floor graph to explain if their costume is pretty, scary, funny, or an occupation. Once their "real graph" is discussed, children return to their desks to draw their costume on a four-inch square. Their photograph is pasted to this costume drawing, and their drawings are taped to a graph on the wall. Once again discussion ensues, and each child is asked to make a comment about the graph. One comment might be, "There are three more funny costumes than pretty ones." These comments are written on strips of paper, and the picture of the youngster who made the comment is glued to the strip of paper. These strips may be placed in strategic spots around the graph. Children are motivated by this kind of activity and certainly find it relevant.

Darlene A. Walsh, *Rhode Island 1991 Teacher of the Year*
Greenbush Elementary School, West Warwick, Rhode Island

10 MOTIVATION AND THE LEARNING ENVIRONMENT

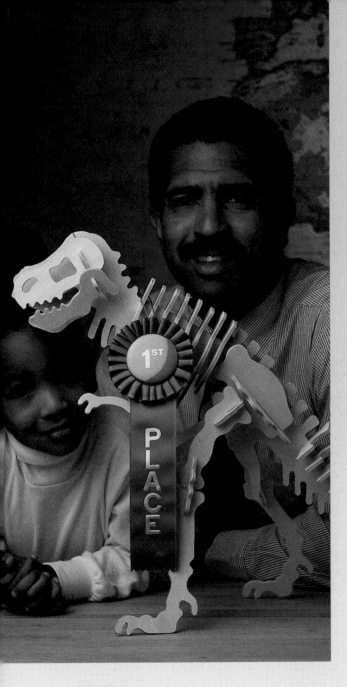

In the previous chapter we saw that motivation is an extremely complex concept. Many factors seem to affect the goals we choose and our energy and persistence in working toward them. We saw that arousal, curiosity, interests, anxiety, goals, needs, beliefs, and attributions all can affect motivation.

How do we put all this information together in teaching? How do we create environments that encourage motivation? These are the questions we will consider in the next several pages. First we focus on the kind of motivation that is most important in classrooms—the motivation to learn. Then we examine how motivation is influenced by the academic work of the class, the value of the work, and the setting in which the work must be done. Having considered the task and the setting, we turn to a very important influence on student motivation—the teacher. Finally, we discuss a number of strategies for developing motivation as a constant state in your classroom and as a permanent trait in your students.

When you finish this chapter, you should be well prepared to do the following:

- Define motivation to learn.
- Explain how the ambiguity and risk of the learning task affect motivation and what can happen when students try to reduce risk and ambiguity.
- Discuss how the value of a task affects motivation to learn.
- Explain how evaluation procedures and grouping arrangements can influence motivation.
- Design a unit using cooperative learning.
- Describe potential effects on students of teachers' positive and negative expectations.
- Devise a strategy for teaching your subject to an uninterested student.

MOTIVATION TO LEARN

Teachers are concerned about developing a particular kind of motivation in their students—the motivation to *learn*. This chapter examines how to design teaching environments that encourage such motivation. Before we consider the factors that support motivation to learn, let's take a closer look at this concept. Jere Brophy (1988) describes **student motivation to learn** as follows:

> Student motivation to learn is a student tendency to find academic activities meaningful and worthwhile and to try to derive the intended academic benefits from them. Motivation to learn can be construed as both a general trait and a situation-specific state. (pp. 205–206)

The general *trait* of motivation to learn is evident most often in people who find learning intrinsically rewarding. They simply value knowing and expanding their store of information. Learning is interesting and satisfying for them. Other students have the trait as part of a sense of duty. They believe they should get the maximum benefit from any experience, even if they did not choose the experience in the first place. The *state* of motivation to learn exists when students take lesson activities seriously. They try to understand and improve, not just finish the work or get the grade. They pay attention, work hard, and persist, even if they are not particularly interested in the topic.

Brophy's description of motivation to learn is consistent with the distinction, discussed in the last chapter, between learning goals and performance goals. Motivation to learn means working toward learning goals. The point is to understand and improve, not just to perform well. You may remember that when students work toward learning goals, they are more likely to seek challenge and persist in the face of failure.

Many elements make up motivation to learn. These include planning, concentration on the goal, metacognitive awareness of what you intend to learn and how you intend to learn it, the active search for new information, clear perceptions of feedback, pride and satisfaction in achievement, and no anxiety or fear of failure (Johnson & Johnson, 1985). Motivation to learn thus involves more than wanting or intending to

Student Motivation to Learn The tendency to work hard on academic activities because one believes they are worthwhile.

learn. It includes the quality of the student's mental efforts. For example, reading the text 10 times may be very persistent, but motivation to learn implies more thoughtful, active study strategies, like summarizing, elaborating the basic ideas, outlining in your own words, drawing graphs of the key relationships, and so on (Brophy, 1988).

Students who are motivated to learn focus on the task at hand. Nicholls and Miller (1984) refer to these learners as **task-involved learners,** because they are concerned with mastering the task and are not worried about how their performance "measures up" compared to others in the class. We often say that these people "get lost in their work." **Ego-involved learners,** on the other hand, are preoccupied with themselves. They are concerned about looking smarter and performing better than others in the class. If this seems impossible, they may adopt the

FIGURE 10.1 **Motivation to Learn** Motivation to learn is a complex collection of beliefs and behaviors. The characteristics listed in the left column are associated with motivation to learn. Characteristics in the right column diminish or undermine motivation to learn.

	Optimum Characteristics of Motivation to Learn	Characteristics that Diminish Motivation to Learn
SOURCE OF MOTIVATION (Chapter 9, pp. 336–337)	INTRINSIC: Personal factors such as needs, interests, curiosity, enjoyment	EXTRINSIC: Environmental factors such as rewards, social pressure, punishment
TYPE OF GOAL SET (Chapter 9, pp. 347–348)	LEARNING GOAL: Personal satisfaction in meeting challenges and improving; tendency to choose moderately difficult and challenging goals	PERFORMANCE GOAL: Desire for approval of performance in others' eyes; tendency to choose very easy or very difficult goals
ACHIEVEMENT MOTIVATION (Chapter 9, pp. 359–360)	Motivation to ACHIEVE: mastery orientation	Motivation to AVOID FAILURE: prone to anxiety
LIKELY ATTRIBUTIONS (Chapter 9, pp. 353–356)	Successes and failures attributed to CONTROLLABLE effort and ability	Successes and failures attributed to UNCONTROLLABLE causes
BELIEFS ABOUT ABILITY (Chapter 9, pp. 357–358)	INCREMENTAL VIEW: Belief that ability is improvable through hard work and added knowledge and skills.	ENTITY VIEW: Belief that ability is a stable, uncontrollable trait
TYPE OF INVOLVEMENT (Chapter 10, pp. 369–370)	TASK-INVOLVED: Concerned with mastering the task.	EGO-INVOLVED: Concerned with self in others' eyes

Task-Involved Learners
Students who focus on mastering the task or solving the problem.

Ego-Involved Learners
Students who focus on how well they are performing and how they are judged by others.

failure-avoiding strategies described in the previous chapter (pretending not to care, not trying, etc.); or they may simply give up (Jagacinski & Nicholls, 1987; Schunk, 1991a). Some recent research by Sandra Graham and Shari Golan (1991) found that fifth- and sixth-grade students who were ego-involved performed as well as comparable students who were task-involved on simple recall activities, but that task-involved students performed significantly better on materials that required deeper processing and understanding. Being ego-involved with your work appears to interfere with the retrieval stage of information processing.

Figure 10.1 on page 369 summarizes the elements of *motivation to learn.* It would be wonderful if all our students came to us filled with motivation to learn, but they don't. And even if they did, work in school might still seem boring or unimportant to some students. As teachers, we have two major goals. The first is to get students productively involved with the work of the class; in other words, to create a state of motivation to learn. The second and more long-term goal is to develop in our students the trait of being motivated to learn. In this dual task, we need to capitalize on both intrinsic and extrinsic motivation. And we need to know more about the external, environmental factors that can affect motivation—the factors that we as teachers can control. First, let us consider what we require students to do, the learning task itself.

ACADEMIC TASKS

To understand how a task can affect students' motivation, we need to analyze the task. The **academic tasks** that teachers set for their students can be characterized in several ways. Tasks have a particular content, for example. Whether assigned in history or geometry or home economics, tasks involve facts, concepts, opinions, and principles. Tasks also involve certain operations; students must memorize, infer, classify, apply, and so on. Because tasks involve both content and operations, as students work on a task they are learning content and practicing operations. Tasks also vary in terms of how clear-cut or ambiguous they are and how much risk is involved in doing them (Doyle, 1983). Finally, tasks have a certain value to students. Since the *content* of tasks in your classroom depends on the subjects and grades you teach, we will consider the other elements of *operations, risk, ambiguity,* and *value.*

Task Operations

Doyle (1983) has suggested that there are four general categories of academic tasks, defined by the operations required.

1. *Memory tasks* simply require students to recognize or reproduce information they have encountered before, as in matching states and capitals or reciting lines from a play.

2. *Routine* or *procedural tasks* involve using an algorithm (prescribed set of steps) to solve a problem. If students apply the procedure correctly, they will get the right answer: if they use the formula πr^2, for example, they will find the area of a circle.

Academic Tasks The work the student must accomplish, including the content covered and the mental operations required.

3. *Comprehension tasks* require students to go a step beyond—to transform information, choose the best among many approaches, combine several ideas to solve a new problem, or write a passage in a particular style.
4. *Opinion tasks* ask students to state a preference, such as which character in a story is the bravest.

It seems obvious, but is worth repeating, that students will learn the operations they practice. For example, to learn to write poetry, you obviously must do some writing. Simply memorizing definitions or steps will not make you a poet. The kind of operation in a task determines how ambiguous and risky the task is, and this, in turn, affects student motivation, as you will see.

Risk and Ambiguity

Some tasks are riskier than others, because failure is more likely. For example, opinion tasks are very low-risk tasks—there are no right or wrong answers. Simple memory or procedural tasks also involve few risks, because getting the right answer is easy: you just follow the steps. But the stakes can be very high with longer and more complex memory or procedural tasks. Reciting 100 lines from Shakespeare is risky, especially if you are graded on how well you do, because there is a great deal to memorize. Involved procedural tasks, such as solving quadratic equations, can also be risky, because there are many possibilities for mistakes.

Another characteristic of tasks is level of ambiguity—how straightforward the expected answer is. Opinion and understanding tasks are ambiguous: it is hard to predict the right answer (if there is one) or how to find it. If you were asked, as I was in my freshman government class, to

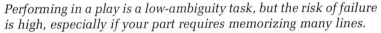

Performing in a play is a low-ambiguity task, but the risk of failure is high, especially if your part requires memorizing many lines.

write a paper on the central problem of the democratic form of government, you wouldn't be certain about what the right answer was or even if there *was* a right answer. (This may involve the teacher's opinion, in which case you'd be on treacherous ground.) Memory and procedural tasks, on the other hand, are straightforward and unambiguous. If you are reciting a soliloquy from *Hamlet,* the "right" answer is clear, even though the task is difficult. Figure 10.2 summarizes how tasks can be categorized by risk and ambiguity.

What does this have to do with motivation? Most students want to lower the risk and decrease the ambiguity involved in schoolwork, because their grades are at stake. This is especially true for highly anxious students or those who are trying to avoid failure. Many times teachers plan a complicated comprehension task that is both ambiguous and risky. They want their students to learn to think and solve problems. But the students want more guidance. They may ask for models, rules, minimums, or formulas: "How many references do you want?" "How many pages?" "Will we have to know dates and names?" "Give us a model to follow." In other words, students negotiate the task. These negotiations can lead to management problems. If the students are very confused, they may become restless, turn to other students for help, get discouraged, or lose interest in the task.

FIGURE 10.2 **Ambiguity and Risk Associated with Academic Tasks in Classrooms** Academic tasks can be characterized by their levels of risk and ambiguity. Because students often find high-ambiguity/high-risk tasks very threatening, they need extra support and fewer pressures when completing them.

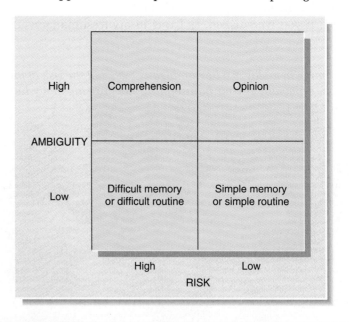

Source: Adapted from W. Doyle, Academic work. *Review of Educational Research, 53,* p. 183. Copyright 1983 by the American Educational Research Association. Reprinted by permission of the publisher.

Under this kind of pressure, the teacher often responds by stating the three main points that should be addressed, giving a minimum number of references or a page limit, and providing books that would be helpful. This transforms the comprehension task into a procedural one. Risk and ambiguity are reduced and motivation may seem to increase, at least temporarily. But the task itself is not as interesting. Doing well on the procedural task is not as rewarding, because achievement does not lead to a sense of increased competence. So the results of the "task negotiation" may be a temporary *state* of motivation, but it is motivation to perform, to get the grade, not motivation to learn. And little has been done to foster the long-term development of the *trait* of motivation to learn. Furthermore, since students learn the operations that they practice, these students have learned how to do a procedure—and how to negotiate with teachers (Doyle, 1983). But they probably have not improved the problem-solving or critical-thinking skills that the teacher had intended to develop. Certainly creativity will not be encouraged. These are only a few examples of what can happen when students press to reduce risk and teachers go along with it.

Obviously, some balance is needed. Tasks that help students learn to remember will not necessarily help them learn to comprehend and understand. Tasks that are clear-cut and low-risk may encourage immediate motivation but undermine the development of long-term motivation and persistence in the face of frustration. Teachers must make wise choices, then stick with them, even when students try to negotiate changes. Instructions should be clear, but not too restricting. The penalties for taking a risk or making a mistake should not be too great. Finally, tasks must have some value to students. Let's take a closer look now at the value of classroom tasks.

Task Value

As you recall from the previous chapter, many theories suggest that the strength of our motivation in a particular situation is determined by our expectation that we can succeed and the value of that success to us. We can think of a task as having three kinds of value to the students (Eccles & Wigfield, 1985). **Attainment value** is the importance of doing well on the task. This aspect of value is closely tied to the needs of the individual (for example, the need to be competent, well-liked, etc.) and the meaning of success to that person. For instance, if someone has a strong need to appear smart and believes that a high grade on a test shows you are smart, then the test has high attainment value for that person.

A second kind of value is **intrinsic** or **interest value.** This is simply the enjoyment one gets from the activity itself. Some people like the experience of learning. Others enjoy the feeling of hard physical effort or of solving puzzles. Finally, tasks have **utility value;** that is, they help us achieve a short-term or long-term goal. You probably are reading this page, in part, because you want to earn credit for a college course that is necessary to reach your long-range goal of becoming a teacher.

You see from our discussion of task value that it is very difficult to separate personal and environmental influences on motivation. The two

Attainment Value The importance of doing well on a task; how success on the task meets personal needs.

Intrinsic or Interest Value The enjoyment a person gets from a task.

Utility Value The contribution of a task to meeting one's goals.

influences interact constantly. The task we ask students to accomplish is an aspect of the environment; it is *external* to the student. But the value of accomplishing the task is bound up with the *internal* needs, beliefs, and goals of the individual.

CLASS STRUCTURE AND MOTIVATION

Let's turn our attention from the task to the setting in which students must work. Classrooms are special settings for learning. They have their own unique characteristics, many of which can affect student motivation. Here we will examine two characteristics—the evaluative climate and the goal structure.

Evaluative Climate

Students' efforts and products are constantly evaluated. Doyle (1983) suggests that students look upon most classroom work as "an exchange of performance for grades" (p. 181). Grading here refers to more than marks on a report card. Students must take tests, answer questions in class, and complete assignments. On all these tasks they are evaluated, either formally with a grade or informally as the teacher forms impressions. The greater the emphasis on competitive evaluation and grading, the more students will focus on performance goals rather than learning goals and the more they will be ego-involved as opposed to task-involved.

Of course, not all students are caught up in an exchange of performance for grades. Low-achieving students who have little hope of either "making the grade" *or* mastering the task may simply want to finish. They complete the worksheet any way they can so it will be over. One study of first graders doing seatwork found that low-achieving students made up answers, filled in the page with patterns, or copied from other students, just to get through the work. As one student said when she finished, "I don't know what it means, but I did it" (Anderson, Brubaker, Alleman-Brooks, & Duffy, 1985, p. 132). On closer examination, the researchers found that the work was often much too hard for these students. For example, the instructions on the worksheet might be to draw a line between the two words that had the same meaning. Since the low-achieving students could not even read most of the words on the sheet, they had little hope of matching definitions. So they settled for making interesting patterns, connecting words at random.

How can teachers prevent students from simply focusing on the grade or doing the work just to "get finished"? The most obvious answer is to deemphasize grades and emphasize learning in the class. Students need to understand the value of the work. Instead of saying, "You will need to know this for the test," tell students how the information will be useful in solving problems they want to solve. Suggest that the lesson will answer some interesting questions. Communicate that understanding is more important than finishing.

Unfortunately, many teachers do not follow this advice. Brophy (1988) reports that when he and several colleagues spent about 100 hours observing how six teachers introduced their lessons, they found that most

One approach to encouraging motivation is to engage students in "authentic" tasks—activities that have practical value such as planning the roadways in a town.

introductions were routine, apologetic, or unenthusiastic. The introductions described procedures, made threats, emphasized finishing, or promised tests on the material. A few examples are the following:

> "You don't expect me to give you baby work to do every day, do you?"
>
> "My talkers are going to get a third page to do during lunch."
>
> "If you are done by 10 o'clock, you can go outside." (Brophy, 1988, p. 204)

During 100 hours, only nine introductions included statements that described the value of the work or suggested that it would be interesting. And these often were brief. One example is, "Answer the comprehension questions with complete sentences. All these stories are very interesting. You'll enjoy them" (Brophy, 1988, p. 203).

While many teachers are similar to the six Brophy studied, there are exceptions. Hermine Marshall (1987) described a few elementary-school teachers who seem to establish a *learning orientation* in their classrooms. They stress understanding instead of performing, being graded, or finishing work. Later in the chapter we will examine strategies for establishing such an orientation in your class.

Goal Structures: Cooperation and Competition

You may remember a teacher who made you want to work hard—someone who made a subject come alive. Or you may remember how many hours you spent practicing as a member of a team, orchestra, choir, or theater troupe. If you do, then you know the motivational power of relationships with other people. David and Roger Johnson (1985) describe the power this way:

> Motivation to learn is inherently interpersonal. It is through interaction with other people that students learn to value learning for its own sake, enjoy the process of learning, and take pride in their

acquisition of knowledge and development of skill. Of the interpersonal relationships available in the classroom, peers may be the most influential on motivation to learn. (p. 250)

Students in the classroom function as part of a large group. Johnson and Johnson (1985) have given considerable attention to this in their work on motivation. They have found that motivation can be greatly influenced by the ways we relate to the other people who are also involved in accomplishing a particular goal. Johnson and Johnson have labeled this interpersonal factor the **goal structure** of the task. There are three such structures: cooperative, competitive, and individualistic, as shown in Figure 10.3.

Cooperative Learning

Several studies have shown that when the task involves complex learning and problem-solving skills, cooperation leads to higher achievement than competition, especially for low-ability students (Johnson & Johnson, 1985; Slavin 1990b). In one study, achievement for all students was increased when the group was rewarded based on the average learning of the group members (Slavin, 1983). In addition, **cooperative learning** seems to result in improved ability to see the world from another person's point of view, better relations among different ethnic groups in schools and classrooms, increased self-esteem, and greater acceptance of handi-

Goal Structure The way students relate to others who are also working toward a particular goal.

Cooperative Learning Arrangement in which students work in mixed-ability groups and are rewarded on the basis of the success of the group.

FIGURE 10.3 Different Goal Structures Each goal structure is associated with a different relationship between the individual and the group. This relationship influences motivation to reach the goal.

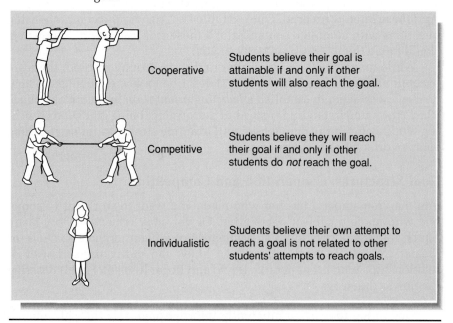

Cooperative — Students believe their goal is attainable if and only if other students will also reach the goal.

Competitive — Students believe they will reach their goal if and only if other students do *not* reach the goal.

Individualistic — Students believe their own attempt to reach a goal is not related to other students' attempts to reach goals.

Source: Adapted from D. Johnson and R. Johnson (1975), *Learning together and alone: cooperation, competition, and individualization.* Adapted by permission of Allyn and Bacon.

Students working in pairs or teams at the computer can support each other's learning. Motivation is greater since immediate help from team members is available when a student has problems.

capped and low-achieving students (Slavin, 1990). Students learn to negotiate and to be more tolerant of others. The interaction with peers that students enjoy so much becomes a part of the learning process. The result? The need for belonging described by Maslow is more likely to be met.

Many activities can be approached cooperatively. For example, students can work together in conducting local surveys. How do people feel about the plan to build a new mall that will bring more shopping and more traffic? Would the community support or oppose the building of a nuclear power plant?

But cooperative learning is not limited to specific or elaborate activities like these. Many of the most ordinary assignments can be enhanced by cooperation. If students must learn 10 new definitions in a biology class, why not let students divide up the terms and definitions and teach one another? Be sure, however, that everyone in the group can handle the task; sometimes a cooperative effort ends with one or two students doing the work of the entire group. Work groups should be monitored to make sure that each person is contributing and that hostilities, if they develop, are resolved in a positive way.

Setting Up Cooperative Groups. In setting up learning groups, it often makes sense to balance the number of boys and girls. Some research indicates that when there are just a few girls in a group, they tend to be left out of the discussions unless they are the most able or assertive members. By contrast, when there are only one or two boys in the group, they tend to dominate and be "interviewed" by the girls unless these boys are less able than the girls or very shy. In general, for very shy and introverted students, individual learning may be a better approach (Webb, 1980, 1985). Whatever the case, teachers must monitor groups to make sure everyone is contributing and learning.

Even if the group as a whole is successful in reaching the goal, there is still no guarantee that every student has benefited equally. In practice, the effects of learning in a group vary, depending on what actually happens in the group and who is in it. If only a few people take responsi-

TABLE 10.1 Using Individual Learning Expectations

The idea behind individual learning expectations, or ILEs, is that students ought to be judged in relation to their own abilities and not compared to others. The focus is on improvement, not on comparisons among students.

To calculate an ILE score, the teacher simply averages the student's grades or test scores from previous work. These scores are usually on a 100-point scale. Letter grades can be converted to points based on the school's system—for example, A = 90 points, B = 80 points, and so on. The student's average score is her or his initial base score. The ILE score becomes the standard for judging each student's work.

If the teacher is using the STAD system of cooperative learning, then students earn points for their group based on the following system:

Test Score	Points Earned for Group
A perfect score	3
10 or more points above ILE score	3
5 to 9 points above ILE score	2
4 points below to 4 points above ILE score	1
5 or more points below ILE score	0

bility for the work, these people will learn, but the nonparticipating members probably will not. Students who ask questions, get answers, and attempt explanations are more likely to learn than students whose questions go unasked or unanswered. In fact, there is evidence that the more a student provides elaborated, thoughtful explanations to other students in a group, the more the *explainer* learns. Giving good explanations appears to be even more important for learning than receiving explanations (Webb, 1989). In order to explain, you have to organize the information, put it into your own words, think of examples and analogies (which connects the information to things you already know), and test your understanding by answering questions. These are excellent learning strategies (King, 1990).

Student Teams–Achievement Divisions (STAD) Cooperative learning with heterogeneous groups and elements of competition and reward.

Individual Learning Expectation (ILE) Constantly recomputed average score in a subject.

STAD. Robert Slavin and his associates have developed a system for overcoming the disadvantages of the cooperative goal structure while maintaining its advantages. The system is called **Student Teams–Achievement Divisions,** or **STAD** (Slavin, 1986, 1990b). Each team has about five members, with a mix of abilities, ethnic backgrounds, and sexes. The teacher calculates an **individual learning expectation (ILE)** score, or base score, for each team member. This score represents the student's average level of performance. Details about how to determine the base scores are given in Table 10.1.

Students work in their teams to study and prepare for twice-weekly quizzes, but they take the quizzes individually, just as in a regular class. Based on test performance, each team member can earn from one to three points for the group. Table 10.1 shows how points are awarded by comparing each student's current test score to his or her base (ILE) score (Slavin, 1980b). As you can see from the table, every student has an equal chance to contribute the maximum number of points to the team total. Thus, every student, not just the most able or motivated, has reason to work hard. This system avoids the problem of students' unequal contributions to a group project. Every week the group earning the greatest number of points is declared the winner. Team accomplishments should be recognized in a class newsletter or a bulletin board display.

Every few weeks the teams can be changed so that students have a chance to work with many different class members. Every two weeks or so the teacher must recompute each student's ILE score by averaging the old base score with grades on the recent tests. With this system, improvement pays off for all students. Those with less ability can still earn the maximum for their team by scoring 10 or more points above their own base score. Those with greater ability are still challenged, because they must score well above their own average or make a perfect score to contribute the maximum to the group total.

TGT. **Teams-Games-Tournaments** or **TGT** is similar to STAD. After the teacher's presentation, students move into their heterogeneous groups to help each other answer problems or questions about the material. Instead of taking written tests, however, each student meets once a week at a "tournament table" with two other students of comparable ability from the other teams. The three students at each tournament table compete, answering questions similar to the problems practiced in their study teams. The winner at each table earns 6 points for his or her team. Each week the participants at the tournament tables are adjusted—the winners are "bumped" up to a higher-ability table to keep the competition fair. This way, every student has the chance to contribute equally to the team's total score (Slavin, 1990b).

Some recent research on TGT raises a caution. Bette Chambers and Philip Abrami (1991) found that members of successful teams did learn more than members of unsuccessful teams, but they also were happier about the outcome and rated their ability higher than members of losing teams. For low-achieving students who tend to be anxious, failure-accepting, or helpless, being on a losing team could make matters worse. Chambers and Abrami suggest experimenting with cooperation both within *and* between teams. For example, the whole class might earn recognition if each team reaches a specified level of learning.

CIRC. A recent addition to the list of cooperative learning techniques is **Cooperative Integrated Reading and Composition (CIRC).** This system supports the traditional approach of using ability-based reading groups. Students are assigned to teams made up of pairs from each reading group in the class. While the teacher works with one reading group, the teams work in their pairs using many of the methods of *reciprocal teaching* described in chapter 7—reading aloud, making predictions, asking questions, summarizing, and writing about the stories they are reading. Teams help each other prepare for tests, write and edit work, and often "publish" team books. Teams are rewarded based on the average performance of all their members on all the reading and writing assignments. Thus there is

In cooperative learning programs such as STAD or Teams-Games-Tournaments, student groups compete. Within each group, members help each other to learn the required material and prepare for assessment.

Teams-Games-Tournaments (TGT) Learning arrangement in which team members prepare cooperatively, then meet comparable individuals of competing teams in a tournament game to win points for their team.

Cooperative Integrated Reading and Composition (CIRC) Cooperative learning technique; pairs of students from each reading group work together on reading and writing projects, then teams are rewarded on the basis of their work.

Can Teachers' Expectations Affect Students' Learning?

The answer to this question is more complicated than it might seem. There are two ways to investigate the question. One is to give teachers unfounded expectations about their students and note if these baseless expectations have any effects. The other approach is to identify the naturally occurring expectations of teachers and study the effects of these expectations. The answer to the question of whether teacher expectations can affect student learning depends in part on which approach is taken to study the question.

Point: Teachers' expectations have less effect than we think.

The original Rosenthal and Jacobson experiment used the first approach—giving teachers groundless expectations and noting the effects. The study was heavily criticized for the experimental

and statistical methods used (Elashoff & Snow, 1971; Weinberg, 1989). A careful analysis of the results revealed that, even though first- through sixth-grade students participated in the study, the self-fulfilling prophecy effects were confined mostly to those in grades one and two. When other researchers tried to replicate the study, they did not find evidence of a self-fulfilling prophecy effect, even for children in these lower grades (Claiborn, 1969; Wilkins & Glock, 1973). Critics argued that even if higher expectations do lead to greater learning in the early grades, this does not prove that lower expectations will lead to decreased learning. Besides, the critics pointed out, giving teachers false expectations is an unnatural situation. Several studies found that when teachers did not believe the information they were given, no expectation effects occurred. After re-

---

equal opportunity for success, group support for learning, and *individual accountability for final performance.* These three elements are characteristic of many cooperative learning strategies (Slavin, 1990b).

Reciprocal Questioning. Another cooperative approach can be used with a wide range of ages and subjects. **Reciprocal questioning** requires no special materials or testing procedures. After a lesson or presentation by the teacher, students work in pairs or triads to ask and answer questions about the material. The teacher provides question stems like the following taken from King (1990):

> How would you use . . . to . . . ?
> What is a new example of . . . ?
> Explain why . . . ?
> How are . . . and . . . similar?
> What do you think would happen if . . . ?
> What are the strengths and weaknesses of . . . ?

Students are taught how to develop specific questions on the material using these generic question stems. The students create questions, then take turns asking and answering. This process has proven more effective than traditional discussion groups, because it seems to encourage deeper thinking about the material.

We have examined the academic task and the goal structure as two influences on student motivation to learn. In this chapter we will explore the ways that teachers can influence student motivation. Before we look

Reciprocal Questioning
Approach where groups of two or three students ask and answer each other's questions after a lesson or presentation.

at intentional effects, however, let's look at some unintentional effects teachers sometimes have on their students' motivation to learn.

TEACHER EXPECTATIONS

Over 25 years ago, a study by Robert Rosenthal and Lenore Jacobson (1968) captured the attention of the national media in a way that few studies by psychologists have since. Articles in newspapers across the country reported the seemingly remarkable effects of "Pygmalion in the classroom," a term taken from the title of the book about the experiment. The study also caused great controversy within the professional community. Debate about the meaning of the results prompted much research (Braun, 1976; Brophy, 1982; Cooper & Good, 1983; Good, 1988; Mendels & Flanders, 1973; Rosenthal, 1987).

What did Rosenthal and Jacobson say that caused such a stir? They chose several students at random in a number of elementary-school classrooms, then told the teachers that these students probably would make significant intellectual gains during the year. The students did indeed make larger gains than normal that year. The researchers presented data suggesting the existence of a self-fulfilling prophecy in the classroom. A **self-fulfilling prophecy** is essentially a groundless expectation that comes true simply because it has been expected. In the classroom this means that a teacher's beliefs about students' abilities or behaviors bring about the very behaviors the teacher expects. The **Point/Counterpoint** section above examines the debate over the existence of a self-fulfilling-prophecy or **Pygmalion effect.**

Self-Fulfilling Prophecy A groundless expectation that is confirmed because it has been expected.

Pygmalion Effect Exceptional progress by a student as a result of high teacher expectations for that student; named for mythological king, Pygmalion, who made a statue, then caused it to be brought to life.

Two Kinds of Expectation Effects

Actually, two kinds of expectation effects can occur in classrooms. The first is the self-fulfilling prophecy described above. In this situation the teacher's beliefs about the student's abilities have no basis in fact, but student behavior comes to match the initially inaccurate expectation. The second kind of expectation effect occurs when teachers are fairly accurate in their initial reading of students' abilities and respond to students based on those readings. So far, so good. There is nothing wrong with forming and acting on accurate estimates of student ability. Indeed, many teachers do this almost automatically. The problems arise when students show some improvement but teachers do not alter their expectations to take account of the improvement. This is called a **sustaining expectation effect,** because the teacher's unchanging expectation sustains the student's achievement at the expected level. The chance to raise expectations, provide more appropriate teaching, and thus encourage greater student achievement is lost. In practice, sustaining effects are more common than self-fulfilling prophecy effects (Cooper & Good, 1983).

Teacher expectations may affect students in the following manner. Teachers begin by forming expectations about how individual students will behave or how well each will do in the class. The teachers then treat each student according to these expectations. If they expect a student to do well, that student may be given more encouragement or more time to answer a question. Students given more time and more encouragement answer correctly more often. If this pattern is repeated daily for months, the students given more time and encouragement will do better academically and score better on achievement tests. Over time, the students' behavior moves closer and closer to the kind of performance originally expected by the teachers (Good & Brophy, 1984; Jussim, 1986). The same cycle of expectation, teacher behavior, and student response can occur with groups within a class or with whole classes.

A student's achievement, motivation, aspiration level, and self-concept may all be affected by a teacher's expectations. Of course, students differ. Some are more sensitive than others to the teacher's opinions. In general, students who are young, dependent, conforming, or who really like the teacher are most likely to have their self-esteem affected by the teacher's views (Brophy, 1982).

Sources of Expectations

Braun (1976) has developed a model based on research findings to explain the origins of teacher expectations and the ways in which these expectations are communicated to students and then perpetuated by student behavior. Figure 10.4 shows the basic elements of this model.

Braun lists 10 possible sources of teacher expectations. Intelligence test scores are an obvious source, especially if teachers do not interpret the scores appropriately. Sex also influences teachers; most teachers expect more behavior problems from boys than from girls. The notes from previous teachers and the medical or psychological reports found in cumulative folders (permanent record files) are another obvious source of expectations. Knowledge of ethnic background also seems to have an

This student might not have become her school's valedictorian if low teachers' expectations had diminished her motivation to learn.

Sustaining Expectation Effect Student performance maintained at a certain level because teachers don't recognize improvements.

FIGURE **10.4** **Teacher Expectations and Changes in Student Behavior**
Braun's model does not include the beliefs and experiences of
the teacher as an influence on a teacher's expectations. Do
you think teacher bias might play a part in the cycle of teacher
expectations?

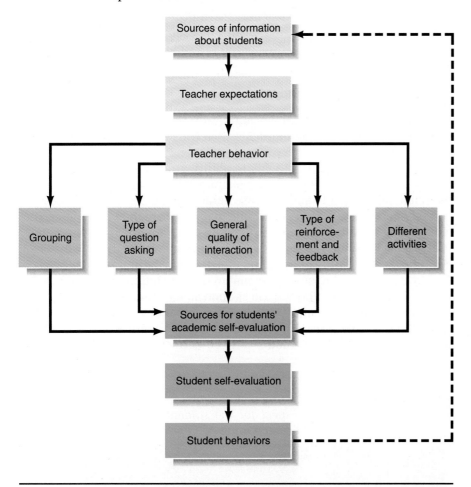

Source: Adapted from C. Braun (1976), Teacher expectations: Sociopsychological dynamics.
Review of Educational Research, 46, 185–213. Copyright © 1976 American Educational
Research Association, Washington, D.C.

influence, as does knowledge of older brothers and sisters. The influence
of students' physical characteristics is shown in several studies, indicating that teachers hold higher expectations for attractive students. Previous achievement, socioeconomic class, and the actual behaviors of the
student are also often used as sources of information.

Teacher Behavior and Student Reaction

In Figure 10.4, you see five areas in which teacher behavior toward
students varies. The first and last of these, grouping and different activities, involve instructional strategies.

Instructional Strategies. As we have seen, different grouping processes may well have a marked effect on students. It appears that even very young students assigned to low reading groups are aware of their grouping and tend to prefer friends from higher-ability groups. Teachers also seem to prefer students in the higher reading groups (McGinley & McGinley, 1970). And some teachers leave little to the imagination; they make their expectations all too clear. For example, Alloway (1984) recorded comments like these directed to low-achieving groups:

"I'll be over to help you slow ones in a minute."
"The blue group will find this hard."

In these remarks the teacher not only tells the students that they lack ability, the teacher also communicates that finishing the work, not understanding, is the goal.

Once teachers assign students to ability groups, they usually assign different learning activities. To the extent that teachers choose activities that challenge students and increase achievement, these differences are probably necessary. Activities become inappropriate, however, when students who are ready for more challenging work are not given the opportunity to try it because teachers believe they cannot handle it. This is an example of a sustaining expectation effect. It may be appropriate to teach at a slower pace and to cover less material with certain students, but the pace and quantity should increase as soon as the students are ready.

Other problems occur when teachers make accurate predictions about students' abilities but at the outset select inappropriate teaching methods. For example, a teacher may be correct in predicting that one

When teachers take the time to give individual feedback to students, they communicate respect for the student and also the expectation that the student can continue to improve.

group of students will have great difficulty with a particular lesson and another group will learn the new material easily. The teacher may decide against spending much time with either group, since one group "can't benefit from help" and the other "doesn't need help." But in this way both groups are robbed of the chance to do their best (Brophy, 1982).

Teacher-Student Interactions. However the class is grouped and whatever activities are assigned, the quantity and the quality of student-teacher interactions are likely to affect the students. These are central aspects of students' experiences in the classroom.

Students who are expected to achieve tend to be asked more and harder questions, to be given more chances and a longer time to respond, and to be interrupted less often than students who are expected to do poorly (Allington, 1980; Good & Brophy, 1984; Rosenthal, 1973). Teachers also give these high-expectation students cues and prompts, communicating their belief that the students can answer the question (Rosenthal, 1973). Teachers tend to be more encouraging in general toward those students for whom they have high expectations. They smile at these students more often and show greater warmth through such nonverbal responses as leaning toward the students and nodding their heads as the students speak (Woolfolk & Brooks, 1983, 1985). In contrast, with students for whom expectations are low, teachers ask easier questions, allow less time for answering, and are much less likely to give prompts.

It appears that feedback and reinforcement are also somewhat dependent on teacher expectations. Good and Brophy (1984) have noted that teachers demand better performance from high-achieving students, are less likely to accept a poor answer from them, and praise them more for good answers. Teachers are more likely, on the one hand, to accept or even reinforce inadequate answers from low-achieving students or, on the other, to criticize these students for wrong answers. Even more disturbing, low-achieving students receive less praise than high-achieving students for similar correct answers. On tests when an answer is "almost right," the teacher is more likely to give the benefit of the doubt (and thus the better grade) to high-achieving students (Finn, 1972).

This inconsistent feedback can be very confusing for low-ability students. Imagine how hard it would be to learn if your wrong answers were sometimes praised, sometimes ignored, and sometimes criticized and your right answers received little recognition (Good 1983a & b).

The Effects of Teacher Behavior on Students. Teacher behaviors can communicate to students just how they are viewed by a very significant person, their teacher. Think about students' attributions. If youngsters see the inevitable mistakes that accompany learning as a consequence of their own lack of ability, they are likely to lower their level of aspiration. Decreased motivation follows lowered expectations. The student and the teacher set lower standards, persistence is discouraged, and poorer performance results. Students start saying "I don't know" or nothing at all rather than risk failure again. Here the teacher's attributions enter the picture: the teacher accepts the poor performance and attributes it to lack of ability. The lower expectation for the student thus seems to be confirmed, and as the dotted line in Figure 10.4 shows, the cycle continues.

"What do I get for just neatness?"
(© Bernhardt)

Guidelines

Avoiding the Negative Effects of Teacher Expectations

Use information about students from tests, cumulative folders, and other teachers very carefully.

Examples

1. Some teachers avoid reading cumulative folders at the beginning of the year.
2. Be critical and objective about the reports you hear from other teachers.

Be flexible in your use of grouping strategies.

Examples

1. Review work of students in different groups often and experiment with new groupings.
2. Use different groups for different subjects.
3. Use mixed-ability groups in cooperative exercises.

Make sure all the students are challenged.

Examples

1. Don't say, "This is easy, I know you can do it."
2. Offer a wide range of problems, and encourage all students to try a few of the harder ones for extra credit. Try to find something positive about these attempts.

Be especially careful about how you respond to low-achieving students during class discussions.

Examples

1. Give them prompts, cues, and time to answer.
2. Give ample praise for good answers.
3. Call on low achievers as often as high achievers.

Use materials that show a wide range of ethnic groups.

Examples

1. Check readers and library books. Is there ethnic diversity?
2. If few materials are available, ask students to research and create their own, based on community or family sources.

Make sure that your teaching does not reflect racial, ethnic, or sexual stereotypes or prejudice.

Examples

1. Use a checking system to be sure you call on and include all students.

2. Monitor the content of the tasks you assign. Do boys get the "hard" math problems to work at the board? Do you avoid having students with limited English give oral presentations?

Be fair in evaluation and disciplinary procedures.

Examples

1. Make sure equal offenses receive equal punishment. Find out from students in an anonymous questionnaire whether you seem to be favoring certain individuals.
2. Try to grade student work without knowing the identity of the student. Ask another teacher to give you a "second opinion" from time to time.

Communicate to all students that you believe they can learn—and mean it.

Examples

1. Return papers that do not meet standards with specific suggestions for improvements.
2. If students do not have the answers immediately, wait, probe, and then help them think through an answer.

Involve all students in learning tasks and in privileges.

Examples

1. Use some system to make sure you give each student practice in reading, speaking, and answering questions.
2. Keep track of who gets to do what job. Are some students always on the list while others seldom make it?

Monitor your nonverbal behavior.

Examples

1. Do you lean away or stand farther away from some students? Do some students get smiles when they approach your desk while others get only frowns?
2. Does your tone of voice vary with different students?
3. Do you avoid touching some students in your class?

Even when student performance does not fit expectations, the teacher may rationalize and attribute the performance to external causes outside of the student's control. For example, a teacher may assume that the low-ability student who did well on a test must have cheated and that the high-ability student who failed must have been upset that day. In both cases, behavior that seems "out of character" is dismissed. It may take many instances of supposedly uncharacteristic behavior to change the teacher's beliefs about a particular student's abilities. Thus, expectations often remain in the face of contradictory evidence (Brophy, 1982).

You may be promising yourself that you will never communicate low expectations to your students, especially now that you know about the dangers involved. Of course, not all teachers form inappropriate expectations or act on their expectations in unconstructive ways (Babad, Inbar, & Rosenthal, 1982). But avoiding the problem may be more difficult than it seems. In general, low-expectation students tend also to be the most disruptive students. (Of course, low expectations can reinforce their desire to disrupt or misbehave.) Teachers may call on these students less, wait a shorter time for their answers, and give them less praise for right answers, partly to avoid the wrong, careless, or silly answers that can cause disruptions, delays, and digressions (Cooper, 1979). The challenge is to deal with these very real threats to classroom management without communicating low expectations to some students or fostering their own low expectations of themselves. The Guidelines on page 386 may help you avoid some of these problems.

STRATEGIES TO ENCOURAGE MOTIVATION TO LEARN

The influences on students' motivation to learn in a particular situation can be summarized in three basic questions: Can I succeed at this task? Do I want to succeed at this task? What do I need to do to succeed? (Eccles & Wigfield, 1985). As reflected in these questions, we want students to have confidence in their ability, so they will approach learning with energy and enthusiasm. We want them to see the value of the tasks involved and work to learn, not just try to get the grade or get finished. We want students to believe that success will come when they apply good learning strategies instead of believing that their only option is to use self-defeating, failure-avoiding, face-saving strategies. When things get difficult, we want students to try to solve the problem and stay focused on the task, not get so worried about failure that they "freeze."

Necessary Conditions in Classrooms

Until four basic conditions are met, no motivational strategies will succeed. Once these requirements are in place, there are numerous strategies to help students gain confidence, value learning, and stay involved with the task (Brophy, 1988; Lepper, 1988).

First, the classroom must be relatively organized and free from constant interruptions and disruptions. (Chapter 11 will give you the information you need to make sure this requirement is met.) Second, the teacher must be a patient, supportive person who never punishes, criticizes, or embarrasses students for *mistakes.* Everyone in the class should see mistakes as opportunities for learning (Clifford, 1990, 1991). Third, the work must be challenging but reasonable. If work is too easy or too difficult, students will have little motivation to learn. They will focus on finishing, not on learning. Finally, the learning tasks must be worthwhile. If you ask students to do busywork, to memorize definitions they will never use, to learn the material only because it is on the test, or to repeat work they already understand, then there can be little motivation to learn (Brophy 1983; Brophy & Kher, 1986; Stipek, 1988).

Table 10.2 on page 391 summarizes the basic requirements and strategies for encouraging student motivation to learn, all of which are discussed at length in the next few pages.

Can I Do It? Building Confidence and Positive Expectations

Let's assume these conditions are met in your classroom. What's next? One of the most important factors in building expectations for success is past success. No amount of encouragement or "cheerleading" will substitute for real accomplishment. To ensure genuine progress:

1. *Begin work at the students' level* and move in small steps. The pace should be brisk, but not so fast that students have to move to the next step before they understand the previous one. This may require assigning different tasks to different students. One possibility is to have very easy and very difficult questions on every test and assignment, so all students are sure to pass some questions and fail others. This provides both success and challenge for everyone. When grades are required, make sure everyone in class has a chance to make at least a C if they work hard.

2. Make sure *learning goals* are clear, specific, and possible to reach in the near future. When long-term projects are planned, break the work into subgoals and help students feel a sense of progress toward the long-term goal. For example, a big research paper could be broken down into identifying a topic and a few basic references, doing an outline, taking notes, finding additional references and learning the form for a bibliography, writing an introduction, doing a first draft, and finally writing the polished paper. If possible, give students a range of goals at different levels of difficulty and let them choose.

3. *Stress self-comparison,* not comparison with others. Help students see the progress they are making by showing them how to use self-management strategies like those described in chapter 6. Give specific feedback and corrections. Tell students what they are doing right as well as what is wrong and *why* it is wrong. Periodically, give students a question or problem that was once hard for them but now seems easy. Point out how much they have improved. Show the connections between their efforts and their accomplishments.

4. Communicate to students that *academic ability is improvable* and specific to the task at hand. In other words, the fact that a student has trouble in algebra doesn't necessarily mean that geometry will be difficult or that he or she is a bad English student. And even when a task is hard, students can improve if they stick with it. Don't undermine your efforts to stress improvement by displaying only the 100 percent papers on the bulletin board.

5. *Model good problem solving,* especially when you yourself have to try several approaches to get a solution. Students need to see that learning is not smooth and error-free, even for the teacher.

Do I Want to Do It? Seeing the Value of Learning

Teachers can use intrinsic and extrinsic motivation strategies to help students see the value of the learning task. In this process the age of the student must be taken into consideration. For younger children, intrinsic or *interest value* is a greater determinant of motivation that attainment or utility value. Because younger students have a more immediate, concrete focus, they have trouble seeing the value of an activity that is linked to distant goals such as getting a good job—or even preparing for the next grade. Older students, on the other hand, have the cognitive ability to think more abstractly and connect what they are learning now with goals and future possibilities, so *utility value* is more important to these students (Eccles & Wigfield, 1985).

Intrinsic and Attainment Value. To establish attainment value, we must *connect the learning task with the needs of the students.* First, it must be possible for students to meet their needs for safety, belonging, and achievement in our classes. The classroom should not be a frightening or lonely place. Second, we must be sure that sexual or ethnic stereotypes do not interfere with motivation. For example, if students subscribe to rigid notions of masculinity and femininity, we must make it clear that both women and men can be high achievers in all subjects and that no subjects are the territory of only one sex. It is not "unfeminine" to be strong in mathematics, science, shop, or sports. It is not "unmasculine" to be good in literature, art, music, or French.

There are many strategies for encouraging intrinsic (interest) motivation. Several of the following are taken from Brophy (1988).

1. Tie class activities to *student interests* in sports, music, current events, pets, common problems or conflicts with family and friends, fads, television and cinema personalities, or other significant features of their lives (Schiefele, 1991). But be sure you know what you are talking about. For example, if you use a verse from the group U2 to make a point, you had better have some knowledge of the music and the group members. When possible, give students choices of research paper or reading topics so they can follow their own interests.

2. *Arouse curiosity.* Point out puzzling discrepancies between students' beliefs and the facts. For example, Stipek (1988) describes a teacher who asked her fifth-grade class if there were "people" on some of the other planets. When the students said yes, the teacher asked if people needed oxygen to breathe. Since the students had just learned this fact, they responded yes to this question also. Then the teacher told them that there is no oxygen in the atmosphere of the other

Learning to read and write is more interesting when students are personally invested in the task. Here, students are encouraged to write their own books and submit work in the "Authors' Basket."

planets. This surprising discrepancy between what the children knew about oxygen and what they believed about life on other planets led to a rousing discussion of the atmospheres of other planets, the kinds of beings that could survive in these atmospheres, and so on. A straight lecture on the atmosphere of the planets might have put the students to sleep, but this discussion led to real interest in the subject.

3. *Make the learning task fun.* Many lessons can be taught through simulations or games. For example, when my daughter was in the eighth grade, all the students in her grade spent three days playing a game her teachers had designed called ULTRA. Students were divided into groups and formed their own "countries." Each country had to choose a name, symbol, national flower, and bird. They wrote and sang a national anthem and elected government officials. The teachers allocated different resources to the countries. To get all the materials needed for the completion of assigned projects, the countries had to establish trade with one another. There was a monetary system and a stock market. Students had to work with their fellow citizens to complete cooperative learning assignments. Some countries "cheated" in their trades with other nations, and this allowed debate about international relations, trust, and war. Liz says she had fun—but she also learned how to work in a group without the teacher's supervision and gained a deeper understanding of world economics and international conflicts.

4. Make use of *novelty and familiarity.* Don't overuse a few teaching approaches or motivational strategies. We all need some variety. Varying the goal structures of tasks (cooperative, competitive, individualistic) can help, as can using different teaching media. When the material being covered in class is abstract or unfamiliar to students, try to connect it to something they know and understand. For example, talk about the size of a large area, such as the Acropolis in Athens, in terms of football fields. Brophy (1988) describes one teacher who read a brief passage from *Spartacus* to personalize the unit on slavery in the ancient world.

Instrumental Value. Sometimes it is difficult to encourage intrinsic motivation, and so teachers must rely on the utility or "instrumental" value of tasks. That is, it is important to learn many skills because they will be needed in more advanced classes or because they are necessary for life outside school.

1. When these connections are not obvious, you should *explain the connections* to your students. Jeanette Abi-Nader (1991) describes one project, the PLAN program, that makes these connections come alive for Hispanic high school students. The three major strategies used in the program to focus students' attention on their future are: (1) working with mentors and models—often PLAN graduates—who give advice about how to choose courses, budget time, take notes, and deal with cultural differences in college; (2) storytelling about the achievements of former students—sometimes the college term papers of former students are posted on PLAN bulletin boards; and (3) filling the classroom with future-oriented talk such as "When you go to college, you will encounter these situations . . ." or "You're at a parents' meeting—you want a good education for your children—and you are the ones who must speak up; that's why it is important to learn public speaking skills" (p. 548).

2. In some situations teachers need to *provide incentives and rewards* for learning. Chapter 6 details the use of extrinsic reinforcement through the application of positive and negative consequences, self-management systems, and other behavioral approaches, so we need not spend time on those topics again here. Remember, though, that giving rewards when students are already interested in the activity may undermine intrinsic motivation. As Stipek (1988) has noted, if teachers began testing and grading students on their memory of the television programs they watched the previous evening, even television viewing would lose some of its intrinsic appeal.

What Do I Need to Do to Succeed? Staying Focused on the Task

When students encounter difficulties, as they must if they are working at a challenging level, they need to keep their attention on the task. If the focus shifts to worries about performance, fear of failure, or concern with "looking smart," then motivation to learn is lost. Here are some ideas for keeping the focus on learning.

1. Give students frequent *opportunities to respond* through questions and answers, short assignments, or demonstrations of skills. Make sure

---

TABLE 10.2 Strategies to Encourage Motivation to Learn

Fulfill basic requirements (p. 387)
- Provide an organized class environment
- Be a supportive teacher
- Assign challenging work, but not too difficult
- Make tasks worthwhile

Build confidence and positive expectations (p. 388)
- Begin work at the students' level
- Make learning goals clear, specific, and attainable
- Stress self-comparison, not competition
- Communicate that academic ability is improvable
- Model good problem solving

Show the value of learning (p. 389)
- Connect the learning task to the needs of the students

- Tie class activities to the students' interests
- Arouse curiosity
- Make the learning task fun
- Make use of novelty and familiarity
- Explain connections between present learning and later life
- Provide incentives and rewards, if needed

Help students stay focused on the task (p. 391)
- Give students frequent opportunities to respond
- Provide opportunities for students to create a finished product
- Avoid heavy emphasis on grading
- Reduce task risk without oversimplifying the task
- Model motivation to learn
- Teach learning tactics

This table refers to the entire Strategies to Encourage Motivation section of the text.

you check the students' answers so you can correct problems quickly. You don't want students to practice errors too long. Computer learning programs give students the immediate feedback they need to correct errors before they become habits.

2. When possible, have students *create a finished product.* They will be more persistent and focused on the task when the end is in sight. We all have experienced the power of the need for closure. For example, I often begin a house-painting project thinking I will work for just an hour and find myself still painting hours later because I want to see the finished product.

3. *Avoid a heavy emphasis on grades and competition.* You will force students to be ego-involved rather than task-involved. Anxious students are especially hard hit by highly competitive evaluation.

FIGURE 10.5   Motivational Strategies of Beginning Teachers   First-year teachers tend to rely on reward and punishment strategies to motivate students, even though these are not necessarily the most effective approaches.

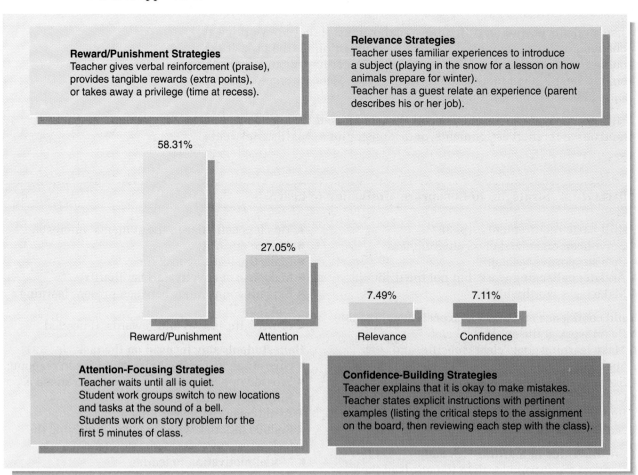

Source: Adapted from T. J. Newby (1991), Classroom motivation: Strategies of first-year teachers. *Journal of Educational Psychology,* *83,* 195–200. Copyright 1991 by the American Psychological Association. Reprinted by permission.

4. *Reduce task risk without oversimplifying the task.* When tasks are risky (failure is likely and the consequences of failing are grave), student motivation suffers. For difficult, complex, or ambiguous tasks, provide students with plenty of time, support, resources, help, and the chance to revise or improve work.

5. *Model motivation to learn* for your students. Talk about your interest in the subject and how you deal with difficult learning problems.

6. *Teach the particular learning tactics* that students will need to master the material being studied. Show students how to learn and remember so they won't be forced to fall back on self-defeating strategies or rote memory.

Table 10.2 on page 391 summarizes these ideas for helping students have confidence in their abilities, value learning, and stay focused on the right task.

How Do Beginning Teachers Motivate Students?

Timothy Newby (1991) trained classroom observers to record the motivational strategies of 30 first-year elementary-school teachers over a 16-week period. He found that the teachers used about 10 different strategies per hour—half were rewards and punishments. Figure 10.5 gives examples of the four types of strategies used by these beginning teachers. As you can see, commenting on the relevance of the lessons and building student confidence each accounted for about 7 percent of strategies, focusing student attention made up 27 percent, and rewards and punishments accounted for 58 percent.

Another interesting finding is that commenting on relevance was positively correlated with students being on task, while using rewards/punishments was negatively correlated. So beginning teachers tended to use less effective strategies more often. It may be that these new teachers turned to extrinsic reinforcement (rewards and punishments) only when it became difficult to keep the students interested in their work. Even if this is true, the study still suggests that tying work to students' interests and emphasizing relevance can encourage motivation.

SUMMARY

MOTIVATION TO LEARN

Student motivation to learn is both a trait and a state. It involves taking academic work seriously, trying to get the most from it, and applying appropriate learning strategies in the process. Students who are motivated to learn set learning rather than performance goals and are task-involved rather than ego-involved.

ACADEMIC TASKS

The tasks that teachers set affect motivation. Tasks that are difficult and require critical thinking are risky and ambiguous. Students often seek to lower the risk and ambiguity in tasks through negotiation with the teacher.

Tasks can have attainment, intrinsic, or utility value for students. Attainment value is the importance of succeeding to the student. Intrinsic value is the enjoyment the students get from the task. Utility value is determined by how much the task contributes to reaching short-term or, long-term goals.

CLASS STRUCTURE AND MOTIVATION

The evaluative climate of the class—that is, the relative emphasis on competition and grading—influences motivation. The more competitive the grading, the more students set performance goals and focus on "looking competent"; that is, the more they are ego-involved.

Cooperative learning arrangements can encourage motivation and increase learning, especially for low-achieving students. There are a number of approaches, including STAD, TGT, CIRC, and reciprocal questioning. Many cooperative learning strategies are designed to allow each student equal access to success, social support for learning, and individual accountability for final performance.

TEACHER EXPECTATIONS

Several studies have pointed to the important role teachers' expectations play in motivating students. Some teachers tend to treat students differently, depending on their own views of how well the students are likely to do. Students may behave accordingly, fulfilling teachers' predictions or staying at an expected level of achievement.

STRATEGIES TO ENCOURAGE MOTIVATION TO LEARN

Strategies to encourage motivation to learn should help students feel confidence in their abilities to improve, value the tasks of learning, and stay involved in the process without being threatened by fear of failure.

KEY TERMS AND CONCEPTS

WHAT WOULD YOU DO?

PRESCHOOL AND KINDERGARTEN

How would you create an environment that communicates the value of learning to young children without becoming too directive or academic in your teaching?

ELEMENTARY AND MIDDLE SCHOOL

You are talking to the parents of one of your lower-achieving students. You really like the student, but he seems not to apply himself to the work. Suddenly the boy's mother says, "We think our son is doing badly in your class because you don't like him. You just seem to expect him to fail!" What would you do?

There are students from four different ethnic groups in your class. Each group seems to stick together, never making friends with students from the other groups. How would you structure the class to help the students feel more comfortable together?

JUNIOR HIGH AND HIGH SCHOOL

You want to prepare your senior classes for the kind of independent work they will face in college, so you assign a research project. As soon as you make the assignment, the questions begin: "How many sources?" "How many pages?" "What exactly do you mean by 'support your conclusions with evidence'?" "What kind of evidence?" How do you make the assignment clear without turning it into a "spoon feeding"?

How could you use cooperative learning strategies with ninth-grade students?

COOPERATIVE LEARNING ACTIVITY

With four or five other members of your educational psychology class, develop a self-monitoring procedure for identifying the expectations that you communicate to your students.

MAKING COOPERATIVE LEARNING WORK

You have decided to use small-group cooperative learning in your classroom, but your students do not seem to be able to help each other well. They rely on you for everything. What would you do to help them benefit more from cooperative learning?

GROUP SKILLS

Students are often asked to work in small groups without learning the skills necessary to be successful in those situations. Before my students work in groups, they are given a summary of their role. This summary includes:

1. *"Needs to . . ."*—This area defines the role, the responsibilities that need to be carried out by the student.
2. *"Sounds like . . ."*—This section gives examples of words or phrases that should be used by the student serving in this role.
3. *"Looks like . . ."*—This part includes reminders of important gestures, including eye contact, leaning forward to show interest, and other ways to show other group members that you are interested and involved.

Group evaluation is based on how well individual members are able to implement all three areas in their role. The role description provides key words for students who are more reluctant to be involved and reinforces all group members for ensuring that everyone is involved.

The last technique that has worked successfully in my classroom is called "The Fishbowl Technique." A small group is placed in the middle of the classroom. They are given an activity that includes role descriptions. The other members of the class are divided into three or four groups and are given a specific group skill to evaluate. They closely watch the small group, looking for an example of the designated skill. They might be looking for "specific examples when someone encouraged another member to speak" or "specific examples of statements that moved the group closer to a solution."

This activity provides immediate positive feedback to the small group. It also serves as a model for successful group work, including the importance of total member involvement and the benefit of high-quality discussions.

Lawrence Leebens, *Curriculum Resource Coordinator*
Forest Hills Elementary School, Eden Prairie, Minnesota

FOCUSING ON LEARNING

What strategies have you found successful in helping your students to focus on learning rather than on the grade they will receive?

MODEL LEARNING'S IMPORTANCE

Learning is a lifelong process. My school is a community school for lifelong learners. The entire concept of the school centers around learning, not grades.

Within my classroom, I am very open with the students about my deficiencies, but I tell them that I am still learning and achieving. I model by using a dictionary to compensate for my poor spelling and I ask a proofreader to help me in my writing. I have even gone as far as joining beginning band. I attempted to play the flute and failed miserably. The students saw that I was discouraged, but they also saw me try again. I am now trying my hand at the electric piano.

Julie A. Addison, *Sixth-Grade Teacher*
Roxborough Elementary School, Littleton, Colorado

TAKE RESPONSIBILITY FOR LEARNING

We talk a lot in my classroom about the responsibility for learning being with the students. I stress that making mistakes is the way we learn, and that a low grade may be the chance for a great learning experience. We then have the opportunity to go over the material again and really concentrate on what we're learning.

We discuss the importance of everyone doing their best, and that we're all individuals. Therefore, what's "best" for one person may not be "best" for another. One person's best job may earn an A while another person's best may earn a C.

Building self-esteem is one of the greatest ways to encourage students to concentrate on learning for learning's sake instead of worrying about the grade they get. Another strategy I use is cooperative learning and other group or partner work. When children are working together, they tend to enjoy themselves more and be less concerned about a letter grade.

Deborah H. Platt, *Third-Grade Teacher*
Eugene Field Elementary School, Mitchell, South Dakota

NON-GRADED PRACTICE

I set up a series of units in which the students select a required number of activities to complete. No grades are given, but completion of each unit is required before a student receives an "expert" award. Topics are chosen by the students and have included sign language, Australia, whales, Mexico, bats, and Greenland. Activities have included cooperative learning activities, independent and paired reading, construction of picture books, guest lecturers, movies, crafts, map skills, brainstorming, writing summaries, and cooking experiences. I find the students to be highly motivated, and we all have fun.

Joanne S. Groseclose, *Virginia 1991 Teacher of the Year*
Marion Intermediate School, Marion, Virginia

HIGH EXPECTATIONS

One of the strategies that I employ to help my students concentrate on learning rather than on the grade they will receive is to hold very high expectations of each pupil. I tell students that they all can be successful and that their success is based on a step-by-step process in which skills are developed. Moreover, students who get A's are not endowed with a magical gift, but are often successful because of the assiduity they put into their studies. In class I focus on each pupil's effort in various ways, such as writing comments on papers pointing out specific areas where their diligence was reflected to make them aware that it was the hard work channeled into their studies that has been shown, not luck. This is an integral part of the process to deemphasize grades and call attention to learning so that students persevere even though they may not be as successful in getting the grade desired. Additionally, grading systems structured to reflect individual effort are very important.

Phyllis N. Marshall, *Seventh-Grade Teacher*
Hoech Middle School, St. Ann, Missouri

CONTROLLING TEACHER BIAS

It is natural and inevitable for teachers to form impressions of their students. How do you control your biases toward favorite students and toward students for whom you have little regard or low expectations?

FOCUS ON GOOD QUALITIES

Every child is special, regardless of faults. All parents trust teachers with their children's self-esteem. As an educator, part of my job is to find a good quality in each student in my class and focus on that quality. As a teacher, I also need to ignore the forewarnings from previous teachers and form my own opinions. Too often children are labeled as "good" or "bad." Many times a student reacts to different teachers in very different ways. I have had "warnings" about students in the past only to find out that we get along just fine and respect each other, and there isn't a behavior problem.

Candice J. Gallagher, *Fourth-Grade Teacher*
Fredericktown Intermediate School, Fredericktown, Ohio

11 CLASSROOM MANAGEMENT AND COMMUNICATION

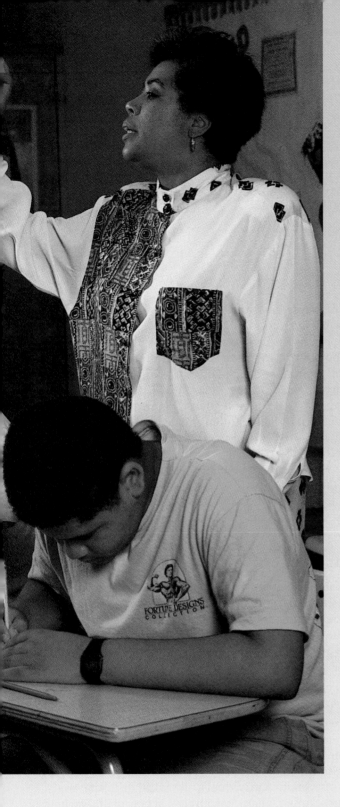

Classroom management is certainly one of the main concerns of teachers, particularly beginning teachers, as well as of administrators and parents. Even students expect teachers to be effective managers. When class time is consumed by management problems, students are uncomfortable, and little real learning takes place.

The very nature of classes, teaching, and students makes good management a critical ingredient of success; we will look at why this is true. Next we will turn to the goals of classroom management. Successful managers create more time for learning, involve more students, and help students to become self-managing. To accomplish these goals, teachers must establish a good working atmosphere.

Once established, a positive working environment must be maintained throughout the year. One of the best ways to do this is to try to prevent problems from occurring at all. But when problems arise—as they always do—an effective response is important. What will you do when students challenge you openly in class, when one student asks your advice on a difficult personal problem, or when another withdraws from all participation? We will examine the ways that teachers can communicate effectively with their students in these and many other situations.

By the time you have finished this chapter, you should be able to do the following:

- Describe the special managerial demands of classrooms and relate these demands to students of different ages.

- Create a list of rules and procedures for a class.

- Develop a plan for organizing your first week of teaching.

- Explain Kounin's suggestions for preventing management problems.

- Describe how you might respond to a student who seldom completes work.

- Describe how and when you might use group consequences, token economies, and contingency contracts to enhance classroom management.

- Suggest two different approaches for dealing with a conflict between teacher and student or between two students.

WHAT DO YOU THINK?

When you imagine facing 25 or 30 students on the first day of class, what are your concerns? List the management problems that you find most difficult. What are your strengths in dealing with classroom management problems?

CLASSROOMS NEED MANAGERS

In 1985 the Gallup organization conducted the 17th annual Gallup Poll of the public's attitude toward the public schools. For the 16th time in those 17 years, "lack of proper discipline" was named as the number one problem facing the schools. From 1986 to 1991 "use of drugs" took over first place on the list of problems, but "lack of discipline" was not far behind as the number two concern. In the 1991 poll "drug use" and "lack of discipline" were virtually tied for first place (Elam, Rose, & Gallup, 1991). In a survey of teachers, chronic student misbehavior was noted as the main source of job stress by 58 percent of respondents (Feitler & Tokar, 1982). The behaviors that most teachers find troubling are not acts of violence but the more common problems of class disruption, incomplete work, nonparticipation, cheating, repeated tardiness, and absences. In order to understand the causes and consequences of these problems, let's take a closer look at the classroom itself.

The Ecology of Classrooms

The word *ecology* is usually associated with nature. But classrooms are ecological systems, too. The environment of the classroom and the inhabitants of that environment—students and teachers—are constantly interacting. Each aspect of the system affects all others. The characteristics of classrooms, the tasks of teaching, and the needs of students all influence classroom management.

Characteristics of Classrooms. Classes are particular kinds of environments. They have "distinctive properties affecting participants regardless of how students are organized for learning or what educational philosophy the teacher espouses" (Doyle, 1986, p. 394). Let's look at six of these features described by Doyle.

Classrooms are *multidimensional.* They are crowded with people, tasks, and time pressures. Many individuals, all with differing goals, preferences, and abilities, must share resources, accomplish various tasks, use and reuse materials without losing them, move in and out of the room, keep track of what is happening, and so on. In addition, actions can have multiple effects. Calling on low-ability students may encourage their participation and thinking but may slow the discussion and lead to management problems if the students cannot answer.

A related feature is *simultaneity.* Everything happens at once. A teacher explaining a concept must also notice if students are following the explanation, decide whether two whispering youngsters should be ignored or stopped, determine if there is enough time to start the next topic, and decide who should answer the question that Jill just asked.

The next characteristic, *immediacy,* has to do with the fast pace of classroom life. Teachers have literally hundreds of exchanges with students during a single day.

In this rapid-fire existence, events are quite *unpredictable.* Even when plans are carefully made, the overhead projector is in place, and the handouts are ready, the lesson can still be interrupted by a burned-out bulb in the projector, a child who suddenly becomes ill, or a loud, angry discussion right outside the classroom window.

The way the teacher handles these unexpected intrusions is seen and judged by all, because classrooms are *public.* Students are always noticing if the teacher is being "fair." Is there favoritism? What happens when a rule is broken?

Finally, classrooms have *histories.* The meaning of a particular teacher's or student's actions depends in part on what has happened before. The 15th time a student arrives late requires a different response from the teacher than the first late arrival. In addition, the history of the first few weeks of school affects life in the class all year.

So much is happening at once in a typical classroom that teachers, especially beginning teachers, may feel distracted or overwhelmed.

The Basic Task: Gain Their Cooperation. No productive activity can take place in a group without the cooperation of all members. This obviously applies to classrooms. Even if some students don't participate, they must allow others to do so. (You have probably seen one or two students bring an entire class to a halt.) So the basic management task for teachers is to achieve order by gaining and maintaining student cooperation in class activities (Doyle, 1986). Given the multidimensional, simultaneous, immediate, unpredictable, public, and historical nature of classrooms, this is quite a challenge.

Gaining student cooperation means much more than dealing effectively with misbehavior. It means planning activities, having materials ready, making appropriate behavioral and academic demands on students, giving clear signals to students, accomplishing transitions smoothly, foreseeing problems and stopping them before they start, selecting and sequencing activities so that order and flow are maintained—and much more. Also, different activities require different managerial skills. For example, a new or complicated activity may be a greater threat to classroom order than a familiar or simple activity.

Age-Related Needs. Another necessary consideration is the age-related needs of students. Obviously, gaining the cooperation of kindergarteners is not the same task as gaining the cooperation of high school seniors. Jere Brophy and Carolyn Evertson (1978) have identified four general stages of classroom management, defined by age-related needs. Let's look briefly at each.

During kindergarten and the first few years of elementary school, children are learning how to go to school. They are being socialized into a new role. Direct teaching of classroom rules and procedures is

Students in this class appear to understand the rules for participating in this activity—raise your hand before speaking. It is impressive that they continue to follow the rules, even when they are clustered around the teacher and must be tempted to call out.

Classroom Management
Techniques used to maintain a healthy learning environment, relatively free of behavior problems.

important during this stage. Little learning will take place until the children master these basics. Luckily, most children this age are willing to accept adults as authority figures—to follow instructions and try to please.

Children in the middle elementary years are usually familiar with the student role, even if they are not always perfect examples of it. Many school and classroom routines have become relatively automatic. Specific new rules and procedures for a particular activity may have to be taught directly, however. And you may hear the familiar refrain, "My teacher last year didn't do it that way!" Still, at this stage you will spend more time monitoring and maintaining the management system than teaching it directly.

Toward the end of elementary school and the beginning of high school, friendships and status within peer groups take on tremendous importance. Pleasing the teacher may be replaced by pleasing peers. Some students begin to test and defy authority. The management challenges at this stage are to deal productively with these disruptions and to motivate students who are becoming less concerned with teachers' opinions and more interested in their social lives.

By the end of high school, the focus of most students returns to academics. By this time, unfortunately, many of the students with the most overwhelming behavioral problems have dropped out. Classroom management at this stage involves managing the curriculum, fitting academic material to students' interests and abilities, and helping students become more self-managing in their learning. The first few classes each semester may be devoted to teaching particular procedures for using materials and equipment or for keeping track of and submitting assignments. But most students know what is expected.

The Goals of Classroom Management

The aim of **classroom management** is to maintain a positive, productive learning environment. But order for its own sake is an empty goal. As we discussed in chapter 6, it is unethical to use class management techniques simply to keep students docile and quiet. What, then, is the point of working so hard to manage classrooms? There are at least three reasons why management is important.

More Time for Learning. As a child, I once used a stopwatch to time the commercials during a TV quiz show. I was amazed to find that half of the program was devoted to commercials. Actually, very little quizzing took place. If you used a similar approach in classrooms, timing all the different activities throughout the day, you might be surprised by how little actual teaching takes place. Many minutes each day are lost through interruptions, disruptions, late starts, and rough transitions. Sometimes the causes are unavoidable, as with fire drills, but often they could be prevented (Karweit, 1989; Karweit & Slavin, 1981).

Obviously, students will learn only the material they have a chance to learn. If a class does not reach the last three chapters in a textbook, you can't expect the students to learn the information in those chapters.

Almost every study examining time and opportunity to learn has found a significant relationship between amount of content covered and student learning (Berliner, 1988). In fact, the correlations between content covered and student learning are usually larger than the correlations between specific teacher behaviors and student learning (Rosenshine, 1979). So one important goal of classroom management is to expand the sheer number of minutes available for learning. This is sometimes called **allocated time.**

But simply making more time for learning will not automatically lead to achievement. To be valuable, time must be used effectively. As you saw in the chapters on cognitive learning, the way students process information is a central factor in what they learn and remember. Basically, students will learn what they practice and what they pay attention to (Doyle, 1983). Time spent actively attending to specific learning tasks is often called **engaged time,** or sometimes **time on task.**

Again, however, just being engaged doesn't guarantee learning. Students may be engaged but be struggling with such difficult material that they learn very little. When students are working with a high rate of success—really learning and understanding—we call the time spent **academic learning time.** A second goal of class management is to increase *academic learning time* by keeping students actively engaged in worthwhile, appropriate learning activities. Figure 11.1 on page 404, taken from Weinstein and Mignano (1993), shows how the 1,000+ hours of time mandated for school in most states can become only about 333 hours of quality academic learning time for a typical student.

Access to Learning. Each classroom activity has its own rules for participation. Sometimes these rules are clearly stated by the teacher, but often they are implicit and unstated. Teacher and students may not even be aware that they are following different rules for different activities (Berliner, 1983). And the differences are sometimes quite subtle. For example, in a reading group students may have to raise their hands to make a comment, but in a show-and-tell circle in the same class they may simply have to catch the teacher's eye.

As we saw in chapter 5, the rules defining who can talk; what they can talk about; and when, to whom, and how long they can talk are often called **participation structures.** In order to participate successfully in a given activity, students must understand the participation structure. Some students, however, seem to come to school less able to participate than others. The participation structures they learn at home in interactions with siblings, parents, and other adults do not match the participation structures of school activities (Tharp, 1989). But teachers are not necessarily aware of this conflict. Instead the teachers see that a child doesn't quite fit in, always seems to say the wrong thing at the wrong time, or is very reluctant to participate, and they are not sure why.

What can we conclude? In order to involve all your students in smoothly run activities, you must make sure that everyone knows how to participate in each specific activity. The key is awareness. What are your rules and expectations? Are they understandable, given your

Allocated Time Time set aside for learning.

Engaged Time Time spent actively learning.

Time on Task Time spent actively engaged in the learning task at hand.

Academic Learning Time Time when students are actually succeeding at the learning task.

Participation Structures Rules defining how to participate in different activities.

FIGURE 11.1 **Who Knows Where the Time Goes?** The over 1,000 hours per year of instruction mandated by most states can represent only 300 or 400 hours of quality academic learning time.

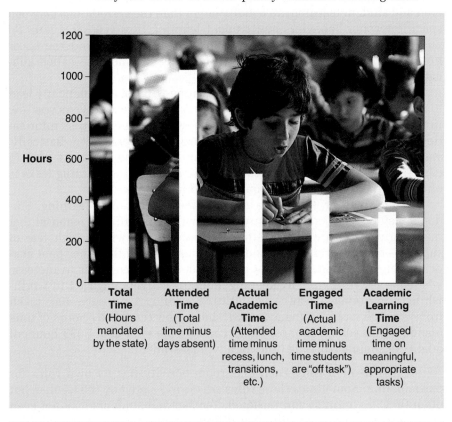

Source: Adapted by permission of the authors from C. Weinstein and A. Mignano (1993), *Organizing the elementary school classroom: Lessons from Research and Practice.* New York: McGraw-Hill.

students' cultural backgrounds and home experiences? What unspoken rules or values may be operating? Are you *clear and consistent* in signaling your students about how to participate? To reach the second goal of good classroom management—giving all students access to learning—you must make sure everyone knows *how* to participate in class activities.

Self-Management
Management of your own behavior and acceptance of responsibility for your own actions.

Management for Self-Management. The third goal of any management system is to help students become better able to manage themselves. Encouraging **self-management** requires extra time. Teaching students how to take responsibility instead of taking care of everything yourself may seem inefficient, but the investment can be well worth the effort. When elementary and secondary teachers have very effective class management systems but neglect to set student self-management as a goal, their students often find that they have trouble working independently after they graduate from these "well-managed" classes.

PLANNING FOR GOOD MANAGEMENT

In making plans for your class, much of what you have already learned in this book should prove helpful. You know, for example, that problems are prevented when individual variations, such as those discussed in chapters 2, 3, 4, and 5, are taken into account in instructional planning. Sometimes students become disruptive because the work assigned is not at their level. Students who are bored by lessons well below their ability levels may also be interested in finding more exciting activities to fill their time.

In one sense, teachers are preventing discipline problems whenever they make an effort to motivate students. A student involved in mastering course objectives is usually not involved in a clash with the teacher or other students at the same time. All plans for motivating students are steps toward preventing problems.

Some Research Results

What else can teachers do to be good managers? For several years, educational psychologists at the University of Texas at Austin studied classroom management quite thoroughly (Emmer, Evertson, & Anderson, 1980; Emmer, Evertson, Sanford, Clements, & Worsham, 1989; Evertson, 1988; Evertson, Emmer, Clements, Sanford, & Worsham, 1989). Their general approach was to visit a large number of classrooms, making intensive observations the first weeks of school and less-frequent visits later in the year. After several months there were dramatic differences among the classes. Some had very few management problems, while others had many. The most and least effective teachers were identified on the basis of the behavior of their classes later in the year.

Next, the researchers looked at their observation records of the first weeks of class to see how the effective teachers got started. Other comparisons were made between the teachers who ultimately had well-behaved, high-achieving classes and those whose classes were fraught with problems. On the basis of these comparisons, management principles were developed. The researchers then taught these principles to a new group of teachers. The results were quite positive. Teachers who applied the principles had fewer problems; their students spent more time working and less time disrupting; and achievement was higher.

The findings of these studies formed the basis for two books on classroom management (Emmer et al., 1989; Evertson et al., 1989). Many of the ideas in the following pages are taken from these books.

Rules and Procedures Required

At the elementary-school level, teachers must lead 20 to 30 students of varying abilities through many different activities each day. Without efficient rules and procedures, a great deal of time is wasted answering the same question over and over. "My pencil broke. How can I do my math?" "I'm finished with my story. What should I do now?" "Steven hit me!" "I left my homework in my locker."

At the secondary-school level, teachers must deal daily with over 100 students who use dozens of materials and often change rooms for each class. Secondary-school students are also more likely to challenge teachers' authority. The effective managers studied by Emmer, Evertson, and their colleagues had planned procedures and rules for coping with these situations.

Procedures. How will materials and assignments be distributed and collected? Under what conditions can students leave the room? How do students respond to the bell at the beginning and end of a period? How will grades be determined? What are the special routines for handling equipment and supplies in science, art, or vocational classes? **Procedures** describe how activities are accomplished in classrooms, but they are seldom written down; they are simply the ways of getting things done in class. Carol Weinstein and Andy Mignano (1993) suggest that teachers establish procedures to cover the following areas:

1. *Administrative routines,* such as taking attendance.
2. *Student movement,* such as entering and leaving the room or going to the rest room.
3. *Housekeeping,* such as watering plants or storing personal items.
4. *Routines for accomplishing lessons,* such as how to collect assignments or return homework.
5. *Interactions between teacher and student,* such as how to get the teacher's attention when help is needed.
6. *Talk among students,* such as giving help or socializing.

You might use these six areas as a frame for planning your class procedures and routines. The Guidelines should help you as you plan.

Rules. **Rules** specify expected and forbidden actions in the class. They are the dos and don'ts of classroom life. Unlike procedures, rules are often written down and posted. In establishing rules, you should consider what kind of atmosphere you want to create. What student behaviors will help you teach effectively? What limits do the students need to guide their behavior? The rules you set should be consistent with school rules and also in keeping with *principles of learning.* For example, we know from the research on small-group learning that students benefit when they explain work to peers. They learn as they teach. A rule that forbids students to help each other may be inconsistent with good learning principles. Or a rule that says, "No erasures when writing" may make students focus more on preventing mistakes than on communicating clearly in their writing (Weinstein & Mignano, 1993).

Having a few general rules that cover many specifics is better than listing all the dos and don'ts. But if specific actions are forbidden, such as chewing gum in class or smoking in the rest rooms, then a rule should make this clear.

Rules for Elementary School. Evertson and her colleagues (1989) give five examples of general rules for elementary-school classes.

1. *Be polite and helpful.* This applies to behavior toward adults (including substitute teachers) and children. Examples of polite behavior

Procedures Prescribed steps for an activity.

Rules Statements specifying expected and forbidden behaviors; dos and don'ts.

Guidelines

Establishing Class Procedures

Determine procedures for student upkeep of desks, classroom equipment, and other facilities.

Examples

1. Some teachers set aside a cleanup time each day or once a week in self-contained classes.
2. You might demonstrate and have students practice how to push chairs under the desk, take and return materials stored on shelves, sharpen pencils, use the sink or water fountain, assemble lab equipment, and so on.
3. In some classes a rotating monitor is in charge of equipment or materials.

Decide how students will be expected to enter and leave the room.

Examples

1. How will students know what they should do as soon as they enter the room? Some teachers have a standard assignment ("Have your homework out and be checking it over").
2. Under what conditions can students leave the room? When do they need permission?
3. If students are late, how do they gain admission to the room?
4. Many teachers require students to be in their seats and quiet before they can leave at the end of class. The teacher, not the bell, dismisses class.

Establish a signal and teach it to your students.

Examples

1. In the classroom, some teachers flick the lights, sound a chord on a piano or recorder, move to the podium and stare silently at the class, use a phrase like "Eyes, please," take out their grade books, or move to the front of the class.

2. In the halls, a raised hand, one clap, or some other signal may mean "Stop."
3. On the playground, a raised hand or whistle may mean "Line up."

Set procedures for student participation in class.

Examples

1. Will you have students raise their hands for permission to speak or simply require that they wait until the speaker has finished?
2. How will you signal that you want everyone to respond at once? Some teachers raise a cupped hand to their ear. Others preface the question with "Everyone. . . ."
3. Make sure you are clear about differences in procedures for different activities: reading group, learning center, discussion, teacher presentation, seatwork, film, peer learning group, library, and so forth.
4. How many students at a time can be at the pencil sharpener, teacher's desk, learning center, sink, bookshelves, reading corner, or bathroom?

Determine how you will communicate, collect, and return assignments.

Examples

1. Some teachers reserve a particular corner of the board for listing assignments. Others write assignments in colored chalk. For younger students it may be better to prepare assignment sheets or folders, color-coding them for math workbook, reading packet, and science kit.
2. Some teachers collect assignments in a box or bin; others have a student collect work so they can introduce the next activity.

include waiting your turn, saying "please" and "thank you," and not fighting or calling names.
2. *Respect other people's property.* This might include picking up litter; returning library books; not marking on walls, desks, or buses; and getting permission before using other people's things.
3. *Listen quietly while others are speaking.* This applies to the teacher and other students, in large-class lessons or small-group discussions.

"This class will stimulate your ideas and thoughts. And remember — no talking."

How does this teacher's "no talking" rule fit her goal of stimulating thinking? (By permission of James Warren.)

4. *Do not hit, shove, or hurt others.* Make sure you give clear explanations of what you mean by hurt. Does this apply to hurt feelings as well as hurt bodies?
5. *Obey all school rules.* This reminds students that all school rules apply in your classroom. Then students cannot claim, for example, that they thought it was okay to chew gum or listen to a radio in your class, even though these are against school rules, "because you never made a rule against it for us."

Whatever the rule, students need to be taught the behaviors that the rule includes and excludes. Examples, practice, and discussion will be required before learning is complete.

As you've seen, different activities often require different rules. This can be confusing for elementary students until they have thoroughly learned all the rules. To prevent confusion, you might consider making signs that list the rules for each activity. Then you can post the appropriate sign before the activity as a reminder. This provides clear and consistent cues about participation structures so all students, not just the "well-behaved," know what is expected. Of course, these rules must be explained and discussed before the signs can have their full effect.

Rules for Secondary School. Emmer and colleagues (1989) suggest six examples of rules for secondary students:

1. *Bring all needed materials to class.* The teacher must specify type of pen, pencil, paper, notebook, texts, and so on.
2. *Be in your seat and ready to work when the bell rings.* Many teachers combine this rule with a standard beginning procedure for the class,

such as a warm-up exercise on the board or a requirement that students have paper with a proper heading ready when the bell rings.

3. *Respect and be polite to everyone.* This covers fighting, verbal abuse, and general troublemaking.

4. *Respect other people's property.* This means property belonging to the school, the teacher, or other students.

5. *Listen and stay seated while someone else is speaking.* This applies when the teacher or other students are talking.

6. *Obey all school rules.* As with the elementary class rules, this covers many behaviors and situations, so you do not have to repeat every school rule for your class. It also reminds the students that you will be monitoring them inside and outside your class. Make sure you know all the school rules. Some secondary students are very adept at convincing teachers that their misbehavior "really isn't against the rules."

Consequences. As soon as you decide on your rules and procedures, you must consider what you will do when a student breaks a rule or does not follow a procedure. It is too late to make this decision after the rule has been broken. For many infractions, the logical consequence is having

---

TABLE 11.1 Seven Categories of Penalties for Students

1. *Expressions of disappointment* If students like and respect their teacher, then a serious, sorrowful expression of disappointment may cause students to stop and think about their behavior.

2. *Loss of privileges* Students can lose free time. If they have not completed homework, for example, they can be required to do it during a free period or recess.

3. *Exclusion from the group* Students who distract their peers or fail to cooperate can be separated from the group until they are ready to cooperate. Some teachers give a student a pass for 10 or 15 minutes. The student must go to another class or study hall where the other students and teachers ignore the offending student for that time.

4. *Written reflections on the problem* Students can write in journals, write essays about what they did and how it affected others, or write letters of apology—if this is appropriate. Another possibility is to ask students to describe objectively what they did; then the teacher and the student can sign and date this statement. These records

are available if parents or administrators need evidence of the students' behavior.

5. *Detentions* Detentions can be very brief meetings after school, during a free period, or at lunch. The main purpose is to talk about what has happened. (In high school, detentions are often used as punishments; suspensions and expulsions are available as more extreme measures.)

6. *Visits to the principal's office* Expert teachers tend to use this penalty rarely, but they do use it when the situation warrants. Some schools require students to be sent to the office for certain offenses, such as fighting. If you tell a student to go to the office and the student refuses, you might send a message to the office saying the student has been sent. Then the student has the choice of either going to the office or facing the principal's penalty for "disappearing" on the way.

7. *Contact with parents* If problems become a repeated pattern, most teachers contact the student's family. This is done to seek support for helping the student, not to blame the parents or punish the student.

Source: Adapted by permission of the authors from C. Weinstein and A. Mignano (1993), *Organizing the elementary classroom: Lessons from Research and Practice.* New York: McGraw-Hill.

to go back and "do it right." Students who run in the hall may have to return to where they started and walk properly. Incomplete papers can be redone. Materials left out should be put back. Sometimes consequences are more complicated. In their case studies of four expert elementary-school teachers, Weinstein and Mignano (1993) found that the teachers' negative consequences fell into seven categories, as shown in Table 11.1 on page 409.

In the first chapter I described Ken, an expert teacher who worked with his students to establish a students' and teacher's "Bill of Rights" instead of defining rules. These "rights" cover most situations that might require a "rule" and help the students move toward the goal of becoming self-managing. The rights for one recent year's class are listed in Table 11.2. The main point here is that decisions about penalties (and rewards)

TABLE 11.2 A Bill of Rights for Students and Teachers

Students' Bill of Rights

Students in this class have the following rights:

To whisper when the teacher isn't talking or asking for silence.
To celebrate authorship or other work at least once a month.
To exercise outside on days there is no physical education class.
To have 2-minute breaks.
To have healthy snacks during snack time.
To participate in choosing a table.
To have privacy. No one may touch anyone else's possessions
  without permission.
To be comfortable.
To chew gum without blowing bubbles or making a mess.
To make choices about the day's schedule.
To have free work time.
To work with partners.
To talk to the class without anyone else talking.
To work without being disturbed.

Teacher's Bill of Rights

The teacher has the following rights:

To talk without anyone else talking, or moving about, or disturbing
  the class.
To work without being disturbed.
To have everyone's attention while giving directions.
To punish someone who is not cooperating.
To send someone out of the group, or room, or to the office.

Source: Adapted by permission of the authors from C. Weinstein and A. Mignano (1993), *Organizing the elementary classroom: Lessons from Research and Practice.* New York: McGraw-Hill.

must be made early on, so students know before they break a rule or use the wrong procedure what this will mean for them. I encourage my student teachers to get a copy of the school rules and their cooperating teacher's rules, then plan their own.

Getting Started: The First Weeks of Class

Having a plan and knowing how you will respond to problems is a first step toward having a well-managed class—which brings us to another very important question. What do effective teachers really do during those first critical days and weeks? One study carefully analyzed the first weeks' activities of effective and ineffective elementary teachers and found striking differences (Emmer, Evertson, & Anderson, 1980).

Effective Managers for Elementary Students. In the effective teachers' classrooms, the very first day was well organized. Name tags were ready. There was something interesting for each child to do right away. Materials were set up. The teachers had planned carefully to avoid any last-minute tasks that might take them away from their students. These teachers dealt with the children's pressing concerns first. "Where do I put my things? How do I pronounce my teacher's name? How do I get the teacher's attention? Can I whisper to my neighbor? Where is the bathroom?" The effective teachers had a workable, easily understood set of rules and taught the students the most important rules right away. They taught the rules like any other subject, with lots of explanation, examples, and practice.

Throughout the first weeks, the effective managers continued to spend quite a bit of time teaching rules and procedures. Some used

This teacher is preventing problems by posting the class rules.

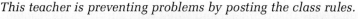

guided practice to teach procedures; others used rewards to shape behavior. Most taught students to respond to a bell or some other signal to gain their attention. These teachers worked with the class as a whole on enjoyable academic activities. They did not rush to get students into small groups or to get them started in readers. This whole-class work gave the teachers a better opportunity to continue monitoring all students' learning of the rules and procedures. Misbehavior was stopped quickly, firmly, but not harshly.

In the poorly managed classrooms, the first weeks were quite different. Rules were not workable; they were either too vague or very complicated. For example, one teacher made a rule to "be in the right place at the right time." Students were not told what this meant, so their behavior could not be guided by the rule. Neither positive nor negative behaviors had clear, consistent consequences. After students broke a rule, ineffective managers might give a vague criticism, such as "Some of my children are too noisy," or issue a warning but not follow through with the threatened consequence.

In the poorly managed classes, procedures for accomplishing routine tasks varied from day to day and were never taught or practiced. Instead of dealing with these obvious needs, ineffective managers spent time on procedures that could have waited. For example, one teacher had the class practice for a fire drill the first day but left unexplained other procedures that would be needed every day. Students wandered aimlessly and had to ask each other what they should be doing. Often the students talked to one another because they had nothing productive to do. Ineffective teachers frequently left the room. Many became absorbed in paperwork or in helping just one student. They had not made plans for how to deal with late-arriving students or interruptions. One ineffective manager tried to teach students to respond to a bell as a signal for attention but later let the students ignore it. All in all, the first weeks in these classrooms were disorganized and filled with surprises for teachers and students alike.

Effective Managers for Secondary Students. What about getting started in a secondary-school class? It appears that many of the differences between effective and ineffective elementary-school teachers hold at the secondary level as well. Again, effective managers focus on establishing rules, procedures, and expectations on the first day of class. These standards for academic work and class behavior are clearly communicated to students and consistently enforced during the first weeks of class. Student behavior is closely monitored, and infractions of the rules are dealt with quickly. In classes with lower-ability students, work cycles are shorter; students are not required to spend long, unbroken periods on one type of activity. Instead, they are moved smoothly through several different tasks each period. In general, effective teachers carefully follow each student's progress, so students cannot avoid work without facing consequences (Emmer & Evertson, 1982).

With all this close monitoring and consistent enforcement of the rules, you may wonder if effective secondary teachers must be grim and humorless. Not necessarily. The effective managers in one study also smiled and joked more with their students (Moskowitz & Hayman, 1976). As any experienced teacher can tell you, there is much more to smile about when the class is cooperative and well behaved.

MAINTAINING EFFECTIVE MANAGEMENT

A good start is only that—a beginning. Effective teachers build on this beginning. They maintain their management system by keeping students engaged in productive work and preventing problems. We already discussed several ways to keep students engaged. In the chapters on motivation, for example, we noted such approaches as stimulating curiosity, relating lessons to student interests, encouraging cooperative learning, establishing learning goals instead of performance goals, and having positive expectations. What else can teachers do?

Encouraging Engagement

The format of a lesson affects student involvement. In general, as teacher supervision increases, student engaged time also increases (Emmer & Evertson, 1981). A recent study, for example, found that elementary students working directly with a teacher were on task 97 percent of the time, while students working on their own were on task only 57 percent of the time (Frick, 1990). This does not mean that teachers should eliminate independent work for students. It simply means that this type of activity usually requires careful monitoring. *Independent* does not necessarily mean "left completely alone without guidance."

When the task provides continuous cues for the student about what to do next, involvement will be greater. Activities with clear steps are likely to be more absorbing, since one step leads naturally to the next. When students have all the materials they need to complete a task, they tend to stay involved (Kounin & Doyle, 1975). And as you now know, if their curiosity is piqued, students will be motivated to continue seeking an answer.

Of course, teachers can't supervise every student all the time or rely on curiosity. Something else must keep students working and completing assignments on their own. In their study of elementary and secondary teachers, Evertson, Emmer, and their colleagues found that effective class managers at both levels had well-planned systems for encouraging students to manage their own work (Evertson et al., 1989; Emmer et al., 1989). The Guidelines on page 414 are based on their findings.

Prevention Is the Best Medicine

What else can you do to maintain your management system? The ideal way to manage problems, of course, is to prevent them in the first place. In a classic study, Jacob Kounin (1970) also studied classroom management by comparing effective teachers, whose classes were relatively free of problems, with ineffective teachers, whose classes were continually plagued by chaos and disruption. Observing both groups in action,

Guidelines

Keeping Students Engaged

Make basic work requirements clear.

Examples

1. Specify and post the routine work requirements for headings, paper size, pen or pencil use, and neatness.
2. Establish and explain rules about late or incomplete work and absences. If a pattern of incomplete work begins to develop, deal with it early; speak with parents if necessary.
3. Make due dates reasonable, and stick to them unless the student has a very good excuse for lateness.

Communicate the specifics of assignments.

Examples

1. With younger students, have a routine procedure for giving assignments, such as writing them on the board in the same place each day. With older students, assignments may be dictated, posted, or given in a syllabus.
2. Remind students of coming assignments.
3. With complicated assignments, give students a sheet describing what to do, what resources are available, due dates, and so on. Older students should also be told your grading criteria.
4. Demonstrate how to do the assignment, do the

first few questions together, or provide a sample worksheet.

Monitor work in progress.

Examples

1. When you make an assignment in class, make sure each student gets started correctly. If you check only students who raise their hands for help, you will miss those who think they know what to do but don't really understand, those who are too shy to ask for help, and those who don't plan to do the work at all.
2. Check progress periodically. In discussions, make sure everyone has a chance to respond.

Give frequent academic feedback.

Examples

1. Elementary students should get papers back the day after they are handed in.
2. Good work can be displayed in class and graded papers sent home to parents each week.
3. Students of all ages can keep records of grades, projects completed, and extra credits earned.
4. For older students break up long-term assignments into several phases, giving feedback at each point.

Kounin found that they were not very different in the way they handled discipline once problems arose. The difference was that the successful managers were much better at preventing problems. Kounin concluded that effective classroom managers were especially skilled in four areas: "withitness," overlapping activities, group focusing, and movement management (Doyle, 1977). More recent research confirms the importance of these factors (Emmer & Evertson, 1981; Evertson, 1988).

Withitness. **Withitness** means communicating to students that you are aware of everything that is happening in the classroom, that you aren't missing anything. "With-it" teachers seem to have eyes in the back of their heads. They avoid becoming absorbed or interacting with only a few students, since this encourages the rest of the class to wander. They are always scanning the room, making eye contact with individual students, so the students know they are being monitored (Brooks, 1985).

These teachers prevent minor disruptions from becoming major. They also know who instigated the problem, and they make sure the right

Withitness According to Kounin, awareness of everything happening in a classroom.

people are dealt with. In other words, they do not make what Kounin called *timing errors* (waiting too long before intervening) or *target errors* (blaming the wrong student and letting the real perpetrators escape responsibility for their behavior).

If two problems occur at the same time, effective managers deal with the more serious one first. For example, a teacher who tells two students to stop whispering but ignores even a brief shoving match at the pencil sharpener communicates to students a lack of awareness. Students begin to believe they can get away with almost anything if they are clever (Charles, 1988).

Overlapping and Group Focus. **Overlapping** means keeping track of and supervising several activities at the same time. Success in this area also requires constant monitoring of the class. In many ways, a teacher must continually manage what Dunkin and Biddle (1974) have called a three-ring circus. For example, a teacher may have to check the work of an individual and at the same time keep a small group working by saying, "Right, go on" (Charles, 1985).

Maintaining a **group focus** means keeping as many students as possible involved in appropriate class activities and avoiding narrowing in on just one or two students. All students should have something to do during a lesson. For example, the teacher might ask everyone to write the answer to a question, then call on individuals to respond while the other students compare their answers. Choral responses might be required while the teacher moves around the room to make sure everyone is participating (Charles, 1985). Some teachers have their students use small blackboards or colored cards for responding in groups. This lets the teacher check for understanding as well. For example, during a grammar lesson the teacher might say, "Everyone who thinks the answer is *have run,* hold up the red side of your card. If you think the answer is *has run,* hold up the green side" (Hunter, 1982). This is a way teachers can ensure that all students are involved and check that they all understand the material.

Movement Management. **Movement management** involves keeping lessons and the group moving with smooth transitions, an appropriate (and flexible) pace, and variety. The effective teacher avoids abrupt transitions, such as announcing a new activity before gaining the students' attention or starting a new activity in the middle of something else. In these situations, one-third of the class will be doing the new activity, many will be on the old lesson, several will be asking other students what to do, some will be taking the opportunity to have a little fun, and most will be confused.

Another transition problem Kounin noted is the *slowdown,* or taking too much time to start a new activity. Sometimes teachers give too many directions. Problems also arise when teachers have students work one at a time while the rest of the class waits and watches. Charles (1985, p. 26) gives this example:

> During a science lesson the teacher began, "Row 1 may get up and get their beakers. Row 2 may get theirs. Now Row 3. Now, Row 1 may line up to put some bicarbonate of soda in their beakers. Row 2 may

Overlapping Supervising several activities at once.

Group Focus Ability to keep as many students as possible involved in activities.

Movement Management Ability to keep lessons and groups moving smoothly.

follow them," and so forth. When each row had obtained their bicarbonate of soda the teacher had them go row by row to add water. This left the remainder of the class sitting at their desks with no direction, doing nothing or else beginning to find something with which to entertain themselves.

. . . After every student had the necessary substances in their beakers the teacher proceeded: "Okay Roy, now pour in the vinegar while we watch. Good. Now Susie, it's your turn. Patti, you're next." The teacher had individuals doing the activity when it would have made more sense to have the class do it together.

A teacher who successfully demonstrates withitness, overlapping activities, group focus, and movement management tends to have a class filled with actively engaged students who do not escape his or her all-seeing eye. This need not be a grim classroom. It is more likely a busy place where students are actively learning and gaining a sense of self-worth rather than misbehaving in order to get attention and achieve status.

Dealing with Discipline Problems

Being an effective manager does not mean publicly correcting every minor infraction of the rules. This kind of public attention may actually reinforce the misbehavior, as we saw in chapter 6. Teachers who frequently correct students do not necessarily have the most well-behaved classes (Irving & Martin, 1982). The key is to know what is happening and what is important so you can prevent problems. Emmer and colleagues (1989) suggest four simple ways to stop misbehavior quickly:

1. Make eye contact with or move closer to the offender. Other nonverbal signals, such as pointing to the work students are supposed to be doing, might be helpful. Make sure the student actually stops the inappropriate behavior and gets back to work. If you do not, students will learn to ignore your signals.
2. If students are not performing a class procedure correctly, remind the students of the procedure and have them follow it correctly.
3. In a calm, unhostile way, ask the student to state the correct rule or procedure and then to follow it.
4. Tell the student in a clear, assertive, and unhostile way to stop the misbehavior. (We will discuss assertive messages to students in more detail later in the chapter.)

If you must impose penalties, the Guidelines on page 417, taken from Weinstein and Mignano (1993), give ideas about how to do it. The examples are taken from the actual words of the four expert teachers described in their book.

Special Problems with Secondary Students

Many secondary students never complete their work. Besides encouraging student responsibility, what else can teachers do to deal with this frustrating problem? Since students at this age have many assignments

"SURE THERE'S A WAY TO DISCIPLINE THEM. YELL AT THEM."

Maybe there's a better way. Research on class management offers some alternatives. (© 1990 by Sidney Harris— Phi Delta Kappan.)

Guidelines

Imposing Penalties

Delay the discussion of the situation until you and the students involved are calmer and more objective.

Examples

1. Say calmly to a student, "Sit there and think about what happened. I'll talk to you in a few minutes," or "I don't like what I just saw. Talk to me during your free period today."
2. Say, "I'm really angry about what just happened. Everybody take out journals; we are going to write about this." After a few minutes of writing, the class can discuss the incident.

Impose penalties privately.

Examples

1. Make arrangements with students privately. Stand firm in enforcing arrangements.
2. Resist the temptation to "remind" students in public that they are not keeping their side of the bargain.

3. Move close to a student who must be disciplined and speak so that only the student can hear.

After imposing a penalty, reestablish a positive relationship with the student immediately.

Examples

1. Send the student on an errand or ask him or her for help.
2. Compliment the student's work or give a real or symbolic "pat on the back" when the student's behavior warrants. Look hard for such an opportunity.

Set up a graded list of penalties that will fit many occasions.

Example

1. For not turning in homework: (1) receive reminder; (2) receive warning; (3) hand homework in before close of school day; (4) stay after school to finish work; (5) participate in a teacher-student-parent conference to develop an action plan.

and teachers have many students, both teacher and students may lose track of what has and hasn't been completed. The teacher must keep accurate records so everyone will be sure what the students are actually doing. But the most important thing is to enforce the established consequences for incomplete work. Do not pass a student because you know he or she is "bright enough" to pass. Make it clear to these students that the choice is theirs: they can do the work and pass or refuse to do the work and face the consequences.

There is also the problem of students who continually break the same rules, always forgetting materials, for example, or speaking without raising their hands. What should you do? Seat these students away from others who might be influenced by them. Try to catch them before they break the rules, but if rules are broken, be consistent in applying established consequences. Do not accept promises to do better next time. Teach the students how to monitor their own behavior; some of the self-management techniques described in chapter 6 should be helpful. Finally, remain friendly with the students. Try to catch them in a good moment so you can talk to them about something other than their rule breaking.

The defiant, hostile student can pose serious problems. If there is an outbreak, try to get out of the situation as soon as possible; everyone loses in a public power struggle. One possibility is to give the student a chance

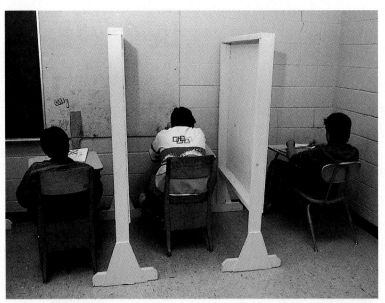

Is detention effective? That depends on whether it is an attractive alternative to class or a true penalty. This detention room seems to offer little chance for socializing, so it may discourage future misbehavior.

to save face and cool down by saying, "It's your choice to cooperate or not. You can take a minute to think about it." If the student complies, the two of you can talk later about controlling the outbursts. If the student refuses to cooperate, you can tell him or her to wait in the hall until you get the class started on work; then step outside for a private talk. If the student refuses to leave, send another class member for the assistant principal. Again, follow through. If the student complies before help arrives, do not let him or her off the hook. If outbursts occur frequently, you might have a conference with the counselor, parents, or other teachers. If the problem is an unreconcilable clash of personalities, the student should be transferred to another teacher.

Violence or destruction of property is a difficult and potentially dangerous problem. The first step is to send for help and get the names of participants and witnesses. Then get rid of any crowd that may have gathered; an audience will only make things worse. Do not try to break up a fight without help. Make sure the school office is aware of the incident. Usually the school has a policy for dealing with these situations.

SPECIAL PROGRAMS FOR CLASSROOM MANAGEMENT

In some situations you may want to consider using a much more formal classroom management system. Three possibilities, all based on behavioral principles, are group consequences, token programs, and contingency contracts.

Group Consequences

A teacher can base reinforcement for the class on the cumulative behavior of all members of the class, usually by adding each student's points to a class or a team total. The **good behavior game** is an example of this approach. A class is divided into two teams. Specific rules for good behavior are cooperatively developed. Each time a student breaks one of the rules, that student's team is given a mark. The team with the fewest marks at the end of the period receives a special reward or privilege (longer recess, first to lunch, and so on). If both teams earn fewer than a preestablished number of marks, both teams receive the reward. Most studies indicate that even though the game produces only small improvements in academic achievement, it can produce definite improvements in the behaviors listed in the good behavior rules.

You can also use **group consequences** without dividing the class into teams; that is, you can base reinforcement on the behavior of the whole class. Wilson and Hopkins (1973) conducted a study using group consequences to reduce noise levels. Radio music served effectively as the reinforcer for students in a home economics class. Whenever noise in the class was below a predetermined level, students could listen to the radio; when the noise exceeded the level, the radio was turned off. Given the success of this simple method, such a procedure might be considered in any class where music does not interfere with the task at hand.

Finally, group rewards can be based on the behavior of an individual student. For example, the entire class can get an extra free time if a particular problem student cooperates in the lesson or if two nonparticipating students volunteer at least one comment or answer during class discussion.

Group consequences are recommended for situations in which students care about the approval of their peers. If the misbehavior of several students seems to be encouraged by the attention and laughter of other students, then group consequences could be helpful. Also, using positive group consequences can help build cooperation among students (Jenson, Sloane, & Young, 1988).

However, caution is needed in group approaches. The whole group should not suffer for the misbehavior or mistakes of one individual if the group has no real influence over that person. Recently I saw an entire class break into cheers when the teacher announced that one boy was transferring to another school. The chant "No more points! No more points!" filled the room. The "points" referred to the teacher's system of giving one point to the whole class each time anyone broke a rule. Every point meant 5 minutes of recess lost. The boy who was transferring had been responsible for many losses. He was not very popular to begin with, and the point system, though quite effective in maintaining order, had led to rejection and even greater unpopularity.

Peer pressure in the form of support and encouragement, however, can be a positive influence. Teachers might show students how to give support and constructive feedback to classmates. If a few students seem to enjoy sabotaging the system, those students may need separate arrangements.

Good Behavior Game
Arrangement where a class is divided into teams and each team receives demerit points for breaking agreed-upon rules of good behavior.

Group Consequences
Rewards or punishments given to a class as a whole for adhering to or violating rules of conduct.

Token Reinforcement Programs

Often it is difficult to provide positive consequences for all the students who deserve them. A **token reinforcement system** can help solve this problem by allowing all students to earn tokens for both academic work and positive classroom behavior. The tokens may be points, checks, holes punched in a card, chips, play money, or anything else that is easily identified as the student's property. Periodically the students exchange the tokens they have earned for some desired reward (Martin & Pear, 1992).

Depending on the age of the student, the rewards could be small toys, school supplies, free time, special class jobs, or other privileges. When a "token economy," as this kind of system is called, is first established, the tokens should be given out on a fairly continuous schedule, with chances to exchange the tokens for rewards often available. Once the system is working well, however, tokens should be distributed on an intermittent schedule and saved for longer periods of time before they are exchanged for rewards. In order to establish an intermittent schedule, the teacher might set a timer for various lengths of time, then give a token to every student who is working when the timer goes off. Of course, the students would not know when the next signal was coming, so they would have to work steadily. An alarm watch would make a good timer for this purpose.

Another variation is to allow students to earn tokens in the classroom and exchange them for rewards at home. These plans are very successful when parents are willing to cooperate. Usually a note or report form is sent home daily or twice a week. The note indicates the number of points earned in the preceding time period. The points may be exchanged for minutes of television viewing, access to special toys, or private time with parents. Points can also be saved up for larger rewards such as trips. Do not use this procedure, however, if you suspect the child might be severely punished for poor reports.

Token reinforcement systems are complicated and time-consuming. Generally, they should be used in only three situations: (1) to motivate students who are completely uninterested in their work and have not responded to other approaches; (2) to encourage students who have consistently failed to make academic progress; and (3) to deal with a class that is out of control. Some groups of students seem to benefit more than others from token economies. Mentally retarded students, slow learners, children who have failed often, students with few academic skills, and students with behavior problems all seem to respond to the concrete, direct nature of token reinforcement.

But before you try a token system, you should be sure that your teaching methods and materials are right for the students. Sometimes class disruptions or lack of motivation indicate that teaching practices need to be changed. Maybe the class rules are unclear or are enforced inconsistently. Maybe the teacher provides too little social reinforcement, praise, or warmth. Maybe the text is too easy or too hard. Maybe the pace is wrong. If these problems exist, a token system may improve the situation temporarily, but the students will still have trouble learning the academic material (Jenson, Sloane, & Young, 1988).

Token Reinforcement System System where tokens earned for academic work and positive classroom behavior can be exchanged for some desired reward.

Guidelines

Setting Up a Token Reinforcement Program

Before presenting the program to students, make sure you have all the details worked out.

Examples

1. Establish rules that clearly specify requirements, such as how many problems done correctly will earn a point.
2. Make sure your system is workable and not too complicated. You might discuss it with another teacher to identify possible sources of problems.

You may want to have different goals for different groups of students.

Examples

1. Focus on cooperative behaviors for students who are disruptive.
2. For high-achieving students, give tokens for enrichment work, peer tutoring, or special projects.
3. Match the token to the age of the student—colored chips for younger children, points for older students.

Offer a variety of rewards at different "prices."

Examples

1. Offer rewards that can be purchased for only two or three tokens, so that all students will be motivated to try.

2. Offer rewards that make more extensive efforts or saving up tokens worthwhile.

Gradually increase the requirements for each token.

Examples

1. Begin with one token for each correct answer, then give a token for every three correct answers, and so on.
2. Offer tokens for 5 minutes of attention to assignments, then eventually for a whole day of attentive work.

Gradually change from tangible rewards and privileges to time focused on enjoyable learning experiences.

Examples

1. With young students, start with candy or small toys, but move to assisting the teacher and free reading time.
2. With older students, start with such things as magazines and move toward free time to spend on special projects, the chance to tutor younger children, or the opportunity to work in the computer lab.

Contingency Contract Programs

In a **contingency contract** program, the teacher draws up an individual contract with each student describing exactly what the student must do to earn a particular privilege or reward. In some programs, students participate in deciding on the behaviors to be reinforced and the rewards that can be gained. The negotiating process itself can be an educational experience, as students learn to set reasonable goals and abide by the terms of a contract.

An example of a contract for completing assignments that is appropriate for intermediate and upper-grade students is presented in Figure 11.2 on page 422. This chart serves as a contract, assignment sheet, and progress record. Something like this might even help you keep track of your assignments and due dates in college.

The few pages devoted to token reinforcement and contingency contracts here can offer only an introduction to these programs. If you want

Contingency Contract A contract between teacher and individual student specifying what the student must do to earn a particular privilege or reward.

FIGURE 11.2   A Contingency Contract for Completing Assignments This contract can serve as a visual reminder of due dates for projects and assignments. Whenever the "actual completion" line is above the "planned completion" line, work is on time and the contract is met.

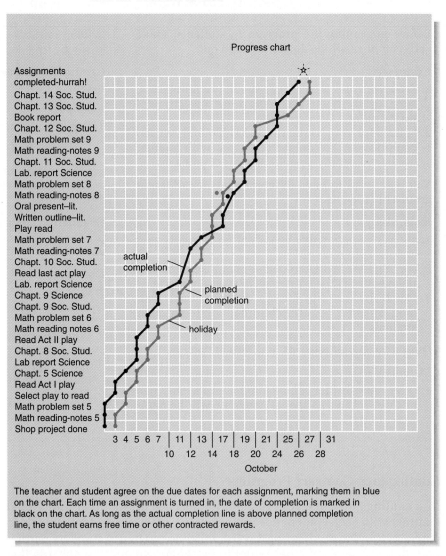

The teacher and student agree on the due dates for each assignment, marking them in blue on the chart. Each time an assignment is turned in, the date of completion is marked in black on the chart. As long as the actual completion line is above planned completion line, the student earns free time or other contracted rewards.

Source: Figure from *Achieving Educational Excellence Using Behavioral Strategies* by Beth Sulzer-Azaroff and G. Roy Mayer, copyright © by Holt, Rinehart and Winston, Inc.; reprinted by permission of the publisher.

to set up a large-scale reward program in your classroom, you should probably seek professional advice. Often the school psychologist, counselor, or principal can help. In addition, remember that, applied inappropriately, external rewards can undermine the students' motivation to learn (Deci, 1975; Lepper & Greene, 1978).

THE NEED FOR COMMUNICATION

Communication between teacher and students is essential when problems arise. Communication is more than "teacher talks—student listens." It is more than simply the words exchanged between individuals. We communicate in many ways. Our actions, movements, voice tone, facial expressions, and many other nonverbal behaviors send messages to our students. Many times the messages we *intend* to send are not the messages our students receive.

Message Sent—Message Received

Teacher: Carl, where is your homework?

Carl: I left it in my Dad's car this morning.

Teacher: Again? You will have to bring me a note tomorrow from your father saying that you actually did the homework. I won't grade it without the note.

Message Carl Receives: You are lying. I can't trust you. I need proof you did the work.

Teacher: Sit at every other desk. Put all your things under your desk. Jane and Laurel, you are sitting too close together. One of you move!

Message Jane & Laurel Receive: I expect you two to cheat on this test.

A new student comes to Ms. Lincoln's kindergarten. The child is messy and unwashed. Ms. Lincoln puts her hand lightly on the girl's shoulder and says, "I know you will like it here." Her muscles tense, and she leans away from the child.

Message Student Receives: I don't like you. I think you are bad.

In all interactions, a message is sent and a message is received. Sometimes teachers believe they are sending one message, but their voices, body positions, choices of words, and gestures may communicate a different message.

Students may hear the hidden message and respond to it without ever stopping to think, "The teacher said . . . but I know she means. . . ." For example, a student may respond with hostility if she or he feels insulted by the teacher (or by another student) but may not be able to say exactly where the feeling of being insulted came from. Perhaps it was in the teacher's tone of voice, not the words actually spoken. In such cases, the teacher may feel attacked for no reason. "What did I say? All I said was. . . ." The first principle of communication is that people respond to what they *think* was said or meant, not necessarily to the speaker's intended message.

There are many exercises you can try in your college courses or in your classroom to practice sending and receiving messages accurately. Students in my classes have told me about one instructor who encourages accurate communication by using the paraphrase rule. Before any participant, including the teacher, is allowed to respond to any other participant in a class discussion, he or she must summarize what the previous speaker said. If the summary is wrong, indicating the speaker was misunderstood, the speaker must explain again. The respondent then tries again to paraphrase. The process continues until the speaker agrees that the listener has heard the intended message.

Paraphrasing is more than a classroom exercise. It can be the first step in communicating with students. Before teachers can deal appropriately with any student problem, they must know what the real problem is. A student who says, "This book is really dumb! Why did we have to read it?" may really be saying, "The book was too difficult for me. I couldn't read it, and I feel dumb." A teacher who responds to the *why* question with a justification for the choice of reading material has missed the point. The student may feel even worse as a result: "Now I'm not just dumb, I've also missed out on this thing the teacher thinks is so important. I'll never catch up. I might as well just give up!"

Diagnosis: Whose Problem Is It?

As a teacher, you may find many student behaviors unacceptable, unpleasant, or troubling. It is often difficult to stand back from these problems, take an objective took, and decide on an appropriate response. According to Thomas Gordon (1981), the key to good teacher-student relationships is determining why you are troubled by a particular behavior and whose problem it is. The teacher must begin by asking who "owns" the problem. The answer to this question is critical. If it is really the student's problem, the teacher must become a counselor and supporter, helping the student find his or her own solution. But if the teacher does "own" the problem, it *is* the teacher's responsibility to find a solution through problem solving with the student.

Diagnosing who owns the problem is not always straightforward. Let's look at three troubling situations to get some practice in this skill:

1. A student writes obscene words and draws sexually explicit illustrations in a school encyclopedia.
2. A student tells you that his mother and father had a bad fight and he hates his father.
3. A student quietly reads a newspaper in the back of the room.

Why are these behaviors troubling? If you cannot accept the student's behavior because it has a serious effect on you as a teacher—if you are blocked from reaching your goals by the student's action—then *you* own the problem. It is your responsibility to confront the student and seek a solution. A teacher-owned problem appears to be present in the first situation described above—the young pornographer—because teaching materials are damaged.

If you feel annoyed by the behavior because it is getting in the student's own way or because you are embarrassed for the child, but the behavior does not directly interfere with your teaching, then it is probably the student's problem. The test question is this: Does this student's action tangibly affect you or prevent you from fulfilling your role as a teacher? The student who hates his father would not prevent you from teaching, even though you might wish the student felt differently. The problem is really the student's, and he must find his own solution. (In both the first and second situations, teachers may want to help students confront moral or emotional problems. Nevertheless, teachers must still clarify *whose* emotions and values are involved, how they are involved, and why.)

Situation 3 is more difficult to diagnose. I have had lengthy debates in my class about whose problem it is when a student reads a newspaper in class. One argument is that the teacher is not interfered with in any way, so it is the student's problem. Another argument is that teachers might find the paper reading distracting during a lecture, so it is *their* problem, and they must find a solution. In a gray area such as this, the answer probably depends on how the teacher actually experiences the student's behavior. Having decided who owns the problem, it is time to act.

Counseling: The Student's Problem

Let's pick up the situation in which the student found the reading assignment "dumb." How might a teacher handle this positively?

Student: This book is really dumb! Why did we have to read it?

Teacher: You're pretty upset. This seemed like a worthless assignment to you. [Teacher paraphrases the student's statement, trying to hear the emotions as well as the words.]

Student: Yeah! Well, it wasn't really worthless. I mean, I don't know if it was. I couldn't read it.

Teacher: It was just too hard to read, and that bothers you.

Student: Sure, I felt really dumb. I know I can write a good report, but I need some help with the book.

Teacher: I think I can give you some hints that will make the book easier to understand. Can you see me after school today?

Student: O.K.

Here the teacher used **empathetic listening** to allow the student to find a solution. (As you can see, this approach relies heavily on paraphrasing.) By trying to hear the student and by avoiding the tendency to jump in too quickly with advice, solutions, criticisms, reprimands, or interrogations, the teacher keeps the communication lines open. Here are a few *unhelpful* responses the teacher might have made:

I chose the book because it is the best example of _____ in our library. You will need to have read it before your English II class next year. [The teacher justifies the choice; this prevents the student from admitting that this "important" assignment is too difficult.]

Did you really read it? I bet you didn't do the work, and now you want out of the assignment. [The teacher accuses; the student hears, "The teacher doesn't trust me!" and must defend herself or himself or accept the teacher's view.]

Empathetic Listening
Hearing the intent and emotions behind what another says and reflecting them back by paraphrasing.

Your job is to read the book, not ask me why. I know what's best. [The teacher pulls rank, and the student hears, "You are too dumb or immature to decide what is good for you!" The student can rebel or passively accept the teacher's judgment.]

Empathetic, or active, listening can be a helpful response when students bring problems to you. You must reflect back to the student what you hear him or her saying. This reflection is more than a parroting of the student's words; it should capture the emotions, intent, and meaning behind them. Sokolove, Garrett, Sadker, and Sadker (1986, p. 241) have summarized the components of active listening:

1. Blocking out external stimuli;
2. Attending carefully to both the verbal and nonverbal messages;
3. Differentiating between the intellectual and the emotional content of the message;
4. Making inferences regarding the speaker's feelings.

When students realize they really have been heard and not evaluated negatively for what they have said or felt, they feel freer to trust the teacher and to talk more openly. Sometimes the true problem surfaces later in the conversation.

Confrontation and Assertive Discipline

Now let's assume a student is doing something that actively interferes with teaching. The teacher decides the student must stop. The problem is the teacher's. Confrontation, not counseling, is required.

"I" Messages. Gordon (1974) recommends sending an **"I" message** in order to intervene and change a student's behavior. Basically, this means telling a student in a straightforward, assertive, and nonjudgmental way what she or he is doing, how it affects you as a teacher, and how you feel about it. The student is then free to change voluntarily, and often does so. Here are two "I" messages:

When you leave your locker open, I sometimes bump into it and hurt myself.

When you all call out answers, I cannot concentrate on each answer, and I feel frustrated.

Assertive Discipline. Lee and Marlene Canter (1976; Canter, 1989) suggest other approaches for dealing with a teacher-owned problem. They call their method **assertive discipline.** Teachers are assertive when they make their expectations clear and follow through with established consequences. Students then have a straightforward choice: they can follow the rules or accept the consequences. Many teachers are ineffective with students because they are either wishy-washy and passive or hostile and aggressive.

The passive style can take several forms. Instead of telling the student directly what to do, the teacher tells, or often asks, the student to *try* or to *think about* the appropriate action. The passive teacher might comment

"I" Message Clear, nonaccusatory statement of how something is affecting you.

Assertive Discipline Clear, firm, unhostile response style.

In giving an "I message" to a student, it is important to give an "eye message" as well. State your case calmly but directly, and focus on the student.

on the problem behavior without actually telling the child what to do differently: "Why are you doing that? Don't you know the rules?" or "Sam, are you disturbing the class?" Or teachers may clearly state what should happen but never follow through with the established consequences, giving the students "one more chance" every time. Finally, teachers may ignore behavior that should receive a response or may wait too long before responding.

A hostile response style involves different mistakes. Teachers may make "you" statements that condemn the student without stating clearly what the student should be doing—"You should be ashamed of the way you're behaving!" or "You never listen!" or "You are acting like a baby!" Teachers may also threaten students angrily but follow through too seldom, perhaps because the threats are too vague—"You'll be very sorry you did that when I get through with you!"—or too severe. For example, one teacher observed by Canter and Canter (1976) told a student in a physical education class that he would have to sit on the bench for three weeks. A few days later the team was short one member and the teacher let the student play, never returning him to the bench to complete the three-week sentence. Often a teacher who has been passive becomes hostile and explodes when students persist in misbehaving.

In contrast with both the passive and hostile styles, an assertive response communicates to the students that you care too much about them and the process of learning to allow inappropriate behavior to persist. Assertive teachers clearly state what they expect. To be most effective, the teachers often look into a student's eyes when speaking, address the student by name, and perhaps touch the student's shoulder. The teacher's voice is calm, firm, and confident. They are not sidetracked by accusations such as "You just don't understand!" or "You don't like

Point/Counterpoint

Does Assertive Discipline Work?

Lee Canter, the developer of "assertive discipline," describes his observations of effective teachers:

> I found that, above all, the master teachers were assertive; that is they *taught* students how to behave. They established clear rules for the classroom, they communicated those rules to the students, and they taught students how to follow them. (1989, p. 58)

Is assertive discipline effective?

Point: Research results do not support assertive discipline.

In an article entitled "What research really shows about Assertive Discipline," Gary Render, Je Neil Padilla, and H. Mark Krank (1989) note that very little unbiased information is available about the effectiveness of this approach. Even though reports claim that 500,000 people have been trained in assertive discipline, Render and his colleagues were able to find only 16 systematic studies of assertive discipline. Their analysis of these studies led them to conclude that

> The claims made by Canter (1988) . . . are simply not supported by the existing and available literature. We would agree that Assertive Discipline could be helpful in severe cases where students are behaving inappropriately more than 96 percent of the time, as in the study by Mandlebaum (1983). We would also argue that teachers such as the one in that study would benefit from any intervention. However, we can find no evidence that Assertive Discipline is an effective approach deserving schoolwide or districtwide adoption. (p. 72)

A second criticism of assertive discipline is that, while it may stop misbehavior in the short run, the long-term effects on students are damag-

me!" Assertive teachers do not get into a debate about the fairness of the rules. They expect changes, not promises or apologies.

Even though many teachers and school administrators have given enthusiastic testimonies about the assertive discipline approach, some educators and psychologists question its effectiveness. The **Point/Counterpoint** section above further explores the issue.

Conflict and Negotiations. If "I" messages or assertive responses fail and a student persists in misbehaving, teacher and student are in a conflict. Several pitfalls now loom. The two individuals become less able to perceive each other's behavior accurately. Research has shown that the angrier you get with another person, the more you see the other as the villain and yourself as an innocent victim. Since you feel the other person is in the wrong, and since he or she feels just as strongly that the conflict is all your fault, very little mutual trust is possible. A cooperative solution to the problem is almost impossible. In fact, by the time the discussion has gone on a few minutes, the original problem is lost in a sea of charges, countercharges, and self-defense (Johnson, 1990).

There are three methods of resolving a conflict between teacher and student. One is for the teacher to impose a solution. This may be necessary during an emergency, as when a defiant student refuses to go to the hall to discuss a public outbreak. The second method is for the teacher to give in to the student's demands; you might be convinced by a particu-

ing. Richard Curwin and Allen Mendler (1988) remind teachers that classroom management systems not only manage behavior, they also teach students lessons about their own self-worth, their ability to act responsibly and solve problems, how much control they have over their own lives, and how to use that control. What lessons are taught by systems such as assertive discipline? "If Richard shapes up after the third mark on the chalkboard because the fourth means a call home to an abusive parent, did the program improve his self-control, or did it simply transfer the inner turmoil of a child caught in a dysfunctional family?" (Curwin & Mendler, 1988, p. 68).

Counterpoint: Practitioners know that assertive discipline works.

In response to the assertion by Render and his colleagues that research does not support assertive discipline, Sammie McCormack (1989) says, "The decision to implement a program should be based on many factors, in addition to research; from a practitioner's standpoint, Assertive Discipline works" (p. 77). McCormack reports the reactions of more than 8,700 teachers from four school districts and a confederation of schools in Oregon. In these schools, 78 to 99 percent of the teachers saw improvements in student behavior as a consequence of using assertive discipline. McCormack does not explain how these particular samples were selected or if teachers in other schools had different reactions.

In response to Curwin and Mendler's (1988) concerns that classroom management models such as assertive discipline may undermine students' self-worth and sense of responsibility, Lee Canter (1988) notes that several studies have found improvements in both teachers' and students' self-concepts after the introduction of assertive discipline. Further, Canter states that the basis of assertive discipline is giving students choices and that it is through making choices and accepting the consequences that students learn about responsibility.

larly compelling student argument. But generally it is a bad idea to be talked out of a position.

Problems arise when either the teacher or the student gives in completely. In each case, someone is the loser and has no impact on the final decision. Gordon recommends a third approach, which he calls the *no-lose method.* Here the needs of both the teacher and the students are taken into account in the solution. No one person is expected to give in completely, and all participants retain respect for themselves and each other. The no-lose method is a six-step problem-solving strategy:

1. *Define the problem.* What exactly are the behaviors involved? What does each person want? (Use active listening to help students pinpoint the real problem.)
2. *Generate many possible solutions.* Brainstorm, but remember, don't allow any evaluations of ideas yet.
3. *Evaluate each solution.* Any participant may veto any idea. If no solutions are found to be acceptable, brainstorm again.
4. *Make a decision.* Choose one solution through consensus—no voting. In the end, everyone must be satisfied with the solution.
5. *Determine how to implement the solution.* What will be needed? Who will be responsible for each task? What is the timetable?
6. *Evaluate the success of the solution.* After trying the solution for a while, ask, Are we satisfied with our decision? How well is it working? Should we make some changes?

SUMMARY

CLASSROOMS NEED MANAGERS

Classrooms are by nature multidimensional, full of simultaneous activities, fast-paced and immediate, unpredictable, public, and affected by the history of students' and teachers' actions. A manager must juggle all these elements every day.

Productive classroom activity requires students' cooperation. Maintaining cooperation is a different task for different age groups. Young students are learning how to "go to school" and need to learn the general procedures of school. Older students need to learn the specifics required for working in different subjects. Working with adolescents requires teachers to understand the power of the adolescent peer group.

The goals of effective classroom management are to make ample time for learning; improve the quality of time use by keeping students actively engaged; make sure participation structures are clear, straightforward, and consistently signaled; and encourage student self-management.

PLANNING FOR GOOD MANAGEMENT

The most effective teachers set rules and establish procedures for handling predictable problems. Procedures should cover administrative tasks, student movement, housekeeping, routines for running lessons, interactions between students and teachers, and interactions among students. Consequences should be established for following and breaking the rules and procedures, so that the teacher and the students know what will happen.

MAINTAINING EFFECTIVE MANAGEMENT

For effective classroom management it seems essential to spend the first days of class teaching basic rules and procedures. Students should be occupied with organized, enjoyable activities and learn to function cooperatively in the group.

Quick, firm, clear, and consistent responses to infractions of the rules characterize effective teachers.

To create a positive environment and prevent problems, teachers must take individual differences into account, maintain student motivation, and reinforce positive behavior.

Successful problem preventers are skilled in four areas described by Kounin: "withitness," overlapping, group focusing, and movement management. When penalties have to be imposed, teachers should impose them calmly and privately.

SPECIAL PROGRAMS FOR CLASSROOM MANAGEMENT

There are several special procedures that may be helpful in maintaining positive management, including group consequences, token economies, and contingency contracts. A teacher must use these programs with caution, emphasizing learning and not just "good" behavior.

THE NEED FOR COMMUNICATION

Communication between teacher and student is essential when problems arise. All interactions between people, even silence or neglect, communicate some meaning.

Techniques such as paraphrasing, empathetic listening, determining whether the teacher or the student "owns" the problem, assertive discipline, avoidance of passive and hostile responses, and active problem solving with students help teachers open the lines of positive communication.

KEY TERMS AND CONCEPTS

academic learning time, p. 403
allocated time, p. 403
assertive discipline, p. 426
classroom management, p. 402
contingency contract, p. 421
empathetic listening, p. 425
engaged time, p. 403

good behavior game, p. 419
group consequences, p. 419
group focus, p. 415
"I" message, p. 426
movement management, p. 415
overlapping, p. 415
participation structures, p. 403

procedures, p. 406
rules, p. 406
self-management, p. 404
time on task, p. 403
token reinforcement system,
 p. 420
withitness, p. 414

WHAT WOULD YOU DO?

PRESCHOOL AND KINDERGARTEN

Your class is larger than ever this year, and it is very difficult to get everyone dressed for play outside. How would you handle the situation?

ELEMENTARY AND MIDDLE SCHOOL

It takes your class 15 minutes to settle down each morning and begin work. What would you do?

A few students in your class always seem to be out of step with the rest of the class. They call out when they shouldn't, interrupt others, and get up and walk around when they should be seated and working. What would you do?

JUNIOR HIGH AND HIGH SCHOOL

You tell a student to put away a radio, and she says, "Try and make me!" What would you do?

One of your students, who is bright and able, has stopped doing homework. What would you do?

COOPERATIVE LEARNING ACTIVITY

With four or five other members in your educational psychology class, plan the rules and procedures for a class you might teach.

SETTING CLASSROOM RULES

Do you involve students in setting classroom rules? Why or why not? How do you do it?

CONSISTENCY AND CARING

Beginning teachers and veteran teachers need to establish clear and reasonable classroom rules. One successful way to develop these rules is to have one or two brainstorming sessions with students at the beginning of the year. With kindergarten youngsters as well as high school seniors, students who are given an opportunity to set classroom standards will feel an ownership of the rules and be more apt to follow them. It is the teacher's task to enforce the rules with consistency.

The teacher who is judged fair by her/his students will receive their respect. Finally, the teacher who has established rules but also responds to students with a smile, a kind word, a helping hand, and genuine concern has achieved the right relationship with her/his students. Students want what we all want, to be cared about. Youngsters will react positively and respectfully to the teacher they believe genuinely cares about their welfare.

Darlene A. Walsh, Rhode Island 1991 Teacher of the Year
Greenbush Elementary School, West Warwick, Rhode Island

CAN YOU BE ACCEPTED AND RESPECTED?

Many beginning teachers want so much to be accepted by their students that any distinction between being friendly and being friends becomes blurred. Others go to the opposite extreme and interpret advice to be assertive as a warning that they must be grim disciplinarians. What advice would you give new teachers about establishing appropriate relationships with students?

WHO'S IN CHARGE?

Everyone wants to be received favorably and to be well liked. But students expect an authority figure to be in charge of the class. They need someone they can turn to if they have a problem, someone who can guide them through difficult times. Someone who acts and talks to them as a peer will have trouble being believed and respected as the person in charge. The students will feel they have as much authority and independence as the teacher. A teacher can certainly joke and have fun with students, but he or she needs to know where and when to draw the line—without any arguments—*before* the situation gets out of hand. Be firm, fair, caring, supportive, and understanding, and your students will not only like you, they will respect you.

Ida Pofahl, Second-Grade Teacher
Denison Elementary School, Denison, Iowa

RESPECT WORKS

My observations lead me to believe that discipline problems occur when students do not respect their teacher. My strongest suggestion is to *earn* your students' respect, and not to assume that students will automatically respect you simply because of your position. You can earn their respect with your competence, preparation, flexibility, and understanding. *Show* them (don't tell them) that you respect each of them as individuals. There are few discipline problems between people who respect and care for each other.

R. Chris Rohde, Chemistry Teacher
Chippewa Falls Senior High School, Chippewa Falls, Wisconsin

STICK TO YOUR GUNS

There's no substitute for well-organized, enthusiastic teaching. If your students are interested and you are well prepared, behavior is easier to manage. Start with these assumptions: you like to teach; your students want to learn; you have something important to give them. Establish, from the beginning, the division of roles: you are the teacher, fully in charge; they are the students, there to learn. A folksy, chummy, pal-like demeanor diminishes your authority. Whatever your game plan for discipline, whether it be names posted, seating changed, extra assignments, removal from class, or after-school detainment, administer it consistently—this means consistency in your expectations and in what you will not tolerate. Carry out your plan with firmness, but without shouting. Do it fairly, without sarcasm or shaming. And from the beginning, try hard to create a climate of optimism and cheerfulness, expecting the very best effort from everyone.

Harriet Chipley, *Elementary Art Teacher*
Lookout Mountain Elementary School, Lookout Mountain, Tennessee

STRATEGIES FOR DISCIPLINE PROBLEMS

A critical part of successful classroom management is having a strategy to deal with discipline problems. How do you deal with students who regularly hand in incomplete work or no work at all?

CONSISTENT CONSEQUENCES

The rules of the classroom must be clear and consistently enforced. At the beginning of the year, students discuss at length with me the rules and the consequences of violating them. I remind students of a rule when it is disobeyed and restate the consequences. In my classroom students are allowed to miss only one homework assignment. After that, they must stay after school in detention if their homework is incomplete. I consistently enforce this rule, with no exceptions or excuses. If students receive more than two detentions for incomplete work, I call their parent(s) and discuss the assignments for completeness. I also stress that completing their homework is part of their job and is necessary to pass fifth grade. Because of my consistency I have few problems with managing homework.

I was not as strict in enforcing these rules in my first year of teaching. Consequently, many students did not complete homework. I have also found that a homework chart, signed by me each afternoon and by a parent in the evening, is helpful to some chronic problem students.

Marcia E. Miller, *Fifth-Grade Teacher*
Walker Elementary School, Charlottesville, Virginia

TEACH RESPONSIBILITY

First of all, the teacher should assign work that can realistically be done in the allotted time and is appropriate to the child's independent working level.

To keep track of completed work, I have a Completed Work folder for each reading and math group. As each child finishes an assignment, he/she puts the work in the appropriate folder. Sometime during the day I quickly go through the folders and make a check next to the child's name and assignment on a checksheet that I have attached to the folder. A more responsible group of children will be able to use the checksheet appropriately.

I try to put some time in each day's schedule for "catching up." At this time I allow the students who haven't finished their work to complete it. I am available, if possible, to answer questions and give help. The other children have a special time when they can choose to go to the various centers in the room . . . library, art, listening, writing, and so on. Most of the children soon decide to make good use of their time during the assigned time period so that they can also enjoy some "free time" activities. I try to make this less of a punitive time period; I've chosen to make it much more positive, and it seems to work better. I also find that using older students and other volunteers to help during this time period make it much more profitable for all.

Eileen D. Akers, *First-Grade Teacher*
Jackson-Via Elementary School, Charlottesville, Virginia

12 PLANNING TO TEACH

Each Sunday night, thousands of teachers across the country sit planning the coming week. Often they begin by outlining the main activities: discussion on Monday, film on Tuesday, and so on. Although this seems like a reasonable way to proceed, an important step may be missing. The teacher may not have asked, "What is the purpose of these activities?"

Because teachers so frequently begin in the middle by selecting activities rather than at the beginning by determining purposes, I have devoted a large part of this chapter to objectives. We look first at some basic definitions of instructional objectives, their function in the classroom, different kinds of written objectives, and some criticisms of written objectives. Next we consider how to select objectives for a lesson or a whole course, using task analysis and taxonomies of learning outcomes as a basis for selection.

Once a teacher has a clear set of purposes in mind, the next step is to decide how to structure the lesson. We discuss several teaching strategies based on the size of the group and the role of the teacher. These strategies include lecturing, recitation, group discussion, seatwork, inquiry methods, and individualized instruction. In the final section we consider how to match the physical environment of the classroom to the objectives and activities of the lesson.

By the time you have finished this chapter, you should be able to do the following:

- Describe the functions and levels of teacher planning.
- Give several reasons for using instructional objectives.
- Write objectives, applying Mager's or Gronlund's approach.
- Use task analysis to develop a sequence of objectives.
- Create objectives for cognitive, affective, and psychomotor learning.
- Plan objectives for an entire course.
- Describe situations in which each of the possible formats would be most appropriate—lecture, recitation, group discussion, seatwork, inquiry, or individualized instruction.
- Draw classroom floor plans that fit your learning goals and teaching methods.

WHAT DO YOU THINK?

Think about the classes you have attended in the past week. What were the objectives of those classes? What were you supposed to be able to do after the class that you could not do before? How did your professor make the point of the class clear?

TEACHER PLANNING

In the past few years educational researchers have become very interested in teachers' planning. They have interviewed teachers about how they plan, asked teachers to "think out loud" while planning or to keep journals describing their plans, and even studied teachers intensively for months at a time. What have they found?

First, planning is a very important step in teaching. In many ways, the plan determines what students will learn, because planning transforms the available time and curriculum materials into activities, assignments, and tasks for students. What students encounter in class activities will determine to a large extent what they learn. When a teacher decides to devote 7 hours to language arts and 15 minutes to science in a given week, the students in that class will learn more language than science. In fact, differences as dramatic as this do occur. Nancy Karweit (1989) reported that in one school the time allocated to mathematics ranged from 2 hours and 50 minutes a week in one class to 5 hours and 55 minutes a week in a class down the hall (Clark & Peterson, 1986; Clark & Yinger, 1988; Doyle, 1983).

Second, teachers engage in several levels of planning—by the year, term, unit, week, and day. All the levels must be coordinated. Accomplishing the year's plan requires breaking the work into terms, the terms into units, and the units into weeks and days. Planning done at the beginning of the year is particularly important, because many routines and patterns are established early. For experienced teachers, unit planning seems to be the most important level, followed by weekly and then daily planning (Clark & Peterson, 1986; Clark & Yinger, 1988).

Third, plans reduce but do not eliminate uncertainty in teaching. Even the best plans cannot (and should not) control everything that happens in class. There is some evidence that when teachers "over-plan"—fill every minute and stick to the plan no matter what—their students do not learn as much as students whose teachers are flexible (Shavelson, 1987). Chris Clark (1983) suggests that beginning teachers think of their plans as "flexible frameworks for action, as devices for getting started in the right direction, as something to depart from or elaborate on, rather than as rigid scripts" (p. 13).

Finally, there is no *one* model for effective planning. For experienced teachers, planning is a creative problem-solving process (Shavelson, 1987). Experienced teachers know how to accomplish many lessons and

"We did that last year—how come we have to do it again this year?"
© *W. A. Vanselow*—Phi Delta Kappan.

segments of lessons. They know what to expect and how to proceed, so they don't necessarily continue to follow the detailed lesson-planning models they learned during their teacher-preparation programs. But many experienced teachers think it was helpful to learn this detailed system as a foundation (Clark & Peterson, 1986). Next we will examine one approach to planning. The main steps in this planning model are setting learning objectives, specifying evaluation procedures, and designing learning activities.

OBJECTIVES FOR LEARNING

The eight items listed in the overview at the beginning of this chapter are examples of learning objectives. Although there are many different approaches to writing objectives, each assumes that the first step in teaching is to decide what changes should take place in the learner—what is the goal of teaching. This leads us to a general definition of an **instructional objective:** it is a clear and unambiguous description of your educational intentions for your students.

The Value of Objectives

The effects of providing students with instructional objectives are not clear-cut. Having objectives seems to improve achievement, but only under certain conditions. First, objectives can promote learning with loosely organized and less-structured activities such as lectures, films, and research projects. With very structured materials such as programmed instruction, objectives seem less important (Tobias & Duchastel, 1974). Second, if the importance of some information is not clear from the learning materials and activities themselves, instructional objectives will probably help focus students' attention and thus increase achievement (Duchastel, 1979). Finally, having objectives at the beginning of a reading passage seems to help students remember very specific verbal information from the passage. But when the task involves simply getting the gist of the passage or transferring the information to a new situation, objectives are not as effective. In these situations, it is better to use questions that focus on meaning, inserting the questions right before the passage to be read (Hamilton, 1985).

Improved Communication. In day-to-day classroom interaction, a good number of a teacher's verbal and nonverbal messages may be ambiguous. For example, a teacher may know that one goal of teaching is to foster good citizenship. This kind of vague purpose is an example of what Dyer (1967) years ago called "word magic." Goals stated in word magic sound great. But no one really knows what they mean. What will the students be doing when they are good citizens? Specifying learning objectives can help teachers clarify the changes they believe are important for their students. This will improve communication between teacher and student.

Planning and Testing. Each day teachers must plan to do something; they must select or create activities and put those activities into some

Instructional Objective
Clear statement of what students are intended to learn through instruction.

order. A reasonable approach is to select activities that will help students learn something worth knowing—or, in other words, help them master important objectives. Even if a teacher never specifies objectives, students will become aware of them when the tests or assignments are graded. If, for example, the top grades go to students who are best at memorizing facts, the students will realize that the objective was to memorize facts. If, on the other hand, the objectives are supplied in advance, both students and teacher will know what the criteria are.

Kinds of Objectives

One of the factors that distinguish the various approaches to writing objectives is the level of specificity required. At a very general, abstract level are the grand goals society may have for graduates of public schools—such as increased intellectual development and effective citizenship. But very general goals become meaningless as potential guidelines for instruction. On the other hand, objectives that are too specific may teach poor study habits by focusing the students' attention on specific facts and encouraging them to skip anything that is not mentioned in the objective (TenBrink, 1986).

Most psychologists and educators agree that we need something between grand generalities and specific item-by-item instructions for each student. But here the agreement ends. Objectives written by people with behavioral views focus on observable and measurable changes in the learner. **Behavioral objectives** use terms such as *list, define, add,* or *calculate.* Objectives written by cognitivists, on the other hand, emphasize internal changes. Their objectives are more likely to include words such as *understand, recognize, create,* or *apply.* Not surprisingly, **cognitive objectives** tend to be more general and less clearly measurable than behavioral objectives. They also tend to be less restricting.

There is a way to consider both the cognitive and behavioral perspectives in writing objectives. Look at the examples in Table 12.1. The more general cognitive objectives in the left-hand column have been **operationalized** to form the more specific behavioral objectives in the right-hand column; that is, the more general objectives have been made measurable.

Behavioral Objectives
Instructional objectives stated in terms of observable behaviors.

Cognitive Objectives
Instructional objectives stated in terms of higher-level thinking operations.

Operationalize Make measurable by making specific.

TABLE 12.1 Objectives: General and Specific

General Objectives	More Specific Objectives
The student reasons in solving simple arithmetic problems.	The student solves simple arithmetic problems written in a new form: $3 + 4 = ?$ and $3 + 4 = x.$
The student understands the concept of meter in poetry.	The student scans poems in various meters and correctly identifies the meters.
The student appreciates teamwork.	The student passes the ball when appropriate.

Suppose your goals are for students to reason, understand, and appreciate. How can you tell if they have accomplished these goals? One way is to give the students a specific, measurable task that will provide evidence for the change. Let's look at one well-developed method of writing specific measurable objectives.

Mager: Start with the Specific. Robert Mager has developed a very influential system for writing instructional objectives. Mager's idea is that objectives ought to describe what students will be doing when demonstrating their achievement and how you will know they are doing it (Mager, 1975). Mager's objectives are generally regarded as behavioral.

According to Mager, a good objective has three parts. First, it describes the intended student behavior—what must the student *do*? Second, it lists the conditions under which the behavior will occur—how will this behavior be recognized or tested? Third, it gives the criteria for acceptable performance on the test. Table 12.2 shows how the system works. This system, with its emphasis on final behavior, requires a very explicit statement. Mager contends that such an effort is worthwhile. He believes that often students can teach themselves if they are given well-stated objectives.

Gronlund: Start with the General. Norman Gronlund (1991) offers a different approach. He believes that an objective should be stated first in general terms (*understand, solve, appreciate,* etc.). Then the teacher should clarify by listing a few sample behaviors that would provide evidence that the student has attained the objective. Gronlund's system is often used for writing cognitive objectives.

Look at the example in Table 12.3, taken from Cangelosi (1990). The goal here really is *problem solving.* The teacher does not want the student to stop with *discriminating, stating, computing,* and so on. Instead, the teacher looks at performance on these sample tasks to decide if the student can solve real-life problems. The teacher could just as well have chosen six different tasks to indicate ability to solve problems.

Gronlund's emphasis on specific objectives as samples of more general student ability is important. A teacher could never list all the behaviors that might be involved in solving problems in the subject area. But stating an initial general objective makes it clear that ability to solve problems is the purpose.

TABLE 12.2 Mager's Three-Part System

Part	Central Question	Example
Student behavior	Do what?	Mark statements with an *F* for fact or an *O* for opinion
Conditions of performance	Under what conditions?	Given an article from a newspaper
Performance criteria	How well?	75% of the statements are correctly marked

Source: From R. F. Mager, *Preparing instructional objectives,* 1975, by Fearon, Belmont, CA. Reprinted by permission of David S. Lake Publishers.

TABLE 12.3   Gronlund's Combined Method for Creating Objectives

General Objective

For sixth-grade mathematics: Student can efficiently solve real-life problems that require finding sizes of surface areas.

Specific Examples

1. Discriminates between the surface area of a figure and other quantitative characteristics of that figure (e.g., height and volume).
2. States the formula for the area of a rectangle.
3. Given the dimensions of a rectangle, computes its area.
4. Given the dimensions of a right triangle, computes its area.
5. Given the dimensions of a right cylinder, computes its surface area.
6. When confronted with a real-life problem, determines whether computing the area of a surface will help solve that problem.

Source: Adapted from *Designing tests for evaluating student achievement* by James S. Cangelosi, p. 6. Copyright © 1990 by Longman Publishing Group. Reprinted with permission from Longman Publishing Group.

The most recent research on instructional objectives tends to favor approaches similar to Gronlund's. It seems reasonable to state a few central objectives in general terms and clarify them with samples of specific behaviors, as in Table 12.3 (Hamilton, 1985; Popham, 1988).

Criticisms and Advantages

Not all educators believe writing objectives is valuable. According to some critics, because trivial, short-term goals are easier to specify than higher-level, more relevant goals, instructional objectives are likely to be trivial and irrelevant. Many critics feel that the use of instructional objectives has a potential effect of spoon-feeding students. If only low-level abilities are specified as outcomes, and if tests are merely a collection of instructional objectives turned into questions, spoon-feeding is indeed likely. The students' opportunities to question and explore may well be limited. But this does not have to be the case. Consider this objective, prepared for a relatively high-level secondary course in history:

> In class, without access to notes, given three presidential elections between 1900 and 1944, write a 200-word essay describing how domestic policy might have changed if the defeated presidential candidate had been elected.

For the test the teacher selects the elections of 1900, 1912, and 1940. Since these particular years were not specified in the objective, students must know a number of facts. What president was chosen in each election year between 1900 and 1944? Who ran against each? What was the

Guidelines

Developing Instructional Objectives

Avoid "word magic"—phrases that sound noble and important but say very little.

Examples

1. Keep the focus on specific changes that will take place in the students' knowledge or skills.
2. Ask students to explain the meaning of the objectives. If they can't give specific examples of what you mean, the objectives are not communicating your intentions to your students.

Suit the activities to the objectives.

Examples

1. If the goal is the memorization of vocabulary, give the students memory aids and practice exercises.

2. If the goal is the ability to develop well-thought-out positions, consider position papers, debates, learn projects, or mock trials.
3. If you want students to become better writers, give many opportunities for writing and rewriting.

Make sure your tests are related to your objectives.

Examples

1. Write objectives and rough drafts for tests at the same time.
2. Weight the tests according to the importance of the various objectives and the time spent on each.

---

domestic policy advocated by each candidate? What were key events during each president's term in office? Besides understanding these facts and concepts, the students would have to be able to make inferences, give evidence to support hypotheses, and think divergently (come up with many possible right answers). This is hardly spoon-feeding! The Guidelines should help you whether you decide to make thorough use of objectives or just to prepare them for certain assignments.

TASK ANALYSIS

When teachers try to decide what students should learn, they face an overwhelming number of possibilities. Several solutions to this dilemma have been proposed. Here we will look at one of the most influential methods of determining learning objectives: task analysis.

The procedure involved in **task analysis** was originally developed by R. B. Miller (1962) to help the armed services train personnel. Miller's system begins with a definition of the final performance requirement, what the trainee (or student) must be able to do at the end of the program or unit. Then the objectives that will lead to the final goal are specified. The procedure simply breaks skills and processes down into subskills and subprocesses.

In the classroom, the teacher begins by asking: "What will the students have to do before they can reach the final goal I have in mind?" The answer to this question may help identify several underlying skills. Let's say five skills are identified. The teacher then asks: "What must the students be able to do to succeed at each of these five skills?" The answer

Task Analysis System for breaking down a task hierarchically into basic skills and subskills.

There are many subskills involved in doing a research paper. A task analysis reveals the importance of using library card catalogues. Can the students do this?

this time should produce a number of subskills for each of the basic skills. This working backward should give a full picture of all the abilities a student must have to accomplish the objective successfully.

Consider the example of task analysis in Figure 12.1 in which students must write a position paper based on library research. If the teacher assigned the position paper without analyzing the task in this way, what could happen? Some of the students might not know how to use the card catalog. They might search through one or two encyclopedias, then write a summary of the issues based only on the encyclopedia articles. Another group of students might know how to use the card catalog, tables of contents, and indexes but have difficulty reaching conclusions. They might hand in lengthy papers listing summaries of different ideas. Another group of students might be able to draw conclusions, but their written presentations might be so confusing and grammatically incorrect that the teacher could not understand what they were trying to say. Each of the groups would have failed, but for different reasons.

A task analysis gives a picture of the logical sequence of steps leading toward the final goal. An awareness of this sequence can help teachers make sure that students have the necessary skills *before* they embark on an assignment. In addition, when students have difficulty, the teacher can pinpoint problem areas. The process can also work in reverse. Student errors can highlight the subskills required to complete a task successfully. Teachers can use the information from student errors to analyze the task before presenting it to another class.

FIGURE 12.1   Task Analysis for a Library Assignment This incomplete task analysis reveals some of the specific knowledge and skills required to write a position paper based on library research. Many of the skills are interrelated, but all are necessary.

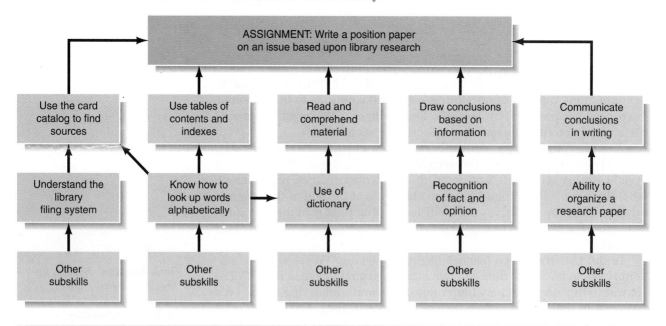

TAXONOMIES

Several decades ago, as interest in defining educational objectives was increasing, a group of experts in educational evaluation led by Benjamin Bloom studied the idea of defining objectives very systematically. They developed a **taxonomy,** or classification system, of educational objectives. Objectives were divided into three domains: cognitive, affective, and psychomotor. A handbook describing the objectives in each area was eventually published. In real life, of course, behaviors from these three domains occur simultaneously. While students are writing (psychomotor), they are also remembering or reasoning (cognitive), and they are likely to have some emotional response to the task as well (affective).

The Cognitive Domain

Six basic objectives are listed in Bloom's taxonomy of the thinking or **cognitive domain** (Bloom, Engelhart, Frost, Hill, & Krathwohl, 1956):

1. *Knowledge:* Remembering or recognizing something without necessarily understanding, using, or changing it.
2. *Comprehension:* Understanding the material being communicated without necessarily relating it to anything else.
3. *Application:* Using a general concept to solve a particular problem.
4. *Analysis:* Breaking something down into its parts.
5. *Synthesis:* Creating something new by combining different ideas.
6. *Evaluation:* Judging the value of materials or methods as they might be applied in a particular situation.

It is common in education to consider these objectives as a hierarchy, each skill building on those below, but this is not entirely accurate. For example, some subjects, such as mathematics, do not fit this structure very well (Pring, 1971). Still, you will hear many references to lower-level and higher-level objectives. As a rough way of thinking about objectives, this level idea can be helpful.

Consider how Bloom's taxonomy might suggest objectives for a course. Table 12.2 gave one example of a specific objective at the *analysis* level in a social studies class—distinguishing between fact and opinion in news stories. At the *synthesis* level, an objective for the class could be written this way:

Given a list of three facts, write a two-paragraph news story taking a position on an issue and documenting the position with the facts.

At the level of *evaluation,* the objective might be written like this:

Given two articles that present contradictory views of a recent event, decide which article gives the fairer presentation and justify your choice.

Taxonomy Classification system.

Cognitive Domain In Bloom's taxonomy, memory and reasoning objectives.

The taxonomy of objectives can also be helpful in planning evaluation, since different types of test items are appropriate for objectives at the various levels. Gronlund (1988) suggests that knowledge objectives can best be measured by true-false, short-answer, matching, or multiple-choice tests. Such tests will also work with the comprehension, application, and analysis levels of the taxonomy. For measuring synthesis and evaluation objectives, however, the essay test is more appropriate. Essay tests will also work at the middle levels of the taxonomy.

The Affective Domain

The objectives in the taxonomy of the **affective domain,** or domain of emotional response, run from least committed to most committed (Krathwohl, Bloom, & Masia, 1956). At the lowest level, a student would simply pay attention to a certain idea. At the highest level, the student would adopt an idea or a value and act consistently with that idea. There are five basic objectives in the affective domain.

1. *Receiving:* Being aware of or attending to something in the environment; the I'll-listen-to-the-concert-but-I-won't-promise-to-like-it level.
2. *Responding:* Showing some new behavior as a result of experience; at this level a person might applaud after the concert or hum some of the music the next day.
3. *Valuing:* Showing some definite involvement or commitment; at this point a person might choose to go to a concert instead of a film.
4. *Organization:* Integrating a new value into one's general set of values, giving it some ranking among one's general priorities; this is the level at which a person would begin to make long-range commitments to concert attendance.
5. *Characterization by value:* Acting consistently with the new value; at this highest level, a person would be firmly committed to a love of music and demonstrate it openly and consistently.

Like the basic objectives in the cognitive domain, these five objectives are very general. To write specific learning objectives, you must state what students will actually be doing when they are receiving, responding, valuing, and so on. For example, an objective for a nutrition class at the valuing level might be stated:

> After completing the unit on consumer action, at least 50 percent of the class will support the junk-food boycott project by giving up candy for a month.

There are at least two ways in which assessing affective objectives may be helpful. Evaluation of these objectives can serve diagnostic purposes, to see what values students bring to class. Final evaluation may also help teachers gauge their success in bringing about a desired change in attitudes or values.

Suppose, for example, that an important goal in a science class is commitment to ethics in conducting and reporting research. If the teacher learns at the beginning of the course that students approve of falsifying scientific results to further one's position, the teacher will have a ready-made affective goal to pursue throughout the course. If the teacher learns

Affective Domain
Emotional objectives.

that students still feel this way at the end of a course, the teacher may wish to approach that topic a little differently the next time.

But it is difficult to measure the attainment of affective objectives. How can the teacher in the nutrition example be sure that students have given up candy in support of a junk-food boycott? The best method may be to ask them to report anonymously on their candy consumption; if students have to sign their names to their responses, the process may counteract the desire to reach another affective goal, honesty. Also, if students are graded on their success in boycotting candy, this process might really encourage the students to give false reports. In most cases, it is best not to grade affective measures.

The Psychomotor Domain

Until recently, the **psychomotor domain,** or realm of physical ability objectives, has been overlooked for the most part by teachers not directly involved with physical education. There are several taxonomies in this domain (e.g., Harrow, 1972; Simpson, 1972). These taxonomies generally move from basic perceptions and reflex actions to skilled, creative movements. James Cangelosi (1990) provides a useful way to think about objectives in the psychomotor domain as either (1) voluntary muscle capabilities that require endurance, strength, flexibility, agility, or speed; or (2) the ability to perform a specific skill.

Objectives in the psychomotor domain should be of interest to a wide range of educators, including those in fine arts, vocational-technical education, and special education. Many other subjects, such as chemistry, physics, and biology, also require specialized movements and well-developed hand and eye coordination. Using lab equipment, the "mouse" on a computer, or art materials means learning new physical skills. Here are two psychomotor objectives:

> Four minutes after completing a 1-mile run in 8 minutes or under, your heart rate will be below 120.

> Without referring to notes or diagrams, assemble the appropriate laboratory apparatus to distill ———.

Learning in the psychomotor area means developing a particular performance ability. How do you assess a student's performance? The obvious answer is to ask the student to demonstrate the skill and observe the student's proficiency. In some cases, the performance of the skill results in a product, so assessment of the product can be substituted for observation of the actual performance. An art student learning to use the potter's wheel, for example, should be able to produce a pot that is symmetrical, stands by itself, and meets a number of other criteria.

When students are actually demonstrating skills or performing, you need a checklist or rating scale to help you focus on the important aspects of the skill being evaluated. A checklist usually gives the measurable dimensions of performance, along with a series of blank spaces for

What does the coach mean by "appreciating team work"? This learning objective could be operationalized as "passing the ball to another player when that person is in a better position to score a point."

Psychomotor Domain
Physical ability objectives.

TABLE 12.4   Checklist to Evaluate Student's Performance of a Two-Arm Press

The student, stationed in front of a barbell with only a light weight that would offer little resistance, is directed to demonstrate one two-arm press.

Scoring key: (11 points possible) +1 for each blank checked on the following form:

_____ feet properly positioned under the bar throughout the entire lift
_____ proper grip and hand spread
_____ back straight throughout
_____ head facing forward throughout
_____ clean initiated with knees flexed
_____ clean initiated with elbows extended
_____ clean properly executed
_____ pauses with bar just above the chest
_____ executes press properly
_____ returns bar to position just above chest and pauses
_____ gently returns bar to floor, flexing knees on the way down

Source: Adapted from *Designing test for evaluating student achievement* by James S. Cangelosi, p. 125. Copyright © 1990 by Longman Publishing Group. Reprinted with permission from Longman Publishing Group.

judgments. Table 12.4 provides an example. A rating scale generally follows the same plan but has a numerical scale to rate each aspect of performance.

The Big Picture: Course Objectives

Once you have learned to write and evaluate objectives in the cognitive, affective, and psychomotor domains, your job is not over. You will be teaching more than single skills and lessons. You must plan an integrated program of study and then evaluate progress in that program. In planning objectives for an entire unit, many teachers develop a **behavior-content matrix** that relates course content to students' cognitive, affective, and psychomotor behaviors. The first step is to decide the general objectives for the course, stated in broad terms. The teacher then breaks down each general objective into two components. The first is student behavior—that is, knowledge of facts, knowledge of concepts, ability to generalize, and so on. The second component is course content—that is, the subjects to be covered in the course. If one of the general objectives in an English class was to enhance appreciation of American literature, student behaviors might include knowledge (of authors, historical periods, book titles, themes, and styles); ability to compare (different styles, different themes); and ability to criticize. The course content component would include the different novels, poems, short stories, and so on that you wished to cover.

In drawing up the matrix or chart, as in Figure 12.2, the teacher lists student behaviors across the top, usually from simplest to most complex,

Behavior-Content Matrix
A planning method that integrates expected student behaviors with course topics to arrive at specific objectives.

FIGURE 12.2   **A Behavior-Content Matrix for a Unit on Decimals**   Here the teacher has decided to emphasize knowledge and comprehension of "Renaming" and knowledge of "Definitions" in this unit on decimals. The numbers indicate how many objectives are to be written for each behavior and content combination.

Content	Behaviors				Total Objectives
	Knowledge	Comprehension	Application	Analysis	
Multiplication		1	1	1	3
Addition and Subtraction			1	1	2
Division		1	1	1	3
Renaming	2	2		1	5
Definitions	2			1	3
Total Objectives	4	4	3	5	16

Source: Reprinted by permission from J. R. Hills (1976), *Measurement and evaluation in the classroom.* Columbus, OH: Merrill, p. 8.

and content areas down the side. At each square where a particular behavior intersects with a particular content area, the teacher can write instructional objectives. In this way, the teacher makes sure all important behaviors and topics are *considered* as possible objectives. Priorities can be set, with several objectives for some squares and none for others, depending on the outcomes the teacher is seeking. At test time, the teacher can emphasize key areas by asking more questions from the most important squares.

If you develop a behavior-content matrix for a course, you may avoid many of the potential problems with instructional objectives, such as trivializing and spoon-feeding. A behavior-content mix also lets you see all the objectives of a course at once and organize them in the most logical sequence.

BASIC TEACHING STRATEGIES FOR REACHING OBJECTIVES

Let's assume you have developed the objectives for your class and have a general idea of the goals for the entire year. What next? You still need to decide what to do on Monday. This section describes a variety of general teaching strategies or formats for turning objectives into action in the classroom. These strategies are not complete models of teaching but rather building blocks that can be used to construct lessons and units. In the next chapter we will examine larger, more complete models of teaching that incorporate many different strategies. We begin with the strategy many people associate most directly with teaching—lecturing.

Lecturing

Some studies have found that lecturing takes up one-sixth to one-fourth of all classroom time. High school teachers, of course, lecture more than teachers in the lower grades. You will probably learn about how to lecture in your methods classes. Many different approaches are available, and the one you choose will depend on your objectives and the subject you are teaching. You will certainly want to keep in mind the age of your students, because the younger your students, the briefer and simpler your explanations should be. You may also want to follow a basic three-part format suggested by Kindsvatter, Wilen, and Ishler (1988), shown in Table 12.5.

Lecturing is appropriate for communicating a large amount of material to many students in a short period of time. The teacher can integrate information from many sources and give students a more complete understanding of a subject in less time than it would take for the students to integrate all the information themselves. Lecturing is a good method for introducing a new topic, giving background information, and motivating students to learn more on their own. Lecturing also helps students learn to listen accurately and critically and gives the teacher a chance to make on-the-spot changes to help students understand when they are confused (Gilstrap & Martin, 1975; Kindsvatter, Wilen, & Ishler, 1988). Lectures are therefore most appropriate for cognitive and affective objectives at the lower levels of the taxonomies described earlier—for knowledge, comprehension, application, receiving, responding, and valuing.

The lecture method also has some disadvantages. You may find that some students have trouble listening for more than a few minutes at a time and simply tune you out. Lecturing puts the students in a passive position and may prevent them from asking or thinking of questions.

TABLE 12.5 Three Phases in the Lecture Method

Entry: Preparation for Learning

A. State objectives and rationale.
B. Provide a context for the new material to be presented.
C. Focus attention on key concept, generalization, or principle that encompasses the lecture.

Presentation

A. Sequence content from simpler to complex understandings.
B. Enhance presentation with visual aids.
C. Stimulate attention with verbal and nonverbal behaviors.

Closure: Review of Learning

A. Integrate with students' knowledge and experiences.
B. Transition to next lesson or activity.

Source: Dynamics of effective teaching by Richard Kindsvatter, William Willen, and Margaret Ishler, p. 221. Copyright © 1988 by Longman Publishing Group. Reprinted with permission from Longman Publishing Group.

Lecturing Organized explanation of a topic by a teacher.

Also, students learn and comprehend at different paces, whereas a lecture proceeds at the lecturer's own pace (Gilstrap & Martin, 1975). If your objectives include having students solve a problem; develop arguments; write essays, poems, or short stories; create paintings; or evaluate work, then you must go beyond lecturing to methods that require more direct student involvement.

Recitation and Questioning

Recitation is a common approach to teaching that has been with us for many years (Stodolsky, 1988). Teachers pose questions and students answer. The teacher's questions generally follow some sort of plan to develop a framework for the subject matter involved. The students' answers are often followed by reactions from the teacher, such as statements of praise, correction, or requests for further information. The pattern from the teacher's point of view consists of *structure* (setting a framework), *solicitation* (asking questions), and *reaction* (praising, correcting, and expanding) (Clark et al., 1979). These steps are repeated over and over.

Let us consider the heart of **recitation,** the soliciting or questioning phase, by looking at the different kinds of questions that may be asked, when to ask them, and how to respond to student answers.

Kinds of Questions. Some educators have estimated that high school teachers ask an average of 395 questions per day (Gall, 1970). What are these questions like? Many can be categorized in terms of Bloom's taxonomy of objectives in the cognitive domain. Table 12.6 on page 450 offers examples of questions at the different taxonomic levels.

Another way to categorize questioning is in terms of **convergent questions** (only one right answer) or **divergent questions** (many possible answers). Questions about concrete facts are convergent: Who ruled England in 1540? Who wrote the original *Peter Pan*? Questions dealing with

Recitation is a common format for teaching. Here the arrangement of the room and the students' chairs makes questioning easier and helps the students stay focused on the topic.

Recitation Format of teacher questioning, student response, and teacher feedback.

Convergent Questions Questions having a single correct answer.

Divergent Questions Questions having no single correct answer.

TABLE 12.6 Classroom Questions for Objectives in the Cognitive Domain

Category	Type of Thinking Expected	Examples
Knowledge (recognition)	Recalling or recognizing information as learned	Define. . . . What is the capital of . . .? What did the text say about . . .?
Comprehension	Demonstrating understanding of the material; transforming, reorganizing, or interpreting	Explain in your own words. . . . Compare. . . . What is the main idea of . . .? Describe what you saw. . . .
Application	Using information to solve a problem with a single correct answer	Which principle is demonstrated in . . .? Calculate the area of. . . . Apply the rule of . . . to solve. . . .
Analysis	Critical thinking; identifying reasons and motives; making inferences based on specific data; analyzing conclusions to see if supported by evidence	What influenced the writings of . . .? Why was Washington, D.C. chosen . . .? Which of the following are facts and which are opinions? Based on your experiment, what is the chemical . . .?
Synthesis	Divergent, original thinking; original plan, proposal, design, or story	What's a good name for this . . .? How could we raise money for . . .? What would the United States be like if the South had won . . .?
Evaluation	Judging the merits of ideas, offering opinions, applying standards	Which U.S. senator is the most effective? Which painting do you believe to be better? Why? Why would you favor . . .?

Source: Adapted by permission from M. Sadker and D. Sadker (1986), Questioning skills. In J. Cooper (Ed.), *Classroom teaching skills: A handbook* (3rd ed.). Lexington, MA: D. C. Heath, pp. 143–160.

opinions or hypotheses are divergent: Why did the United States go to war in 1898? What do you think of nuclear power plants?

Quite a bit of space in education textbooks has been devoted to urging teachers to ask more **higher-level questions** (analysis, synthesis, and evaluation) and divergent questions. Is this really a better way of questioning? Research has provided several surprises.

Fitting the Questions to the Students. Stallings and Kaskowitz (1975) and Soar (1973) found that the frequency of knowledge questions, comprehension-level questions, convergent questions, and single-word answers is positively related to student learning. In these studies, high-level questions were negatively related to student learning. But we should keep three facts in mind in interpreting these results. The students were in primary grades; they were from low socioeconomic backgrounds; and their achievement was measured with test questions at the knowledge and comprehension levels. Other investigators have reached different

Higher-Level Questions
Questions that ask students to apply knowledge to new situations or to analyze, synthesize, or evaluate ideas.

conclusions. For example, Redfield and Rousseau (1981) examined 14 studies and concluded that higher-level questions can lead to achievement gains when teachers are trained to use this approach appropriately.

It appears that both types of questions can be effective (Gall, 1984). Different patterns seem to be better for different students, however. The best pattern for younger students and for lower-ability students of all ages is simple questions allowing a high percentage of correct answers, ample encouragement, help when the student does not have the correct answer, and praise. For high-ability students, the successful pattern includes harder questions at both higher and lower levels and more critical feedback (Berliner, 1987; Good, 1988).

Whatever their age or ability, all students should have some experience with thought-provoking questions and, if necessary, help in learning how to answer them. As we saw in chapter 8, to master critical thinking and problem-solving skills, students must have a chance to practice the skills. They also need time to think about their answers. But research shows that teachers wait an average of only 1 second for students to answer (Rowe, 1974). Consider the following slice of classroom life (Sadker & Sadker, 1986a, p. 170):

Teacher: Who wrote the poem "Stopping by Woods on a Snowy Evening"? Tom?

Tom: Robert Frost.

Teacher: Good. What action takes place in the poem? Sally?

Sally: A man stops his sleigh to watch the woods get filled with snow.

Teacher: Yes. Emma, what thoughts go through the man's mind?

Emma: He thinks how beautiful the woods are. . . . (She pauses for a second)

Teacher: What else does he think about? Joe?

Joe: He thinks how he would like to stay and watch. (Pauses for a second)

Teacher: Yes—and what else? Rita? (Waits half a second) Come on, Rita, you can get the answer to this. (Waits half a second) Well, why does he feel he can't stay there indefinitely and watch the woods and the snow?

Sarah: Well, I think it might be—(Pauses a second)

Teacher: Think, Sarah. (Teacher waits for half a second) All right then—Mike? (Waits again for half a second) John? (Waits half a second) What's the matter with everyone today? Didn't you do the reading?

Very little thoughtful responding can take place in this situation. When teachers learn to pose a question, then wait at least 5 seconds before calling on a student to answer, students tend to give longer answers; more students are likely to participate, ask questions, and volunteer appropriate answers; student comments involving analysis, synthesis, inference, and speculation tend to increase; and the students generally appear more confident in their answers (Berliner, 1987; Rowe, 1974; Sadker & Sadker, 1986a; Tobin, 1987). This seems like a simple improvement in teaching, but 5 seconds of silence is not that easy to handle. It takes practice. You might try asking students to jot down ideas or even discuss the question with another student. This makes the wait more comfortable and gives students a chance to think. Of course, if it is clear that students are lost or don't understand the question, waiting longer will not help. When your question is met with blank stares, rephrase the question or ask if anyone can explain the confusion.

A word about selecting students to answer questions. If you call only on volunteers, then you may get the wrong idea about how well students understand the material. And the same people volunteer over and over again. Many expert teachers have some systematic way of making sure that they call on everyone—they pull names from a jar or check names off a list as each student speaks (Weinstein & Mignano, 1993). Another possibility is to put each student's name on an index card, then shuffle the cards and go through the deck as you call on people. You can use the card to make notes about students' answers or extra help they may need.

Responding to Student Answers. What do you do after the student answers? The most common response, occurring about 50 percent of the time in most classrooms, is simple acceptance—"OK" or "Uh-huh" (Sadker & Sadker, 1986a). But there are better reactions, depending on whether the student's answer is correct, partially correct, or wrong. If the answer is quick, firm and correct, simply accept the answer or ask another question. If the answer is correct but hesitant, give the student feedback about why the answer is correct: "That's right, Chris, because the Senate does not have the power to. . . ." This allows you to explain the material again. If this student is unsure, others may be confused as well. If the answer is partially or completely wrong but the student has made an honest attempt, you should probe for more information, give clues, simplify the question, review the previous steps, or reteach the material. If the student's wrong answer is silly or careless, however, it is better simply to correct the answer and go on. Whatever you do, don't let misunderstandings go uncorrected (Good, 1988; Rosenshine & Stevens, 1986).

Group Discussion

Group discussion is in some ways similar to the recitation strategy. A teacher may pose questions, listen to student answers, react, and probe for more information. But in a true group discussion the teacher tries to assume a less dominant role. Students ask questions, answer each other's questions, and respond to each other's answers.

Again, choices about when to use group discussion can best be made with an understanding of the advantages and disadvantages of the method in relation to your objectives. On the positive side, the students are directly involved and have the chance to participate. Group discussion helps students learn to express themselves clearly, to justify opinions, and to tolerate different views. Group discussion also gives students a chance to ask for clarification and get more information. Students also can assume responsibility by sharing the leadership of the group with the teacher.

Thus, group discussions are appropriate for objectives like evaluation of ideas, development of tolerant attitudes, and synthesis of personal viewpoints. Discussions are also useful when students are trying to understand difficult concepts that go against common sense. As we saw in chapter 8, many scientific concepts, like the role of light in vision or Newton's laws of motion, are difficult to grasp because they contradict commonsense notions. By thinking together, challenging each other, and suggesting and evaluating possible explanations, students are more likely to reach a genuine understanding.

Of course, there are disadvantages. Class discussions are quite unpredictable and may easily digress into exchanges of ignorance. Some members of the group may have great difficulty in participating and may become anxious if forced to speak. In addition, you may have to do a good

Guidelines

Leading Class Discussions

Invite the participation of shy children.

Examples

1. "What's your opinion, Joel? We need to hear from some other students."
2. Don't wait until there is a deadly silence to ask shy students to reply. Most people, even those who are confident, hate to break a silence.

Direct student comments and questions back to another student.

Examples

1. "That's an unusual idea, Steve. Kim, what do you think of Steve's idea?"
2. "That's an important question, John. Maura, do you have any thoughts about how you'd answer that?"
3. Encourage students to look at and talk to one another rather than wait for your opinion.

Make sure you understand what a student has said. If you are unsure, other students may be unsure as well.

Examples

1. Ask a second student to summarize what the first student said; then the first student can try again to explain if the summary is incorrect.
2. "Karen, I think you're saying. . . . Is that right, or have I misunderstood?"

Probe for more information.

Examples

1. "That's a strong statement. Do you have any evidence to back it up?"
2. "Tell us how you reached that conclusion. What steps did you go through?"

Bring the discussion back to the subject.

Examples

1. "Let's see, we were discussing . . . and Sarah made one suggestion. Does anyone have a different idea?"
2. "Before we continue, let me try to summarize what has happened thus far."

Give time for thought before asking for responses.

Example

"How would your life be different if television had never been invented? Jot down your ideas on paper, and we will share reactions in a minute." After a minute: "Jean, will you tell us what you wrote?"

When a student finishes speaking, look around the room to judge reactions.

Examples

1. If other students look puzzled, ask them to describe why they are confused.
2. If students are nodding assent, ask them to give an example of what was just said.

deal of preparation to ensure that participants have a common background of knowledge on which to base the discussion. And large groups are often unwieldy. In many cases, a few students will dominate the discussion while the others daydream (Kindsvatter, Wilen, & Ishler, 1988).

Seatwork and Homework

There is little research on the effects of **seatwork,** or independent classroom desk work, but it is clear that this technique is often overused. In fact, a study found that American elementary students spend 51 percent of mathematics time in school working alone, while Japanese students spend 26 percent and Taiwanese students spend only 9 percent (Stigler, Lee, & Stevenson, 1987). Some educators point to these differences as part of the explanation for Asian students' superiority in mathematics. Seatwork should follow up a lesson and give students supervised practice. It should not be the main mode of instruction.

In the 1980s several studies reported strong positive correlations between the amount of homework students were assigned and their grades (Keith, 1982). Many schools responded by requiring that more homework be assigned. But just assigning more homework is not necessarily a good idea. Several conditions must be met to make the work worthwhile (Walberg, Pascal, & Weinstein, 1985).

The assignments of seatwork and homework must be meaningful extensions of class lessons, not just busywork. Unfortunately, many workbook pages and "dittos" do little to teach important objectives. Before you assign work, ask yourself, "Does doing this work help students learn anything that matters?" For example, consider this task, cited in the report of the Commission on Reading of the National Institute of Education (Anderson, Hiebert, Scott, & Wilkinson, 1985):

> Read each sentence. Decide which consonant letter is used the most. Underline it each time.

What's the point? This sort of activity communicates to students that reading isn't very important or useful.

Carol Weinstein and Andy Mignano (1993) describe several alternatives to workbooks and dittos, such as silent reading and reading aloud to a partner, "real" writing for an audience, letters, journals, transcribing conversations and punctuating them properly, making up problems, working on long-term projects and reports, brainteasers and puzzles, and computer activities. One of my favorites is a group story. Two students begin a story on the computer. Then two more add a paragraph. The story grows with each new pair's addition. The students are reading and writing, editing and improving.

To benefit from seatwork or homework, students must stay involved and do the work. The first step toward involvement is getting students started correctly by making sure they understand the assignment. It may help to do the first few questions as a class, to clear up any misconceptions. This is especially important for homework assignments, because students may have no one to consult if they have problems with the

Seatwork Independent classroom work.

assignment. A second way to keep students involved is to hold them accountable for completing the work correctly, not just for filling in the page. This means the work should be checked, the errors corrected, and the results counted toward the class grade (Brophy & Good, 1986).

Seatwork particularly requires careful monitoring. As you saw in the previous chapter, effective teachers supervise students, keeping them actively involved in the materials so that the time spent on seatwork is not wasted. Being available to students doing seatwork is more effective than offering students help before they ask for it. To be available, you should move around the class and avoid spending too much time with one or two students. Short, frequent contacts are best (Brophy & Good, 1986; Rosenshine, 1977).

Sometimes you may be working with a small group while other students do seatwork. In these situations it is especially important for students to know what to do if they need help. One expert teacher described by Weinstein and Mignano (1993) taught students a rule, "Ask three, then me." Students have to consult three classmates before seeking help from the teacher. This teacher also spends time early in the year showing students *how* to help each other—how to ask questions and how to explain.

Students should see the connection between the seatwork or homework and the lesson. Tell them *why* they are doing the work. The objectives should be clear, all the materials that might be needed should be provided, and the work should be easy enough that students can succeed on their own. Success rates should be high—near 100 percent. When seatwork is too difficult, students often resort to guessing or copying just to finish (Anderson, 1985).

Inquiry Methods

John Dewey described the basic **inquiry teaching** format in 1910. There have been a number of adaptations of this strategy, but the form usually includes the following elements (Pasch, Sparks-Langer, Gardner, Starko, & Moody, 1991):

> The teacher presents a puzzling event, question, or problem.
> The students:
>
> - formulate hypotheses to explain the event or solve the problem.
> - collect data to test the hypotheses.
> - draw conclusions.
> - reflect on the original problem and on the thinking processes needed to solve it.

At times, teachers present a problem and students ask yes/no questions to gather data and test hypotheses. This allows the teacher to monitor students' thinking and guide the process. Here is an example:

1. Teacher presents discrepant event (after clarifying ground rules). The teacher blows softly across the top of an 8½" × 11" sheet of paper, and the paper rises. She tells students to figure out *why* it rises.

Inquiry Teaching Approach in which teacher presents a puzzling situation and students solve the problem by gathering data and testing conclusions.

2. Students ask questions to gather more information and to isolate relevant variables. Teacher answers only "yes" or "no." Students ask if temperature is important (no). They ask if the paper is of a special kind (no). They ask if air pressure has anything to do with the paper rising (yes). Questions continue.

3. Students test causal relationships. In this case, they ask if the nature of the air on top causes the paper to rise (yes). They ask if the fast movement of the air results in less pressure on the top (yes). Then they test out the rule with other materials—for example, thin plastic.

4. Students form a generalization (principle): "If the air on the top moves faster than the air on the bottom of a surface, then the air pressure on top is lessened, and the object rises." Later lessons expand students' understanding of the principles and physical laws through further experiments.

5. The teacher leads students in a discussion of their thinking processes. What were the important variables? How did you put the causes and effects together? and so on. (Pasch et al., 1991, pp. 188–189)

Inquiry teaching allows students to learn content and process at the same time (Kindsvatter, Wilen, & Ishler, 1988). In the example above, students learned about the effects of air pressure and how airplanes fly. In addition, they learned the inquiry process itself—how to solve problems, evaluate solutions, and think critically.

The inquiry approach has much in common with guided discovery learning and shares its advantages and disadvantages. Like discovery learning, inquiry methods require great preparation, organization, and monitoring to be sure everyone participates and learns.

Individualized Instruction

The defining characteristic of **individualized instruction** is that each student works with learning plans designed to fit his or her own needs, interests, and abilities. To accomplish this goal, individualized instruction takes many forms; students may even work in small or large groups so long as the activities are designed to match the needs of the individuals involved. So individualized instruction does not necessarily require independent or solitary work. Let's consider how you would modify lessons to meet individual needs.

Modifying Lessons to Fit Individual Needs. To tailor a learning activity to an individual student, a teacher might vary one or more of the following elements: (1) the pace of learning; (2) the instructional objectives; (3) the activity or the materials; (4) the reading level; or (5) the methods by which students are to demonstrate what they have learned.

Perhaps the simplest form of individualized instruction is to let students work at their own pace on the same assignment. If you use this form of individualized instruction, the material must be broken down into a sequence of objectives and learning activities or assignments. After meeting one objective, a student can move on to the next.

Individualized Instruction
Approach tailored to individual students' needs, interests, abilities, and work pace.

The second variable in individualized instruction is the choice of learning objectives. If you establish a set of objectives, then pretest the class on the objectives, you may find that many students are already able to do much of the work. Instead of insisting that each student move through the same sequence of objectives, you can tailor the objectives to the needs, interests, and abilities of different students or different groups of students. Clearly, to accommodate a heterogeneous group of students you need a variety of objectives across many ability levels.

A third variable in individualized instruction is the learning activity itself. Even if students are moving toward the same objectives, they might use different means to achieve those goals. One student might rely on the textbook, while others might read library books or newspaper stories or use audiovisual resources. Students with reading problems, students who have impaired vision, or students who have difficulty remembering what they read might listen to tapes or play simulation games together. Gifted students might do independent library or field research. Individual contracts are also possibilities. In your methods courses you may learn about other approaches, such as learning centers.

A fourth variable has just been touched on—reading level. All your students may be capable of working toward the same objective, but some may require material at a lower reading level than others. Most of the students in a high school class may be able to write a two-page paper comparing the Great Depression and the present economic situation, for example, but some of them may need background reading material at the junior high level or even lower. It is not always possible to find such a wide range of reading materials. Information sources other than the printed word—tapes, films, photographs, cartoons, and so on—may have to be included.

The way in which students are required to demonstrate their new learning is the fifth variable that can be tailored to fit the needs of individual students. Students who have difficulty with written expression might first be given oral tests, or they might be asked to tape their answers to written tests. Gifted students might demonstrate learning by completing major papers or projects. For other students, frequent tests might be better. Students may also demonstrate some learning nonverbally by drawing pictures, graphing relationships, making a model, or assembling a collage.

Research on Individualized Instruction. In practice, the results of individualized instruction have not always matched the expectations. When used as the only form of instruction for elementary and secondary students, these approaches are not superior to traditional methods. But individualized methods do seem quite effective for college students (Bangert, Kulik, & Kulik, 1983). It is possible that completely individualized systems leave elementary and secondary students on their own too much. Only the most motivated and self-directed students can stay involved, and many students don't get the direct teaching and explanation they need. The teacher's time is absorbed with preparing and correcting individual assignments, leaving less time for demonstrating, presenting, explaining, and reteaching.

This doesn't mean that teachers should make every student work at the same pace, on the same objectives and activities, or at the same reading level as every other student. Many elements of individualized instruction can be incorporated into regular class lessons. For example, students can work at their own pace on assignments matched to their ability but study and practice together in cooperative, mixed-ability learning groups like those described in chapter 10. This variation of cooperative learning, called **team-assisted individualization,** has proven very effective in elementary-school mathematics classes (Slavin & Karweit, 1985).

Good teachers have been individualizing for years. Teachers individualize, for example, when they make sure that the books chosen for library assignments match the reading levels of the students. Individualized assignments can provide remediation and enrichment, if carefully designed and monitored. At times it makes sense to send some children into a different grade for instruction in one subject. Two second-grade students, for example, joined my daughter's sixth-grade class for science.

Mastery Learning

A method that is consistent with the goals of individualized instruction is called **mastery learning,** based on the assumption that given enough time and the proper instruction, most students can master any learning objective (Bloom, 1968; Guskey & Gates, 1986).

To use the mastery approach, a teacher must break a course down into small units of study. Each unit might involve mastering several specific objectives. "Mastery" usually means a score of 80 percent or more on a test. The teacher informs the students of the objectives and the criteria for meeting each. Students who do not reach the minimum level of mastery or who reach this minimum but want to improve their performance (thus raising their grade) can recycle through the unit and take another form of the unit test.

Under a mastery system grades can be determined by the actual number of objectives mastered, the number of units completed, the proficiency level reached on each unit, or some combination of these measures. Students can work at their own pace, finishing the entire course quickly if they are able or taking a long time to reach a few objectives. Of course, if only a few objectives are met by the end of the marking period, the student's grade will reflect this.

The **Keller Plan,** also called the **Personalized System of Instruction (PSI),** is a form of mastery learning used most often in college. It has a number of basic components (Sherman, Ruskin, & Semb, 1982). First, course readings are broken down into small units, each with specific goals and study guides. Students move at their own pace through the units and then come to class for testing. Proctors, usually students who have successfully completed the course, administer an oral or written test for the unit in class and give immediate feedback. If students have mastered the unit (generally with a score of 80 percent or better), they can go on to the next. If not, they must repeat the unit and take another test. Grades depend on the number of units successfully completed and perhaps to a

Team-Assisted Individualization Arrangement where students work at their own pace on individualized assignments, but practice together in cooperative, mixed-ability groups.

Mastery Learning Method where students move through brief units of work by demonstrating mastery on one unit before going to the next.

Keller Plan, or Personalized System of Instruction (PSI) Program with small units, specific goals, self-pacing, and feedback.

small extent on a midterm and a final examination. Lectures and demonstrations are used more to motivate students than to present information.

There are some problems with the mastery learning approach. Because all students do not cover the same material, a mastery learning course must be self-contained and cannot serve as a prerequisite for other courses. Using a mastery approach to teach Algebra I, for example, would not ensure that all students had the prerequisites for Algebra II, since some students in Algebra I might never get past solving an equation with one unknown. If the entire school uses a mastery system, however, some of these problems are eliminated.

Another problem with mastery learning is that teachers must have a variety of materials to allow students to recycle through objectives they failed to meet the first time. Usually, just repeating the same materials won't help. It is also important to have several tests for each unit. Students quickly figure out that taking the test and failing is better preparation for passing the unit than studying all the material, because an attempt at the test tells them exactly what to study before taking the next test (Cox & Dunn, 1979). This discovery can lead to memorizing and learning a few specifics but not to a real understanding of the material.

In practice, mastery learning has not helped to erase achievement differences among students, as some proponents have hoped. Individual differences in achievement persist, unless the teacher holds back the faster students while the slower ones catch up (Arlin, 1984). Left to work at their own pace, some students will learn much more and leave a unit with much better understanding than others. Some will work much harder to take advantage of the learning opportunities (Grabe & Latta, 1981). Some will be frustrated instead of encouraged by the chance to recycle ("You mean I have to do it again?"). And finally, the word *mastery* may be misleading. Completing a mastery unit successfully usually means that the students are ready to move to the next unit, not that they are "masters" of the information (Cox & Dunn, 1979).

Computers, Videodiscs, and Beyond

No discussion of teaching strategies would be complete without considering the role of computers in teaching and learning. The uses of computers and other instructional technology are so broad and varied, we can only touch on a few key points here. Because this is such an important topic for today's teachers, I encourage you to learn all you can about it. Some of my student teachers have gotten teaching positions in difficult times partly because they knew how to use computers in their classroom.

Many of your students will have been working with computers to do word processing, graphics, or games since their preschool years. Other students will have had little chance to use computers. Some schools will have computers in every classroom. Videodisc encyclopedias will make a tremendous amount of information available to students. Communications networks will connect your class with students around the country and with museums, research labs, or colleges. But in other schools, there will be a few old model computers in a lab down the hall. Given this wide range in students' sophistication and in schools' resources, what

Students in many classrooms today are familiar with computers as tools and as tutors.

Drill-and-Practice Programs Computer programs of exercises and activities that allow students to practice skills.

Computer Tutorials Programs that teach material by questioning students and responding to their answers.

Computer Simulations Programs that require students to apply knowledge and skills to solve lifelike problems.

can we say about using technology to teach? There are two main uses of computers in schools: as *teachers* to help students learn content and problem-solving skills and as *tools* to help students and teachers with such tasks as word processing, computing, locating and managing information, doing graphics, or programming computers.

Computers as Teachers. The most widely available computer learning programs are **drill-and-practice programs** in arithmetic, reading, spelling, and other basic skills. A sophisticated drill-and-practice program can give students immediate feedback about answers; diagnose problems and misconceptions that the student may be experiencing; keep records about individual progress; and maintain students' motivation by using graphics, sounds, and other "arcadelike" features to keep students engaged. Not all drill-and-practice software takes advantage of these features, however. Some programs are simply electronic workbooks and share many of the disadvantages of printed workbooks.

Computer tutorials teach new material using text, graphics, activities, and exercises. These programs try to act like teachers, asking students questions and responding to their answers. The responses can be tailored to the individual student; the pace and difficulty can be altered and different materials presented, depending on the student's performance. One problem with computer tutorials is that it may be difficult to find and use needed information. Moving backward and forward can be awkward, and students can't always keep all the information they need in front of them at the same time, because the computer screen limits what is visible (Vargas, 1986).

Computer simulations create situations in which students must learn and apply learning or problem-solving strategies. For example, an elementary school in upstate New York was faced with an all too typical set of somewhat contradictory demands: improve students' knowledge of social studies and their ability to write and use reference skills, and get them computer literate while you're at it. Unfortunately, the school day was already filled with reading, language, and math, and the school had available only 14 computers. Faced with these conditions, the school's computer coordinator put together a social studies unit built around the computer simulation program "Where in the USA Is Carmen San Diego?" The unit begins with the whole class playing the game as it is presented on a large monitor, practicing the note-taking and fact-finding skills that will be useful in successfully "capturing the criminal." After several days of guided instruction in using reference materials to unravel the clues that appear in the game, students pair off and as a team continue working with the program.

The importance of note taking is soon apparent to students as they are quickly assigned the task of designing a "wanted" poster for a criminal they have encountered in the program. To do this, students must use the facts about each criminal presented in the program. Use of a graphics program to design the posters extends students' experiences with computers. Such extensions continue as students begin using a data base to organize information they acquire concerning one of the states they "visited" while playing "Carmen." Students next learn to write business letters and to use a word processing program as they compose letters to state departments of tourism requesting information on different states. The culminating activity for the student is the preparation of a report about the state he or she researched.

Integrated instructional systems (IIS) are relatively new, but they have great potential. Mark Sherry (1990) lists the following characteristics of an IIS:

1. Most of the instruction in such a system is done on the computer.
2. Students work individually or in small groups at many microcomputers connected in networks.
3. The IIS includes a management system that will keep records of student performance, print reports, and make assignments for individual students based on the students' progress.
4. The teaching programs cover several subjects and grade levels; often an IIS is set up for the whole school.
5. Once a school sets up an IIS, the manufacturer will continue to provide revisions and upgrades of the materials, but the school must pay for these services.
6. The computer learning programs are linked to school curricula.

In 1990 Educational Products Information Exchange (EPIE) Institute published the *IIS Report,* an evaluation of integrated instructional systems. The findings were generally positive—students and teachers like working with IISs. But few schools are using the systems as effectively as they might, in part because teachers don't receive the training they need.

Computers and Learning. Are computers effective teachers? The answer in any given situation depends on the quality of the programs and how they are used, but in general, computer-assisted instruction appears to be moderately more effective than conventional methods (Niemiec & Walberg, 1987). And as microcomputers become less expensive, the cost of learning on computers is coming down as well. For example, in one study, third- and fifth-grade students who used the Milliken Math Sequences, a drill-and-practice program, scored higher on a standard test of mathematics achievement than students taught with the traditional methods of teacher presentation—practice problems from the textbook, flash cards, and math drill games. In addition, the cost per pupil was less for the computer-assisted approach (Flecter, Hawley, & Piele, 1990).

Given all the possibilities for using instructional technology and the rapid pace of advances in the field, it would be foolhardy to specify exactly how students should use computers. However, there are three general principles related to computer use. First, because teachers are concerned about being fair and equitable, they often have all their students use the same software at the same time. Yet one of the most important benefits of computers is the wide variety of ways they can be used to encourage children to develop different skills at different times. For some this will be accomplished through the use of drill and practice programs; for others, through learning a programming language or word processing.

"I DON'T GET IT! THEY MAKE US LEARN READING, WRITING AND ARITHMETIC TO PREPARE US FOR A WORLD OF VIDEOTAPES, COMPUTER TERMINALS AND CALCULATORS!"

H. Schwadron—Phi Delta Kappan.

Integrated Instructional System (IIS) System of programs that teaches several subjects at multiple grade levels and keeps records on individual students' progress.

Whatever Happened to the Computer Revolution?

Since the early 1980s we have heard and read about the need to make computers an integral part of the educational process from preschool through graduate school. Both the need for a computer-literate student body and the promise of a revolutionary form of education where every child will be a winner have captured the attention of the parents, educators, businesses, and the media. Is there a computer revolution in American schools?

Point: New technologies have reshaped education.

National surveys indicate that schools have heard and responded to the call for an infusion of computers. More than 380,000 computers were purchased by schools in 1987 alone, bringing the total number of computers in precollegiate education at that time to over 2 million (Goodspeed, 1988). Quality Education Data of Denver, a market research firm, reports that during the 1987–88 academic year, 95 percent of U.S. schools owned at least one computer. The number of computers in schools quadrupled in four years between 1984 and 1988.

In addition to purchasing computers, schools are also investing heavily in teacher training. As reported in *Educational Technology*'s 1987 survey, 25 states budgeted over $25 million for computer-related training for their practicing teachers. A commitment to integrating computers into the school curriculum is also evident. This same survey reported that 17 states were involved in projects to produce their own instructional software, geared specifically to their state's curriculum, and that 30 states were developing curriculum projects to incorporate commercially available software. As to furthering the use of computers in teaching, the survey found that 13 states and the District of Columbia now require

Second, the notion that computers individualize instruction has been interpreted by many educators to mean that the computer should be used by one student at a time. As a result, computers have been underutilized as a means of providing small-group and large-group learning experiences. Research on cooperative or collaborative learning indicates that this approach may have numerous benefits for both cognitive and social development (Slavin, 1984; Webb, 1982). Cooperative learning via the computer has only recently been the focus of extensive research, yet the results thus far are encouraging (Lieber & Semmel, 1988; Robinson, DePascale, & Deno, 1988).

Finally, a general goal of education is to prepare students to be contributing members of our society. Computer experience for students should be consistent with the ways computers are currently used in the adult world outside of school. While this orientation does not preclude the use of drill-and-practice or tutorial software, or the learning of programming languages, it does place greater emphasis on use of computers as tools. If we consider tools in the sense put forth by Bruner, "as amplifiers of human capacities and implementers of human activity" (1966, p. 81), then this use of computers will allow students access to a powerful and creative means of personal development.

Computers and Teaching. First and foremost, teachers should focus on those aspects of computing that will enable them to do their job well by making work easier, more interesting, and more effective. The elec-

that teacher certification candidates complete at least one educational computing course as part of their professional training. An additional 21 states reported that they strongly encourage certification candidates to take such a course.

Counterpoint: In classrooms it's business as usual.

A glance at the preceding paragraphs with their rather impressive percentages and statistics could lead you to believe that the goal of computer integration is being achieved and the promised educational revolution is progressing quite well. In reality, it appears that this is not the case. James Mecklenburger (1990) notes that the students in public and private schools in the United States outnumber the available computers by 20, 30, or even 40 to 1. And many of these computers are completely outdated, so the actual figures may be more like 400 or even 1,000 students for every truly capable computer. A report by the National Assessment of Educational Progress in-

dicates that although most of the 24,000 students contacted could identify the components of a computer system, few had practical knowledge of how to use the machine (Rothman, 1988). Knowledge of programming was found to be almost nonexistent in this group of students.

This report, coupled with the results of other research projects (for example, Eaton & Olson, 1986; Mathinos & Woodward, 1991), has led many to wonder if the computer revolution will ever materialize. Mecklenburger notes:

Virtually every student-sized and classroom-sized application of information technology imaginable—from student-produced television programs to students using supercomputers, from teachers reducing their clerical burdens to teachers making fascinating electronic presentations—exists *somewhere* in America. . . . Yet chalkboards, lectures, and textbooks continue to dominate instruction almost *everywhere*. (p. 106)

tronic gradebook, test generator, spreadsheet, data base, and word processor are similar or identical to applications that dominate business and professional uses of computers. Yet teachers have been encouraged to focus their energies primarily on using the computer with the students rather than using it themselves. The time has come for teachers to be encouraged and allowed to profit personally from the presence of computers in schools.

Given the seemingly tremendous potential of computers, can you expect to find a "computer revolution" in the classrooms where you will teach? The **Point/Counterpoint** section above examines this question.

SETTINGS FOR ACHIEVING OBJECTIVES

In recent years psychologists have become interested in the role of the physical environment in classroom learning. Many teachers have discovered how to match the setting to objectives and activities. To understand the impact of the physical environment on learning in classrooms, you should be familiar with two basic ways of organizing space: interest areas and personal territories. These two ways of organizing space are not mutually exclusive; many teachers use a design that combines the two. Individual students' desks are placed in the center, with interest areas in the back or around the periphery of the room. This allows the flexibility needed for both large- and small-group activities.

Interest-Area Arrangements

The design of interest areas can influence the way the areas are used by students. For example, working with a classroom teacher, Carol Weinstein (1977) was able to make changes in interest areas that helped the teacher meet her objectives of having more girls involved in the science center and having all students experiment more with a variety of manipulative materials. In a second study, changes in a library corner led to more involvement in literature activities throughout the class (Morrow & Weinstein, 1986).

Teachers are often puzzled about how to design interest areas that match their objectives for the students. Here are several suggestions.

What Activities Should the Classroom Accommodate? For example, if you are in a self-contained elementary classroom, you might wish to set up interest areas for reading, arts and crafts, science, and math. If you are teaching one particular subject on the junior or senior high level, you may wish to divide your room into several areas, perhaps for audiovisual activities, small-group instruction, quiet study, and projects. List these activities in a column, and next to each note whether any pose special spatial requirements. For example, art and science should be near the sink; science should also be near windows if you wish to grow plants; a quiet study area should not be in front of the door; small-group instruction should be near the board.

Draw Floor Plans and Choose the Best. Use graph paper if possible, and draw to scale. As you work, keep in mind these principles:

1. *Take note of the fixed features.* What are the "givens" of the room that you must deal with—doors, windows, outlets? You don't want an audiovisual center in a corner without an electrical outlet!

2. *Have easy access to materials and a well-organized place to store them.* Materials should have clearly labeled places of their own, and these places must be easy to reach if you want students to use the materials. Shelves toward the center of the room seem to be more likely to attract attention than those placed in the corners. There should be enough shelves so that materials need not be stacked on one another.

3. *Provide students with clean, convenient surfaces on which to use equipment.* The closer these surfaces are to the materials, the better.

4. *Make sure work areas are private and quiet, and segregate activities.* Tables or work areas should not be placed in the middle of traffic lanes, and a person should not have to pass through one area to get to another. Noisy activities should be placed as far as possible from quiet ones. You can increase the feeling of quiet and privacy by placing partitions such as bookcases or pegboards between areas or within large areas.

5. *Arrange things so you can see your students and they can see all instructional presentations.* If you plan to put up partitions, make sure they are low enough for you to see over them comfortably. If possible, students should be able to see instruction without moving their chairs or desks.

6. *Avoid dead spaces and "racetracks."* Check to see that you have not placed all the interest areas around the outside of the room, leaving a large dead space in the middle. You also want to avoid placing a few items of furniture right in the middle of this large space, creating a "racetrack" around the furniture. Such arrangements encourage rowdiness, perhaps because they resemble playgrounds and so communicate to the pupils that running is permissible.

7. *Provide choices.* Different people have different spatial needs. Some people prefer closed, small spaces in which to work; others may find such places too confining.

8. *Provide flexibility.* At times you may wish to have students work alone, in small groups, or with many others. If you cannot arrange to have spaces for all these possibilities at one time, try to ensure that your design is flexible enough so that it can be changed to meet the requirements of new activities.

9. *Give students a place to keep their personal belongings.* This is especially important if students don't have personal desks.

Once you have chosen your room design, try the new arrangement, evaluate it, and make any needed changes. The goal of these suggestions is to remove as much physical friction from the classroom system as possible, so that students can easily select and use materials. The only way to know whether you have reached this goal is to monitor the use of the environment, identify problems, and try again. Incidentally, enlist the aid of your students. They have to live in the room, too, and designing a classroom can be a very challenging educational experience.

Personal Territories

Can the physical setting influence teaching and learning in classrooms organized by territories? Firsthand experience in college tells me that the most interested students sit at the front, and those who yearn for an early escape station themselves as close to the door as possible. In an extensive research project examining elementary and secondary classes, Adams and Biddle (1970) found that verbal interaction between teacher and students was concentrated in the center front of the classroom and in a line directly up the center of the room. The data were so dramatic that Adams and Biddle coined the term **action zone** to refer to this area of the room. Later research modified this finding. Even though most rooms have an action zone where participation is greatest, this area is not always front and center. In some classes it may be on one side or near a particular learning center (Good, 1983a).

Front-seat location does seem to increase participation for students who are predisposed to speak in class, whereas a seat in the back will make it more difficult to participate and easier to sit back and daydream (Woolfolk & Brooks, 1983). To "spread the action around," Weinstein and Mignano (1993) suggest that teachers move around the room when possible, establish eye contact with students seated far away, and direct comments to students seated at a distance.

Action Zone Area of a classroom where the greatest amount of interaction takes place.

Many teachers vary the seating in their classrooms so the same students are not always consigned to the back of the room. Another reason to change seating is to make the arrangement more appropriate for particular objectives and activities, as we've discussed. But since too much rearranging can be a waste of time and an invitation to chaos, Musgrave (1975) distinguishes between **home-base formations,** semipermanent arrangements that are suitable for a wide number of teaching and learning situations, and "special formations," which give needed variety and are suited to a particular lesson.

Figure 12.3 shows several home-base formations other than rows and columns. Horizontal rows share many of the advantages of row and column arrangements. Both are useful for independent seatwork, presentations, and recitations; they encourage students to focus on the teacher; and they simplify housekeeping. Horizontal rows permit students to work more easily in pairs. This formation is also best for demonstrations, since students are closer to the teacher. However, it is a poor arrangement if a teacher wishes to encourage large-group interaction.

FIGURE 12.3 **Some Home-Base Formations** These home-base formations work well for whole-class instruction and also allow for some cooperative work.

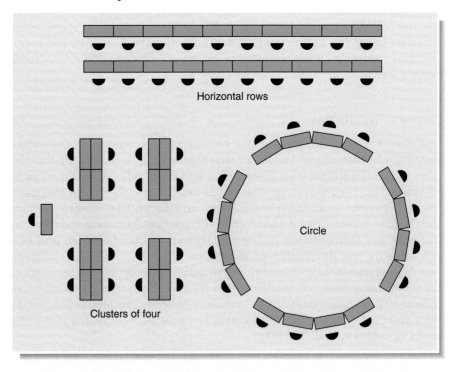

Horizontal rows

Clusters of four

Circle

Home-Base Formations
Arrangements for students' desks that allow flexibility in activities.

Source: Adapted from G. R. Musgrave, *Individualized instruction: Teaching strategies focusing on the learner,* pp. 49, 52, 54. Copyright © 1975. Reprinted with permission of Allyn and Bacon.

FIGURE 12.4 **Some Special Formations** These special seating plans are appropriate when certain activities, such as a debate or demonstration, require room rearrangements.

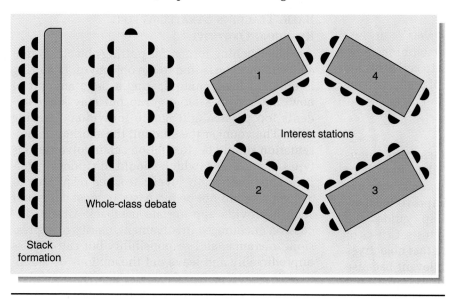

Interest stations

Whole-class debate

Stack formation

Source: Adapted from G. R. Musgrave, *Individualized instruction: Teaching strategies focusing on the learner,* pp. 48, 63, 65. Copyright © 1975. Reprinted with permission of Allyn and Bacon.

Clusters of four or circle arrangements are best for student interaction. Circles are especially useful for discussions but still allow for independent seatwork. Clusters permit students to talk, help one another, share materials, and work on group tasks. Both arrangements, however, are poor for whole-group presentations and may make class control more difficult.

Figure 12.4 shows several special formations. The debate arrangement and interest stations are probably familiar. The stack formation, where students sit close together near the focus of attention (the back row may even be standing), should be used only for short periods of time, since it is not comfortable for a long period and can lead to discipline problems. On the other hand, the stack can create a feeling of group cohesion and is helpful when the teacher wants students to watch a demonstration, brainstorm on a class problem, or see a small visual aid.

Although the physical environment can hinder or aid the realization of a teacher's goals in ways that are real and important, it is not all-powerful. Arranging desks in a circle will not guarantee increased participation in a discussion. A cozy reading area will not solve reading problems. Nevertheless, it is essential that teachers consider the classroom space at the same time that they focus on the objectives and teaching methods. All play an important role in the establishment of an optimal learning environment.

SUMMARY

TEACHER PLANNING

Planning on several different levels is an important step in teaching. The plan determines how time and materials will be turned into activities for students. There is no single model of planning, but all plans should allow for flexibility.

OBJECTIVES FOR LEARNING

Instructional objectives state a teacher's intentions for what students will learn. Objectives help provide structure, let students know what they are studying for or working toward, improve teacher-student communication, and help guide the teacher in writing fair and balanced tests. Critics of instructional objectives have argued that objectives are time-consuming, tend to be irrelevant because trivial objectives are easier to create, and place too many restrictions on students' inclination to explore on their own. Two approaches to writing objectives are Mager's specific behavior objectives and Gronlund's combination of general and specific objectives. Many educators believe that Gronlund's approach is the most helpful.

TASK ANALYSIS

Using task analysis, a teacher identifies all the skills and subskills necessary to master a goal or objective. Specific objectives are written for each subskill, forming a logical sequence of steps.

TAXONOMIES

Bloom and others have developed taxonomies categorizing basic objectives in the cognitive, affective, and psychomotor domains. A taxonomy encourages systematic thinking about relevant objectives and ways to evaluate them. One straightforward method for planning an entire unit is a behavior-content matrix, which can help a teacher integrate desired student behaviors with specific items of course content.

BASIC TEACHING STRATEGIES FOR REACHING OBJECTIVES

The teaching format for putting objectives into action should be suited to the objectives. Lecturing is efficient for communicating a large amount of new material to a large group but may keep students too passive and ignore individual learning rates. The younger the student, the shorter the presentation should be. Recitation can involve various types of questions, which should fit students' abilities and motivation levels; teacher responses to answers should not be too hasty in most cases and should provide appropriate feedback. Group discussion encourages involvement, clarity of expression, tolerance, and responsibility but can digress unpredictably and leave out the anxious or unmotivated. Homework and seatwork are useful if they involve real work, are specific, engage students, and are well supervised. Inquiry methods require students to gather data and test hypotheses in order to solve perplexing problems.

In individualized instruction the teacher can vary the pace, objectives, activities, reading level, or method by which students demonstrate learning. Mastery learning is one approach to individualized instruction. The course is divided into units and students move from one unit to the next when they reach a predetermined mastery level.

SETTINGS FOR ACHIEVING OBJECTIVES

There are two basic kinds of spatial organization, territorial (the traditional classroom arrangement) and functional (dividing space into interest or work areas). Flexibility is often the key. Access to materials, convenience, privacy when needed, ease of supervision, and a willingness to reevaluate plans are important considerations in the teacher's choice of physical arrangements.

KEY TERMS AND CONCEPTS

action zone, p. 465
affective domain, p. 444
behavioral objectives, p. 438
behavior-content matrix, p. 446
cognitive domain, p. 443
cognitive objectives, p. 438
computer simulations, p. 460
computer tutorials, p. 460
convergent questions, p. 449
divergent questions, p. 449
drill-and-practice programs,
  p. 460

higher-level questions, p. 450
home-base formations, p. 466
individualized instruction,
  p. 456
inquiry teaching, p. 455
instructional objective,
  p. 437
integrated instructional system
  (IIS), p. 461
Keller Plan or Personalized
  System of Instruction (PSI),
  p. 458

lecturing, p. 448
mastery learning,
  p. 458
operationalize, p. 438
psychomotor domain,
  p. 445
recitation, p. 449
seatwork, p. 454
task analysis, p. 441
taxonomy, p. 443
team-assisted
  individualization, p. 458

WHAT WOULD YOU DO?

PRESCHOOL AND KINDERGARTEN

You have designed your kindergarten room with a nice open-space area in the middle so the whole group can meet for stories and sharing. You find that there is too much running, scuffling, and other activity in this area when you are not using it for group time. What would you do?

ELEMENTARY AND MIDDLE SCHOOL

You want your students to help one another during seatwork, while you teach a small group. How would you organize the work and the desks to make this possible?

Your cooperating teacher wants a full lesson plan for each subject. What would you include in the plan to make it useful for you?

JUNIOR HIGH AND HIGH SCHOOL

You want your students to form and defend a position, but still to be open and tolerant of the beliefs of others. What would you do in your class to move toward these objectives? Specifically, what teaching format(s) would you use, and how would you arrange the physical environment of the room to support your objectives?

Identify three instructional objectives for a lesson in your subject to be used in a mixed-ability 10th-grade class. How would you make these learning objectives clear to your students?

COOPERATIVE LEARNING ACTIVITY

With four or five other members of your educational psychology class, plan a unit. Include objectives, lesson formats, and room arrangements.

TEACHERS' CASEBOOK

GROUP PARTICIPATION

You want to use more group discussion in your classes, but a few students do all the discussing and the rest tune out. What would you do to get more high-quality participation in group discussions?

SPEAKING AND LISTENING SKILLS

Every student wants to feel that what they have to offer to a discussion is important and is heard. Building a successful discussion group, therefore, requires speaking skills as well as listening skills, so both need to be developed concomitantly.

I start many of my small-group discussions with a quick fluency exercise. Students are given a few chips or markers and asked to brainstorm ideas on a given topic. Each student then turns in a marker for every idea that they contribute to the topic. All students are encouraged to use all their markers. This activity promotes equal involvement for all students in the group and emphasizes the concept that all ideas are equally accepted. The process also encourages fast responders to "hold back" ideas until later to ensure that they are involved throughout the duration of the activity.

Lawrence Leebens, *Curriculum Resource Coordinator*
Forest Hills Elementary, Eden Prairie, Minnesota

THE VALUE OF LESSON PLANS

A beginning teacher at your school tells you in confidence that he does not see the value of writing the lesson plans as required by the school administration. What would you say?

REFLECTIVE PROFESSIONALISM A MUST

I would first ask the teacher what he understood the purpose of the directive to be and what he thought it entailed. If he thought writing lesson plans involved the detailed format used in teacher training classes, I would show him how to simplify the process with a coding system or abbreviated statement of goals, materials needed, and so forth. If he thought writing lesson plans meant recording the page numbers of the textbook/manual/worksheet in the plan book, I'd tell him about some exciting, insightful ways of teaching. I would share how much more I enjoy teaching now that I integrate learning, encourage the students to become their own teachers, use textbooks as one of many resources, have the students create their own written application of what they have learned, and use alternative forms of assessment.

Writing down plans and taking the time to evaluate them makes teachers reflective professionals. Writing the plans makes it possible for the teacher to document what has been done and demonstrate accountability, to protect the children in case of teacher absence or extended emergency leave so that they can have continuity in their learning, to provide data for integrating previous information with current lessons, and to have ready reference for parent conferences about material covered and the purpose of the material.

Betty Garner, *Art Teacher*
Pattonville I.D.E.A.L. Center, Maryland Heights, Missouri

GUIDES FOR CREATIVE WORK

The most effective teacher is one who provides for individual needs, supplies interesting enrichment experiences, and affords opportunities for remediation that are motivating and effective. It is valuable to write down these plans to keep track of what is being done in your classroom. Not only do these written plans serve as an effective guide for keeping record of the skills being taught and the materials being used, they are also a valuable resource that can be tapped in the future when ideas are needed.

Effective teachers teach students and go beyond textbooks. Written plans provide documentation of what skills have been presented. In this time of accountability, a teacher needs to keep accurate records and not rely exclusively upon memory.

Malcolm Jarrell, *Remedial Mathematics and Reading Elementary Teacher*
Jackson-Via School, Charlottesville, Virginia

SEATWORK

A common criticism of seatwork is that it is busywork: students get bored, their attention wanders, and the time is wasted in the end. How can seatwork assignments be structured so that they are valid, positive learning experiences?

ADAPTABLE, NOT BORING

My classroom uses a workshop board where the seatwork is posted in numerical order. Some tasks are similar for all of the students and some are for various academic levels. Many of the tasks require creative thinking so the child is not just doing busywork. Also there are some activities that the children do with a partner so ideas can be shared. If a task becomes boring, I give a child a new approach to practice that skill.

Kathryn Daniels, *Second-Grade Teacher*
Fredericktown Elementary School, Fredericktown, Ohio

A DIFFICULT BUT WORTHWHILE ENDEAVOR

Seatwork can be a valid teaching tool if properly planned. The success of a seatwork assignment hinges on several variables that teachers must take into account—the who, what, where, when, how, and why of the students and the assignment: the personalities of the students and the gestalt of the whole class; the background knowledge students bring to the subject and to the task; the physical environment and its conduciveness to the task; how fatigued, distracted, or stimulated students are at the particular time of day; the procedure and the essential materials and their accessibility; and the existing motivation for the task as well as the extra reinforcement necessary to encourage self-directed work.

In addition, teachers need a thorough knowledge of the subject matter, legitimate long-range goals, and specific, behaviorally stated short-range objectives. Seatwork then becomes one of the comprehensive, productive, daily assignments that are the culmination of this kind of extensive planning. As for the students, they must see a legitimate correlation between an assignment's purpose and its actual completion. There must be a predetermined criterion for success, and actual completion of the task must also be reinforced. Seatwork can and should be exciting and motivating.

Laura Atkinson, *Special Education Teacher*
Chapel Hill, North Carolina

SHOULD STUDENTS KNOW YOUR OBJECTIVES?

Do you tell your students what your objectives are? Do you tell them what your performance standards are as well? Why or why not?

PURPOSES AND STANDARDS MAKE THE DIFFERENCE

We all—adults and children—need to know that what we're learning serves some purpose. Without this, learning becomes trivial. If reasons are stated in terms children can understand, they are much more willing to tackle the work. They also need to know what's expected of them: is this particular lesson simply to introduce them to a new concept, or will they be expected to master the concept, and if so, in what kind of time framework? They must know, too, when their efforts are acceptable, and why.

Ida Pofahl, *Second-Grade Teacher*
Denison Elementary School, Denison, Iowa

13 EFFECTIVE TEACHING/ EFFECTIVE LEARNING

eachers make many decisions affecting the lives of students. These decisions range from how to position desks to how long to spend teaching reading or reviewing homework each day. Even when students are working independently or in small unsupervised groups, they are influenced by decisions the teacher has made about such things as materials, grouping, and timing.

In this chapter we examine in depth what is known about the role of the teacher in student learning. Are there particular characteristics that distinguish effective from ineffective teachers?

Next we turn to the teaching of basic skills. Research in recent years has identified a cluster of principles that can guide the teaching of basic, explicit information and procedures. But students must master more than basic skills. Recent studies of teaching emphasize the role of the learner in constructing what is learned. These cognitive/constructivist views challenge the basic skills teaching approach. We will explore effective teaching beyond the basics and discuss how to match teaching strategies to the demands of the subject matter and the aptitudes of the students.

By the time you finish this chapter, you are likely to have many new ideas about methods and approaches to try in the classroom. More specifically, you should be able to do the following:

- Describe a number of characteristics that effective teachers seem to share.

- List steps that can ensure clarity in presentation.

- Give examples of lessons based on the principles of direct instruction, on the Hunter model, and on the Missouri Mathematics Program.

- Summarize the criticisms of direct instruction and offer an alternative based on the cognitive/constructivist perspective.

- Plan a unit in your subject for a low-ability class.

- Choose one lesson in your own area and explain how you would go about presenting it to the students you will be teaching.

WHAT DO YOU THINK?

In the first chapter of this book I asked you to list the characteristics of teachers you found truly outstanding. Review (or redo) that list now. Can you add or delete any characteristics based on what you have learned so far? Consider what you now know about student learning and why the teacher characteristics you listed might promote learning.

THE SEARCH FOR THE KEYS TO SUCCESS

The search for the secret of effective teaching is not a new one. But until recently it hasn't been very successful. In the 1960s and 1970s, several widely publicized studies concluded that teachers have very little impact on student learning (Coleman, Campbell, Wood, Weinfeld, & York, 1966; Jencks et al., 1972). Based on these reports, it seemed that factors such as social class and student ability were the main influences on learning. Many people wondered . . .

Do Teachers Make a Difference?

A closer look at the Coleman and Jencks reports reveals many problems in the design of this research (Good, 1983a & b). These studies looked mainly for correlations between such things as the verbal ability or social class of the teachers and the intellectual skills of the students. School-wide averages were generally used. The studies did not try to relate what actually happened in individual classrooms to the achievement of students, nor did they examine the effects of individual teachers within each school. And because the research was purely correlational, we have no basis for inferring any causal relationships. So the studies did not answer the basic question: Do individual teachers make a difference in the day-to-day learning of their students?

Partly in response to the Coleman and Jencks reports, many researchers set out to answer this question. Their efforts have had profound implications for teaching. As a result of their research, for example, many states have changed regulations for teacher certification. The findings of these studies are required reading in many teacher-preparation programs and are included on most national tests for teachers. The first part of this chapter describes what we have learned from this explosion of research on teachers and teaching.

Methods for Studying Effective Teaching

How would you go about identifying the keys to effective teaching? You might ask students, principals, college professors of education, or experienced teachers to list the characteristics of good teachers. Or you could do intensive case studies of a few classrooms over a long period. You might observe classrooms, rate different teachers on certain traits, and then see which traits were associated with teachers whose students achieved the most or were the most motivated to learn. (To do this, of course, you would have to decide how to measure achievement and motivation.) You could identify teachers whose students, year after year, learned more than students working with other teachers; then you could watch the more successful teachers, and note what they do. You might also train teachers to apply several different strategies to teach the same lesson and then determine which strategy led to the greatest student learning. You could videotape teachers, then ask them to view the tapes and report what they were thinking about as they taught and what influenced their decisions while teaching.

All these approaches and more have been used to investigate effective teaching. Often a series of studies takes an approach called the **descriptive-correlational-experimental loop.** Researchers make careful observations, identify relationships between teaching and learning, use these relationships as the basis for developing teaching approaches, then test these approaches in experimental studies. Let's examine some of the specific knowledge about effective teaching gained from these projects.

CHARACTERISTICS OF EFFECTIVE TEACHERS

Some of the earliest research on effective teaching focused on personal qualities of the teachers themselves. Researchers thought that the key to success in teaching must lie in the characteristics of teachers (Medley, 1979). Although this assumption proved incorrect, or at least incomplete, it did teach us some lessons about three teacher characteristics: knowledge, clarity, and warmth.

Teachers' Knowledge

Do teachers who know more about their subject have a more positive impact on their students? When we look at teachers' knowledge of facts and concepts, as measured by test scores and college grades, the relationship to student learning is unclear and may be indirect. Teachers who know more facts about their subject do not necessarily have students who learn more. But teachers who know more may make clearer presentations. They are ready for any student questions and do not have to be evasive or vague in their answers. So knowledge is necessary but not sufficient for effective teaching.

Knowing about Knowing. What else is needed? Today researchers are studying other aspects of teachers' knowledge. One conclusion is that, in addition to knowing the important facts, concepts, and procedures in their academic discipline, teachers must know how to transform their knowledge into curriculum—into lessons, explanations, assignments, games, tests, questions, examples, demonstrations, and all the other activities of teaching (Wilson, Shulman, & Richert, 1987). Good teachers

Descriptive-Correlational-Experimental Loop Research in which observation identifies variables that might be related, relationships are studied, and teaching approaches based on significant correlations are tested in experiments.

can make facts, procedures, and concepts understandable for students, but to do so, the teachers must know more about their subject than facts, procedures, and concepts. Charles Anderson (1989) suggests that they must also know the *structure, function,* and *development* of the material they teach. He gives three examples of beginning teachers who *lack* this knowledge:

1. Ann has been very successful in her teacher education program, making grades of 4.0 in every course before student teaching. Now Ann, a biology major, is student teaching in a middle school life science class. I visit her for the first time as her university supervisor.

Today Ann is teaching about atoms, molecules, elements, and compounds, and she does not look like a 4.0 student. Her teaching is uninspired and didactic, her way of distinguishing molecules from compounds is not quite right, and some of her examples are fictitious (He_2, Zn_2).

When I talk to Ann after the lesson she acknowledges her disappointment in her performance and talks about how difficult she finds it to come up with good examples. When she asks for help I ask a question back: How are you going to use these concepts [molecules, atoms, elements, etc.] later in the year? Ann says that she doesn't know; it's just something that you have to teach. Her mentor teacher, however, quickly names several topics where these concepts play an important role: photosynthesis, digestion, respiration, ecological matter cycling. As he does this he mentions examples of elements and compounds that the middle school students will need to be familiar with. (Anderson, 1989, p. 94)

2. A group of elementary student teachers is meeting to discuss mathematics teaching. The discussion is led by Deborah Ball, who challenges them to develop a word problem that can be solved with the expression, "1¾ divided by ½." Only one student suggests an appropriate example: "How many half cakes are in 1¾ cakes?" Most students suggest problems that go through a variety of contortions to arrive at 3½, which they all know to be the correct answer. The following is typical: "I buy 1¾ pizzas that are split into four slices each and divide them equally with my friend. How many slices does each of us get?" (Note that this problem actually involves division by two rather than division by ½. The logic of the problem is: 1¾ = 7/4 divided by 2 = 3½ fourths.) (Anderson, 1989, p. 95)

3. Several secondary biology majors are discussing their plans for teaching one-week units. Most of the unit plans share a common problem: They include far too much content for the time available. One student, for example, plans to cover the following topics in five-day units on fishes: evolution of fishes, classes of fishes (named in Latin) and their characteristics, adaptation of fishes to their environment, structure, and function of fish body systems (down to the level of parts of the brain). The methods course instructors immediately begin suggesting ways to reduce and simplify the content that she plans to teach. She demurs, "But it's all interconnected!" (Anderson, 1989, p. 96)

Problems Transforming Knowledge. What is wrong here? Ann had trouble finding good examples and resorted to making up fictitious molecules because she did not know the *structure* of the material she was teaching. She did not understand the relationships among the different concepts, ideas, procedures, and areas of application in biology. Like most college students, she probably had studied and been tested on units of work in isolation without being encouraged to identify relationships across different courses in biology or even across different chapters in the same textbook. Consequently, she had trouble seeing relationships across units in her own class, from the unit on "molecules" to the unit on "digestion," for example. In the language of information processing, she did not have well-organized, richly elaborated, deeply processed knowledge.

The second example, develop a problem that can be solved with the expression "1¾ divided by ½," highlights another necessary kind of knowledge. Teachers must know the *function* of the information they teach. What is it used for? What problems will it solve? How will students encounter the need for the information in other classes or in everyday life? Too often we teach students a fact or procedure without teaching them how, why, when, or when not to use it.

The problem in the final example, of teaching *too much* about fishes, could be solved if the teacher had a better understanding of *how knowledge develops* in individuals. How do students move from a simple to a highly developed understanding of a particular concept or idea? How can a teacher simplify complicated ideas without reducing them to definitions or steps to be memorized? Anderson (1989) believes that "teachers must somehow relate their own understanding to the alternate forms or levels of understanding that their students bring with them to class. They must deal with multitudes of wrong answers and half-right answers, somehow sorting out what is legitimate and what is problematic in each" (p. 97).

Educational psychology cannot give you the structure, function, or development of the subjects you will teach. Unfortunately, few of your college courses in specific subject areas will provide this kind of knowledge either. I tell my students to try to construct these understandings for themselves and press their professors for explanations of the structure, function, and development of the material they are presenting. Teaching experience, especially tutoring slower students, can help as well.

Organization and Clarity

Students discussing a teacher are likely to say things like, "Oh, she can really explain," "He's so disorganized," or "Those two! They're impossible to follow!" When Barak Rosenshine and Norma Furst (1973) reviewed about 50 studies of teaching, they concluded that clarity was the most promising teacher behavior for future research on effective teaching. Recent studies confirm the importance of clarity. Teachers who give clear presentations and explanations tend to have students who learn more and who rate their teachers more positively (Hines, Cruickshank, & Kennedy, 1982, 1985; Land, 1987).

"AND THEN, OF COURSE, THERE'S THE POSSIBILITY OF BEING JUST THE SLIGHTEST BIT *TOO* ORGANIZED."

Glen Dines—Phi Delta Kappan.

What does it mean to be "clear"? Clear teachers are precise and specific, not vague. They avoid words and phrases that are ambiguous (*somewhere, someplace*); approximate or indeterminate (*fairly, nearly, maybe, often, in general*); or "bluffing" (*as anyone can see, so to speak, you know*). Teachers with more knowledge of the subject tend to be less vague in their explanations to the class. The less vague the teacher, the more the students learn (Land, 1987). Lack of knowledge may cause teachers to be vague—or to be anxious and nervous, which also causes them to be vague. Either way, students get lost.

Planning for Clarity. Recent research offers guidelines for greater clarity in teaching (Berliner, 1987; Evertson et al., 1989; Hines, Cruickshank, & Kennedy, 1982, 1985). When planning a lesson, try to anticipate the problems your students will have with the material. Turn to teachers' manuals and experienced teachers for help with this. You might also do the written parts of the lesson yourself to identify potential problems. Have definitions ready for new terms, and prepare several relevant examples for concepts. Think of analogies that will make ideas easier to understand. For example, "electric current is like flowing water." Organize the lesson in a logical sequence; include checkpoints incorporating oral or written questions or problems to make sure the students are following the explanations.

Plan a clear introduction to the lesson. Tell students what they will be learning and how they should learn it. Often teachers are vague about both the "what" and the "how." For example, an ineffective reading teacher in a study by Duffy, Roehler, Meloth, and Vavrus (1986) began her lesson on using context in reading by saying:

> Today we are going to learn about context. This skill will help you in your reading. (p. 206)

This is a vague and general statement of "what" the students will learn. An effective teacher in the same study began her lesson with an explicit, precise description:

> At the end of today's lesson, you will be able to use the other words in a sentence to figure out the meaning of an unknown word. The skill is one that you use when you come to a word that you don't know and you have to figure out what the word means. (p. 206)

Being precise about "how" to do the work is even harder. One study found that teachers seldom, if ever, explain the cognitive processes they want their students to use in a seatwork activity. Bright students figure out the right process, but slower students often guess or give up. For example, an ineffective teacher might introduce a seatwork activity on words with prefixes by saying, "Here are some words with prefixes. Write the meaning of each in the blanks." An effective teacher, on the other hand, would demonstrate (1) how to divide the words into a prefix and a root, (2) how to determine the meaning of the root and the prefix, and

(3) how to put the two meanings together to make sense of the whole word (Berliner, 1987).

Clarity during the Lesson. Make clear connections between facts or concepts by using **explanatory links** such as *because, if . . . then,* or *therefore.* For example, when a teacher says, "The Northern economy was based on manufacturing and the North had an advantage in the Civil War," students are given two facts, but no connection between them. If there is a relationship between the two ideas, it should be indicated with an explanatory link as in, "The North had an advantage in the Civil War because its economy was based on manufacturing." Explanatory links tie ideas together and make them easier to learn (Berliner, 1987).

In general, stick with your plan and do not digress. Signal transitions from one major topic to another with phrases such as *"The next area . . . ,"* *"Now we will turn to . . ,"* or *"The second step is. . . ."* You might help students follow the lesson by outlining topics or listing key points on the board or on an overhead projector. Continually monitor the group to see if everyone is following the lesson. Look for confident nods or puzzled stares. You should be able to tell if most students are keeping up.

Throughout the lesson, choose words that are familiar to the students. Define new terms and relate them to what the students already know. Be precise. Avoid vague words and ambiguous phrases: steer clear of "the *somes*"—*something, someone, sometime, somehow;* "the *not verys*"—*not very much, not very well, not very hard, not very often;* and other unspecific fillers, such as *most, not all, sort of, and so on, of course, as you know, I guess, in fact, or whatever,* and *more or less.* Use specific (and, if possible, colorful) names instead of *it, them,* and *thing.* Also, refrain from using pet phrases such as *you know, like,* and *Okay?* Another idea is to record a lesson on tape to check yourself for clarity.

Warmth and Enthusiasm

As you know well, some teachers are much more enthusiastic than others. Some studies have found that ratings of teachers' enthusiasm for their subject are correlated with student achievement gains (Rosenshine & Furst, 1973). Warmth, friendliness, and understanding seem to be the teacher traits most strongly related to student attitudes (Murray, 1983; Ryans, 1960; Soar & Soar, 1979). In other words, teachers who are warm and friendly tend to have students who like them and the class in general. But notice, these are correlational studies. The results do not tell us that teacher enthusiasm causes student learning or that warmth causes positive attitudes, only that the two variables tend to occur together. Teachers trained to demonstrate their enthusiasm have students who are more attentive and involved but not necessarily more successful on tests of content (Gillett & Gall, 1982).

The research we have looked at has identified teacher knowledge, clarity, organization, and enthusiasm as important characteristics of effective teachers. The Guidelines on page 480 summarize the practical implications of this work for the classroom.

Sometimes, to be clear about abstract concepts, the teacher must use models, diagrams, and illustrations.

Explanatory Links Words and phrases such as "because" and "in order to" that specify the relationships between ideas.

Guidelines

Teaching Effectively

Organize your lessons carefully.

Examples

1. Provide objectives that help students focus on the purpose of the lesson.
2. Begin lessons by writing a brief outline on the board, or work on an outline with the class as part of the lesson.
3. If possible, break the presentation into clear steps or stages.
4. Review periodically.

Strive for clear explanations.

Examples

1. Use concrete examples or analogies that relate to the students' own lives. Have several examples for particularly difficult points.
2. Give explanations at several levels so all students, not just the brightest, will understand.

3. Focus on one idea at a time and avoid digressions.

Communicate an enthusiasm for your subject and the day's lesson.

Examples

1. Tell students why the lesson is important. Have a better reason than "This will be on the test" or "You will need to know it next year." Emphasize the value of the learning itself.
2. Be sure to make eye contact with the students.
3. Vary your pace and volume in speaking. Use silence for emphasis.

Constantly broaden your knowledge in your area.

Examples

1. Read journals that report new research and suggest new ideas.
2. Go to workshops and conventions; take a course at a nearby college.

The outcome of much of the research on effective teaching in the 1970s and 1980s was to combine findings about teacher characteristics and teaching behaviors into models of effective teaching. In these models, the emphasis was on teaching basic skills.

TEACHING THE BASICS

The models described in this section fit a specific set of circumstances because they are based on a particular approach to research. The studies that provide the foundation for these models identified existing teaching practices that are effective in American classrooms. Effectiveness usually was defined as average improvement in standardized test scores for a whole class or school. So the results hold for large groups, but not necessarily for every student in the group. Even when the average achievement of a group improves, the achievement of some individuals may actually decline.

Given these conditions, you can see that the models described below apply best to the teaching of **basic skills**—clearly structured knowledge and skills, such as science facts, mathematics computations, reading vocabulary, and grammar rules (Rosenshine & Stevens, 1986). These skills involve tasks that are relatively unambiguous; they can be taught

Basic Skills Clearly structured knowledge that is needed for later learning and that can be taught step by step.

step-by-step and tested by standardized tests. The teaching approaches described below are not necessarily appropriate for objectives such as helping students to write creatively, solve complex problems, or mature emotionally.

Basic Skills: Direct Instruction

Several psychologists have identified a teaching approach that is related to improved student learning. Barak Rosenshine calls this approach **direct instruction** (1979) or **explicit teaching** (1986). Tom Good (1983a) uses the term **active teaching** for a similar approach. The goal of direct instruction is the mastery of basic skills as measured by the tests commonly given in schools. In Rosenshine's words:

> Direct instruction refers to academically focused, teacher-directed classrooms using sequenced and structured materials. It refers to teaching activities where goals are clear to students, time allocated for instruction is sufficient and continuous, coverage of content is extensive, the performance of students is monitored, . . . and feedback to students is immediate and academically oriented. In direct instruction the teacher controls instructional goals, chooses materials appropriate for the student's ability, and paces the instructional episode. Interaction is . . . structured, but not authoritarian. Learning takes place in a convivial academic atmosphere. (1979, p. 38)

We will look at three elaborations on the basic model of direct instruction—Rosenshine's six teaching functions, Hunter's "mastery teaching," and the Missouri Mathematics Program of Good and Grouws.

Rosenshine's Six Teaching Functions. Rosenshine and his colleagues (Rosenshine, 1988; Rosenshine & Stevens, 1986) have identified six teaching functions based on the research on effective instruction. These could serve as a checklist or a framework for teaching basic skills.

1. *Review and check the previous day's work.* Reteach if students misunderstood or made errors.
2. *Present new material.* Make the purpose clear, teach in small steps, provide many examples and nonexamples.
3. *Provide guided practice.* Question students, give practice problems, and listen for misconceptions and misunderstandings. Reteach if necessary. Continue guided practice until students answer about 80 percent of the questions correctly.
4. *Give feedback and correctives* based on student answers. Reteach if necessary.
5. *Provide independent practice.* Let students apply the new learning on their own, either in seatwork or in homework. The success rate during independent practice should be about 95 percent. This means that students must be well prepared for the work by the presentation and guided practice and that assignments must not be too difficult. The point is for the students to practice until the skills become over-

Direct Instruction/Explicit Teaching Instruction for mastery of basic skills.

Active Teaching Teaching characterized by high levels of teacher explanation, demonstration, and interaction with students.

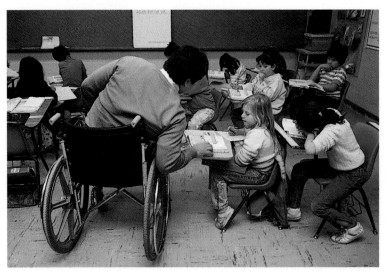

When students are doing seatwork, the teacher should monitor and assist. Students need to know how to get the teacher's attention and what to do while they wait for the teacher to come to them. Some teachers encourage students to ask fellow classmates for help, or to go on to the rest of the seatwork.

learned and automatic. Hold students accountable for the work they do—check it.

6. *Review weekly and monthly to consolidate learning.* Include some review items as homework. Test often, and reteach material missed on the tests.

These six functions are not steps to be followed in a particular order, but are elements of effective instruction. For example, feedback, review, or reteaching should occur whenever necessary and should match the abilities of the students.

Hunter's Mastery Teaching Program. Even before the research on basic skills became influential, Madeline Hunter had developed a system for designing lessons that had much in common with direct instruction. The most recent version of this system is the Hunter Mastery Teaching program (Hunter, 1982, 1991). Like Rosenshine, Hunter emphasizes review, guided practice, checking for understanding, and independent practice, but she also includes ideas about how to get students ready to learn and how to present material effectively. Table 13.1 is a summary of Hunter's approach.

Good and Grouws—The Missouri Mathematics Program. Tom Good and Doug Grouws have spent years studying mathematics teachers who consistently improve the achievement of their students. On the basis of this research, Good and Grouws have developed a model for teaching elementary- and middle-school students. Again, the program emphasizes review, guided practice, checking for understanding, and independent practice.

TABLE 13.1 The Hunter Mastery Teaching Program: Selected Principles

Get students set to learn.

Make the best use of the prime time at the beginning of the lesson.

Give students a review question or two to consider while you call the roll, pass out papers, or do other "housekeeping" chores. Follow up—listen to their answers, and correct if necessary.

Create an *anticipatory set* to capture the students' attention. This might be an advance organizer, an intriguing question, or a brief exercise. For example, at the beginning of a lesson on categories of plants you could ask, "How is pumpkin pie similar to cherry pie but different from sweet potato pie?" Answer: Pumpkins and cherries are both fruits, unlike sweet potatoes.

Communicate the lesson objectives (unless withholding this information for a while is part of your overall plan).

Provide information effectively.

Determine the basic information and organize it. Use this basic structure as scaffolding for the lesson.

Present information clearly and simply. Use familiar terms, examples, illustrations.

Model what you mean. If appropriate, demonstrate or use analogies—"If the basketball Ann is holding were the sun, how far away do you think I would have to hold this pea to represent Pluto . . . ?"

Check for understanding, and give guided practice.

Ask a question and have every student signal an answer—"Thumbs up if this statement is true, down if it's false."

Ask for a choral response: "Everyone, is this a dependent or an independent clause?"

Sample individual responses: "Everyone, think of an example of a closed system. Jon, what's your example?"

Allow for independent practice.

Get students started right by doing the first few few questions together.

Make independent practice brief. Monitor responses, giving feedback quickly.

Good and Grouws believe that the presentation or development portion of the math lesson is critical. The most successful teachers emphasize understanding and meaning in their presentations. They do not simply teach procedures and rules but strive to make students comprehend the material. Demonstrations, illustrations, concrete examples, diagrams, models, and clear explanations are important aspects of their

---

TABLE 13.2   Missouri Mathematics Program: Key Instructional Elements

Opening (first 8 minutes except Mondays)

1. Briefly review the concepts and skills associated with the homework.
2. Collect and deal with homework assignments.
3. Ask students to do several mental computation exercises. ("Think: what's 4×4? Now, what's 40×4?")

Development (about 20 minutes)

1. Briefly focus on prerequisites—the skills and concepts that will be needed in the lesson.
2. Focus on meaning and on promoting student understanding by using explanations, demonstrations, and illustrations. Keep the pace lively.
3. Assess student comprehension frequently. Use both rapid short-answer questions (but give students enough time to respond) and single practice problems.
4. Repeat and elaborate on meaning as necessary. Use examples and analogies.

Seatwork (about 15 minutes)

1. Provide uninterrupted successful practice. Most students should get at least 80 percent of their items correct.

2. Maintain momentum—keep the ball rolling; get everyone involved, then sustain involvement.
3. Alert your students—let students know their work will be checked at the end of the period.
4. Require accountability—check the students' work.

Homework Assignment

1. Assign homework at the end of each math class except Fridays. The work should take about 15 minutes.
2. Include one or two review problems in homework assignments.

Special Reviews

1. Weekly review/maintenance: during the first 20 minutes each Monday. Focus on skills and concepts covered the previous week.
2. Monthly review/maintenance on every fourth Monday. Focus on skills and concepts covered since the last monthly review.

Source: Adapted by permission of the author from T. Good, D. Grouws, and H. Ebmeier (1983), *Active mathematics teaching.* New York: Longman.

presentations (Good & Grouws, 1979; Good, Grouws, & Ebmeier, 1983; Kutz, 1991). A model for a math lesson is given in Table 13.2.

Criticisms of Direct Instruction

Critics say that direct instruction is limited to lower-level objectives, that it is based on traditional teaching methods that ignore innovative models, and that it discourages students' independent thinking. Some educational psychologists claim that the direct instruction model tells teachers to "do what works" without grounding the suggestions in a theory of student learning. Other critics disagree, saying that direct instruction *is* based on a theory of student learning—but it is the *wrong* theory. The learning theory underlying direct instruction, they believe, is a purely behavioral or transmission view—teachers break material into small segments, present each segment clearly, and reinforce or correct, thus *transmitting* accurate understandings from teacher to student. The student is seen as an "empty vessel" waiting to be filled with knowledge. These images of teaching and learning are wrong, say the opponents of direct instruction (Anderson, 1989a; Berg & Clough, 1991; Davis, Maher, & Noddings, 1990).

These criticisms of direct instruction echo the criticisms of behavioral learning theories. As support for behavioral views of learning declined and cognitive perspectives became more influential, the study of teaching discovered a critical variable long overlooked—the student!

REDISCOVERING THE STUDENT IN TEACHING

Linda Anderson (1989a) describes an alternative to the behavioral/transmission model of learning. You probably will recognize that it is based on a cognitive perspective:

> Learning is a constructive process in which knowledge structures are continually changed to assimilate and accommodate new information. The learner is more than a passive vessel for knowledge structures; rather, the learner is like a traffic cop who sometimes lets the traffic of information flow automatically and sometimes steps in actively to direct the process of sense making. (p. 91)

This concept of learning grows from the work of Piaget, Vygotsky, the information processing theorists, and other cognitive psychologists. It is sometimes called a **constructivist view of learning** or a **cognitive-mediational view.** Whatever the name, the key idea is that students actively *construct* their own knowledge; the mind of the student *mediates* inputs from the outside world to determine what the student will learn. Learning is active mental work, not passive reception of teaching. In this work, other people play an important role by providing support, challenging thinking, and serving as coaches or models, but the student is the key to learning.

If we accept the "traffic cop" view of learning described above, then an important implication for teaching follows: "No matter how talented teachers are in instructional presentations, they cannot replace the traffic cop in each student's mind. Nor should they try to do so if students are to become independent of teacher direction in their thinking" (Anderson, 1989a, p. 91). With the recognition that students control their own learning, the study of *how students learn from instruction* became a central question in research on teaching. In the 1980s and 1990s the study of teaching turned the cameras and microphones around to capture what the students were doing while the teacher was teaching. A series of studies conducted in New Zealand provide an excellent example of this new focus on the student.

The New Zealand Studies

Graham Nuthall and Adrienne Alton-Lee (1990) in New Zealand have conducted a series of studies that focus on how and what students learn. The researchers take a long-term view, trying to pinpoint what helps students construct accurate understandings and remember them a year later. The design of the studies includes careful development of student

Constructivist View of Learning View that emphasizes the active role of the learner in building understanding and making sense of information.

Cognitive-Mediational View View that emphasizes the role of the student's cognitive information processing system in interpreting, shaping, and filtering inputs from the external world.

tests based on the actual material being taught in the class; records of everything that happens in class—teacher presentations, handouts, blackboard diagrams, assignments, and so on; and in-depth case studies of selected students. The class activities and the case-study students are video- and audiotaped. Individual transmitting microphones pick up the case-study students' private speech, and an observer is assigned to each of these students to keep detailed records of the student's activities. At regular intervals the class is tested and the teacher and the case-study students are interviewed.

Some Findings. What have Nuthall and Alton-Lee learned about how students learn? Here are a few findings:

1. Students learn very different things from the same lesson. The class average test score "is more likely to misrepresent rather than reflect the learning of an individual student" (p. 555).
2. Quantity of *academic learning time* (the amount of time a student spends engaged with challenging but understandable tasks) is closely related to learning.
3. Watching demonstrations and looking at charts seem to be powerful influences on the students and promote learning that is remembered for a long time.
4. Students' prior knowledge in a subject area, including erroneous knowledge, is particularly important in shaping what they learn. For example, students' misconceptions make a significant difference in what the students will learn and remember. Sometimes students in the study "learned" a concept temporarily but remembered their misconception as *fact* a year later.

Conditions for Learning from Teaching. Nuthall and Alton-Lee developed a theory of student learning based on these and other findings. They believe that three clusters of factors must come together for memo-

Students need opportunities to apply what they have learned to new problems so that they practice self-regulation and independence in learning.

rable learning to take place. Unless all three overlap, learning will not be strong and enduring. (1) The student must have *resources* to learn. These include such personal, social, and technical resources as sufficient prior knowledge, support from home, materials and equipment, and relevant experiences. (2) The student must have many *opportunities* to learn. This means sufficient time spent with demonstrations, discussions, and projects; opportunities to clarify concepts; and challenges that will displace misconceptions. (3) The student must *take advantage of these resources and opportunities;* students must pay attention, talk to the teachers and other students, and express their understanding of key concepts orally or in writing.

In order to improve teaching, we must provide resources and opportunities for learning, *and* we must help students benefit from resources and take advantage of learning opportunities. This means helping students become more effective learners.

What Makes an Effective Learner?

The concept of self-regulated learning integrates much of what is known about effective learning and motivation. **Self-regulated learners** have a combination of academic learning skills and self-control that makes learning easier, so they are more motivated to learn. How can teachers encourage their students to become active, successful, self-regulated learners so the students will take advantage of learning opportunities and use learning resources? In order to be effective, expert, self-regulated learners, students need both the *skill* and the *will* to learn (McCombs & Marzano, 1990). Three factors influence skill and will—knowledge, motivation, and self-discipline or volition.

Learners' Knowledge. To be self-regulated learners, students need knowledge about themselves, the subject, the task, and strategies for learning. First, "expert" students know about *themselves* and how they learn best. For example, they know their preferred learning styles, what is easy and what is hard for them, how to cope with the hard parts, what their interests and talents are, and how to use their strengths. These experts also know quite a bit about the *subject* being studied—and the more they know, the easier it is to learn more. They probably understand that different learning *tasks* require different approaches on their part. A simple memory task, for example, might require a mnemonic strategy, while a complex comprehension task might be approached by means of concept maps of the key ideas. These expert students not only know what each task requires, they can also apply the *strategy* needed. They can skim or read carefully. They can use mnemonics or reorganize the material. In short, they have mastered a large repertoire of learning strategies and tactics (Wang & Palincsar, 1989; Weinstein, 1991).

Motivation. Self-regulated learners know why they are learning. They are serious about getting the intended benefit from the subject. As we saw in chapters 9 and 10, students who value a goal and believe they can attain it with a reasonable amount of effort are likely to be motivated. They are especially likely to work hard if they believe that through

Self-Regulated Learners
Students whose academic learning abilities and self-discipline make learning easy so motivation is maintained.

effort they can become smarter—more competent. Interest, curiosity, co-operation, a safe learning environment, realistic goals, valued outcomes—all these factors and more encourage student motivation. But knowledge and motivation are not always enough. Self-regulated learners need volition or self-discipline.

Volition. It is Halloween night. I have been writing almost all day. I want to keep writing because the deadline for this chapter is (very) near. I have knowledge and motivation, but to keep going I need a good dose of volition. **Volition** is an old-fashioned word for willpower. Self-regulated learners know how to protect themselves from distractions—where to study, for example, so they are not interrupted. They know how to cope when they feel anxious, drowsy or lazy (Corno, 1987). And they know what to do when tempted to stop working and watch *L.A. Law*—the temptation I'm facing now—that, and a large bowl of Halloween candy.

Obviously, not all of your students will be self-regulated learners. In fact, some psychologists suggest that you think of this capacity as an individual difference characteristic. Some students are much better at it than others. A major goal of teaching is to help students become more self-regulating. The models described in the next few pages are based on a cognitive/constructivist view of learning and emphasize the development of student self-regulation.

COGNITIVE/CONSTRUCTIVIST MODELS: TEACHING FOR SELF-REGULATION

In earlier chapters you have already seen examples of several approaches to teaching that could be called *cognitive/constructivist:* reciprocal teaching, discovery learning, inquiry methods, and critical thinking. In this section we will examine two additional models of teaching in this general category. These approaches seek to promote complex thinking and problem solving, and they aspire to develop self-regulated learners.

In a talk to educators, Barak Rosenshine commented on changing thinking about teaching: "Before, we were asking students questions. Now we see we need to teach students how to ask questions. That's a watershed" (Association for Supervision and Curriculum Development, 1990, p. 5). Let's start our consideration of constructivist models of teaching by examining Rosenshine's latest view of effective teaching beyond the basics.

Rosenshine's Factors That Support Complex Learning

Earlier in this chapter we discussed Rosenshine's six teaching functions—his summary of effective teaching strategies for direct instruction in "explicit" basic skills. In 1990 he reviewed the research on teaching reading and language arts in first grade through college and identified nine factors that support student learning of "implicit" skills such as reading comprehension, creative writing, and complex problem solving. Table 13.3 summarizes these factors.

Volition Willpower; self-discipline.

TABLE 13.3 Factors That Support Complex Learning

- *Procedural facilitators.* These provide a "scaffold" to help students learn implicit skills. For example, students can be taught to use "signal words" such as who, what, where, when, why, and how to generate questions after reading a passage.
- *Modeling use of facilitators.* The teacher, in the above example, might model the generation of questions about the reading.
- *Thinking out loud.* This models the teacher's expert thought processes, showing students the revisions and choices the learner makes in using procedural facilitators to work on problems.
- *Anticipating difficult areas.* During the modeling and presentations phase of instruction, for example, the teacher anticipates and discusses potential student errors.
- *Providing prompt or cue cards.* Procedural facilitators were written on "prompt cards" that students kept for reference as they worked. As

students practiced, the cards gradually became unnecessary.
- *Regulating the difficulty.* Tasks involving implicit skills were introduced by beginning with simpler problems, providing for student practice after each step, and gradually increasing the complexity of the task.
- *Providing half-done examples.* Giving students half-done examples of problems and having them work out the conclusions can be an effective way to teach students how to ultimately solve problems on their own.
- *Reciprocal teaching.* Having the teacher and students rotate the role of teacher. The teacher provides support to students as they learn to lead discussions and ask their own questions.
- *Providing checklists.* Students can be taught self-checking procedures to help them regulate the quality of their responses.

Source: Reprinted with permission from Association for Supervision and Curriculum Development (1990), Effective teaching redux, *ASCD Update, 32*(6), p. 5. Copyright © 1990 by ASCD. All rights reserved.

Constructing Mathematics

Critics of direct instruction believe that traditional mathematics instruction often teaches students an unintended lesson—that they "cannot understand mathematics," or worse, that mathematics doesn't have to make sense, you just have to memorize the formulas. Arthur Baroody and Herbert Ginsburg (1990, p. 62) give this example:

Sherry, a junior high student, explained that her math class was learning how to convert measurements from one unit to another. The interviewer gave Sherry the following problem:

To feed data into the computer, the measurements in your report have to be converted to one unit of measurement: feet. Your first measurement, however, is 3 feet 6 inches. What are you going to feed into the computer?

Sherry recognized immediately that the conversion algorithm taught in school applied: (a) Retrieve the equivalent measures (12 inches = 1 foot); (b) let x = the unknown; (c) set up a proportion (6 inches/12 inches = x/1 foot); (d) cancel units of measure appearing in both the numerator and denominator (6/12 = x/1 foot); and (e) cross multiply, and simplify the expression (12 times x = 6 times 1 foot; 12x = 6 feet; 12x/12 = 6 feet/12; x = 0.5 feet). By adding the result of the conversion (0.5 feet) to the whole number of feet (3), it can be determined that 3 feet 6 inches equals 3.5 feet. However, because she really did not understand the rationale behind the conversion algorithm, Sherry had difficulty in remembering the steps and how to execute them. After some time she came up with an improbable answer (it was less than 3 feet). Sherry knew she was in trouble and became flustered. At this point, the interviewer tried to help by asking her if there was any other way of solving the problem. Sherry responded sharply, "No!" She explained, "That's the way it *has* to be done." The interviewer tried to give Sherry a hint: "Look at the numbers in the problem, is there another way we can think about them that might help us figure out the problem more easily?" Sherry grew even more impatient, "This is the way I learned in school, so it has to be the way."

Sherry believed that there was only one way to solve a problem. Though Sherry knew that 6 inches was one-half a foot and that the fraction one-half was equivalent to the decimal expression .5, she did not use this knowledge to solve the problem informally and quickly ("3 feet 6 inches is 3½ or 3.5 feet"). Her beliefs prevented her from effectively using her existing mathematical knowledge to solve the problem.

A constructivist approach to mathematics teaching creates an environment in which students can make sense of mathematics and can use mathematics to make sense of the world. To accomplish these goals, teaching begins with the student's current understanding. A major challenge for teachers is to capitalize on the student's natural ways of thinking about mathematics. For example, young children create concrete,

Concrete materials (called "manipulatives") play an important role in mathematics learning. This student practices math addition facts by selecting a cardboard number for the yellow square (2) and a number for the green square (3), then counting 2 blocks and 3 blocks to match the numbers, then adding the two sets of blocks to get the answer—5.

direct representations of problems and use counting to solve problems. To answer a question such as "Melissa has three cookies—how many more does she need to have six altogether?" young children might use counters (sticks, fingers, pebbles, etc.) to represent three cookies, keep adding until there are six, then count how many were added (Peterson, Fennema, & Carpenter, 1989).

Teachers can capitalize on the natural use of counting strategies to see how many different ways students can solve a problem. The emphasis is on mathematical thinking and not on math "facts" or on learning the one best (teacher's) way to solve the problem. Here is an example of how one teacher encouraged mathematical thinking while doing the lunch count:

> During the first few minutes of the day, Ms. White asked how many children wanted hot lunches that day. Eighteen children raised their hands. Six children were going to eat cold lunches. Ms. White asked, "How many children are going to eat lunch here today?"
>
> By starting with 18 and counting on, several children got to the answer of 24. One child got out counters and counted out a set of 18 and another set of 6. He then counted all of them and said "24."

TABLE 13.4 A Constructivist Approach to Mathematics: Five Components

1. Promote students' autonomy and commitment to their answers

Examples:

- Question student answers, whether they are right or wrong.
- Insist that students at least try to solve a problem and be able to explain what they tried

2. Develop students' reflective processes

Examples:

- Ask students to restate the problem in their own words.
- Question students to guide them to try different ways to resolve the problem.
- Ask students to explain what they are doing and why.
- Ask students what they mean by the terms they are using.

3. Construct a case history of each student

Examples:

- Note general tendencies in the way the student approaches problems.
- Note common misconceptions and strengths.

4. If the student is unable to solve a problem, intervene to negotiate a possible solution with the student

Examples:

- Based on the case study and your understanding of how the student is thinking about the problem, guide the student to think about a possible solution.
- Ask questions such as "Is there anything you did in the last one that will help you here?" or "Can you explain your diagram?"
- If the student is becoming frustrated, ask more direct, product-oriented questions.

5. When the problem is solved, review the solution

Examples:

- Encourage students to reflect on what they did and why.
- Note what students did well and build confidence.

Source: Adapted by permission from J. Confrey (1990), What constructivism implies for teaching. In R. Davis, C. Maher, and N. Noddings (Eds.), *Constructivist views on the teaching and learning of mathematics.* Monograph 4 of the National Council of Teachers of Mathematics, Reston, VA.

Ms. White then asked, "How many more children are eating hot lunch than are eating cold lunch?"

Several children counted back from 18 to 12. The child with the blocks matched 18 blocks with 6 blocks and counted the blocks left over.

Ms. White asked the children who volunteered to tell the rest of the class how they got the answer. Ms. White continued asking for different solutions until no one could think of a new way to solve the problem. (Peterson, Fennema, & Carpenter, 1989, p. 45)

Jere Confrey (1990b) analyzed an expert mathematics teacher in a class for high school girls who have difficulty with mathematics. Confrey identified five components in a model of this teacher's approach to teaching. These components are summarized in Table 13.4 on page 491.

INTEGRATIONS: BEYOND MODELS TO OUTSTANDING TEACHING

We have examined two ways of conducting research on teaching—one that focuses on what the teacher is doing to teach and one that focuses on what the student is doing to learn. Of course, in practice teaching and learning cannot be separated—they are always connected. Perhaps you identified some of the connections in response to the "What Do You Think?" question at the beginning of this chapter when I asked why the outstanding teacher characteristics you listed might promote student learning. Let's take a minute to consider how the models of teaching described in this chapter could influence the ways students process information, learn, and remember.

What aspects of direct instruction might explain its success? Linda Anderson (1989b) offers one clue. She suggests that lessons that help students perceive links among main ideas will help students construct accurate understandings. Well-organized presentations, clear explanations, the use of explanatory links, and reviews all can help students perceive connections among ideas. If done well, therefore, a direct instruction lesson could be a resource that students use to construct understanding. For example, reviews activate prior knowledge so the student is ready to understand. Brief, clear presentations and guided practice avoid overloading the students' information processing systems and taxing their memories. Numerous examples and explanations give many pathways and associations for building networks of concepts. Guided practice also can give the teacher a snapshot of the students' thinking and of their misconceptions so these can be dealt with.

What direct instruction cannot do is ensure that students learn. If badly done, it may encourage students to memorize and mimic but never to "own" the knowledge. To help students reach this goal, Eleanor Duckworth believes that teachers must pay very close attention to understanding their students' understandings (Meek, 1991). This process is the basis for cognitive/constructive models of teaching.

Nel Noddings (1990) ends her chapter on "Constructivism in Mathematics Education" with this example of "a teacher's constructivist thinking":

Suppose I am concentrating on the central problem of getting my students' thinking out into the open. As I mark a set of tests, I realize that, alas, students are not showing their work as I have instructed them to do. Then I look at what I'm doing—taking off points here and there for small or large errors. Aha! Suppose I switch to a positive scheme of grading? The next day, and before every written exercise thereafter, I remind students that I'll be searching for thoughts to reward. They will get points for useful pictures, charts, formulas, statements that suggest either hypotheses or doubts, challenges to the question itself. And then I do this. No more −2s and −10s. Their papers will, rather, be peppered with +2s and +10s together with remarks encouraging attempts or explaining why an attempt failed. The result should be lots more student talk on paper. (It worked for me, by the way.) This is just one example of constructivist thinking applied to an everyday problem of schoolteaching, but it illustrates the power of constructivism as a cognitive and methodological position. (p. 18)

As I read this paragraph, it struck me that it is also an example of the power of reinforcement to encourage behavior. If we want our students to construct knowledge, we must be sure that our teaching makes this possible and that our evaluation systems reward such a process. Assessment and grading must not undermine the very processes we are trying to establish. Perhaps a behaviorist would say that cognitive approaches are successful because they reward thinking and self-regulated learning—not a bad goal for teaching.

Matching Methods to Learning Goals

Penelope Peterson (1979) compared the more traditional teacher-centered direct instruction with more open, constructivist methods. She concluded that teacher-centered instruction leads to better performance on achievement tests; while the open, informal methods like discovery learning or inquiry approaches are associated with better performance on tests of creativity, abstract thinking, and problem solving. In addition, the open methods are better for improving attitudes toward school and stimulating curiosity, cooperation among students, and lower absence rates (Walberg, 1990). According to these conclusions, when the goals of teaching involve problem solving, creativity, and mastering processes and when the students are average or above in their knowledge of a subject, many approaches besides direct instruction should be effective.

These guidelines are in keeping with Tom Good's conclusion that teaching should become less direct (1) as students mature and (2) when the goals involve affective development and problem solving or critical thinking (Good, 1983a). Of course, every subject, even college English or chemistry, can require some direct instruction. If you are teaching when to use *who* and *whom* or how to set up laboratory apparatus, direct instruction may be the best approach. Noddings (1990) reminds teachers that students may need some direct instruction in how to use various manipulative materials to get the possible benefits from them. Students working in cooperative groups may need guidance, modeling, and practice in how to ask questions and give explanations. And to solve difficult problems, students may need some direct instruction in possible problem-solving strategies. The message for teachers is to match instructional methods to learning goals.

Matching Methods to Students' Abilities

In chapters 4 and 5 we explored several ways that students differ: intelligence, gender, cognitive style, socioeconomic status, race and ethnicity, and culture. In chapter 9 we discussed student differences in need for achievement, locus of control, and anxiety. In analyzing effective teaching, we must ask whether one method of teaching can be equally effective with everyone. Even without turning to research for an answer, you might say no—and you would be right.

Aptitude-Treatment Interactions. The term **aptitude-treatment-interaction,** or ATI, refers to the ways individual differences—verbal ability, anxiety, cognitive style, or need to achieve—interact with particular teaching methods. The result is as we have seen: No single method is effective for everyone (Cronbach & Snow, 1977). You encountered a few examples of ATIs in chapter 9 when we discussed how approaches like programmed instruction and competitive grading can have very different effects on nonanxious and highly anxious students.

Studies by Penelope Peterson and colleagues at the University of Wisconsin provide examples of ATI research (Peterson, Janicki, & Swing, 1980). In one of these studies, two experienced social studies teachers taught each of their three ninth-grade classes with an inquiry, lecture-recitation, or public issues approach. The students in each class varied in verbal ability, anxiety level, attitude toward social studies, and personality factors; some, for example, expressed their need to achieve by conforming, while others were motivated to work independently. Results indicated that student differences did interact with the teaching method. As you can see in Figure 13.1, students with high verbal ability performed best on a test after the lecture-recitation lessons, and students with lower verbal ability performed best after the public issues lessons.

The interaction shown in Figure 13.1 is only one of the results of Peterson's study. Several other **higher-order interactions** were identified. Higher-order interactions involve more than two variables, more than ability and method, for example. These interactions become increasingly complex and difficult to interpret. For example, Peterson found a three-way interaction involving student anxiety, student ability, and type of instruction. Anxiety did not affect how well high-ability students responded to any of the teaching methods, but it was a factor for low-ability students. High-anxiety, low-ability students did poorly with the public issues approach but responded well to the inquiry method. Low-anxiety, low-ability students had the opposite reaction, performing better with public issues than with inquiry.

As you can see, using these relationships as guidelines for teaching would be quite difficult (Good & Stipek, 1983). With the exception (dis-

Aptitude-Treatment Interaction (ATI) Interaction of individual differences in learning with particular teaching methods.

Higher-Order Interactions Interactions involving more than two variables.

FIGURE 13.1   **An Aptitude-Treatment Interaction in the Teaching of Social Studies**   This figure shows that no one teaching approach is best in social studies. For example, in this sample, lecture-recitation was best for students with good verbal abilities while it was the worst method for students with weaker verbal abilities.

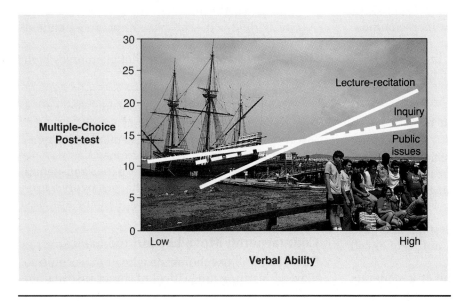

Source: Adapted from P. Peterson, T. C. Janicki, and S. R. Swing, Aptitude-treatment interaction effects of three social studies teaching approaches. *American Educational Research Journal, 17,* p. 354. Copyright 1980 by the American Educational Research Association. Adapted by permission of the publisher.

cussed below) of student ability, most aptitudes interact differently with treatments, depending on the situation or study. There is one important general implication of the ATI research: When students are having difficulty learning with one teaching approach, it makes sense to try something else. If you can form some hypotheses about your students' particular needs and the reasons your current approach does not fit these needs, you should be able to find a better alternative. Once more, flexibility is the key.

   Ability Differences and Prior Knowledge. There is one area of ATI research where findings have fairly clear and consistent implications for teaching. This is the research that has focused on academic ability and prior knowledge. In ATI research the term *ability* refers not to a theoretical notion of potential but instead to having the necessary prior knowledge to understand new material (Cronbach & Snow, 1977; Good & Stipek, 1983).

   If we look at ATI studies involving prior knowledge, we can identify some consistent findings. When students are quite knowledgeable about a particular subject, many methods can be successful. But when students have little prior knowledge, the method makes a difference. The less students know, the more they need instructional support, probably in the

Point/Counterpoint

What Is the Best Way to Help At-Risk Students?

There are many ideas and models for teaching low-achieving students—students often referred to as "at risk" for failure. Some recommendations are based on direct instruction and basic skills teaching. Another approach bases its recommendations on cognitive theories of learning, and these recommendations question the value of direct instruction. What are the teaching strategies offered by each approach?

Point: Adapt direct instruction for students' needs.

Research on effective teachers of low achievers (Ebmeier & Ziomek, 1982; Emmer et al., 1989; Slavin, Karweit, & Madden, 1989) has identified these approaches as helpful:

- Break instruction into small steps and provide short activities, chosen and sequenced by the teacher.
- Cover material thoroughly and at a moderate

pace. Give plenty of practice, immediate clear feedback, and specific praise.
- Have students work as a whole class or in groups so the teacher can supervise. Avoid individualized, self-paced, or independent work.
- Keep a level of difficulty that guarantees high rates of success.
- Ask convergent questions—one correct answer.
- Make sure to call on everyone and stay with a student until a question is answered.
- Avoid interruptions, open-ended questions, and nonacademic conversations.
- Emphasize short, frequent paper-and-pencil exercises. Games, arts, crafts, discovery learning activities, and interest centers are less helpful for learning.

Counterpoint: Move beyond the basics.

Educators and psychologists who hold a cognitive view of learning are critical of direct instruction.

form of improved materials, help in focusing and sustaining attention, systematic feedback, and explicit teaching or direct instruction (Rosenshine & Stevens, 1986; Sigmund Tobias, 1981, 1982). One goal of this extra instructional support is to reduce the information processing demands on the students (Corno, 1980; Snow, 1977). Appropriate materials and methods help the students organize the information, direct their attention to its critical features, and relieve some of the burden on their memories.

Lesson Formats for Low-Ability Classes. In most secondary-school subjects, teachers follow a lesson format that involves an opening, a presentation of the content of the lesson, student work on problems or questions based on the presentation, and a closing. In a low-ability class, however, this standard format can invite problems, because the students are expected to pay attention to one activity for long blocks of time.

Teachers who are successful with low-ability classes tend to have more than one cycle of presentation and student seatwork in each period (Ebmeier & Ziomek, 1982). The teacher may make a short presentation, have the students work briefly, continue the lesson with more content development and then more student practice on the skill being developed, and perhaps give another presentation followed by student seatwork (Evertson, 1982). This pattern keeps the students attentive by giving small doses of both information and individual work. The different activities are short enough to be within the students' attention spans, and the teacher can make sure every student understands each step.

For example, Barbara Means and Michael Knapp (1991) decry the "basics" approach to teaching low achievers:

A recent summary of critiques of conventional approaches to teaching academic skills to at-risk students, offered by a group of national experts in reading, writing, and mathematics education, concluded that such approaches tend to:

- underestimate what students are capable of doing;
- postpone more challenging and interesting work for too long—in some cases, forever; and
- deprive students of a meaningful or motivating context for learning or for employing the skills that are taught. (pp. 283–284)

What do critics of direct instruction offer in its place? The following are some principles recommended by Means and Knapp (1991):

- Focus on complex, meaningful problems. Keep the level of tasks high enough that the purpose of the task is apparent and makes sense to students.
- Embed basic skills instruction in the context of more global tasks such as class record keeping or letter writing.
- Make connections with students' out-of-school experience and culture.
- Model powerful thinking strategies for students; for example, think aloud as you try to figure out a difficult text passage.
- Encourage multiple approaches to academic tasks. Have students describe how they reached their answers.
- Provide scaffolding to enable students to accomplish complex tasks; for example, perform the calculations for students as they set up an algebra problem correctly.
- Make dialogue the central medium for teaching and learning. Reciprocal teaching is one example.

To give students a greater sense of responsibility for their own work, Emmer and colleagues (1989) have suggested short daily assignments. Students keep a record of grades on every assignment and of average grades for each week so they can see the results of their work (or lack of work). Class participation is part of the grading system, with daily or weekly grades awarded for appropriate contributions. In addition, students can be taught some of the learning and metacognitive strategies that more successful students tend to apply automatically. It is especially important to give low-achieving students techniques for monitoring their own learning and problem-solving processes so they can tell when they should use a particular strategy and if they are applying it correctly (Brown, Campione, & Day, 1981).

With all this emphasis on structure, the atmosphere of the class should remain as friendly and supportive as possible. Students who have failed repeatedly are more likely to need the kind of genuine, constant encouragement and nurturing that is effective with younger students (Good & Brophy, 1991). But you should know that not all educators agree with these findings. The **Point/Counterpoint** section above gives two perspectives on teaching strategies for these students.

Teaching High Achievers. The research on aptitude-treatment interactions indicates that a wider range of methods and approaches can be effective with high achievers. During lecture-discussion sessions these students tend to learn more if the teacher keeps the pace of the class rapid

Guidelines

Adapting Teaching to Different Students and Situations

Vary the amount of structure to fit the needs of the students.

Examples

1. Give clear directions and very specific objectives (written or oral) when working with younger, more-anxious, or more-dependent students.
2. Encourage independence in older and higher-achieving students by providing less structure for some assignments. Give them a topic and suggest they propose a reading list and tentative outline.

Allow students in junior and senior high school ample opportunity to explore a limited amount of material in depth. Focus on one novel for several weeks or on one essay or one historical figure for several days.

Examples

1. Hold debates after students finish reading an essay. The next day, have students change sides and defend the opposite position.
2. Have thought-provoking questions ready for discussion. Was Robert E. Lee right to take on leadership of the Confederate army, even though he was opposed to the dissolution of the country? How might the world be different today if Lincoln, the Kennedys, or Martin Luther King, Jr., had not been assassinated?

3. Ask students to write proposals for turning a novel into a film and to present their proposals to the class as if to prospective producers.
4. Have different groups of students take the positions of a novel's protagonist(s) and antagonist(s) and defend their actions, debate their differences, or draw up a profile of their most important traits.

Use unexpected events as vehicles for teaching.

Examples

1. Teach new words and concepts related to electricity and sound transmission when students are excited by an electrical storm.
2. Discuss seeing events from several different perspectives after a disappointing loss in sports or after the announcement of schoolwide election results.

Be flexible: if one approach does not work with some students, try a different strategy.

Examples

1. If teacher praise does not seem motivating to a student, try a self-management approach or provide more challenging work.
2. If a student does not understand a concept, use more concrete examples or let a peer explain it.

and the tasks challenging, asks both factual questions and questions requiring higher-level thinking, sets high standards, and points out errors clearly (Brophy & Evertson, 1976). The more nurturing style of teaching seems less important in encouraging learning in high achievers, although this does not hold for every individual. Presentations can be longer, and more material can be covered in one session. Guided practice sessions can be shorter. Less review and independent practice is necessary (Rosenshine, 1986).

Teaching and Learning: Conclusions

If you teach your fifth-grade students fractions using a constructivist approach, will they automatically understand fractions? Not if your explanations are confused and vague. Not if you lose control of the class. Not if you fear fractions, become very anxious, and make no sense as a result. Could a dynamic, knowledgeable, well-organized, enthusiastic teacher have positive results using a weak strategy to teach mathematics? It is very possible. Could a biology teacher produce students who did well on achievement tests at the end of the year but hated the subject so much that they vowed never to take another biology course as long as they lived? Again, it is possible.

Teaching is complicated. Some of the methods that are supposed to work for every situation simply do not. As a teacher, you will have to make judgments based on your students and the subjects you teach. The Guidelines on page 498 should help you make some of these decisions.

The models presented in this chapter should give you some frameworks for experimenting in your own class. But your own judgment of the impact of each strategy on your students should be your criterion for using or abandoning any of the approaches.

SUMMARY

THE SEARCH FOR THE KEYS TO SUCCESS

For years researchers have tried to unravel the mystery of effective teaching. Studies reported in the 1960s and early 1970s focused on general ability levels and social class of teachers and average measures of student ability. Later research has tried to determine whether individual teachers make a difference in the daily lives and learning of their students.

CHARACTERISTICS OF EFFECTIVE TEACHERS

Results of research on teacher characteristics indicate that thorough and expert knowledge of a subject, organization and clarity in presentation, and enthusiasm all play important parts in effective teaching. But no one way of teaching has been found to be right for each class, lesson, or day.

TEACHING THE BASICS

Direct instruction seems most appropriate for teaching basic skills. A framework for direct instruction might involve reviewing yesterday's work, presenting new material, giving guided practice, giving feedback and corrections, providing independent practice, and reviewing weekly and monthly. Hunter's mastery teaching and the Missouri Mathematics Program are also elaborations on direct instruction in the basics. Critics of direct instruction, however, suggest that it is based on a misleading theory of student learning, one that sees students as passive recipients of knowledge from the teacher.

REDISCOVERING THE STUDENT IN TEACHING

The study of teaching today has responded to these criticisms—and to the findings from cognitive research on learning—by turning attention to the student's role in learning.

COGNITIVE/CONSTRUCTIVIST MODELS: TEACHING FOR SELF-REGULATION

Cognitive/constructivist models of teaching emphasize the creation of environments in which students can develop their understandings of the content and become more independent, self-regulated learners in the process. Beyond the basics—for abstract problem solving, affective development, and creativity; for older students; and for complex subjects like high school English—more open, inquiry-type approaches seem to be effective.

INTEGRATIONS: BEYOND MODELS TO OUTSTANDING TEACHING

Teachers must deal with a wide range of student aptitudes for learning. Aptitude-treatment interaction research has attempted to determine how particular methods affect students of different abilities. One clear implication is that teachers must be flexible and must be willing to try a new approach if one is not working well. Degree of prior knowledge can influence the effectiveness of teaching methods. Students with little prior knowledge need much more support and structure in learning.

Low-ability students need an emotionally supportive atmosphere and lessons broken up into small doses of presentation and seatwork—not too much of any one task at once. A wider range of methods and a faster pace are more appropriate for high achievers. Though there are no guarantees about effectiveness, it is clear that effective classrooms are pleasant, convivial, and fun.

KEY TERMS AND CONCEPTS

active teaching, p. 481
aptitude-treatment interaction
  (ATI), p. 494
basic skills, p. 480
cognitive-mediational view,
  p. 485

constructivist view of learning,
  p. 485
descriptive-correlational-
  experimental loop, p. 475
direct instruction/explicit
  teaching, p. 481

explanatory links, p. 479
higher-order interactions,
  p. 494
self-regulated learners, p. 487
volition, p. 488

WHAT WOULD YOU DO?

PRESCHOOL AND KINDERGARTEN

You have a very well supplied science corner in your class, but your students seldom visit it. When they do, they don't seem to take advantage of the learning possibilities available with the manipulatives. How would you help students benefit from the materials?

ELEMENTARY AND MIDDLE SCHOOL

You are given a math workbook and text series and told that you must use these materials as the basis for your math teaching. What would you do to incorporate these materials into lessons that help students understand mathematical thinking and problem solving?

One of the teachers in your building is really disorganized and confusing. Your students have to go to this teacher for science and they hate it. The saddest part is that many of your students seem to have decided that science is impossibly difficult and they are just "too dumb" to learn it. What would you do?

JUNIOR HIGH AND HIGH SCHOOL

You have been assigned a "developmental" class—25 students who are several years behind. How would you help them become better learners?

The range of abilities in your fourth-period class is really wide. You want to use an inquiry-based approach that requires problem solving and writing in journals. What would you do to make this approach work in fourth period?

COOPERATIVE LEARNING ACTIVITY

With four or five other members of your educational psychology class, brainstorm ways to "understand your students' understanding" in a particular content area. What would you do before, during, and after a class in this unit to make your students' knowledge and thinking processes visible to you and to them?

TEACHERS' CASEBOOK

MAKING EXPLANATIONS WORK

How do you know when an explanation "works"? What do you do if students greet your well-planned presentation with blank stares?

SENSE AND APPLICATION

I know that an explanation "works" when my students are able to apply it to other knowledge or work. Anytime I am greeted with blank stares, or for that matter, even one blank stare, I try another angle. A great presentation is worthless if it doesn't make sense to the audience. Frequently I will try a more involved, hands-on approach or I will tie the new learning in to something they know well. I might, for example, apply math concepts to batting records of famous baseball players, if my students' interests were so directed.

Sarah Gustafson, *Florida 1991 Teacher of the Year*
The Okeechobee Center, Okeechobee, Florida

ACTIVE INVOLVEMENT

Blank stares indicate that I have not effectively presented material that will lead to key student understanding. Students need to be *actively* involved in all areas of the curriculum from introduction of a concept to the completion of a lesson. As a teacher I must create activities that rely on my students' own experience base and then constantly check for understanding in creative and engaging ways. I immediately recognize the success of an explanation when students "attack" the task at hand, providing their own creative and divergent approaches to problem solving.

If I'm still unsuccessful after modifying my approach, I will move on to something else. I will rethink the activity and consult other resources and colleagues before reteaching the lesson.

Bruce D. Fisher, *California 1991 Teacher of the Year*
Fortuna Elementary School, Fortuna, California

STORY PROBLEMS

Students often have difficulty with story problems in math because they are not representing the problems so they can "see" the appropriate solution strategies. What are some techniques you use to help students represent problems?

LET STUDENTS WORK TOGETHER

When we do story problems for homework I make it an in-class assignment and let the students work together. They are free to check any answers with me. On a test I use problems that they can identify with personally. They spend money at a street fair, baby-sit at different rates, work for so much an hour. I often let them use calculators. With story problems, I am more concerned about having students solve that problem than with the actual computation.

Donald Falk, *Math Teacher*
Fredericktown Intermediate School, Fredericktown, Ohio

A VARIETY OF STRATEGIES

I strongly urge students to sketch out some sort of model for each word problem. Brainstorming is an important problem-solving tool. I reward appropriate strategies even if the final answer is inaccurate. Also, we explore a variety of strategies that will effectively solve each problem. I often attack problem solving by employing cooperative learning. This model of teaching gives students exposure to each other's ideas and strategies.

Stephen C. Ellwood IV, *Maine 1991 Teacher of the Year*
St. Francis Elementary School, St. Francis, Maine

ROLE PLAYING

Role playing is an excellent way to help children visualize and understand the process of solving story problems. For instance, if a story problem involves two characters, I select two students for the roles. I set the scene by reading the story. To personalize it, each student plays himself and decides what lines he would say in that particular situation. (In the beginning, students may require some prompting.) Then I write the story on the chalkboard in equation form and explain it. A second story problem is presented, and new volunteers are selected for role playing. A volunteer is also selected to write the story on the board as an equation. The students soon learn to write their own story problems in this form. Should a student fail to understand the process, he can draw a picture or retell the story to me. Invariably the child will "see" the solution.

Nancy R. Gonzalez, *Bilingual First-Grade Teacher*
Robert Frost School, Mount Prospect, Illinois

STUDENT WRITING

Sometimes students get bogged down in the mechanics of writing. . . . How do you encourage students to write creatively and imaginatively while also helping them learn correct grammar and vocabulary?

WRITE FOR A REASON

In order for students to write well, they must write for a reason. I have found that students are willing to write if they have something to say and believe that someone, either myself as their teacher or any other real audience, cares what they have to say. My students write to explain, to argue a point of view, to prove a hypothesis. My focus is on their message. Eventually their need to present a clear description or persuasive argument will lead to a concern with the clarity and logic of their message. First and foremost, my students are encouraged to write in order to discover and clarify their ideas. Editing is done only to strengthen the intelligibility of the ideas, and revisions are always acceptable. Students want to be heard. Clear writing, reflecting our shared symbolic conventions, allows them to be.

Karen B. Kreider, *Pennsylvania 1991 Teacher of the Year*
Central High School, Philadelphia, Pennsylvania

STRATEGIES TO INVOLVE STUDENTS

We know that effective teaching relies in part on students' active involvement in lessons. What strategies do you use to keep students involved? How do you keep the rest of the class engaged when only a few are answering questions?

WINNING TECHNIQUES

Keeping all students involved is always a challenge. One way to meet the challenge is to make sure that all students believe they may be called on at any time. In my experience, secondary-school students should be selected to answer questions randomly. The question should be asked first, before anyone is called on. After the first student has responded, that answer can be used to generate a new question for others.

Another technique to help keep students focused on the task is to walk around the classroom while asking questions. Students tend to daydream less if the teacher is standing nearby. A third technique is to have students write individual responses to questions. After they've all had enough time to write their responses, an individual student can be called on. This way, all students think through the question and answer it, even if they don't respond orally.

Jane C. Dusell, *English Teacher*
Medford Senior High School, Medford, Wisconsin

14 STANDARDIZED TESTING

Would it surprise you to learn that published tests such as the college entrance exams and IQ tests are creations of the 20th century? In the 19th and early 20th centuries, college entrance was generally based on grades, essays, and interviews. From your own experience, you know that testing has come a long way since then. In fact, many educators and psychologists believe standardized testing has come too far. Critics want to reshape testing as a way of reshaping the curriculum and reforming education. We will explore these new ideas.

In spite of the criticisms, schools still use many standardized tests, so teachers must be knowledgeable about testing. How will you interpret standardized test scores? What would you like to know about testing? How should you prepare yourself or your students for tests? How should you make up tests? This chapter will focus on the first question, interpreting standardized tests, leaving the others for chapter 15. An understanding of how standardized test scores are determined, what they really mean, and how they can be used (or misused) will give you a framework for ensuring that the tests you give are appropriate.

First we consider testing in general, including the various methods of interpreting test scores. Then we look at the different kinds of standardized tests used in schools. Finally, we examine the criticisms of testing and the alternatives being proposed. By the time you have completed this chapter, you should be able to do the following:

- Calculate mean, median, mode, and standard deviation.

- Define percentile ranks, standard deviations, z scores, T scores, and stanine scores.

- Explain how to improve reliability and validity in testing.

- Interpret the results of achievement, aptitude, and diagnostic tests in a realistic manner.

- Take a position on the testing issue and defend your position.

- Describe how to prepare students (and yourself) for taking standardized tests.

- Explain the strengths and weaknesses of alternative forms of assessment such as portfolios.

MEASUREMENT AND EVALUATION

All teaching involves **evaluation.** At the heart of evaluation is judgment—making decisions based on values. In the process of evaluation, we compare information to criteria and then make judgments. Teachers must make all kinds of judgments. "Should we use a different text this year?" "Is the film appropriate for my students?" "Will Sarah do better if she repeats the first grade?" "Should Terry get a B− or a C+ on the project?"

Measurement is evaluation put in quantitative terms—the description of an event or characteristic in numbers. Measurement tells how much, how often, or how well by providing scores, ranks, or ratings. Instead of saying, "Sarah doesn't seem to understand addition," a teacher might say, "Sarah answered only 2 of the 15 problems correctly on her addition worksheet." Measurement also allows a teacher to compare one student's performance on one particular task with a standard or with the performances of the other students.

Not all the evaluative decisions made by teachers involve measurement. Some decisions are based on information that is difficult to express numerically: student preferences, information from parents, previous experiences, even intuition. But measurement does play a large role in many classroom decisions, and properly done, it can provide unbiased data for evaluations.

The answers given on any type of test have no meaning by themselves; we must make some kind of comparison to interpret test results. Two basic types of comparison are possible. A test score can be compared to the scores obtained by other people who have taken the same test (this is a norm-referenced comparison). If you took a college entrance exam, the score you received told you (and the admissions offices of colleges) how your performance compared to performances of many other people who had previously taken the same test or one like it. The second type of comparison is to a fixed standard or minimum passing score (criterion-referenced). Most tests required for a driver's license are based on this kind of comparison.

Norm-Referenced Tests

In **norm-referenced testing,** the people who have taken the test provide the *norms* for determining the meaning of a given individual's score. You

Evaluation Decision making about student performance and about appropriate teaching strategies.

Measurement Evaluation expressed in quantitative (number) terms.

Norm-Referenced Testing Testing in which scores are compared with the average performance of others.

can think of a norm as being the typical level of performance for a particular group. By comparing the individual's raw score (the actual number correct) to the norm, we can determine if the score is above, below, or around the average for that group.

There are at least three types of **norm groups** (comparison groups) in education. One frequently used norm group is the class or school itself. When a teacher compares the score of one student in a 10th-grade American history class with the scores of all the other students in the class, the class itself is the norm group. If the teacher happens to have three American history classes, all of about the same ability, then the norm group for evaluating individual performance might be all three classes.

Norm groups may also be drawn from wider areas. Sometimes, for example, school districts develop achievement tests. When students take this kind of test, their scores are compared to the scores of all other students at their grade level throughout the district. Finally, some tests have national norm groups. When students take the college entrance exam, their scores are compared with the scores of students all over the country.

Norm-referenced tests are constructed with certain objectives in mind, but the test items themselves tend to cover many different abilities rather than assess a limited number of specific objectives. Norm-referenced tests are especially useful in measuring overall achievement when students have come to understand complex material by different routes. Norm-referenced tests are also appropriate when only the top few candidates can be admitted to a program.

Norm-referenced measurement also has its limitations. Results of a norm-referenced test do not tell you whether students are ready to move on to more advanced material. Knowing that a student is in the top 3 percent of the class on a test of algebraic concepts will not tell you if he or she is ready to move on to trigonometry. *Everyone* in the class may have failed to achieve sufficient mastery of algebraic concepts.

Norm-referenced tests are also not particularly appropriate for measuring affective and psychomotor objectives. To measure individuals' psychomotor learning, a clear description of standards is necessary. Even the best gymnast in any school performs certain exercises better than others and needs specific guidance about how to improve. In the affective area, attitudes and values are personal; comparisons among individuals are not really appropriate. For example, what is an "average" performance on a measure of political values or opinions? Finally, norm-referenced tests tend to encourage competition and comparison of scores. Some students compete to be the best. Others, realizing that being the best is impossible, may compete to be the worst! Either goal has its casualties.

Criterion-Referenced Tests

When test scores are compared not to those of others but to a given criterion or standard of performance, this is **criterion-referenced testing**.

Norm Group A group whose average score serves as a standard for evaluating any student's score on a test.

Criterion-Referenced Testing Testing in which scores are compared to a set performance standard.

To get a driver's license, you must pass a criterion-referenced test—that is, you must reach a certain standard of performance.

To decide who should be allowed to drive a car, it is important to determine just what standard of performance is appropriate for selecting safe drivers. It does not matter how your test results compare to the results of others. If your performance on the test was in the top 10 percent but you consistently ran through red lights, you would not be a good candidate for receiving a license, even though your score was high.

Criterion-referenced tests measure the mastery of very specific objectives. The results of a criterion-referenced test should tell the teacher exactly what the students can do and what they cannot do, at least under certain conditions. For example, a criterion-referenced test would be useful in measuring the ability to add three-digit numbers. A test could be designed with 20 different problems. The standard for mastery could be set at 17 out of 20 correct. (The standard is often somewhat arbitrary but may be based on such things as the teacher's experience.) If two students receive scores of 7 and 11, it does not matter that one student did better than the other, since neither met the standard of 17. Both need more help with addition.

In the teaching of basic skills there are many such instances when comparison to a preset standard is more important than comparison to the performance of others. It is not very comforting to know, as a parent, that your child is better than most of the students in class in reading if all the students are unable to read material suited for their grade level. Sometimes standards for meeting the criterion must be set at 100 percent correct. You would not like to have your appendix removed by a surgeon who left surgical instruments inside the body only 10 percent of the time.

But criterion-referenced tests are not appropriate for every situation. Not every subject can be broken down into a set of specific objectives that exhausts all possible learning outcomes. Moreover, although standards are important in criterion-referenced testing, they often tend to be arbitrary, as you have already seen. When deciding whether a student has mastered the addition of three-digit numbers comes down to the difference between 16 or 17 correct answers, it seems difficult to justify one

---

TABLE 14.1   Deciding on the Type of Test to Use

Norm-referenced tests may work best when you are

- Measuring general ability in certain areas, such as English, algebra, general science, or American history.
- Assessing the range of abilities in a large group.
- Selecting top candidates when only a few openings are available.

Criterion-referenced tests may work best when you are

- Measuring mastery of basic skills.
- Determining if students have prerequisites to start a new unit.
- Assessing affective and psychomotor objectives.
- Grouping students for instruction.

particular standard over another. Finally, at times it is valuable to know how the students in your class compare to other students at their grade level both locally and nationally. Table 14.1 offers a comparison of norm-referenced and criterion-referenced tests.

WHAT DO TEST SCORES MEAN?

On the average, more than 1 million standardized tests are given per school day in classes throughout this country (Lyman, 1986). Most of these are norm-referenced standardized tests. **Standardized tests** are the official-looking pamphlets and piles of forms purchased by school systems and administered to students. More specifically, a standardized test is "a task or set of tasks given under standard conditions and designed to assess some aspect of a person's knowledge, skill, or personality" (Green, 1981, p. 1001). The tests are meant to be given under carefully controlled conditions so that students all over the country undergo the same experience when they take the tests. Standard methods of developing items, administering the test, scoring it, and reporting the scores are all implied by the term *standardized test.*

Basic Concepts

In standardized testing the test items and instructions have been tried out to make sure they work and then rewritten and retested as necessary. The final version of the test is administered to a **norming sample,** a large sample of subjects as similar as possible to the students who will be taking the test in school systems throughout the country. This norming sample serves as a comparison group for all students who take the test.

The test publishers provide one or more ways of comparing each student's raw score (number of correct answers) with the norming sample. Let's took at some of the measurements on which comparisons and interpretations are based.

Frequency Distributions. A **frequency distribution** is simply a listing of the number of people who obtain each score or fall into each range of scores on a test or other measuring device. For example, on a spelling test 19 students made these scores: 100, 95, 90, 85, 85, 85, 80, 75, 75, 75, 70, 65, 60, 60, 55, 50, 50, 45, 40. A graph, in this case a **histogram,** or bar graph, of the spelling test scores is shown in Figure 14.1 on page 510. As you can see, one student made a score of 100, three made 85, and so on. This kind of information is often expressed as a simple graph where one axis (the *x* or horizontal axis) indicates the possible scores and the other axis (the *y* or vertical axis) indicates the number of subjects who attained each score.

Measurements of Central Tendency and Standard Deviation. You have probably had a great deal of experience with means. A **mean** is simply the arithmetical average of a group of scores. To calculate the mean, you add the scores and divide the total by the number of scores in

Standardized Tests Tests given, usually nationwide, under uniform conditions and scored according to uniform procedures.

Norming Sample Large sample of students serving as a comparison group for scoring standardized tests.

Frequency Distribution Record showing how many scores fall into set groups.

Histogram Bar graph of a frequency distribution.

Mean Arithmetical average.

FIGURE 14.1   **Histogram of a Frequency Distribution** This bar graph or histogram shows the number of people who earned each score on a test. You can quickly see, for example, that three people earned a 75 and three people earned an 85.

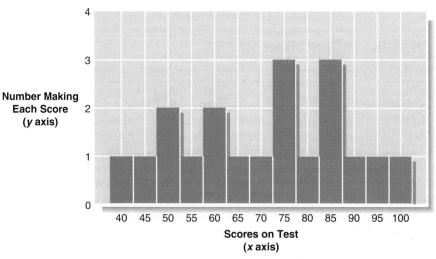

Number Making
Each Score
(*y* axis)

Scores on Test
(*x* axis)

the distribution. For example, the total of the 19 spelling scores is 1,340, so the mean is 1,340/19, or 70.53. The mean offers one way of measuring **central tendency,** the score that is typical or representative of the whole distribution of scores.

Two other measures of central tendency are the median and the mode. The **median** is the middle score in the distribution, the point at which half the scores are larger and half are smaller. The median of the 19 scores is 75. Nine scores in the distribution are greater than or equal to 75, and nine are less. The **mode** is the score that occurs most often. The distribution in Figure 14.1 actually has two modes, 75 and 85. This makes it a **bimodal distribution.**

The measure of central tendency gives a score that is representative of the group of scores, but it does not tell you anything about how the scores are distributed. Two groups of scores may both have a mean of 50 but be alike in no other way. One group might contain the scores 50, 45, 55, 55, 45, 50, 50; the other group might contain the scores 100, 0, 50, 90, 10, 50, 50. In both cases the mean, median, and mode are all 50, but the distributions are quite different.

The **standard deviation** is a measure of how widely the scores vary from the mean. The larger the standard deviation, the more spread out the scores in the distribution. The smaller the standard deviation, the more the scores are clustered around the mean. For example, in the distribution 50, 45, 55, 55, 45, 50, 50, the standard deviation is much smaller than in the distribution 100, 0, 50, 90, 10, 50, 50. Another way of saying this is that distributions with very small standard deviations have less **variability** in the scores.

The standard deviation is relatively easy to calculate if you remember your high school math. It does take time, however. The process is similar

Central Tendency Typical score for a group of scores.

Median Middle score in a group of scores.

Mode Most frequently occurring score.

Bimodal Distribution Frequency distribution with two modes.

Standard Deviation Measure of how widely scores vary from the mean.

Variability Degree of difference or deviation from mean.

to taking an average, but square roots are used. To calculate the standard deviation, you follow these steps:

1. Calculate the mean (written as $\bar{X}$) of the scores.
2. Subtract the mean from each of the scores. This is written as $(X - \bar{X})$.
3. Square each difference (multiply each difference by itself). This is written $(X - \bar{X})^2$.
4. Add all the squared differences. This is written $\Sigma (X - \bar{X})^2$.
5. Divide this total by the number of scores. This is written $\dfrac{\Sigma (X - \bar{X})^2}{N}$.
6. Find the square root. This is written $\sqrt{\dfrac{\Sigma (X - \bar{X})^2}{N}}$, which is the formula for calculating the standard deviation.

Knowing the mean and the standard deviation of a group of scores gives you a better picture of the meaning of an individual score. For example, suppose you received a score of 78 on a test. You would be very pleased with the score if the mean of the test were 70 and the standard deviation were 4. In this case, your score would be 2 standard deviations above the mean, a score well above average.

Consider the difference if the mean of the test had remained at 70 but the standard deviation had been 20. In the second case, your score of 78 would be less than 1 standard deviation from the mean. You would be much closer to the middle of the group, with an above-average but not a high score. Knowing the standard deviation tells you much more than simply knowing the **range** of scores. One or two students may do very well or very poorly no matter how the majority scored on the tests.

The Normal Distribution. Standard deviations are very useful in understanding test results. They are especially helpful if the results of the tests form a **normal distribution.** You may have met the normal distribution before. It is the bell-shaped curve, the most famous frequency distribution because it describes many naturally occurring physical and social phenomena. Many scores fall in the middle, giving the curve its puffed appearance. You find fewer and fewer scores as you look out toward the end points, or *tails,* of the distribution. The normal distribution has been thoroughly analyzed by statisticians. The mean of a normal distribution is also its midpoint. Half the scores are above the mean, and half are below it. In a normal distribution, the mean, median, and mode are all the same point.

Another convenient property of the normal distribution is that the percentage of scores falling within each area of the curve is known, as you can see in Figure 14.2 on page 512. A person scoring within 1 standard deviation of the mean obviously has a lot of company. Many scores pile up here. In fact, 68 percent of all scores are located in the area plus and minus 1 standard deviation from the mean. About 16 percent of the scores are higher than 1 standard deviation above the mean. Of this higher group, only 2.5 percent are better than 2 standard deviations above the mean. Similarly, only about 16 percent of the scores are less than 1 standard deviation below the mean, and of that group only about 2.5 percent are worse than 2 standard deviations below. At 2 standard deviations from the mean in either direction, the scorer has left the pack behind.

Range Distance between the highest and the lowest score in a group.

Normal Distribution The most commonly occurring distribution, in which scores are distributed evenly around mean.

FIGURE 14.2   **The Normal Distribution**   The normal distribution or bell-shaped curve has certain predictable characteristics. For example, 68 percent of the scores are clustered within 1 standard deviation below to 1 standard deviation above the mean.

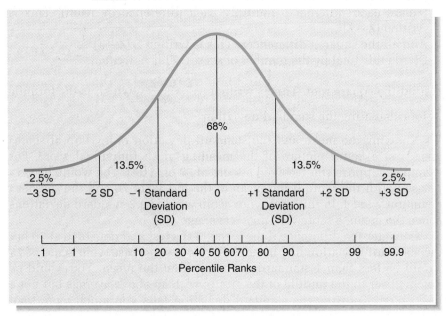

The SAT college entrance exam offers one example of a normal distribution. The mean of the SAT is 500 and the standard deviation is 100. If you know people who made scores of 700, you know they did very well. Only about 2.5 percent of the people who take the test do that well, because only 2.5 percent of the scores are better than 2 standard deviations above the mean in a normal distribution.

Types of Scores

Now you have enough background for a discussion of the different kinds of scores you may encounter in reports of results from standardized tests.

Percentile Rank Scores. The concept of ranking is the basis for one very useful kind of score reported on standardized tests: a **percentile rank** score. In percentile ranking, each student's raw score is compared with the raw scores obtained by the students in the norming sample. The percentile rank shows the percentage of students in the norming sample who scored at or below a particular raw score. If a student's score is the same as or better than three-quarters of the students in the norming sample, the student would score in the 75th percentile, or have a percentile rank of 75. You can see that this does *not* mean that the student had a raw score of 75 correct answers or even that the student answered 75 percent of the questions correctly. Rather, the 75 refers to the percentage of people in the norming sample whose scores on the test were equal to

Percentile Rank
Percentage of those in the norming sample who scored at or below individual's score.

or below this student's score. A percentile rank of 50 means that a student has scored as well as or better than 50 percent of the norming sample and achieved an average score.

Figure 14.3 illustrates one problem in interpreting percentile scores. Differences in percentile ranks do not mean the same thing in terms of raw score points in the middle of the scale as they do at the fringes. The graph shows Joan's and Alice's percentile scores on the fictitious Test of Excellence in Language and Arithmetic. Both students are about average in arithmetic skills. One equaled or surpassed 50 percent of the norming sample; the other, 60 percent. But in the middle of the distribution, this difference in percentile ranks means a raw score difference of only a few points. Their raw scores actually were 75 and 77. In the language test, the difference in percentile ranks seems to be about the same as the difference in arithmetic, since one ranked at the 90th percentile and the other at the 99th. But the difference in their raw scores on the language test is much greater. It takes a greater difference in raw score points to make a difference in percentile rank at the extreme ends of the scale. On the language test the difference in raw scores is about 10 points.

Grade-Equivalent Scores. **Grade-equivalent scores** are generally obtained from separate norming samples for each grade level. The average

FIGURE 14.3 Percentile Ranking on a Normal Distribution Curve One problem with percentile scores is that they have different meanings at different places on the scale. For example, a difference of a few raw score points near the mean might translate into a 10 point percentile difference, while it would take 6 or 7 points to make a 10 point percentile difference farther out on the scale.

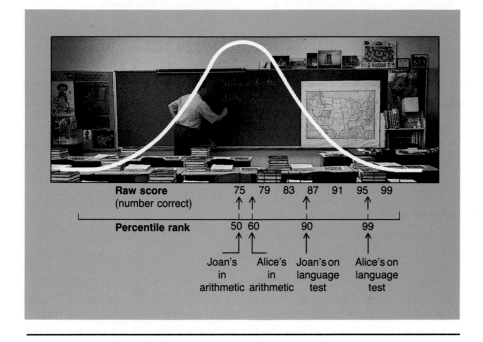

Grade-Equivalent Score
Measure of grade level based on comparison with norming samples from each grade.

of the scores of all the 10th graders in the norming sample defines the 10th-grade equivalent score. Suppose the raw-score average of the 10th-grade norming sample is 38. Any student who attains a raw score of 38 on that test will be assigned a grade-equivalent score of 10th grade. Grade-equivalent scores are generally listed in numbers, such as 8.3, 4.5, 7.6, 11.5, and so on. The whole number gives the grade and the decimals stand for tenths of a year, but they are usually interpreted as months.

Suppose a student with the grade-equivalent score of 10 is a 7th grader. Should this student be promoted immediately? Probably not. Different forms of tests are used at different grade levels, so the 7th grader may not have had to answer items that would be given to 10th graders. The high score may represent superior mastery of material at the 7th-grade level rather than a capacity for doing advanced work. Even though an average 10th grader could do as well as our 7th grader on this particular test, the 10th grader would certainly know much more than this test covered. Also, grade-equivalent score units do not mean the same thing at every grade level. For example, a 2nd grader reading at the 1st-grade level would have more trouble in school than an 11th grader who reads at the 10th-grade level.

Because grade-equivalent scores are misleading and so often misinterpreted, especially by parents, most educators and psychologists strongly believe *they should not be used at all.* There are several other forms of reporting available that are more appropriate.

Standard Scores. As you may remember, one problem with percentile ranks is the difficulty in making comparisons among ranks. A discrepancy of a certain number of raw-score points has a different meaning at different places on the scale. With standard scores, on the other hand, a difference of 10 points is the same everywhere on the scale.

Standard scores are based on the standard deviation. A very common standard score is called the **z score.** A z score tells how many standard deviations above or below the average a raw score is. In the example described earlier, in which you were fortunate enough to get a 78 on a test where the mean was 70 and the standard deviation was 4, your z score would be +2, or 2 standard deviations above the mean. If a person were to score 64 on this test, the score would be 1.5 standard deviation units *below* the mean, and the z score would be −1.5. A z score of 0 would be no standard deviations above the mean—in other words, right on the mean.

To calculate the z score for a given raw score, just subtract the mean from the raw score and divide the difference by the standard deviation. The formula is:

$$z = \frac{\chi - \bar{\chi}}{SD}$$

Since it is often inconvenient to use negative numbers, other standard scores have been devised to eliminate this difficulty. The ***T score*** has a mean of 50 and uses a standard deviation of 10. If you multiply the z score by 10 (which eliminates the decimal) and add 50 (which gets rid of

Standard Scores Scores based on the standard deviation.

***z* Score** Standard score indicating number of standard deviations above or below the mean.

***T* Score** Standard score with a mean of 50 and a standard deviation of 10.

the negative number), you get the equivalent *T* score as the answer. The person whose *z* score was –1.5 would have a *T* score of 35:

First multiply by 10: –1.5 × 10 = –15
Then add 50: –15 + 50 = 35

The scoring of the College Entrance Examination Board test is based on a similar procedure. The mean of the scores is set at 500, and a standard deviation of 100 is used.

Before we leave this section on types of scores, we should mention one other widely used method. **Stanine scores** (the name comes from "standard nine") are standard scores. There are only nine possible scores on the stanine scale, the whole numbers 1 through 9. The mean is 5, and the standard deviation is 2. Each unit from 2 to 8 is equal to half a standard deviation. Stanine scores also provide a method of considering a student's rank, since each of the nine scores includes a specific range of percentile scores in the normal distribution. For example, a stanine score of 1 is assigned to the bottom 4 percent of scores in a distribution. A stanine of 2 is assigned to the next 7 percent. Of course, some raw scores in this 7 percent range are better than others, but they all get a stanine score of 2.

Each stanine score represents a wide range of raw scores. This has the advantage of encouraging teachers and parents to view a student's score in more general terms instead of making fine distinctions based on a few points. Figure 14.4 compares the four types of standard scores we have considered, showing how each would fall on a normal distribution curve.

FIGURE 14.4   **Four Types of Standard Scores on a Normal Distribution Curve**   Using this figure, you can translate one type of standard score into another.

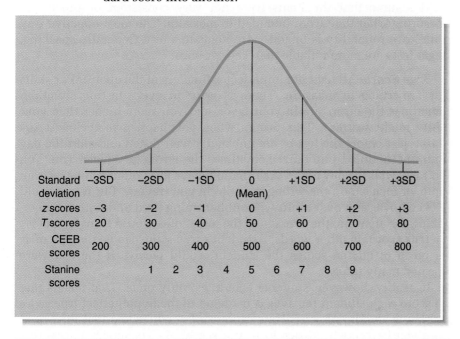

Standard deviation	–3SD	–2SD	–1SD	0 (Mean)	+1SD	+2SD	+3SD
z scores	–3	–2	–1	0	+1	+2	+3
T scores	20	30	40	50	60	70	80
CEEB scores	200	300	400	500	600	700	800
Stanine scores		1 2	3 4	5 6	7 8	9	

Stanine Scores Whole-number scores from 1 to 9, each representing a wide range of raw scores.

Interpreting Test Scores

One of the most common problems with the use of tests is misinterpretation of scores. Often this takes the form of believing that the numbers are precise measurements of a student's ability. No test provides a perfect picture of a person's abilities; a test is only one small sample of behavior. Two factors are important in developing good tests: reliability and validity. Both must be considered when we interpret test scores.

Reliability. If you took a standardized test on Monday, then took the same test again one week later and received about the same score each time, you would have reason to believe the test was reliable. If 100 people took the test one day and then repeated it again the following week and the ranking of the individual scores was about the same for both tests, you would be even more certain the test was reliable. (Of course, this assumes that no one looks up answers or studies before the second test.) A reliable test gives a consistent and stable "reading" of a person's ability from one occasion to the next, assuming the person's ability remains the same. A reliable thermometer works in a similar manner, giving you a reading of 100°C each time you measure the temperature of boiling water. Measuring a test's **reliability** in this way, by giving the test on two different occasions, indicates *stability* or *test-retest reliability*. If a group of people takes two equivalent versions of a test and the scores on both tests are comparable, this indicates *alternate-form reliability.*

Reliability can also refer to the internal consistency or the precision of a test. This type of reliability, known as *split-half reliability,* is calculated by comparing performance on half of the test questions with performance on the other half. If, for example, someone did quite well on all the odd-numbered items and not at all well on the even-numbered items, we could assume that the items were not very consistent or precise in measuring what they were intended to measure. The most effective way to improve reliability is to add more items to a test. Generally speaking, longer tests are more reliable than shorter ones.

True Score. All tests are imperfect estimators of the qualities or skills they are trying to measure. There is error in every testing situation. Sometimes the errors are in your favor, and you score higher than your ability might warrant. This occurs when you happen to review a key section just before the test or are unusually well rested and alert the day of an unscheduled pop quiz. Sometimes the errors go against you. You don't feel well the day of the examination, have just gotten bad news from home, or focused on the wrong material in your review. But if you could be tested over and over again without becoming tired and without memorizing the answers, the average of the test scores would bring you close to a **true score.** In other words, a student's true score can be thought of as the mean of all the scores the student would receive if the test were repeated many times.

In reality, however, students take a test only once. That means that the score each student receives is made up of the hypothetical true score plus some amount of error. How can error be reduced so that the actual score can be brought closer to a true score? As you might guess, this

Reliability Consistency of test results.

True Score Hypothetical average of all of an individual's scores if repeated testing under ideal conditions were possible.

returns us to the question of reliability. The more reliable the test, the less error in the score actually obtained. On standardized tests, test developers take this into consideration and make estimations of how much the students' scores would probably vary if they were tested repeatedly. This estimation is called the **standard error of measurement.** It represents the standard deviation of the distribution of scores from our hypothetical repeated testings. Thus, a reliable test can also be defined as a test with a small *standard error of measurement.* In their interpretation of tests, teachers must also take the margin for error into consideration.

Confidence Interval. Teachers should never base an opinion of a student's ability or achievement on the exact score the student obtains. Many test companies now report scores using a **confidence interval** or "standard error band" that encloses the student's actual score. This makes use of the standard error of measurement and allows a teacher to consider the range of scores within which a student's true score might be.

Let us assume, for example, that two students in your class take a standardized achievement test in Spanish. The standard error of measurement for this test is 5. One student receives a score of 79; the other, a score of 85. At first glance, these scores seem quite different. But when you consider the standard error bands around the scores instead of the scores alone, you see that the bands overlap. The first student's true score might be anywhere between 74 and 84 (that is, the actual score of 79 plus and minus the standard error of 5). The second student's true score might be anywhere between 80 and 90. If these two students took the test again, they might even switch rankings. It is crucial to keep in mind the idea of standard error bands when selecting students for special programs. No child should be rejected simply because his or her obtained score misses the cutoff by one or two points. The student's true score might well be above the cutoff point.

Validity. If a test is sufficiently reliable, the next question is whether it is *valid*. A test has **validity** if it measures what it is supposed to measure or predicts what it is supposed to predict. To be a valid test of Spanish grammar and vocabulary, the questions must measure just those things and not reading speed or lucky guessing. Tests of mathematics achievement ought to measure what students have learned in mathematics and not level of anxiety about math. A test is judged to be valid in relation to a specific purpose.

There are several ways to determine whether a test is valid for a specific purpose (Gronlund, 1988). If the purpose of a test is to measure the skills covered in a particular course or unit, the inclusion of questions on all the important topics and on no extraneous topics would provide *content-related evidence* of validity. Have you ever taken a test that dealt only with a few ideas from one lecture or a few pages of the textbook? That test certainly would *not* have content-related evidence of validity.

Some tests are designed to predict outcomes. The SATs, for example, are intended to predict performance in college. If SAT scores correlate with academic performance in college as measured by, say, grade-point average in the first year, then we have *criterion-related evidence* of valid-

Standard Error of Measurement Hypothetical estimate of variation in scores if testing were repeated.

Confidence Interval Range of scores within which an individual's particular score is likely to fall.

Validity Degree to which a test measures what it is intended to measure.

ity for the SAT. In other words, the test scores are fairly accurate predictors of how well the student would do in college.

Most standardized tests are designed to measure some psychological characteristic or "construct" such as reasoning ability, reading comprehension, achievement motivation, intelligence, creativity, and so on. It is a bit more difficult to gather *construct-related evidence* of validity, yet this is a very important requirement. Construct-related evidence of validity is gathered over many years. It is seen in a pattern of scores. For example, older children can answer more questions on intelligence tests than younger children. This fits with our construct of intelligence. If the average 5-year-old answered as many questions correctly on a test as the average 13-year-old, we would doubt that the test really measured intelligence. Construct-related evidence for validity can also be demonstrated when the results of a test correlate with the results of other well-established and valid measures of the same construct.

Guidelines

Increasing Test Reliability and Validity

Make sure the test actually covers the content of the unit of study.

Examples

1. Compare test questions to course objectives. A behavior-content matrix might be useful here.
2. Use local achievement tests and local norms when possible.
3. Check to see if the test is long enough to cover all important topics.
4. Are there any difficulties your students experience with the test, such as not enough time, level of reading, and so on? If so, discuss these problems with appropriate school personnel.

Make sure students know how to use all the test materials.

Examples

1. Several days before the testing, do a few practice questions with a similar format.
2. Demonstrate the use of the answer sheets, especially computer-scored answer sheets.
3. Check with new students, shy students, slower students, and students who have difficulty reading to make sure they understand the questions.
4. Make sure students know if and when guessing is appropriate.

Follow instructions for administering the test exactly.

Examples

1. Practice giving the test before you actually use it.
2. Follow the time limits exactly.

Make students as comfortable as possible during testing.

Examples

1. Do not create anxiety by making the test seem like the most important event of the year.
2. Help the class relax before beginning the test, perhaps by telling a joke or having everyone take a few deep breaths. Don't be tense yourself!
3. Make sure the room is quiet.
4. Discourage cheating by monitoring the room. Don't become absorbed in your own paper-work.

Remember that no test scores are perfect.

Examples

1. Interpret scores using bands instead of a single score.
2. Ignore small differences between scores.

A number of factors may interfere with the validity of tests given in classroom situations. One problem has already been mentioned—a poorly planned test with little or no relation to the important topics. Standardized achievement tests must also be chosen so that the items on the test actually measure content covered in the classes. This match is absent more often than we might assume. One group of teachers in St. Louis found that fewer than 10 percent of the items in their curriculum overlapped with both the textbooks and the standardized tests they were using (Fiske, 1988). Also, students must have the necessary skills to take the test. If students score low on a science test not because they lack knowledge about science but because they have difficulty reading the questions, do not understand the directions, or do not have enough time to finish, the test is not a valid measure of science achievement.

A test must be reliable in order to be valid. If, for example, an intelligence test yields different results each time it is given to the same child over a few months, then by definition it is not reliable. And it couldn't be a valid measure of intelligence because intelligence is assumed to be fairly stable, at least over a short period of time. However, reliability will not guarantee validity. If that intelligence test gave the same score every time for a particular child but didn't predict school achievement, speed of learning, or other characteristics associated with intelligence, then performance on the test would not be a true indicator of intelligence. The test would be reliable but invalid. The Guidelines should help you increase the reliability and validity of the standardized tests you give.

TYPES OF STANDARDIZED TESTS

Several kinds of standardized tests are used in schools today. If you have seen cumulative folders, with testing records for individual students over several years, you know the many ways students are tested in this country. There are three broad categories of standardized tests: achievement, diagnostic, and aptitude (including interest). As a teacher, you will probably encounter achievement and aptitude tests most frequently.

Achievement Tests: What Has the Student Learned?

The most common standardized tests given to students are **achievement tests.** These are meant to measure how much a student has learned in specific content areas such as reading comprehension, language usage, computation, science, social studies, mathematics, and logical reasoning.

Achievement tests can be designed to be administered to a group or individually. Group tests can be used for screening—to identify children who might need further testing or as a basis for grouping students according to achievement levels. Individual achievement tests are generally given to determine a child's academic level more precisely or to help diagnose learning problems.

Norm-referenced achievement tests that are commonly given to groups include the California Achievement Test, the Metropolitan Achievement Test, the Stanford Achievement Test, the Comprehensive Test of Basic

"I hate taking a test without an eraser." (© Martha Campbell.)

Achievement Tests
Standardized tests measuring how much students have learned in a given content area.

Skills, the SRA Achievement Series, and the Iowa Test of Basic Skills. Individually administered norm-referenced tests include Part II of the Woodcock-Johnson Psycho-Educational Battery: Tests of Achievement; the Wide-Range Achievement Test; the Peabody Individual Achievement Test; and the Kaufman Assessment Battery for Children. These tests vary in their reliability and validity.

Using Information from a Norm-Referenced Achievement Test. What kind of specific information do achievement tests results offer teachers? Test publishers usually provide individual profiles for each student, showing scores on each subtest. Figure 14.5 is an example of an individual profile for an eighth grader, Susie Pak, on the California

FIGURE 14.5   An Individual Test Record   Test publishers provide several kinds of report forms for individual students and for entire classes. The form below gives both norm-referenced and criterion-referenced information about an eighth-grade girl.

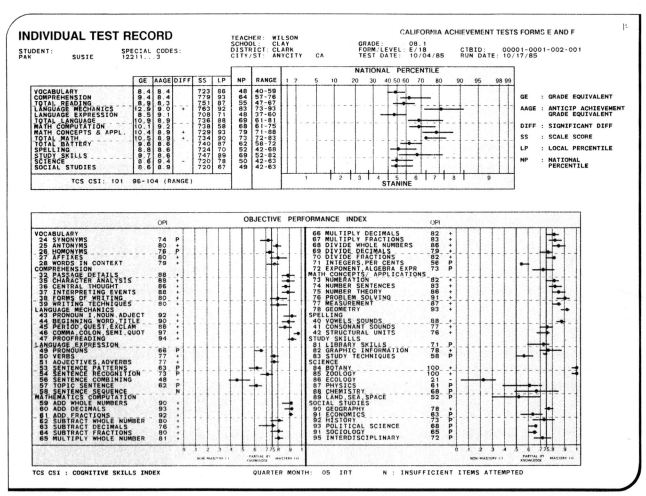

Achievement Test. Note that the Individual Test Record reports the scores in many different ways. At the top of the form, after the identifying information about Susie's teacher, school, district, grade, and so on, is a list of the various tests—Vocabulary, Comprehension, Total Reading (Vocabulary and Comprehension combined), Language Mechanics, and so on. Beside each test are several different ways of reporting her score:

GE: Susie's grade-equivalent score.

AAGE: Anticipated achievement grade-equivalent score, which is the *average* grade-equivalent score on this test for students around the country who are at Susie's grade level.

DIFF: An indication of whether the difference between Susie's actual and anticipated grade-equivalent scores is statistically significant (+ means her actual grade-equivalent score is significantly higher than the average; – means her score is significantly lower than the average).

SS: Susie's standard score.

LP: Susie's local percentile score; this tells us where Susie stands in relation to other students at her grade level in her district.

NP: Susie's national percentile score, telling us where Susie stands in relation to students at her grade level across the country.

RANGE: The range of national percentile scores in which Susie's true score is likely to fall. You may remember from our discussion of *true scores* that this range, or *confidence interval,* is determined by adding and subtracting the standard error of the test from Susie's

Standardized testing is a part of most students' experience. For the test to be a valid measure of the students' knowledge, the students must be familiar with procedures for taking a test—how to use the machine-scored sheets, what to do if they don't know an answer, and so on.

actual score. There is a 95 percent chance that Susie's true score is within this range.

Beside the scores is a graph showing Susie's national percentile and stanine scores, with the standard error bands indicated around the scores. Bands that show any overlap are probably not significantly different. But when there is no overlap between bands for two test scores, we can be reasonably certain that Susie's achievement levels in these two areas are actually different.

Interpreting Achievement Test Scores. Let's look at Susie's scores more carefully. In language mechanics she has a grade-equivalent score of 12.9, which is equal to a standard score of 763. This is at the 92nd percentile for Susie's district and at the 83rd percentile nationally. Her true national percentile score is probably in the range from 73 to 93 (that is, plus and minus 1 standard error of measurement from the actual score of 83). By looking at the graph, we can see that Susie's language mechanics score is equal to a stanine of 7. We can also see that her score bands on vocabulary and comprehension overlap a bit, so her achievement in these areas is probably similar, even though there seems to be a difference when you look at the NP scores alone. Comparing language mechanics and expression, on the other hand, we see that the bands do not overlap. Susie probably is stronger in mechanics than in expression.

You may also have noticed that the difference between Susie's actual and anticipated grade-equivalent scores in language mechanics is significant. She scored significantly higher than the average student in her grade on this part of the test. But as discussed earlier, it is best not to interpret grade-equivalent scores literally. Susie is much better than the average 8th grader in language mechanics (in fact, she is as good as or better than 92 percent of students at her grade level locally), but it's very unlikely that she could handle 12th-grade English classes.

The profile in Figure 14.5 tells us a number of things. First, we can see that Susie is apparently strongest in language mechanics and math concepts and applications and weakest in language expression and science. She is significantly below the average for her grade level only in science. By comparing the two columns under LP (local percentiles) and NP (national percentiles), we can see that the eighth graders in Susie's district are achieving below the national level on every test except math computations. This is evident because Susie's performance places her generally in the 70th to 90th percentile range for her district but only in the 50th to 70th percentile range nationally. For example, Susie's performance in vocabulary is well above average for her district (86th percentile) but only average (48th percentile) for eighth graders nationally.

The scores we have just described are all norm-referenced. However, results from standardized tests like the one Susie took can also be interpreted in a criterion-referenced way. The bottom portion of Susie's Individual Test Record in Figure 14.6 breaks down the larger categories of the top section and shows criterion-referenced scores that indicate mastery, partial knowledge, or nonmastery for specific skills like use of synonyms and antonyms, character analysis in reading comprehension, and abilities in geometry and physics. Teachers could use these results to get a relatively good idea of Susie's strengths and weaknesses with these specific skills and thus to determine her progress toward objectives in a given subject.

Diagnostic Tests: What Are the Student's Strengths and Weaknesses?

If teachers want to identify more general learning problems, they may need to refer to results from the various diagnostic tests that have been developed. Most **diagnostic tests** are given to students individually by a highly trained professional. The goal is usually to identify the specific problems a student is having. Achievement tests, both standardized and teacher-made, identify weaknesses in academic content areas like mathematics, computation, or reading; individually administered diagnostic tests identify weaknesses in learning processes. There are diagnostic tests to assess the ability to hear differences among sounds, remember spoken words or sentences, recall a sequence of symbols, separate figures from their background, express relationships, coordinate eye and hand movements, describe objects orally, blend sounds to form words, recognize details in a picture, coordinate movements, and many other abilities needed to receive, process, and express information.

Elementary-school teachers are more likely than secondary teachers to receive information from diagnostic tests. There are few such tests for older students. If you become a high school teacher, your students are more likely to be given aptitude tests.

Aptitude Tests: How Well Will the Student Do in the Future?

Both achievement and aptitude tests measure developed abilities. Achievement tests may measure abilities developed over a short period of time, such as during a week-long unit on map reading, or over a longer period of time, such as a semester. **Aptitude tests** are meant to measure abilities developed over many years and to predict how well a student will do in learning unfamiliar material in the future. The greatest difference between the two types of tests is that they are used for different purposes—achievement tests to measure final performance (and perhaps give grades), and aptitude tests to predict how well people will do in particular programs like college or professional school (Anastasi, 1988).

Scholastic Aptitude. The purpose of a scholastic aptitude test, like the SAT or ACT, is to predict how well a student is likely to do in college. Colleges use such scores to help decide on acceptances and rejections. The SAT may have seemed like an achievement test to you, measuring what you had already learned in high school. Although the test is designed to avoid drawing too heavily on specific high school curricula, the questions are very similar to achievement test questions.

Standardized aptitude tests such as the SAT (and the SCAT and PSAT for younger students) seem to be fairly reliable in predicting future achievement. Since standardized tests are less open to teacher bias, they may be even fairer predictors of future achievement than high school grades are. Indeed, some psychologists believe grade inflation in high

Diagnostic Tests Individually administered tests to identify special learning problems.

Aptitude Tests Tests meant to predict future performance.

schools has made tests like the SAT even more important. Others believe that the SATs are not good predictors of success in college for women or members of cultural or ethnic minority groups. The controversy continues.

IQ and Scholastic Aptitude. In chapter 4 we discussed one of the most influential aptitude tests of all, the IQ test. The IQ test as we know it could well be called a test of scholastic aptitude. IQ scores are distributed based on the results of the major individual tests. Now that you understand the concept of standard deviation, you will be able to appreciate several statistical characteristics of the tests. For example, the IQ score is really a standard score with a mean of 100 and a standard deviation of 15 (for the Wechsler Scales; the Cognitive Abilities section of the Woodcock-Johnson Psycho-Educational Battery; and the Global Scale of the Kaufman Assessment Battery for Children) or 16 (for the Stanford-Binet and the McCarthy Scales for Children). Thus, about 68 percent of the general population would score between +1 and −1 standard deviations from the mean, or between about 85 and 115. Only about 2.5 percent of the general population would have a score higher than 2 standard deviations above the mean—that is, above 130 on the Wechsler Scales.

A difference of a few points between two students' IQ scores should not be viewed as important. Scores between 90 and 109 are within the average range. In fact, scores between 80 and 119 are considered to range from low average to high average. To see the problems that may arise, consider the following conversation:

> **Parent:** We came to speak with you today because we are shocked at our son's IQ score. We can't believe he has only a 99 IQ when his sister scored much higher on the same test. We know they are about the same. In fact, Sam has better marks than Lauren did in the fifth grade.
>
> **Teacher:** What was Lauren's score?
>
> **Parent:** Well, she did much better. She scored a 103!

Clearly, brother and sister have both scored within the average range. The standard error of measurement on the WISC-R (Weschler Intelligence Scale for Children) varies slightly from one age to the next, but the average standard error is 3.19. So the bands around Sam's and Lauren's IQ scores—about 96 to 102 and 100 to 106—are overlapping. Either child could have scored 100, 101, or 102. The scores are so close that on a second testing Sam might score slightly higher than Lauren.

Vocational Aptitude and Interest. In schools, the guidance counselor is generally the person most concerned with students' career decisions. It is the responsibility of people in the guidance office to know what aptitude test scores really mean and how to help each student make an appropriate decision. **Vocational aptitude tests** and **vocational interest tests** may provide useful information for educational planning. But as with any tests, interpretation must be cautious.

If you teach in a junior high or high school, your school may administer vocational aptitude tests to the students. One test designed to measure aptitudes relevant to career decisions is the **Differential Aptitude**

Vocational Aptitude Tests
Tests designed to measure abilities needed in particular occupations.

Vocational Interest Tests
Tests indicating possible areas of career interest.

Differential Aptitude Test (DAT) A vocational aptitude test that measures such abilities as mechanical reasoning, clerical speed and accuracy, and number ability.

In many subjects, the most reasonable test is to demonstrate the ability to produce a finished product.

Test (DAT). Students in grades 8 through 12 may take the test. Questions cover seven areas: (1) verbal reasoning, (2) numerical ability, (3) abstract reasoning, (4) clerical speed and accuracy, (5) mechanical reasoning, (6) space relations, and (7) spelling and language. The test results on the DAT are converted into percentiles, and a percentile band is reported for each subtest. After the tests have been scored, the guidance counselors in a school should be able to help students relate their DAT profile scores to career-planning decisions.

In many high schools vocational interest tests are also given. Three examples are the Kuder Preference Record, the Strong-Campbell Interest Blank, and Part III of the Woodcock-Johnson Psycho-Educational Battery: Tests of Interest Level. In these tests students may be asked to indicate which of several activities (such as collecting books, collecting shells, or collecting postcards) they would like most and which they would like least. The pattern of the students' answers is then compared to the answer patterns of adults working in different occupations. Remember that the results on such a test indicate interests, not aptitude or talent and that no career option should be permanently closed to an adolescent on the basis of an occupational interest test.

ISSUES IN STANDARDIZED TESTING

Today many important decisions about students, teachers, and schools are based in part on the results of standardized tests. Test scores may affect high school graduation, admission to special programs, placement in special education classes, teacher certification, and school funding. Because the decisions affected by test scores are so critical, many educators call this process **high-stakes testing.** Some groups are working to increase the role of testing—by establishing a national examination, for

High-Stakes Testing
Standardized tests whose results have powerful influences when used by school administrators, other officials, or employers to make decisions.

example—while others are working to cut back the use of standardized tests in schools (O'Neil, 1991).

In the next few pages we will consider two basic questions: What role should testing play in making decisions about people? Do some students have an unfair advantage in taking tests?

The Uses of Testing in American Society

Tests are not simply procedures used in research. Many decisions about individuals are made every day based on the results of tests. Should Liz be issued a driver's license? How many and which students from the eighth grade would benefit from an accelerated program in science? Who belongs in a special class for the mentally retarded? Who will be admitted to college or professional school? In answering these questions, it is important to distinguish between the quality of the test itself and how the test is used. Even the best instruments can be and have been misused. In earlier years, for example, many students were inappropriately classified as mentally retarded on the basis of valid and reliable individual intelligence tests. The problem was not with the tests but instead with the fact that the test score was the only information used to classify students. Much more information must be considered before a student can be identified as retarded.

Behind all the statistics and terminology are issues related to values and ethics. Who will be tested? What are the consequences of choosing one test over another for a particular purpose with a given group? What is the effect on students of being tested? How will the test scores of minority-group students be interpreted? What do we really mean by intelligence, competence, and scholastic aptitude; and do our views agree with those implied by the tests we use to measure these constructs? How will test results be integrated with other information about the individual to make judgments? Answering these questions requires choices based on values as well as accurate information about what tests can and *cannot* tell us. Let's look at three uses of testing: testing readiness, testing minimum competency, and testing teachers.

Readiness Testing. In 1988 Georgia became the first state to require that children pass a test before moving from kindergarten to first grade (Fiske, 1988; Linn, 1986). The test quickly became a symbol of the misuse of tests. Public outcry led to modifications of the policy and spurred many educators to reform the **readiness testing** process. In fact, the uproar over this group-administered, machine-scored, norm-referenced test for kindergarten children "probably did more to advance readiness assessment reform in this country than all other causes combined" (Engel, 1991, p. 41).

Critics of readiness tests (Engel, 1991; Meisels, 1989; Shepard & Smith, 1989) believe:

1. Group-administered paper-and-pencil tests are inappropriate for preschool children and thus should not be the basis for decisions about school entry.
2. Using readiness tests narrows the preschool curriculum, making it more academic and less developmentally appropriate.

Readiness Testing Testing procedures meant to determine if an individual is ready to proceed to the next level of education or training.

School "readiness" is a controversial construct. Individualized assessment is one response to criticisms of group-administered, machine-scored, norm-referenced tests for kindergarten placement.

3. The evidence shows that delaying entry into first grade or retaining students in kindergarten is not effective. Students who are retained do no better than similar students who are not held back.

In spite of these criticisms, today almost every state uses testing at the state or district level to determine if a child is "ready" for first grade or to place a child in a special "developmental kindergarten" (Kirst, 1991a). Several states as well as a few test publishers are trying to develop appropriate ways to determine readiness. Engel (1991) suggests that such procedures would be ongoing assessments about many different aspects of readiness—cognitive, social/emotional, physical, and so on. These assessments would be indirect; that is, they would be completed by adults rather than requiring the children to answer questions directly on paper. The observations should provide useful information for teaching and should be conducted in a comfortable natural setting, often as part of the preschool program itself.

Minimum Competency Testing. *A Nation at Risk* (National Commission on Excellence in Education, 1983) reported that about 23 million American adults were functionally illiterate. About 13 percent of the teenagers in the United States (and up to 40 percent of minority youth) were also functionally illiterate. And in many studies comparing U.S. students with students from other industrialized nations, the American students have placed low in academic achievement (Educational Testing Service, 1992).

In response to this problem, many people believe that **minimum competency testing** should be used to determine high school graduation. Some people even suggest that a national examination would be helpful. "Escalating concern over low achievement, coupled with a growing belief that each pupil needs to be able to aim for a national standard of performance, has some policymakers, business leaders, and educators favoring a national exam (or set of exams) for all students" (O'Neil, 1991). Seventy-

Minimum Competency Testing Standardized tests meant to determine if students meet minimum requirements to graduate or to proceed in school.

seven percent of the people surveyed in the 1991 Gallup Poll of the public's attitude toward the public schools said they favored requiring the public schools in their community to use standardized national tests to measure the academic achievement of students (Elam, Rose, & Gallup, 1991). This idea is still under discussion and the debate rages.

Will requiring minimum competency tests or a national exam improve the situation? As usual, experts disagree. Barbara Lerner (1981) believes the close monitoring and clear standards required by minimum competency testing would encourage teachers and students to spend more time teaching and learning the basics. Since academic engaged time is one of the few factors that seems clearly associated with learning, this increased attention should improve achievement. Besides, "no other approach is demonstrably superior to it" (Lerner, 1981, p. 1062).

However, many psychologists and teachers believe such tests are undesirable. Their argument is that teachers would have less and less freedom in deciding what and how to teach. The tests would control the curriculum. In working to get everyone to the minimum level, teachers would have to ignore the faster students. A few slower students might monopolize the teacher's attention. New ways of organizing classes would be necessary to prevent holding everyone back (Kirst, 1991a & b). And finally, tests might discriminate against minority students.

This last factor had a great impact when Florida instituted a **functional literacy** test for high school graduation. Although the citizens of the state were in favor of the testing, a federal judge ordered the process stopped on the grounds that the tests perpetuated the effects of past discrimination against minority students. Evidence presented during the trial *Debra P.* v. *Turlington* indicated that 20 percent of African-American seniors and only 2 percent of white seniors were denied diplomas on the basis of the tests. Many of the African-American students had spent some of their early school careers in segregated schools. The judge felt that denying them diplomas punished these students for having gone to inferior schools and thus violated their right to equal protection under the law (Haney, 1981).

Testing Teachers. Almost 90 percent of the people surveyed in the 1985 Gallup Poll believed that teachers should have to pass a basic competency test before being hired. When teachers answered the same question a year earlier, 63 percent agreed that testing was a good idea (Gallup, 1984). By 1985, 30 states, mostly in the southern and western sections of the United States, reported that they had some kind of teacher-assessment program, and a dozen more states indicated that serious discussions were under way.

Edward Haertel (1991) notes that, like other standardized tests, "the teacher competency tests now in common use have been strenuously and justifiably criticized for their content, their format, and their impacts, as well as the virtual absence of criterion-related validity evidence supporting their use" (p. 3). In other words, high test scores do not predict good teaching.

New models of teacher assessment are in the planning and development stages. For example, the revision of the National Teacher Examina-

Functional Literacy A level of reading, writing, and communication ability that allows the individual to function independently in society.

tion (NTE) is nearing completion as I am writing this page and may be available by the time you read these words. The revised NTE is a battery of tests given in three stages. Stage I tests basic skills early in the prospective teacher's education program. Stage II, given at the end of the undergraduate program, tests subject matter knowledge and knowledge of teaching. Stage III is a performance-based assessment conducted mostly through classroom observations.

Like the alternatives to standardized tests we will examine shortly, the NTE and other new teacher tests will make greater use of authentic performances and products. Teacher candidates might complete a lesson-planning exercise and then be interviewed about what they planned and why. They might be asked to submit a portfolio containing an overview of a unit, details of two consecutive lessons, copies of student handouts, lists of the resources selected for background, a videotape of teaching samples showing large- and small-group lessons, and other examples of the teacher's actual work.

These procedures are not yet refined, but many look promising. Of course, every innovation has its shortcomings. Can these portfolios and performances be evaluated objectively? Will we see an explosion of businesses that specialize in helping teachers build a beautiful portfolio? Will the wealthier teachers and teacher candidates have the best portfolios and videos (Kirst, 1991b)?

Advantages in Taking Tests—Fair and Unfair

In this section we will consider three basic issues: Are standardized tests biased against minority students? Can students gain an advantage on admissions tests through coaching? Can they be taught test-taking skills?

Bias in Testing. As you saw in chapter 5, the average performance of students of lower socioeconomic status and from minority groups is below that of middle-class white students on most standardized measures of mental abilities, although the discrepancies are decreasing for some minority groups (Burton & Jones, 1982). Are tests such as the individual measures of intelligence or college admissions tests biased against minorities? This is a complex question.

Research on test bias shows that most standardized tests predict school achievement equally well for all groups of students. Items that might appear on the surface to be biased against minorities are not necessarily more difficult for minorities to answer correctly (Sattler, 1988). Even though standardized aptitude and achievement tests are not biased against minorities in predicting school performance, however, many people believe there are factors related to the specific content and procedures of such tests that put minority students at a disadvantage. Here are a few factors they suggest:

1. The language of the test and the tester is often different from the languages of the students.
2. The questions asked tend to center on experiences and facts more familiar to the dominant culture than to minority-group students.

Guidelines

Taking a Test

Use the night before the test effectively.

Examples

1. Study the night before the exam, ending with a final look at a summary of the key points, concepts, and relationships.
2. Get a good night's sleep. If you know you generally have trouble sleeping the night before an exam, try getting extra sleep on several previous nights.

Set the situation so you can concentrate on the test.

Examples

1. Give yourself plenty of time to eat and get to the exam room.
2. Don't sit near a friend. It may make concentration difficult. If your friend leaves early, you may be tempted to do so too.

Make sure you know what the test is asking.

Examples

1. Read the directions carefully. If you are unsure, ask the instructor or proctor for clarification.
2. Read each question carefully to spot tricky words, such as *not, except, all of the following but one.*

3. On an essay test, read every question first, so you know the size of the job ahead of you and can make informed decisions about how much time to spend on each question.
4. On a multiple-choice test, read every alternative, even if an early one seems right.

Use time effectively.

Examples

1. Begin working right away and move as rapidly as possible while your energy is high.
2. Do the easy questions first.
3. Don't get stuck on one question. If you are stumped, mark the question so you can return to it easily later, and go on to questions you can answer more quickly.
4. If you are unsure about a question, answer it but mark it so you can go back if there is time.
5. On a multiple-choice test, if you know you will not have time to finish, fill in all the remaining questions with the same letter if there is no penalty for guessing.
6. If you are running out of time on an essay test, do not leave any questions blank. Briefly outline a

---

3. Answers that support middle-class values often are rewarded with more points.
4. On individually administered intelligence tests, being very verbal and talking a lot is rewarded, which favors students who feel comfortable in the situation.
5. Minority-group children may not be oriented toward individual achievement and may not appreciate the value of doing well on tests.

Concern about cultural bias in testing has led some psychologists to try to develop **culture-fair** or **culture-free tests.** These efforts have not been very successful. On many of the so-called culture-fair tests, the performance of students from lower socioeconomic backgrounds and minority groups has been the same as or worse than their performance on the standard Wechsler and Binet Intelligence scales (Sattler, 1988).

Coaching and Test-Taking Skills. Courses to prepare students for college entrance exams are becoming more popular. As you probably know from experience, both commercial and public school coaching programs are available. It is difficult to evaluate the effects of these courses. In general, research has indicated that short high school training programs yield average gains of 10 points in SAT verbal scores and 15 points in SAT math scores, whereas longer commercial programs show gains of anywhere from 50 to as much as 200 points for some people

Culture-Fair/Culture-Free Tests Tests without cultural bias.

few key points to show the instructor you "knew" the answer but needed more time.

Know when to guess on multiple-choice or true-false tests.

Examples

1. Always guess when only right answers are scored.
2. Always guess when you can eliminate some of the alternatives.
3. Don't guess if there is a penalty for guessing, unless you can confidently eliminate at least one alternative.
4. Are correct answers always longer? shorter? in the middle? more likely to be one letter? more often true than false?
5. Does the grammar give the right answer away or eliminate any alternatives?

Check your work.

Examples

1. Even if you can't stand to look at the test another minute, reread each question to make sure you answered the way you intended.
2. If you are using a machine-scored answer sheet, check occasionally to be sure the number of the question you are answering corresponds to the number of the answer on the sheet.

On essay tests, answer as directly as possible.

Examples

1. Avoid flowery introductions. Answer the question in the first sentence and then elaborate.
2. Don't save your best ideas till last. Give them early in the answer.
3. Unless the instructor requires complete sentences, consider listing points, arguments, and so on by number in your answer. It will help you organize your thoughts and concentrate on the important aspects of the answer.

Learn from the testing experience.

Examples

1. Pay attention when the teacher reviews the answers. You can learn from your mistakes, and the same question may reappear in a later test.
2. Notice if you are having trouble with a particular kind of item; adjust your study approach next time to handle this type of item better.

(Owen, 1985). Kulik, Kulik, and Bangert (1984) analyzed the results of 40 different studies on aptitude and achievement test training and found that there were more substantial gains when students practiced on a parallel form of a test for brief periods. The design of the coaching program, therefore, may be the critical factor.

Two other types of training can make a difference in test scores. One is simple familiarity with the procedures of standardized tests. Students who have a lot of experience with standardized tests do better than those who do not. Some of this advantage may be due to greater self-confidence, less tendency to panic, familiarity with different kinds of questions (for example, analogies like house : garage : : _____ : car), and practice with the various answer sheets (Anastasi, 1988). Even brief orientations about how to take tests can help students who lack familiarity and confidence.

A second type of training that appears to be very promising is instruction in general cognitive skills such as solving problems, carefully analyzing questions, considering all alternatives, noticing details and deciding which are relevant, avoiding impulsive answers, and checking work. These are the kinds of metacognitive and study skills we have discussed before. Training in these skills is likely to generalize to many tasks (Anastasi, 1988). The Guidelines give some ideas about how to be a more effective test-taker.

To Test or Not to Test?

Student teachers are often astounded by the amount of time they must spend every spring preparing their students for "test week." Schools have been known to abandon innovations such as "whole language" and hands-on science teaching and to adopt drill-and-practive test-based programs in their place, just because test scores fell when these innovations were introduced. Yet there is talk of more, not less, testing and the development of a National Achievement Test. Should standardized testing be continued?

Point: Testing should be stopped.

Critics of standardized testing state that these tests measure disjointed facts and skills that have no use or meaning in the real world. Often test questions do not match the curriculum of the schools, so the tests can't measure how well students have learned the curriculum. Even so, there is great pressure on teachers to produce high test scores. Teachers' jobs, principals' raises, and even

the value of real estate in the school district are affected by the schools' test scores. So teachers find themselves "teaching to the test." Because tests are best at measuring lower-level objectives, facts, and basic skills, these facts and skills become the content of the curriculum. Too often, the results of tests are used to label students as low achievers, and self-fulfilling prophecies are set into motion. Mary Lee Smith (1991) found the following effects of standardized testing on teachers:

- When test scores are made public, teachers often feel embarrassed, angry, or ashamed. They sometimes change students' answers, excuse poor students from taking the test, drill students on the answers, or give unallowed "help" because the pressure for high scores is so great.
- Teachers feel alienated from the test process, because when test scores are published, no one takes into account the fact that some of

NEW DIRECTIONS IN STANDARDIZED TESTING

Standardized tests continue to be controversial, as you can see in the **Point/Counterpoint** section above. In response to dissatisfaction with traditional forms of assessment, new approaches have emerged to deal with some of the most common testing problems. But each of these approaches has its own problems. We will examine proposed procedures for measuring learning potential, for making assessment more "authentic," and for improving the SAT.

Assessing Learning Potential

Learning Potential Assessment Device
Innovative method for testing the student's ability to benefit from teaching, consistent with Vygotsky's theory of cognitive development.

One criticism of traditional forms of intelligence testing is that such tests are merely samples of performance at one particular point in time. These tests, critics say, fail to capture the child's potential for future learning. Reuven Feuerstein's **Learning Potential Assessment Device** attempts to look at the process of learning rather than its product (Feuerstein, 1979). The child is presented with various reasoning and memory tasks. When necessary, the examiner teaches the child how to solve the problems and then assesses how well the child has benefited from instruction. This approach reflects Vygotsky's ideas about the zone of proximal develop-their students live in poverty or are just learning English.

- Teachers are concerned that the tests take away valuable teaching time and make their students too anxious. Preparing for, giving, and recovering from the tests took an average of 100 hours of instructional time in the schools Smith studied.

Counterpoint: Tests can provide valuable information.

Defenders of standardized tests note that it is the responsibility of the school to select an appropriate test. Standardized tests are designed to sample what is *typically* taught, so the fit with any particular school's curriculum will not be perfect. Thus, a standardized test is only one source of information. To redesign the curriculum so that it matches the test or to make placement decisions based only on a test score is to overuse and misuse the test. No test is reliable and valid enough to serve as the only basis for making important decisions. But tests do provide useful information.

To make good use of test results, Blaine Worthen and Vicki Spandel (1991) suggest the following:

Don't test unless there is an important decision to make. Then choose a good test that will give useful information about the decision.

Never use the test as the only basis for the decision. Supplement with other information, including the teacher's judgment.

Assume every test score is imperfect. Take the score as an estimate.

Know what the test actually measures. Just because it is called a test of reading comprehension does not mean that a test measures everything about reading comprehension.

Know your students. A test of math achievement that uses word problems can be a test of reading comprehension for students whose English is limited.

Don't use test results to compare students or foster competition. Use the results to benefit students.

---

ment—the range of functioning where a child cannot solve problems independently but can benefit from guidance. Results of the test have been difficult to interpret. Nevertheless, it offers a thought-provoking and radically different approach to intelligence testing.

Authentic Assessment

One of the major criticisms of standardized tests is that they test low-level skills that have no equivalent in the real world. Students are asked to solve problems or answer questions they will never encounter again; and they are expected to do so alone, without relying on any tools or resources, while working under extreme time limits. Critics say that real life just isn't like this. Important problems take time to solve, and often require using resources, consulting other people, and integrating basic skills with creativity and high-level thinking. (Kirst, 1991a; Wolf, Bixby, Glenn, & Gardner, 1991).

How can standardized tests assess complex, important, real-life outcomes? This has been called the problem of **authentic assessment.** Some states are developing procedures to conduct authentic assessments. For example, Kentucky recently passed the Educational Reform Act of 1990. The act identifies six objectives for students, including

Authentic Assessment
Measurement of important abilities using procedures that simulate the application of these abilities to real-life problems.

533

such goals as applying knowledge from mathematics, the sciences, the arts, the humanities, and the social sciences to problems the students will encounter throughout their lives as they become self-sufficient individuals and responsible members of families, work groups, and communities.

According to Jack Foster (1991), the secretary of the Education and Humanities Cabinet for the governor of Kentucky, "The task now is to create prototypes of complex tasks that students can perform to demonstrate all these objectives in an interactive context. The tasks must have multiple objectives and require higher levels of thinking than is demanded by most paper-and-pencil tests" (p. 35). The state assessments will be tied to ongoing school and class assessments that guide instruction. The process will be criterion-referenced rather than norm-referenced, because students' performances will be compared to expected "benchmark" levels of attainment at grades 3, 5, 8, and 12.

Many of the suggestions for improving standardized tests will require new forms of testing and more thoughtful, time-consuming scoring. Standardized tests of the future may be more like the writing sample you may have submitted for college entrance and less like the multiple-choice college entrance tests you also had to take. Newer tests will feature more **constructed-response formats.** This means that students will *create* responses (essays, problem solutions, graphs, diagrams, etc.) rather than simply *selecting* the (one and only) correct answer. This will allow tests to measure higher-level and divergent thinking.

Changes in the SAT

Even the SAT is changing. The new SAT will have tests of verbal reasoning, mathematical reasoning, and subject matter. The verbal test will emphasize reading. The reading passages will be more engaging and more similar to the material that high school students have read in their classes. Each passage will be longer, and students will have to answer more questions about the passage. The verbal test will still have sentence completion and analogy questions, but the antonyms questions will be dropped. On the mathematical portion, students will generate their own answers (constructed-response format) for 20 percent of the questions. Hand-held calculators will be allowed but not required. There will be a writing test that is two-thirds multiple-choice questions and one-third essay. The new SAT is projected to be ready by spring 1994, and a new PSAT should be out by fall 1993, so students who take the PSAT in fall 1993 will encounter the same format when they take their SATs later (Smith, 1991).

With a move to more authentic assessment, standardized tests and classroom tests can be better coordinated. This brings us to classroom testing and grading—the topics of the next chapter.

Constructed-Response Format Assessment procedures that require the student to create an answer instead of selecting an answer from a set of choices.

SUMMARY

MEASUREMENT AND EVALUATION

Evaluation of student learning can be based on measurements from norm-referenced tests, in which a student's performance is compared to the average performance of others, or from criterion-referenced tests, in which scores are compared to a preestablished standard.

WHAT DO TEST SCORES MEAN?

Standardized tests are most often norm-referenced. They have been pilot tested, revised, and then administered in final form to a norming sample, which becomes the comparison group for scoring. Important aspects of measurement in standardized testing are the frequency distribution, the central tendency, and the standard deviation. The mean (arithmetical average), median (middle score), and mode (most common score) are all measures of central tendency. The standard deviation reveals how scores spread out around the mean.

A normal distribution is a frequency distribution represented as a bell-shaped curve. Many scores cluster in the middle; the farther from the midpoint, the fewer the scores. Half the scores are above the mean; half are below.

There are several basic types of standardized test scores: percentile rankings, which indicate the percentage of others who scored at or below an individual's score; grade-equivalent scores, which indicate how closely a student's performance matches average scores for a given grade; and standard scores, which are based on the standard deviation. T and z scores are both common standard scores. A stanine score is a standard score that incorporates elements of percentile rankings.

Care must be taken in the interpretation of test results. Each test is only a sample of a student's performance on a given day. The score is only an estimate of a student's hypothetical true score. Some tests are more reliable than others—that is, they yield more stable and consistent estimates. The standard error of measurement takes into account the possibility for error and is one index of test reliability.

Some tests are more valid than others, in the sense that they measure what they are supposed to measure and the meaning of the scores is clear. Evidence of validity can be related to content, criterion, or construct. Tests must be reliable to be valid, but reliability does not guarantee validity.

TYPES OF STANDARDIZED TESTS

Three kinds of standardized tests are used frequently in schools: achievement, diagnostic, and aptitude. Profiles from norm-referenced achievement tests can also be used in a criterion-referenced way to help a teacher assess a student's strengths and weaknesses in a particular subject.

ISSUES IN STANDARDIZED TESTING

Controversy over standardized testing has focused on the role and interpretation of tests, the validity of readiness tests as a guide for decisions about young children, the fairness and usefulness of minimum competency testing, the testing of teachers, and the degree of bias against minority-group students inherent in tests.

The way test results are used is a major issue for teachers. Teachers should use results to improve instruction, not to stereotype students or to justify lowered expectations. Performance on standardized tests can be improved if students are given experience with this type of testing and training in study skills and problem solving.

NEW DIRECTIONS IN STANDARDIZED TESTING

Today there is great interest in authentic assessment—designing procedures that assess students' abilities to solve important real-life problems, think creatively, and act responsibly. Standardized tests of the future will be more varied and will use more constructed-response formats, requiring students to generate rather than select answers.

KEY TERMS

achievement tests, p. 519

aptitude tests, p. 523

authentic assessment, p. 533

bimodal distribution, p. 510

central tendency, p. 510

confidence interval, p. 517

constructed-response format,
  p. 534

criterion-referenced testing,
  p. 507

culture-fair/culture-free tests,
  p. 530

diagnostic tests, p. 523

differential aptitude test (DAT),
  p. 524

evaluation, p. 506

frequency distribution, p. 509

functional literacy, p. 528

grade-equivalent score, p. 513

high-stakes testing, p. 525

histogram, p. 509

Learning Potential Assessment
  Device, p. 532

mean, p. 509

measurement, p. 506

median, p. 510

minimum competency testing,
  p. 527

mode, p. 510

normal distribution, p. 511

norm group, p. 507

norming sample, p. 509

norm-referenced testing, p. 506

percentile rank, p. 512

range, p. 511

readiness testing, p. 526

reliability, p. 516

standard deviation, p. 510

standard error of measurement,
  p. 517

standardized tests, p. 509

standard scores, p. 514

stanine scores, p. 515

true score, p. 516

T score, p. 514

validity, p. 517

variability, p. 510

vocational aptitude tests, p. 524

vocational interest tests, p. 524

z score, p. 514

WHAT WOULD YOU DO?

PRESCHOOL AND KINDERGARTEN

Your district is considering establishing a first-grade readiness testing program. As the lead teacher for the kindergarten, you are asked to speak to the school board about the issue. What points would you make?

ELEMENTARY AND MIDDLE SCHOOL

Your students seem very nervous about the spring testing. The local paper has carried stories about the school's "low" scores last year and there is pressure on everyone to do better this time. How would you prepare your students?

The parents of one of your students are angry with you because their child was not selected for the special accelerated math group. Selection was based on both standardized test scores and class performance. How would you explain the school's decision?

JUNIOR HIGH AND HIGH SCHOOL

Parents of one of your students want their child to receive credit for ninth-grade math without taking the course because she received a grade-equivalent score of 10.7 on her standardized math test in the spring of eighth grade. What would you say to the parents?

One of your students is very upset because the vocational interest test he took suggests that he "should be a forest ranger" and he wants to be a lawyer. What would you say to this student?

COOPERATIVE LEARNING ACTIVITY

With four or five other members of your educational psychology class, analyze the test printout in Figure 14.6. If you were Susie's English teacher, how would you use this information in teaching? What could teachers in other subjects learn from this test report?

ACHIEVEMENT TESTS AND ESL STUDENTS

Your district is giving standardized achievement tests. Two of your students have recently moved to the United States and are still having problems reading quickly. Although they are bright students, you know they will score low on the test because they must work slowly. What would you do?

SPECIAL TREATMENT

The first step I would take is to speak with the person administering the test and make him or her aware of the situation. In many instances, it would be possible to arrange for those two students to meet with a guidance counselor or other staff member and have that person orally read the test to the students. By doing this you would get a better idea of the students' actual abilities. This would also help to ensure that misplacement in a remedial program did not occur.

Candice J. Gallagher, *Fourth-Grade Teacher*
Fredericktown Intermediate School, Fredericktown, Ohio

EXTRA EFFORT NEEDED

I would give each student an *additional* answer sheet on which I would direct them to continue the test beyond the time limit. For example, had they completed 28 questions, I would tell them to begin on line 29 of the *second* answer sheet. The students would be given a specific amount of time, but under no condition would the additional time exceed the original allotted time. The teacher should copy the answers from the first answer sheet to the second. Both sheets should be submitted and corrected, and the ESL students will each have two scores.

Louise Harrold Melucci, *Fourth-Grade Teacher*
Greenwood School, Warwick, Rhode Island

GUIDE TO GENERAL ABILITY

Since the students are not discouraged enough to give up working on the test, they should be encouraged to finish what is possible. Achievement tests are used to measure general ability rather than just reading skills. Children should not be penalized for being slow readers. The results of most standardized tests have item analyses that the teacher can and should study for correct and incorrect answers. By analyzing the questions answered, the teacher can see the children's strengths and weaknesses. Though the composite scores may be lowered, there will still be enough information to be useful.

Ida Pofahl, *Second-Grade Teacher*
Denison Elementary School, Denison, Iowa

COACHING FOR TESTS?

Do you do anything special to prepare students for standardized tests such as the College Boards? Why or why not?

PSYCHOLOGY OF THE GAME

Most of my students have experienced considerable success in their educational careers. They are accustomed to doing very well on their tests. I believe my most important role is to assure them that it is "okay" not to be able to answer all the questions on a standardized test. They do not fully understand that the test will purposely establish percentiles by asking some very difficult questions. I am convinced that many bright students become frustrated as they are taking the test and lose confidence in their ability and preparation. In many ways, I must become more of a coach than a teacher and must concentrate on the psychology of the "game."

R. Chris Rohde, *Chemistry Teacher*
Chippewa Falls Senior High School, Chippewa Falls, Wisconsin

CHEATING

Several students tell you that three other students in your class were cheating during a statewide standardized test. What would you do?

COMMUNICATION FIRST

I would first meet individually with the students who reported the incident to try to verify that the accusations deserved further investigation. I would then talk with the students accused of cheating to hear their side of the story. If the cheating did in fact occur, I would visit with my administrator and determine what course of action to follow. I would stress to all students involved the importance of honesty, trust, and truthfulness. If the accusations were proven to be true, parents would also need to be involved in some way.

Deborah H. Platt, *Third-Grade Teacher*
Eugene Field Elementary School, Mitchell, South Dakota

MONITOR CLOSELY

The observers should be talked with separately. If they were very convincing, then I would tell the accused what had been observed. Depending on the situation and what was said, I might give the option to retake the test (if that was a possibility) in a closely monitored situation; or if the child admitted that cheating occurred, then the test results would need to note what had occurred. I would be careful not to accuse or throw out test results unless I was reasonably sure that cheating did occur.

Ruth Ann Dearth, *English and Reading Teacher*
Fredericktown Junior High School, Fredericktown, Ohio

SEEK THE TRUTH

My first step would be to talk to the students involved and to attempt to arrive at the truth. If I was sure that the accusation was correct, I would involve the parents and declare the test results to be invalid for those students. Then I would try to find out why those students felt the pressure to cheat.

Joanne S. Groseclose, *Virginia 1991 Teacher of the Year*
Marion Intermediate School, Marion, Virginia

TESTING ADVANTAGES AND DISADVANTAGES

Achievement tests have become a way of life in schools. But the tests are an expense to the schools and a source of anxiety to the students (and teachers). What are the advantages and disadvantages of these tests? How can the results be used?

MEASURE INDIVIDUAL GROWTH

The advantages: (1) Achievements provide a basis of comparison for evaluating strengths and correcting weaknesses of students, classes, schools, and districts. (2) They provide support for teacher judgment. (3) They serve as tools for evaluating the worth of texts, instructional materials, and curriculum.

The disadvantages: (1) Tests do not always test what is taught. (2) Some administrators use tests to evaluate teachers and principals, pitting school against school and teacher against teacher. (3) Some teachers are pressured into teaching the tests, thereby invalidating the results. (4) Some students are not "test takers" and some are "super-guessers," making results unreliable. (5) Test results are too often just filed and forgotten.

Joan H. Lowe, *Fifth-Grade Teacher*
Russell Elementary School, Hazelwood, Missouri

15 CLASSROOM EVALUATION AND GRADING

When you think about elementary or secondary school, you probably vividly remember being tested and graded. In this chapter, we will look at both tests and grades, focusing not only on the effects these are likely to have on students but also on practical means of developing more efficient methods for testing and grading.

We begin with a consideration of the many types of tests teachers prepare each year, including some new approaches to assessment. Then we examine the effects grades are likely to have on students. Because there are so many grading systems, we also spend some time identifying the advantages and disadvantages of one system over another. Finally, we turn to the very important topic of communication with students and parents. How will you justify the grades you give?

By the time you have finished this chapter, you should be able to do the following:

- Make a plan for testing students on a unit of work.

- Evaluate tests that accompany textbooks and teachers' manuals.

- Create multiple-choice and essay test items for your subject area.

- Describe authentic assessment approaches, including portfolios, performances, and exhibitions.

- Discuss the potential positive and negative effects of grades on students.

- Give examples of criterion-referenced and norm-referenced grading systems.

- Assign grades to a hypothetical group of students and defend your decisions in a class debate.

- Role-play a conference with parents who do not understand your grading system or their child's grades.

WHAT DO YOU THINK?

Think back on your report cards and grades over the years. Did you ever receive a grade that was lower than you expected? How did you feel about the teacher, the subject, and school in general as a result of the lower grade? How did you explain the grade to yourself and to others? What could the teacher have done to help you understand and profit from the experience?

FORMATIVE AND SUMMATIVE ASSESSMENT

As a teacher, you may or may not help in designing the grading system for your school or your class. Many school districts have a standard approach to grading. Still, you will have choices—about how you use your district's grading system and how you assess your students' learning. Will you give tests? How many? What kinds? Will students do projects or keep portfolios of their work? How will homework influence grades? Will you grade on students' current academic performance or on their degree of improvement? How will you use the information from student assessments?

There are two general uses or functions for assessment: formative and summative. **Formative assessment** occurs before or during instruction. It has two basic purposes: to guide the teacher in planning and to help students identify areas that need work. In other words, formative assessment helps *form* instruction. Often students are given a formative test prior to instruction, a **pretest** that helps the teacher determine what students already know. Sometimes a test is given during instruction to see what areas of weakness remain so teaching can be directed toward the problem areas. This is generally called a **diagnostic test** but should not be confused with the standardized diagnostic tests of more general learning abilities. A classroom diagnostic test identifies a student's areas of achievement and weakness in a particular subject. Older students are often able to apply the information from diagnostic tests to "reteach" themselves. For example, armed with the knowledge that you have difficulty interpreting standardized test reports like the one on page 520, you could reread the section on this topic in chapter 14, read the interpretation section of a test manual, or ask another student or the instructor for an explanation.

Pretests and diagnostic tests are not graded. And since formative tests do not count toward the final grade, students who tend to be very anxious on "real" tests may find this low-pressure practice in test taking especially helpful.

A variation of formative measurement is ongoing measurement, often called **data-based instruction** (Lovitt, 1977). This approach uses daily "probes," or brief tests of specific skills, to give a very precise picture of a student's current performance. This method has been used primarily

Formative Assessment Ungraded testing used before or during instruction to aid in planning and diagnosis.

Pretest Formative test for assessing students' knowledge, readiness, and abilities.

Diagnostic Test Formative test to determine students' areas of weakness.

Data-Based Instruction Assessment method using daily probes of specific-skill mastery.

with students who have learning problems, since it provides systematic evaluation of both student performance and the teaching methods used. If a student shows inadequate progress on the daily probes, the teacher should consider modifying or switching instructional strategies.

Summative assessment occurs at the end of instruction. Its purpose is to let the teacher and the students know the level of accomplishment attained. Summative assessment, therefore, provides a *summary* of accomplishment. The final exam is a classic example.

The distinction between formative and summative assessment is based on how the results are used. The same evaluation procedure can be used for either purpose. If the goal is to obtain information about student learning for planning purposes, the assessment is formative. If the purpose is to determine final achievement (and help determine a course grade), the assessment is summative.

GETTING THE MOST FROM TRADITIONAL ASSESSMENT APPROACHES

When most people think of assessment, they usually think of testing. As you will see shortly, teachers today have many other options, but testing is still a significant activity in most classrooms. Let's consider your options for assessing students using the traditional testing approach. In this section we will examine how to plan effective tests, how to evaluate the tests that accompany standard curriculum materials, and how to write your own test questions.

Planning for Testing

Both instruction and evaluation are most effective when they are well organized and planned. In chapter 12 you saw that creating a behavior-content matrix can help teachers develop thoughtful learning objectives. The same process can be applied in planning classroom evaluations. When you have a good plan you are in a better position to judge the tests provided in teacher's manuals and texts and to write tests yourself.

Using a Behavior-Content Matrix. Here is how you might use a behavior-content matrix to design a unit test. First you will need to decide how many items students can complete during the testing period and then make sure that the items you write cover all the objectives you have set for the unit. More important objectives should have more items (Berliner, 1987).

An example of a plan that might be appropriate for a 40-question unit test in government is given in Figure 15.1 on page 544. From the test plan, you can see that this teacher has decided the most important topic is *major political issues* and has accordingly allotted a total of 15 questions to it. The least important topic is *methods of inquiry*. Also, the teacher wants to emphasize students' ability to make *generalizations* (14 questions) while giving considerable attention to *understanding concepts* and *locating information. Interpreting graphs* is the least important skill, but it is not to be overlooked.

Summative Assessment
Testing that follows instruction and assesses achievement.

FIGURE 15.1   **Test Plan for a Unit on Government**   In making a test plan, begin by deciding on the totals (the numbers in bold) and then allocate the number of questions to each particular type and skill combination.

Topics	Skills Tested				
	Understanding Concepts	Making Generalizations	Locating Information	Interpreting Graphs	Total Questions
Social trends	4	4	1	1	**10**
National political events	2	3	3	2	**10**
Methods of inquiry	1	1	2	1	**5**
Major political issues	3	6	4	2	**15**
Total questions	**10**	**14**	**10**	**6**	**40**

By preparing such a plan, a teacher can avoid a situation where she or he has written 15 great questions (out of 40), only to discover that all 15 ask students to deal with the same concept or topic. Making a test plan will also improve the validity of tests. You will be able to ask a reasonable number of questions that measure the skills you hoped to develop about each key topic.

When to Test? Frank Dempster (1991) examined the research on reviews and tests and reached these useful conclusions for teachers:

1. Frequent testing encourages the retention of information and appears to be more effective than a comparable amount of time spent reviewing and studying the material.
2. Tests are especially effective in promoting learning if you give students a test on the material soon after they learn it, then retest on the material later. The retestings should be spaced farther and farther apart.
3. The use of cumulative questions on tests is a key to effective learning. Cumulative questions ask students to apply information they learned in several previous units to solve a new problem.

Judging Textbook Tests. Most elementary and secondary texts today come complete with supplemental materials such as teaching manuals, handout masters, and ready-made tests. Using these tests can save time, but is this good teaching practice? The answer depends on your objectives for your students, the way you taught the material, and the quality of the tests provided (Airasian, 1991). If the textbook test matches your testing plan and the instruction you actually provided for your students, then it may be the right test to use. Table 15.1 gives key points to consider in evaluating textbook tests.

What if there are no tests available for the material you want to cover or the tests provided in your teacher's manuals are not appropriate for

---

TABLE 15.1 Key Points to Consider in Judging Textbook Tests

- The decision to use a textbook test must come *after* you identify the important topics and behaviors taught.
- Textbook tests are designed for the typical classroom; but few classrooms are typical, and most teachers deviate somewhat from the text to accommodate pupils' needs.
- The more instruction deviates from the textbook objectives and lesson plans, the less valid a textbook test is likely to be for assessing pupil achievement.
- The main criterion for judging the adequacy of a textbook test is the match between the test questions and what pupils were taught. Consult your behavior-content matrix.

   - Are questions similar to your objectives and instructional emphases?
   - Do questions require pupils to perform the behaviors they were taught?
   - Do questions cover all or most of the important objectives taught?
   - Is the language level and terminology appropriate?

Source: Adapted from P. Airasian (1991), *Classroom assessment* (New York: McGraw-Hill), p. 176. Reproduced with permission of McGraw-Hill, Inc.

your students? Then it's time for you to create your own tests. We will consider the two major kinds of tests—objective and essay.

Objective Testing

Multiple-choice questions, matching exercises, true-false statements, and short-answer or fill-in items are all types of **objective testing.** The word *objective* in relation to testing means "not open to many interpretations," or "not subjective." The scoring of these types of items is relatively straightforward compared to the scoring of essay questions, because the answers are more clear-cut than essay answers.

Gronlund (1988) suggests that teachers first try to write multiple-choice questions, then switch to other formats if writing good multiple-choice items is not possible for the material. For example, if related concepts need to be linked, such as terms and definitions, then a *matching item* is a better format than multiple-choice. If it is difficult to come up with several wrong answers for a multiple-choice item, try a *true-false question* instead. Alternatively, ask the student to supply a short answer that completes a statement (*fill in the blank*). Variety in objective testing can lower students' anxiety, because the entire grade does not depend on one type of question that a particular student may find difficult. Here we will look closely at the multiple-choice format, since it is the most versatile—and the most difficult to use well.

Using Multiple-Choice Tests. People often assume that multiple-choice items are appropriate only for asking factual questions. But

Objective Testing
Multiple-choice, matching, true-false, short-answer, and fill-in tests; scoring answers does not require interpretation.

Guidelines

Writing Objective Test Items

The stem should be clear and simple, and present only a single problem. Unessential details should be left out.

Poor

There are several different kinds of standard or derived scores. An IQ score is especially useful because . . .

Better

An advantage of an IQ score is . . .

The problem in the stem should be stated in positive terms. Negative language is confusing. If you must use words such as *not, no,* or *except,* underline them or type them in all capitals.

Poor

Which of the following is not a standard score?

Better

Which of the following is NOT a standard score?

Do not expect students to make extremely fine discrimination among answer choices.

Poor

The percentage of area in a normal curve falling between +1 and −1 standard deviations is about:
a. 66%. **b.** 67%. **c.** 68%. **d.** 69%.

Better

The percentage of area in a normal curve falling between +1 and −1 standard deviations is about:
a. 14%. **b.** 34%. (**c.**) 68%. **d.** 95%.

As much wording as possible should be included in the stem so that phrases will not have to be repeated in each alternative.

Poor

A percentile score
a. indicates the percentage of items answered correctly.
b. indicates the percent of correct answers divided by the percent of wrong answers.
c. indicates the percent of people who scored at or above a given raw score.
d. indicates the percent of people who scored at or below a given raw score.

Better

A percentile score indicates the percentage of
a. items answered correctly.
b. correct answers divided by the percent of wrong answers.
c. people who scored at or above a given raw score.
(**d.**) people who scored at or below a given raw score.

Each alternative answer should fit the grammatical form of the stem, so that no answers are obviously wrong.

Poor

The Stanford-Binet test yields an
a. IQ score. **c.** vocational preference.
b. reading level. **d.** mechanical aptitude.

multiple-choice items can test higher-level objectives as well, although writing higher-level items is difficult (Carter, 1984). A multiple-choice item can assess more than recall and recognition if it requires the student to deal with new material by *applying* or *analyzing* the concept or principle being tested. For example, the following multiple-choice item is designed to evaluate students' ability to recognize unstated assumptions—one of the skills involved in analyzing an idea:

An educational psychology professor states, "A *z* score of +1 on a test is equivalent to a percentile rank of approximately 84." Which of the following assumptions is the professor making?

1. The scores on the test range from 0 to 100.
2. The standard deviation of the test scores is equal to 3.4.
3. The distribution of scores on the test is normal. (CORRECT ANSWER)
4. The test is valid and reliable.

Better

The Stanford-Binet is a test of
a. intelligence.
b.) reading level.
c. vocational preference.
d. mechanical aptitude.

Categorical words such as *always, all, only,* **or** *never* **should be avoided unless they can appear consistently in all the alternatives. Most smart test takers know the categorical answers are usually wrong.**

Poor

A student's true score on a standardized test is
a. never equal to the obtained score.
b. always very close to the obtained score.
c. always determined by the standard error of measurement.
d. usually within a band that extends from +1 to −1 standard errors of measurement on each side of the obtained score.

Better

Which one of the statements below would most often be correct about a student's true score on a standardized test?
a. It equals the obtained score.
b. It will be very close to the obtained score.
c. It is determined by the standard error of measurement.
d.) It could be above or below the obtained score.

You should also avoid including two distractors that have the same meaning. If only one answer can be right and if two answers are the same, then these two must both be wrong. This narrows down the choices considerably.

Poor

The most frequently occurring score in a distribution is called the
a. mode.   c. arithmetical average.
b. median.   d. mean.

Better

The most frequently occurring score in a distribution is called the
a.) mode.   c. standard deviation.
b. median.   d. mean.

Using the exact wording found in the textbook is another technique to avoid. Poor students may recognize the answers without knowing what they mean.

Avoid overuse of *all of the above* **and** *none of the above.* **Such choices may be helpful to students who are simply guessing. In addition, using** *all of the above* **may trick a quick student who sees that the first alternative is correct and does not read on to discover that the others are correct, too.**

Obvious patterns on a test also aid students who are guessing. The position of the correct answer should be varied, as should its length.

All test items require skillful construction, but good multiple-choice items are a real challenge.

Writing Multiple-Choice Questions. Some students jokingly refer to multiple-choice tests as "multiple-guess" tests—a sign that these tests are often poorly designed. Your goal in writing test items is to design them so that they measure student achievement rather than test-taking and guessing skills.

The **stem** of a multiple-choice item is the part that asks the question or poses the problem. The choices that follow are called *alternatives.* The wrong answers are called **distractors,** because their purpose is to distract students who have only a partial understanding of the material. If there were no good distractors, students with only a vague understanding would have no difficulty in finding the right answer.

Stating the correct answer so that it is the *only* right answer or clearly the *best* answer is tricky. You probably have been on the student side of discussions about whether the correct answer was really correct or

Stem The question part of a multiple-choice item.

Distractors Wrong answers offered as choices in a multiple-choice item.

whether several of the answers might be correct. The teacher is just as unhappy as the students when half the class selects the same wrong answer. Often this means the item was poorly constructed. The Guidelines on pages 546–547, adapted from Gronlund (1988), should make writing multiple-choice questions easier.

Essay Testing

The best way to measure some learning objectives is to require students to create answers on their own. An essay question is appropriate in these cases. The most difficult part of essay testing is judging the quality of the answers; but writing good, clear questions is not particularly easy, either. We will look at several factors involved in writing, administering, and grading essay tests, with most of the specific suggestions taken from Gronlund (1988). We will also consider factors that can bias the scoring of essay questions and ways you can overcome these problems.

Constructing Essay Tests. Because answering takes time, true essay tests cover less material than objective tests. Thus, for efficiency, essay tests should generally be limited to the evaluation of the more complex learning outcomes.

An essay question should give students a clear and precise task and should indicate the elements to be covered in the answer. Gronlund suggests the following as an example of an essay question that might appear in an educational psychology course to measure an objective at the *synthesis* level of Bloom's taxonomy in the cognitive domain:

> For a course that you are teaching or expect to teach, prepare a complete plan for evaluating student achievement. Be sure to include the procedures you would follow, the instruments you would use, and the reasons for your choices.

This question requires students to apply information and values derived from course material to produce a complex new product.

Gronlund (1988) has offered a variety of specific suggestions for constructing and administering essay tests. First, students should be given ample time for answering. If more than one essay is being completed in the same class period, you may want to suggest time limits for each. Remember, however, that time pressure increases anxiety and may prevent accurate evaluation of some students.

Whatever your approach, do not include a large number of essay questions in an attempt to make up for the limited amount of material an essay test can cover. It would be better to plan on more frequent testing than to include more than two or three essay questions in a single class period. Combining an essay question with a number of objective items is one way to avoid the problem of limited sampling of course material.

Evaluating Essays: Dangers. In 1912 Starch and Elliot began a classic series of experiments that shocked educators into critical consideration of subjectivity in testing. These researchers wanted to find out the extent to which teachers were influenced in scoring essay tests by personal values, standards, and expectations. For their initial study they sent copies of English examination papers written by two high school students to English teachers in 200 high schools. Each teacher was asked to score the papers according to his or her school's standards. A percentage scale was to be used, with 75 percent as a passing grade.

The results? Neatness, spelling, punctuation, and communicative effectiveness were all valued to different degrees by different teachers. The scores on one of the papers ranged from 64 to 98 percent, with a mean of 88.2. The average score for the other paper was 80.2, with a range between 50 and 97. The following year Starch and Elliot (1913a & b) published similar findings in a study involving history and geometry papers. The most important result of these studies was the discovery that the problem of subjectivity in grading was not confined to any particular subject area. The main difficulties were the individual standards of the grader and the unreliability of scoring procedures.

Certain qualities of an essay may influence grades. For example, in a study of grading practices at 16 law schools, Linn, Klein, and Hart (1972) found that neatly written, verbose, jargon-filled essays with few grammatical and construction errors were given the best grades. Evidence indicates that teachers may reward quantity rather than quality in essays. In a series of studies, many high school and college English teachers rated pairs of student essays that were identical in every way but linguistic style. One essay was quite verbose, with flowery language, complex sentences, and passive verbs. The other essay was written in the simple, straightforward language most teachers claim is the goal for students of writing. The teachers consistently rated the verbose essay higher.

Evaluating Essays: Methods. Gronlund (1988) offers several strategies for grading essays to avoid problems of subjectivity and inaccuracy. When possible, a good first step is to construct a model answer; then you can assign points to its various parts. Points might also be given for the organization of the answer, as well as the internal consistency. You can then assign grades such as 1 to 5 or A, B, C, D, and F and sort the papers into piles by grade. As a final step, skim the papers in each pile to see if they are comparable in quality. These techniques will help ensure fairness and accuracy in grading.

When grading essay tests with several questions, it makes sense to grade all responses to one question before moving on to the next. This helps prevent the quality of a student's answer to one question from influencing your evaluation of the student's other answers. After you finish reading and scoring the first question, shuffle the papers so that no students end up having all their questions graded first, last, or in the middle (Hills, 1976).

You may achieve greater objectivity if you ask students to put their names on the back of the paper, so that grading is anonymous. A final check on your fairness as a grader is to have another teacher who is equally familiar with your goals and subject matter grade your tests without knowing what grades you have assigned. This can give you valuable insights into areas of bias in your grading practices.

Educators concerned with the writing process have developed an approach to evaluating written work known as **holistic scoring.** The

Holistic Scoring
Evaluation of a piece of written work as a whole, without separate grades for individual elements.

TABLE 15.2 Comparing Objective and Essay Tests		
	Objective Tests	**Essay Tests**
Useful for measuring . . .	Outcomes at the knowledge, comprehension, application, and analysis levels of Bloom's taxonomy	Synthesis and evaluation outcomes; also comprehension, application, and analysis outcomes
Number of items/range of material covered	Large number of items/broad coverage of course content	Relatively small number of items/ limited but often in-depth coverage
Preparation problems	Difficult and time consuming	Difficult for good items, but easier than objective items
Scoring	Objective, simple, and highly reliable	Subjective, difficult, and less reliable
Sources of score distortions	Students' level of reading ability; guessing	Students' writing ability; bluffing
Probable effect on learning	Encourage students to remember, interpret, and analyze the ideas of others.	Encourage students to organize, integrate, and express their own ideas

Source: N. E. Gronlund (1988), *Constructing achievement tests* (3rd ed.), p. 73. Reprinted with permission of Allyn and Bacon.

philosophy underlying the holistic approach is that a written passage is greater than the sum of its parts. When teachers focus on the specific parts of an essay, such as vocabulary, grammar, spelling, or inclusion of particular details, they may miss important qualities like the essential message and persuasiveness. Rather than assigning separate grades for style, grammar, and content, for example, the holistic approach would evaluate the essay as a whole and give just one grade (Vacc, 1989). To make sure holistic scores are reliable, White (1984) has recommended that teachers read essays in one session and at the outset choose sample essays for each grade level to serve as models—choose one essay as a model for an A, one for a B, and so on.

Now that we have examined both objective and essay testing, we can compare the two approaches. Table 15.2 presents a summary of the important characteristics of each.

INNOVATIONS IN ASSESSMENT

We have been considering how to make traditional testing more effective; now let's look at a few new approaches to classroom assessment. One of the main criticisms of standardized tests—that they control the curriculum, emphasizing recall of facts instead of thinking and problem solving—is a major criticism of classroom tests as well. Few teachers would dispute these criticisms. Even if you follow the guidelines we have been discussing, traditional testing can be limiting. What can be done? One solution is to apply the concept of authentic assessment to classroom evaluation.

Authentic Classroom Tests

Authentic tests ask students to apply skills and abilities as they would in real life; for example, to use fractions to enlarge or reduce recipes. Grant Wiggins makes this argument:

> If tests determine what teachers actually teach and what students will study for—and they do—then the road to reform is a straight but steep one: test those capabilities and habits we think are essential, and test them in context. Make [tests] replicate, within reason, the challenges at the heart of each academic discipline. Let them be—authentic. (1989, p. 41)

Wiggins goes on to say that if our instructional goals for students include the abilities to write, speak, listen, create, think critically, do research, solve problems, or apply knowledge, then our tests should ask students to write, speak, listen, create, think, solve, and apply. How can this happen?

Many educators suggest we look to the arts and sports for analogies to solve this problem. If we think of the "test" as being the recital, exhibition, game, mock court trial, or other performance, then teaching to the test is just fine. All coaches, artists, and musicians gladly "teach" to these "tests" because performing well on these tests is the whole point of instruction. Authentic assessment asks students to perform. The performances may be thinking performances, physical performances, creative performances, or other forms.

It may seem odd to talk of thinking as a performance, but there are many parallels. Serious thinking is risky, because real-life problems are not well defined. Like a sculptor looking at a lump of clay, a student facing a difficult problem must experiment, observe, redo, imagine and test solutions, apply both basic skills and inventive techniques, make interpretations, decide how to communicate results to the intended audi-

One way to determine whether students have understood a principle is to require them to apply their knowledge to build a model.

Authentic Tests
Assessment procedures that test skills and abilities as they would be applied in real-life situations.

ence, and often accept criticism and improve the solution (Wolf, in press; Wolf, Bixby, Glenn, & Gardner, 1991). Table 15.3 lists some characteristics of authentic tests.

Performance in Context: Portfolios and Exhibitions

The concern with authentic assessment has led to the development of several new approaches based on the goal of *performance in context*. Instead of circling answers to factual questions that are removed from the situations where the facts are needed, students are required to solve real problems. Facts are used in a context where they apply—for example, the student uses grammar facts to write a persuasive letter to a software company requesting donations for the class computer center. The follow-

---

TABLE 15.3   Characteristics of Authentic Tests

A. Structure and Logistics

1. Are more appropriately public; involve an audience, a panel, and so on.
2. Do not rely on unrealistic and arbitrary time constraints.
3. Offer known, not secret, questions or tasks.
4. Are more like portfolios or a *season* of games (not one-shot).
5. Require some collaboration with others.
6. Recur—and are *worth* practicing for, rehearsing, and retaking.
7. Make assessment and feedback to students so central that school schedules, structures, and policies are modified to support them.

B. Intellectual Design Features

1. Are "essential"—not needlessly intrusive, arbitrary, or contrived to "shake out" a grade.
2. Are "enabling"—constructed to point the student toward more sophisticated use of the skills or knowledge.
3. Are contextualized, complex intellectual challenges, not "atomized" tasks, corresponding to isolated "outcomes."
4. Involve the student's own research or use of knowledge, for which "content" is a means.
5. Assess student habits and repertoires, not mere recall or plug-in skills.
6. Are *representative* challenges—designed to emphasize *depth* more than breadth.

7. Are engaging and educational.
8. Involve somewhat ambiguous ("ill-structured") tasks or problems.

C. Grading and Scoring Standards

1. Involve criteria that assess essentials, not easily counted (but relatively unimportant) errors.
2. Are graded not on a "curve" but in reference to performance standards (criterion-referenced, not norm-referenced).
3. Involve demystified criteria of success that appear to *students* as inherent in successful activity.
4. Make self-assessment a part of the assessment.
5. Use a multifaceted scoring system instead of one aggregate grade.
6. Exhibit harmony with shared schoolwide aims—a *standard*.

D. Fairness and Equity

1. Ferret out and identify (perhaps hidden) strengths.
2. Strike a *constantly* examined balance between honoring achievement and native skill or fortunate prior training.
3. Minimize needless, unfair, and demoralizing comparisons.
4. Allow appropriate room for student learning styles, aptitudes, and interests.
5. Can be—should be—attempted by *all* students, with the test "scaffolded up," not "dumbed down," as necessary.

Source: Grant Wiggins (1989), Teaching to the Authentic Test, *Educational Leadership, 45*(7), p. 44. Reprinted with permission of the Association for Supervision and Curriculum Development. Copyright © by ASCD. All rights reserved.

ing example of a test of performance is taken from the Connecticut Core of Common Learning.

> Many local supermarkets claim to have the lowest prices. But what does this really mean? Does it mean that every item in their store is priced lower, or just some of them? How can you really tell which supermarket will save you the most money? Your assignment is to design and carry out a study to answer this question. What items and prices will you compare and why? How will you justify the choice of your "sample"? How reliable is the sample, etc.? (Wolf, Bixby, Glenn, & Gardner, 1991, p. 61)

Students completing this "test" will use mathematical facts and procedures in the context of solving a real-life problem. In addition, they will have to think critically and write persuasively.

Portfolios and exhibitions are two new approaches to assessment that require performance in context. With these new approaches it is difficult

If you give prizes in your classes, make sure that there are categories for all kinds of accomplishments.

FIGURE 15.2 **A Student Reflects on Learning: Self-Analysis of Work in a Portfolio** Not only has this student's writing improved, but the student has become a more self-aware and self-critical writer.

> 2
>
> Today I looked at all my stories in my writing folder. I read some of my writing since September. I noticed that I've improved some stuff. Now I edit my stories, and revise. Now I use periods, quotation mark. Sometimes my stories are longer I used to misspell my words and now I look in a dictionary or ask a friend and now I write exciting and scary stories and now I have very good endings. Now I use capitals I used to leave out words and write short simple stories.

Guidelines

Creating Portfolios

Students should be involved in selecting the pieces that will make up the portfolio.

Examples

1. During the unit or semester, ask each student to select work that fits certain criteria, such as "my most difficult problem," "my best work," "my most improved work," or "three approaches to. . . ."
2. For their final submissions, ask students to select pieces that best show how much they have learned.

A portfolio should include information that shows student self-reflection and self-criticism.

Examples

1. Ask students to include a rationale for their selections.
2. Have each student write a "guide" to his or her portfolio, explaining how strengths and weaknesses are reflected in the work included.
3. Include self- and peer critiques, indicating specifically what is good and what might be improved.
4. Model self-criticism of your own productions.

The portfolio should reflect the students' activities in learning.

Examples

1. Include a representative selection of projects, writings, drawings, etc.

2. Ask students to relate the goals of learning to the contents of their portfolios.

The portfolio can serve different functions at different times of the year.

Examples

1. Early in the year, it might hold unfinished work or "problem pieces."
2. At the end of the year, it should contain only what the student is willing to make public.

Portfolios should show growth.

Examples

1. Ask students to make a "history" of their progress along certain dimensions and to illustrate points in their growth with specific works.
2. Ask students to include descriptions of activities outside class that reflect the growth illustrated in the portfolio.

Teach students how to create and use portfolios.

Examples

1. Keep models of very well done portfolios as examples, but stress that each portfolio is an individual statement.
2. Examine your students' portfolios frequently, especially early in the year when they are just getting used to the idea. Give constructive feedback.

to tell where instruction stops and assessment starts, because the two processes are interwoven.

Portfolios. A **portfolio** is

> a purposeful collection of student work that exhibits the student's efforts, progress, and achievements in one or more areas. The collection must include student participation in selecting contents, the criteria for judging merit, and evidence of student self-reflection. (Paulson, Paulson, & Meyer, 1991, p. 60)

Portfolio A collection of the student's work in an area, showing growth, self-reflection, and achievement.

Portfolios often include work in progress, revisions, student self-analyses, and reflections on what the student has learned. For example, one student's self-reflection is presented in Figure 15.2 on page 553.

Written work or artistic pieces are common contents of portfolios, but students might also include graphs, diagrams, snapshots of displays, peer comments, audio- or videotapes, laboratory reports, computer programs—anything that demonstrates learning in the area being taught and evaluated (Belanoff & Dickson, 1991; Camp, 1990; Wolf, Bixby, Glenn, & Gardner, 1991). The Guidelines give some ideas for using portfolios in your teaching.

Exhibitions. An **exhibition** is a performance test with two additional features. First, it is public, so students preparing exhibitions must take the audience into account; communication and understanding are essential. Second, an exhibition often requires many hours of preparation, because it is the culminating experience of a whole program of study. Ted Sizer (1984) proposed that "exhibitions of mastery" replace traditional tests in determining graduation or course completion requirements. Grant Wiggins (1989) believes that an exhibition of mastery "is meant to be more than a better test. Like the thesis and oral examination in graduate

FIGURE 15.3 A Final Exhibition for High School Students In this example of an exhibition, students must complete an eight-part portfolio, a research project, oral tests, and oral presentations.

Include a range of assignments and activities in students' grades. How well can this student explain why you need "fuzzy" absorbent string between the two straws to make a good bubble?

The Rite of Passage Experience (R.O.P.E.) at Walden III, Racine, Wisconsin

All seniors must complete a portfolio, a study project on U.S. history, and 15 oral and written presentations before a R.O.P.E. committee composed of staff, students, and an outside adult. Nine of the presentations are based on the materials in the portfolio and the project; the remaining six are developed for presentation before the committee. All seniors must enroll in a yearlong course designed to help them meet these requirements.

The eight-part *portfolio*, developed in the first semester, is intended to be "a reflection and analysis of the senior's own life and times." The requirements include:
• a written autobiography,
• a reflection on work (including a resume),
• an essay on ethics,
• a written summary of coursework in science,
• an artistic product or a written report on art (including an essay on artistic standards used in judging artwork).

The *project* is a research paper on a topic of the student's choosing in American history. The student is orally questioned on the paper in the presentations before the committee during the second semester.

The *presentations* include oral tests on the previous work, as well as six additional presentations on the essential subject areas and "personal proficiency" (life skills, setting and realizing personal goals, etc.). The presentations before the committee usually last an hour, with most students averaging about 6 separate appearances to complete all 15.

A diploma is awarded to those passing 12 of the 15 presentations and meeting district requirements in math, government, reading, and English.

Note: This summary is paraphrased from both the R.O.P.E. Student Handbook and an earlier draft of Archbald and Newmann's (1988) *Beyond Standardized Testing*.

Source: Grant Wiggins (1989), Teaching to the authentic test, *Educational Leadership, 46* (7), p. 42. Reprinted with permission of the Association for Supervision and Curriculum Development. Copyright © 1989 by ASCD. All rights reserved.

Exhibition A performance test or demonstration of learning that is public and usually takes an extended time to prepare.

To Test or Not to Test, Part II

We have seen the advantages and disadvantages of standardized tests, but what about classroom testing? Are traditional multiple-choice and essay tests useful in classroom assessment?

Point: Traditional tests are a poor basis for classroom assessment.

In his article "Standards, Not Standardization: Evoking Quality Student Work," Grant Wiggins (1991) makes a strong case for giving students standards of excellence against which they can judge their accomplishments. But these standards should not be higher scores on multiple-choice tests. When scores on traditional tests become the standard, the message to students is that only right answers matter and the thinking behind the answers is unimportant. Wiggins notes:

> We do not judge Xerox, the Boston Symphony, the Cincinnati Reds, or Dom Perignon vine-

yards on the basis of indirect, easy to test, and common indicators. Nor would the workers in those places likely produce quality if some generic, secure test served as the only measure of their success in meeting a standard. Demanding *and getting* quality, whether from students or adult workers, means framing standards in terms of the work that we undertake and value. And it means framing expectations about that work which make quality a necessity, not an option. Consider:

- the English teacher who instructs peer-editors to mark the place in a student paper where they lost interest in it or found it slapdash and to hand it back for revision at that point;
- the professor who demands that all math homework be turned in with another student having signed off on it, where one earns the grade for one's work *and* the

school, it indicates whether a student has *earned* a diploma, is ready to leave high school" (p. 47). Figure 15.3 on page 555 is an example of a final exhibition required for graduation in a Racine, Wisconsin, high school. You can see that a portfolio, a research project, and oral work are elements of the exhibition.

Evaluating Performances

Checklists and rating scales are helpful when you assess performances, because assessments of performances, portfolios, and exhibitions are criterion-referenced, not norm-referenced (Cangelosi, 1990). In other words, the students' products and performances are compared to established public standards, not ranked in relation to other students' work (Cambourne & Turbill, 1990; Wiggins, 1991). Sometimes model products are used as standards. For example, the expectations for accomplishment in design and technology for students in Great Britain include these criteria at Level 4 (average 11-year-old):

Pupils should be able to:

1. Use hand tools and simple equipment appropriate to the materials to be worked, safely, and with a broad degree of accuracy (for example, use scissors to cut cardboard, a saw to cut wood, a computer keyboard to enter data);

grade for the work that each person (willingly!) countersigned. (p. 22)

Counterpoint: Traditional tests can play an important role.

Most psychologists and educators would agree with Wiggins that setting clear, high, authentic standards is important, but many also believe that traditional tests are useful in this process. Learning may be more than knowing the right answers, but right answers are important. While schooling is about learning to think and solve problems, it is also about knowledge. Students must have something to think about—facts, ideas, concepts, principles, theories, explanations, arguments, images, opinions. Well-designed traditional tests can evaluate students' knowledge effectively and efficiently (Airasian, 1991; Kirst, 1991b).

Some educators believe that traditional testing should play an even greater role than it currently does. Educational policy analysts suggest that American students, compared to students in many other developed countries, lack essential knowledge because American schools emphasize process—critical thinking, self-esteem, problem solving—more than content. In order to teach more about content, teachers will need to determine how well their students are learning the content, and traditional testing provides useful information about content learning.

Tests are also valuable in motivating and guiding students' learning. There is research evidence that frequent testing encourages learning and retention (Nungester & Duchastel, 1982). In fact, students generally learn more in classes with more rather than fewer tests (Dempster, 1991).

2. Use under supervision making and assembling procedures appropriate to the range of tools and materials;
3. Use simple plans, drawings, and diagrams to assist making (for example, use their working sketches and diagrams to make a vehicle that moves); and
4. Suggest a possible solution to a problem that arises during making (for example, suggest different means of dealing with wheel spin in a vehicle they have designed). (Wolf, Bixby, Glenn, & Gardner, 1991, p. 71)

Performance assessment requires great judgment on the part of teachers and clear communication to students about what is good and what needs improving. In some ways the approach is similar to the clinical method first introduced by Binet to assess intelligence: it is based on observing the student perform a variety of tasks and comparing his or her performance to a standard. Just as Binet never wanted to assign a single number to represent the child's intelligence, teachers using authentic assessments do not try to assign one score to the student's performance. Ranking and rating are not the goals—improvement of learning is. If you look back to Table 15.3 on page 552 you will see other grading characteristics of performance tests.

Should innovations in classroom assessment make traditional testing obsolete? The **Point/Counterpoint** section above addresses this question.

EFFECTS OF GRADES AND GRADING ON STUDENTS

There is some evidence that high standards, a competitive class atmosphere, and a large percentage of lower grades are associated with increased absenteeism and increased dropout rates (Moos & Moos, 1978; Trickett & Moos, 1974). This seems especially likely with disadvantaged students (Wessman, 1972). Highly competitive classes may be particularly hard on anxious students or students who lack self-confidence. So while high standards and competition do tend generally to be related to increased academic learning, it is clear that a balance must be struck between high standards and a reasonable chance to succeed.

It may sound as though low grades and failure should be avoided in school. But the situation is not that simple. After reviewing many years of research on the effects of failure from several perspectives, Margaret Clifford (1990, 1991) concluded that failure can have both positive and negative effects on subsequent performance, depending on the situation and the personality of the students involved.

For example, one study required subjects to complete three sets of problems. On the first set, the experimenters arranged for subjects to experience either 0, 50, or 100 percent success. On the second set, it was arranged for all subjects to fail completely. On the third set of problems, the experimenters merely recorded how well the subjects performed. Those who had succeeded only 50 percent of the time before the failure experience performed the best. It appears that a history of complete failure or 100 percent success may be bad preparation for learning to cope with failure, something we must all learn. Some level of failure may be helpful for most students, especially if teachers help the students see connections between hard work and improvement. Efforts to protect students from failure and guarantee success may be counterproductive. Clifford (1990) gives this advice to teachers:

> It is time for educators to replace easy success with challenge. We must encourage students to reach beyond their intellectual grasp and allow them the privilege of learning from mistakes. There must be a tolerance for error-making in every classroom, and gradual success rather than continual success must become the yardstick by which learning is judged. (p. 23)

The more able your students, the more challenging and important it will be to help them learn to "fail successfully" (Foster, 1981).

So far, we have been talking about the effects of failing a test or perhaps a course. But what about the effect of failing an entire grade—that is, of being "held back"? Holmes and Matthews (1984) contend that being held back injures students' self-esteem. In their view, students generally do better academically when promoted. Other researchers have found some advantage for children who are retained in first, second, or third grade, but the advantage may not last. In one study that followed many students for several years, children who could have been retained but were promoted did about as well as similar children who were held back. No matter what, students who have trouble should get help, whether they are promoted or retained. The best approach may be to promote the students along with their peers but to give them special remediation during the summer or the next year (Peterson, DeGracie, & Ayabe, 1987; Shepard & Smith, 1989).

Effects of Feedback

The results of several studies of feedback fit well with the notion of "successful" or constructive failure. These studies have concluded that it is more helpful to tell students when they are wrong than when they are right, but that the most productive approach is to tell them *why* they are wrong so they can learn more appropriate strategies (Bangert-Drowns, Kulik, Kulik, & Morgan, 1991). Students often need help in figuring out why their answers are incorrect. Without such feedback, they are likely to make the same mistakes again. Yet this type of feedback is rarely given. In one study, only about 8 percent of the teachers noticed a consistent type of error in a student's arithmetic computation and informed the student (Bloom & Bourdon, 1980).

Early research indicated that written comments by teachers on completed assignments can lead to improved performance in the future (Page, 1958). In more recent work the emphasis has been on identifying characteristics of effective written feedback. With older students (late elementary through high school), written comments are most helpful when they are personalized and when they provide constructive criticism. This means the teacher should make specific comments on errors or faulty strategies but balance this criticism with suggestions about how to improve as well as with comments on the positive aspects of the work (Butler & Nisan, 1986; Elawar & Corno, 1985). Working with sixth-grade teachers, Elawar and Corno (1985) found that feedback was dramatically improved when the teachers used these four questions as a guide: "What is the key error? What is the probable reason the student made this error? How can I guide the student to avoid the error in the future? What did the student do well that could be noted?" (p. 166). Here are some examples of teachers' written comments that proved helpful (Elawar & Corno, 1985, p. 164):

Juan, you know how to get a percent, but the computation is wrong in this instance. . . . Can you see where? (Teacher has underlined the location of errors.)

You know how to solve the problem—the formula is correct—but you have not demonstrated that you understand how one fraction multiplied by another can give an answer that is smaller than either $(\frac{1}{2} \times \frac{1}{2} = \frac{1}{4})$.

Extensive written comments may be inappropriate for younger students, but brief written comments are a different matter. These comments should help students correct errors and should recognize good work, progress, and increasing skill.

Guidelines

Minimizing the Detrimental Effects of Grading

Avoid reserving high grades and high praise for answers that conform to your ideas or to those in the textbook.

Examples

1. Give extra points for correct and creative answers.
2. Withhold your opinions until all sides of an issue have been explored.
3. Reinforce students for disagreeing in a rational, productive manner.
4. Give partial credit for partially correct answers.

Make sure each student has a reasonable chance to be successful, especially at the beginning of a new task.

Examples

1. Pretest students to make sure they have prerequisite abilities.
2. Individualize instruction based on pretest results.
3. When appropriate, provide opportunities for students to retest to raise their grades, but make sure the retest is as difficult as the original.

Balance written and oral feedback.

Examples

1. Consider giving short, lively written comments with younger students and more extensive written comments with older students.
2. When the grade on a paper is lower than the student might have expected, be sure the reason for the lower grade is clear.
3. Tailor comments to the individual student's performance; avoid writing the same phrases over and over.
4. Note specific errors, possible reasons for errors, ideas for improvement, and work done well.

Make grades as meaningful as possible.

Examples

1. Tie grades to the mastery of important objectives.
2. Give ungraded assignments to encourage exploration.
3. Experiment with performances and portfolios.

Base grades on more than just one criterion.

Examples

1. Use essay questions as well as multiple-choice items on a test.
2. Grade oral reports and class participation.

Grades and Motivation

Is there really a difference between working for a grade and working to learn? The answer depends in part on how a grade is determined. If grades are based on tests that require detailed memorization of facts, dates, and definitions, the students' study time will probably be spent learning these details. There will be little opportunity to explore the thought questions that may be found at the end of the chapter. But would students actually explore these questions if their work were not graded?

As a teacher, you can use grades to motivate the kind of learning you intend students to achieve in your course. If you test only at a simple but detailed level of knowledge, you may force students to choose between higher aspects of learning and a good grade. But when a grade reflects meaningful learning, working for a grade and working to learn become the same thing. The Guidelines above summarize the effects grades can have on students.

GRADING AND REPORTING: NUTS AND BOLTS

In determining a final grade, the teacher must make a major decision. Should a student's grade reflect the amount of material learned and how well it has been learned, or should the grade reflect the student's status in comparison with the rest of the class? In other words, should grading be criterion-referenced or norm-referenced?

Criterion-Referenced versus Norm-Referenced Grading

In **criterion-referenced grading,** the grade represents a list of accomplishments. If clear objectives have been set for the course, the grade may represent a certain number of objectives met satisfactorily. When a criterion-referenced system is used, criteria for each grade generally are spelled out in advance. It is then up to the student to earn the grade she or he wants to receive. Theoretically, in this system all students can achieve an A if they master the necessary number of specified objectives.

In **norm-referenced grading,** the major influence on a grade is the student's standing in comparison with others who also took the course. If a student studies very hard but almost everyone else does too, the student may receive a disappointing grade, perhaps a C.

Criterion-Referenced Systems. Criterion-referenced grading has the advantage of relating judgments about a student to the achievement of clearly defined instructional objectives. Some school districts have developed reporting systems where report cards list objectives along with judgments about the student's attainment of each. Reporting is done at the end of each unit of instruction. The junior high report card shown in Figure 15.4 on page 562 demonstrates the relationship between evaluation and the goals of the unit.

In practice, many school systems would look askance at a teacher who turned in a roster filled with A's and explained that all the students had obtained the course objectives. Administrators might say that if all the objectives could be so easily attained by all the students, then more or tougher objectives were needed. Nevertheless, a criterion-referenced system may be acceptable in some schools.

Norm-Referenced Systems. One very popular type of norm-referenced grading is **grading on the curve.** As noted in the previous chapter, the characteristics of the normal curve, or normal distribution, are well known. For example, we know that two-thirds of the distribution (68 percent) are clustered within 1 standard deviation of the mean. In grading on the curve, the middle of the normal distribution or "average" performance becomes the anchor on which grading is based. In other words, teachers look at the average level of performance, assign what they consider an "average grade" for this performance, and then grade superior performances higher and inferior performances lower.

If grading were done strictly on the normal curve, there would be an equal number of A's and F's, a larger number of B's and D's, and an even larger number of C's. The grades would have to form a bell-shaped curve. For example, a teacher might decide to give 10 percent A's and F's, 20

Criterion-Referenced Grading Assessment of each student's mastery of course objectives.

Norm-Referenced Grading Assessment of students' achievement in relation to one another.

Grading on the Curve Norm-referenced grading that compares students' performance to an average level.

FIGURE 15.4   **Criterion-Referenced Grades at the Secondary Level**   This is one example of a criterion-referenced report card. Other forms are possible, but all criterion-referenced reports indicate a student's progress toward specific goals.

JERICHO JUNIOR HIGH SCHOOL
JERICHO, NEW YORK

EVALUATION

Teacher _____   Student _____
Counselor _____   Dates (from) _____ (to) _____
Unit: Analogy as a Thought Process   Grade _____   Subject: English

Code: 1 The student has met the objective.
       2 The student has demonstrated progress toward meeting the objective.
       3 The student has not at this time met the objective.
       4 The student has not demonstrated whether or not the objective has been met.
       5 The objective does not apply at this time.

BASIC INFORMATION:
____ a. The student can identify comparisons that use *like, as, than*, and *is*.
____ b. The student can identify comparisons that do not use *like, as, than,* or *is*. *(The teacher threw the student out of class. Student = ball.)*
____ c. The student can recognize the similarity in two unlike items.

UNDERSTANDING:
____ a. The student can distinguish between the *is* of indentity and the *is* of comparison. *(I am John. I am a block of wood.)*
____ b. The student can distinguish between the literal sense of a poem and the meaning suggested by its imagery.

APPLICATION:
____ a. The student can compose original sentences that make a comparison without using words such as *like, as,* or *than*.
____ b. Given a comparison, the student can extend it into a paragraph.

percent B's and D's, and 40 percent C's. This is a very strict interpretation of grading on the curve, and it makes sense only if achievement in the class follows the normal curve.

Grading on the curve can be done with varying levels of precision. The simplest approach is to rank-order the students' raw scores on a test and use this ranked list of scores as the basis for assigning grades. Such a distribution might look like this: 92 91 91 90 83 80 78 76 72 68 65 61 57 54 53 49 48 47 46 43 38 36 29 29. Knowing that two-thirds of the scores in a normal distribution should be in the middle, you might bracket off the middle two-thirds of the scores and plan to give those students C's (or B's, if you believed B was an average grade for the class in question). Some people prefer to use the middle one-third of the students rather than the middle two-thirds as the basis for the average grade. Based on these two approaches, grades might be assigned as follows:

Middle Two-Thirds Assigned C's

A	B	C	D	F
92	91 91 90	83 80 78 76 72 68 65 61 57 54 53 49 48 47 46 43	38 36	29 29

Middle One-Third Assigned C's

A	B	C	D	F
92	91 91 90 83 80 78 76	72 68 65 61 57 54 53 49	48 47 46 43 38 36	29 29

This approximation to grading on the curve is very rough indeed. In these examples the distance between one letter grade and another is sometimes one point! Given the amount of error in testing, this assignment of grades is probably not fair. You can correct some of these problems by introducing common sense into the process. For example, you may believe the following grade assignment is fairer:

Adjusted Grades

A	B	C	D	F
92 91 91 90	83 80 78 76 72	68 65 61 57 54 53	49 48 47 46 43 38 36	29 29

In this case the instructor has used the natural gaps in the range of scores to locate boundaries between grades. Between the A and B categories are 7 points, between the B and C, 4 points, and so on.

Preparing Report Cards

Whatever grading system you use, you will undoubtedly give several tests. And you will probably assign homework or projects. Let's assume your unit evaluation plan includes two short tests (mostly multiple-choice questions with one essay), homework, a portfolio, and a unit test. If you use a criterion-referenced system for testing and grading, how will you convert scores on these individual performances to the overall indications of mastery on a report card such as that in Figure 15.4? What about using a norm-referenced system? How do you combine results from individual tests and assignments to yield a final distribution of scores for the unit grade?

Let us consider criterion-referenced grading first. If you adopt this system, you cannot average or combine test scores or homework grades in a mathematical way. Since each test and assignment measures the mastery of a particular objective (or set of objectives), it would be meaningless to average, say, the students' mastery of addition of two-digit numbers with their mastery of measurement with a ruler, although both might be objectives in arithmetic. On the report card, the various objectives are listed, and the student's level of proficiency in each is indicated.

Norm-referenced grading is a different story. In order to assign grades, the teacher must merge all the scores from tests and other assignments into one final score. Final grades are assigned based on how each student's final score compares with that of the rest of the students. But the usual procedure of simply adding up all the scores and averaging the total is often not appropriate, and it can be misleading. For example, assume two students took two tests. The tests are equally important in the overall unit. The students' scores are shown below (from Chase, 1978, p. 328).

	Test 1 Class mean = 30 Standard deviation = 8	Test 2 Class mean = 50 Standard deviation = 16	Total Raw score
Leslie	38	50	88
Jason	30	66	96

If we compute an average or if we rank the students based on their totals, Jason will be ahead of Leslie. But if we look at the class mean and standard deviation for each test, we see a different picture. On one test, Leslie's score was 1 standard deviation above the mean, and on the other her score was at the mean; Jason's record is exactly the same.

	Test 1	Test 2
Leslie	+ 1 SD	Mean
Jason	Mean	+1 SD

If these two tests are really equally important, Jason and Leslie have identical records in relation to the rest of the class on these tests. To compare students' performances on several tests, the scores for each must be converted to a standard scale like a T score. As you may recall from chapter 14, a T score is a standard score. The mean is automatically 50 and the standard deviation is 10. Most teachers do not calculate T scores for all their students, but the example illustrates the importance of using common sense in grading. Gross totals do not always reflect how well one student is doing in relation to others in the class.

The Point System

One popular system for combining grades from many assignments is a point system. Each test or assignment is given a certain number of total points, depending on its importance. A test worth 40 percent of the grade could be worth 40 points. A paper worth 20 percent could be worth 20 points. Points are then awarded on the test or paper based upon specific criteria. An A+ paper, one that meets all the criteria, could be given the full 20 points; an average paper might be given 10 points. If tests of comparable importance are worth the same number of points, are equally difficult, and cover a similar amount of material, we can expect to avoid

	Test 1 20% 20 points	Test 2 20% 20 points	Unit Test 30% 30 points	Homework 15% 15 points	Portfolio 15% 15 points	
Student						**Total**
Amy	10	12	16	6	7	___
Lee	12	10	14	7	6	___
Luis	20	19	30	15	13	___
Wayne	18	20	25	15	15	___
Étienne	6	5	12	4	10	___
Frieda	10	12	18	10	9	___
Grace	13	11	22	11	10	___
Houston	7	9	12	5	6	___
Isaac	14	16	26	12	12	___
Liz	20	18	28	10	15	___
Keith	19	20	25	11	12	___
Linda	14	12	20	13	9	___
Melody	15	13	24	8	10	___
Ned	8	7	12	8	6	___
Olivia	11	12	16	9	10	___
Peter	7	8	11	4	8	___

TABLE 15.4 Points Earned on Five Assignments

some of the problems encountered with Jason and Leslie, when the means and standard deviations of two supposedly comparable tests varied so greatly.

Let us assume a grade book indicates the scores shown in Table 15.4. How would you assign grades to students for this unit of work? Here are several possibilities:

1. Find the total number of points for each student and rank the students. Assign grades by looking for natural gaps of several points or imposing a curve (a certain percentage of A's, B's, and so on).

2. Convert each score to a percentage and average the percentages. Rank the students on percentages and proceed as above to look for gaps or impose a curve. Compare the results of this approach with the results of the one above.

3. Rank the students on each assignment. Then calculate each student's average rank for all five assignments. (If two students tie for one rank, they split the difference between that rank and the one below. For example, if two students tie for third place, they each get 3.5 and there is no fourth place.) Use the average rankings to determine overall ranks, then look for gaps or impose a curve on the overall ranks.

Percentage Grading

There is another approach to assigning grades to a group of students like those in Table 15.4. The teacher can assign grades based on how much knowledge each student has mastered—what percentage of the total knowledge he or she understands. To do this, the teacher might score tests and other classwork with percentage scores (based on how much is correct—50 percent, 85 percent, etc.) and then average these scores to reach a course score. These scores are converted into letter grades according to predetermined cutoff points. Then any number of students can earn any grade. This procedure is very common; you may have experienced it yourself as a student. Let us look at it more closely, because it has some frequently overlooked problems.

The grading symbols of A, B, C, D, and F are probably the most popular means of reporting at the present time. School systems often establish equivalent percentage categories for each of these symbols. The percentages vary from school district to school district, but two typical ones are as follows:

90–100% = A; 80–89% = B; 70–79% = C; 60–69% = D; below 60% = F

94–100% = A; 85–93% = B; 76–83% = C; 70–75% = D; below 70% = F

As you can see, although both districts have an A to F five-point grading system, the average achievement required for each grade is different.

But can we really say what is the total amount of knowledge available in, for example, eighth-grade science? Are we sure we can accurately measure what percentage of this body of knowledge each student has attained? To use **percentage grading** appropriately, we would have to know exactly what there was to learn and exactly how much of that each student *had* learned. These conditions are seldom met, even though teachers use the cutoff points to assign grades as if measurement were so accurate that a one-point difference was meaningful: "In spite of decades of research in educational and psychological measurement, which has produced more defensible methods, the concept [of percentage grading], once established, has proved remarkably resistant to change" (Zimmerman, 1981, p. 178).

Any grading system prescribed or suggested by the school can be influenced by particular concerns of the teacher. So don't be fooled by the seeming security of absolute percentages. Your own grading philosophy will continue to operate, even in this system. Because there is more concern today with specifying objectives and criterion-referenced evaluation, especially at the elementary-grade levels, several new methods for evaluating student progress against predetermined criteria have evolved. We will look at one: the contract system.

The Contract System

When applied to the whole class, the **contract system** indicates the type, quantity, and quality of work required for each number or letter grade in the system. Students agree or "contract" to work for particular grades by meeting the specified requirements. For example, the following standards might be established:

F: Not coming to class regularly or not turning in the required work.

D: Coming to class regularly and turning in the required work on time.

Percentage Grading
System of converting class performances to percentage scores and assigning grades based on predetermined cutoff points.

Contract System System in which each student agrees to work for a particular grade according to agreed-upon standards.

C: Coming to class regularly, turning in the required work on time, and receiving a check mark on all assignments to indicate they are satisfactory.

B: Coming to class regularly, turning in the required work on time, and receiving a check mark on all assignments except at least three that achieve a check-plus, indicating superior achievement.

A: As above, plus a successful oral or written report on one of the books listed for supplementary reading.

This example calls for more subjective judgment than would be ideal. However, contract systems reduce student anxiety about grades and can eliminate subjective judgment to whatever extent the teacher wants by specifying the quantity and quality required for various grades. The contract system can also be applied to individual students, in which case it functions much like an independent study plan.

Unfortunately, the system can also lead to overemphasis on quantity of work. Teachers may be too vague about the standards that differentiate acceptable from unacceptable work. It is sometimes difficult to tell a student that a particular assignment is completely unsatisfactory ("Is it that bad?"), so many teachers accept almost every piece of work. In addition, if a school system requires a five-point grading system and all students contract for and achieve the highest grade, the teacher will wish that the principal had approved the system *before* the grades came out.

A teacher can modify the contract system by including a **revise option.** For example, a check might be worth 75 points and a check-plus 90 points; a check-plus earned after revision could be worth 85 points— more than a check but less than a check-plus earned the first time around. This system allows students to improve their work but also rewards getting it right the first time. Some quality control is possible, since students earn points not just for quantity but also for quality. In addition, the teacher may be less reluctant to judge a project unsatisfactory since students can improve their work (King, 1979).

Grading on Effort and Improvement

Grading on effort and improvement is not really a complete grading system but rather a theme that can run through most grading methods. Should teachers grade students based on how much they learn or on the final level of learning? One problem with using improvement as a standard for grading is that the best students improve the least, since they are already the most competent. Do you want to penalize these students because they knew quite a bit initially and the teaching and testing have limited how much learning they can demonstrate? After all, unless you assign extra work, these students will run out of things to do.

One solution is to use the **individual learning expectation (ILE)** system described on page 378. With this system students earn improvement points on tests or assignments for scoring above their personal base (average) score in that subject or for making a perfect score. The teacher can count these improvement points when figuring a final grade or simply use them as a basis for giving other classroom rewards.

Most teachers display student work, but often the same students' work is always chosen. One way to avoid this problem is to ask each student to pick his or her "best" or "most improved" work, then display these selections.

Revise Option In a contract system, the chance to revise and improve work.

Individual Learning Expectation (ILE) Personal average score.

Guidelines

Using Any Grading System

Explain your grading policies to students early in the course and remind them of the policies regularly.

Examples

1. Give older students a handout describing the assignments, tests, grading criteria, and schedule.
2. Explain to younger students in a low-pressure manner how their work will be evaluated.

Set reasonable standards.

Examples

1. Discuss workload and grading standards with more experienced teachers.
2. Give a few formative tests to get a sense of your students' abilities before you give a graded test.
3. Take tests yourself first to gauge the difficulty of the test and to estimate the time your students will need.

Base your grades on as much objective evidence as possible.

Examples

1. Plan in advance how and when you will test.
2. Keep a portfolio of student work. This may be useful in student or parent conferences.

Be sure students understand test directions.

Examples

1. Outline the directions on the board.
2. Ask several students to explain the directions.
3. Go over a sample question first.

Correct, return, and discuss test questions as soon as possible.

Examples

1. Have students who wrote good answers read their responses for the class; make sure they are not the same students each time.
2. Discuss why wrong answers, especially popular wrong choices, are incorrect.
3. As soon as students finish a test, give them the answers to questions and the page numbers where answers are discussed in the text.

As a rule, do not change a grade.

Examples

1. Make sure you can defend the grade in the first place.
2. DO change any clerical or calculation errors.

Guard against bias in grading.

Examples

1. Ask students to put their names on the backs of their papers.
2. Use an objective point system or model papers when grading essays.

Keep pupils informed of their standing in the class.

Examples

1. Write the distribution of scores on the board after tests.
2. Schedule periodic conferences to go over work from previous weeks.

Give students the benefit of the doubt. All measurement techniques involve error.

Examples

1. Unless there is very good reason not to, give the higher grade in borderline cases.
2. If a large number of students miss the same question in the same way, revise the question for the future and consider throwing it out for that test.

Source: Adapted by permission of the author from A. M. Drayer (1979), *Problems in middle and high school teaching: A handbook for student teachers and beginning teachers.* Boston: Allyn and Bacon, pp. 182–187. Reprinted with permission of Allyn and Bacon.

Dual Marking System
System of assigning two grades, one reflecting achievement, the other effort, attitude, and actual ability.

Many teachers try to include some judgment of effort in final grades. But effort is difficult to assess. Are you certain your perception of each student's effort is correct? Clement (1978) suggests a system for including a judgment about effort in the final grade called the **dual marking system.** Students are assigned two grades. One (usually a letter) indicates the actual level of achievement. The other, a number, indicates the relation-ship of the achievement to the student's ability and effort. For example, a grade of B could be qualified as follows (Clement, 1978, p. 51):

B_1: Outstanding effort, better achievement than expected, good attitude

B_2: Average effort, satisfactory in terms of ability

B_3: Lower achievement than ability would indicate, poor attitude

Of course, this system assumes that the teacher can adequately judge true ability and effort. A grade of D_1, D_2, or F_2 could be quite insulting. A grade of A_3 or F_1 should not be possible. But the system does have the advantage of recognizing hard work and giving feedback about a seeming lack of effort. An A_2 might tell very bright students: "You're doing well, but I know you could do better." This could help the students to expect more of themselves and not slip by on high ability. The overall grade—A, B, C—still reflects achievement and is not changed (or biased) by teachers' subjective judgment of effort.

Cautions: Being Fair

The attributions a teacher makes about the causes of student successes or failures can affect the grades that students receive. Teachers are more likely to give higher grades for effort (a controllable factor) than for ability (an uncontrollable factor). Lower grades are more likely when teachers attribute a student's failure to lack of effort instead of to lack of ability (Weiner, 1979). It is also possible that grades can be influenced by a **halo effect**—that is, by the tendency to view particular aspects of a student based on a general impression, either positive or negative. As a teacher, you may find it difficult to avoid being affected by positive and negative halos. A very pleasant student who seems to work hard and causes little trouble may be given the benefit of the doubt (B– instead of C+), whereas a very difficult student who seems to refuse to try might be a loser at grading time (D instead of C–). The Guidelines on page 568 give ideas for using any grading system in a fair and reasonable way.

BEYOND GRADING: COMMUNICATION

No number or letter grade conveys the totality of a student's experience in a class or course. Both students and teachers sometimes become too focused on the end point—the grade. But children and adolescents spend the majority of their waking hours for many months of the year in school, where teachers are the relevant adults; and this gives teachers the oppor-tunity and the responsibility to know their students as people.

Conferences with parents are often expected of teachers in elemen-tary school and can be equally important in junior high and high school. At every level, the success of the conference depends on a number of factors. At the simplest level, both parties must be present. Schedule conferences at a time convenient for parents and confirm appointments in writing or by phone.

Clearly, the more skilled teachers are at communicating, the more effective they will be at conducting these conferences. Listening and

"I hope this isn't another ploy to up your grade, Haskell."

How would you evaluate Haskell's "effort"?
© Art Bouthillier.

Halo Effect Tendency for a general impression of a person to influence our perception of any aspect of that person.

problem-solving skills such as those discussed in chapter 11 can be particularly important. Especially when dealing with parents or students who are angry or upset, make sure you really hear the *concerns* of the participants, not just their words.

The conference should not be a time for lecturing parents or students. As the professional, the teacher needs to take a leadership role while remaining sensitive to the needs of the other participants. The atmosphere should be friendly and unrushed. Any observations about the student should be as factual as possible, based on observation or information from assignments. Information gained from a student or a parent alone should be kept confidential. Table 15.5 offers some helpful ideas for planning and conducting conferences.

TABLE 15.5 Conducting a Successful Parent-Teacher Conference

Plan ahead.

What are your goals?
Problem solving?
Sharing test results?
Asking questions that you want answered?
Providing information you want to share? Emphasize the positive.
Describing your "next steps" in the classroom?
Making suggestions for use at home?

Begin with a positive statement.

"Howard has a great sense of humor."
"Giselle really enjoys materials that deal with animals."
"Sandy is sympathetic when somebody has a problem."

Listen actively.

Empathize with the parents.
Accept their feelings: "You seem to feel frustrated when Lee doesn't listen."

Establish a partnership.

Ask parents to follow through on class goals at home: "If you ask to see the homework checklist and go over it at home with Iris, I'll review it and chart her progress at school."

Plan follow-up contacts.

Write notes or make phone calls to share successes.
Keep parents informed *before* problems develop.

End with a positive statement.

"José has made several friends this year."
"Courtney should be a big help in the social studies play that a group is developing."

Source: Adapted by permission from D. P. Fromberg & M. Driscoll (1985), *The successful classroom: Management strategies for regular and special education teachers.* New York: Teachers College Press, p. 181.

An important federal law, the Buckley Amendment, is likely to have an effect on you as a teacher. Also called the Family Educational Rights and Privacy Act of 1974 and the Educational Amendments Act of 1974, this law states that all educational agencies must make test results and any other information in students' records available to the students and/or their parents. If the records contain information students or parents believe is incorrect, they can challenge such entries and have the information removed if they win the challenge. This means that the information in a student's records must be based on firm, defensible evidence. Tests must be valid and reliable. Your grades must be justified by thorough testing and observation. Comments and anecdotes about students must be accurate and fair.

SUMMARY

FORMATIVE AND SUMMATIVE ASSESSMENT

Two important and challenging tasks for teachers are assessing students and assigning grades. Many schools have established policies about testing and grading practices, but individual teachers decide how these practices will be carried out. In the classroom, assessment may be formative (ungraded, diagnostic) or summative (graded). Formative assessment helps form instruction, and summative assessment summarizes students' accomplishments.

GETTING THE MOST FROM TRADITIONAL ASSESSMENT APPROACHES

Assessment requires planning. Teachers can use a behavior-content matrix to plan tests so that test questions match course objectives. With the goals of assessment in mind, teachers are in a better position to design their own tests or evaluate the tests provided by textbook publishers.

Two traditional formats for testing are the objective test and the essay test. Objective tests, which can include multiple-choice, true-false, fill-in, and matching items, should be written with specific guidelines in mind. Writing and scoring essay questions requires careful planning plus criteria to discourage bias in scoring.

INNOVATIONS IN ASSESSMENT

Critics of traditional testing believe that teachers should use authentic tests and other authentic assessment procedures. This approach requires students to perform tasks and solve problems that are similar to the real-life performances that will be expected of students outside of school. Portfolios and exhibitions are two examples of authentic assessment.

EFFECTS OF GRADES AND GRADING ON STUDENTS

Students need experience in coping with failure, so standards must be high enough to encourage effort. Occasional failure can be positive if appropriate feedback is provided. Grades can encourage students' motivation to learn if grades are tied to meaningful learning.

GRADING AND REPORTING: NUTS AND BOLTS

Grading can be either criterion-referenced or norm-referenced. Criterion-referenced report cards usually indicate how well each of several objectives has been met by the individual student. One popular norm-referenced system is grading on the curve, based on a ranking of students in relation to the average performance level.

Tests and papers are often scored on a point system. Many schools use percentage grading systems, but the difficulty of the tests and the scoring criteria often influence the results. The difference between a B and a C may only be a matter of one or two points on paper, but the effect of the difference can be large for a student.

Alternatives to traditional grading are the contract, ILE, and dual marking approaches. Whatever system you use, you will have to decide whether you want to grade on effort, improvement, or some combination and whether you want to limit the number of good grades available.

Many factors besides quality of work can influence grades: the teacher's beliefs about the student's ability or effort or the student's general classroom behavior, for example.

BEYOND GRADING: COMMUNICATION

Not every communication from the teacher needs to be tied to a grade. Communication with students and parents can be important in helping a teacher understand students and create effective instruction. Students and parents have a legal right to see all the information in the students' records.

KEY TERMS AND CONCEPTS

authentic tests, p. 551

contract system, p. 566

criterion-referenced grading,
  p. 561

data-based instruction, p. 542

diagnostic test, p. 542

distractors, p. 547

dual marking system, p. 568

exhibition, p. 555

formative assessment, p. 542

grading on the curve, p. 561

halo effect, p. 569

holistic scoring, p. 549

individual learning expectation
  (ILE), p. 567

norm-referenced grading, p. 561

objective testing, p. 545

percentage grading, p. 566

portfolio, p. 554

pretest, p. 542

revise option, p. 567

stem, p. 547

summative assessment, p. 543

WHAT WOULD YOU DO?

PRESCHOOL AND KINDERGARTEN

The parents of several children in your class want a report about how their daughters and sons are "progressing" in preschool. How would you respond to their requests? What kind of assessment and reporting would be helpful for your young students?

ELEMENTARY AND MIDDLE SCHOOL

Your school requires that you give letter grades to your fourth-grade students. How would you determine these letter grades?

During a parent-teacher conference, a mother and father accuse you of playing favorites and giving their child low grades "just because he's different." How would you respond?

JUNIOR HIGH AND HIGH SCHOOL

Several students are very unhappy with the grades on their term projects. They come to you for an explanation and to try to get you to raise their grades. What would you do?

Your school requires percentage grading, but you would prefer a different system. How would you make a case for your alternative?

COOPERATIVE LEARNING ACTIVITY

With four or five other members of your educational psychology class, plan how you would use portfolios in your teaching. What would be the content? How would you evaluate the work and give students feedback?

TEACHERS' CASEBOOK

If you could choose any method of grading your students or giving feedback on their performance, what would you do?

INFORMAL FEEDBACK

Students thrive on positive input from respected adults. Therefore, analyzing an assignment and discussing it would result in the greatest achievement. Unfortunately, we do not provide resources in public education that permit such intensive evaluation techniques.

Many times informal feedback can be very effective. Too often we assign a grade but fail to really communicate a genuine interest in the work submitted. Taking time to recognize extended effort or a particularly good thought process may create more incentive to excel. Simply assigning letter grades or numerical values can hinder academic growth and probably never has more than a neutral effect on student achievement.

Marc Gray, *Science Teacher*
Highland Middle School, Louisville, Kentucky

DEPENDS ON SUBJECT

The appropriate form of feedback depends on the subject matter. For math skills, constant checking works well. For problem solving, group discussion with justifications is beneficial. For content areas, I prefer the tell-me-all-you-know method. For reading and language, conferencing works well. The teacher can better understand the pupil if they discuss and share ideas.

Jan Reynolds, *Fifth-Grade Teacher*
Fredericktown Intermediate School, Fredericktown, Ohio

A BLESSING AND A CURSE

Evaluating student performance is both the blessing and the curse of teaching. Evaluation allows a teacher to measure the progress his/her class has made, to quantify the growth in their development, and to publicize the results of their labors. However, teacher evaluation can also shatter egos, stunt intellectual curiosity, and promote unnatural competition among students. Although grading is a pitfall-filled process for even veteran teachers, it is also a necessary component of education. My dream evaluation system would allow me to offer my students individual feedback based on each one's unique abilities, competencies, and needs. Sometimes the feedback would be oral, sometimes written. Both would rely heavily on close observation of the student's performance in independent and group work. Instead of arbitrary grades, anecdotal entries would allow me to comment on individual progress. However, human beings do not seem to work well in a vacuum. For this reason, I believe some group evaluation measures in which all students attempt to demonstrate the same task or exhibit the same knowledge in a competitive manner is also necessary. Students need to measure their progress against each other in order to ascertain growth. Letter grades, although useful in classifying students and awarding scholarships, are not really adequate indicators of student achievement. If students are to assume responsibility for their own learning, they must feel that they are viewed as individuals, not just as letters in a gradebook.

Jane C. Dusell, *English Teacher*
Medford Area Senior High School, Medford, Wisconsin

CONFERENCE AND PROGRESS REPORTS

I would use frequent individual student conferences as well as in-depth written progress reports. In both cases students are made aware of the areas in which they are doing well and those in which they are having difficulty. A plan is developed between

574

student and teacher to specify ways to improve. Parents receive a copy of the progress report and the improvement plan. Advantages include student involvement, especially in the designing of improvement plans, and parental notification in a form more detailed than just a letter grade.

Carol Gibbs, *Sixth-Grade Teacher*
Happy Valley School, Rossville, Georgia

BE HONEST, BE FAIR

I'm not sure there is an ideal grading system. Children are very sharp. They know how they are doing before we ever try to evaluate them. The best way to evaluate children is to be honest and fair with them.

In the primary grades, I evaluate children on their performance at their levels of ability and maturity. I let parents know that "at this level (above, below, or at grade level), your child is doing this." This way, even the child who is performing below grade level can be acknowledged for effort and progress.

In the upper grades, you need a more sophisticated and formal grading system, but one that the students understand. It must be one that does not defeat them before they start. Since we all have good days and bad days, perhaps we could give students an option of selecting five of their best pieces of work in a unit or eliminating the lowest grade on one or two out of five papers.

Carolyn R. Cook, *Kindergarten Teacher*
Ramona Elementary School, Ramona, California

INTERPRETING SCORES FOR STUDENTS AND PARENTS

You have just given a 50-item final exam. One of your students gets only 35 items correct—a score well below the average for the class. On your scale the 35 is a D, but the student and the student's parents are upset. They argue that 35 out of 50 is 70 percent and should be a C. What do you say to them?

STANDARDS ARE IMPORTANT

Parents need to feel confident that the teacher is concerned for the best interest of their child. Confrontation and strong words never bring consensus; thus, the classroom teacher must maintain her/his composure and explain that mastery of skills and concepts is vital. The teacher should explain that she or he cannot change the test grade without lowering her/his expectations and standards.

Perhaps a schedule of activities could be set up to help the student practice skills and review concepts, so that mastery might be achieved. Parents need to understand that grades mean nothing unless they represent some meaningful standard.

Darlene A. Walsh, *Rhode Island 1991 Teacher of the Year*
Greenbush Elementary School, West Warwick, Rhode Island

SHOWING THE EVIDENCE

I would show all the scores in the class—numbers only, without any names—to the parents and student. I would explain which scores are A's, B's, C's, and so on and point out that 35 right answers out of a possible 50 was just not an average grade or C on this particular test. I think the parents and student need to *see* the scores of the entire class. In this case, a picture is worth a thousand words.

Louise Harrold Melucci, *Fourth-Grade Teacher*
Greenwood School, Warwick, Rhode Island

APPENDIX: RESEARCH IN EDUCATIONAL PSYCHOLOGY

In order to achieve a better understanding of educational psychology you must know how information in the field is created and how to judge the information you encounter. In this appendix we will explore the value and limitations of research, the major road to knowledge in educational psychology. Then we will examine a specific problem to determine how research might answer questions posed by teachers. Finally, we will describe how to judge a research study by evaluating a real experiment.

ASKING AND ANSWERING QUESTIONS

To get a better understanding of a few of the basic methods for asking and answering questions in educational psychology, we can examine a question that may interest you: Do students' expectations about the competence of a new teacher influence the way the students behave toward the teacher? To be more specific, do students pay more attention to a teacher they expect to be good? Suppose, for our purposes here, that an educational psychologist decided to look for an answer to this question. What methods might be used to gather information?

Forming a Research Question

The first step might be to frame a clear and specific question. In this case, we might begin with something like this: Do students' beliefs about a teacher's competence affect the amount of attention they pay to the teacher? Notice how specific the wording is. We will have problems if the question is too vague—for example, Do students' beliefs about a teacher affect the way they behave in class? There is too much territory to cover in answering the question. We need to be specific about what kinds of beliefs—beliefs about the teacher's competence, not age, intelligence, or marital status. And we need to be specific about what kind of behavior—attention to the teacher, not enthusiasm for the subject or anxiety about a new year.

Choosing Variables and Selecting Measurement Techniques

At this point we are ready to identify the variables to be studied. A **variable** is any characteristic of a person or environment that can change under different conditions or that can differ from one person to the next. In our hypothetical study, we have decided to examine two variables—student beliefs about the teacher's competence and student attention to the teacher.

The next thing we must do is decide how we will define what we mean by *beliefs* and *attention*. This question leads to the issue of measurement, because our definitions will be useful only if they give us something we can measure.

To study any variable systematically, there must be a way to measure changes or compare different levels of the variable. To simplify matters, let us concentrate at this point on just one of the variables—student attention. We will need to find a way to measure the degree of attention shown by the students. The method chosen will depend in part on the design of the study and on the limitations imposed by the situation. Here we will look at four basic approaches to measurement: (1) self-report, (2) direct observation, (3) testing, and (4) teacher or peer ratings.

Using the **self-report** method, we could ask the students questions about how attentive they thought they were being. Answers could be given in writing or face to face, in an interview with the students.

If we decided instead to use **direct observation,** we could send researchers into the classroom to watch the students and assess their attention. These investigators might simply rate the students (on a scale of one to five, perhaps, from very attentive to very inattentive), or they could use a stopwatch to count the number of seconds each student watched the teacher. Observers could also work from a videotape of the class, replaying the tape several times so that each student could be observed and his or her level of attention rechecked. These are only a few of the systems that could be designed using observers to measure attention.

A **test** would be a little more difficult to construct in this case. Many variables are measured with tests, especially those involving learning or achievement. But since attention is a process rather than a product, it is difficult to design a test to measure it. One approach, however, would be to use a "vigilance task." We could see if the students were paying attention by having the teacher give an unpredictable signal, such as "Stand up," during the lesson. The measure of attention in this case would be the number of people who stood up immediately (Woolfolk & Woolfolk, 1974).

Finally, we might decide to use **teacher ratings** or **peer ratings.** We could measure attention by asking the teacher or the students to rate the attention of every student in the class.

Clearly, each of these approaches has advantages and disadvantages. Using self-reports or ratings of teachers or peers means relying on the judgments of the participants themselves. Using observers or tests can be disruptive to the class, at least initially. Videotaping is difficult and expensive. Let us assume, however, that we have chosen direct observation from videotapes. We will train the observers to time student attention with a stopwatch to

Variable Any characteristic that can vary.

Self-Report Research method where subjects respond directly to questions.

Direct Observation Method where researchers watch and record behavior without any intervention.

Test Series of questions or tasks for measuring a variable.

Teacher Ratings Teacher evaluations of students on a given variable.

Peer Ratings Student evaluations of one another on a given variable.

determine how many seconds each student looks at the teacher during a 10-minute lesson. Note that our system of measurement has given us our definition of attention: the number of seconds each student looks at the teacher during a 10-minute lesson. This seems to offer a reasonably good definition. If the measurement system did not offer a good definition, we would need to find another way of measuring.

To define and measure our first variable—students' beliefs about the teacher's competence—we could also choose from a number of methods. Let us assume, at least for the time being, that we have selected a rating system. Students' answers to the question "How competent do you think this teacher is?" should give us a good idea of student opinion.

One other definition may be in order here, although in this particular study it seems rather obvious. Since we will be studying student beliefs and student attentiveness, the subjects in our investigation will be students. As you probably know, **subjects** is the term for the people (or animals) whose behavior is being measured. We would want to specify the grade, sex, and type of student to be studied. For our hypothetical study, we will select male and female sixth graders in a predominantly middle-class school.

Stating a Hypothesis and Choosing an Approach

At this point we have our research question, the variables to be studied, the definition of these variables, the system for measuring them, and the subjects to be studied. We are now ready to add two new details: a **hypothesis** or guess about the relationship between the two variables, and a decision about what kind of approach we will use in our study. To some extent, the hypothesis will dictate the approach.

At the most general level, there are two approaches to answering research questions. The first is to describe the events and relationships in a particular situation as they take place in real life. The second approach is to change one aspect of a situation and note the effects of the change. These two approaches are generally called *descriptive* and *experimental.*

A Descriptive Approach. One hypothesis we might establish in our study of student beliefs and attention is that students pay more attention to a teacher they believe to be competent. To test this hypothesis, we could go into several sixth-grade classrooms and ask students to rate their teachers on competence. Ideally, we would conduct the study in a middle school where sixth graders usually have more than one teacher each day. We could then observe the students and measure their level of attention to each teacher. At this point we could get some idea about whether the two variables—believing that a teacher is competent and paying attention to that teacher—go together.

Let's assume, for the sake of the argument, that the two variables do go together. What we have now is a **correlation.** If two variables tend to occur together, they are correlated. We have just assumed such a correlation between beliefs and attention. Other variables that are often correlated are height and weight, income and education, and colder temperatures and falling leaves. A taller person, for example, is likely to weigh more than a shorter person. A richer person is likely to have completed more years of education than a poorer person. And, for the sake of the argument, we are now assuming that a student who believes a teacher to be competent is more likely to pay attention to that teacher.

Subjects People or animals studied.

Hypothesis Prediction or assumption that provides the basis for investigation.

Correlation Statistical description of how closely two variables are related.

But what does this correlation give us? If educational psychologists know that two variables are correlated, they can then make predictions about one of the variables based on knowledge of the other variable. For example, because the IQ scores of parents and children are correlated, educators can predict a child's IQ based on that of the mother or father. The prediction may not be correct every time, because the correlation between parents' IQs and children's IQs is not perfect. But the prediction is likely to be correct or nearly correct much more often than a prediction based on no information at all. Several studies have found a correlation between a teacher's enthusiasm and student learning. If we have information about a teacher's enthusiasm, we can make a prediction about the achievement level of the students in his or her class.

This last example brings us to a very important point about correlation and prediction, mentioned briefly in chapter 1. Knowing that two variables tend to occur together does not tell us that one variable is actually *causing* the other. Although enthusiastic teachers may tend to have students who achieve more than the students of unenthusiastic teachers, we cannot say that teacher enthusiasm leads to or causes student achievement. We know only that teacher enthusiasm and student achievement tend to occur together. Perhaps teaching students who are achieving more makes a teacher more enthusiastic. Perhaps a third factor—the interesting materials a teacher has chosen to work with, for example—causes both teacher enthusiasm and student achievement.

Although being able to predict levels of one variable from information about levels of another is useful, teachers are often interested in finding out what factors actually *will* cause a desired change in behavior. For this, they would need a different kind of research—research based on experimental manipulation.

An Experimental Approach. Returning to our original question about student beliefs and attention, suppose we made a different hypothesis. Rather than just hypothesizing that student attention and beliefs about teacher competence go together, we could hypothesize that one of the factors actually causing students to pay attention is the belief that a teacher is competent. In this case, the hypothesis states a causal relationship. To test this hypothesis, we must change one of the variables to see if this change actually causes changes in the other variable. In our study, this assumed cause—known as the **independent variable**—is the belief that the teacher is competent. The purpose of our experiment will be to see if changes in this variable really cause changes in the other variable—the **dependent variable** of student attention to the teacher.

Assume that we create three comparable groups of students by randomly assigning the students to the groups. Since the selection and assignment of students to groups is totally **random**—by chance, based on no particular plan—the three groups should be very similar.

We then tell one group of students that the teacher they are about to meet is a "very good" teacher; we tell the second group that the teacher they will have is "not a very good" teacher; and we tell the third group nothing about the teacher they are going to have. This final group serves as the **control group**. It will give us information about what happens when there is no experimental manipulation. At some point in the experiment we would ask the students what they believed about the teacher to make sure they had accepted the description they were given.

Independent Variable
Variable changed to determine its effects on other variables.

Dependent Variable
Variable measured to determine if its changes are results of changes in the independent variable.

Random Without any definite pattern; following no rule.

Control Group Subjects receiving no special treatment and serving as a basis for comparison.

Next, the teacher, actually the same person in all three cases, teaches the same lesson to each group. Of course the teacher should not be told about the experimental manipulation. We videotape the students in each group as they listen to the teacher. Later, raters viewing the tapes measure the number of seconds each student in the three groups has looked at the teacher. (You may have noticed that although the definition and measurement of the attention variable remain the same as they were in the descriptive study, the definition and measurement of the belief variable have changed. As you can see, such a change is necessary to turn the study into an experiment.)

What kind of results can we expect? If we find that students who believed the teacher was competent paid attention most of the time, students who believed the teacher was not very good paid very little attention, and students who were given no information paid a moderate amount of attention, have we proved our hypothesis? No! In psychology and in educational psychology it is assumed that hypotheses are never really proven by one study, because each study tests the hypothesis in only one specific situation. Hypotheses are "supported" but never proven by the positive results of a single study. Have we supported the hypothesis that student beliefs affect student attention? The answer to this question depends on how well we designed and carried out the study.

Since this is just a hypothetical study, we can assume, once again for the sake of the argument, that we did everything just right. If you read the following list of requirements for a "true experiment," set forth by Van Mondrans, Black, Keysor, Olsen, Shelley, and Williams (1977), you will see that we were indeed on the right track:

> The "true experiment" is usually defined as one in which the investigator can (a) manipulate at least one independent variable; (b) randomly select and assign subjects to experimental treatments; and (c) compare the treatment group(s) with one or more control groups on at least one dependent variable. (p. 51)

With a real experiment, however, we would need to know more about exactly how every step of the investigation was conducted. And we would also want to know whether other researchers could come up with the same results if they did the same experiment.

IS THE RESEARCH VALID?

Being able to evaluate research studies has a dual payoff. The kind of thinking needed is in and of itself valuable. It is the same kind of thinking needed to evaluate any complex idea, plan, argument, or project. In all these cases, you need to search for errors, oversights, inconsistencies, or alternative explanations. The analytical ability necessary to evaluate research is useful in any occupation, from law to business to motorcycle maintenance. The second payoff is more specifically valuable for teachers. As an educator, you will have to evaluate research done in your school district or reported in professional journals to determine if the findings are relevant to your own situation.

To be valid, the results of an experiment must pass several tests. Changes in the dependent variable must be due solely to the manipulation of the independent variable. In the following pages, we will look at eight questions that can be asked in an evaluation of a research experiment.

1. *Were the groups to be studied reasonably equal before the experiment began?* If the subjects vary greatly from group to group, any changes found at the end of the experiment may be the results of the original differences in the groups and not of changes in the independent variable. Random assignment of subjects to groups usually takes care of this problem. If instead of randomly selecting the subjects in our own study we had used three different sixth-grade classes, our results would be questionable. Maybe one class already had more generally attentive students. Had they been given the teacher labeled "very good" in the experiment, their high degree of attention would have been relatively meaningless. With random selection from a number of sixth-grade classes, however, each group is likely to have gotten an equal share of the generally attentive and generally inattentive students.

2. *Were all the variables except the independent variable controlled so that the only real difference in the treatment of each group was the change in the independent variable?* We have just seen that the subjects in each group must be equivalent. This principle is equally true of everything else in the experiment. If different procedures were used with each group, it would be difficult to determine which of the differences caused the results. In our study, for example, if we had used different teachers or different lessons in each group, we would have run into this problem in evaluating the results. The students' attention to the teacher could have been based on many things other than the initial statement given by the experimenter about the teacher's competence (the independent variable).

3. *Were the measurement procedures applied consistently to each group?* Unreliable results may at times be caused by an inconsistent measurement system. In our study, if we had used a different videotape rater for each group, we could not have trusted our results. Perhaps one rater would give credit for student attention when students had their faces pointed toward the teacher even if their bodies were turned away. Perhaps another rater would give credit only if the students' entire bodies were directed toward the teacher. Ideally, one rater should make all the measurements. If more are used, there must be some test of the raters' ability to agree on the results. One way to check this would be to see if they agreed when measuring the same students' behaviors.

4. *Are the results of the study due to the experimental procedures rather than to the novelty of the situation?* It is always possible that subjects will respond in some special way to any change, at least temporarily. This possibility was pointed out dramatically by studies conducted at the Western Electric Plant in Hawthorne, Illinois. Investigators were trying to determine which changes in the plant environment would lead to greater worker productivity. As it turned out, everything they tried, every change in the working conditions, seemed to lead to greater productivity, at least for a while (Roethlisberger & Dickson, 1939). In other words, the workers were reacting not to the actual changes but to something new happening. Because the experiment took place in Hawthorne, Illinois, such results are now said to be examples of the **Hawthorne effect.** Our control group helped us avoid this problem. Although the independent variable of a "good" or "bad" teacher label was not applied to the control group, these students were given the special treatment of being in an experiment. If

Hawthorne Effect Change resulting from subjects' knowledge that they are being studied.

their attention ratings had been particularly high, we might have suspected the Hawthorne effect for all three groups.

5. *Has the investigator who designed the study biased the results in any way?* There are numerous obvious and subtle ways in which an investigator can influence the participants in an experiment. The investigator may have no intention of doing so but may still communicate to the subjects what he or she expects them to do in a given situation (Rosenthal, 1976). In our study, for example, if the investigator had told the teacher involved what the purpose of the experiment was, the teacher might have expected less attention from one of the groups and unintentionally done something to increase or decrease the attention actually given. If the investigator had told the videotape raters the purpose of the experiment, the same thing might have happened. Without meaning to, they might have looked harder for attention in one of the groups. In order to eliminate these problems, both teacher and raters would have to be unaware of the independent variable that was being studied.

6. *Is it reasonably certain that the results did not occur simply by chance?* To answer this question, researchers use statistics. The general agreement is that differences among the groups can be considered "significant" if these differences could have occurred by chance only 5 times out of 100. In reading a research report, you might see the results stated in the following manner: "The difference between the groups was significant ($p < .05$)." Unless you are planning to do your own scientific research, the most important part of this is probably the word *significant.* The mathematical statement means that the probability (p) of such a difference occurring by chance factors alone is less than ($<$) 5 in 100 (.05).

7. *Will the findings in this particular study be likely to fit other, similar situations?* This is really a question of generalization. How similar does a new situation have to be to get the same results? Consider our own experiment. Would we get similar results (a) with much older or younger students? (b) with students who are more or less intelligent? (c) with students who already know the teacher? (d) with different teachers or different lessons? (e) with the removal of videotape cameras? (f) with a lesson that lasts more than 10 minutes?

We cannot answer these questions until the study has been repeated with many different subjects in many different situations. This brings us to the question of **replication.**

8. *Has the study been replicated?* A study has been replicated if it has been repeated and the same results are found. Replication may involve exactly the same study conditions, or it may involve changes in conditions that will give us a better idea of the extent to which the findings can be applied to other situations. If results have been replicated in well-designed studies, the findings form the basis for principles and laws.

Since our own study was only hypothetical, we cannot get a replication of it. But we can look at a similar study done by Feldman and Prohaska (1979). Analyzing this study should be useful to you in two ways. First, it will provide a model for considering other research articles you will find in textbooks and in professional journals. Second, the results of the study itself will probably be of interest because they suggest ways in which student expectations may cause teachers to be more or less effective.

Replication Repetition of a research study to see if the same results are obtained.

A SAMPLE STUDY: THE EFFECT OF STUDENT EXPECTATIONS

Feldman and Prohaska's 1979 study concerns student expectations about a teacher's competence and the effect of these expectations on the students' and the teacher's behavior. (Remember that we were looking only at student behavior in our hypothetical study.) You may want to read the study in the *Journal of Educational Psychology* (vol. 71, no. 4, 1979). At the beginning of the article you will find specific information: the names of the authors, the university where they work, the name of the article, the name of the journal, and the basic facts about the study. The basic facts describing the design and results of the study are usually included in a brief summary, called an **abstract,** found at the beginning of such an article.

Essential Data

The subjects in Feldman and Prohaska's first experiment were undergraduate female volunteers from an introductory psychology class. Each subject was randomly assigned to a positive-expectation group or a negative-expectation group, but was not told which group she was in.

Each subject arrived separately at the experimental center and was told she would have to wait a few minutes before she could see the teacher. While she waited, she met another student who had supposedly just been working with the teacher and was now completing a questionnaire evaluating the teacher. Actually, this student, a male, was a **confederate** of the experimenter—an assistant pretending to be one of the subjects. The confederate played one of two roles, depending on whether he was meeting a subject from the positive-expectation group or the negative-expectation group. (The subjects, of course, did not know what group they were in.) When the confederate met a subject from the positive group, he told her the teacher had been really good, effective, and friendly. He then gave her a completed questionnaire (which also said good things about the teacher) and asked her to turn it in for him, since he had to leave. When the confederate met a subject from the negative group, he said very uncomplimentary things about the teacher and gave the subject a questionnaire with very negative comments on it.

The subject then went into a room and met the teacher, who was the same person for both groups. The teacher did not know the subject had been given any expectations at all. While she was teaching two minilessons, she and the subject were secretly videotaped. After the two lessons, the subject took a short quiz on the material and filled out a questionnaire just like the one she had seen the confederate completing. The same procedure was repeated for each subject.

Finally, the videotapes of all the subjects were shown to trained coders who were unaware of the actual experimental conditions. These coders measured three things: (1) percentage of time each subject looked at the teacher, (2) each subject's forward body lean toward the teacher, and (3) each subject's general body orientation toward the teacher. Taken together, these student behaviors could be called paying attention. When the coders rated the same subject's videotape, their ratings of the three behaviors were highly correlated. Thus we can assume that the coders agreed about how to use the measurement technique.

Results showed that the subjects who expected the teacher to be "bad" rated the lesson as significantly more difficult, less interesting, and less

Abstract Brief summary of a study's key procedures and results.

Confederate Assistant pretending to be a subject in an experiment.

effective than the subjects who expected the teacher to be "good." They also found the teacher to be less competent, less intelligent, less likable, and less enthusiastic than the other subjects did. Furthermore, the subjects who expected the teacher to be "bad" learned significantly less as measured by the short quiz. They also leaned forward less often and looked at the teacher less than the subjects who expected the teacher to be good.

How would you evaluate this study? The full report (Feldman & Prohaska, 1979) gives many more details, but based on our summary alone, what can you tell about the validity of the findings?

Judging Validity

If you look at the eight questions for evaluating a research study, it appears that conditions 1, 3, 5, and 6 have been met. (Do you agree?) We cannot yet be certain about condition 2—equal treatment of the subjects—because in this first experiment we have no detailed information about the way the teacher behaved toward the subjects. We know only that the teacher was instructed to give the same lesson, in the same way, to each subject. But what if the differences in the subjects' behavior toward the teacher—the differences that were found in the study—caused the teacher to give the lesson in different ways to different students? Perhaps after the first minute or so, subjects were reacting to real differences in the way the teacher delivered the lesson.

Feldman and Prohaska looked at this very real possibility in their second experiment. They found that students' nonverbal behavior (leaning forward or looking at the teacher) actually could affect how well the teacher taught the lesson. Although this may, to some extent, lessen the validity of their first experiment, it is a worthy finding in and of itself.

You may have noticed that we have not yet discussed conditions 4, 7, and 8. Feldman and Prohaska did not include a control group. The fact that the two experimental groups reacted in significantly different ways, however, shows that they were not simply reacting to the novelty of the situation. If both groups had been particularly eager or bored, we might have had good reason to expect the Hawthorne effect.

We can't know anything about conditions 7 and 8, of course, until further research has been conducted. We can say, however, that two respected educational psychologists have reported findings that seem to support our initial hypothesis. In some cases, at least, student expectations about a teacher's competence do have an effect, not only on the students' behavior but also on the teacher's behavior.

The last two questions are equally difficult to answer. It is almost always possible to offer alternative explanations for the findings of any study. In a well-controlled study, an attempt is made to eliminate as many of these alternative explanations as possible. The question of educational versus statistical significance is also one on which reasonable people might easily differ. How large a difference between the test scores of the two groups is large enough to warrant a change in educational practice? This question must be answered in part by the individual teacher. Do the potential gains offered by the findings seem worthwhile enough to make whatever change is called for?

GLOSSARY

Abstract Brief summary of a study's key procedures and results.

Academic Learning Time Time when students are actually succeeding at the learning task.

Academic Socialization The ways that children are taught how to be students, the value of learning, and their own role in schooling.

Academic Tasks The work the student must accomplish, including the content covered and the mental operations required.

Accommodation Altering existing schemes or creating new ones in response to new information.

Achievement Motivation Desire to excel; impetus to strive for excellence and success.

Achievement Tests Standardized tests measuring how much students have learned in a given content area.

Acronym Technique for remembering names, phrases, or steps by using the first letter of each word to form a new, memorable word.

Action Zone Area of a classroom where the greatest amount of interaction takes place.

Active Teaching Teaching characterized by high levels of teacher explanation, demonstration, and interaction with students.

Adaptation Adjustment to the environment.

Adolescent Egocentrism Assumption that everyone else shares one's thoughts, feelings, and concerns.

Advance Organizer Statement of inclusive concepts to introduce and sum up material that follows.

Affective Domain Emotional objectives.

Affective Education Education focusing on emotional growth.

Aggression Bold, direct action that is intended to hurt someone else or take property; unprovoked attack.

Algorithm Step-by-step procedure for solving a problem; prescription for solutions.

Allocated Time Time set aside for learning.

Analogical Thinking Heuristic in which one limits the search for solutions to situations that are similar to the one at hand.

Anorexia Nervosa Eating disorder characterized by very limited food intake.

Antecedents Events that precede an action.

Anxiety General uneasiness, a feeling of tension.

Applied Behavior Analysis The application of behavioral learning principles to understand and change behavior.

Aptitude Tests Tests meant to predict future performance.

Aptitude-Treatment Interaction (ATI) Interaction of individual differences in learning with particular teaching methods.

Arousal Physical and psychological reactions causing a person to be alert, attentive, wide awake.

Articulation Disorders Any of a variety of pronunciation difficulties, such as the substitution, distortion, or omission of sounds.

Artificial Intelligence The capability of a computer or computer system to simulate human thinking and problem solving.

Assertive Discipline Clear, firm, unhostile response style.

Assimilation Fitting new information into existing schemes.

Attainment Value The importance of doing well on a task; how success on the task meets personal needs.

Attention Focus on a stimulus.

Attention Deficit–Hyperactive Disorder Current term for disruptive behavior disorders marked by overactivity, excessive difficulty sustaining attention, or impulsiveness.

Attribution Theories Descriptions of how individuals' explanations, justifications, and excuses influence their motivation and behavior.

Authentic Assessment Measurement of important abilities using procedures that simulate the application of these abilities to real-life problems.

Authentic Tests Assessment procedures that test skills and abilities as they would be applied in real-life situations.

Automaticity The result of learning to perform a behavior or thinking process so thoroughly that the performance is automatic and does not require effort.

Autonomy Independence.

Basic Skills Clearly structured knowledge that is needed for later learning and that can be taught step by step.

Behavior Modification Systematic application of antecedents and consequences to change behavior.

Behavior-Content Matrix A planning method that integrates expected student behaviors with course topics to arrive at specific objectives.

Behavioral Learning Theories Explanations of learning that focus on external events as the cause of changes in observable behaviors.

Behavioral Objectives Instructional objectives stated in terms of observable behaviors.

Being Needs Maslow's three higher-level needs, sometimes called growth needs.

Between-Class Ability Grouping System of grouping in which students are assigned to classes based on their measured ability or achievements.

Bilingualism Speaking two languages fluently.

Bimodal Distribution Frequency distribution with two modes.

Blended Families Parents, children, and stepchildren merged into families through remarriages.

Bottom-Up Processing Perceiving based on noticing separate defining features and assembling them into a recognizable pattern.

Brainstorming Generating ideas without stopping to evaluate them.

Bulimia Eating disorder characterized by overeating, then getting rid of the food by self-induced vomiting or laxatives.

Case Study Intensive study of one person or one situation.

Central Tendency Typical score for a group of scores.

Cerebral Palsy Condition involving a range of motor or coordination difficulties due to brain damage.

Chain Mnemonics Memory strategies that associate one element in a series with the next element.

Chunking Grouping individual bits of data into meaningful larger units.

Classical Conditioning Association of automatic responses with new stimuli.

Classification Grouping objects into categories.

Classroom Management Techniques used to maintain a healthy learning environment, relatively free of behavior problems.

Coding System A hierarchy of ideas or concepts.

Cognitive Behavior Modification Procedures based on both behavioral and cognitive learning principles for changing your own behavior by using self-talk and self-instruction.

Cognitive Development Gradual, orderly changes by which mental processes become more complex and sophisticated.

Cognitive Domain In Bloom's taxonomy, memory and reasoning objectives.

Cognitive Monitoring Monitoring of our thinking and learning strategies.

Cognitive Objectives Instructional objectives stated in terms of higher-level thinking operations.

Cognitive Styles Different ways of perceiving and organizing information.

Cognitive View of Learning A general approach that views learning as an active mental process of acquiring, remembering, and using knowledge.

Cognitive-Mediational View View that emphasizes the role of the student's cognitive information processing system in interpreting, shaping, and filtering inputs from the external world.

Collective Monologue Form of speech in which children in a group talk but do not really interact or communicate.

Compensation The principle that changes in one dimension can be offset by changes in another.

Components In an information-processing view, basic problem-solving processes underlying intelligence.

Computer Simulations Programs that require students to apply knowledge and skills to solve lifelike problems.

Computer Tutorials Programs that teach material by questioning students and responding to their answers.

Concept General category of ideas, objects, people, or experiences whose members share certain properties.

Concept Mapping Student's diagram of his or her understanding of a concept.

Concrete Operations Mental tasks tied to concrete objects and situations.

Conditional Knowledge "Knowing when and why" to use declarative and procedural knowledge.

Conditioned Response (CR) Learned response to a previously neutral stimulus.

Conditioned Stimulus (CS) Stimulus that evokes an emotional or physiological response after conditioning.

Confederate Assistant pretending to be a subject in an experiment.

Confidence Interval Range of scores within which an individual's particular score is likely to fall.

Consequences Events that follow an action.

Conservation Principle that some characteristics of an object remain the same despite changes in appearance.

Constructed-Response Format Assessment procedures that require the student to create an answer instead of selecting an answer from a set of choices.

Constructivist View of Learning View that emphasizes the active role of the learner in building understanding and making sense of information.

Context The physical or emotional backdrop associated with an event.

Contiguity Association of two events because of repeated pairing.

Contingency Contract A contract between teacher and individual student specifying what the student must do to earn a particular privilege or reward.

Continuous Reinforcement Schedule Presenting a reinforcer after every appropriate response.

Contract System System in which each student agrees to work for a particular grade according to agreed-upon standards.

Control Group Subjects receiving no special treatment and serving as a basis for comparison.

Convergent Questions Questions having a single correct answer.

Convergent Thinking Narrowing possibilities to the single answer.

Cooperative Integrated Reading and Composition (CIRC) Cooperative learning technique; pairs of students from each reading group work together on reading and writing projects, then teams are rewarded on the basis of their work.

Cooperative Learning Arrangement in which students work in mixed-ability groups and are rewarded on the basis of the success of the group.

Correlation Statistical description of how closely two variables are related.

Creativity Imaginative, original thinking or problem solving.

Criterion-Referenced Grading Assessment of each student's mastery of course objectives.

Criterion-Referenced Testing Testing in which scores are compared to a set performance standard.

Critical Thinking Evaluating conclusions by logically and systematically examining the problem, the evidence, and the solution.

Cueing Providing a stimulus that "sets up" a desired behavior.

Cultural Deficit Model A model that explains the school achievement problems of ethnic-minority students by assuming that their culture is inadequate and does not prepare them to succeed in school.

Culturally Compatible Classrooms Classrooms in which procedures, rules, grouping strategies, attitudes, and teaching methods do not cause conflicts with the students' culturally influenced ways of learning and interacting.

Culture The knowledge, values, attitudes, and traditions that guide the behavior of a group of people and allow them to solve the problems of living in their environment.

Culture-Fair/Culture-Free Tests Tests without cultural bias.

Data-Based Instruction Assessment method using daily probes of specific-skill mastery.

Decay The weakening and fading of memories with the passage of time.

Decentering Focusing on more than one aspect of an object or situation at a time.

Declarative Knowledge Verbal information; facts; "knowing that" something is the case.

Deductive Reasoning Drawing conclusions by applying rules or principles; logically moving from a general rule or principle to a specific solution.

Deficiency Needs Maslow's four lower-level needs, which must be satisfied first.

Defining Attributes Distinctive features shared by members of a category.

Dependent Variable Variable measured to determine if its changes are results of changes in the independent variable.

Descriptive Research Studies that collect detailed information about specific situations, often using observation, surveys, interviews, recordings, or a combination of these methods.

Descriptive-Correlational-Experimental Loop Research in which observation identifies variables that might be related, relationships are studied, and teaching approaches based on significant correlations are tested in experiments.

Development Orderly, adaptive changes we go through from conception to death.

Developmental Crisis A specific conflict whose resolution prepares the way for the next stage.

Developmentally Appropriate Education Educational programs and activities designed to meet the cognitive, emotional, social, and physical needs of students.

Deviation IQ Score based on statistical comparison of individual's performance with the average performance of others in that age group.

Diagnostic Test Formative test to determine students' areas of weakness, or individually administered tests to identify special learning problems.

Dialect Rule-governed variation of a language spoken by a particular group.

Differential Aptitude Test (DAT) A vocational aptitude test that measures such abilities as mechanical reasoning, clerical speed and accuracy, and number ability.

Direct Instruction/Explicit Teaching Active, teacher-directed instruction for mastery of basic skills.

Direct Observation Method where researchers watch and record behavior without any intervention.

Disability The inability to do something specific such as walk or hear.

Discovery Learning Bruner's approach, in which students work on their own to discover basic principles.

Discriminate Make a different voluntary response to similar stimuli.

Discrimination Responding differently to similar, but not identical stimuli.

Disequilibrium In Piaget's theory, the "out-of-balance" state that occurs when a person realizes that his or her current ways of thinking are not working to solve a problem or understand a situation.

Distractors Wrong answers offered as choices in a multiple-choice item.

Distributed Practice Practice in brief periods with rest intervals.

Divergent Questions Questions having no single correct answer.

Divergent Thinking Coming up with many possible solutions.

Domain-Specific Knowledge Information that is useful in a particular situation or that applies only to one specific topic.

Down Syndrome Retardation caused by presence of extra chromosome.

Drill-and-Practice Programs Computer programs of exercises and activities that allow students to practice skills.

Dual Marking System System of assigning two grades, one reflecting achievement, the other effort, attitude, and actual ability.

Educational Psychology Discipline concerned with teaching and learning processes; applies the methods and theories of psychology and has its own as well.

Educationally Blind Needing Braille materials in order to learn.

Eg-Rule Method Teaching or learning by moving from specific examples to general rules.

Ego-Involved Learners Students who focus on how well they are performing and how they are judged by others.

Egocentric Assuming that others experience the world the way you do.

Elaboration Adding and extending meaning by connecting new information to existing knowledge.

Elaborative Rehearsal Keeping information in working memory by associating it with something else you already know.

Empathetic Listening Hearing the intent and emotions behind what another says and reflecting them back by paraphrasing.

Empathy Ability to feel emotion as experienced by others.

Engaged Time Time spent actively learning.

English as a Second Language (ESL) Designation for programs and classes to teach English to students who are not native speakers of English.

Entity View of Ability Belief that ability is a fixed characteristic that cannot be changed.

Epilepsy Disorder marked by seizures and caused by abnormal electrical discharges in the brain.

Episodic Memory Long-term memory for information tied to a particular time and place, especially memory of the events in a person's life.

Equilibration Search for mental balance between cognitive schemes and information from the environment.

Ethnic Pride A positive self-concept about one's racial or ethnic heritage.

Ethnicity A cultural heritage shared by a group of people.

Ethnography A descriptive approach to research that focuses on life within a group and tries to understand the meaning of events to the people involved.

Evaluation Decision making about student performance and about appropriate teaching strategies.

Exceptional Students Students who have abilities or problems so significant that the students require special education or other services to reach their potential.

Executive Control Processes Processes such as selective attention, rehearsal, elaboration, and organization that influence encoding, storage, and retrieval of information in memory.

Exemplar A specific example of a given category that is used to classify an item.

Exhibition A performance test or demonstration of learning that is public and usually takes an extended time to prepare.

Expectancy × Value Theories Explanations of motivation that emphasize individuals' expectations for success combined with their valuing of the goal.

Experimentation Research method in which variables are manipulated and the effects recorded.

Expert Teachers Experienced, effective teachers who have developed solutions for common classroom problems. Their knowledge of teaching process and content is extensive and well organized.

Explanatory Links Words and phrases such as "because" and "in order to" that specify the relationships between ideas.

Expository Teaching Ausubel's method—teachers present material in complete, organized form, moving from broadest to more specific concepts.

Extinction Gradual disappearance of a learned response.

Extrinsic Motivation Motivation created by external factors like rewards and punishments.

Faces of Intellect In Guilford's theory, the three basic categories of thinking—operations, contents, and products.

Failure-Accepting Students Students who believe their inevitable failures are due to low ability and there is little they can do about it.

Failure-Avoiding Students Students who avoid failure by sticking to what they know, by not taking risks, or by claiming not to care about their performance.

Field Dependence Cognitive style in which patterns are perceived as wholes.

Field Independence Cognitive style in which separate parts of a pattern are perceived and analyzed.

Fine-Motor Skills Voluntary body movements that involve the small muscles.

Finger Spelling Communication system that "spells out" each letter with a hand position.

Fixed-Interval Reinforcement Schedule Reinforcing a behavior after a predictable, fixed amount of time.

Fixed-Ratio Reinforcement Schedule Reinforcing a behavior after a fixed number of responses.

Formal Operations Mental tasks involving abstract thinking and coordination of a number of variables.

Formative Assessment Ungraded testing used before or during instruction to aid in planning and diagnosis.

Frequency Distribution Record showing how many scores fall into set groups.

Functional Fixedness Inability to use objects or tools in a new way.

Functional Literacy A level of reading, writing, and communication ability that allows the individual to function independently in society.

Gender Biases Different views of males and females, often favoring one gender over the other.

General Knowledge Information that is useful in many different kinds of tasks; information that applies to many situations.

Generalization Responding in the same way to similar stimuli.

Generativity Sense of concern for future generations.

Gestalt German for pattern or whole; Gestalt theorists hold that people organize their perceptions into coherent wholes.

Gifted Student A very bright, creative, and talented student.

Goal Structure The way students relate to others who are also working toward a particular goal.

Goal-Directed Actions Deliberate actions toward a goal.

Good Behavior Game Arrangement where a class is divided into teams and each team receives de-merit points for breaking agreed-upon rules of good behavior.

Grade-Equivalent Score Measure of grade level achievement based on comparison with norming samples from each grade.

Graded Membership The extent to which something belongs to a category.

Grading on the Curve Norm-referenced grading that compares students' performance to an average level.

Gross-Motor Skills Voluntary body movements that involve the large muscles.

Group Consequences Rewards or punishments given to a class as a whole for adhering to or violating rules of conduct.

Group Focus Ability to keep as many students as possible involved in activities.

Guided Discovery An adaptation of discovery learning, in which the teacher provides some direction.

Halo Effect Tendency for a general impression of a person to influence our perception of any aspect of that person.

Handicap A disadvantage in a particular situation, sometimes caused by a disability.

Hawthorne Effect Change resulting from subjects' knowledge that they are being studied.

Hemispheric Specialization A property of the human brain—the right and left halves or hemispheres of the brain are involved with different functions, so that control of certain behaviors tends to be dominated by the right or by the left side, depending on the function.

Heuristic General strategy used in attempting to solve problems.

Hierarchy of Needs Maslow's model of seven levels of human needs, from basic physiological requirements to the need for self-actualization.

High-Road Transfer Application of abstract knowledge learned in one situation to a different situation.

High-Stakes Testing Standardized tests whose results have powerful influences when used by school administrators, other officials, or employers to make decisions.

Higher-Level Questions Questions that ask students to apply knowledge to new situations or to analyze, synthesize, or evaluate ideas.

Higher-Order Interactions Interactions involving more than two variables.

Histogram Bar graph of a frequency distribution.

Holistic Scoring Evaluation of a piece of written work as a whole, without separate grades for individual elements.

Holophrases Single words that express complex ideas.

Home-Base Formations Arrangements for students' desks that allow flexibility in activities.

Humanistic View Approach to motivation that emphasizes personal freedom, choice, self-determination, and striving for personal growth.

Hyperactivity Behavior disorder marked by atypical, excessive restlessness and inattentiveness.

Hypothesis Prediction or assumption that provides the basis for investigation.

Hypothetico-Deductive Reasoning A formal-operations problem-solving strategy in which an individual begins by identifying all the factors that might affect a problem and then deduces and systematically evaluates specific solutions.

"I" Message Clear, nonaccusatory statement of how something is affecting you.

Identity (Piaget) Principle that a person or object remains the same over time.

Identity (Erikson) The complex answer to the question "Who am I?"

Identity Achievement Strong sense of commitment to life choices after free considerations of alternatives.

Identity Diffusion Uncenteredness; confusion about who one is and what one wants.

Identity Foreclosure Acceptance of parental life choices without consideration of options.

Impulsive Characterized by cognitive style of responding quickly but often inaccurately.

Incremental View of Ability Belief that ability is a set of skills that can be changed.

Incubation Unconscious work toward a solution while one is away from the problem.

Independent Variable Variable changed to determine its effects on other variables.

Individual Learning Expectation (ILE) Constantly recomputed personal average score in a subject.

Individualized Education Program (IEP) Annually revised program for an exceptional student, detailing present achievement level, goals, and strategies, drawn up by teachers, parents, specialists, and (if possible) student.

Individualized Instruction Approach tailored to individual students' needs, interests, abilities, and work pace.

Inductive Reasoning Formulating general principles based on knowledge of examples and details.

Industry Eagerness to engage in productive work.

Information Processing Human mind's activity of taking in, storing, and using information.

Initiative Willingness to begin new activities and explore new directions.

Inquiry Teaching Approach in which teacher presents a puzzling situation and students solve the problem by gathering data and testing conclusions.

Insight Sudden realization of a solution.

Instructional Events Model Gagné's theory of learning that relates phases of instruction to stages of information processing.

Instructional Objective Clear statement of what students are intended to learn through instruction.

Integrated Instructional System (IIS) System of computer programs that teaches several subjects at multiple grade levels and keeps records on individual students' progress.

Integrity Sense of self-acceptance and fulfillment.

Intelligence Ability or abilities to acquire and use knowledge for solving problems and adapting to the world.

Intelligence Quotient (IQ) Score comparing mental and chronological ages.

Interference The process that occurs when remembering certain information is hampered by the presence of other information.

Intermittent Reinforcement Schedule Presenting a reinforcer after some but not all responses.

Intrinsic Motivation Motivation associated with activities that are their own reward.

Intrinsic or Interest Value The enjoyment a person gets from a task.

Intuitive Thinking Making imaginative leaps to correct perceptions or workable solutions.

Keller Plan, or Personalized System of Instruction (PSI) Instruction based on small units, specific goals, self-pacing, and feedback.

Keyword Method System of associating new words or concepts with similar-sounding cue words.

Law of Effect Law stating that any action producing a satisfying effect will be repeated in similar situations.

Learned Helplessness The expectation, based on previous experiences with a lack of control, that all one's efforts will lead to failure.

Learning Process through which experience causes permanent change in knowledge or behavior.

Learning Goal A personal intention to improve abilities and understand, no matter how performance suffers.

Learning Potential Assessment Device Innovative method for testing the student's ability to benefit from teaching, consistent with Vygotsky's theory of cognitive development.

Learning Strategies General plans for approaching learning tasks.

Learning Style Preferences Preferred ways of studying and learning, such as using pictures instead of text, working with other people versus alone, learning in structured or in unstructured situations, and so on.

Learning Styles Individual differences that affect classroom learning.

Learning Tactics Specific techniques for learning, such as using mnemonics or outlining a passage.

Least Restrictive Placement Placement of each child in as normal an educational setting as possible.

Lecturing Organized explanation of a topic by a teacher.

Levels of Processing Theory Theory that recall of information is based on how deeply it is processed.

Limited English Proficiency (LEP) Descriptive term for students who have limited mastery of English.

Linguistic Comprehension Understanding of the meaning of sentences.

Loci Method Technique of associating items to be remembered with specific places.

Locus of Control "Where" people locate responsibility for success and failures—inside or outside themselves.

Long-Term Memory Permanent store of knowledge.

Low Vision Vision limited to close objects.

Low-Road Transfer Spontaneous and automatic transfer of highly practiced skills.

Mainstreaming Teaching disabled children in regular classes for part or all of their school day.

Maintenance Rehearsal Keeping information in working memory by repeating it to yourself.

Massed Practice Practice for a single extended period.

Mastery Learning Method where students move through brief units of work by demonstrating mastery on one unit before going to the next.

Mastery-Oriented Students Students who focus on learning goals because they value achievement and see ability as improvable.

Maturation Genetically programmed, naturally occurring changes over time.

Mean Arithmetical average.

Meaningful Verbal Learning Focused and organized relationships among ideas and verbal information.

Means-Ends Analysis Heuristic in which goal is divided into subgoals.

Measurement Evaluation expressed in quantitative (number) terms.

Median Middle score in a group of scores.

Melting Pot A metaphor for the absorption and assimilation of immigrants into the mainstream of society so that ethnic differences vanish.

Memory Strength The durability of a memory; if information is well learned, it is more durable.

Mental Age In intelligence testing, a score based on average abilities for that age group.

Mental Retardation Significantly below-average intellectual and adaptive social behavior, evident before age 18.

Metacognition Knowledge about our own thinking processes.

Metalinguistic Awareness Understanding about one's own use of language.

Minimum Competency Testing Standardized tests meant to determine if students meet minimum requirements to graduate or to proceed in school.

Minority Group A group of people who have been socially disadvantaged—not always a minority in actual numbers.

Mnemonics Techniques for remembering; also, the art of memory.

Mode Most frequently occurring score.

Modeling Changes in behavior, thinking, or emotions that occur through observing another person—a model.

Monolinguals Individuals who speak only one language.

Moral Dilemmas Situations in which no choice is clearly and indisputably right.

Moral Reasoning The thinking processes involved in judgments about questions of right and wrong.

Moratorium Identity crisis; suspension of choices because of struggle.

Morphemes Smallest units in language that have meaning.

Motivation Internal state that arouses, directs, and maintains behavior.

Movement Management Ability to keep lessons and groups moving smoothly.

Multicultural Education Education that teaches the value of cultural diversity.

Multiple Intelligences In Gardner's theory of intelligence, a person's seven separate abilities: logical-mathematical, verbal, musical, spatial, bodily-kinesthetic, interpersonal, intrapersonal.

Negative Correlation A relationship between two variables in which a high value on one is associated with a low value on the other. Example: height and distance from top of head to the ceiling.

Negative Reinforcement Strengthening behavior by removing an aversive stimulus when the behavior occurs.

Norm Group A group whose average score serves as a standard for evaluating any student's score on a test.

Norm-Referenced Grading Assessment of students' achievement in relation to one another.

Norm-Referenced Testing Testing in which scores are compared with the average performance of others.

Normal Distribution The most commonly occurring distribution, in which scores are distributed evenly around the mean.

Norming Sample Large sample of students serving as a comparison group for scoring standardized tests.

Novice Teachers Inexperienced teachers just beginning their career. They may be excellent teachers but have not yet developed a repertoire of solutions for common teaching problems or systems of well-organized knowledge about the many aspects of teaching.

Object Permanence The understanding that objects have a separate, permanent existence.

Objective Testing Multiple-choice, matching, true-false, short-answer, and fill-in tests; scoring answers does not require interpretation.

Observational Learning Learning by observation and imitation of others.

Operant Conditioning Learning in which voluntary behavior is strengthened or weakened by consequences or antecedents.

Operants Voluntary (and generally goal-directed) behaviors emitted by a person or an animal.

Operationalize Make measurable by making specific.

Operations Actions a person carries out by thinking them through instead of literally performing the actions.

Optimal Level An element of Fischer's skill theory of cognitive development; the highest level of performance that a person can attain under the most supportive conditions.

Organization Ongoing process of arranging information and experience into mental systems or categories; ordered and logical network of relations.

Orthopedic Devices Devices such as braces and wheelchairs that aid the physically handicapped.

Overextension Using one word to cover a range of concepts.

Overgeneralization Inclusion of nonmembers in a category; overextending a concept.

Overlapping Supervising several activities at once.

Overlearning Practicing a task past the point of mastery to combat forgetting and improve transfer.

Overregularize Apply a learned rule to all situations, including inappropriate ones.

Part Learning Breaking a list of rote items into shorter lists.

Participant Observation A method for conducting descriptive research in which the researcher becomes a participant in the situation in order to better understand life in that group.

Participation Structures The formal and informal rules for how to take part in a given activity.

Peer Ratings Student evaluations of one another on a given variable.

Peg-Type Mnemonics Systems of associating items with cue words.

Percentage Grading System of converting class performances to percentage scores and assigning grades based on predetermined cutoff points.

Percentile Rank Percentage of those in the norming sample who scored at or below individual's score.

Perception Interpretation of sensory information.

Performance Goal A personal intention to seem competent or perform well in the eyes of others.

Personal Development Changes in personality that take place as one grows.

Phonemes Distinctive sounds of a language.

Physical Development Changes in body structure and function over time.

Portfolio A collection of the student's work in an area, showing growth, self-reflection, and achievement.

Positive Correlation A relationship between two variables in which the two increase or decrease together. Example: calorie intake and weight gain.

Positive Practice Practicing correct responses immediately after errors.

Positive Reinforcement Strengthening behavior by presenting a desired stimulus after the behavior.

PQ4R A method for studying text that involves six steps: Preview, Question, Read, Reflect, Recite, Review.

Pragmatics Area of language involving the effects of contexts on meaning.

Premack Principle Principle stating that a more-preferred activity can serve as reinforcer for a less-preferred activity.

Preoperational The stage before a child masters logical mental operations.

Presentation Punishment Decreasing the chances that a behavior will occur again by presenting an aversive stimulus following the behavior; also called Type I punishment.

Pretest Formative test for assessing students' knowledge, readiness, and abilities.

Primary Reinforcers Stimuli with reinforcing properties built into the organism itself.

Principle Established relationship between factors.

Private Speech Children's self-talk, which guides their thinking and action. Eventually these verbalizations are internalized as silent inner speech.

Proactive Interference Old information interfering with new.

Problem Any situation in which you are trying to reach some goal and must find a means to do so.

Problem Solving Creating new solutions for problems.

Procedural Knowledge Knowledge that is demonstrated when we perform a task; "knowing how."

Procedural Memory Long-term memory for how to do things.

Procedures Prescribed steps for an activity.

Productions The contents of procedural memory; rules about what actions to take, given certain conditions.

Prompt A reminder that follows a cue to make sure the person reacts to the cue.

Propositional Network Set of interconnected concepts and relationships in which long-term knowledge is held.

Prototype Best representative of a category.

Psychomotor Domain Physical ability objectives.

Psychosocial Describing the relation of the individual's emotional needs to the social environment.

Puberty The period in early adolescence when individuals begin to reach physical and sexual maturity.

Punishment Process that weakens or suppresses behavior.

Pygmalion Effect Exceptional progress by a student as a result of high teacher expectations for that student; named for mythological king, Pygmalion, who made a statue, then caused it to be brought to life.

Race A group of people who share common biological traits that are seen as self-defining by the people of the group.

Random Without any definite pattern; following no rule.

Range Distance between the highest and the lowest score in a group.

Readiness Testing Testing procedures meant to determine if an individual is ready to proceed to the next level of education or training.

Receptors Parts of the human body that receive sensory information.

Reciprocal Determinism An explanation of behavior that emphasizes the mutual effects of the individual and the environment on each other.

Reciprocal Questioning Approach in which groups of two or three students ask and answer each other's questions after a lesson or presentation.

Reciprocal Teaching A method, based on modeling, to teach reading comprehension strategies.

Recitation Format of teacher questioning, student response, and teacher feedback.

Reconstruction Recreating information by using memories, expectations, logic, and existing knowledge.

Reflective Thoughtful and inventive. Reflective teachers think back over situations to analyze what they did and why and to consider how they might improve learning for their students.

Reflective Cognitive Style Characterized by cognitive style of responding slowly, carefully, and accurately.

Regular Education Initiative An educational movement that advocates giving regular education teachers, not special education teachers, responsibility for teaching mildly (and sometimes moderately) handicapped students.

Reinforcement Use of consequences to strengthen behavior.

Reinforcer Any event that follows a behavior and increases the chances that the behavior will occur again.

Relearning Filling in the gaps and encoding more completely material that is not totally unfamiliar.

Reliability Consistency of test results.

Removal Punishment Decreasing the chances that a behavior will occur again by removing a pleasant stimulus following the behavior; also called Type II punishment.

Replication Repetition of a research study to see if the same results are obtained.

Reprimands Criticisms for misbehavior; rebukes.

Resistance Culture Group values and beliefs about refusing to adopt the behaviors and attitudes of the majority culture.

Resource Room Classroom with special materials and a specially trained teacher.

Respondents Responses (generally automatic or involuntary) elicited by specific stimuli.

Response Observable reaction to a stimulus.

Response Cost Punishment through loss of reinforcers.

Response Set Rigidity; tendency to respond in the most familiar way.

Restructuring Conceiving of a problem in a new or different way.

Resultant Motivation Whichever is the stronger tendency—the need to achieve or the need to avoid failure.

Retrieval Process of searching for and finding information in long-term memory.

Retroactive Interference New information interfering with old.

Reversibility A characteristic of Piagetian logical operations—the ability to think through a series of steps, then mentally reverse the steps and return to the starting point; also called reversible thinking.

Reversible Thinking Thinking backward, from the end to the beginning.

Revise Option In a contract system, the chance to revise and improve work.

Ripple Effect "Contagious" spreading of behaviors through imitation.

Rote Memorization Remembering information by repetition without necessarily understanding the meaning of the information.

Rule-Eg Method Teaching or learning by moving from general principles to specific examples.

Rules Statements specifying expected and forbidden behaviors; dos and don'ts.

Satiation Requiring a person to repeat a problem behavior past the point of interest or motivation.

Scaffolding Support for learning and problem solving. The support could be clues, reminders, encouragement, breaking the problem down into steps, providing an example, or anything else that allows the student to grow in independence as a learner.

Schema-Driven Problem Solving Recognizing a problem as a "disguised" version of an old problem for which one already has a solution.

Schemata (singular, **Schema**) Basic structures for organizing information; concepts.

Schemes Mental systems or categories of perception and experience.

Script Schema or expected plan for the sequence of steps in a common event such as buying groceries or ordering take-out pizza.

Seatwork Independent classroom work.

Second-Language Acquisition The process of learning a second language, very similar to the process of first-language learning.

Secondary Reinforcers Stimuli that acquire their reinforcing properties through learning.

Self-Actualization Fulfilling one's potential.

Self-Concept Our perceptions about ourselves.

Self-Efficacy A person's sense of being able to deal effectively with a particular task; beliefs about personal competence in a particular situation.

Self-Esteem The value each of us places on our own characteristics, abilities, and behaviors.

Self-Fulfilling Prophecy A groundless expectation that is confirmed because it has been expected.

Self-Instruction Talking oneself through the steps of a task.

Self-Management Management of your own behavior and acceptance of responsibility for your own actions; use of behavioral learning principles to change your own behavior.

Self-Regulated Learners Students whose academic learning abilities and self-discipline make learning easier so motivation is maintained.

Self-Reinforcement Providing yourself with positive consequences, contingent on accomplishing a particular behavior.

Self-Report Research method where subjects respond directly to questions.

Semantic Memory Memory for meaning.

Semantics The meaning of words and combinations of words.

Semilingual Not proficient in any language; speaking one or more languages inadequately.

Semiotic Function The ability to use symbols—language, pictures, signs, gestures, etc.—to represent actions or objects mentally.

Sensorimotor Involving the senses and motor activity.

Sensory Register System of receptors holding sensory information very briefly.

Serial-Position Effect The tendency to remember the beginning and the end but not the middle of a list.

Seriation Arranging objects in sequential order according to one aspect, such as size, weight, or volume.

Derry, S. J. (1991). Strategy and expertise in solving word problems. In C. McCormick, G. Miller, & M. Pressley (Eds.), *Cognitive strategies research: From basic research to educational applications*. New York: Springer-Verlag.

Derry, S. J. (1989). Putting learning strategies to work. *Educational Leadership, 47*(5) 4–10.

Derry, S. J., & Murphy, D. A. (1986). Designing systems that train learning ability: From theory to practice. *Review of Educational Research, 56*, 1–39.

Deshler, D. D., & Schumaker, J. B. (1986). Learning strategies: An instructional alternative for low-achieving adolescents. *Exceptional Children, 52*, 583–590.

Dias, R. M. (1983). Thought and two languages: The impact of bilingualism on cognitive development. *Review of Research in Education, 10*, 23–54.

Dinnel, D., & Glover, J. A. (1985). Advance organizers: Encoding manipulations. *Journal of Educational Psychology, 77*, 514–522.

Doctorow, M., Wittrock, M. C., & Marks, C. (1978). Generative processes in reading comprehension. *Journal of Educational Psychology, 70*, 109–118.

Donaldson, M. (1985). The mismatch between school and children's minds. In N. Entwistle (Ed.), *New directions in educational psychology. Vol. I: Learning and teaching*. Philadelphia: Falmer Press.

Dorans, N. J., & Livingston, S. A. (1987). Male-female differences in SAT Verbal ability among students of high SAT Mathematical ability. *Journal of Educational Measurement, 24*, 65–71.

Dorval, R., & Eckerman, C. O. (1984). Developmental trends in the quality of conversation achieved by small groups of acquainted peers. *Monographs of the Society for Research in Child Development, 49* (2, Serial No. 206).

Doyle, W. (1977). The uses of nonverbal behaviors: Toward an ecological model of classrooms. *Merrill-Palmer Quarterly, 23*, 179–192.

Doyle, W. (1983). Academic work. *Review of Educational Research, 53*, 287–312.

Doyle, W. (1985, May/June). Recent research on classroom management: Implications for teacher preparation. *Journal of Teacher Education*, pp. 31–35.

Doyle, W. (1986). Classroom organization and management. In M. Wittrock (Ed.), *Handbook of research on teaching* (3rd ed., pp. 392–431). New York: Macmillan.

Duchastel, P. (1979). Learning objectives and the organization of prose. *Journal of Educational Psychology, 71*, 100–106.

Duffy, G., Roehler, L. R., Meloth, M. S., & Vavrus, L. G. (1986). Conceptualizing instructional explanation. *Teaching and Teacher Education, 2*, 197–214.

Duncker, K. (1945). On solving problems. *Psychological Monographs, 58* (5, Whole No. 270).

Dunkin, M. J., & Biddle, B. J. (1974). *The study of teaching*. New York: Holt, Rinehart & Winston.

Dunn, K., & Dunn, R. (1978). *Teaching students through their individual learning styles*. Reston, VA: National Council of Principals.

Dunn, K., & Dunn, R. (1987). Dispelling outmoded beliefs about student learning. *Educational Leadership, 44*(6), 55–63.

Dunn, R. (1987). Research on instructional environments: Implications for student achievement and attitudes. *Professional School Psychology, 2*, 43–52.

Dunn, R., Beaudry, J. S., & Klavas, A. (1989). Survey of research on learning styles. *Educational Leadership, 47*(7), 50–58.

Dunn, R., Dunn, K., & Price, G. E. (1984). *Learning Style Inventory*. Lawrence, KS: Price Systems.

Dush, D. M., Hirt, M. L., & Schroeder, H. (1983). Self-management modification with adults: A meta-analysis. *Psychological Bulletin, 94*, 408–422.

Dweck, C. S. (1986). Motivational processes affecting learning. *American Psychologist, 41*, 1040–1047.

Dweck, C. S., & Bempechat, J. (1983). Children's theories on intelligence: Consequences for learning. In S. Paris, G. Olson, & W. Stevenson (Eds.), *Learning and motivation in the classroom* (pp. 239–256). Hillsdale, NJ: Erlbaum.

Dyer, H. S. (1967). The discovery and development of educational goals. *Proceedings of the 1966 Invitational Conference on Testing Problems*. Princeton, NJ: Educational Testing Service.

Eaton, J. F., Anderson, C. W., & Smith, E. L. (1984). Students' misconceptions interfere with science learning: Case studies of fifth-graders. *Elementary School Journal, 84*, 365–379.

Eaton, S., & Olson, J. (1986). "Doing computers?" The micro in the elementary curriculum. *Journal of Curriculum Studies, 18*(3), 342–344.

Ebbinghaus, H. (1913). *Memory*. New York: Teachers College, Columbia University.

Ebmeier, H. H., & Ziomek, R. L. (1982, March). *Increasing engagement rates of low and high achievers*. Paper presented at the annual meeting of the American Educational Research Association, New York.

Eccles, J., & Wigfield, A. (1985). Teacher expectations and student motivation. In J. Dusek (Ed.), *Teacher expectancies* (pp. 185–226). Hillsdale, NJ: Erlbaum.

Educational Testing Service (1962). *Hidden Figures Test* (Cf-1). Princeton, NJ.

Educational Testing Service. (1992). *The second international assessment of educational progress*. Princeton, NJ: ETS.

Eimas, P. D. (1985). The perception of speech in early infancy. *Scientific American, 252*, 46–52.

Eiseman, J. W. (1981). What criteria should public school moral education programs meet? *The Review of Education, 7*, 213–230.

Eisner, E. (1986). A secretary in the classroom. *Teaching and Teacher Education, 2*, 325–328.

Elam, S. E., Rose, L. C., & Gallup, A. M. (1991). The 23rd annual Gallup Poll of the public's attitudes toward the public schools. *Phi Delta Kappan, 73*(1) 41–56.

Elashoff, J. D. & Snow, R. E. (1971). *Pygmalion reconsidered*. Worthington, OH: Charles A. Jones.

Elawar, M. C., & Corno, L. (1985). A factorial experiment in teachers' written feedback on student homework: Changing teacher behavior a little rather than a lot. *Journal of Educational Psychology, 77*, 162–173.

Electronic Learning (1987). Educational technology 1987: A report on EL's seventh annual survey of the states. *Electronic Learning, 7*(2), 39–44, 53–57, 83.

Elkind, D. (1981). Obituary—Jean Piaget (1896–1980). *American Psychologist, 36*, 911–913.

Elkind, D. (1986). *The miseducation of children: Superkids at risk*. New York: Knopf.

Elkind, D. (1989). Developmentally appropriate education for 4-year-olds. *Theory Into Practice, 28*(1), 47–52.

Elkind, D. (1991). Formal education and early childhood education: An essential difference. In K. M. Cauley, F. Linder, & J. H. MacMillan (Eds.), *Annual Editions: Educational Psychology 91/92* (pp. 27–37). Guilford, CN: Duskin.

Emmer, E. T., & Evertson, C. M. (1981). Synthesis of research on classroom management. *Educational Leadership, 38*, 342–345.

Emmer, E. T., & Evertson, C. M. (1982). Effective classroom management at the beginning of the school year in junior high school classes. *Journal of Educational Psychology, 74,* 485–498.

Emmer, E. T., Evertson, C. M., & Anderson, L. M. (1980). Effective classroom management at the beginning of the school year. *Elementary School Journal, 80,* 219–231.

Emmer, E. T., Evertson, C., Sanford, J. P., Clements, B., & Worsham, M. (1989). *Classroom management for secondary teachers* (2nd ed.). Englewood Cliffs, NJ: Prentice-Hall.

Emmer, E. T., & Millett, G. (1970). *Improving teaching through experimentation: A laboratory approach.* Englewood Cliffs, NJ: Prentice-Hall.

Engel, P. (1991). Tracking progress toward the school readiness goal. *Educational Leadership, 48*(5), 39–42.

Engelmann, S., & Englemann, T. (1981). *Give your child a superior mind.* New York: Simon & Schuster.

Epstein, H. (1978). Growth spurts during brain development: Implications for educational policy and practice. In J. Chall & A. Mirsky (Eds.), *Education and the brain.* The seventy-seventh yearbook of the National Society for the Study of Education, Part II. Chicago: University of Chicago Press.

Epstein, H. (1980). EEG developmental stages. *Developmental psychobiology, 13,* 629–631.

Erikson, E. (1963). *Childhood and society* (2nd ed.). New York: Norton.

Erikson, E. H. (1968). *Identity, youth, and crisis.* New York: Norton.

Erikson, E. H. (1980). *Identity and the life cycle* (2nd ed.). New York: Norton.

Erickson, F., & Shultz, J. (1982). *The counselor as gatekeeper: Social interaction in interviews.* New York: Academic Press.

Espe, C., Worner, C., & Hotkevich, M. (1990). Whole language—What a bargain. *Educational Leadership, 47*(6), 45.

Evertson, C. M. (1982). Differences in instructional activities in high and low achieving junior high classes. *Elementary School Journal, 82,* 329–350.

Evertson, C. M. (1988). Managing classrooms: A framework for teachers. In D. Berliner & B. Rosenshine (Eds.), *Talks to teachers* (pp. 54–74). New York: Random House.

Evertson, C. M., Emmer, E. T., Clements, B. S., Sanford, J. P., & Worsham, M. E. (1989). *Classroom management for elementary teachers* (2nd ed.). Englewood Cliffs, NJ: Prentice-Hall.

Evertson, C. M., & Green, J. (1986). Observation as inquiry and method. In M. Wittrock (Ed.), *Handbook of research on teaching* (3rd ed., pp. 162–213). New York: Macmillan.

Fagot, B. I., Hagan, R., Leinbach, M. D., & Kronsberg, S. (1985). Differential reactions to assertive and communicative acts of toddler boys and girls. *Child Development, 56,* 1499–1505.

Faw, H. W., & Waller, T. G. (1976). Mathemagenic behaviors and efficiency in learning from prose. *Review of Educational Research, 46,* 691–720.

Feiman-Nemser, S. (1983). Learning to teach. In L. Shulman & G. Sykes (Eds.), *Handbook of teaching and policy* (pp. 150–170). New York: Longman.

Fein, G. (1978). *Child development.* Englewood Cliffs, NJ: Prentice-Hall.

Feitler, F., & Tokar, E. (1982). Getting a handle on teacher stress: How bad is the problem? *Educational Leadership, 39,* 456–458.

Feldman, R., & Prohaska, T. (1979). The student as Pygmalion: Effects of student expectancy of the teacher. *Journal of Educational Psychology, 71,* 485–493.

Fennema, E., & Peterson, P. (1988). Effective teaching for boys and girls: The same or different? In D. Berliner & B. Rosenshine (Eds.), *Talks to teachers* (pp. 111–127). New York: Random House.

Fennema, E., & Sherman, J. (1977). Sex-related differences in mathematics achievement, spatial visualization and affective factors. *American Educational Research Journal, 14*(1), 51–71.

Ferguson, D. L., Ferguson, P. M., & Bogdan, R. C. (1987). If mainstreaming is the answer, what is the question? In V. Richardson-Koehler (Ed.), *Educators' handbook: A research perspective.* New York: Longman.

Fetterman, N., & Rohrkemper, M. (1986, April). *The utilization of failure: A look at one social/instructional environment.* Paper presented at the annual meeting of the American Educational Research Association, San Francisco.

Feuerstein, R. (1979). *The dynamic assessment of retarded performers: The Learning Potential Assessment Device, theory, instruments, and techniques.* Baltimore: University Park Press.

Finn, J. (1972). Expectations and the educational environment. *Review of Educational Research, 42,* 387–410.

Fischer, K. W. (1980). A theory of cognitive development: The control and construction of hierarchies of skills. *Psychological Review, 87,* 477–531.

Fischer, K. W., & Knight, C. C. (1990). Cognitive development in real children: Levels and variations. In R. McClure (Ed.), *Learning and thinking styles: Classroom interactions.* Washington, DC: National Education Association.

Fiske, E. B. (1981, October 27). Teachers reward muddy prose, study finds. *The New York Times,* p. C1.

Fiske, E. B. (1988, April 10). America's test mania. *The New York Times* (Education Life Section), pp. 16–20.

Flavell, J. H. (1985). *Cognitive development* (2nd ed.). Englewood Cliffs, NJ: Prentice-Hall.

Flavell, J. H., Friedrichs, A. G., & Hoyt, J. D. (1970). Developmental changes in memorization processes. *Cognitive Psychology, 1,* 324–340.

Flecter, J. D., Hawley, D. E., & Piele, P. K. (1990). Costs, effects, and utility of microcomputer assisted instruction in the classroom. *American Educational Research Journal, 27,* 783–806.

Floden, R. E., & Klinzing, H. G. (1990). What can research on teacher thinking contribute to teacher preparation? A second opinion. *Educational Researcher, 19*(4), 15–20.

Forrest, D. L., & Waller, T. G. (1980, April). *What do children know about their reading and study skills?* Paper presented at the annual meeting of the American Educational Research Association, Boston.

Foster, J. D. (1991). The role of accountability in Kentucky's Educational Reform Act of 1990. *Educational Leadership, 48*(5), 34–36.

Foster, W. (1981, August). *Social and emotional development in gifted individuals.* Paper presented at the Fourth World Conference on Gifted and Talented, Montreal.

Fox, L. H. (1981). Identification of the academically gifted. *American Psychologist, 36,* 1103–1111.

Frederiksen, N. (1984). Implications of cognitive theory for instruction in problem solving. *Review of Educational Research 54,* 363–407.

Frick, T. W. (1990). Analysis of patterns in time: A method of recording and quantifying temporal relations in education. *American Educational Research Journal, 27,* 180–204.

Fromberg, D. P., & Driscoll, M. (1985). *The successful classroom: Management strategies for regular and special education teachers.* New York: Teachers College Press.

Frymier, J. (1988). Understanding and preventing teen suicide: An interview with Barry Garfinkel. *Phi Delta Kappan, 70,* 290–293.

Fuller, F. G. (1969). Concerns of teachers: A developmental conceptualization. *American Educational Research Journal, 6,* 207–226.

Furman, W., & Bierman, K. L. (1984). Children's conceptions of friendship: A multimethod study of developmental changes. *Developmental Psychology, 20,* 925–931.

Furst, E. J. (1981). Bloom's taxonomy of educational objectives for the cognitive domain: Philosophical and educational issues. *Review of Educational Research, 51,* 441–454.

Furth, H., & Wachs, H. (1974). *Thinking goes to school: Piaget's theory in practice.* New York: Oxford University Press.

Gage, N. L. (1991). The obviousness of social and educational research results. *Educational Researcher, 20*(A), 10–16.

Gagné, E. D. (1985). *The psychology of school learning.* Boston: Little, Brown.

Gagné, R. M. (1985). *The conditions of learning and theory of instruction* (4th ed.). New York: Holt, Rinehart & Winston.

Gagné, R. M., & Driscoll, M. P. (1988). *Essentials of learning for instruction* (2nd ed.). Englewood Cliffs, NJ: Prentice-Hall.

Gagné, R. M., & Smith, E. (1962). A study of the effects of verbalization on problem solving. *Journal of Experimental Psychology, 63,* 12–18.

Galambos, S. J., & Goldin-Meadow, S. (1990). The effects of learning two languages on metalinguistic development. *Cognition, 34,* 1–56.

Gall, M. D. (1970). The use of questions in teaching. *Review of Educational Research, 40,* 707–721.

Gall, M. D. (1984). Synthesis of research on teachers' questioning. *Educational Leadership, 41,* 40–47.

Gallini, J. K. (1991). Schema-based strategies and implications for instructional design in strategy training. In C. McCormick, G. Miller, & M. Pressley (Eds.), *Cognitive strategies research: From basic research to educational applications.* New York: Springer-Verlag.

Gallup, A. M. (1984). Gallup Poll of teachers' attitudes toward the public schools. *Phi Delta Kappan, 66,* 97–107.

Gallup, A. M. (1985). The 17th annual Gallup Poll of the public's attitudes toward the public schools. *Phi Delta Kappan, 67,* 35–47.

Gallup, A. M. (1986). The 18th annual Gallup Poll of the public's attitudes toward the public schools. *Phi Delta Kappan, 68*(1), 43–59.

Gallup, A. M., & Clark, D. L. (1987). The 19th annual Gallup Poll of the public's attitudes toward the public schools. *Phi Delta Kappan, 69*(1), 17–30.

Gallup, A. M., & Elam, S. M. (1988). The 20th annual Gallup Poll of the public's attitudes toward the public schools. *Phi Delta Kappan, 70*(1), 33–46.

Gallup, G. (1982). Fifteenth annual Gallup Poll of public attitudes toward the public schools. *Phi Delta Kappan, 64*(1), 34–46.

Garcia, R. L. (1991). *Teaching in a pluralistic society: Concepts, models, and strategies.* New York: HarperCollins.

Gardner, H. (1982a). *Art, mind, and brain: A cognitive approach to creativity.* New York: Basic Books.

Gardner, H. (1982b). *Developmental psychology* (2nd ed.). Boston: Little, Brown.

Gardner, H. (1983). *Frames of mind: The theory of multiple intelligences.* New York: Basic Books.

Gardner, H., & Hatch, T. (1989). Multiple intelligences go to school. *Educational Researcher, 18*(8), 4–10.

Garger, S., & Guild, P. (1984). Learning styles: The crucial differences. *Curriculum Review, 23,* 9–12.

Garner, R. (1990). When children and adults do not use learning strategies: Toward a theory of settings. *Review of Educational Psychology, 60,* 517–530.

Garner, R., & Kruas, C. (1982). Monitoring of understanding among 7th graders: An investigation of good comprehender–poor comprehender differences on knowing and regulating reading behaviors. *Educational Research Quarterly, 6,* 5–12.

Garrett, S. S., Sadker, M., & Sadker, D. (1986). Interpersonal communication skills. In J. Cooper (Ed.), *Classroom teaching skills* (3rd ed.). Lexington, MA: D. C. Heath.

Gartner, A., & Lipsky, D. K. (1987). Beyond special education: Toward a quality system for all students. *Harvard Educational Review, 57,* 367–395.

Gelman, R. (1979). Preschool thought. *American Psychologist, 34,* 900–905.

Gelman, R., & Baillargeon, R. (1983). A review of some Piagetian concepts. In P. Mussen (Ed.), *Carmichael's manual of child psychology. Vol. 3: Cognitive development* (E. Markman & J. Flavell, Volume Eds.). New York: Wiley.

Gelman, R., Meck, E., & Merkin, S. (1986). Young children's numerical competence. *Cognitive Development, 1,* 1–29.

Gelman, S. A., & Ebeling, K. S. (1989). Children's use of non-egocentric standards in judgments of size. *Child Development, 60,* 920–932.

Gentner, D. (1975). Evidence for the psychological reality of semantic components: The verbs of possession. In D. Norman & D. Rumelhart (Eds.), *Explorations in cognition.* San Francisco: Freeman.

Gibbs, J. W., & Luyben, P. D. (1985). Treatment of self-injurious behavior: Contingent versus noncontingent positive practice overcorrection. *Behavior Modification, 9,* 3–21.

Gick, M. L., & Holyoak, K. L. (1983). Schema induction and analogical transfer. *Cognitive Psychology, 15,* 1–38.

Gick, M. L. (1986). Problem-solving strategies. *Educational Psychologist, 21,* 99–120.

Gillett, M., & Gall, M. (1982, March). *The effects of teacher enthusiasm on the at-task behavior of students in the elementary grades.* Paper presented at the annual meeting of the American Educational Research Association, New York.

Gilligan, C. (1982). *In a different voice: Psychological theory and women's development.* Cambridge, MA: Harvard University Press.

Gilligan, C., & Attanucci, J. (1988). Two moral orientations: Gender differences and similarities. *Merrill-Palmer Quarterly, 34,* 223–237.

Gilstrap, R. L., & Martin, W. R. (1975). *Current strategies for teachers: A resource for personalizing education.* Pacific Palisades, CA: Goodyear.

Ginsburg, H. (1985). Piaget and education. In N. Entwistle (Ed.), *New directions in educational psychology. Vol. 1: Learning and teaching.* Philadelphia: Falmer Press.

Ginsburg, H., & Opper, S. (1988). *Piaget's theory of intellectual development* (3rd ed.). Englewood Cliffs, NJ: Prentice-Hall.

Glaser, R. (1981). The future of testing: A research agenda for cognitive psychology and psychometrics. *American Psychologist, 36,* 923–936.

Gleitman, H. (1987). *Basic psychology* (2nd ed.). New York: Norton.

Gleitman, H. (1991). *Psychology* (3rd ed.). New York: Norton.

Glover, J. A., Ronning, R. R., & Bruning, R. H. (1990). *Cognitive psychology for teachers.* New York: Macmillan.

Goin, M. T., Peters, E. E., & Levin, J. R. (1986, April). *Effects of pictorial mnemonic strategies on the reading performance of students classified as learning disabled.* Paper presented at the annual meeting of the Council for Exceptional Children, New Orleans.

Goleman, D. (1988, April 10). An emerging theory on blacks' I.Q. scores. *The New York Times* (Education Life Section), 22–24.

Good, T. L. (1983a). Classroom research: A decade of progress. *Educational Psychologist, 18,* 127–144.

Good, T. L. (1983b). Research on classroom teaching. In L. Shulman & G. Sykes (Eds.), *Handbook of teaching and policy* (pp. 42–80). New York: Longman.

Good, T. L. (1988). Teacher expectations. In D. Berliner & B. Rosenshine (Eds.), *Talks to teachers.* New York: Random House.

Good, T. L., & Brophy, J. E. (1984). *Looking in classrooms* (3rd ed.). New York: Harper and Row.

Good, T. L., & Brophy, J. E. (1991). *Looking in classrooms* (5th ed.). New York: Harper Collins.

Good, T. L., & Grouws, D. (1979). The Missouri mathematics effectiveness project: An experimental study in fourth grade classrooms. *Journal of Educational Psychology, 71,* 355–362.

Good, T. L., Grouws, D., & Ebmeier, H. (1983). *Active mathematics teaching.* New York: Longman.

Good, T. L., & Marshall, S. (1984). Do students learn more in heterogeneous or homogeneous groups? In P. Peterson, L. C. Wilkinson, & M. Hallinan (Eds.), *The social context of instruction: Group organization and group processes* (pp. 15–38). Orlando, FL: Academic Press.

Good, T. L., & Stipek, D. J. (1983). Individual differences in the classroom: A psychological perspective. In G. Fenstermacher & J. Goodlad (Eds.), *1983 National Society for the Study of Education Yearbook.* Chicago: University of Chicago Press.

Good, T., & Weinstein, R. (1986). Schools make a difference: Evidence, criticisms, and new directions. *American Psychologist, 41,* 1090–1097.

Goodman, Y. M., & Goodman, K. S. (1990). Vygotsky in a whole-language perspective. In L. Moll (Ed.), *Vygotsky and education: Instructional implications and applications of sociohistorical psychology* (pp. 223–250). New York: Cambridge University Press.

Goodspeed, J. (1988). Two million microcomputers now used in U.S. schools. *Electronic Learning, 7*(8), 16.

Gordon, E. W. (1991). Human diversity and pluralism. *Educational Psychologist, 26,* 99–108.

Gordon, S. (1986). What kids need to know: Most parents and school systems fail to provide teenagers with relevant sex education. *Psychology Today, 20*(10), 22–26, 74.

Gordon, T. (1974). *Teacher effectiveness training.* New York: Peter H. Wyden.

Gordon, T. (1981). Crippling our children with discipline. *Journal of Education, 163,* 228–243.

Grabe, M., & Latta, R. M. (1981). Cumulative achievement in a mastery instructional system: The impact of differences in resultant achievement motivation and persistence. *American Educational Research Journal, 18,* 7–14.

Graham, S. (1991). A review of attribution theory in achievement contexts. *Educational Psychology Review, 3,* 5–39.

Graham, S., & Barker, G. (1990). The downside of help: An attributional-developmental analysis of helping behavior as a low ability cue. *Journal of Educational Psychology, 82,* 7–14.

Graham, S., & Golan, S. (1991). Motivational influences on cognition: Task involvement, ego involvement, and depth of information processing. *Journal of Educational Psychology, 83,* 187–194.

Grant, C. A., & Sleeter, C. E. (1989). Race, class, gender, exceptionality, and educational reform. In J. Banks & C. McGee Banks (Eds.), *Multicultural education: Issues and perspectives* (pp. 49–66). Boston: Allyn & Bacon.

Green, B. F. (1981). A primer of testing. *American Psychologist, 36,* 1001–1012.

Green, J., & Weade, R. (1985). Reading between the lines: Social cues to lesson participation. *Theory into Practice, 24,* 14–21.

Gregorc, A. F. (1982). *Gregorc Style Delineator: Development, technical, and administrative manual.* Maynard, MA: Gabriel Systems.

Gresham, F. (1981). Social skills training with handicapped children. *Review of Educational Research, 51,* 139–176.

Grinder, R. E. (1981). The "new" science of education: Educational psychology in search of a mission. In F. H. Farley & N. J. Gordon (Eds.), *Psychology and education: The state of the union.* Berkeley, CA: McCutchan.

Gronlund, N. E. (1985). *Measurement and evaluation in teaching* (5th ed.). New York: Macmillan.

Gronlund, N. E. (1988). *How to construct achievement tests* (4th ed.). Englewood Cliffs, NJ: Prentice-Hall.

Gronlund, N. E. (1991). *How to write and use instructional objectives* (4th ed.). New York: Macmillan.

Grossman, H. G. (Ed.). (1983). *Classification in mental retardation.* Washington, DC: American Association on Mental Deficiency.

Guilford, J. P. (1988). Some changes in the Structure-of-Intellect model. *Educational and Psychological Measurement, 48,* 1–4.

Guskey, T. R., & Gates, S. L. (1986). Synthesis of research on mastery learning. *Education Leadership, 43,* 73–81.

Guttmacher (Alan) Institute (1984). *Issues in brief* (Vol. 4, No. 2). Washington, DC: Alan Guttmacher Institute.

Haertel, E. H. (1991). New forms of teacher assessment. *Review of Research in Education, 17,* 3–30.

Hakuta, K. (1986). *Mirror of language: The debate on bilingualism.* New York: Basic Books.

Hakuta, K., & Garcia, E. E. (1989). Bilingualism and education. *American Psychologist, 44,* 374–379.

Hale-Benson, J. E. (1986). *Black children: Their roots, culture, and learning styles* (rev. ed.). Baltimore: Johns Hopkins University Press.

Hall, J. W. (1991). More on the utility of the keyword method. *Journal of Educational Psychology, 83,* 171–172.

Hallahan, D. P., & Kauffman, J. M. (1991). *Exceptional children: Introduction to special education* (5th ed.). Boston: Allyn & Bacon.

Hamilton, R. J. (1985). A framework for the evaluation of the effectiveness of adjunct questions and objectives. *Review of Educational Research, 55,* 47–86.

Haney, W. (1981). Validity, vaudeville, and values: A short history of social concerns over standardized testing. *American Psychologist, 36,* 1021–1034.

Hansen, R. A. (1977). Anxiety. In S. Ball (Ed.), *Motivation in education.* New York: Academic Press.

Hansford, B. C., & Hattie, J. A. (1982). The relationship between self and achievement/performance measures. *Review of Educational Research, 52,* 123–142.

Hardman, M. L., Drew, C. J., Egan, M. W., & Wolf, B. (1990). *Human Exceptionality* (3rd ed.). Boston: Allyn & Bacon.

Harris, K. R. (1990). Developing self-regulated learners: The role of private speech and self-instruction. *Educational Psychologist, 25,* 35–50.

Harris, K. R., Graham, S., & Pressley, M. (in press). Cognitive strategies in reading and written language. In N. Singhh & I. Beale (Eds.), *Current perspectives in learning disabilities: Nature, theory, and treatment.* New York: Springer-Verlag.

Harris, K. R., & Pressley, M. (in press). The nature of cognitive strategy instruction: Interactive strategy construction. *Exceptional Children.*

Harrison, A. O., Wilson, M. N., Pine, C. J., & Buriel, R. (1990). Family ecologies of ethnic minority children. *Child Development, 61,* 347–362.

Harrow, A. J. (1972). *A taxonomy of the psychomotor domain: A guide for developing behavior objectives.* New York: David McKay.

Hartup, W. W. (1989). Social relationships and their developmental significance. *American Psychologist, 44,* 120–126.

Harter, S. (1990). Issues in the assessment of self-concept of children and adolescents. In A. LaGreca (Ed.), *Through the eyes of a child* (pp. 292–325). Boston: Allyn & Bacon.

Harvard University (1985, June). Preschool: It does make a difference. *Harvard Education Letter, 1*(6), 1–3.

Harvard University (1986, January). Girls' math achievement: What we do and don't know. *Harvard Education Letter, 2*(1), 1–5.

Harvard University (1986, March). When the student becomes the teacher. *Harvard Education Letter, 2*(3), 5–6.

Harvard University (1988, March). Cultural differences in the classroom. *Harvard Education Letter, 4*(2), 1–4.

Haskins, R. (1989). Beyond metaphor: The efficacy of early childhood education. *American Psychologist, 44,* 274–282.

Hayes, J. R., Waterman, D. A., & Robinson, C. S. (1977). Identifying relevant aspects of a problem text. *Cognitive Science, 1,* 297–313.

Hayes, S. C., Rosenfarb, I., Wulfert, E., Munt, E. D., Korn, Z., & Zettle, R. D. (1985). Self-reinforcement effects: An artifact of social standard setting? *Journal of Applied Behavior Analysis, 18,* 201–214.

Herman, J. (1988, April). *The faces of meaning: Teachers', administrators', and students' views of the effect of ACOT.* Paper presented at the annual meeting of the American Educational Research Association and the International Association for Computing in Education, New Orleans.

Hess, R., Chih-Mei, C., & McDevitt, T. M. (1987). Cultural variation in family beliefs about children's performance in mathematics: Comparisons among People's Republic of China, Chinese-American, and Caucasian-American families. *Journal of Educational Psychology, 79,* 179–188.

Hess, R., & McDevitt, T. (1984). Some cognitive consequences of maternal intervention techniques. A longitudinal study. *Child Development, 55,* 1902–1912.

Hess, R. D., & Shipman, V. C. (1965). Early experience and the socialization of cognitive modes in children. *Child Development, 36,* 869–886.

Hetherington, E. M. (1989). Coping with family transitions: Winners, losers, and survivors. *Child Development, 60,* 1–14.

Heward, W. L., & Orlansky, M. D. (1984). *Exceptional children* (2nd ed.). Columbus, OH: Charles E. Merrill.

Hilgard, E. R., Atkinson, R. L., & Atkinson, R. C. (1979). *Introduction to psychology* (7th ed.). New York: Harcourt Brace Jovanovich.

Hill, K. T., & Eaton, W. O. (1977). The interaction of test anxiety and success-failure experiences in determining children's arithmetic performance. *Developmental Psychology, 13,* 205–211.

Hill, K. T., & Wigfield, A. (1984). Test anxiety: A major educational problem and what can be done about it. *Elementary School Journal, 85,* 105–126.

Hill, W. E. (1990). *Learning: A survey of psychological interpretations* (5th ed.). New York: Harper & Row.

Hiller, J. J. (1971). Verbal response indicators of conceptual vagueness. *American Educational Research Journal, 8,* 151–161.

Hills, J. R. (1976). *Measurement and evaluation in the classroom.* Columbus, OH: Charles E. Merrill.

Hines, C. V., Cruickshank, D. R., & Kennedy, J. J. (1982, March). *Measures of teacher clarity and their relationships to student achievement and satisfaction.* Paper presented at the annual meeting of the American Educational Research Association, New York.

Hines, C. V., Cruickshank, D. R., & Kennedy, J. J. (1985). Teacher clarity and its relation to student achievement and satisfaction. *American Educational Research Journal, 22,* 87–99.

Hinsley, D., Hayes, J. R., & Simon, H. A. (1977). From words to equations. In P. Carpenter & M. Just (Eds.), *Cognitive processes in comprehension.* Hillsdale, NJ: Erlbaum.

Hodgkinson, H. L. (1985). *All one system: Demographics of education, kindergarten through graduate school.* Washington, DC: Institute of Educational Leadership.

Hoffman, L. W. (1977). Changes in family roles, socialization, and sex differences. *American Psychologist, 32*(8), 644–657.

Hoffman, M. L. (1978). Empathy: Its development and prosocial implications. In C. B. Keasey, (Ed.), *Nebraska Symposium on Motivation, 1977.* Lincoln, NE: University of Nebraska Press.

Hoffman, M. L. (1979). Development of moral thought, feeling, and behavior. *American Psychologist, 34,* 958–966.

Hoffman, M. L. (1983). Affective and cognitive processes in oral internal moralization. In T. Higgins, D. Ruble, & W. Hartup (Eds.), *Social cognition and social development.* Cambridge: Cambridge University Press.

Hoffman, M. L. (1984). Empathy, its limitations and its role in a comprehensive moral theory. In W. Kurtines & J. Gewirtz (Eds.), *Morality, moral behavior, and moral development.* New York: Wiley.

Hoge, D. R., Smit, E. K., & Hanson, S. L. (1990). School experiences predicting changes in self-esteem of sixth- and seventh-grade students. *Journal of Educational Psychology, 82,* 117–126.

Holmes, C. T., & Matthews, K. M. (1984). The effects of non-promotion on elementary and junior high school pupils: A meta-analysis. *Review of Educational Research, 54,* 225–236.

Houston, J. P. (1991). *Fundamentals of learning of memory* (4th ed.). New York. Harcourt Brace Jovanovich.

Howard, K. (1990, spring). Making the writing portfolio real. The *Quarterly of the National Writing Project, 27,* 4–8.

Hoy, W. K., & Woolfolk, A. E. (1990). Organizational socialization of student teachers. *American Educational Research Journal, 27,* 279–300.

Hoy, W. K., & Woolfolk, A. E. (in press). Teachers' sense of efficacy and the organizational health of schools. *Elementary School Journal.*

Huessman, L. R., Eron, L. D., Klein, R., Brice, P., & Fischer, P. (1983). Mitigating the imitation of aggressive behaviors by changing children's attitudes about media violence. *Journal of Personality and Social Psychology, 44,* 899–910.

Huessman, L. R., Lagarspetz, K., & Eron, L. (1984). Intervening variables in the TV violence-aggression relation: Evidence from two countries. *Developmental Psychology, 20,* 746–775.

Hundert, J., & Bucher, B. (1978). Pupil's self-scored arithmetic performance: A practical procedure for maintaining accuracy. *Journal of Applied Behavior Analysis, 11,* 304.

Hunt, J. McV. (1961). *Intelligence and experience.* New York: Ronald.

Hunter, M. (1982). *Mastery teaching.* El Segundo, CA: TIP Publications.

Hunter, M. (1991). Hunter design helps achieve the goals of science instruction. *Educational Leadership, 48*(4), 79–81.

Hyde, J. (1981). How large are cognitive gender differences? *American Psychologist, 36,* 292–301.

Hyde, J. S., Fennema, E., & Lamon, S. J. (1990). Gender differences in mathematical performance: A meta-analysis. *Psychological Bulletin, 107,* 139–155.

IIS Report (1990). Water Mill, NY: Educational Products Information Exchange Institute.

Irving, O., & Martin, J. (1982). Withitness: The confusing variable. *American Educational Research Journal, 19,* 313–319.

Irwin, J. W. (1986). *Teaching reading comprehension.* Englewood Cliffs, NJ: Prentice-Hall.

Isenberg, J. (1991). Societal influences on children. In K. M. Cauley, F. Linder, & J. H. MacMillan (Eds.), *Annual Editions:*

Educational Psychology 91/92 (pp. 38–44). Guilford, CN: Duskin.

Jacklin, C. N., Dipietro, J. A., & Maccoby, E. E. (1984). Sex-typing behavior and sex-typing pressure in child-parent interactions. *Sex Roles, 13,* 413–425.

Jacklin, C. N., & Maccoby, E. E. (1972, April). *Sex differences in intellectual abilities: A reassessment and a look at some new explanations.* Paper presented at the annual meeting of the American Educational Research Association, Chicago.

Jagacinski, C. M., & Nicholls, J. G. (1987). Competence and affect in task involvement and ego involvement: The impact of social comparison information. *Journal of Educational Psychology, 76,* 107–114.

Jencks, C., Smith, M., Acland, H., Bane, M., Cohen, D., Gintis, H., Heyns, B., & Michelson, S. (1972). *Inequality: A reassessment of the effect of family and schooling in America.* New York: Basic Books.

Jenson, W. R., Sloane, H. N., & Young, K. R. (1988). *Applied behavior analysis in education: A structured teaching approach.* Englewood Cliffs, NJ: Prentice-Hall.

Johnson, D. W. (1990). *Reaching out: Interpersonal effectiveness and self-actualization* (4th ed.) Englewood Cliffs, NJ: Prentice-Hall.

Johnson, D., & Johnson, R. (1975). *Learning together and alone: Cooperation, competition, and individualization.* Englewood Cliffs, NJ: Prentice-Hall.

Johnson, D., & Johnson, R. (1985). Motivational processes in cooperative, competitive, and individualistic learning situations. In C. Ames & R. Ames (Eds.), *Research on motivation in education. Vol. 2: The classroom milieu* (pp. 249–286). New York: Academic Press.

Johnson, J. S., & Newport, E. L. (1989). Critical period effects in second language learning: The influence of maturational state on the acquisition of English as a second language. *Cognitive Psychology, 21,* 60–69.

Jones, V. F., & Jones, L. S. (1986). *Comprehensive classroom management: Creating positive learning environments* (2nd ed.). Boston: Allyn & Bacon.

Jordan, N., & Goldsmith-Phillips, J. (in press). *Assessment of learning disabilities.* Boston: Allyn & Bacon.

Joshua, S., & Dupin, J. J. (1987). Taking into account students conceptions in instructional strategy: An example in physics. *Cognition and Instruction, 4,* 117–135.

Joyce, B., & Weil, M. (1986). *Models of teaching.* Englewood Cliffs, NJ: Prentice-Hall.

Jussim, L. (1986). Self-fulfilling prophecies: A theoretical and integrative review. *Psychological Review, 93,* 429–445.

Kagan, S. (1983). Social orientation among Mexican-American children: A challenge to traditional classroom structures. In E. Garcia (Ed.), *The Mexican-American child: Language, cognition, and social development.* Tempe, AZ: Center for Bilingual Education.

Kanfer, F. H., & Gaelick, L. (1986). Self-management methods. In F. Kanfer & A. Goldstein (Eds.), *Helping people change: A textbook of methods* (3rd ed.). New York: Pergamon.

Kaplan, B. (1984). *Development and growth.* Hillsdale, NJ: Erlbaum.

Kaplan, J. S. (1991). *Beyond behavior modification* (2nd ed.). Austin, TX: Pro-Ed.

Karweit, N. (1989). Time and learning: A review. In R. E. Slavin (Ed.), *School and classroom organization.* Hillsdale, NJ: Erlbaum.

Karweit, N., & Slavin, R. (1981). Measurement and modeling choices in studies of time and learning. *American Educational Research Journal, 18,* 157–171.

Kash, M. M., & Borich, G. (1978). *Teacher behavior and pupil self-concept.* Reading, MA: Addison-Wesley.

Kaufman, P. (1976). The effects of nonverbal behavior on performance and attitudes in a college classroom. *Dissertation Abstracts International, 37* (1-A), 235.

Kazdin, A. E. (1984). *Behavior modification in applied settings.* Homewood, IL: Dorsey Press.

Keefe, J. W. (1982). Assessing student learning styles: An overview. In *Student learning styles and brain behavior.* Reston, VA: National Association of Secondary School Principals.

Keefe, J. W., & Languis, M. L. (1983). *Operational definitions.* Paper presented to the NASSP Learning Styles Task Force. Reston, VA: National Association of Secondary School Principals.

Keefe, J. W., & Monk, J. S. (1986). *Learning style profile examiner's manual.* Reston, VA: National Association of Secondary School Principals.

Keith, T. Z. (1982). Time spent on homework and high school grades: A large-sample path analysis. *Journal of Educational Psychology, 74,* 248–253.

Kiewra, K. A. (1988). Cognitive aspects of autonomous note taking: Control processes, learning strategies, and prior knowledge. *Educational Psychologist, 23,* 39–56.

Kindsvatter, R., Wilen, W., & Ishler, M. (1988). *Dynamics of effective teaching.* New York: Longman.

King, A. (1990). Enhancing peer interaction and learning in the classroom through reciprocal questioning. *American Educational Research Journal, 27,* 664–687.

King, G. (1979, June). Personal communication. University of Texas at Austin.

Kirk, S., & Gallagher, J. J. (1983). *Educating exceptional children* (4th ed.). Boston: Houghton Mifflin.

Kirst, M. (1991a). Interview on assessment issues with Lorrie Shepard. *Educational Researcher, 20*(2), 21–23.

Kirst, M. (1991b). Interview on assessment issues with James Popham. *Educational Researcher, 20*(2), 24–27.

Klatzky, R. L. (1980). *Human memory: Structures and processes* (2nd ed.). San Francisco: Freeman.

Klausmeier, H. J. (1976). Instructional design and the teaching of concepts. In J. Levin & V. Allen (Eds.), *Cognitive learning in children: Theories and strategies.* New York: Academic Press.

Knapp, M., Turnbull, B. J., & Shields, P. M. (1990). New directions for educating children of poverty. *Educational Leadership, 48*(1), 4–9.

Kneedler, P. (1985). California assesses critical thinking. In A. Costa (Ed.), *Developing minds: A resource book for teaching thinking.* Alexandria, VA: Association for Supervision and Curriculum Development.

Kneedler, R. (1984). *Special education for today.* Englewood Cliffs, NJ: Prentice-Hall.

Knight, S. L., & Waxman, H. C. (1991). Students' cognitions and classroom instruction. In H. Waxman & H. Walberg (Eds.), *Effective teaching: Current research.* Berkeley, CA: McCutchan.

Knupfer, N. (1988, April). *Providing teacher guidance for instructional computing: A model for implementation.* Paper presented at the annual meeting of the American Educational Research Association, New Orleans.

Kogan, N. (1983). Stylistic variation in childhood and adolescence: Creativity, metaphor, and cognitive style. In P. Mussen (Ed.), *Handbook of child psychology* (4th ed.), Vol. 3, pp. 630–706). New York: Wiley.

Kohlberg, L. (1963). The development of children's orientations toward moral order: Sequence in the development of moral thought. *Vita Humana, 6,* 11–33.

Kohlberg, L. (1975). The cognitive-developmental approach to moral education. *Phi Delta Kappan, 56,* 670–677.

Kohlberg, L. (1981). *The philosophy of moral development.* New York: Harper and Row.

Kohlberg, L. (1984). *Essays on moral development.* San Francisco: Harper and Row.

Kohlberg, L., Yaeger, J., & Hjertholm, E. (1969). Private speech: Four studies and a review of theories. *Child Development, 39,* 691–736.

Kolata, G. B. (1980). Math and sex; Are girls born with less ability? *Science, 210,* 1234–1235.

Kounin, J. (1970). *Discipline and group management in classrooms.* New York: Holt, Rinehart & Winston.

Kounin, J. S., & Doyle, P. H. (1975). Degree of continuity of a lesson's signal system and task involvement of children. *Journal of Educational Psychology, 67,* 159–164.

Kozulin, A. (1990). *Vygotsky's psychology: A biography of ideas.* Cambridge, MA: Harvard University Press.

Krathwohl, D. R., Bloom, B. S., & Masia, B. B. (1956). *Taxonomy of educational objectives. Handbook II: Affective domain.* New York: David McKay.

Kroger, J. (1989). *Identity in adolescence: The balance between self and other.* New York: Routledge.

Krumboltz, J. D., & Krumboltz, H. B. (1972). *Changing children's behavior.* Englewood Cliffs, NJ: Prentice-Hall.

Kulik, C. C., & Kulik, J. A. (1982). Effects of ability grouping on secondary school students: A meta-analysis of evaluation findings. *American Educational Research Journal, 19,* 415–428.

Kulik, J. A., & Kulik, C. C. (1984). Effects of accelerated instruction on students. *Review of Educational Research, 54,* 409–425.

Kulik, J. A., Kulik, C. C., & Bangert, R. L. (1984, April). Effects of practice on aptitude and achievement test scores. *American Educational Research Journal, 21,* 435–447.

Kupersmidt, J. B., Coie, J. D., & Dodge, K. A. (1990). The role of poor peer relations in the development of disorder. In S. Asher & J. Coie (Eds.), *Peer rejection in childhood* (pp. 274–305). New York: Cambridge.

Kutz, R. E. (1991). *Teaching elementary mathematics.* Boston: Allyn & Bacon.

Lamb, M. E. (1982). Parent-infant interaction, attachment, and socioemotional development in infancy. In R. Emde & R. Harmon (Eds.), *The development of attachment and affiliative systems.* New York: Plenum.

Land, M. L. (1987). Vagueness and clarity. In M. Dunkin (Ed.), *The international encyclopedia of teaching and teacher education* (pp. 392–397). New York: Pergamon.

Laosa, L. (1984). Ethnic, socioeconomic, and home language influences on early performance on measures of ability. *Journal of Educational Psychology, 76,* 1178–1198.

Larrivee, B. (1985). *Effective teaching behaviors for successful mainstreaming.* New York: Longman.

Lefcourt, H. (1966). Internal versus external control of reinforcement: A review. *Psychological Bulletin, 65,* 206–220.

Lefton, L. A. (1991). *Psychology* (4th ed.). Boston: Allyn & Bacon.

Leinhardt, G. (1986). Expertise in mathematics teaching. *Educational Leadership, 43,* 28–33.

Leinhardt, G. (1988). Situated knowledge and expertise in teaching. In J. Calderhead (Ed.), *Teachers' professional learning.* London: Farmer Press.

Leinhardt, G., & Greeno, J. D. (1986). The cognitive skill of teaching. *Journal of Educational Psychology, 78,* 75–95.

Leinhardt, G., & Smith, D. (1985). Expertise in mathematics instruction: Subject matter knowledge. *Journal of Educational Psychology, 77,* 247–271.

Leming, J. S. (1981). Curriculum effectiveness in value/moral education. *Journal of Moral Education, 10,* 147–164.

Lepper, M. R. (1988). Motivational considerations in the study of instruction. *Cognition and Instruction, 5,* 289–309.

Lepper, M. R., & Greene, D. (1978). *The hidden costs of rewards: New perspectives on the psychology of human motivation.* Hillsdale, NJ: Erlbaum.

Lerner, B. (1981). The minimum competency testing movement: Social, scientific, and legal implications. *American Psychologist, 36,* 1057–1066.

Lever, J. (1978). Sex differences in the complexity of children's play and games. *American Sociologist Review, 43,* 471–483.

Levin, J. R. (1985). Educational applications of mnemonic pictures: Possibilities beyond your wildest imagination. In A. A. Sheikh (Ed.), *Imagery in the educational process.* Farmingdale, NY: Baywood.

Levin, J. R., McCormick, C. B., Miller, G. E., Kessler, J., & Pressley, M. (1981). *Mnemonic versus nonmnemonic vocabulary learning strategies for children.* Report from the Project on Studies in Language: Reading and Communication. University of Wisconsin.

Lieber, J., & Semmel, M. (1988, April). *The relationship of group configuration to educational outcomes using microcomputers.* Paper presented at the annual meeting of the American Educational Research Association, New Orleans.

Lindsay, P. H., & Norman, D. A. (1977). *Human information processing: An introduction to psychology* (2nd ed.). New York: Academic Press.

Linn, M. C., & Hyde, J. S. (1989). Gender, mathematics, and science. *Educational Researcher, 18,* 17–27.

Linn, R. L. (1986). Educational testing and assessment: Research needs and policy issues. *American Psychologist, 41,* 1153–1160.

Linn, R., Klein, S., & Hart, F. (1972). The nature and correlates of law school essay grades. *Educational and Psychological Measurement, 32,* 267–279.

Lipscomb, T. J., MacAllister, H. A., & Bregman, N. J. (1985). A developmental inquiry into the effects of multiple models on children's generosity. *Merrill-Palmer Quarterly, 31,* 335–344.

Lohman, D. L. (1989). Human intelligence: An introduction to advances in theory and research. *Review of Educational Research, 59,* 333–374.

Lortie, D. (1977). The balance of control and autonomy in elementary school teaching. In D. Erickson (Ed.), *Educational organization and administration* (pp. 335–371). Berkeley, CA: McCutchan.

Lovitt, T. C. (1977). *In spite of my resistance, I've learned from children.* Columbus, OH: Charles E. Merrill.

Luiten, J., Ames, W., & Ackerson, G. (1980). A meta-analysis of the effects of advance organizers on learning and retention. *American Educational Research Journal, 17,* 211–218.

Lyman, H. B. (1986). *Test scores and what they mean* (4th ed.). Englewood Cliffs, NJ: Prentice-Hall.

McClelland, D. (1973). Testing for competence rather than for intelligence. *American Psychologist, 28,* 1–14.

McClelland, D. (1985). *Human motivation.* Glenview, IL: Scott, Foresman.

McClelland, D., Atkinson, J. W., Clark, R. W., & Lowell, E. L. (1953). *The achievement motive.* New York: Appleton-Century-Crofts.

McClelland, D., & Pilon, D. (1983). Sources of adult motives in patterns of parent behavior in early childhood. *Journal of Personality and Social Psychology, 44,* 564–574.

McCombs, B. L., & Marzano, R. J. (1990). Putting the self in self-regulated learning: The self as agent in integrating skill and will. *Educational Psychologist, 25,* 51–70.

McCormack, S. (1989). Response to Render, Padilla, and Krank: But practitioners say it works! *Educational Leadership, 46*(6), 77–79.

McCormick, C. B., & Levin, J. R. (1987). Mnemonic prose-learning strategies. In M. Pressley & M. McDaniel (Eds.), *Imaginary and related mnemonic processes.* New York: Springer-Verlag.

McGinley, P., & McGinley, H. (1970). Reading groups as psychological groups. *Journal of Experimental Education, 39,* 36–42.

McGuire, J. (1988). Gender stereotypes of parents with two-year-olds and beliefs about gender differences in behavior. *Sex Roles, 19,* 233–240.

McKenzie, T. L., & Rushall, B. S. (1974). Effects of self-recording on attendance and performance in a competitive swimming training environment. *Journal of Applied Behavior Analysis, 7,* 199–206.

McLaughlin, T. F., & Gnagey, W. J. (1981, April). *Self-management and pupil self-control.* Paper presented at the annual meeting of the American Educational Research Association, Los Angeles.

MacMillan, D. L. (1982). *Mental retardation in school and society.* Boston: Little, Brown.

McNemar, Q. (1964). Lost: Our intelligence? Why? *American Psychologist, 19,* 871–882.

Macionis, J. J. (1991). *Sociology* (3rd ed.). Englewood Cliffs, NJ: Prentice-Hall.

Madsen, C. H., Becker, W. C., & Thomas, D. R. (1968). Rules, praise, and ignoring: Elements of elementary classroom control. *Journal of Applied Behavior Analysis, 1,* 139–150.

Madsen, C. H., Becker, W. C., Thomas, D. R., Koser, L., & Plager, E. (1968). An analysis of the reinforcing function of "sit down" commands. In R. K. Parker (Ed.), *Readings in educational psychology.* Boston: Allyn & Bacon.

Maehr, M. L. (1974). *Sociocultural origins of achievement.* Monterey, CA: Brooks/Cole.

Mager, R. (1975). *Preparing instructional objectives* (2nd ed.). Palo Alto, CA: Fearon.

Mahoney, M. J., & Thoresen, C. E. (1974). *Self-control: Power to the person.* Monterey, CA: Brooks/Cole.

Maier, N. R. F. (1933). An aspect of human reasoning. *British Journal of Psychology, 24,* 144–155.

Maker, C. J. (1987). Gifted and talented. In V. Richardson-Koehler (Ed.), *Educators' handbook: A research perspective* (pp. 420–455). New York: Longman.

Manaster, G. (1989). *Adolescent development: A psychological interpretation.* Itasca, IL: F. E. Peacock.

Mandlebaum, L. H., Russell, S. C., Krouse, J., & Gonter, M. (1983). Assertive discipline: An effective classwide behavior management program. *Behavior Disorders, 8*(4), 258–264.

Manning, B. H. (1991). *Cognitive self-instruction of classroom processes.* Albany, NY: State University of New York Press.

Maratsos, M. P. (1989). Innateness and plasticity in language acquistion. In M. L. Rice & R. L. Schiefelbusch (Eds.), *The teachability of language* (pp. 105–125). Baltimore, MD: Brooks/Cole.

Marcia, J. (1980). Ego identity development. In J. Adelson (Ed.), *The handbook of adolescent psychology.* New York: Wiley.

Marcia, J. (1987). The identity status approach to the study of ego identity development. In T. Honess & K. Yardley (Eds.), *Self and identity: Perspectives across the life span.* London: Routledge & Kagan Paul.

Markman, E. M. (1977). Realizing that you don't understand: A preliminary investigation. *Child Development, 48,* 986–992.

Markman, E. M. (1979). Realizing that you don't understand: Elementary school children's awareness of inconsistencies. *Child Development, 50,* 643–655.

Marsh, H. W. (1987). The big-fish-little-pond effect on academic self-concept. *Journal of Educational Psychology, 79,* 280–295.

Marsh, H. W. (1990). Influences of internal and external frames of reference on the formation of math and English self-concepts. *Journal of Educational Psychology, 82,* 107–116.

Marsh, H. W., & Holmes, I. W. M. (1990). Multidimensional self-concepts: Construct validation of responses by children. *American Educational Research Journal, 27,* 89–118.

Marsh, H. W., & Shavelson, R. (1985). Self-concept: Its multifaceted, hierarchical structure. *Educational Psychologist, 20,* 107–123.

Marshall, H. H. (1987). Motivational strategies of three fifth-grade teachers. *Elementary School Journal, 88,* 135–150.

Marshall, H. H. (1989). The development of self-concept. *Young Children, 44*(5), 44–51.

Marshall, S. (1984). Sex differences in children's mathematics achievement: Solving computations and story problems. *Journal of Educational Psychology, 76,* 194–204.

Martin, G., & Pear, J. (1992). *Behavior modification: What it is and how to do it* (4th ed.). Englewood Cliffs, NJ: Prentice-Hall.

Martindale, C. (1991). *Cognitive psychology: A neural-network approach.* Pacific Grove, CA: Brooks/Cole.

Maslow, A. H. (1970). *Motivation and personality* (2nd ed.). New York: Harper and Row.

Mathinos, D., & Woodward, A. (1991). Instructional computing in an elementary school: The rhetoric and reality of an innovation. *Journal of Curriculum Studies.*

Mayer, R. E. (1979). Can advance organizers influence meaningful learning? *Review of Educational Research, 49,* 371–383.

Mayer, R. E. (1982). Memory for algebra story problems. *Journal of Educational Psychology, 74,* 199–216.

Mayer, R. E. (1983a). Can you repeat that? Qualitative and quantitative effects of repetition and advance organizers on learning from science prose. *Journal of Educational Psychology, 75,* 40–49.

Mayer, R. E. (1983b). *Thinking, problem solving, cognition.* San Francisco: Freeman.

Mayer, R. E. (1984). Twenty-five years of research on advance organizers. *Instructional Science, 8,* 133–169.

Mayer, R. E. (1992). *Thinking, problem solving, cognition* (2nd ed.). New York: Freeman.

Means, B., & Knapp, M. S. (1991). Cognitive approaches to teaching advanced skills to educationally disadvantaged students. *Phi Delta Kappan, 73,* 282–289.

Mecklenburger, J. A. (1990). Educational technology is not enough. *Phi Delta Kappan, 72,* 105–108.

Medley, D. M. (1979). The effectiveness of teachers. In P. Peterson & H. Walberg (Eds.), *Research on teaching: Concepts, findings, and implications.* Berkeley, CA: McCutchan.

Meek, A. (1991). On thinking about teaching: A conversation with Eleanor Duckworth. *Educational Leadership, 48*(6), 30–34.

Meichenbaum, D. (1977). *Cognitive behavior modification: An integrative approach.* New York: Plenum.

Meichenbaum, D. (1986). Cognitive behavior modification. In F. Kanfer & A. Goldstein (Eds.), *Helping people change: A textbook of methods* (3rd ed., pp. 346–380). New York: Pergamon.

Meichenbaum, D., Burland, S., Gruson, L., & Cameron, R. (1985). Metacognitive assessment. In S. Yussen (Ed.), *The growth of reflection in children.* Orlando, FL: Academic Press.

Meisels, S. J. (1989). High-stakes testing in kindergarten. *Educational Leadership, 46*(7), 16–22.

Mendels, G. E., & Flanders, J. P. (1973). Teacher's expectations and pupil performance. *American Educational Research Journal, 10,* 203–212.

Mercer, C. (1982). Learning disabilities. In H. Haring (Ed.), *Exceptional children and youth.* Columbus, OH: Charles E. Merrill.

Metcalfe, B. (1981). Self-concept and attitude toward school. *British Journal of Educational Psychology, 51,* 66–76.

Meyer, B. J. F., Brandt, D. M., & Bluth, G. J. (1980). Use of top-level structure in text: Key for reading comprehension of ninth-graders. *Reading Research Quarterly, 15,* 72–103.

Miller, G. A. (1956). The magical number seven, plus or minus two: Some limits on our capacity for processing information. *Psychological Review, 63,* 81–97.

Miller, G. A., Galanter, E., & Pribram, K. H. (1960). *Plans and the structure of behavior.* New York: Holt, Rinehart & Winston.

Miller, K., & Gelman, R. (1983). The child's representation of number: A multidimensional scaling analysis. *Child Development, 54,* 1470–1479.

Miller, R. B. (1962). Analysis and specification of behavior for training. In R. Glaser (Ed.), *Training research and education: Science edition.* New York: Wiley.

Milliken math sequences. (1980). (Computer program.) St. Louis, MO: Milliken Publishing.

Mills, J. R., & Jackson, N. E. (1990). Predictive significance of early giftedness: The case of precocious reading. *Journal of Educational Psychology, 82,* 410–419.

Mitchell, B. M. (1984). An update on gifted and talented education in the U.S. *Roeper Review, 6,* 161–163.

Moely, B. E., Hart, S. S., Santulli, K., Leal, L., Johnson, T., Rao, N., & Burney, L. (1986). How do teachers teach memory skills? In J. Levin & M. Pressley (Eds.), *Educational Psychologist, 21* (Special issue on learning strategies), 55–72.

Moos, R. H., & Moos, B. S. (1978). Classroom social climate and student absences and grades. *Journal of Educational Psychology, 70,* 263–269.

Morgan, M. (1985). Self-monitoring of attained subgoals in private study. *Journal of Educational Psychology, 77,* 623–630.

Morris, C. G. (1988). *Psychology: An introduction* (6th ed.). Englewood Cliffs, NJ: Prentice-Hall.

Morris, C. G. (1991). *Psychology: An introduction* (7th ed.). Englewood Cliffs, NJ: Prentice-Hall.

Morrow, L. (1983). Home and school correlates of early interest in literature. *Journal of Educational Research, 76,* 221–230.

Morrow, L., & Weinstein, C. (1986). Encouraging voluntary reading: The impact of a literature. *Reading Research Quarterly, 21,* 330–346.

Moshman, D., Glover, J. A., & Bruning, R. H. (1987). *Developmental Psychology.* Boston: Little, Brown.

Moskowitz, B. A. (1978). The acquisition of language. *Scientific American, 239,* 92–108.

Moskowitz, G., & Hayman, M. L. (1976). Successful strategies of inner-city teachers; A year-long study. *Journal of Educational Research, 69,* 283–289.

Murray, H. G. (1983). Low inference classroom teaching behavior and student ratings of college teaching effectiveness. *Journal of Educational Psychology, 75,* 138–149.

Musgrave, G. R. (1975). *Individualized instruction: Teaching strategies focusing on the learner.* Boston, MA: Allyn & Bacon.

Mussen, P., Conger, J. J., & Kagan, J. (1984). *Child development and personality* (6th ed.). New York: Harper and Row.

National Center for Education Statistics. (1990). *Digest of Education Statistics.* Washington, DC: Center for Education Statistics.

National Commission on Excellence in Education. (1983). *A nation at risk: The imperative for educational reform.* Washington, DC: U.S. Government Printing Office.

National Governors Association (1989). *Results in education: 1989.* Washington, DC: NGA.

National Science Foundation (1988). *Women and minorities in science and engineering* (NSF 88-301). Washington, DC: National Science Foundation.

Naveh-Benjamin, M. (1991). A comparison of training programs intended for different types of test-anxious students: Further support for an information-processing model. *Journal of Educational Psychology, 83,* 134–139.

Naveh-Benjamin, M., McKeachie, W. J., & Lin, Y. (1987). Two types of test-anxious students: Support for an information processing model. *Journal of Educational Psychology, 79,* 131–136.

Neimark, E. (1975). Intellectual development during adolescence. In F. D. Horowitz (Ed.), *Review of child development research* (Vol. 4). Chicago: University of Chicago Press.

Neisser, U. (1979). The concept of intelligence. In R. Sternberg & D. Detterman (Eds.), *Human intelligence: Perspectives on its theory and measurement.* Norwood, NJ: Ablex.

Nelson, K. (1981). Individual differences in language development: Implications for development and language. *Developmental Psychology, 17,* 170–187.

Nelson, K. (1986). *Event knowledge.* Hillsdale, NJ: Erlbaum.

Newby, T. J. (1991). Classroom motivation: Strategies of first-year teachers. *Journal of Educational Psychology, 83,* 195–200.

Newcomb, M. D., & Bentler, P. M. (1989). Substance use and abuse among children and teenagers. *American Psychologist, 44,* 242–248.

Newcombe, N., & Baenninger, M. (1990). The role of expectations in spatial test performance: A meta-analysis. *Sex Roles.*

Newsweek (1984, September 24). Why teachers fail, pp. 64–70.

Newsweek (Summer, 1991). The end of innocence, pp. 62–64. Special Edition: How Kids Grow.

Nicholls, J. G., & Miller, A. (1984). Conceptions of ability and achievement motivation. In R. Ames & C. Ames (Eds.), *Research on motivation in education. Vol. 1: Student Motivation* (pp. 39–73). New York: Academic Press.

Niemiec, R., & Walberg, H. J. (1987). Comparative effects of computer-assisted instruction: A synthesis of reviews. *Journal of Educational Computing Research, 3,* 19–37.

Noddings, N. (1990). Constructivism in mathematics education. In R. Davis, C. Maher, & N. Noddings (Eds.), *Constructivist views on the teaching and learning of mathematics* (pp. 7–18). Monograph 4 of the National Council of Teachers of Mathematics, Reston, VA.

Norman, D. P. (1982). *Learning and memory.* San Francisco: Freeman.

Novak, J. D., & Musonda, D. (1991). A twelve-year longitudinal study of science concept learning. *American Educational Research Journal, 28,* 117–154.

Nucci, L. (1987). Synthesis of research on moral development. *Educational Leadership, 44*(5), 86–92.

Nungester, R. J., & Duchastel, P. C. (1982). Testing versus review: Effects on retention. *Journal of Educational Psychology, 74,* 18–22.

Nuthall, G., & Alton-Lee, A. (1990). Research on teaching and learning: Thirty years of change. *Elementary School Journal, 90,* 546–570.

Oakes, J. (1990). Opportunities, achievement, and choice: Women and minority students in science and math. *Review of Research in Education, 16,* 153–222.

Ogbu, J. (1987). Variability in minority school performance: A problem in search of an explanation. *Anthropology and Education Quarterly, 18,* 312–334.

Ogden, J. E., Brophy, J. E., & Evertson, C. M. (1977, April). *An experimental investigation of organization and management techniques in first-grade reading groups.* Paper presented at the annual meeting of the American Educational Research Association, New York.

O'Leary, K. D. (1980). Pills or skills for hyperactive children? *Journal of Applied Behavior Analysis, 13,* 191–204.

O'Leary, K. D., Kaufman, K. F., Kass, R. E., & Drabman, R. S. (1970). The effects of loud and soft reprimands on the behavior of disruptive students. *Exceptional Children, 37,* 145–155.

O'Leary, K. D., & O'Leary, S. (Eds.). (1977). *Classroom management: The successful use of behavior modification* (2nd ed.). Elmsford, NY: Pergamon.

O'Leary, K. D., & Wilson, G. T. (1987). *Behavior therapy: Application and outcome.* Englewood Cliffs, NJ: Prentice-Hall.

O'Leary, S. G., & O'Leary, K. D. (1976). Behavior modification in the schools. In H. Leitenberg (Ed.), *Handbook of behavior modification and behavior therapy.* Englewood Cliffs, NJ: Prentice-Hall.

Ollendick, T. H., Dailey, D., & Shapiro, E. S. (1983). Vicarious reinforcement: Expected and unexpected effects. *Journal of Applied Behavior Analysis, 16,* 485–491.

Olsen, L. (1988). *Crossing the schoolhouse border: Immigrant students and the California public schools.* San Francisco: California Tomorrow.

O'Neil, J. (1990a). Link between style, culture proves divisive. *Educational Leadership, 48*(2), 8.

O'Neil, J. (1990b). Piecing together the restructuring puzzle. *Educational Leadership, 47*(7), 4–10.

O'Neil, J. (1991). Drive for national standards picking up steam. *Educational Leadership, 48*(5), 4–8.

Osborn, A. F. (1963). *Applied imagination* (3rd ed.). New York: Scribner's.

Ovando, C. J. (1989). Language diversity and education. In J. Banks & C. McGee Banks (Eds.), *Multicultural education: Issues and perspectives* (pp. 208–228). Boston: Allyn & Bacon.

Owen, L. (1985). *None of the above: Behind the myth of scholastic aptitude.* Boston: Houghton Mifflin.

Page, E. B. (1958). Teacher comments and student performances: A 74-classroom experiment in school motivation. *Journal of Educational Psychology, 49,* 173–181.

Paivio, A. (1971). *Imagery and verbal processes.* New York: Holt, Rinehart & Winston.

Paivio, A. (1986). *Mental representations: A dual-coding approach.* New York: Oxford University Press.

Palincsar, A. S. (1986). The role of dialogue in providing scaffolded instruction. In J. Levin & M. Pressley (Eds.), *Educational Psychologist, 21* (Special issue on learning strategies), 73–98.

Palincsar, A. S., & Brown, A. L. (1984). Reciprocal teaching of comprehension-fostering and monitoring activities. *Cognition and Instruction, 1,* 117–175.

Pallas, A. M., & Alexander, K. (1983). Sex differences in quantitative SAT performance: New evidence on the differential coursework hypothesis. *American Educational Research Journal, 20,* 165–182.

Pallas, A. M., Natriello, G., & McDill, E. L. (1989). The changing nature of the disadvantaged population: Current dimensions and future trends. *Educational Researcher, 18*(5), 16–22.

Paris, S. (1988, April). *Fusing skill and will: The integration of cognitive and motivational psychology.* Paper presented at the annual meeting of the American Educational Research Association, New Orleans.

Paris, S. G., Lipson, M. Y., & Wixson, K. K. (1983). Becoming a strategic reader. *Contemporary Educational Psychology, 8,* 293–316.

Pasch, M., Sparks-Langer, G., Gardner, T. G., Starko, A. J., & Moody, C. D. (1991). *Teaching as decision making: Instructional practices for the successful teacher.* New York: Longman.

Pauk, W. (1989). *How to study in college* (4th ed.). Boston: Houghton Mifflin.

Paulman, R. G., & Kennelly, K. J. (1984). Test anxiety and ineffective test taking: Different names, same construct? *Journal of Educational Psychology, 76,* 279–288.

Paulson, F. L., Paulson, P. R., & Meyer, C. A. (1991). What makes a portfolio a portfolio? *Educational Leadership, 48*(5), 60–63.

Pearson, P. D. (1989). Commentary: Reading the whole language movement. *Elementary School Journal, 90,* 231–241.

Peeck, J., van den Bosch, A. B., & Kreupeling, W. J. (1982). Effect of mobilizing prior knowledge on learning from text. *Journal of Educational Psychology, 74,* 771–777.

Pelham, W. E. (1981). Attention deficits in hyperactive and learning-disabled children. *Exceptional Education Quarterly, 2,* 13–23.

Pelham, W. E., & Murphy, H. A. (1986). Attention deficit and conduct disorders. In M. Hersen (Ed.), *Pharmacological and behavioral treatment: An integrative approach* (pp. 108–148). New York: Wiley.

Penfield, W. (1969). Consciousness, memory, and man's conditioned reflexes. In K. Pribram (Ed.), *On the biology of learning.* New York: Harcourt Brace Jovanovich.

Peper, R. J., & Mayer, R. E. (1986). Generative effects of note taking during science lectures. *Journal of Educational Psychology, 78,* 34–38.

Perkins, D. N. (1986). Thinking frames. *Educational Leadership, 43,* 4–11.

Perkins, D. N. (1987). Thinking frames: An integrative perspective on teaching cognitive skills. In J. B. Baron & R. J. Sternberg (Eds.), *Teaching thinking skills: Theory and practice* (pp. 41–85). New York: Freeman.

Perkins, D. N., & Salomon, G. (1989). Are cognitive skills context-bound? *Educational Researcher, 18,* 16–25.

Peters, E. E., & Levin, J. R. (1986). Effects of a mnemonic imagery strategy on good and poor reader's prose recall. *Reading Research Quarterly, 21,* 179–192.

Peterson, P. (1979). Direct instruction reconsidered. In P. Peterson & H. Walberg (Eds.), *Research on teaching: Concepts, findings, and implications.* Berkeley, CA: McCutchan.

Peterson, P. L., & Comeaux, M. A. (1989). Assessing the teacher as a reflective professional: New perspectives on teacher evauation. In A. Woolfolk (Ed.), *Research perspectives on the graduate preparation of teachers* (pp. 132–152). Englewood Cliffs, NJ: Prentice-Hall.

Peterson, P., Fennema, E., & Carpenter, T. (1989). Using knowledge of how students think about mathematics. *Educational Leadership, 46*(4), 42–46.

Peterson, P., Janicki, T. C., & Swing, S. R. (1980). Aptitude-treatment interaction effects of three social studies teaching approaches. *American Educational Research Journal, 17,* 339–360.

Peterson, S. E., DeGracie, J. S., & Ayabe, C. R. (1987). A longitudinal study of the effects of retention/promotion on academic achievement. *American Educational Research Journal, 24,* 107–118.

Pfeffer, C. R. (1981). Developmental issues among children of separation and divorce. In I. Stuart & L. Abt (Eds.), *Children of separation and divorce.* New York: Van Nostrand Reinhold.

Pfeffer, C. R. (1986). *The suicidal child.* New York: Guilford Press.

Pfiffner, L. J., Rosen, L. A., & O'Leary, S. G. (1985). The efficacy of an all-positive approach to classroom management. *Journal of Applied Behavior Analysis, 18,* 257–261.

Piaget, J. (1954). *The construction of reality in the child* (M. Cook, Trans.). New York: Basic Books.

Piaget, J. (1963). *Origins of intelligence in children.* New York: Norton.

Piaget, J. (1965). *The moral judgment of the child.* New York: Free Press.

Piaget, J. (1970a). Piaget's theory. In P. Mussen (Ed.), *Handbook of child psychology* (3rd ed.). New York: Wiley.

Piaget, J. (1970b). *The science of education and the psychology of the child.* New York: Orion Press.

Piaget, J. (1974). *Understanding causality* (D. Miles and M. Miles, Trans.). New York: Norton.

Pine, G. J., & Hilliard, A. G., III (1990). Rx for racism: Imperatives for America's schools. *Phi Delta Kappan, 71,* 593–600.

Popham, W. J. (1988). *Educational evaluation* (2nd ed.). Englewood Cliffs, NJ: Prentice-Hall.

Posner, M. I. (1973). *Cognition: An introduction.* Glenview, IL: Scott, Foresman.

Powell, R. R., Garcia, J., & Denton, J. J. (1985, March). *The portrayal of minorities and women in selected elementary science series.* Paper presented at the annual meeting of the American Educational Research Association, Chicago.

Powers, S. I., Hauser, S. T., & Kilner, L. A. (1989). Adolescent mental health. *American Psychologist, 44,* 200–208.

Prawat, R. S. (1991). The value of ideas: The immersion approach to the development of thinking. *Educational Researcher, 20,* 3–10.

Prawat, R. S., Anderson, A., Diamond, B., McKeague, D., & Whitmer, S. (1981, April). *Teacher thinking about the affective domain: An interview study.* Paper presented at the annual meeting of the American Educational Research Association, Los Angeles.

Premack, D. (1965). Reinforcement theory. In D. Levine (Ed.), *Nebraska symposium on motivation* (Vol. 13). Lincoln, NE: University of Nebraska Press.

Pressley, M. (1982). Elaboration and memory development. *Child Development, 53,* 296–309.

Pressley, M. (1986). The relevance of the good strategy user model to the teaching of mathematics. In J. Levin & M. Pressley (Eds.), *Educational Psychologist, 21* (Special issue on learning strategies), 139–161.

Pressley, M. (1991). Comparing Hall (1988) with related research on elaborative mnemonics. *Journal of Educational Psychology, 83,* 165–170.

Pressley, M., Barkowski, J. G., & Schneider, W. (1987). Cognitive strategies: Good strategy users coordinate metacognition and knowledge. In R. Vasta & G. Whitehurst (Eds.), *Annals of Child Development.* Vol. 4. Greenwich, CT: JAI Press.

Pressley, M., Levine, J., & Delaney, H. D. (1982). The mnemonic keyword method. *Review of Research in Education, 52,* 61–91.

Price, G., & O'Leary, K. D. (1974). *Teaching children to develop high performance standards.* Unpublished manuscript. State University of New York at Stony Brook.

Pring, R. (1971). Bloom's taxonomy: A philosophical critique. *Cambridge Journal of Education, 1,* 83–91.

Purcell, P., & Stewart, L. (1990). Dick and Jane in 1989. *Sex Roles, 22,* 177–185.

Quality Education Data (1988). *Microcomputer and VCR usage in schools, 1987–1988.* Denver: Quality Education Data.

Quay, H. C., & Peterson, D. R. (1987). *Manual for the revised behavior problem checklist.* Coral Gables, FL.

Rathus, S. A. (1988). *Understanding child development.* New York: Holt, Rinehart & Winston.

Raudenbush, S. (1984). Magnitude of teacher expectancy effects on pupil IQ as a function of the credibility of expectancy induction: A synthesis of findings from 18 experiments. *Journal of Educational Psychology, 76,* 85–97.

Raudsepp, E., & Haugh, G. P. (1977). *Creative growth games.* New York: Harcourt Brace Jovanovich.

Recht, D. R., & Leslie, L. (1988). Effect of prior knowledge on good and poor readers' memory of text. *Journal of Educational Psychology, 80,* 16–20.

Redfield, D. L., & Rousseau, E. W. (1981). A meta-analysis of experimental research on teacher questioning behavior. *Review of Educational Research, 51,* 181–193.

Reed, S. K. (1992). *Cognition* (3rd ed.). Pacific Grove, CA: Brooks/Cole.

Reed, S., & Sautter, R. C. (1990). Children of poverty: The status of 12 million Americans. *Phi Delta Kappan, 71*(10), K1–K12.

Reich, P. A. (1986). *Language development.* Englewood Cliffs, NJ: Prentice-Hall.

Reid, D. K., Hresko, W. P., & Swanson, H. L. (1991). *A cognitive approach to learning disabilities* (2nd ed.). Austin, TX: Pro-Ed.

Reid, M. K., & Borkowski, J. G. (1987). Causal attributions of hyperactive children: Implications for teaching strategies and self control. *Journal of Educational Psychology, 79,* 296–307.

Render, G. F., Padilla, J. N. M., & Krank, H. M. (1989). What research really shows about assertive discipline. *Educational Leadership, 46*(6), 72–75.

Renzulli, J. S. (1982). Dear Mr. and Mrs. Copernicus: We regret to inform you . . . *Gifted Child Quarterly, 26,* 11–14.

Renzulli, J. S., & Smith, L. H. (1978). *The Learning Styles Inventory: A measure of student preferences for instructional techniques.* Mansfield Center, CT: Creative Learning Press.

Resnick, L. B. (1981). Instructional psychology. *Annual Review of Psychology, 32,* 659–704.

Resnick, L. B., & Klopfer, L. E. (1989). Toward the thinking curriculum: An overview. In *Toward the thinking curriculum: Current cognitive research.* Alexandria, VA: Association for Supervision and Curriculum Development.

Reynolds, M. C., & Birch, J. W. (1988). *Adaptive mainstreaming: A primer for teachers and principals* (3rd ed.). New York: Longman.

Reynolds, W. M. (1980). Self-esteem and classroom behavior in elementary school children. *Psychology in the Schools, 17,* 273–277.

Rhode, G., Morgan, D. P., & Young, K. R. (1983). Generalization and maintenance of treatment gains of behaviorally handicapped students from resource rooms to regular classrooms using self-evaluation procedures. *Journal of Applied Behavior Analysis, 16,* 171–188.

Rice, M. L. (1984). Cognitive aspects of communicative development. In R. Schiefelbusch & J. Pickar (Eds.), *The Acquisition of communicative competence.* Baltimore: University Park Press.

Rice, M. L. (1989). Children's language acquisition. *American Psychologist, 44,* 149–156.

Richardson, T. M., & Benbow, C. P. (1990). Long-term effects of acceleration on the social-emotional adjustment of mathematically precocious youths. *Journal of Educational Psychology, 82,* 464–470.

Riley, M. S., & Greeno, J. G. (1991). Developmental analysis of understanding language about quantities and of solving problems. *Cognition and Instruction, 5,* 49–101.

Rist, R. (1970). Student social class and teacher expectations: The self-fulfilling prophecy in ghetto education. *Harvard Educational Review, 40,* 411–451.

Robbins, P. A. (1990). Implementing whole language: Bridging children and books. *Educational Leadership, 47*(6), 50–55.

Robinson, C. S., & Hayes, J. R. (1978). Making inferences about relevance in understanding problems. In R. Revlin & R. E. Mayer (Eds.), *Human reasoning.* Washington, DC: Winston.

Robinson, F. P. (1961). *Effective study.* New York: Harper and Row.

Robinson, S., Depascale, C., & Deno, S. (1988, April). *Technology and group instruction: An investigation of enhanced teacher monitoring, correction and student feedback.* Paper presented at the annual meeting of the American Educational Research Association, New Orleans.

Rodriguez, R. (1987). What is an American education? *Education Week, 7*(1). September 9.

Roethlisberger, F. J., & Dickson, W. J. (1939). *Management and the worker.* Cambridge, MA: Harvard University Press.

Rogers, D. (1985). *Adolescents and youth* (5th ed.). Englewood Cliffs, NJ: Prentice-Hall.

Rogoff, B., & Morelii, G. (1989). Perspectives on children's development from cultural psychology. *American Psychologist, 44,* 343–348.

Rogoff, B., & Wertsch, J. V. (Eds.). (1984). *Children's learning in the "zone of proximal development."* San Francisco: Jossey-Bass.

Rosch, E. H. (1973). On the internal structure of perceptual and semantic categories. In T. Moore (Ed.), *Cognitive development and the acquisition of language.* New York: Academic Press.

Rosch, E. H. (1975). Cognitive representations of semantic categories. *Journal of Experimental Psychology: General, 104,* 192–233.

Rosen, L. A., O'Leary, S. G., Jouye, S. A., Conway, G., & Pfiffner, L. J. (1984). The importance of prudent negative consequences for maintaining the appropriate behavior of hyperactive students. *Journal of Abnormal Child Psychology, 12,* 581–604.

Rosenman, A. A. (1987). The value of multicultural curricula. *Education Week, 7*(10), November 11.

Rosenshine, B. (1977, April). *Primary grades instruction and student achievement.* Paper presented at the annual meeting of the American Educational Research Association, New York.

Rosenshine, B. (1979). Content, time, and direct instruction. In P. Peterson & H. Walberg (Eds.), *Research on teaching: Concepts, findings, and implications.* Berkeley, CA: McCutchan.

Rosenshine, B. (1986). Synthesis of research on explicit teaching. *Educational Leadership, 43*(7), 60–69.

Rosenshine, B. (1988). Explicit teaching. In D. Berliner & B. Rosenshine (eds.), *Talks to teachers* (pp. 75–92). New York: Random House.

Rosenshine, B., & Furst, N. (1973). The use of direct observation to study teaching. In R. Travers (Ed.), *Second handbook of research on teaching.* Chicago: Rand McNally.

Rosenshine, B., & Stevens, R. (1986). Teaching functions. In M. Wittrock (Ed.), *Handbook of research on teaching* (3rd ed., pp. 376–391). New York: Macmillan.

Rosenthal, R. (1973). The Pygmalion effect lives. *Psychology Today,* pp. 56–63.

Rosenthal, R. (1976). *Experimenter effects in behavioral research* (enlarged ed.). New York: Halsted Press.

Rosenthal, R. (1987). Pygmalion effects: Existence, magnitude and social importance. A reply to Wineburg. *Educational Researcher, 16,* 37–41.

Rosenthal, R., and Jacobson, L. (1968). *Pygmalion in the classroom.* New York: Holt, Rinehart, Winston.

Ross, S. M. (1986). *BASIC programming for educators.* Englewood Cliffs, NJ: Prentice-Hall.

Ross, S. M., McCormick, D., Krisak, N., & Anand, P. (1985). Personalizing context in teaching mathematical concepts: Teacher-managed and computer-managed models. *Educational Communication Technology Journal, 33,* 169–178.

Rothman, R. (1988, April 1). "Computer competence" still rare among students, assessment finds. *Education Week,* p. 20.

Rotter, J. (1954). *Social learning and clinical psychology.* Englewood Cliffs, NJ: Prentice-Hall.

Rowe, M. B. (1974). Wait-time and rewards as instructional variables: Their influence on language, logic, and fate control.

Part 1: Wait-time. *Journal of Research in Science Teaching, 11,* 81–94.

Rumelhart, D. & Ortony, A. (1977). The representation of knowledge in memory. In R. Anderson, R. Spiro, & W. Montague (Eds.), *Schooling and the acquisition of knowledge.* Hillsdale, NJ: Erlbaum.

Ruopp, F., & Driscoll, M. (1990, January/February). *Harvard Education Letter, 6*(A), 4–5.

Ryans, D. G. (1960). *Characteristics of effective teachers, their descriptions, comparisons and appraisal: A research study.* Washington, DC: American Council on Education.

Sabers, D. S., Cushing, K. S., & Berliner, D. C. (1991). Differences among teachers in a task characterized by simultaneity, multidimensionality, and immediacy. *American Educational Research Journal, 28,* 68–87.

Sadker, M., & Sadker, D. (1985, March). Sexism in the schoolroom of the '80s. *Psychology Today,* 54–57.

Sadker, M., & Sadker, D. (1986a). Questioning skills. In J. Cooper (Ed.), *Classroom teaching skills* (3rd ed., pp. 143–180). Lexington, MA: D. C. Heath.

Sadker, M., & Sadker, D. (1986b). Sexism in the classroom: From grade school to graduate school. *Phi Delta Kappan, 68,* 512.

Sadker, M., Sadker, D., & Klein, S. (1991). The issue of gender in elementary and secondary education. *Review of Research in Education, 17,* 269–334.

Salili, F., Maehr, M. L., Sorensen, R. L., & Fyans, L. J. (1976). A further consideration of the effect of evaluation on motivation. *American Educational Research Journal, 13*(2), 85–102.

Salomon, G., & Perkins, D. N. (1989). Rocky roads to transfer: Rethinking mechanisms of a neglected phenomenon. *Educational Psychologist, 24,* 113–142.

Sandefur, J. T. (1985). Competency assessment of teachers. *Action in Teacher Education, 7,* (1–2), 1–6.

Sattler, J. (1988). *Assessment of children* (3rd ed.). San Diego: Jerome M. Sattler.

Scarr, S., & Carter-Saltzman, L. (1982). Genetics and intelligence. In R. Sternberg (Ed.), *Handbook of human intelligence.* New York: Cambridge University Press.

Scarr, S., Weinberg, R. A., & Levine, A. (1986). *Understanding development.* New York: Harcourt Brace Jovanovich.

Schab, F. (1980). Cheating in high school: Differences between the sexes (revisited). *Adolescence, 15,* 959–965.

Schiedel, D., & Marcia, J. (1985). Ego integrity, intimacy, sex role orientation, and gender. *Developmental Psychology, 21,* 149–160.

Schiefele, U. (1991). Interest, learning, and motivation. *Educational Psychologist, 26,* 299–324.

Schoenfeld, A. H. (1979). Explicit heuristic training as a variable in problem solving performance. *Journal for Research in Mathematics Education, 10,* 173–187.

Schofield, J. W. (1991). School desegregation and intergroup relations. *Review of Research in Education, 17,* 235–412.

Schon, D. (1983). *The reflective practitioner.* New York: Basic Books.

Schunk, D. H. (1987). Peer models and children's behavioral change. *Review of Educational Research, 57,* 149–174.

Schunk, D. H. (1991a). *Learning theories: An educational perspective.* New York: Merrill.

Schunk, D. H. (1991b). Self-efficacy and academic motivation. *Educational Psychologist, 26,* 207–232.

Schunk, D. H., & Hanson, A. R. (1985). Peer models: Influence on children's self-efficacy and achievement. *Journal of Educational Psychology, 77,* 313–322.

Schwartz, B., & Reisberg, D. (1991). *Learning and memory.* New York: Norton.

Schwartz, J. C., Scarr, S., & McCartney, K. (1983, August). *Center, sitter, and home care before age two: A report on the first*

Bermuda infant care study. Paper presented at the annual meeting of the American Psychological Association, Los Angeles.

Science (1986). Obese children: A growing problem. *Science, 232,* 20–21.

Scruggs, T. E., Mastropieri, M. A., McLoone, B., Levin, J. R., & Morrison, C. R. (1985). *Mnemonic facilitation of learning-disabled students' memory for expository prose.* Unpublished manuscript, Utah State University, Logan.

Seiber, J. E., O'Neil, H. F., & Tobias, S. (1977). *Anxiety, learning, and instruction.* Hillsdale, NJ: Erlbaum.

Seifert, K. L., & Hoffnung, R. J. (1991). *Child and adolescent development.* Boston: Houghton-Mifflin.

Seligman, M. E. P., (1975). *Helplessness: On depression, development, and death.* San Francisco: Freeman.

Selman, R. L. (1981). The child as a friendship philosopher, In S. Asher & J. Gottman (Eds.), *The development of children's friendships.* Cambridge: Cambridge University Press.

Serbin, L., & O'Leary, D. (1975, January). How nursery schools teach girls to shut up. *Psychology Today,* 56–58.

Shantz, C. (1975). The development of social cognition. In E. M. Hetherington (Ed.), *Review of child development research* (Vol. 5). Chicago: University of Chicago Press.

Shavelson, R. J. (1987). Planning. In M. Dunkin (Ed.), *The international encyclopedia of teaching and teacher education* (pp. 483–486). New York: Pergamon Press.

Shavelson, R. J., & Bolus, R. (1982). Self-concept: The interplay of theory and methods. *Psychology, 74,* 3–17.

Shavelson, R. J., Hubner, J. J., & Stanton, G. C. (1976). Self-concept: Validation of construct interpretations. *Review of Educational Research, 46,* 407, 442.

Shepard, L. A., & Smith, M. L. (1989). Academic and emotional effects of kindergarten retention. In L. Shepard & M. Smith (Eds.), *Flunking grades: Research and policies on retention* (pp. 79–107). Philadelphia: Farmer Press.

Sherman, J. G., Ruskin, R. S., & Semb, G. B. (Eds.) (1982). *The Personalized System of Instruction: 48 seminal papers.* Lawrence, KS: TRI Publications.

Sherry, M. (1990). Implementing an integrated instructional system: Critical issues. *Phi Delta Kappan, 72,* 118–120.

Shields, P., Gordon, J., & Dupree, D. (1983). Influence of parent practices upon the reading achievement of good and poor readers. *Journal of Negro Education, 52,* 436–445.

Shostak, R. (1986). Lesson presentation skills. In J. Cooper (Ed.), *Classroom teaching skills* (3rd ed., pp. 114–138). Lexington, MA: D. C. Heath.

Shuell, T. J. (1981a). Dimensions of individual differences. In F. H. Farley & N. J. Gordon (Eds.), *Psychology and education: The state of the union.* Berkeley, CA: McCutchan.

Shuell, T. J. (1981b, April). *Toward a model of learning from instruction.* Paper presented at a meeting of the American Educational Research Association, Los Angeles.

Shuell, T. J. (1986). Cognitive conceptions of learning. *Review of Educational Research, 56,* 411–436.

Shuell, T. J. (1990). Phases of meaningful learning. *Review of Educational Psychology, 60,* 531–548.

Shulman, L. S. (1987). Knowledge and teaching: Foundations of the new reform. *Harvard Educational Review, 19*(2), 4–14.

Shultz, J., & Florio, S. (1979). Stop and freeze: The negotiation of social and physical space in a kindergarten/first grade classroom. *Anthropology and Education Quarterly, 10,* 166–181.

Siegel, L. J. (1983). Psychosomatic and psychophysiological disorders. In R. J. Morris & T. R. Kratochwill (Eds.), *The practice of child therapy.* New York: Pergamon.

Siegler, R. S. (1986). *Children's thinking.* Englewood Cliffs: NJ: Prentice-Hall.

Siegler, R. S. (1991). *Children's thinking* (2nd ed.). Englewood Cliffs, NJ: Prentice-Hall.

Silberman, C. (1966). Technology is knocking at the schoolhouse door. *Fortune, 74,* 120–125.

Simon, D. P., & Chase, W. G. (1973). Skill in chess. *American Scientist, 61,* 394–403.

Simon, P. (1980). *The tongue-tied American: Confronting the foreign language crisis.* New York: Continuum.

Simpson, E. J. (1972). "The classification of educational objectives in the psychomotor domain." *The Psychomotor Domain.* Vol 3. Washington, Gryphon House.

Sisk, D. A. (1988). Children at risk: The identification of the gifted among the minority. *Gifted Education International, 5,* 138–141.

Sizer, T. (1984). *Horace's compromise: The dilemma of the American high school* (updated ed.). Princeton, NJ: Houghton Mifflin.

Skinner, B. F. (1953). *Science and human behavior.* New York: Macmillan.

Slavin, R. E. (1983). *Cooperative learning.* New York: Longman.

Slavin, R. E. (1984). Students motivating students to excel: Cooperative incentives, cooperative tasks, and student achievement. *Elementary School Journal, 85,* 53–64.

Slavin, R. E. (1986). *Educational psychology: Theory into practice.* Englewood Cliffs, NJ: Prentice-Hall.

Slavin, R. E. (1987). Ability grouping and student achievement in elementary schools: A best-evidence synthesis. *Review of Educational Research, 57,* 293–336.

Slavin, R. E. (1990a). Achievement effects of ability grouping in secondary schools: A best-evidence synthesis. *Review of Educational Research, 60,* 471–500.

Slavin, R. E. (1990b). *Cooperative learning.* Englewood Cliffs, NJ: Prentice-Hall.

Slavin, R. E., & Karweit, N. (1985). Effects of whole class, ability grouped, and individualized instruction on mathematics achievement. *American Educational Research Journal, 22,* 351–368.

Slavin, R. E., Karweit, N. L., & Madden, N. A. (1989). *Effective programs for students at risk.* Boston: Allyn & Bacon.

Sleeter, C. E., & Grant, C. A. (1987). An analysis of multicultural education in the United States. *Harvard Educational Review, 57,* 421–444.

Smith, F. (1975). *Comprehension and learning: A conceptual framework for teachers.* New York: Holt, Rinehart & Winston.

Smith, J. (1991). What will the new SAT look like? An interview with Lawrence Hecht. *d'News: The Newsletter of Division D, American Educational Research Association, 1*(2), 1–4.

Smith, J. D., & Caplan, J. (1988). Cultural differences in cognitive style development. *Developmental Psychology, 24,* 46–52.

Smith, M. L. (1991). Put to the test: The effects of external testing on teachers. *Educational Researcher, 20*(5), 8–11.

Smith, S. M., Glenberg, A., & Bjork, R. A. (1978). Environmental context and human memory. *Memory and Cognition, 6,* 342–353.

Smith, S. M., & Neisworth, J. T. (1975). *The exceptional child: A functional approach.* New York: McGraw Hill.

Snider, V. E. (1990). What we know about learning styles from research in special education. *Educational Leadership, 48*(2), 53.

Snow, C. E. (1987). Beyond conversation: Second language learners' acquisition of description and explanation. In J. P. Lantolf & A. Labarca (Eds.), *Research in second language learning: Focus on the classroom* (pp. 3–16). Norwood, NJ: Ablex.

Snow, M. A. (1986). *Innovative second language education: Bilingual immersion programs* (Education Report 1). Los Angeles: Center of Language Education and Research, University of California.

Snow, R. E. (1977). Research on aptitude for learning: A progress report. In L. Shulman (Ed.), *Review of research in education.* Itasca, IL: F. E. Peacock.

Snowman, J. (1984). Learning tactics and strategies. In G. Phye & T. Andre (Eds.), *Cognitive instructional psychology.* Orlando, FL: Academic Press.

Snyderman, M., & Rothman, S. (1987). Survey of expert opinion of intelligence and aptitude testing. *American Psychologist, 42,* 137–144.

Soar, R. S. (1973). *Follow-through classroom process measurement and pupil growth 1970–1971: Final report.* Gainesville, FL: University of Florida.

Soar, R. S., & Soar, R. M. (1979). Emotional climate and management. In P. Peterson & H. Walberg (Eds.), *Research on teaching: Concepts, findings, and implications.* Berkeley, CA: McCutchan.

Sokolove, S., Garrett, J., Sadker, D., & Sadker, M. (1986). Interpersonal communications skills. In J. Cooper (Ed.), *Classroom teaching skills: A handbook.* Lexington, MA: D. C. Heath.

Soloway, E., Lockhead, J., & Clement, J. (1982). Does computer programming enhance problem solving ability? Some positive evidence on algebra word problems. In R. J. Seidel, R. E. Anderson, & S. B. Hunter (Eds.), *Computer literacy.* New York: Academic Press.

Spearman, C. (1927). *The abilities of man: Their nature and measurement.* New York: Macmillan.

Spencer, M. B., & Markstrom-Adams, C. (1990). Identity processes among racial and ethnic-minority children in America. *Child Development, 61,* 290–310.

Sroufe, L. A., Fox, N. E., & Pancake, V. R. (1983). Attachment and dependency in developmental perspective. *Child Development 54,* 1615–1627.

Stallings, J. A., & Kaskowitz, D. H. (1975, April). *A study of follow-through implementation.* Paper presented at the annual meeting of the American Educational Research Association, Washington, DC.

Stanovich, K. E. (1992). *How to think straight about psychology* (3rd ed.) Glenview, IL: Scott, Foresman.

Starch, D., & Elliot, E. C. (1912). Reliability of grading high school work in English. *Scholastic Review, 20,* 442–457.

Starch, D., & Elliot, E. C. (1913a). Reliability of grading work in history. *Scholastic Review, 21,* 676–681.

Starch, D., & Elliot, E. C. (1913b). Reliability of grading work in mathematics. *Scholastic Review, 21,* 254–259.

Starr, R. H., Jr. (1979). Child abuse. *American Psychologist, 34,* 872–878.

Stein, B. S., Littlefield, J., Bransford, J. D., & Persampieri, M. (1984). Elaboration and knowledge acquisition. *Memory and Cognition, 12,* 522–529.

Steinberg, L., Elmen, J. D., & Mounts, N. S. (1989). Authoritative parenting, psychosocial maturity, and academic success among adolescents. *Child Development, 60,* 1424–1436.

Sternberg, R. (1985). *Beyond IQ: A triarchic theory of human intelligence.* New York: Cambridge University Press.

Sternberg, R. (1986). *Intelligence applied: Understanding and increasing your own intellectual skills.* New York: Harcourt Brace Jovanovich.

Sternberg, R. (1990). *Metaphors of mind: Conceptions of the nature of intelligence.* New York: Cambridge University Press.

Sternberg, R., & Davidson, J. (1982, June). The mind of the puzzler. *Psychology Today,* pp. 37–44.

Sternberg, R. J., & Detterman, D. L. (Eds.). (1986). *What is intelligence? Contemporary viewpoints on its nature and definition.* Norwood, NJ: Ablex.

Stigler, J. W., Lee, S., & Stevenson, H. W. (1987). Mathematics classrooms in Japan, Taiwan, and the United States. *Child Development, 58,* 1272–1285.

Stipek, D. J. (1988). *Motivation to learn.* Englewood Cliffs, NJ: Prentice-Hall.

Stodolsky, S. S. (1988). *The subject matters: Classroom activity in math and social studies.* Chicago: University of Chicago Press.

Straus, M. A., Gelles, R. J., & Steinmetz, S. K. (1980). *Behind closed doors: Violence in the American family.* New York: Doubleday.

Strike, K. (1975). The logic of discovery. *Review of Educational Research, 45,* 461–483.

Sulzer-Azaroff, B., & Mayer, G. R. (1986). *Achieving educational excellence using behavioral strategies.* New York: Holt, Rinehart & Winston.

Suzuki, B. H. (1983). The education of Asian and Pacific Americans: An introductory overview. In D. Nakanishi & M. Hirano-Nakanishi (Eds.), *The education of Asian and Pacific Americans: Historical perspectives and prescriptions for the future.* Phoenix, AZ: Oryx Press.

Swanson, H. L., O'Conner, J. E., & Cooney, J. B. (1990). An information processing analysis of expert and novice teachers' problem solving. *American Educational Research Journal, 27,* 533–556.

Tal, Z., & Babad, E. (1990). The teachers' pet phenomenon: Rate of occurrence, correlates, and psychological costs. *Journal of Educational Psychology, 82,* 637–645.

Tanner, J. (1970). Physical growth. In P. Mussen (Ed.), *Carmichael's manual of child psychology* (3rd ed., Vol. 1). New York: Wiley.

Task Force on Pediatric AIDS: American Psychological Association. (1990). Pediatric AIDS and human immunodeficiency virus infection: Psychological issues. *American Psychologist, 44,* 258–264.

Taylor, J. B. (1983). Influence of speech variety on teachers' evaluation of reading comprehension. *Journal of Educational Psychology, 75,* 662–667.

Teacher Magazine (1991, April). You and the system: Who you will teach, p. 32H.

Tenbrink, T. D. (1986). Writing instructional objectives. In J. Cooper (Ed.), *Classroom teaching skills* (3rd ed., pp. 71–110). Lexington, MA: D. C. Heath.

Tennyson, R. D. (1981, April). *Concept learning effectiveness using prototype and skill development presentation forms.* Paper presented at the annual meeting of the American Educational Research Association, Los Angeles.

Tennyson, R. D., & Cocchiarella, M. J. (1986). An empirically based instructional design theory for teaching concepts. *Review of Educational Research, 56,* 40–71.

Terman, L. M., Baldwin, B. T., & Bronson, E. (1925). Mental and physical traits of a thousand gifted children. In L. M. Terman (Ed.), *Genetic studies of genius* (Vol. 1). Stanford, CA: Stanford University Press.

Terman, L. M., & Oden, M. H. (1947). The gifted child grows up. In L. M. Terman (Ed.), *Genetic studies of genius* (Vol. 4). Stanford, CA: Stanford University Press.

Terman, L. M., & Oden, M. H. (1959). The gifted group in mid-life. In L. M. Terman (Ed.), *Genetic studies of genius* (Vol. 5). Stanford, CA: Stanford University Press.

Tharp, R. C., & Gallimore, R. (1988). *Rousing minds to life: Teaching, learning, and schooling in social context.* New York: Cambridge University Press.

Tharp, R. G. (1989). Psychocultural variables and constants: Effects on teaching and learning in schools. *American Psychologist, 44,* 349–359.

Thoma, S. J. (1986). Estimating gender differences in the comprehension and preference of moral issues. *Developmental Review, 6,* 165–180.

Thomas, E. L., & Robinson, H. A. (1972). *Improving reading in every class: A sourcebook for teachers.* Boston: Allyn & Bacon.

Thorndike, E. L. (1913). *Educational psychology.* In *The psychology of learning* (Vol. 2). New York: Teachers College, Columbia University.

Thorndike, R., Hagen, E., & Sattler, J. (1986). *The Stanford-Binet Intelligence Scale* (4th ed.). Chicago: Riverside.

Thurstone, L. L. (1938). Primary mental abilities. *Psychometric Monographs,* No. 1.

Tiedt, P. L., & Tiedt, I. M. (1990). *Multicultural education: A handbook of activities, information, and resources.* Boston: Allyn & Bacon.

Tierney, R. J., Readence, J. E., & Dishner, E. K. (1990). *Reading strategies and practices: A compendium,* (3rd ed.). Boston: Allyn & Bacon.

Timmer, S. G., Eccles, J., & O'Brien, K. (1988). How children use time. In F. Juster & F. Stafford (Eds.), *Time, goods, and well-being.* Ann Arbor, MI: Institute for Social Research, University of Michigan.

Tobias, Sheila. (1982, January). Sexist equations. *Psychology Today,* pp. 14–17.

Tobias, Sigmund. (1979). Anxiety research in educational psychology. *Journal of Educational Psychology, 71,* 573–582.

Tobias, Sigmund. (1981). Adaptation to individual differences. In F. Farley & N. Gordon (Eds.), *Psychology and education: The state of the union.* Berkeley, CA: McCutchan.

Tobias, Sigmund. (1982). When do instructional methods make a difference? *Educational Researcher, 11*(4), 4–10.

Tobias, Sigmund. (1985). Text anxiety: Interference, defective skills, and cognitive capacity. *Educational Psychologist, 20,* 135–142.

Tobias, Sigmund, & Duchastel, P. (1974). Behavioral objectives, sequence, and anxiety in CAI. *Instructional Science, 3,* 232–242.

Tobin, K. (1987). The role of wait time in higher cognitive learning. *Review of Educational Research, 56,* 69–95.

Tomlinson-Keasey, C. (1990). Developing our intellectual resources for the 21st century: Educating the gifted. *Journal of Educational Psychology, 82,* 399–403.

Tomlinson-Keasey, C., & Little, T. D. (1990). Predicting educational attainment, occupational achievement intellectual skill, and personal adjustment among gifted men and women. *Journal of Educational Psychology, 82,* 442–455.

Torrance, E. P. (1972). Predictive validity of the Torrance tests of creative thinking. *Journal of Creative Behavior, 6,* 236–262.

Torrance, E. P. (1986). Teaching creative and gifted learners. In M. Wittrock (Ed.), *Handbook of research on teaching* (3rd ed.). New York: Macmillan.

Torrance, E. P., & Hall, L. K. (1980). Assessing the future reaches of creative potential. *Journal of Creative Behavior, 14,* 1–19.

Travers, R. M. W. (1977). *Essentials of learning* (4th ed.). New York: Macmillan.

Trickett, E., & Moos, R. (1974). Personal correlates of contrasting environments: Student satisfaction with high school classrooms. *American Journal of Community Psychology, 2,* 1–12.

Ure, A. (1861). *The philosophy of manufactures: Or an exposition of the scientific, moral, and commercial economy of the factory system of Great Britain* (3rd ed.). London: H. G. Bohn.

U.S. Bureau of the Census (1990). *Current Population Reports. Series P-20.* Washington, DC: U.S. Government Printing Office.

Vacc, N. N. (1989). Writing evaluation: Examining four teachers' holistic and analytic scores. *Elementary School Journal, 90,* 88–95.

Vaillant, G. E., & Vaillant, C. O. (1981). Natural history of male psychological health, X: Work as a predictor of positive mental health. *The American Journal of Psychiatry, 138,* 1433–1440.

Van Houten, R., & Doleys, D. M. (1983). Are social reprimands effective? In S. Axelrod & J. Apsche (Eds.), *The effects of punishment on human behavior.* San Diego: Academic Press.

Van Mondrans, A. P., Black, H. G., Keysor, R. E., Olsen, J. B., Shelley, M. F., & Williams, D. D. (1977). Methods of inquiry in educational psychology. In D. Treffinger, J. Davis, & R. R. Ripple (Eds.), *Handbook on teaching educational psychology.* New York: Academic Press.

Vargas, J. (1986). Instructional design flaws in computer-assisted instruction. *Phi Delta Kappan, 67,* 738–744.

Vasquez, J. A. (1990). Teaching to the distinctive traits of minority students. *The Clearing House, 63,* 299–304.

Veenman, S. (1984). Perceived problems of beginning teachers. *Review of Educational Research, 54,* 143–178.

Viadero, D. (1990). Battle over multicultural education rises in intensity. *Education Week, 10*(13), 1, 11, 13, 14.

Vygotsky, L. S. (1978). *Mind in society: The development of higher mental process.* Cambridge, MA: Harvard University Press.

Vygotsky, L. S. (1986). *Thought and language.* Cambridge, MA: MIT Press.

Wadsworth, B. J. (1978). *Piaget for the classroom teacher.* New York: Longman.

Wadsworth, B. J. (1989). *Piaget's theory of cognitive development: An introduction for students of psychology and education* (4th ed.). New York: Longman.

Walberg, H. J. (1990). Productive teaching and instruction: Assessing the knowledge base. *Phi Delta Kappan, 72,* 470–478.

Walberg, H. J., Pascal, R. A., & Weinstein, T. (1985). Homework's powerful effects on learning. *Educational Leadership, 42*(7), 76–79.

Walden, E. L., & Thompson, S. A. (1981). A review of some alternative approaches to drug management of hyperactive children. *Journal of Learning Disabilities, 14,* 213–217.

Walker, C., & Shaw, W. (1988). Assessment of eating and elimination disorders. In P. Karoly (Ed.), *Handbook of child health assessment: Biosical perspectives.* New York: Wiley.

Walker, L. J. (1989). A longitudinal study of moral reasoning. *Child Development, 60,* 157–166.

Walker, L. J., & de Vries, B. (1985, August). *Moral stages/moral orientations: Do the sexes really differ?* Paper presented at the annual meeting of the American Psychological Association, Los Angeles.

Walker, L. J., de Vries, B., & Trevethan, S. D. (1987). Moral stages and moral orientations in real-life and hypothetical dilemmas. *Child Development, 58,* 842–858.

Wallerstein, J., & Blakeslee, S. (1989). *Second chances: Men, women, and children a decade after divorce.* New York: Ticknor & Fields.

Walton, G. Identification of the intellectually gifted children in the public school kindergarten. Unpublished doctoral dissertation, University of California, Los Angeles, 1961.

Wang, M. C., & Palincsar, A. S. (1989). Teaching students to assume an active role in their learning. In M. Reynolds (Ed.), *Knowledge base for the beginning teacher.* New York: Pergamon.

Ward, M., & Sweller, J. (1990). Structuring effective worked examples. *Cognition and Instruction, 7,* 1–40.

Waterman, A. S. (Ed.). (1985). *Identity in adolescence: Processes and contents.* San Francisco: Jossey Bass.

Watson, B. (1990). The wired classroom: American education goes on-line. *Phi Delta Kappan, 72,* 109–112.

Webb, N. (1980). A process-outcome analysis of learners in group and individual settings. *Educational Psychology, 15,* 69–83.

Webb, N. (1982). Student interaction and learning in small groups. *Review of Educational Research, 52,* 421–445.

Webb, N. (1985). Verbal interaction and learning in peer-directed groups. *Theory into Practice, 24,* 32–39.

Webb, N. (1989). Peer interaction and learning in small groups. *International Journal of Educational Research, 23,* 253–261.

Weinberg, R. A. (1989). Intelligence and IQ. *American Psychologist, 44,* 98–104.

Weiner, B. (1979). A theory of motivation for some classroom experiences. *Journal of Educational Psychology, 71,* 3–25.

Weiner, B. (1980). The role of affect in rational (attributional) approaches to human motivation. *Educational Researcher, 9,* 4–11.

Weiner, B. (1984). Principles for a theory of student motivation and their application within an attributional framework. In R. Ames & C. Ames (Eds.), *Research on motivation in education* (Vol. 1). Orlando, FL: Academic Press.

Weiner, B. (1990). History of motivational research in education. *Journal of Educational Psychology, 82,* 616–622.

Weiner, B., & Graham, S. (1989). Understanding the motivational role of affect: Lifespan research from an attributional perspective. *Cognition and Emotion, 4,* 401–419.

Weiner, B., Russell, D., & Lerman, D. (1978). Affective consequences of causal ascriptions. In J. H. Harvey, W. J. Ickes, & R. F. Kidd (Eds.). *New directions in attribution research* (Vol. 2). Hillsdale, NJ: Erlbaum.

Weinstein, C. E. (1991, August). *Enhancing strategic learning in a variety of educational settings.* Paper presented at the annual meeting of the American Psychological Association, San Francisco.

Weinstein, C. E., & Mayer, R. E. (1985). The teaching of learning strategies. In M. C. Wittrock (Ed.), *Handbook of research on teaching* (3rd ed.). New York: Macmillan.

Weinstein, C. S. (1977). Modifying student behavior in an open classroom through changes in the physical design. *American Educational Research Journal, 14,* 249–262.

Weinstein, C. S., & Mignano, A. (1993). *Organizing the elementary school classroom: Lessons from research and practice.* New York: McGraw-Hill.

Wertsch, J. V. (1985). Adult-child interaction as a source of self-regulation in children. In S. Yussen (Ed.), *The growth of reflection in children.* Orlando, FL: Academic Press.

Wertsch, J. V. (1991). *Voices of the mind: A sociocultural approach to mediated action.* Cambridge, MA: Harvard University Press.

Wessells, M. G. (1982). *Cognitive psychology.* New York: Harper and Row.

Wessman, A. (1972). Scholastic and psychological effects of a compensatory education program for disadvantaged high school students: Project A B C. *American Educational Research Journal, 9,* 361–372.

White, E. M. (1984). Holisticism. *College Composition and Communication, 35,* 400–409.

White, H. (1986). Damsels in distress: Dependency themes in fiction for children and adolescents. *Adolescence, 21,* 251–256.

White, K. R. (1982). The relation between socioeconomic status and academic achievement. *Psychological Bulletin, 91*(3), 461–481.

White, R. W. (1959). Motivation reconsidered: The concept of competence. *Psychological Review, 66,* 297–333.

White, S., & Tharp, R. G. (1988, April). *Questioning and wait-time: A cross cultural analysis.* Paper presented at the annual meeting of the American Educational Research Association, New Orleans.

Wigfield, A., & Eccles, J. (1989). Test anxiety in elementary and secondary school students. *Educational Psychologist, 24,* 159–183.

Wiggins, G. (1989). Teaching to the authentic test. *Educational leadership, 46*(7), 41–47.

Wiggins, G. (1991). Standards, not standardization: Evoking quality student work. *Educational Leadership, 48*(5), 18–25.

Wiig, E. H. (1982). Communication disorders. In H. Haring (Ed.), *Exceptional children and youth.* Columbus, OH: Charles E. Merrill.

Wilkins, W. E., & Glock, M. D. (1973). *Teacher expectations and student achievement: A replication and extension.* Ithaca, NY: Cornell University Press.

Willerman, L. (1979). *The psychology of individual and group differences.* San Francisco: Freeman.

Williams, J. P. (1976). *Individual differences in achievement test presentation and evaluation anxiety.* Unpublished doctoral dissertation, University of Illinois, Urbana-Champaign.

Williams, M. D. (1991). Observations in Pittsburgh ghetto schools. *Anthropology and Education Quarterly, 12,* 211–220.

Willis, P. (1977). *Learning to labor.* Lexington, MA: D. C. Heath.

Wilson, C. W., Hopkins, B. L. (1973). The effects of contingent music on the intensity of noise in junior high home economics classes. *Journal of Applied Behavior Analysis, 6,* 269–275.

Wilson, S. M., Shulman, L. S., & Richert, A. R. (1987). 150 different ways of knowing: Representations of knowledge in teaching. In J. Calderhead (Ed.), *Exploring teacher thinking* (pp. 104–124). London: Cassell.

Wineburg, S. S. (1987). The self-fulfillment of the self-fulfilling prophecy: A critical appraisal. *Educational Researcher, 16,* 28–37.

Winett, R. A., & Winkler, R. C. (1972). Current behavior modification in the classroom: Be still, be quiet, be docile. *Journal of Applied Behavior Analysis, 15,* 499–504.

Wingate, N. (1986). Sexism in the classroom. *Equity and Excellence, 22,* 105–110.

Winograd, P., & Johnston, P. (1982). Comprehension monitoring and the error-detection paradigm. *Journal of Reading Behavior, 14,* 61–76.

Witkin, H. A., Moore, C. A., Goodenough, D. R., & Cox, R. W. (1977). Field-dependent and fieldindependent cognitive styles and their educational implications. *Review of Educational Research, 47,* 1–64.

Wittrock, M. C. (1978). The cognitive movement in instruction. *Educational Psychologist, 13,* 15–30.

Wlodkowski, R. J. (1981). Making sense out of motivation: A systematic model to consolidate motivational constructs across theories. *Educational Psychologist, 16,* 101–110.

Wolf, D. (in press). *Presence of minds, performances of thought.* New York: College Entrance Examination Board.

Wolf, D., Bixby, J., Glenn, J., III, & Gardner, H. (1991). To use their minds well: New forms of student assessment. *Review of Research in Education, 17,* 31–74.

Women on Words and Images. (1975). *Dick and Jane as victims: Sex stereotyping in children's readers* (expanded ed.). Available from author, P. O. Box 2163, Princeton, NJ.

Wong, L. (1987). *Reaction to research findings: Is the feeling of obviousness warranted?* Dissertation Abstracts International, 48/12, 3709B (University Microfilms #DA 8801059).

Wood, D., Bruner, J., & Ross, S. (1976). The role of tutoring in problem solving. *British Journal of Psychology, 66,* 181–191.

Woolfolk, A. E., & Brooks, D. (1983). Nonverbal communication in teaching. In E. Gordon (Ed.), *Review of research in education* (Vol. 10). Washington, DC: American Educational Research Association.

Woolfolk, A. E., & Brooks, D. (1985). The influence of teachers' nonverbal behaviors on students' perceptions and performance. *Elementary School Journal, 85,* 514–528.

Woolfolk, A. E., & Hoy, W. K. (1988, April). *Efficacy, belief, and control orientations of prospective teachers.* Paper presented at the Annual Meeting of the American Educational Research Association, New Orleans.

Woolfolk, A. E., & Hoy, W. K. (1990). Prospective teachers' sense of efficiency and beliefs about control. *Journal of Educational Psychology, 82,* 81–91.

Woolfolk, A. E., Rosoff, B., & Hoy, W. K. (1990). Teachers' sense of efficacy and their beliefs about managing students. *Teaching and Teacher Education, 6,* 137–148.

Woolfolk, A. E., & Woolfolk, R. L. (1974). A contingency management technique for increasing student attention in a small group. *Journal of School Psychology, 12,* 204–212.

Workman, E. (1982). *Teaching behavioral self-control to students.* Austin, TX: PRO-ED.

Worthen, B. R., & Spandel, V. (1991). Putting the standardized text debate in perspective. *Educational Leadership, 48(5),* 65–70.

Yerkes, R. M., & Dodson, J. D. (1908). The relation of strength of stimulus to rapidity of habit formation. *Journal of Comparative Neurology, 18,* 459–482.

Youniss, J. (1980). *Parents and peers in social development.* Chicago: University of Chicago Press.

Yussen, S. R. (Ed.). (1985). *The growth of reflection in children.* Orlando, FL: Academic Press.

Zimmerman, B. J. (1990). Self-regulated learning and academic achievement: An overview. *Educational Psychologist, 21,* 3–18.

Zimmerman, B. J., & Schunk, D. H. (Eds.). (1989). *Self-regulated learning and academic achievement: Theory, research, and practice.* New York: Springer-Verlag.

Zimmerman, D. W. (1981). On the perennial argument about grading "on the curve" in college courses. *Educational Psychologist, 16,* 175–178.

NAME INDEX

SUBJECT INDEX

Boldface numbers indicate pages on which key terms and concepts are defined.

AAMD (American Association on Mental Deficiency), 122–123
Ability
  beliefs about, 356–358, 360–361
  differences in, 495–496
  entity view of, **356**–357
  high, 497–498
  incremental view of, **357**
  low, 496–497
  matching strategies to, 40–42
  prior knowledge and, 495–496
  underestimating, 43–44
Ability grouping, 120–122, 153
  between-class, **121**
  within-class, **122**
Abstract, **583**
Abstractions, 38, 62–63
Abstract mapping, 44–46
Abstract words, 55
Academic learning time, **403**, 404
Academic socialization, **165**
Academic tasks, **370**–374
Acceleration
  of cognitive development, 42–43
  of gifted students, 127–128
  through grade skipping, 14
Accommodation, **27**
Achievement
  ethnic differences in, 169
  intelligence and, 118–119
  racial differences in, 169
  socioeconomic status and, 163–166
Achievement motivation, **350**–351, 352, 356
Achievement tests, **519**–523, 538
Acronym, **268**
Action zone, **465**
Active involvement, 502
Active listening, 425–426
Active teaching, **481**
Activity, 28
Adaptation, **28**–29
Adolescence, 97–103
  AIDS and, 101, 102
  cognitive development in, 37–40

drug abuse in, 100–101
eating disorders in, 99–100
physical development in, 97–98, 100
psychosocial development in, 70–73
risks in, 99–103
sexuality in, 99
suicide in, 102–103
Adolescent egocentrism, **39**
Adulthood, psychosocial development in, 73–74
Advance organizer, **324**–325, 326
Affective domain, **444**–445
Affective education, **90**–92
  programs in, 91
  teachers on, 90–92
African Americans
  attribution theory and, 356
  black dialect of, 177–178
  discrimination and, 170–171
  education of, 156, 169
  learning styles of, 184
  population of, 167
  socioeconomic status of, 163, 165
Age-related needs, 401–402
Aggression, **84**
  managing, 85, 106, 107
  media and, 85–86
  moral behavior and, 84–86, 106
  socialized, 140
AIDS, 101, 102
Alcohol, 100
Algorithm, **297**
Allocated time, **403**
Alternate-form reliability, 516
Ambiguity, of tasks, 371–373
American Association on Mental Deficiency (AAMD), 122–123
American Psychological Association, 102, 229
Analogical thinking, **298**
Analysis of Learning Potential, 120
Animal research, 43
Anorexia nervosa, **99**–100

Antecedents, **202**, 208–209, 210
Anxiety, **344**–347
Anxiety-withdrawal disorder, 139
Applied behavior analysis, **210**–220
  coping with undesirable behavior in, 215–220
  encouraging behaviors in, 211–215
  reprimands in, 218–219
  response cost and, 219
  social isolation and, 219
Aptitude tests, **523**–525
Aptitude-treatment interaction (ATI), **494**–495
Arousal, **342**–347
Articulation disorders, **138**
Artificial intelligence, **241**
Asian Americans
  bilingualism among, 180
  cultural compatibility of, 168–169
  learning styles of, 184–185
  population of, 167
Assertive discipline, **426**–429
Assertiveness vs. aggression, 84–85
Assessment, 540–575
  authentic, **533**–534, 551–557
  communication and, 569–571, 574, 575
  of creativity, 306–309
  effects on students, 558–560
  formative, **542**–543
  grading, 392, 397, 558–569, 574–575
  innovations in, 550–557
  of learning potential, 120, 532–533
  of performance in context, 552–557
  planning for, 543–545
  summative, **543**
  See also Test(s)
Assimilation, **27**
ATI (aptitude-treatment interaction), **494**–495

Industry, **69**
    encouraging, 70
    identity and, 70
    inferiority vs., 67, 69–70
Infancy
    sensorimotor stage in, 30
    trust vs. mistrust in, 67–68
Inferiority vs. industry, 67, 69–70
Information
    retaining, 249, 250
    retrieval from memory, 256–258
    storing in memory, 255–256
Information processing, **241**–244, 260
Inhibitions, 223
Initiative, **68**
    encouraging, 68–69
    guilt vs., 67, 68–69
    identity and, 70
Inquiry teaching, **455**–456
Insight, **301**
Instruction
    data-based, **542**
    direct, **481**–485, 492, 496–497
    individualized, **456**–458
    for preoperational child, 33
Instructional events model, 326, **327**–328
Instructional objectives, **437**–441, 471
    advantages of, 440–441
    classifications of, 443–447
    criticisms of, 440
    kinds of, 438–440
    value of, 437–438
Instrumental value, 390–391
Integrated instructional systems (IIS), **461**
Integrity, **74**
Intellect, faces of, **112**, 113
Intelligence, **111**–115
    achievement and, 118–119
    artificial, **241**
    components of, 113–114
    Guilford's model of, 112–113, 306
    heredity vs. environment and, 119–120
    measurement of, 116–120
    multiple, **112**–113, 114
    triarchic theory of, **113**–115
Intelligence quotient (IQ), **116**–120, 524
Intelligence tests, 116–120, 127
Interactions
    aptitude-treatment, **494**–495
    higher-order, **494**

Interest areas, 464–465
Interest value, **373**, 389–390
Interference, **250**, 258–259
Intermittent reinforcement schedule, **205**–208
Internalization
    of action, 31
    of moral rules and principles, 83
Interval schedule, 205–207
Intimacy vs. isolation, 67, 73–74
Intrinsic motivation, **337**
Intrinsic value, **373**, 389–390
Intuitive thinking, **320**
Involvement
    active, 502
    ego, 369
    encouraging, 413, 414, 503
    task, 369
Iowa Test of Basic Skills, 520
IQ (intelligence quotient), **116**–120, 524
Isolation
    intimacy vs., 67, 73–74
    social, **219**

Joplin Plan, 122
Journals, student, 3

Kansas Learning Strategies Curriculum, 142
Kaufman Assessment Battery for Children, 120, 520, 524
Keller Plan, **458**–459
Keyword method, **268**–270
Knowledge
    ability and, 495–496
    importance of, 239–240
    kinds of, 240–241
    learners', 487
    memory and, 265–266
    novice, 303
    personalization of, 282
    problem solving and, 301, 303
    problems transforming, 477
    professional, 6–7
    teacher's, 475–476, 480
Kohlberg's theory of moral development, 79–83
Kuder Preference Record, 525
Kuhlman-Anderson Intelligence Tests, 120

Labeling, 72, 110–111
Language
    bilingualism, 2–3, **178**–183, 193
    capacity for, 52

cognitive development and, 47–48
    cultural differences and, 156, 177–183
    deep structure of, 52
    development of, 50–56, 62
    dialect and, 177–178, 179
    holistic, 57–59
    misunderstandings and, 186–187
    playing with, 54
    sociolinguistics and, **185**–187
    surface structure of, 52
    teaching and, 56–59
    whole, **56**–59
Language disorders, 138, 139
Language games, 32
Law of effect, **202**
Laws
    Educational Amendments Act of 1974 (Buckley Amendment), 571
    Education for All Handicapped Children Act (PL 94–142), 143, 144
    Education of the Handicapped Act Amendments of 1986 (PL 99–457), 143–144
    Family Educational Rights and Privacy Act of 1974, 571
    Individuals with Disabilities Education Act of 1990 (PL 101–476), 144
Learned helplessness, **142**, 165, 355
Learners
    ego-involved, **369**–370
    self-regulated, **487**–488
    task-involved, **369**
Learning, **196**–198
    behavioral views, 196–235
    cognitive-mediational view of, **485**, 488–493
    cognitive view of, **238**–283
    complex, 488–489
    computers and, 461–462
    constructivist view of, **485**, 488–493
    cooperative, **376**–381, 396, 462
    discovery, 318, **319**–323, 333
    mastery, **458**–459
    meaningful verbal, **322**
    New Zealand studies of, 485–487
    observational, **220**–224
    overlearning, **318**
    part, **267**

PHOTO CREDITS